AMBULATORY HYSTEROSCOPY

Diagnosis and Treatment

Edited by

Bruno J van Herendael MD
Professor, Gynaecological Endoscopic Surgery
Università degli studi dell, Insubria Varese Italy,
Coordinator Gynaecology, *ZNA Campus*
Stuivenberg Antwerp Belgium,
Director, *Endocopic Training Centre Antwerp*
(ETCA) Antwerp Belgium.

Rafael Valle MD
Professor, *Department of Obstetrics and Gynecology,*
Northwestern University Medical School,
Chicago, IL, USA

Stefano Bettocchi MD
Associate Professor, *University of Bari-Policlinico,*
Bari, Italy

© 2004 Bladon Medical Publishing
12 New Street, Chipping Norton, Oxfordshire OX7 5LJ, UK

First published 2004

All rights reserved. No part of this publication may be reproduced, stored in a retrieval system, or transmitted in any form or by any means, electronic, mechanical, photocopying, recording or otherwise without the prior permission of the copyright owner.

The Authors have asserted their right under the Copyright, Designs and Patents Act, 1988, to be identified as the Authors of this work.

Always refer to the manufacturer's Prescribing Information before prescribing drugs cited in this book.

British Library Cataloguing in Publication Data.
A catalogue record for this title is available from the British Library

ISBN 1-904218-12-1

Bruno J van Herendael, Rafael Valle, Stefano Bettocchi
Ambulatory Hysteroscopy: Diagnosis and Treatment

Design and production:
Design Online Ltd, Oxford

Printed by
Ingoprint
Barcelona, Spain

Distributed by
Plymbridge Distributors Ltd
Estover Road, Plymouth PL6 7PY, UK

Contents

Contributors — viii

Foreword: *J.J. Sciarra* — ix

Preface: *Bruno J. van Herendael, Rafael F. Valle and Stefano Bettocchi* — x

Introduction: The mini endoscopes — xii
Jacques Hamou

Part I: DIAGNOSTIC TESTS AND TECHNIQUES

1 Diagnostic outpatient hysteroscopy service: conventional hysteroscopy — 2
B. J. van Herendael

2 Diagnostic outpatient hysteroscopy service: semi-rigid hysteroscopy — 7
P. J. O'Donovan and Kalaish Nakade

3a Outline of a flexible hysteroscope outpatient service — 12
René Marty

3b Comparison of flexible hysteroscopes: theoretical and practical considerations — 19
Boa-Liang Lin

4 Hysteroscopes and sheaths: rigid scopes — 25
Stefano Bettocchi

5a Set up of an outpatient facility — 29
Corry G.W.A. Stappers-de Kuijer

5b The nurse's role in outpatient hysteroscopy — 34
Donna M. Morrison

6 Techniques for approaching the uterus: classic and vaginoscopical — 40
Stefano Bettocchi

7 Distension media in diagnostic hysteroscopy — 42
J. Hamou

8 The self-retaining office hysteroscope — 46
H. Guedj

Part I: DIAGNOSTIC TESTS AND TECHNIQUES

9   Indications, contraindications and complications of outpatient hysteroscopy   55
Rafael F. Valle and B.J. van Herendael

10   Pre-IVF hysteroscopic evaluation of intrauterine cavity   60
Aygül Demirol and Timur Gürgan

11   Sonography and sonohysterography in outpatient gynecological practice   65
Leeber Cohen

12   Saline infusion sonography: the essentials   74
Linda D. Bradley

13   Observations on the anatomy of the endometrium   84
Bruno J. van Herendael and Stefano Bettocchi

14   Endometrial receptors   93
Hugo Maia Jr, Amélia Maltez, Célia Athayde, Genevieve Coelho and Elsimar M. Coutinho

15   Interpretation of visual appreciation of intrauterine pathology   99
Ramón Labastida, Alicia Ubeda and José Manuel Traver

16   Endometrial cell transportation during hysteroscopy   107
Stefano Bettocchi

Part II: OPERATIVE PROCEDURES

17a Instrumentation and biopsies The reliability of eye-guided biopsies (EGB) — 110
Stefano Bettocchi

17b Instrumentation and biopsies Endometrial cytology and endometrial sampling — 112
René Marty

17c Blind and hysteroscopically guided endometrial sampling: a pathologist's point of view — 117
Maurizio Colafranceschi

18 Liquid distension media and their complications — 124
Rafael F. Valle

19a Bipolar energy — 131
Stefano Bettocchi

19b Mechanical instruments for operative hysteroscopy — 135
Rafael F. Valle

20 Indications and limitations of operative hysteroscopy in the office setting — 140
Stefano Bettocchi

21 New indications for hysteroscopy: sterilization — 143
Rafael F. Valle and B.J. van Herendael

22 Anesthesia and monitoring in an outpatient set up — 152
Bruno Lasters and B.J. van Herendael

Part III: PRACTICAL ASPECTS

23a Disinfection, sterilization, and maintenance of instruments: Europe — 162
Sabine Taylor

23b Disinfection, sterilization, and maintenance of instruments: USA — 166
Donna M. Morrison

24 Office hysteroscopy: reimbursement — 170
Joseph J. Houser

25 Evidence-based comparison of the different diagnostic techniques to approach the cervix and the uterine cavity — 178
B. J. van Herendael

26a Training and accreditation: USA – Hysteroscopy and operative hysteroscopy: learning, training, proctoring, and credentialing — 184
Rafael F. Valle

26b Training and accreditation: USA
Training and credentialing in operative hysteroscopy — 188
Toufic Nakad and Keith Isaacson

27a Training and accreditation: Europe — 192
Walter Costantini

27b Training and accreditation: Europe
European point of view — 200
B.J. van Herendael

28 Training and accreditation: Australia — 202
Peter J. Maher

29 Training and accreditation: The Far East — 208
Bao-Liang Lin

30 Training and accreditation in hysteroscopy: an overview — 209
Arnold Gillespie

31a Record-keeping, documentation, and registry
Photo and video archiving for endoscopy — 211
Luk Rombauts, Scott Pearce and Yves van Belle

31b Record-keeping, documentation, and registry
Documentation of hysteroscopic and endoscopic procedures — 216
T.F. Kruger, I.J. van der Wat, C.F. Hoogendijk and J. P. van der Merwe

Part IV: THE OFFICE AND OUTPATIENT TEAM

32 The nurse's perspective 222
Corry G.W.A. Stappers-de Kuijer

33 Patients' compliance with small diameter scope size 226
B.J. van Herendael

34 Counseling patients 231
Chris Van de Mosselaer

Part V: Epilogue 233

Contributors

Célia Athayde BSc, Coordinator
Research Department, CEPARH, Salvador, Bahia, Brazil

Stefano Bettocchi MD, Associate Professor
University of Bari-Policlinico, Bari, Italy

Linda D. Bradley MD, Director of Hysteroscopic Services
Department of Obstetrics and Gynecology, Cleveland Clinic Foundation, Cleveland, OH, USA

Genevieve Coelho MD, Research Assistant
Endoscopy Unit, CEPARH, Salvador, Bahia, Brazil

Leeber Cohen MD, Associate Professor
Northwestern Medical Faculty Foundation, Department of Obstetrics and Gynecology, Chicago, IL, USA

Maurizio Colafranceschi MD, Professor Pathology
Instituto di Anatomia Patologica, Policlinico Careggi, Firenze, Italy

Walter Costantini MD, Associate Professor,
Director of Obstetric School, University of Milan, and Clinica Mangiagalli, Milan, Italy

Elsimar M. Coutinho MD, President
CEPARH, Salvador, Bahia, Brazil

Aygül Demirol MD, Clinical Director
Women's Health Clinic and IVF Center, Ankara, Turkey

Arnold Gillespie MB BS BSc FRANZCOG FRCOG, Associate Professor
Department of Obstetrics and Gynecology, University of Adelaide, South Australia

Hubert Guedj MD, Consultant
St Jacques Hospital, Paris, France

Timur Gürgan MD, Professor and Head
Division of Reproductive Endocrinology and Infertility, Department of Obstetrics and Gynecology, Faculty of Medicine, Hacettepe University, Ankara, Turkey

J. Hamou MD
Department of Obstetrics and Gynaecology, Hopital A. Béclère, Clamart, France

C.F. Hoogendijk
Department of Obstetrics and Gynaecology, University of Stellenbosch and Tygerberg Hospital, Tygerberg, South Africa

Joseph J. Houser MBA, Director (Marketing)
K. Storz America, Charlton, MA, USA

Keith Isaacson MD, Associate Professor
Department of Obstetrics and Gynecology, Massachusetts General Hospital, Harvard Medical School, Boston, MA, USA

Thinus F. Kruger MBChB(Pret) MMed(Pharm)(Clinical Pharmacology)(Pret) MMed(O&G)(Stell) FCOG(SA) FCOG(Lond) MD, Professor
Department of Obstetrics and Gynaecology, University of Stellenbosch and Tygerberg Hospital, Tygerberg, South Africa

Ramón Labastida MD PhD, Head of Gynaecology Service
Department of Obstetrics and Gynaecology, Institut Universitari Dexeus, Barcelona, Spain

B Lasters MD
Anesthesiology, ZNA Campus Stuivenberg, Antwerp, Belgium

Bao-Liang Lin MD PhD, Director
Department of Obstetrics and Gynecology, 12-1 Shinkawadori, Kawasaki-ku, Kawasaki, Kanagawa-ken, Japan

Peter J. Maher MB BS FRANZCOG FRCOG(Lon), Associate Professor and Director Endosurgery Unit,
Department of Obstetrics and Gynaecology, University of Melbourne, Mercy Hospital for Women, Melbourne, Australia

Hugo Maia Jr MD, Head of Endoscopy Unit
CEPARH, Salvador, Bahia, Brazil

Amélia Maltez MD, Head of Pathology Unit
CEPARH, Salvador, Bahia, Brazil

René Marty MD, Spécialiste Gynécologue-Obstétricien
Attaché Consultant à l'Hôpital Jean Verdier Responsable de l'Unité d'Hystéroscopie Flexible, Centre Hospitalier Universitaire et de Recherche, Paris XIII, France

Donna M. Morrison RN BSN CNOR, Operating Room Nurse Specialist
Prentice Surgical Services, Northwestern Memorial Hospital, Chicago, IL, USA

Toufic Nakad MD, Clinical Instructor
Department of Obstetrics and Gynecology, Massachusetts General Hospital, Harvard Medical School, Boston, MA, USA

Kailash Nakade MD MRCOG, Karl Storz Research Fellow
MERIT Centre, Bradford Royal Infirmary, Bradford, UK

P. O. O'Donovan FRCS FRCOG, Professor
MERIT Centre, Bradford Royal Infirmary, Bradford, UK

Donna M. Morrison RN, BSN, CNOR, Operating Room Nurse Specialist
Prentice Surgical Services, Northwestern Memorial Hospital, Chicago, IL, USA

Scott Pearce
Department of Obstetrics and Gynaecology, Monash University, Clayton, Victoria, Australia

L. Rombauts MD
Department of Obstetrics and Gynaecology, Monash University, and Monash Medical Centre, Clayton, Victoria, Australia

Corry G.W.A. Stappers-de Kuijer RN
Hysteroscopy Training Centre, Spaarne Hospital, Haarlem, The Netherlands

Sabine Taylor MD, Senior Registrar
Department of Obstetrics and Gynaecology, Hopital A. Béclère, France

José Manuel Traver
Department of Obstetrics and Gynaecology, Institut Universitari Dexeus, Barcelona, Spain

Alicia Ubeda, Head of Endoscopic Unit
Department of Obstetrics and Gynaecology, Institut Universitari Dexeus, Barcelona, Spain

Rafael F. Valle, MD, Professor
Department of Obstetrics and Gynecology, Northwestern University Medical School, Chicago, IL, USA

Yves R.M. van Belle MD, Assistant Chief of Department, Chef de Clinique
Department of Obstetrics and Gynaecology, St Janziekenhuis, Brussels, Belgium

Chris Van de Mosselaer, Project Manager
Endoscopic Training Centre, Antwerp, Belgium

J. P. van der Merwe
Department of Obstetrics and Gynaecology, University of Stellenbosch and Tygerberg Hospital, Tygerberg, South Africa

I. J. van der Wat
Parklane Clinic, Parktown, South Africa

Bruno J. van Herendael MD, Professor, Gynaecological Endoscopic Surgery,
Università degli studi dell, Insubria Varese Italy,
Coordinator Gynaecology, *ZNA Campus Stuivenberg Antwerp Belgium,*
Director, *Endocopic Training Centre Antwerp (ETCA) Antwerp Belgium*

Foreword

Hysteroscopy has become an important, if not an essential part of gynecologic practice today. This volume on "Ambulatory Hysteroscopy – Diagnosis and Treatment" is an important new contribution to this ever-expanding field of clinical practice.

In recent years, outpatient procedures have increased in importance in gynecology and gynecologic surgery, and this volume, with its emphasis on office and outpatient procedures is both timely and welcome. It will serve as a manual for the beginner and a reference work for the accomplished practitioner. I have known the editors for many years and they are both experts and authorities in the field of hysteroscopy, with long personal experience. They have assembled an outstanding team of authors who have covered all aspects of both diagnostic and operative hysteroscopy. They have not neglected those useful aspects of hysteroscopy that are not often discussed, with chapters on "How to set up an outpatient facility" and "The nurse's role in outpatient hysteroscopy." In addition, they have also not neglected the complimentary techniques, such as the use of ultrasound and saline infusion sonography as adjunctive techniques to assist the clinician in an accurate diagnosis of intrauterine pathology. In the area of operative hysteroscopy, the editors should be credited in putting together very readable chapters on the intelligent use of operative procedures in the office setting, including the use of anesthesia and monitoring in ambulatory surgery. The editors should also be credited in stressing new operative indications for hysteroscopy, such as hysteroscopic sterilization.

It is important that a significant portion of this volume addresses what the editors call the "practical aspects" of ambulatory hysteroscopy, including evidence-based comparison between the different diagnostic techniques and information on maintenance of equipment, reimbursement and training and accreditation. The latter information is particularly interesting, since it includes up to date material on activities in the United States of America, Europe, Australia and Asia. It is valuable to gynecologists that there is solid information in this volume on record-keeping and documentation, issues that are so important today in clinical practice.

I have the pleasure of personally knowing many of the contributors to this volume and they are all recognized experts. It should be noted that the editors have given us experience from not only both sides of the Atlantic, but from all over the world. This volume, accordingly, is truly a world-class contribution, and the editors deserve credit for their efforts.

This volume is comprehensive, authoritative and exceptionally well illustrated, but of greater importance is the fact that it is extremely easy to read and to use. I predict that it will become an instant classic in the field of gynecology and gynecologic surgery. It is essential reading and is an essential reference for all gynecologists who plan to or who are already practicing ambulatory hysteroscopy.

As a gynecologist who has been in the field of hysteroscopy from its infancy 30 years ago, I congratulate both the editors and the publisher for a very high-quality, unique, scholarly and contemporary scientific publication on ambulatory hysteroscopy.

John J. Sciarra MD
Thomas J. Watkins Professor
Department of Obstetrics and Gynecology
Northwestern University Medical School
and
Former President, International Society for Gynecologic Endoscopy

Preface

It seems strange that most gynecologists conclude their clinical examination with the view of the external os of the cervix as exposed with a speculum. Specula have been found at the archeological site of Pompei. This means that they were in use over 2000 years ago. Recammier in France reinvented these tools and it is striking that they are almost identical with the tools found at Pompei.

So we see the outside of the cervix and even with colposcopy we do not see very much more. So we switch to vaginal ultrasound or fluid-enhanced vaginal ultrasound. This is frustrating for the patient who comes to see us with complaints of abnormal uterine bleeding. Patients want to be helped. They prefer a 'see and treat' concept. They come with a complaint, we – the physicians – are supposed to find a diagnosis that fits their complaint and provide a solution that ends their complaint. This solution should be as radical as possible and the results have to be visible as soon as possible. This does not leave very much room for interpretations or doubts. Solutions in the form of removing mechanical problems are preferred over medical solutions that take more time to produce the desired effect.

Therefore it seems strange that most of us are afraid to progress beyond the uterine cervix and look into the uterine cavity. It is undeniable that hysteroscopy has made great progress in the last two decades. This is due to several factors, particularly the awareness of the benefits of adding visualization to the blind methods of uterine evaluation used for so many years. This is a change in the traditional thinking. Additionally industry – finally aware of the changes and the requests made by physicians – adapted, improved, and developed better instrumentation for diagnosis and therapy. It takes very little. If a small barrel hysteroscope, <5 mm in diameter is used, it takes some saline as a distension medium (in most cases 100 ml are sufficient) and on average some 5 minutes to have a clear view of the cervix and the uterine cavity. So the instruments were made small enough to be introduced atraumatically across the cervical channel into the uterine cavity without requiring cervical dilatation. If the appropriate technique is used, i.e. the vaginoscopic technique developed by Stefano Bettocchi, the patient will be very comfortable and even operative procedures can be performed while the patient witnesses the cause and the solution of her problems. Operative hysteroscopy has benefited greatly from improvements in ancillary instrumentation, as well as in large bore operative endoscopes. As a consequence, many of the procedures previously performed only with such instruments, which required cervical dilatation and some type of anesthesia (be it local, regional or even general), have been transferred to the office setting by utilizing mini endoscopes and small caliber instrumentation. The anesthesia, if local anesthesia is used, will take longer than the actual procedure. These changes have been welcomed by physicians and patients alike, in view of the relative simplicity, expeditious performance, decreased morbidity, and decrease in inconvenience and cost to the patient. While this revolution has occurred in selected medical centers, the adoption of this method of evaluation and treatment by an increased number of physicians has been slow.

So what is it that deters a great number of physicians? Why is the technique not used more frequently? Our conclusion is that the majority of the physicians, not really trained in outpatient procedures, are afraid of inflicting pain on their patients. As we work in a very competitive world the patients may prefer to go to another physician and this engenders a loss of income for the first physician. There is also the fear of not to being able to perform the hysteroscopy well enough with the patient awake and witnessing the procedure and hence giving the impression that one is not qualified. There is also a notion of time. Physicians are afraid to lose some of their precious time and they believe that hysteroscopy is a long procedure – first to set up the patient and then to perform. However, patients (as well as health providers' requests) have also focused on these new ways of evaluating and treating patients in an ambulatory setting and have highlighted physicians' awareness and interest in the concept of office evaluation and treatment.

With these facts in mind we decided to bring together an international group of physicians who were knowledgeable about hysteroscopy and these new trends to compile in this volume the fundamentals and more advanced thoughts and procedures that encompass up-to-date information and state-of-the-art in diagnostic and operative ambulatory hysteroscopy. As it is undeniable that the introduction of sonography (with or without fluid enhancement) has blended with endoscopic procedures to provide an even better evaluation of the uterus as an organ, we have included specific chapters designed to offer the real and logical role of sonographic methods blended with hysteroscopy as a complementary and certainly not competitive method of evaluation. Finally, we also attempted to outline the specific features of teamwork – adding chapters on education, counseling patients, preparation and disinfection of instruments, as well as documentation and costs. Needless to say, principles of guidelines for training and certification, now being requested by insurance companies, hospitals, and local health-care organizations, have been added to complement the overall theme of ambulatory hysteroscopy. Hopefully this volume will help those physicians already involved with ambulatory hysteroscopy to expand their personal field and will stimulate other physicians, not familiar with the approach, to embark and extend their practices following similar guidelines. If this volume benefits physicians and patients alike with a more rational, practical, safe, and less taxing approach to offering hysteroscopic evaluation and treatment in such a way, our purpose in writing this volume will be amply fulfilled.

We need no longer stop at an incomplete examination, but dare we progress and visualize the problems – and why not treat them at the same time?

Bruno J. van Herendael *(Antwerp)*
Rafael F. Valle *(Chicago)*
Stefano Bettocchi *(Bari)*

Introduction: The mini endoscopes

Jacques Hamou

Hysteroscopy provides the gynecologist with valuable and useful information in contemporary gynecologic practice. Direct visualization of the uterine cavity adds a significant dimension and valuable information, and enhances the diagnostic quality provided by indirect techniques such as radiology or transvaginal sonography (TVS). The main reason for the acceptance and the large diffusion of diagnostic outpatient hysteroscopy is the miniaturization of the hysteroscopes.

Until 1980 the slow acceptance of the technique was partially due to the development of the necessary technology to reduce the outer diameter of the diagnostic scopes. What was apparently an easy task proved to be extremely difficult. Another problem to overcome was the anatomic entity formed by the cervical canal. Here mucus was encountered and there is a tendency for the surface to bleed when touched. Forceful passage, with or without previous dilatation, even under general anesthesia inevitably provokes bleeding. To master this bleeding while maintaining visibility requires the use of fluids or a strong flow of carbon dioxide to prevent the blood from obscuring the gynecologist's field of vision. It was the necessity to address these difficulties that led to the development of a new endoscope. The first of the series was the microcolpohysteroscope called the Hamou I (Figure 1).

The properties of this instrument, which include both panoramic and contact vision modes, permit constant visual control in the cervical canal. The various magnification capabilities of this instrument allow the operator to negotiate the cervical canal with precision. The atraumatic crossing of the endocervical canal gives the operator for the first time the possibility of performing hysteroscopy without anesthesia, it diminishes the risk of bleeding, although it is still present with this scope because of the diameter. The use of fluid media is not an issue as carbon dioxide can be used. Because of the ease of performing the procedure hysteroscopy was set to become the routine, atraumatic, reproducible examination it has now become because of the further reduction in diameter of the scopes. It was also the first step towards performing hysteroscopy in the physician's office, as I was able to prove. The first model had an inner diameter of 4 mm with a diagnostic sheath of 5 mm. This diameter was well adjusted for the majority of cases, but soon specific conditions – such as nulliparous women with fertility problems and menopausal women – demanded a specific approach. Slimmer and slimmer hysteroscopes were developed (Figure 2): first a 2.9-mm scope with a 3.7-mm diagnostic sheath and most recently a 1.9-mm scope with a 2.5-mm diagnostic sheath. These very slim scopes now need a construction to protect them from breaking during the procedure.

This section deals with my involvement in creating rigid scopes on the Hopkins rod lens system. We must not forget that flexible scopes (Figure 3) and fiberscopes were developed and improved over the last decades with the same purpose – to make the access to the uterine cavity through the cervical canal as atraumatic and easy as possible.

However, in my opinion they do not yet offer the same quality of image as the rigid scopes. We know that new developments in electronics will open a complete new area

Figure 1
The Hamou I microcolpohysteroscope (Karl Storz Gmbh, Tütlingen, Germany) in the upper part of the figure. Note the side arm allowing for the ×150 magnification for cellular exploration. The optical qualities of the system allow for ×20 magnification when the final lens is at a distance of some 1 cm from the endometrial surface and of ×80 when in contact with the endometrial surface. The nob on the side steers the focusing so that clear vision is always possible. In the middle part the later model called Hamou II, still used today, has the same possibilities except for the ×150 enlargement. Semi-flexible instruments are used to operate.

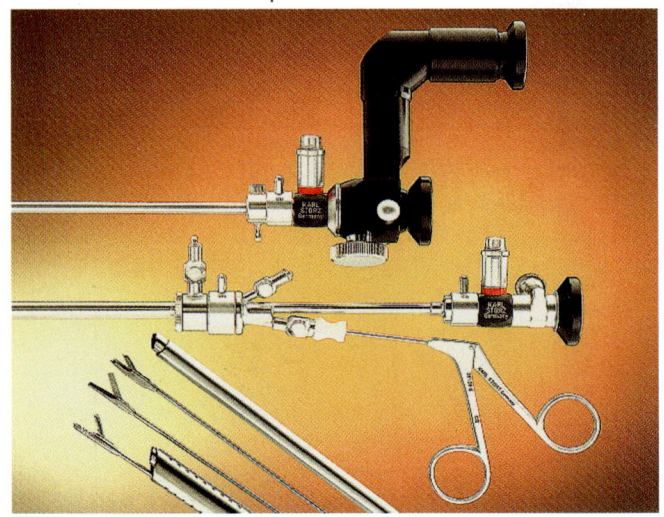

in endoscopy and therefore we have to keep an open mind. At the moment we have to go for the best buy that combines quality of vision and reasonable price.

The other major and logical advance was the surgical, hence operative, approach to intrauterine lesions by hysteroscopy. New and continually evolving endoscopic instruments and specially designed devices are leading the development of this operative branch of hysteroscopy, allowing for intrauterine manipulation under visual control. These techniques add a new dimension in the treatment of uterine pathology and in the exploration of the utero-tubal anatomy, especially now that selected procedures can be performed even without anesthesia in the private office or in an outpatient facility with the patient witnessing the process.

The long history of hysteroscopy is fascinating when one considers the ideas and the difficulties, physical and ethical, that needed to be overcome before we came to the development of the actual hysteroscopy. It all started with the perception of the uterus as an autonomous entity in the body of the female by primitive civilizations. Aubinais has been credited with the first hysteroscopy in 1863. He used transillumination. Desormeaux produced the first true endoscope in 1865 (Figure 4). It consisted of a straight tube containing deflectors. The light was provided by a flame produced by a mixture of alcohol and resin.

The next step took some 40 years, if we do not consider Pantaleoni's efforts – his hysteroscopies were considered too difficult a technique by his pupils, so they omitted to perform the technique. It was David who adapted Nitze's cystoscope by applying an optical system permitting magnification of the field of observation while reducing the external diameter of the instrument. This took place in 1908.

The possibility of visualizing the uterine cavity has interested physicians over the past hundred years, but because of the technical difficulties encountered hysteroscopy did not become a standard procedure until the advent of modern instrumentation. The mini hysteroscope not only offers the possibility of exploring the endocervical canal by atraumatic controlled progression to the uterine cavity that can be observed in panoramic and contact mode, but also gives the gynecologist the possibility of observation with a magnification from 1/1 over 1/20 and 1/60 to 1/150. The last magnification gives the possibility of performing cytology in situ, particularly of the uterine cervix.

It is my firm belief that in the near future diagnostic and operative procedures performed through the mini endoscopes will affect every gynecologist in their daily practice.

Figure 2
The new generation of rigid scopes demonstrate the visible difference between the diameters of the scopes: the upper model is reduced compared with the earlier models but very much more signifant in diameter than the one in the lower part of the picture. Note that the 5 Fr operating channel is more significant in diameter than the diameter of the scope.

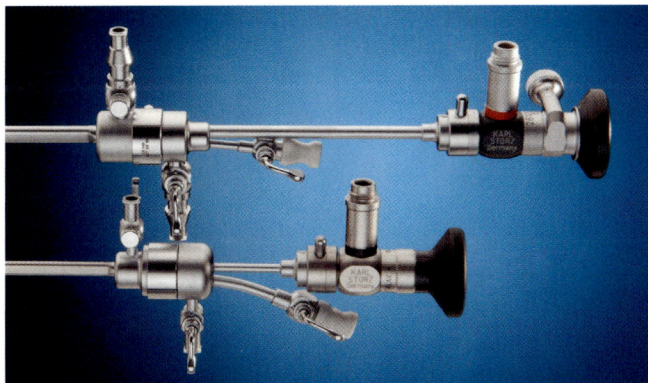

Figure 3
The flexible scope developed especially for hysteroscopic use.

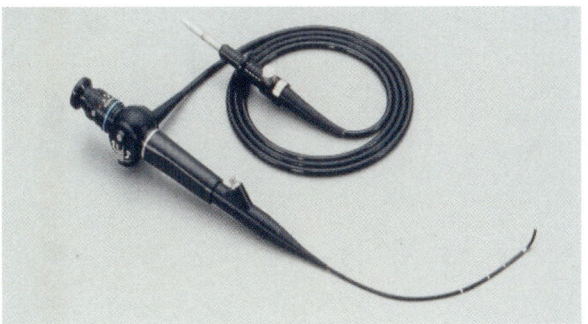

Figure 4
The original viewing apparatus of Desormeaux. Note the chimney that provided for smoke evacuation due to the heavy fumes of the resin.

Part I
DIAGNOSTIC TESTS AND TECHNIQUES

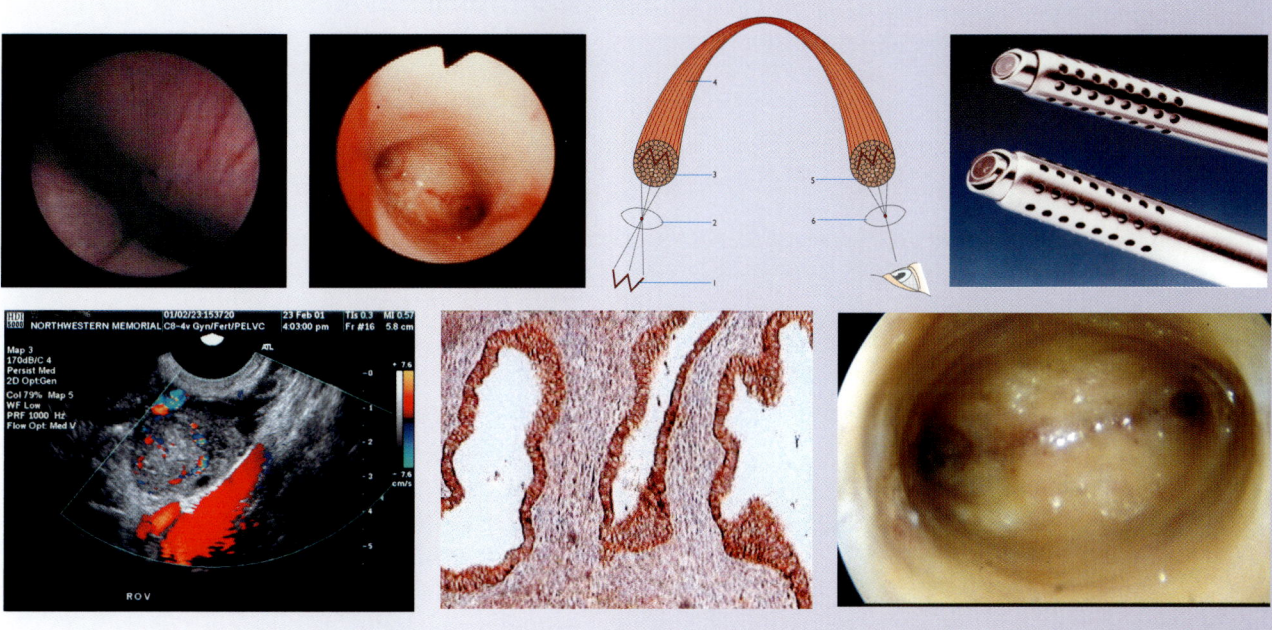

1 Diagnostic outpatient hysteroscopy service: conventional hysteroscopy

B. J. van Herendael

> **Take Home Message**
>
> Modern diagnostic hysteroscopy is performed with the patient in the lithotomy position on a couch that can be moved to a Trendelenburg position. The distension medium of choice is a low molecular weight fluid; usually a normal saline solution. A speculum can be used but the vaginoscopic technique offers more freedom of movement outside the vagina. If small barrel scopes are used (<5 mm diameter) local anesthetic is not necessary. Clamping the cervix should be avoided if at all possible. The physician should be relaxed and should talk to the patient and explain the whole procedure to her. The patient should not be obliged to watch the whole procedure. Fluid distension can be achieved in diagnosis with a saline bag suspended 1.2 m above the seat of the couch. If operative work is foreseen a rotator pump is best used so as to regulate the intrauterine pressure. Be aware that the pressure on the pump only gives an indication of the actual pressure. A maximum pressure of 50 mmHg should not be exceede. A suppository of 100 mg of indamethacin is given as premedication half an hour before the hysteroscopy together with 0.25 mg of atropine to prevent vagal reactions. After the intervention a 50 mg tablet of diclofenac is given and repeated after 3 hours.

The value of hysteroscopy lies in the 'see and treat' concept. Patients want to walk in with their problem and walk out without the problem. In ideal circumstances they want to witness the solution to the problem in real time. Outpatient hysteroscopy is the tool par excellence to fulfil patients' wishes.

From the physician's point of view there is a strong financial factor to be taken into account. Investments have to be made to be able to perform ambulatory hysteroscopy, not just the purchase of the necessary instruments, but time and money also have to be spent in extracurricular training to be able to perform the examination to the satisfaction of both the physician and the patient. Physicians both outside and inside the hospital live in a very competitive world, so another factor is the fear of losing patients to other colleagues. If the patient experiences pain she will probably turn to someone else with her problem if it is not satisfactorily resolved. There is also, to a minor extent, the fact that ultrasound is a very popular diagnostic medium and this tool is readily available in most gynecological practices for obvious reasons: it can be used in a variety of diagnostic procedures both as an aid or as the principal tool. The question then is: does the practice really need yet another diagnostic tool?

The answer is twofold. First, there are typical problems that confine themselves to the uterine cavity, both pathophysiologic or anatomic, that cannot be detected with a 100% positive predictive value by any other approach except for hysteroscopy, as the authors will prove in this book. The second aspect is precisely the 'see and treat' possibility that hysteroscopy gives the physician and the patient.

THE START AND EVOLUTION OF MODERN OUTPATIENT HYSTEROSCOPY

From the first day that hysteroscopy (by rule) became a part of the protocol for D&C in the department back in 1980 there was a strong desire to use the technique out of theater. At that time I was performing outpatient laparoscopy for female sterilization, a far more invasive technique than hysteroscopy, as it was performed with an 11-mm single puncture scoop. My problem was the dilatation of the cervical canal, at that time necessary to allow the passage of large barrel hysteroscopes. Because of the dilatation of the cervical canal, dilatation that destroyed the fine structure of the cervical plicae and crypts, these scopes did not allow for the objective that I had set myself: to use a technique to diagnose and treat patients in the same session. The advent of the Hamou I scope in the early 1980s was a very big step in the right direction. The older, large barrel scopes were used with vacuum cups that fitted the ectocervix, so as to prevent the leakage of CO_2 gas, which was used as the medium to distend the uterine cavity. These cups were very difficult to bring into the vagina and once the vacuum was applied they did hurt the patients.

Now here was a scope of some 6 mm outer diameter that could be brought through the cervical canal by gradually distending it and in doing so enable us to identify problems in the canal and to appreciate the anatomy and the physiology. Classically a tenaculum was used to grasp the cervix so as to align the cervical canal in the axis of the uterine cavity. This tenaculum was used with or without prior anesthesia. I had adapted the technique in such a way that I did not wanted to use the tenaculum, because in my experience the act of putting a tenaculum on the cervix makes the patient restless and anxious, so that they experience more discomfort. I started to use a classical Collins speculum. This speculum has the advantage that it can easily be taken apart when it hampers the movements of the hysteroscope. I was then able to perform hysteroscopy very easily and to the satisfaction of the patients. I could perform biopsies and sterilizations following the diagnostic procedure in the office setting with CO_2 gas. I was also able to teach the technique so that I carried out a reproducible examination in an unprepared patient. However, the frustration was that we were not able to perform the technique in up to 25% of the patients, so we had to select the patients very carefully: we could only perform the technique in pluripara women and not in nulli gravida, perimenopausal, or most menopausal patients. So we jumped at the opportunity when smaller barrel scopes became available – now we had an instrument that was oval in shape and of a maximal outer diameter of 5 mm in length and 3.4 mm in transverse diameter. This included a 5 Fr working channel. Again the technique was easy to learn and reproducible even by junior registrars. When even smaller diameter hysteroscopes became available, CO_2 gas no longer fulfilled the needs of the approach, as the distension became too time-consuming and did not provide good quality vision. A low molecular weight liquid distension medium, a saline solution, was used and has become the standard. The advantage is that not only are we able to make a diagnosis but we are also able to switch to operative procedures without even changing the scope out of its position, just by introducing an instrument while holding the scope stable so that we can perform the procedure immediately.

HOW WE PERFORM OUTPATIENT HYSTEROSCOPY

The experience of many years – some 15 years in diagnostic and 12 in operative procedures – and the mistakes and successes have shown us how to perform outpatient hysteroscopy in the easiest possible way.

THE COUCH AND THE CHAIR

It is possible to perform hysteroscopy in nearly every single condition. However, the best results are obtained when the patient and the physician are relaxed and when both have good visual access to the screen (Figure 1). Therefore it is best to position the patient in a lithotomy position, preferably on an electrically powered couch, although mechanical couches can be used. It should be possible to set the couch higher or lower during the procedure. The physician should be able to set the couch in different positions without having to put down the instruments.

The physician has to seat him or herself very comfortably so that he or she avoids undue strain on the arms and the hands during the procedure. If the physician is in an uncomfortable position this will reflect on the procedure. One then tends to shorten a procedure or to lean on the scope and thus on the patient. In the first instance the procedure will not deliver the expected results. In the

Figure 1
My office. (a) The patient walks from the chair at the desk (foreground) to the couch and can witness the procedure on the screen by simply turning her head to the left. The physician observes the procedure on the screen that is slightly to his right.

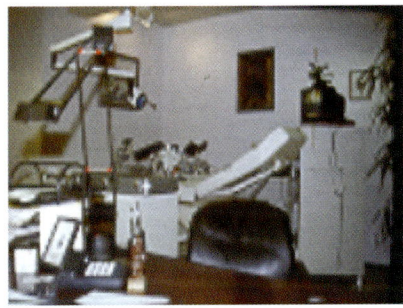

(b) more or less in the axis of the scope. The couch can be lowered or raised electrically by a pedal under the physician's right foot at the foot end of the couch.

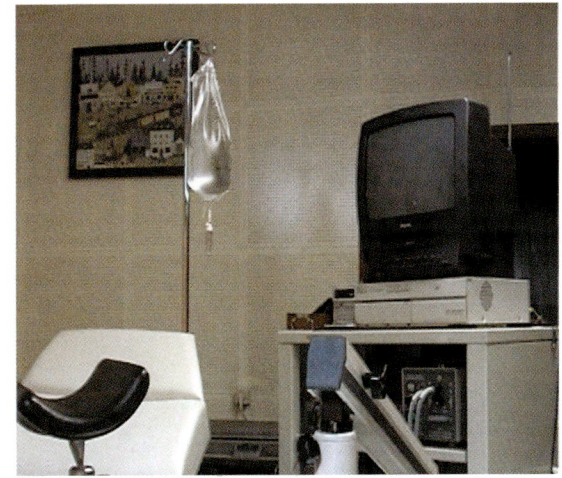

second case the patient will get nervous because of the pain and eventually will not be able to sustain the examination. The best option is to provide a chair with a back rest (Figure 2) and if possible with arm rests that can be adapted to suit the individual physician.

It should also be possible to use the couch to place the patient in the Trendelenburg position if a vagal reaction occurs (Figure 3). Vagal reactions are rare, but unpredictable.

The patient should receive a full explanation of the procedure during the assembling of the scopes and during the whole period of the examination. The physician should point out the stages of the advancement of the scope in the cervical canal, the opening and entering of the isthmus, the entering and inspection of the uterine cavity and the inspection and the aspect (including the flap valve mechanism) of the tubal ostia. If contact hysteroscopy is performed, this procedure should also be commented upon and the results pointed out to the patient. It is of note that no patient should be obliged to watch the entire procedure. If patients so wish they should be allowed to focus on something else. When a specific lesion is seen the attention of the patient can then be called for so that the eventual treatment can be discussed together with the patient. It is our experience that small barrel hysteroscopes do not require local anesthesia. This excludes the need to place a speculum and to infiltrate the cervix. In most cases the cervix needs to be lifted forwards for a paracervical injection and this requires that a tenaculum is placed on the anterior lip of the cervix. Positioning a speculum and applying a tenaculum on the lip of the cervix are stressful and painful moments for patients, so we tend to avoid this so as to be able to perform the hysteroscopy in as relaxed an atmosphere as possible. There is also the fact that patients tend to feel the injection site of the local anesthetic in the cervix many hours after the procedure has finished, reminding them of the procedure. The more technical procedures we can avoid during hysteroscopy the better.

Is there a place for a premedication? Premedication is not necessary for diagnostic hysteroscopy or the small operative maneuvers that could follow a diagnostic hysteroscopy. The removal of small polyps, the cutting of small adhesions or the mechanical or bipolar opening of the outer cervical ostium or the cervical canal do not require premedication. If surgical procedures are foreseen, especially if the intramural part of the tube is involved as in sterilization procedures, it is advisable to use some sort of premedication. I use a nonsteroidal anti-inflammatory drug (NSAID), indomethacin, 100 mg anal suppository 30 minutes before surgery and 0.25 mg of atropine IM. The NSAID prevents most of the pain and the atropine prevents most of the vagal reactions that can occur during the dilatation of the uterine cervix in the menopause or the dilatation of the intramural part of the tube when inserts are used, as in sterilization procedures. After the procedure the patients receive a 50 mg diclofenac enteric-coated tablet per os immediately after the procedure and a second tablet some 3 hours later. Prostaglandins can be used to soften and shorten the cervix. Because the impact on the cervix occurs only after a period of time it is best to give the drugs the evening before the examination. This is inconvenient in a 'see and treat' situation. Dinoprostone gel (PGE2) 0.5 mg or dinoprostone (PGE2) 3-mg vaginal suppositories can be used.

Small operative procedures are very well tolerated even if we open the cervix, os externum, with small scissors. The 'take home message' here is to avoid touching the myometrium in the fundus or the lateral side of the

Figure 2
A chair with a back rest which can be adjusted to suit the individual physician.

Figure 3
The Trendelenburg position.

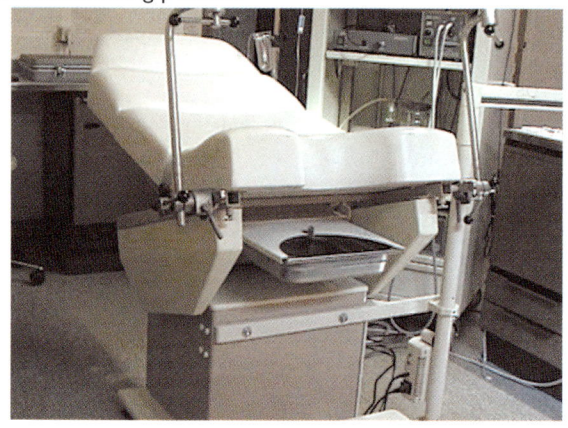

uterus. Anterior end posterior walls are slightly less sensitive but great experience is needed to be able to perform larger operative procedures such as small myomectomies.

THE PHYSICIAN

A physician performing outpatient hysteroscopy should be well aware of the differences that exist as compared with classical hysteroscopy under general anesthesia.

They should be willing to talk the patient through the procedure and to bear with the patient. The insertion of the scope and the dilatation of the uterine cavity require some patience as these acts have to be performed very carefully and therefore require more time than in the anesthetised patient. They should also be prepared to discuss the treatment with the patient and, if the patient wishes, to postpone the treatment even if this treatment could easily be performed in the same session. It is impossible to perform an operative procedure without the patient's agreement. If the patient does not agree, performing the procedure will result in painful sensation for the patient and frustration for the physician. It is recommneded that the physician attends a specific training course for outpatient hysteroscopy, as the handling of the scope and the dilatation of the uterine cavity are different when small barrel scopes are used as compared with classical scopes. In particular, the use of the pump systems is different and requires other settings.

DISTENSION MEDIA

The distension medium of choice is low molecular weight fluid distension medium. In daily practice the most readily available and the most easy to use is normal saline. I use it in 3-litre bags, using a classical pole and the bag at 1.5 m above the patient for diagnostic procedures and small operative maneuvers, such as taking biopsies, removal of small polyps and the use of scissors to open the cervical canal (Figure 4).

For operative procedures I use a rotary pump system that allows a quicker distension of the vagina and more ease in the adaptation of the pressures to the needs of the hysteroscopic maneuver. I use a higher pressure, 100 mmHg, for the distension of the vagina and of the cervical canal and 50 mmHg when working in the uterine cavity. The reduction from 100 to 50 mmHg is made just an instant before the isthmus and thus the internal os opens to avoid the patient experiencing cramp-like pain.

It has to be taken into account that the indicators on the pumps do not show the exact pressure in the vagina or the uterus, as the pumps have difficulty in assessing the exact pressure owing to the diameter of the internal canals in the small barrel scopes.

Figure 4
The bag with the distension medium positioned on a pole above the couch.

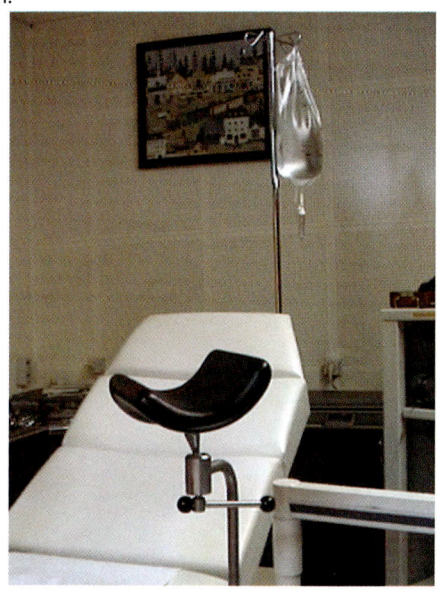

Figure 5
(a) and (b) The opening of the cervix and the fact that the oval tip of the scope is turned so as to adopt the largest diameter to the natural opening of the cervical canal. This is the most delicate moment, as this is the moment the patient will experience most pain and should be talked to and the situation should be explained while the patient witnesses the procedure.

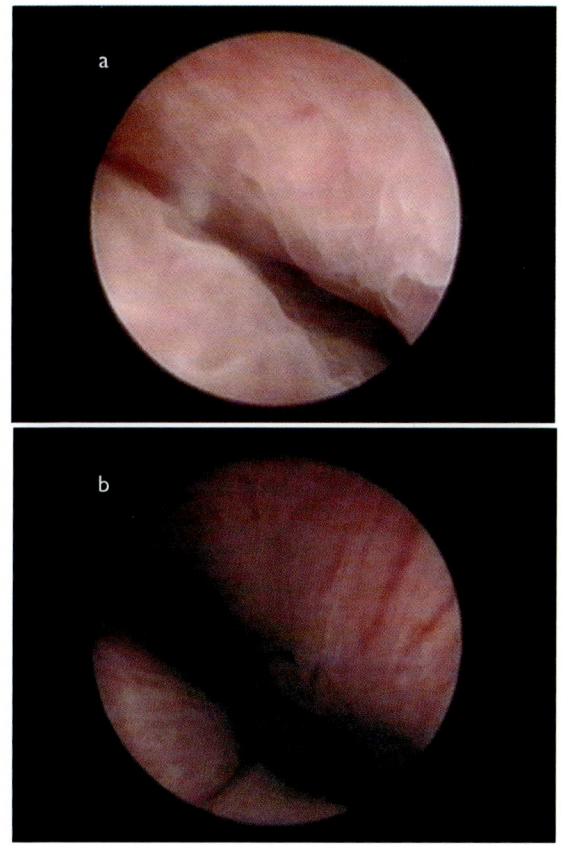

THE HARDWARE

There is a difference between the hospital and the office. In most cases trolleys are used for operative and diagnostic work in hospital, and they tend to be more sophisticated. In the office we can manage with less sophisticated and older equipment. I use hardware that is over 10 years old and it performs just as well; many pictures in this book are from the office (Figure 6). I use analogue video recording in a system that provides both a screen and a video unit of the type that is used in the stores to promote products. This unit is connected to a digital printer which produces hard copy to store in the file or to give the patient so that she can show it to her family physician. The camera is also an older model that still gives a clear picture but does not perform as well as the one used for theater work. The light source is a conventional source.

Figure 6
(a) and (b) The inexpensive video display unit and the simple older video camera and light source used in the author's office.

BIBLIOGRAPHY

Campo R, Van Belle Y, Rombouts L, Brosens I, Gordts S. Office mini-hysteroscopy. *Hum Reprod Update* 1999; **5**: 73–81.

Siegler AM. Office hysteroscopy. *Obstet Gynecol Clin North Am* 1995; **22**: 457–471.

Perez-Medina T, Bajo JM, Martinez-Cortes L, Castellanos P, Perez de Avila I. Six thousand office diagnostic-operative hysteroscopies. *Int J Gynaecol Obstet* 2000; **71**: 33–38.

Bettocchi S, Selvaggi L. A vaginoscopic approach to reduce the pain of office hysteroscopy. *J Am Assoc Gynecol Laparosc* 1997; **4**: 255–258.

Valle RF. Office hysteroscopy. *Clin Obstet Gynecol* 1999; **42**: 276–289.

Naegele F, O'Connor H, Davies A, Badaway A, Mohamed H, Magos A. 2500 Outpatient diagnostic hysteroscopies. *Obstet Gynecol* 1996; **88**: 87–92.

Kremer C, Barik S, Duffy S. Flexible outpatient hysteroscopy without anaesthesia: a safe, successful and well tolerated procedure. *Br J Obstet Gynaecol* 1998; **105**: 672–676.

Valli E, Zupi E, Marconi D, Solima E, Nagar G, Romanini C. Outpatient diagnostic hysteroscopy. *J Am Assoc Gynecol Laparosc* 1998; **5**: 397–402.

Marty R. Diagnostic fibrohysteroscopic evaluation of perimenopausal and postmenopausal uterine bleeding: a comparative study with Belgian and Japanese data. *J Am Assoc Gynecol Laparosc* 1998; **5**: 69–73.

Diagnostic outpatient hysteroscopy service: semi-rigid hysteroscopy

P. J. O'Donovan and Kalaish Nakade

> **Take Home Message**
> Office hysteroscopy with semi-rigid hysteroscopes can be undertaken in a short period of time with minimal morbidity and inconvenience to the patients. The procedures are best carried out in the proliferative phase of the cycle. At present the indications are diagnostic. Newer technologies could allow a limited number of operative procedures.

INTRODUCTION

Since Pantaleoni [1] performed the first hysteroscopy in 1869, many advances have been made in this field. During the last quarter of a century hysteroscopy has become a gold standard for evaluating the uterine cavity. It has replaced blind dilatation and curettage as one of the important investigations in the management of abnormal uterine bleeding [2]. Over the past decade technological advances have led to the development of small caliber hysteroscopes that are <5 mm in outer diameter. This has made it possible to perform hysteroscopy in the office setting with or without the administration of a local anesthetic agent. Office hysteroscopy has many advantages over conventional in-patient procedures. Not only does it reduce the cost for health-care providers, it is also beneficial to patients in terms of recovery and avoidance of risks of general anesthesia. The time taken for the procedure is less than conventional hysteroscopy, as cervical dilatation is not necessary owing to the small diameter of the hysteroscope.

INDICATIONS AND CONTRAINDICATIONS

Indications for outpatient hysteroscopy are similar to conventional hysteroscopy (Table 1). With the use of new micro instruments, and bipolar microelectrodes that work in saline [3], operative procedures are increasingly moved into outpatient settings. The most common indications are abnormal uterine bleeding including menorrhagia, postmenopausal bleeding, and abnormal bleeding while on hormone replacement therapy.

Absolute contraindications to office hysteroscopy are few and similar to conventional in-patient hysteroscopy (Table 1). It is better to avoid hysteroscopy if there is active cervicitis or vaginitis. Chronic pelvic inflammatory disease is a relative contraindication. Active bleeding from the uterus is a relative contraindication as it may obscure the view of the uterine cavity; it is better to delay office hysteroscopy until the bleeding has settled. It is recommended that the surgeon attend a suitable training course, as insertion of micro-hysteroscopes requires less force than conventional hysteroscopes. Any excess force

Table 1
Indications and contraindications for office hysteroscopy

Diagnostic indications	Therapeutic indications	Absolute contraindications	Relative contraindications
Abnormal uterine bleeding	Polypectomy	Active pelvic inflammatory disease	Active uterine bleeding
Directed biopsy	Removal of IUCD	No consent	Chronic pelvic inflammatory disease
Confirmation or location of intrauterine polyps or fibroids	Adhesiolysis	Known genital tract malignancy	Uncooperative patient
	Sterilization		
Before endometrial ablation		Pregnancy	

during insertion may result in a false passage or perforation.

SET UP

It is necessary to have a sufficiently large room to accommodate the surgeon, equipment, and two or three assistants including a nurse. There should be access to oxygen and a resuscitation trolley. A separate room for counseling and recovery is preferable. A suggested lay out of the operating room is shown in Figure 1.

INSTRUMENTS

outpatient hysteroscopy can be performed with a minimal amount of equipment, which should include a hysteroscope, a fiberoptic cable, and a light source. However, it is preferable to have a camera, high resolution monitor, video recorder, and printer. Ideally all this equipment should be mounted on a video trolley.

HYSTEROSCOPE

We use a 1.2-mm semi-rigid micro-hysteroscope with a 2.5-mm sheath (Figures 2 and 3). New terminology has been proposed for these small telescopes [3]. Hysteroscopes with 2–5 mm diameter are called 'mini' hysteroscopes. Micro-hysteroscopy is the term used when the diameter of the outer sheath is 2 mm or less (Table 2). Micro-endoscopes have fiberoptic flexible bundles for image collection rather than the rod lens system used in rigid endoscopes. These small hysteroscopes usually do not need cervical dilatation. The semi-rigid fiberoptic hysteroscopes are more durable and user-friendly, with superior light transmission compared with similar diameter rod lens telescopes [3]. However, extra care is necessary when handling these fine telescopes. Currently, most of them are not autoclavable and a sterilizing solution such as Nu Cidex is required. It is preferable to use saline rather than CO_2 for uterine distension, as mild contamination of the lens by blood or mucus reduces picture quality. Advances in technology have allowed the recent development of rod lens hysteroscopes with diameters of <2 mm. These new generation instruments can be autoclaved; however, further studies are required to determine how these will perform over long periods of time.

DISTENSION MEDIUM

We use normal saline for uterine distension, which flows with gravity from a bag hung on a stand. A 60-ml syringe can also be used. This is an isotonic, nonviscous solution and gives a clear view of the cervical canal and uterine cavity. Use of nonviscous medium like saline does not

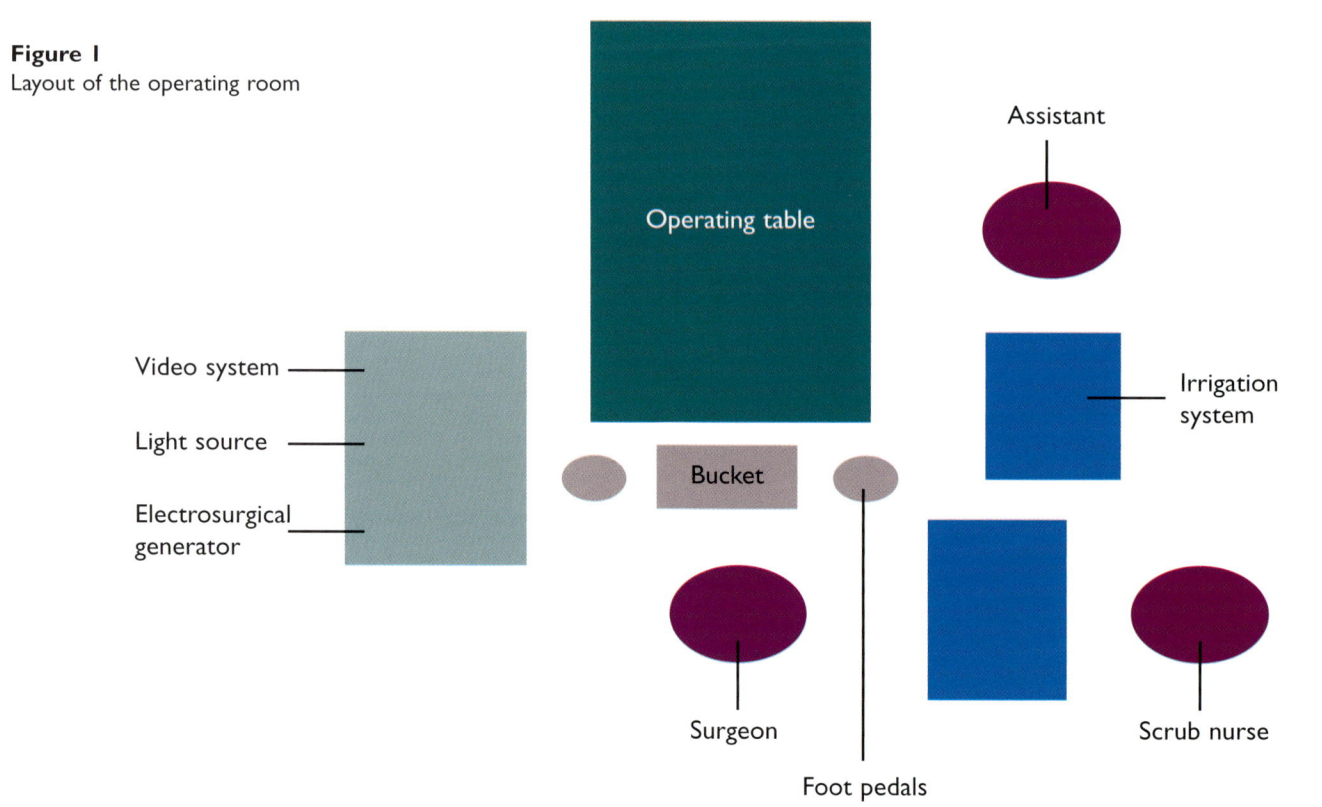

Figure 1
Layout of the operating room

flatten the endometrium and does not create mucous bubbles or foaming. It is advisable to perform the procedure in the early proliferative phase, as it is easy to pick up pathology, whereas in the late proliferative phase the endometrial lining absorbs the solution and this makes it difficult to identify lesions such as endometrial polyps [4]. In certain countries the use of a hysteromat is mandatory, especially in operative hysteroscopy.

Alternatively CO_2 can be used. It is easy to use and safe when used with proper insufflation apparatus [5]. The recommended flow of CO_2 is 100 ml/minute and maximum intrauterine pressure is 200 mmHg. However, for adequate visualization, a flow rate of 40–60 ml/minute and a pressure of 40–80 mmHg are enough. The advantages of CO_2 are that it is readily available, does not clog up surgical instruments, and is well tolerated under local anesthesia. Other distending media such as Dextran 70 and glycine are rarely used for office hysteroscopy.

LIGHT SOURCE AND VIDEO CAMERA

A 150-W cold light source is sufficient; however, a 175-W xenon light source gives good depth of field. A video camera monitor is an advantage as it allows participation and education of the nursing staff and the patient herself. It may be preferable to use a camera with zoom facility, as the image obtained with micro-hysteroscopy is small. A single-chip camera is sufficient for diagnostic purposes. Also an electrically powered chair/table allows easier patient maneuverability.

PERSONNEL

The outpatient hysteroscopy team consists of a surgeon, a nurse facilitator, and a nursing assistant. It is important that the surgeon performing the procedure has had proper training in outpatient hysteroscopy, as this will reduce the complication rates and also the number of failed procedures. The role of the nurse facilitator is very important. Her work involves liaising with hospital and community trusts, acting as a contact person and providing a link between general practitioners (GPs), hospital-based services, and the patients. The nurse facilitator acts as a named nurse for patients. It is advisable that this person has some theater background and also has counseling skills, teaching qualifications, and community awareness skills [6].

PROCEDURE

On arrival in the department the nurse facilitator welcomes the woman. The woman is usually well prepared by pre-hysteroscopy counseling by her GP or the practice nurse. Diazepam 5 mg and mefenamic acid 500 mg are offered, to be taken 1 hour before the procedure. Time is spent with the nurse facilitator, checking the woman's record booklet, providing reassurance, and answering any questions. It has been shown that counseling and information can help preparation and improve recovery [7]. The surgeon then obtains consent. The woman is allowed to have a friend or relative with her throughout the procedure.

With the patient placed in dorsal lithotomy position and after pelvic examination, the vulva and vagina are cleansed with an antiseptic solution. The procedure itself requires minimal manipulation and usually no cervical dilatation is

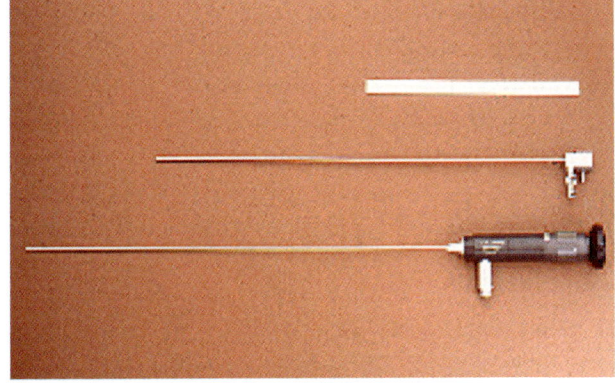

Figure 2
Semi-rigid microhysteroscope (1.2 mm) and outer sheath (2.5 mm).

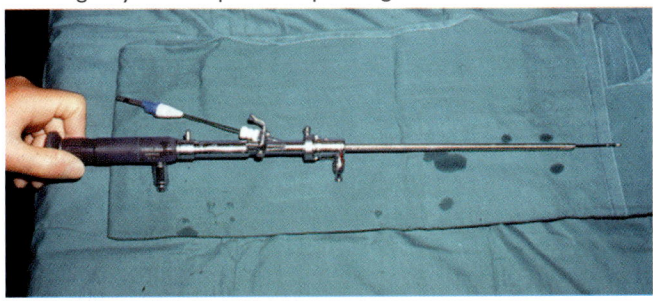

Figure 3
Semi-rigid hysteroscope with operating channel.

Table 2
Classification of endoscopes

Outer sheath diameter (mm)	Endoscope classification
>5	Conventional
2–5	Mini
<2	Micro

required when a scope <4 mm in diameter is used. The endoscope is introduced under direct vision through the endocervical canal. If the endoscope cannot be passed easily and cervical dilation is required, a paracervical block with local anesthetic can be performed. A small dot of anesthetic can be placed at the anterior cervical lip where a tenaculum can be placed. The image is observed on the video monitor. The cervical canal and the whole of the uterine cavity are examined in a systematic fashion. At the end of the procedure the hysteroscope is withdrawn gently, observing the endocervical canal. Endometrial biopsy is then carried out if required.

After the procedure, the woman is able to relax in a comfortable room with a drink. In this relaxing environment, results and recommended treatment and advice are discussed and explanatory leaflets are given. A care plan devised by the clinic nurses is completed to document nursing care throughout the woman's attendance. If in-patient hysteroscopy is required the necessary arrangements are made.

ANESTHESIA

No anesthesia/analgesia is required for most patients undergoing office hysteroscopy [8]. Nonsteroidal anti-inflammatory drugs can be given for mild cramps, which may occasionally accompany the procedure. One study reported that 65% of patients reported that intracervical injection of the local anesthetic was more painful than hysteroscopic examination of the uterus itself [2]. Another study reported that the routine use of a paracervical block for outpatient hysteroscopy in premenopausal women had no advantage [9].

SUCCESS AND FAILURE RATES

The procedure is simple and can be completed in most women. In a series of 2500 diagnostic hysteroscopies with 4-mm hysteroscopes, the procedure was successfully completed in 96% of patients and a complete view of the uterine cavity was obtained in 89% [10]. A series of 1976 patients undergoing outpatient hysteroscopy with a 1.2-mm semi-rigid micro-hysteroscope showed a similar success rate (96.1%). The common causes of failure included cervical stenosis (67.9%), severe discomfort (8.9%), large cervical polyp (5.1%), and vagal reaction (2.6%) [11]. A satisfaction survey of outpatient micro-hysteroscopy revealed a 98% approval rating from patients [12].

OPERATIVE OUTPATIENT MICRO-HYSTEROSCOPY

With the advent of newer smaller instruments it is possible to perform simple procedures such as polypectomy by outpatient hysteroscopy. However, owing to the small image any bleeding encountered during surgery may obscure the field of vision. The use of hysteroscopes with sheaths with a continuous flow channel can solve this problem. Bipolar microelectrodes that work in a saline medium could reduce the need for subsequent in-patient operative hysteroscopy [13,14] (Figure 4).

TRAINING IN OUTPATIENT HYSTEROSCOPY

It is important that the person performing outpatient hysteroscopy is properly trained in the technique, to minimize the complications and failure rates. In the UK, there are recognized training courses in hysteroscopic surgery, which have Royal College approval. A survey of training in minimal access surgery in the West Midlands region in the UK supports the strong link between supervision of appropriate training and complications in minimal access surgery. It stresses the crucial role of the supervisor and the need for formal training [15]. Of the trainees, 26% encountered hysteroscopic complications in their total experience. In general rigid or semi-rigid hysteroscopes are easier to insert and have a shorter learning curve than flexible hysteroscopes.

Figure 4
Bipolar electrodes:

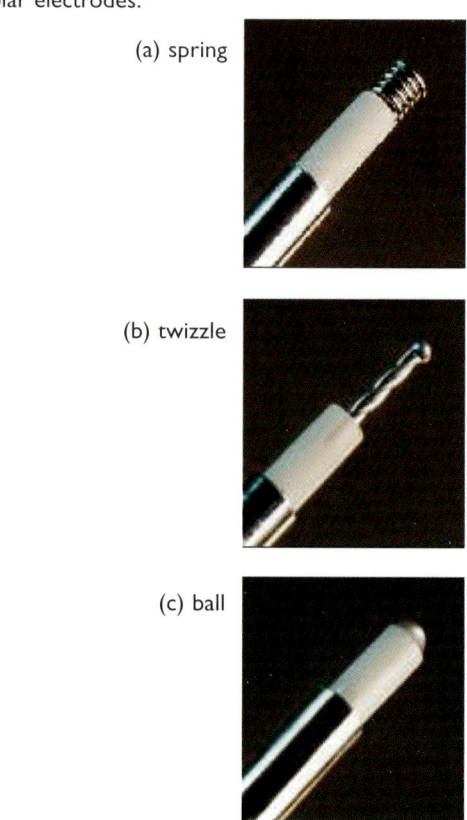

(a) spring

(b) twizzle

(c) ball

SUMMARY

Small caliber endoscopes have it made possible to carry out hysteroscopy in an outpatient setting. As it is simple and easy to use, it has become a 'gold standard' as a screening method for patients with abnormal uterine bleeding. Office hysteroscopy can be undertaken in a short period of time with minimal morbidity and inconvenience for patients. To minimize failure rates it is important to select patients appropriately and to carry out the procedure in the early proliferative phase of the cycle. Outpatient hysteroscopy with semi-rigid micro-hysteroscopes may be better suited to a subgroup of patients where no prior cervical dilation is required such as postmenopausal and nulliparous women. Although at present the main indications for this procedure are diagnostic, with the development of newer technologies such as bipolar microelectrodes it may be possible to perform a limited number of operative hysteroscopic procedures in the outpatient setting.

REFERENCES

1. Pantaleoni DC. On endoscopic examination of the cavity of the womb. *Med Press Circ* 1869; **8**: 26–27.
2. Downes E. Goodbye D & C welcome hysteroscopy. *Br J Hosp Med* 1992; **48**: 75–77.
3. O'Donovan PJ, Gupta JK. Microendoscopy in gynaecology. In: O'Donovan P, Downes E, eds. Recent advances in gynaecological surgery. London: Greenwich Medical Media, 2002: 3–12.
4. Porter MB, Brumsted JR. Office hysteroscopy: complications and management. In: Issacson KB, ed. Office hysteroscopy. Mosby: St Louis, 1996: 45–53.
5. Lindeman HJ, Mohr J. CO_2 hysteroscopy: diagnosis and treatment. *Am J Obstet Gynecol* 1976; **124**: 129–133.
6. Quinn P, Ludkin H. Developing a direct access outpatient hysteroscopy service. *Nursing Standard* 1996; **10**: 40–42.
7. Walsh M. Pain and anxiety in A&E attenders. *Nursing Standard* 1993; **7**: 40–42.
8. Wamsteker K. Office hysteroscopy: complications and management. In: Issacson KB, ed. Office hysteroscopy. Mosby: St Louis, 1996.
9. Vercellini P, Colombo A, Mauro F, Oldeni S, Bramate T, Crosignani PG. Paracervical anaesthesia for outpatient hysteroscopy. *Fertil Steril* 1994; **62**: 1083–1085.
10. Nagele F, O'Connor H, Davies A, Badawy A, Mohamed H, Magos AL. 2500 outpatient diagnostic hysteroscopies. *Obstet Gynecol* 1996; **88**: 87–92.
11. Salah O, Okeahialam M, Jones S, O'Donovan PJ. Outpatient microhysteroscopy: why does it fail? *Gynaecol Endosc* 2001; **10**: 167–171.
12. O'Donovan PJ, Jones SE, Quinn P, Ludkin H. What is the place of outpatient microhysteroscopy in the management of abnormal vaginal bleeding? Experience with 1000 patients using a 1.2 mm semi-rigid hysteroscope. *Gynaecol Endosc* 1997; **6** (Suppl): 226 (Abstract)
13. O'Donovan PJ, Jones SE. Versapoint: operative microhysteroscopy using bipolar electrosurgery in a saline medium. *Gynaecol Endosc* 1997; **6** (Suppl): 73 (Abstract).
14. Vleugles MPH. First clinical results with the new bipolar electrosurgical device versapoint in hysteroscopic surgery. *Gynaecol Endosc* 1997; **6** (Suppl): 74 (Abstract).
15. Chin K, Newton J. Survey of training in minimal access surgery in the West Midland Region of the UK. *Gynaecol Endosc* 1996; **5**: 329–333.

3a Outline of a flexible hysteroscope outpatient service

René Marty

> **Take Home Message**
> Over the last decade flexible hysteroscopes have improved considerably. They can be used without anesthesia in an office setting. The best time to perform diagnostic procedures is the follicular phase. Biopsies can be performed during the same session and with the same scope. Patient compliance is very high, in a series of 35,289 procedures cervical dilatation was needed in only 11% of the patients when fiberscopes of more than 3mm outer diameter were used. There is a tendency to switch to the 3-mm mini flexible hysteroscopes.

INTRODUCTION

Continuing improvements in hysteroscopic techniques enable the physician to work on an outpatient basis. This is possible because of the miniaturization of endoscopes. The practice of office procedures without anesthesia requires the choice of the smallest possible hysteroscope to avoid discomfort for the patient and so that the lowest possible rate of cervical dilatation is employed.

To avoid a painful progression of the tip, it is quite logical to prefer a flexible instrument rather than a rigid one, as it is possible to adapt the hysteroscope precisely to each individual's anatomy for a smooth cervical progression, avoiding endometrial damage and bleeding.

The flexible endoscope gives the possibility of placing the tip of the endoscope in the ideal position to perform a targeted endometrial biopsy, ignoring the difficult areas increases the reliability of the approach.

HISTORICAL ASPECTS

In 1968, Mohri and Yamadori (Japan) contributed to the first publication on a fiberscope [1]. In 1970, Aguëro and colleagues (Mexico) used cold light hysteroscopy with a small balloon and, in 1970, Edström and Ferstöm (Sweden) used cold light hysteroscopy. In 1971, Porto and Gaujoux carried out pneumohysteroscopy with CO_2.

We started the practice of hysteroscopy with a rigid endoscope (Storz) with a sheath of 3 mm diameter and a telescope of 2.3 mm [2]. Then, we discovered the multiple advantages of flexible hysteroscopes and started the exclusive use of fibrohysteroscopes. Our first publication [3] was produced during the First World Congress on Obstetrics and Gynecological Endoscopy and Related Ultrasonography and Imaging in Florence, May 1986. Then we successively evaluated various fiberscopes [4–6].

The first rigid endoscope uterine examination was performed 132 years ago and the first fibrohysteroscope examination was performed 37 years ago. This means that it took 94 years to switch from rigid to flexible hysteroscopy.

The milestones of the development of fibrohysteroscopy are: the replacement of the lenses by optic fibers, the invention of the cold light source, and the use of normal saline instead of CO_2 as a distension medium.

Finally, continuing improvements in optic fibers have made it possible to reduce the diameter of the fibrohysteroscope, to 3 mm, and to obtain superior resolution and brightness of the image.

GENERAL CONSIDERATIONS ON THE OUTPATIENT TECHNIQUE

The mini-fibrohysteroscope enables the physician to work easily on an outpatient basis without anesthesia and with a very low rate of failure to insert: less than 5% with conventional fiberscopes and less than 2% with the 3-mm fiberscope [7].

The technique is specific and differs from the technique employed with a conventional rigid hysteroscope. A tenaculum is rarely needed to hold the cervix. Dilatation of the cervical canal is very rarely employed and, unlike the procedure with rigid hysteroscopes, patients do not require the use of prostaglandin or premedication [8].

To facilitate the observation, the best period is the follicular phase, because the endometrium is thin [9]. Before the procedure, the patient is given a small manual containing a basic explanation. We briefly show and describe the instrumentation used for the procedure: cold light source, camera, mini-fibrohysteroscope, and ancillary instrumentation.

OUR PREFERRED EQUIPMENT FOR OFFICE FIBROHYSTEROSCOPY

Flexible hysteroscopes are manufactured by various companies: Storz, Leisegang, Wolf, Circon, Fujinon, Olympus, and others.

THE FIBERSCOPE

We have chosen the Olympus HYF-XP model for many reasons:

- *The caliber is 3 mm*. This is ultra-slim, allowing a very low rate of cervical dilatation. (<2%).
- *100° field of vision.* Very convenient to observe the two tubal ostia from the isthmus simultaneously, mandatory for orientation during the panoramic view.
- *100° active deflection.* This is the most appropriate angulation to face all the anatomic distinctive features.
- *1.2-mm operating channel.* It is inconceivable that histological confirmation of the visual diagnosis cannot be made. This channel admits all the 3 Fr flexible ancillary instrumentation to perform a directed cytobrushing, a targeted endometrial biopsy, or cannulation of the tubes with a Katayama catheter.
- *In addition*, the HYF-XP (like all Olympus endoscopes) is equipped with a deflection brake. The use of this brake is very helpful to stiffen the tip during a difficult introduction. It allows the gynecologist to maintain the suitable correct position of the tip easily before introducing the flexible biopsy forceps. It makes it possible to freeze the optimal position of the tip before the introduction of the catheter for tubal cannulation.

CAMERA

We use a digital camera: the Olympus OTV S6. The definition is 470,000 pixels and the sensivity is 1 lux at a quarter opening.

COLD LIGHT SOURCE

The cold light source is from Olympus, equipped with a 300 W xenon light.

MONITOR

ESSENTIAL EQUIPMENT

This is listed in Table 1. All the instrumentation must be flexible and must be 3 Fr in size. We do not use a CO_2 insufflator.

GUIDELINES FOR THE PROCEDURE

- The triangle mark in the eyepiece of the hysteroscope must be placed at 0° before the onset of the procedure. This triangle allows the operator to know where the tip is oriented.
- The normal saline is connected to the stopcock of the fiberscope and the operator must check that all the bubbles are flushed out of the tubing.
- Then, the tip of the fiberscope is placed close to the external cervical os and introduced slowly.

Table 1
Essential instrumentation

Minifibrohysteroscopes	HYF-XP	3-mm
Ancillary instrumentation (outer diameter 3 Fr)	Selection of biopsy forceps with various types of jaws: lasso forceps, basket forceps, Katayama 3 Fr catheter, Versapoint	Cytobrush, rat tooth, mouse tooth, alligator
Xenon light source	300 W	
Camera		
Isotonic saline	Bag (with appropriate tubing); distension by gravity ≤1.5 m above the patient	
Optional	Tenaculum	

The procedure is divided into three stages, as described below.

STAGE ONE: PROGRESSION INSIDE THE CERVICAL CANAL

The opening of the virtual cervical cavity is done by the distending medium. The normal saline creates and opens a space that can be used for progression of the hysteroscope. This progression must be done slowly and the operator must keep the hysteroscope in the middle of the cervical canal, avoiding contact with the walls: this allows a painless progression without bleeding. Because of the frontal view of the fiberscope and its softness, the operator avoids causing cervical laceration. There is no risk of perforation. Progress to the internal cervical os is made by snaking the hysteroscope through the cervical canal.

During this first step, a careful exploration of the canal is easy, looking for a pathological aspect of the endometrium. Judicious use of the flexible tip makes it easy to adjust the shape of the hysteroscope to each individual anatomy [10].

Technical hitches and solutions
Insertion of the fiberscope is impossible:
- Timid patients: the only way to deal with this is to perform a paracervical block
- Cervical external os measuring <3 mm: stiffen the tip using the brake and try again
- If failure: sound with a plastic sound and dilate slowly up to 3 mm
- If failure: place a laminaria – in such a case, the patient must be hospitalized for 1 day.

Difficult cervical progression:
- Stenotic cervical canal: stiffen the tip (using the brake)
  – wait a little while after each small progression
  – always remain in the middle of the canal.
- Winding or angled cervical canal: adjust the bending tip during the progression and progress very slowly to adapt the shape of the hysteroscope to the individual anatomy
  – always remain in the middle of the canal.
- Synechia or polyp: this requires a meticulous third stage to complete the evaluation.

STAGE TWO: EVALUATION OF THE UTERINE CAVITY

When the tip of the hysteroscope is at the level of the internal cervical os, it is generally possible to visualize the entire uterine cavity. A global panoramic view of the cavity is mandatory before initiating the exploration (Figure 1).

First panoramic global evaluation
The clinician must locate the two tubal ostia, observe the general shape of the cavity, and look for the presence of any abnormal growth and/or a global or partial distorsion of the uterine walls [11]. The uterine cavity has an arcuate shape and the walls and the surfaces of all the lateral portions are concave. The two horns are clearly visible and sometimes one or both tubal ostia are not identified when the uterine cavity is greatly enlarged or distorted by a myoma. In such circumstances, the endoscopist must insert the fiberscope further in the fundus to identify the ostia.

Close evaluation of each different area
The fundus, anterior and posterior walls, lateral portions of the cornual area, and tubal ostia are explored and, at the end, the lower uterine portion. This exploration is made very easy by using all the potential of the fiberscope to observe any suspicious endometrial area in the entire uterine cavity.

A pathological growth is found or a suspect endometrial area is observed
Then, a directed cytology and/or a targeted endometrial biopsy must be performed in the selected area. With the fiberscope, it is very easy to pass over a pathological growth or a synechia. In every patient, the full endometrial cavity may be explored and faced, utilizing the bending capacity

Figure 1
View of the cavity from the isthmus.

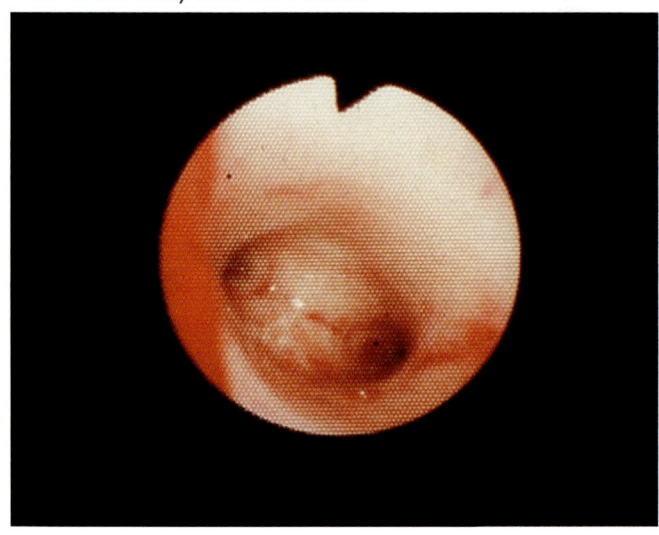

of the tip. An accurate description of the pathology must be reported to the pathologist, accompanied by a sketch.

Tubal ostia
The fiberscope allows a minute and close evaluation of each tubal ostium in all cases (Figure 2). This observation is of major importance in patients treated for infertility. Hysteroscopic tubal cannulation is an excellent method of selecting those patients who may benefit from microsurgery. This cannulation is performed with a 3 Fr Katayama catheter [12].

Technical hitches and solutions
Inadequate panoramic view:
- Presence of mucus, debris, clots or tissue: wash and drain the cavity

Difficult or poor visibility:
- Inadequate visibility: refer to the chapter on 'Distension media'
- One or both tubal ostia not visualized: pull back the fiberscope and look for the existence of a septum, synechia or large myoma, try to bypass the obstacle by moving the flexible tip.

STAGE THREE: WITHDRAWAL OF THE FIBERSCOPE

This is also an important step. The tip is moved from the internal cervical os to the external os and this is an opportunity to discover a missed pathology. During stage one, if the progression is too fast or the tip too close to the cervical wall, it is possible to miss a pathological area. Sometimes, the endoscopist starts the observation only at the internal cervical os.

Missed pathology is always caused by faulty technique. If the progression of the hysteroscope is too fast, a small focal endometrial lesion or a tiny polyp may be overlooked. An anomaly may be missed when the endoscopist begins to observe only when the tip has already arrived at the internal cervical os. This stage is also very important to confirm any deviation of the cervical canal, this information is very important to facilitate a future embryo transfer.

Technical hitches and solutions: the image on the screen
- Red or hazy
  - the tip is on the fundus or a uterine wall: pull back the hysteroscope
  - the tip is pressing on a pathological growth: withdraw the hysteroscope
  - blood or debris on the lens: pull out the fiberscope and wipe and the lens clean.
- White or dazzling
  - the tip is too close to the endometrium: withdraw the hysteroscope and change the approach.

END OF THE PROCEDURE

It is very useful to complete a detailed sheet regarding the hysteroscopic procedure. A drawing must be made if a pathological lesion has been discovered. The area chosen for a targeted endometrial biopsy must be reported. A copy of this sheet must be sent to a pathologist with the tissue sample.

The patient may leave the office 15 minutes after the procedure.

MANAGEMENT OF THE NORMAL SALINE INFUSION

We always use normal saline 0.9% for the distension of the uterine cavity, using gravity. This low viscosity fluid is readily available all over the world and is cheap. It requires appropriate IV tubing for connection to the stopcock of the fibrohysteroscope. Patients' tolerance is better than that for CO_2 distension [13,14]. The saline solution allows the cavity to be washed when there is spotting or clots, provides clear visualization, and does not create bubbles.

If a polypectomy is required during the office evaluation, normal saline is appropriate for the use of a Versapoint® electrode [15,16].

The plastic bag must be placed 1.5 m above the patient and the endoscopist must check that all the bubbles are flushed out of the tubing. The stopcock may be closed when the appropriate uterine distension is obtained. Because of

Figure 2
View close to the tubal ostium.

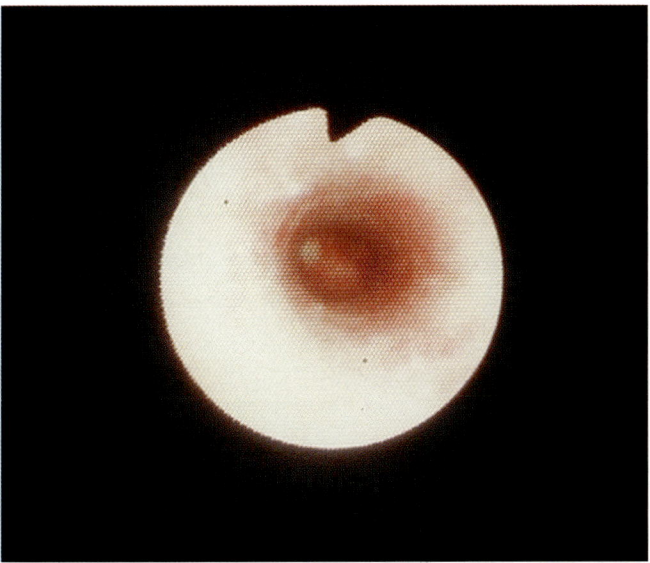

the slight leakage of the normal saline around the hysteroscope, the pressure is always optimal, avoiding the problem of a dangerous overload. This system works as well as continuous flow rigid diagnostic hysteroscopy.

Observation of the endometrial lining is optimized because liquid distension allows small polyps to float and does not flatten the endometrium and, because the endometrium is floating free in the liquid distension, it facilitates the discovery of small pathological areas.

Technical hitches and solutions
No distension:
- Absence of intrauterine pressure: check the tubing and the stopcock
- Insufficient distension: pressure is too low: check and open the stopcock
- Elevate the plastic bag slightly.

Inconstant distension:
- The input flow is less than the leakage – increase the input flow.

LOW PRESSURE TEST SCREENING

We have developed this procedure and suggest that it is used at the end of stage two. An accurate visualization of the uterine cavity depends on the appropriate intrauterine pressure and the appearance of the cavity varies with its dilatation. After panoramic observation, at the end of the stage two, observation must be done at a very low pressure. This is very useful, before the withdrawal of the fiberscope, if a myoma is suspected or when a suspicious endometrial area has been detected during the procedure.

The triple advantage of a very low pressure is:
- The color, undulation, and projections of the endometrial lining are more visible
- The vascular pattern is easier to evaluate
- A rupture of the shape or a rigidity is detected more clearly (submucus myoma or interstitial eventually). In such a case, the gynecologist must ask for sonography and a sonographic examination to check the suspect area detected by the low pressure test.

APPEARANCE OF THE ENDOMETRIAL LINING DURING THE CYCLE

The cyclic appearance of the endometrium may be divided into five stages: regenerative, midproliferative, midcycle, secretory, and involutional. The endoscopist must observe various parameters: undulations and folds, glandular ostia, color, and blood vessels. The endometrial thickness must be appreciated [17]. A good description of the cyclic changes of the endometrium has been provided by Sugimoto [18].

The visual impression gained during the hysteroscopic procedure allows the experienced endoscopist to anticipate the histological dating. We recently published a serie of 225 cases in which there was good correlation between the visual appearance and the results of the biopsy – 58.9% [19]. Postmenopausal endometrial appearance shows a very thin flat smooth endometrial lining.

SPECIAL CASES
POST-CERVICAL SURGERY
This may occur after a local treatment, such as cervical conization, cryotherapy, ultrasound, electrotherapy or laser therapy. The gynecologist must sound carefully and evaluate the external cervical os and the cervical canal with a plastic canal or a rubber probe. A cervical dilatation up to 3 mm could possibly be performed before the endoscopy. If the dilatation is a failure, the only way is to place a laminaria, in such a case, another day hospitalization is necessary.

NULLIPAROUS PATIENTS
We advise sounding at least the external cervical os and, if possible, the first centimeter of the cervical canal. If this fails, the clinician must try to dilate up to 3 mm.

POSTMENOPAUSAL PATIENTS
These patients may have severe cervical atrophy. We suggest exploring the external cervical os and the first centimeter of the cervical canal. If this fails, the patient must receive a preoperative treatment – vaginal oestrogen pellets for 3 weeks before the hysteroscopy [20]. If a 3-mm dilatation of the external cervical os cannot be reached, it will be necessary to perform a cervical dilatation.

PATIENTS WITH SPOTTING OR MODERATE METRORRHAGIA
Irrigation with normal saline will drain and clear the view before initiating the evaluation.

PATIENTS RECEIVING TAMOXIFEN TREATMENT
Most of these patients are postmenopausal. A careful evaluation of the cervix must be made before endoscopy is carried out. In these patients, the detection of an endometrial pathology is mandatory before initiating the treatment and also during follow-up. In our University Hospital, we have included the practice of hysteroscopy in our pretreatment checking. We prefer hysteroscopy to sonography, because the direct view allows a better observation and may show abnormal vascular patterns or

small areas of modified coloration of the endometrium. Of course, targeted endometrial biopsy is recommended to confirm the visual diagnosis [21] (Figure 3).

SYMPTOMATIC PATIENTS RECEIVING HORMONAL REPLACEMENT THERAPY

It is very useful, and often indicated, in patients suffering from spotting or metrorrhagia, to evaluate the endometrium and a targeted endometrial biopsy during the procedure is also mandatory to evaluate the endometrial response and to adjust the hormonal therapy to each individual [22]. If the patient receives a sequential treatment, the first part of the cycle must be chosen, to avoid the thickened endometrium in the second phase (Figure 3).

IVF PROTOCOL

Infertility is the second indication for hysteroscopy after abnormal uterine bleeding. Because the failure rate of embryo transfer is the stage of the in vitro fertilization procedure that has the highest failure rate, hysteroscopic evaluation and re-evaluation are valuable with a failed IVF [23].

It is mandatory to detect any endometrial and structural abnormalities so as to decrease the rate of embryo transfer failure. Systematic evaluation of the uterine cavity is generally scheduled during the first assessment of the patient.

EMBRYO TRANSFER

Sometimes transfer is not possible because the cannula containing the embryo cannot clear the cervical canal if it is very angled or tortuous. For these selected cases, we introduce the cannula into the operating channel of the fiberscope to clear the cervical canal and stop the progression of the tip as soon as the internal cervical os is reached. The reliability of this procedure requires confirmation by some selected cases in the future.

CONCLUSION

During the last decade, considerable improvements have been made as regards flexible hysteroscopes: for many years, we have worked successfully with the HYF-P 3.6 mm, but now the new fibro-mini-hysteroscope HYF-XP 3 mm (Figure 4) seems to be the most suitable endoscope for an ambulatory procedure without anesthesia in an office setting. [We must point out that the National French Survey did not include the 3-mm fibroscope (see Chapter 17b).]

The procedure is simple, safe, and permits an accurate diagnosis that can always be correlated with histology. In addition, the experienced endoscopist may also perform minor operative procedures under normal saline uterine distension using the bi-electrode technique [24]. The rate of impossible insertion is very low and patients' tolerance is good.

Figure 3
Flow chart for review of patients under treatment.

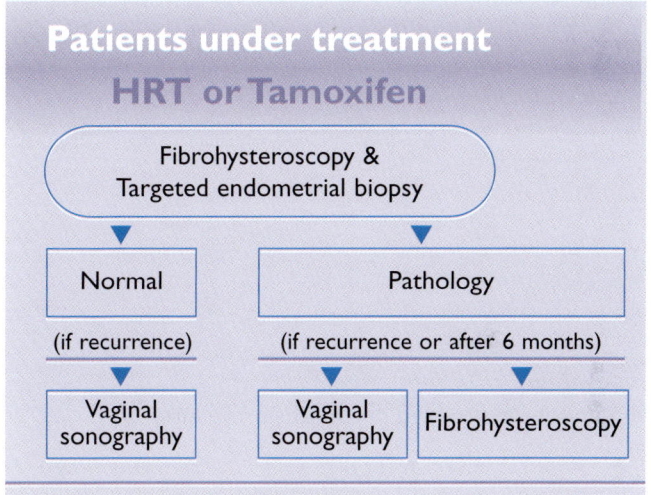

Figure 4
The practical benefits of the recent technical improvements.

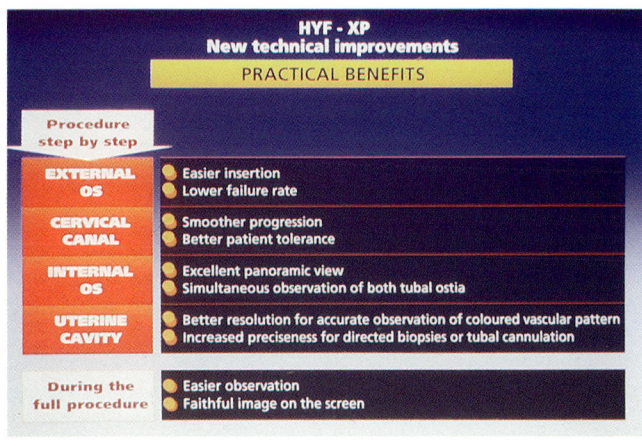

REFERENCES

1. Mohri C, Yamadori F. Problem of observing the human ovum descending in the fallopian tube by a tubaloscope. In: Mohri T, Mohri C, eds. Our 25 Years Experience with Endoscope. Philadelphia: Lippincott, 1968.
2. Marty R. Carbon dioxide hysteroscopy without anesthesia in 478 patients. In: Lindemann HJ, ed. Hysteroscopy Principles and Practice. Philadelphia: Lippincott, 1984: 48–50.
3. Marty R et al. One year of diagnostic and operative experience with the flexible hysteroscope. First World Congress on Obstetrics and Gynecological Endoscopy and Related Ultrasonography and Imaging, Florence, May. Philadelphia: Lippincott, 1986.
4. Marty R. A propos de la fibrohystéroscopis souple et operatoire. *Contracept Fertil Sex V* 1987; **15**: 593.
5. Marty R. Experience with a new flexible hysteroscope. *Int J Gynaecol Obstet* 1988; **27**: 97–99.
6. Marty R. Présentation d'un hystéroscope de la troisième génération: le Fujinon flexible system 2000. *Congrès de la Fédération des Gynécologues Obstétriciens Français* 1988; **17**: 54.
7. Marty R. Technique de l'hystéroscopie souple de consultation. Série de 1000 cas. *La Revue du Praticien* 1997; **2**: 24.
8. Loffer FD. Techniques for diagnostic rigid hysteroscopy. In: Isaacson KB, ed. Office Hysteroscopy. St Louis: Mosby Year Book, 1996: 55–56.
9. Valle RF. A Manual of Clinical Hysteroscopy. New York: Parthenon Publishing, 1998: 50.
10. Marty R. Fibrohysteroscopie au cabinet médical (8 ans de pratique). *Gynecologie Obstétrique Pratique* 1995; **7**: 13–14.
11. Blanc B, Boubli L. Endoscopie Utérine. Paris: Editions Pradel, 1996: 21.
12. Valle RF. A Manual of Clinical Hysteroscopy. New York: Parthenon Publishing, 1998: 72.
13. Goldfarb HA. Comparison of carbon dioxide with continuous flow technique for office hysteroscopy. *J Am Assoc Gynecol Laparosc* 1996; **3**: 571–574.
14. O'Connor H, Nagele F, Bournas N, Richardson R, Magos A. The effects of CO_2 and normal saline on pain and visualization during outpatient hysteroscopy. Selected scientific abstracts of the World Congress of Hysteroscopy. *J Am Assoc Gynecol Laparosc* 1996; 20–21.
15. Benzakine Y. Versapoint. Electrochirurgie bipolaire en milieu physiologique. *Endomag* 1998; 24: 12–13.
16. Kung RC, Vilos GA, Zaltz AP, Thomas B, Penkin P, Stabinsky SA. A new bipolar system for performing operative hysteroscopy in normal saline. *J Am Assoc Gynecol Laparosc* 1999; **6**: 331–336.
17. Marty R. Nine years of experience with flexible hysteroscopy. In: Isaacson KB, ed. Office Hysteroscopy. St Louis: Mosby Year Book, 1996: 61–62.
18. Sugimoto O. Diagnostic and Therapeutic Hysteroscopy. Tokyo: Igaku-Shoin, 1978: 39–49.
19. Marty R, Carbillon L, Karroumy ME, Cedrin I, Hugues JN. Diagnostic flexible minihysteroscopy and infertility. 10th Annual Congress of the International Society for Gynecologic Endoscopy, Chicago, 2001. Book of Abstracts TH2-4: 1.
20. Marty R, Valle RF. Eight years' experience performing procedures with flexible hysteroscopes. *J Am Assoc Gynecol Laparosc* 1995; **3**: 113–118.
21. Marty R. Technique d l'hysteroscopie soule de consultation. Série de 1000 cas. La Revue du Praticien. *Gynécologie et Obstétrique* 1997; **2**: 25.
22. Marty R. Diagnostic fibrohysteroscopic evaluation of perimenopausal and postmenopausal uterine bleeding: a comparative study with Belgian and Japanese data. *J Am Assoc Gynecol Laparosc* 1998; **5**: 69–73.
23. Dicker D, Ashkenazi J, Feldberg D, Fahri J, Ben Rafael Z. The value of repeat hysteroscopic evaluation in patients with failed in vitro fertilization transfer cycles. *Fertil Steril* 1992; **58**: 833–835.
24. Marty R. Flexible hysteroscopy for diagnostic and minor operative procedures (without anesthesia). In: Phillips JM, Brooks PJ, Bradley L, Cooper JM, eds. Diagnostic and Operative Hysteroscopy. Santa FE Springs, CA: AAGL Publications, 2001: 6–9.

Comparison of flexible hysteroscopes: theoretical and practical considerations

Boa-Liang Lin

> **Take Home Message**
> When various flexible scopes are compared there is no great difference in the quality of images. The recorded images are always smaller than those obtained by rigid hysteroscopes. When a continuous flow system is requested a hard outer sheath has to be added to the flexible scope; the system then acts as a rigid scope.

INTRODUCTION

As the cervical canal is narrow and curved, it is difficult to insert a hysteroscope (especially a rigid hysteroscope) into the uterine cavity to carry out an examination. Cervical dilatation and anesthesia are usually required. However, with a flexible hysteroscope, because the distal end is equipped with wire, the direction of the scope can be controlled. Also, because the more recent flexible hysteroscopes have a small caliber, hysteroscopic examination can be performed without using a tenaculum, cervical dilatation and analgesia, or anesthesia [1] (Figure 1).

MECHANICAL CONSTRUCTION [2]
FIBEROPTIC HYSTEROSCOPE

The heart of the flexible fiberoptic hysteroscope is the glass fiber bundle that transmits images from the objective lens at the distal end of the scope to the ocular lens in the eyepiece (Figures 2 and 3).

Figure 1
Comparison between scope insertion of (a) a flexible hysteroscope and (b) a rigid hysteroscope. The most important aspect of performing hysteroscopy is the insertion of a scope easily, safely, and atraumatically into the uterine cavity. With a flexible hysteroscope, because the soft section can be bent and the direction of the tip can be controlled, the scope can be introduced along the curved uterine cavity easily and safely; whereas a rigid scope – because of its straight and rigid structure – is difficult to insert. The possibility of causing a uterine perforation should be kept in mind when a rigid scope is used.

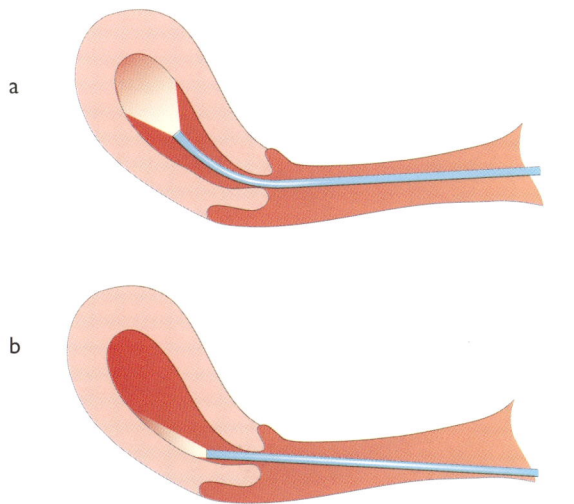

Figure 2
A basic fiberscope optical system. The objective lens at the tip of the fiberscope forms an image of the object that is transmitted through the image-guide fiber (IG) bundle and a duplicate image is formed on the proximal face of the bundle near the eyepiece. (1) object, (2) objective lens, (3) distal face of IG bundle, (4) IG bundle, (5) proximal face of IG bundle, (6) ocular lens.

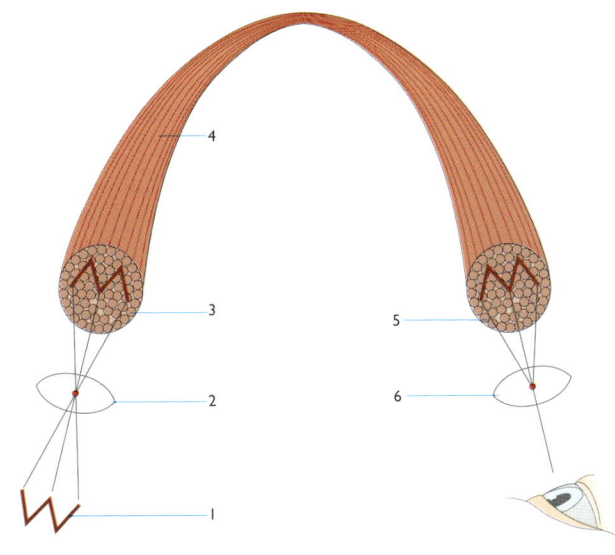

There are two types of optical fiber bundles. Image-guide fiber bundles (IG bundles) are for transmission of the image and light-guide fiber bundles (LG bundles) are for endoscopic illumination.

VIDEO HYSTEROSCOPE

The extremely small CCD (charge-coupled device) is manufactured to fit in the limited space at the distal tip of the endoscope. This CCD image sensor captures the image and transmits it electronically to a television monitor (Figure 3). The resolution of the image is excellent; there is no problem of broken IG bundles, which interfere with the image. A smaller caliber video hysteroscope is currently being developed.

FLEXIBLE HYSTEROSCOPE

The major parts and controls are as follows:
- Distal tip
- Bending section and angulation system
- Insertion tube
- Control section
- Universal cord and light guide connector.

INSTRUMENTATION
FLEXIBLE HYSTEROSCOPES

There are two kinds of flexible hysteroscope:

A. Flexible diagnostic hysteroscopes (Table 1)
- Olympus diagnostic flexible hysteroscope (outer diameter 3.1 mm). The scope can be changed into a continuous flow system or a rigid hysteroscope when equipped with a Lin outer sheath (Figure 4). Figure 5 shows an image obtained with this scope.
- Fujinon soft and rigid flexible diagnostic hysteroscope (outer diameter 3.7 mm) (Figure 6) [3]. Figures 7 and 8 show images obtained with this scope.
- Mochida cordless diagnostic flexible hysteroscope (outer diameter 3.5 mm) (Figure 9).
- Storz diagnostic flexible hysteroscope (outer diameter 2.9 mm and 3.6 mm).
- Circon ACMI diagnostic flexible hysteroscope (outer diameter 3.25 mm).

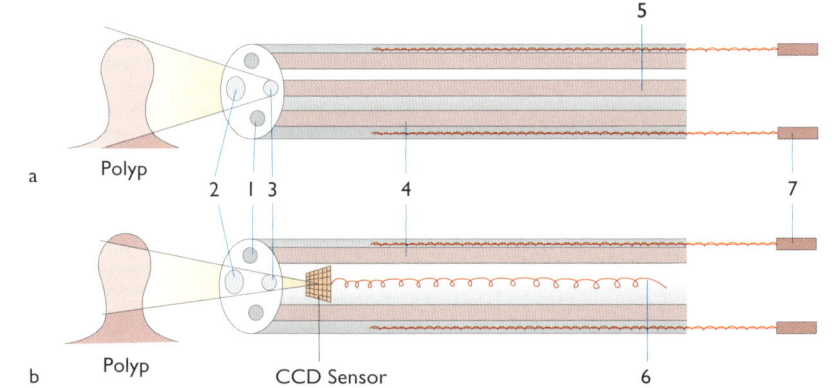

Figure 3
The components of
(a) a fiberoptic hysteroscope and
(b) a video hysteroscope:
  (1) illumination lens,
  (2) irrigation channel,
  (3) objective lens,
  (4) light-guide fiber (LG) bundle,
  (5) image-guide fiber (IG) bundle,
  (6) electric cord,
  (7) angulation control wire.

Figure 4
Olympus diagnostic flexible hysteroscope (HYF-XP, outer diameter 3.1 mm) equipped with a Lin soft outer sheath.

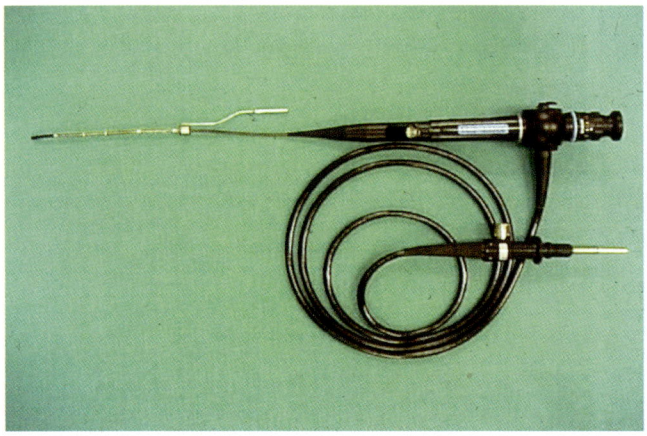

Figure 5
Endometrial polyp (35-mm film, Olympus HYF-XP).

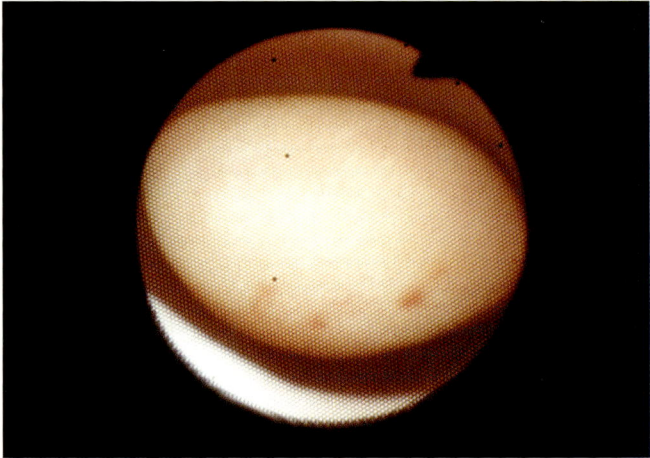

B. Flexible operating hysteroscopes (Table 2)

If it is necessary to perform a direct intrauterine manipulation after using the aforementioned scopes, the following flexible operating hysteroscopes are used.

- Olympus operating flexible hysteroscope (outer diameter 4.9 mm). Figures 10 and 11 illustrate the use of a snare for polypectomy [4]. Lin giant forceps were designed for this scope, increasing its operating ability significantly.
- Fujinon soft and rigid operating flexible hysteroscope (outer diameter 4.9 mm) [5] (Figure 12).
- Mochida cordless operating flexible hysteroscope (outer diameter 4.9 mm) (Figure 9).
- Storz operating flexible hysteroscope (outer diameter 5.3 mm).
- Mochida video hysteroscope (outer diameter 5.3 mm) (Figure 13).

Table 1
Specifications of six different diagnostic flexible hysteroscopes

Type of scope	Olympus diagnostic (HYF-XP)	Fujinon diagnostic (HYS-F)	Storz diagnostic	Storz diagnostic	Circon ACMI diagnostic (AUR-FH)	Mochida cordless diagnostic (FHY-10RBS)
Field of view (in air)	100°	90°	88°	90°	80°	110°
Diameter of distal end	3.0 mm	3.7 mm	2.5 mm	3.5 mm	3.25 mm	3.4 mm
Diameter of insertion tube	3.1 mm	3.7 mm	2.9 mm	3.6 mm	3.25 mm	3.5 mm
Diameter of canal	1.2 mm	1.0 mm	1.2 mm	1.3 mm	1.2 mm	1.2 mm
Bending capacity Up Down	100° 100°	100° 90°	110° 110°	110° 110°	– 160°	130° 130°
Rigid section	(–)	Rigid middle section	(–)	(–)	(–)	(–)

Table 2
Specifications of five different operating flexible hysteroscopes

Type of scope	Olympus operating (HYF-1T)	Fujinon operating (HYS-FT)	Storz operating	Mochida cordless operating (FHY-15RBS)	Mochida video hysteroscope
Field of view (in air)	120°	120°	120°	125°	120°
Diameter of distal end	4.5 mm	4.8 mm	5.0 mm	4.8 mm	5.3 mm
Diameter of insertion tube	4.9 mm	4.9 mm	5.3 mm	4.9 mm	5.1 mm
Diameter of operative canal	2.2 mm	2.2 mm	2.3 mm	2.2 mm	2.0 mm
Bending capacity Up Down	120° 120°	100° 100°	120° 120°	130° 130°	130° 130°
Rigid section	(–)	Axis rotation 180°; bending degree of semi-rigid section 45°	(–)	(–)	(–)

Figure 6
Fujinon diagnostic fiberoptic hysteroscope (HYS-F, outer diameter 3.7 mm) and its tip. This scope is composed of three sections in its functional portion – a soft flexible front, a rigid middle, and a soft rear section. Because of the rigid middle section, the scope can be manipulated and inserted easily into the uterine cavity.

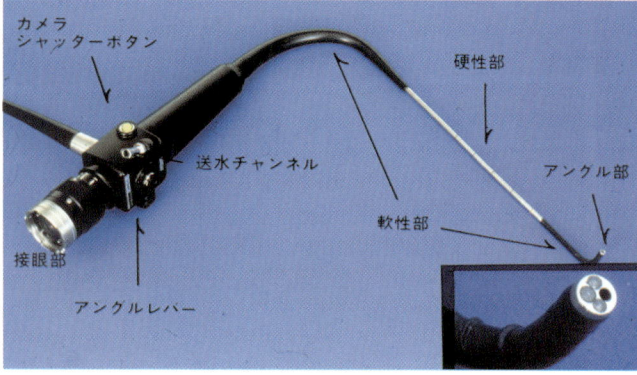

Figure 7
Endometrial polyp (upper) and submucous myoma (lower) (16-mm film, Fujinon HYS-F).

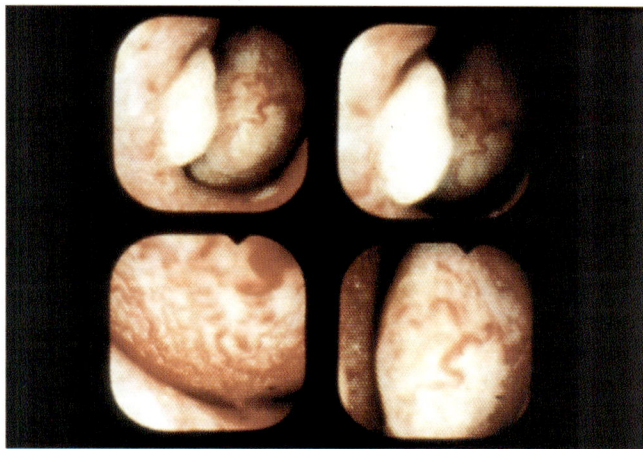

Figure 8
Endometrial carcinoma (small polypoid type) (16 mm film, Fujinon HYS-F).

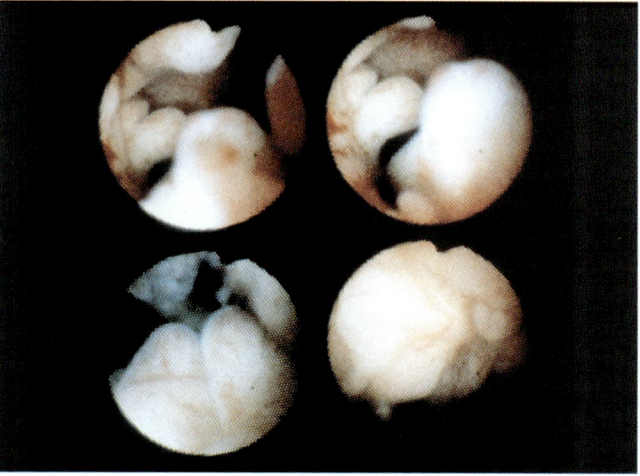

Figure 9
Mochida cordless flexible hysteroscopes. Right: diagnostic (outer diameter 3.5 mm, FHY-10RBS); left: operating (outer diameter 4.9 mm, FHY-15RBS). A long light cord for illumination is not necessary because a small halogen lamp with battery is included in the control section.

Figure 10
An opened snare extending beyond the end of an Olympus operating flexible hysteroscope (HYF-1T, outer diameter 4.9 mm).

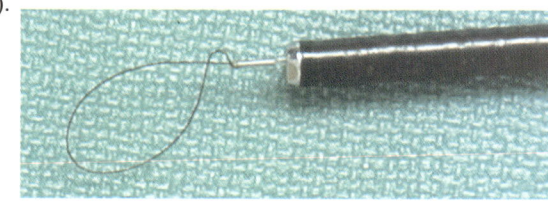

Figure 11
The loop is opened to grasp the pedicle of the polyp. The polyp is extracted when the scope is removed.

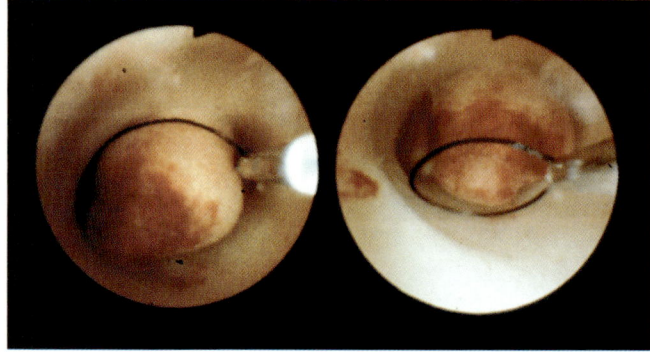

Figure 12
Fujinon operating fiberoptic hysteroscope (HYS-FT, outer diameter 4.9 mm). The functional part of the telescope consists of three sections: a soft flexible front section; a rigid rotating middle section and a semi-rigid, self-retaining rear section. These properties allow for easy maneuvering of the tip of the scope in all directions inside the uterine cavity.

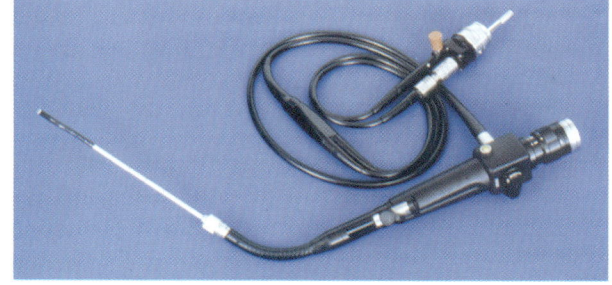

LIN GIANT FORCEPS (Figures 14 and 15) [6]

The clinical applications of these forceps include: (1) directed biopsies, (2) the removal of lost IUDs, and (3) the cutting of intrauterine adhesions.

OUTER SHEATHS (Hakko Shoji Co., Tokyo, Japan)

- A soft outer sheath for a continuous flow system and easy operation of the scope [7] (Figure 16). With a continuous flow system, flexible hysteroscopic intrauterine diagnosis is possible during intrauterine bleeding, but not with heavy bleeding. Also, the soft sheath increases the rigidity of the shaft in a soft hysteroscope, for easy insertion, holding, and controlling of the scope.

- A hard outer sheath for a continuous flow system and performance like a rigid hysteroscope (Figure 17). When equipped with a hard outer sheath, the flexible hysteroscope not only has a continuous flow system but also acts like a rigid scope that can be forced to approach an intrauterine target. In the case of intrauterine adhesions, the adhesions can sometimes be dissected with the tip of a hard outer sheath.

CD RECORDER (Figure 18)

The hysteroscopic findings can be recorded onto a standard PC CD in real time.

Figure 13
Mochida video hysteroscope (outer diameter 5.3 mm). A small CCD is fitted at the distal tip of the scope. The image is captured and transmitted electronically to a television monitor.

Figure 14
A giant Lin biopsy forceps, which is used for directed biopsy, is advanced from a flexible operating hysteroscope.

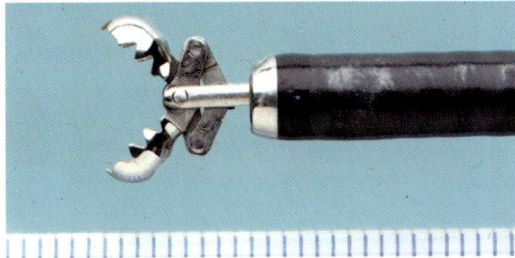

Figure 15
A giant Lin grasping forceps, which is used for removal of lost IUDs or intrauterine foreign bodies, is advanced from a flexible operating hysteroscope.

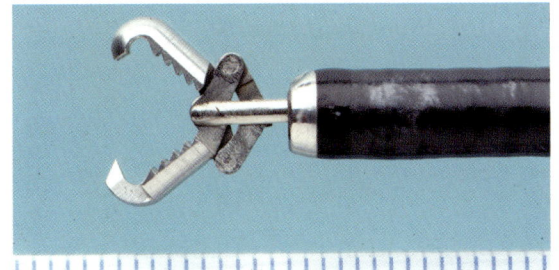

Figure 16
A Lin soft outer sheath (which allows a continuous flow system to be used), placed in front of an Oympus diagnostic flexible hysteroscope (HYF-XP).

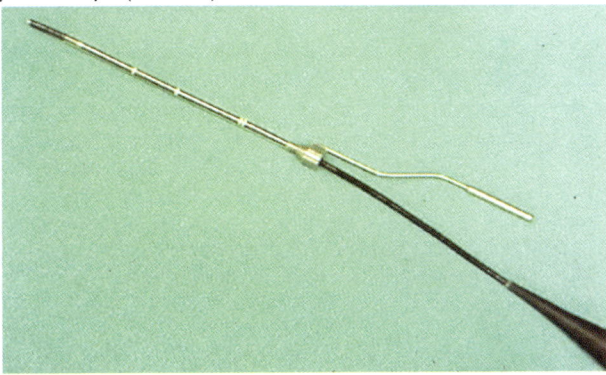

Figure 17
A Lin hard outer sheath placed in front of an Oympus diagnostic flexible hysteroscope (HYF-XP). The fiberoptic hysteroscope can be used like a rigid scope with a continuous flow system.

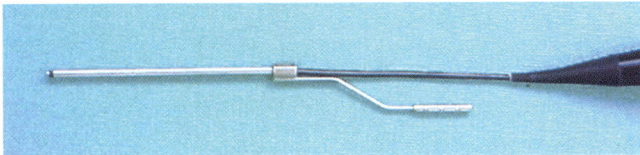

Figure 18
A medical digital video recorder system (MP 3000) can be used to record the hysteroscopic findings. It can convert digital or analog video and audio onto a standard PC CD in real time (CD-R, CR-RW disc).

REFERENCES

1. Marty R, Valle RF. Eight years' experience performing procedures with flexible hysteroscopes. *J Am Assoc Gynecol Laparosc* 1995; **3**: 113–118.
2. Kawahara IZ, Ichikawa HS. Flexible endoscope technology: the fiberoptic endoscope. In: Sivak MV, Aschleutermann D, eds. *Gastroenterologic Endoscopy*, 2nd edition, Vol 1. Philadelphia: WB Saunders, 2000: 16–49.
3. Lin BL, Iwata YY, Liu KH, Valle RF. The Fujinon diagnostic fiber optic hysteroscope. Experience with 1503 patients. *J Reprod Med* 1990; **35**: 685–689.
4. Lin BL, Iwata YY, Mizuhara HS et al. Trial study on endometrial polypectomy by newly developed snare under flexible hysteroscopy. *Nippon Sanka Fujinka Gakkai Zasshi* 1991; **43**: 1728–1730.
5. Lin BL, Iwata YY, Liu KH, Valle RF. Clinical applications of a new Fujinon operating fiberoptic hysteroscope. *J Gynecol Surg* 1990; **6**: 81–87.
6. Lin BL, Iwata YY, Valle RF. Clinical applications of Lin's forceps in flexible hysteroscopy. *J Am Assoc Gynecol Laparosc* 1994; **1**: 383–387.
7. Lin BL, Ishigawa MY, Komiyama MK et al. The development of an outer sheath for hysterofiberscope. *Japanese Journal of Gynecologic and Obstetric Endoscopy* 1997; **13**: 69–72.

Hysteroscopes and sheaths: rigid scopes

Stefano Bettocchi

> **Take Home Message**
> Rigid scopes are based on the Hopkins rod lens system, where glass rods are alternated with air bubbles. This arrangement produces the refractive index of the light and the images obtained are equal to the refractive index of normal light; so the images obtained become very easy to interpret. The use of 30° scopes allows for easy observation in diagnostic hysteroscopy, because the scope does not have to be maneuvered within the uterine cavity – it only has to be turned on its axis to observe the different parts of the uterine cavity including the horns and the tubal ostia. For operative use 12° or 0° scopes are preferred, as this allows for an easier view of the tissues to be operated upon directly in front of the scope and the angle of the incoming instrument is easier to foresee.

Rigid scopes are based on the Hopkins rod lens system, where glass rods are alternated with air bubbles. This arrangement produces the refractive index of the light and the images obtained are equal to the refractive index of normal light; so the images obtained become very easy to interpret. The use of 30° scopes allows for easy observation in diagnostic hysteroscopy, because the scope does not have to be maneuvered within the uterine cavity – it only has to be turned on its axis to observe the different parts of the uterine cavity including the horns and the tubal ostia. For operative use 12° or 0° scopes are preferred, as this allows for an easier view of the tissues to be operated upon directly in front of the scope and the angle of the incoming instrument is easier to foresee.

HISTORY

The modern history of hysteroscopy starts at the beginning of the 1980s, after a decade (the 1970s) of 'first generation' instruments characterized by poor optical quality and a diameter of 5.5–6 mm.

In 1979 Jacques Hamou (Paris, France) designed a 4-mm scope with an enlarged and excellent view (Hamou I and Hamou II; Karl Storz GmbH, Tuttlingen, Germany). These 'second generation' hysteroscopes were based on Hopkins technology, modified by Hamou to obtain a magnification up to 150×. By positioning the tip of the scope close to the area to be observed, the physician can obtain a macro-view: the correct focus is obtained by rotating a screw located on the left side of the eyepiece. The scopes are completed by a single-flow round sheath that brings the final diameter to 5 mm, therefore designed to work only with CO_2 distension.

The characteristics of these hysteroscopes (ease of use, clear and bright vision, magnification) allowed a great number of gynecologists to become familiarized with the hysteroscopic procedure, contributing to the diffusion of the method. Subsequently, with the discovery of the surgical potential of these instruments, operative sheaths were created. These operative hysteroscopes were characterized by a large diameter sheath (around 7–8 mm) with an operative channel of 5 Fr (approximately 1.6 mm). For more than 10 years the hysteroscopes used have been always the same, without any particular improvement in technology.

At the beginning of the 1990s, improvements in fiberoptic technology allowed manufacturers to create the third generation of hysteroscopes, no longer based on lenses but on fiberoptics. These instruments were characterized by a smaller total diameter of the sheath (ranging between 2.5 and 4.5 mm), thanks to the great reduction in the diameter of the scope (between 1 and 2 mm). The success of these fiberscopes was relatively low owing to the poor quality of the images and the tendency to overexpose the images, problems related to the use of fibers instead of lenses.

The real, great, benefit of the fiberscopes was to open the way to a new concept of miniaturized instruments, designed to simplify the technique and to increase patient satisfaction. This led to the fourth generation of hysteroscopes, which appeared on the market during the second half of the 1990s. The main characteristic of these hysteroscopes – which included a rod lens system (Hopkins technology) scope and a continuous flow operative sheath with a 5 Fr channel in a total diameter of 5 mm – was to give the physician the possibility of performing some operative procedures at the time of diagnosis (the 'see and treat' philosophy), while maintaining an excellent optical quality in a liquid distension media.

In 2002 we greeted the arrival of the fifth generation of hysteroscopes, where the main new development has been the reduction in outer diameter (4 mm) together with the realization of the world's first rod lens system scope of 1.9 mm (Bettocchi Office Hysteroscope size 4; Karl Storz GmbH).

SCOPES
HAMOU I
This 4-mm scope has revolutionized the world of hysteroscopy. Designed at the end of the 1970s by Dr Jacques Hamou for Karl Storz Co., it combined the clear and sharp view of the lenses (Hopkins technology) with the possibility of obtaining magnification up to ×150. Even the design of the scope was revolutionary, at that time: a lateral arm with an 'L' shape, containing the lens system for the microscopic view (×150), was located at the right side of the classic eyepiece. A piston, located on the opposite side of the arm, was used to select the magnification. 'Up', gave a classic view through the eyepiece located at the end of the scope, with a magnification ranging between ×1 and ×60; 'down', produced ×150 magnification through the eyepiece located at the end of the lateral arm. The magnification, obtained by putting the tip of the scope close to (or in contact) with the area to be observed and by focusing with the dedicated screw located at the left side of the classic eyepiece, was used to observe the vascularization of the endometrium and the glands opening (up to ×60) or to study the cervical epithelium and its nuclear and cytoplasmatic aspects (×150). Another characteristic of this scope was the view deflected by 30°, obtained by a special prism located at the tip of the scope. The 30° view is particularly useful in the examination of the uterine cavity: by leaving the scope in the middle of the cavity, it is sufficient to rotate the scope on its axis to gradually visualize the entire cavity, without moving the instrument laterally.

HAMOU II (Figure 1)
Introduced a few years later, this was a simplified version of the previous scope. The ×150 lateral arm, dedicated only to the particular observation of the cervical epithelium (MicroColpoHysteroscopy) was eliminated, while the magnification of the scope itself was increased to ×80 always using the lateral screw. The result was a lighter 4-mm scope with a longer lens section (particularly useful in some overweight patients) and an increased endoscopic view.

CHORIONSCOPE/HAMOU III
Created at the end of the 1980s to be used with the Chorionscope, this 30° optic of 2.9 mm is based on a rod lens system and it has also been released in a version modified by Dr Hamou, with a ×80 magnification: practically a miniaturization of the 4-mm Hamou II. With a quality of view that is practically similar to the above-mentioned optics but with a smaller diameter of 1 mm, it has provided the base for development of the actual generation of office hysteroscopes. This scope has been underestimated for a long time, with the general interest focused on the 4-mm lenses until the author designed his innovative sheaths' system.

FIBERSCOPES (OR MINISCOPES)
Regularly available on the market since the beginning of the 1990s, another revolution in hysteroscopy has brought the outer diameter largely below the limit of 4 mm (around 2 mm). This revolution was made possible by using optical fibers instead of a rod lens system. The price paid for this reduction in diameter was a decrease in the quality of view (the so-called 'fly view') and overexposure (whitish view and losd of details) of the image because the tip of the scope was too close to the area to be observed. These defects were related to the technology used. The optical fibers are round and in a hysteroscope can be located in up than 75,000: by so doing between 4 fiber there will be an empty area that will be reproduced on the screen as black (Figure 2). Multiplication of all these 'non-illuminated' areas produces a kind of dark net on the image ('fly view').

Figure 1
The Hamou II scope (Karl Storz).

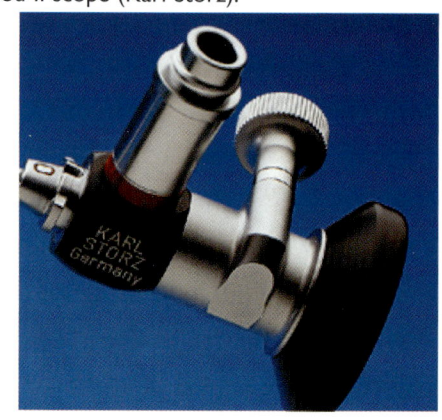

BETTOCCHI OFFICE HYSTEROSCOPE 2 MM

The newest scope available on the market (released in February 2002) is unique: it is the first 2-mm 30° rod lens system scope in the world. Despite its small diameter, the optical characteristics (quality of view, illumination, colors, etc.) are excellent and very similar to those of the 2.9-mm and not too far from the 4-mm scopes. A new continuous flow operative sheath of 4 mm has been developed around this scope (Bettocchi Office Hysteroscope size 4).

SHEATHS

DIAGNOSTIC SHEATHS FOR 4-MM SCOPES (Figure 3)

For a long time these round sheaths have only been available only in a 'single flow' version (to work only with CO_2 distension), characterized by a final diameter of 5 mm. Continuous flow sheaths of 6 mm have only recently been designed to work with liquid distension: too large, anyway, to be introduced in the uterine cavity without a cervical dilatation!

OPERATIVE SHEATHS FOR 4-MM SCOPES (Figure 4)

Due to the presence of a 7 Fr operative channel and two separate channels for irrigation/aspiration, the final diameter of these sheaths ranged between 7 and 8.3 mm. Therefore they were always used together with anesthesia and cervical dilatation.

OPERATIVE SHEATHS FOR 2.9-MM SCOPES (Bettochi Office Hysteroscope size 5) (Figures 5 and 6)

This family of sheaths has been the great innovation of recent years: a continuous flow system and a 5 Fr operative channel have been included in the same diameter of a simple diagnostic scope (5 mm). Another revolutionary characteristic was the oval shape that could be a great help in the introduction of the hysteroscope in a normal cervical canal. The internal cervical os (ICO) is oval (with the main axis horizontal) and not round: thus rotating the hysteroscope by 90° is sufficient to have its main axis corresponding to that of the ICO.

DIAGNOSTIC SHEATHS FOR 2-MM SCOPES

(fiberscopes) (Figure 7)

Thanks to the small diameter of these scopes it has been possible to produce continuous flow sheaths of 3 mm, characterized by a round profile and two separate sheaths (one for irrigation and one for aspiration). With this

Figure 2
Diagram of the view produced by multiple optical fibers (fibers are represented by the grey circles).

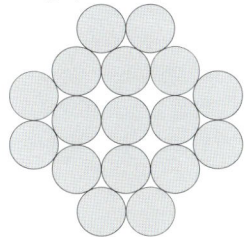

Figure 3
Sheaths for 4-mm diagnostic scopes.

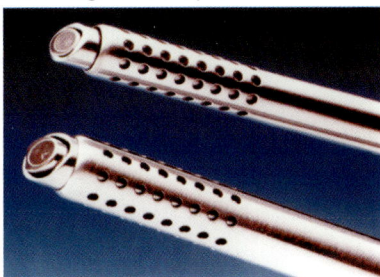

Figure 4
Sheath for 4-mm operative scope.

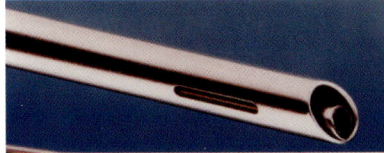

Figure 5
Bettocchi Office Hysteroscope size 5.

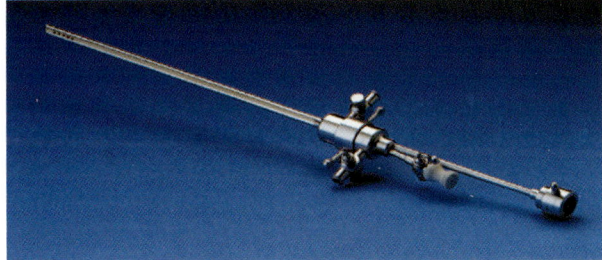

Figure 6
Sheaths for 2.9-mm diagnostic scopes.

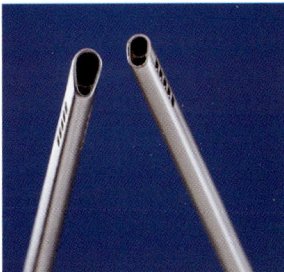

Figure 7
Sheath for 2-mm diagnostic scope.

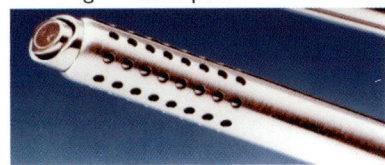

diameter, the main problem for the hysteroscopists, the introduction of the scope in the uterine cavity through a stenotic ICO, is just a memory. On the contrary, using these small diameter hysteroscopes in a multiparous woman, with an enlarged ICO, could produce insufficient dilatation of the uterine cavity because of the loss of distension media. The absence of an operative channel does not allow the physician to perform eye-guided biopsies (EGB) in case he needs an histological confirmation of his visual diagnosis.

Figure 8
Bettocchi Office Hysteroscope size 4.

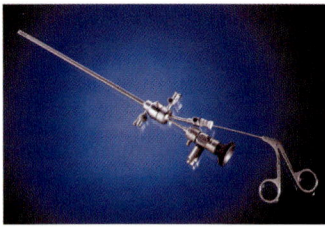

Figure 9
Sheath for 2-mm operative scope.

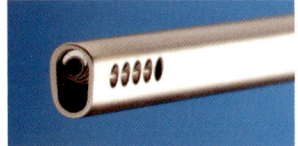

Figure 10
Mechanical instruments for operative hysteroscopes (all 5 Fr instruments from Karl Storz).

    (A) Crocodile grasping forceps with teeth,
    (B) spoon biopsy forceps,
    (C) punch biopsy forceps,
    (D) sharp scissors, (E) blunt scissors,
    (F) 'Tira-bouchon'.

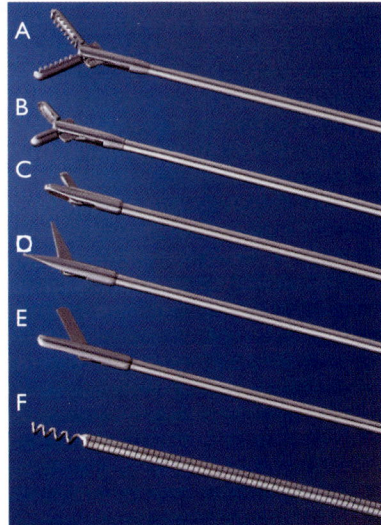

OPERATIVE SHEATHS FOR 2-MM SCOPES *(Bettochi Office Sheaths for fiberscopes and Bettocchi Office Hysteroscope size 4)* (Figures 8 and 9)

This family of sheaths has brought together the innovation of those dedicated to the 2.9-mm scope with the availability of the 2-mm rod lens system scope. Unique features are the continuous flow system, the 5 Fr operative channel and the oval shape in a final diameter corresponding to 4 mm. With this small diameter each cavity could be reached easily, even by trainees, without losing the operative capacity.

MECHANICAL INSTRUMENTS

For a long time mechanical instruments have been the right companions for operative hysteroscopes. Available in different diameters (5 or 7 Fr) depending on the size of the operative channel, for a long time these were based on only three instruments: 'spoon' biopsy forceps (Figure 10B), 'punch' biopsy forceps (Figure 10C) and blunt scissors (Figure 10E). With the increased and new operative features related to the recent generation of operative office hysteroscopes, new instruments have been added to manufacturers' catalogues.

The most innovative development has been the 'crocodile' grasping forceps with teeth (Figure 10A), designed to grasp foreign bodies and lost intrauterine devices (IUDs), but, thanks to the length of the two jaws (double those of spoon biopsy forceps), these forceps can to collect a large amount of tissue during a normal eye-directed biopsy (see the chapter on Eye-guided biopsies). New sharp scissors (Figure 10D) are also available to gently cut delicate areas with a smooth surface, like the anatomical impediments, as well as a 'Tira-bouchon' (Figure 10F) to eventually hold any fibrotic tissue inside the uterine cavity, such as small myomas or large fibrotic polyps.

Set up of an outpatient facility

Corry G.W.A. Stappers-de Kuijer

> **Take Home Message**
> The procedure should preferably take place in a special outpatient unit in hospital or in an outpatient clinic where any unforeseen complications can be managed. The nurse should set up the room where the procedure takes place in order to enssure that the physician has all the necessary equipment and instruments to perform the procedures safely. Both rigid and flexible hysteroscopes can be used. Conventional hysteroscopes need local anesthesia in 11% of patients. Both gas and fluid can be used as a distension medium. High molecular weight dextran induces an anaphylactic reaction in 1 in 10,000 patients. Hysteroscopy should be scheduled preferably in the proliferative phase of the cycle between days 7 and 12 of the cycle. No sedation is required before or during a diagnostic procedure. The use of a video camera helps in explaining the findings to patients and discussing the actions to be taken.

INTRODUCTION

Hysteroscopy is the most reliable method for diagnosis of intrauterine disorders. A diagnostic hysteroscopy could reveal the most probable cause of the patient's complaints. During and after the hysteroscopy there should be enough time to explain the results of the procedure and if necessary the possibilities for trans-cervical treatment should be discussed.

SET UP

A special set up is required for a diagnostic hysteroscopy. The procedure room should preferably be located in a special outpatient unit in a hospital or in an outpatient clinic, so that any unforeseen complications can be managed.

- The hysteroscopy should, if possible, be scheduled to take place during the proliferative phase of the menstrual cycle, preferably between days 7 and 12 of the cycle.
- The results of a PAP smear, blood group, erythrocyte sedimentation rate (ESR) and haemoglobin (Hb) tests should be available at the procedure.
- No sedation is required before or during a diagnostic procedure.
- To prevent myometrial contractions during distension of the uterine cavity a prostaglandin synthetase inhibitor like Naproxen 500 mg can be given the evening and/or 2 hours before the procedure.
- If there are no contraindications it is advisable to give the patient an intramuscular (IM) injection of 0.5 mg atropine 15 min before the procedure, to prevent vagal reactions, which can sometimes occur during manipulation of the internal cervical os.
- If the resistance to the hysteroscope at the internal cervical os is too high for a smooth insertion, the use of local anesthesia is recommended. Prilocaine (Citanest™) 10 mg/ml, has been found to be the most effective local anesthetic. (See also the chapter on Anesthesia.)

EQUIPMENT

a gynecological chair
b video endocamera and monitor
c light source and a light-guide cable
d pressure cuff or an electronic pump for administration of the fluid
e hysteroscopy CO_2 insufflator and tubing.

GYNECOLOGICAL CHAIR

An electrohydraulically adjustable chair is recommended; this will to add to the comfort of both the patient and the doctor.

VIDEO CAMERA AND MONITOR

A video camera is an essential element of modern endoscopy. The application of video systems attached directly to the hysteroscope and connected to a monitor will make the patient more involved. This allows an interaction between the patient and the physician – the physician is able to explain the view and any abnormalities and can discuss the available treatment while the patient is looking at the monitor (Figure 1). The nursing staff and residents can also follow the procedure, which will lead to improved cooperation of the team involved in a patient's care.

The camera is usually connected to a control unit with extra adjustment possibilities (Figure 2). The camera adaptor fits around the eyepiece of the telescope (Figure 3). Most cameras have to be white balanced before the procedure. [Note: there is always the possibility of some remnants of the distension media remaining inside the adaptor; in that case the moving parts may malfunction and the image may be cloudy; this has to be checked before every hysteroscopy session.]

LIGHT SOURCE AND LIGHT-GUIDE CABLE (Figure 4)

A light source of at least 300 W is recommended for video imaging during the procedure. A glass fiber light-guide cable enables the light conduction (Figure 5). [Note: the light-guide cable is composed of rather vulnerable glass fibers; damage or rupture of these fibers caused by forced bending will immediately reduce the light intensity.]

PRESSURE CUFF OR AN ELECTRONIC PUMP FOR THE ADMINISTRATION OF FLUID

When continuous flow hysteroscopes are being used for purely diagnostic procedures the distending liquid can be applied with gravity pressure by positioning a liquid bag

Figure 1

Figure 2
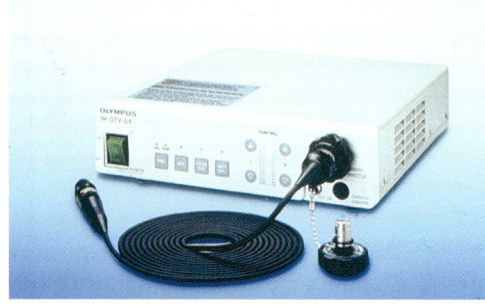

Figure 3

Figure 4
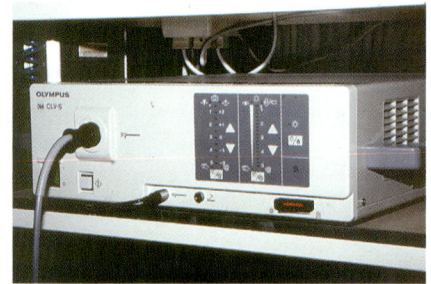

Figure 5

Figure 6
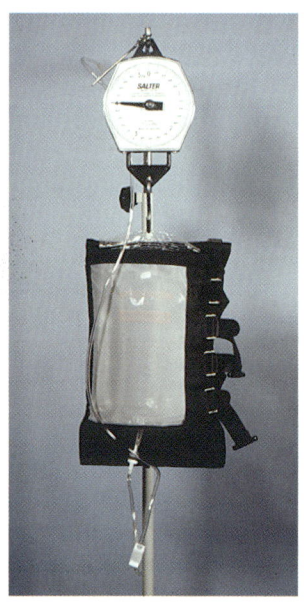

(2–3 liters) 1.5 m above the patient. However, the use of a pressure cuff provides a more rapid and clear visualization (Figure 6).

The use of a pressure cuff is recommended in cases of uterine bleeding or during minor procedures. In these cases the recovered liquid should be collected and monitored to prevent inadvertent intravasation. An electronic delivery pump with scale and automatic fluid loss control can also be used in these cases.

CO_2 INSUFFLATOR

Only equipment that has been specially developed for hysteroscopy should be used for CO_2 insufflation. The use of laparoscopy insufflators is extremely dangerous and can lead to fatal complications.

DISTENSION MEDIA

For distension of the uterine cavity there is a choice of:

a CO_2 gas

b High viscosity fluid (HVF), such as dextran 70 (32% or 29%)

c Low viscosity fluid (LVF): saline, if no electricity is required; or sorbitol 4%, glycine 1.5%, or dextrose 5% if electricity is likely to be used for minor operations.

Figure 7

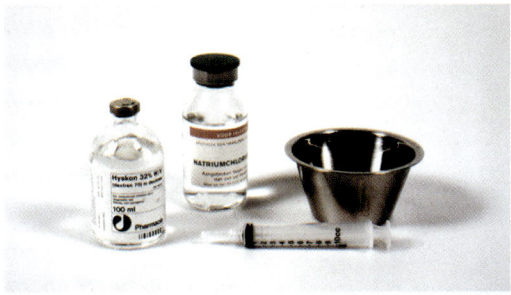

Figure 8

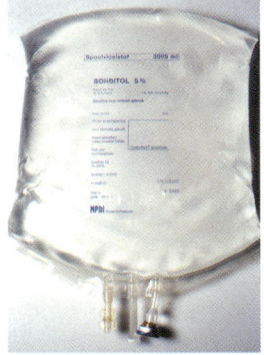

CO_2

- The CO_2 flow rate must be limited to a maximum level of 100 ml/min, in almost all cases a much lower rate of 30–50 ml/min is sufficient.
- The maximum level of the intrauterine pressure must be limited to 150 mmHg (pressures higher than 60 mmHg start to induce cramp-like sensations in patients).
- The hysteroscope and the silicone tubes should be completely dry to prevent blowing air bubbles into the uterine cavity.
- All stopcocks not in use should be closed.
- If there is gas leakage through the stopcocks or the connections with the hysteroflator the uterine cavity will collapse.

HIGH VISCOSITY FLUID

With the development of continuous flow hysteroscopes the use of high viscosity fluid has almost ceased.

To obtain the appropriate viscosity (29% dextran 70) a 100-ml bottle of 32% dextran 70 (Hyskon™) has to be diluted with 10 ml of saline 0.9% or dextrose 5%. Ensure that the liquids are mixed well (Figure 7).

[Note: when using dextran it is very important to clean the instruments immediately after the procedure to prevent caramelization of the dextran, which leads to malfunction of all moving parts of the instruments.]

LOW VISCOSITY FLUIDS

Low viscosity fluids (LVF) have to be used for continuous flow hysteroscopy (CFH) (Figure 8).

For just diagnostic hysteroscopy it is in most cases it is sufficient to hang a 3-litre plastic bag bottle of distension fluid about 1–1.5 m above the patient to obtain good visualization. In cases of poor visualization caused by blood or cervical mucus the use of extra pressure is recommended.

A pressure cuff with an automatic pressure control unit is very beneficial.

The fluid has to be administered at a pressure of 150 mmHg and should preferably be at a

temperature of 37°C. Special equipment for this purpose is available.

With continuous flow there is always the risk of intravasation, therefore all returning fluid must be collected, measured and subtracted from the infused amount. The difference between the administered and collected fluid is the 'fluid loss' and should be considered to have been intravasated. This 'fluid loss' should never be allowed to exceed 1500 ml. The risk of intravasation is less with diagnostic procedures but the safety limits should be kept strictly for major intrauterine surgery.

HYSTEROSCOPES

Hysteroscopes are available in two designs:

a flexible

b ridgided.

FLEXIBLE HYSTEROSCOPES

Flexible hysteroscopes are available with or without a working channel (Figure 9).

The smallest diagnostic hysteroscope is 3.1 mm and generally no anesthesia is required for this instrument. Flexible hysteroscopes produce a picture with a slight honeycomb structure and the image is mostly less bright than that of the rigid hysteroscopes. Flexible hysteroscopes can be used with CO_2 and low viscosity distension media. [Note: HVF should never be used with flexible hysteroscopes or flexible instruments.]

RIDGEID HYSTEROSCOPES

A ridgeid hysteroscope consists of a 3- or 4-mm 30° fore-oblique telescope (Figure 10).

For purely diagnostic procedures a ridgeid 3-mm telescope with a 4.5-mm continuous flow sheath is most commonly used. The application of local anesthesia will be required in approximately 10% of cases. The sheath has two stopcocks – one for the inflow and one for the outflow of the distension medium. There is also a working channel for 3 Fr instruments. The space between the telescope and the sheath is used for the distension medium (Figure 11).

CFContinuous flow hysteroscopes provide a very clear image during the whole procedure. Blood or cervical mucus will not obscure the image because of the rapid flow of the distension medium in front of the telescope.

If minor therapeutic approaches are necessary a 5.5- or 6.5-mm sheath can be used, in combination with 5 or 7 Fr instruments with matching seal caps (Figure 12). Semi-flexible biopsy forceps, grasping forceps, and scissors are available for surgical procedures (Figure 13).

The latest development in hysteroscopes is a 1.9-mm telescope with 4.5-mm continuous flow sheath; this could be an alternative to the flexible hysteroscopes. [Note: 1 Fr (French) = 1.3 mm.]

ADDITIONAL INSTRUMENTS AND REQUIREMENTS (Figure 14)

- Collins speculum
- long tweezers
- forceps
- tenaculum
- half size hegars, 3–7

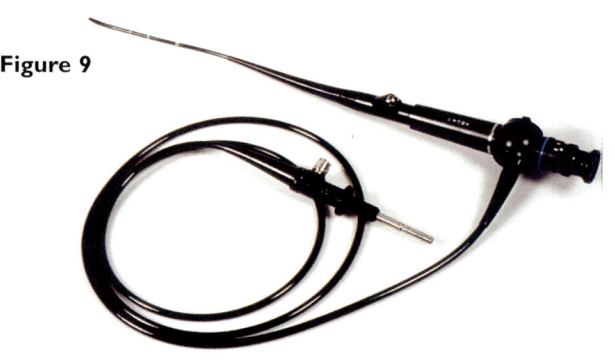

Figure 9

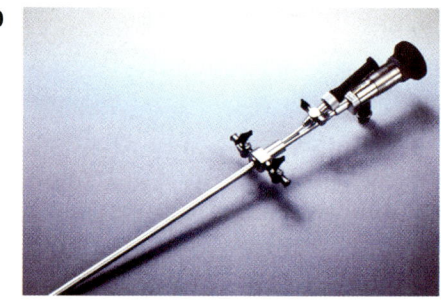

Figure 10

Figure 11

Figure 12

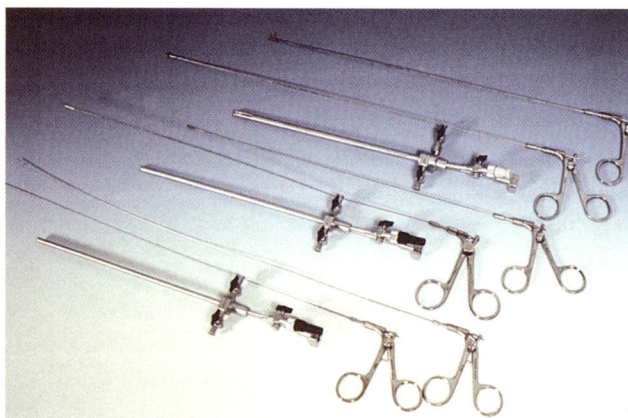

figure 13

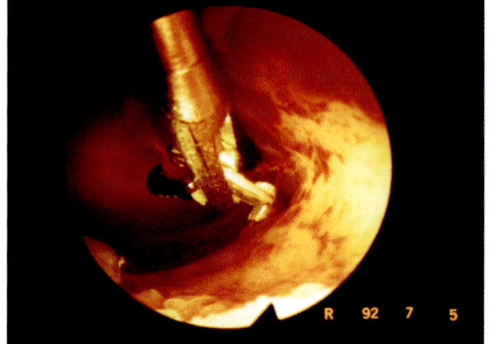

- tubingses with Luer-Lok connections for delivery of LVFlow viscosity fluids
- tubesings with Luer-Lok connections for the returning fluid
- iodine, swabs (5 × 5 and 10 × 10)
- sterile drapes
- local anesthetics
- long needle (0.9 × 70 mm)
- 10-ml syringe (Luer-Lok connection).

SAFETY PRECAUTIONS

Although it is rare, there is always the possibility of allergic reactions to local anesthetics or dextran; thus, a complete emergency set must be available in the procedure room. (See also the chapter on Anesthesia)

PRACTICAL RECOMMENDATIONS

After the procedure the patient generally does not need any recovery time and should be able to go home immediately. If local anesthesia has been administered she should be advised not to drive home by herself.

The patient may have some bloody discharge and she should be advised not to take a bath, not to swim in open water and not to have sexual intercourse as long as this persists.

The possibilities for endosurgical treatment should be discussed.

CONCLUSIONS

The hysteroscopic approach for intrauterine disorders has completely replaced dilatation and curettage [D&C] as a diagnostic toolModern techniques for hysteroscopy allow a rapid and clear visualization of the uterine cavity and intracavitary disorders and allow for minor operative procedures to be carried out via a 'see and treat' philosophy.

BIBLIOGRAPHY

McLucas B. Hyskon complications in hysteroscopic surgery. *Obstet Gynecol Survey* 1991; **46**: 196.

Stappers-de Kuijer CGWA. Specific needs for an ambulatory outpatient hysteroscopy service. HTC-NL Syllabus, 1991.

Wamsteker K, De Blok S. Diagnostic hysteroscopy: technique and documentation. In: Sutton C, Diamond M, eds. Endoscopic Surgery for Gynaecologists. London: WB Saunders, 1998.

Figure 14

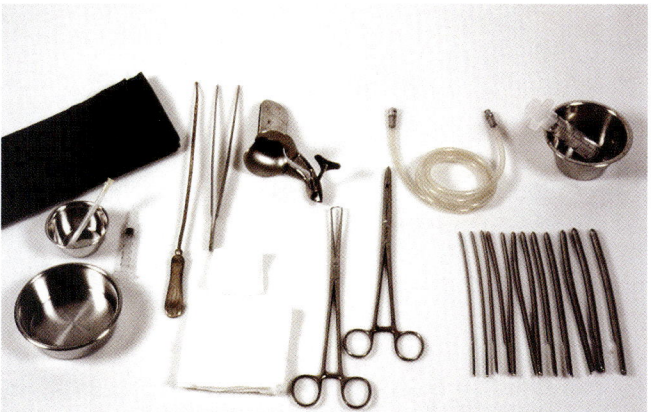

5b The nurse's role in outpatient hysteroscopy

Donna M. Morrison

> **Take Home Message**
> The nurse's role is three-fold: ensuring patient safety, providing patient comfort, and increasing patient satisfaction. The procedure should be reviewed, as should the information given by the physician. The nurse should assess the patient's understanding of the information given. The patient should be told to contact the physician or the staff if unforeseen problems occur before, during, or after the procedure. In the USA the signing of consent forms is mandatory but there is a growing worldwide tendency to apply that rule because of legal and consumer pressure.

INTRODUCTION

The role of the nurse during office hysteroscopy is threefold. The nurse plays a vital role in ensuring patient safety, providing patient comfort, and increasing patient satisfaction. This is accomplished through patient preparation, preparation for the procedure, and preparing self and other office personnel for emergency situations should they arise.

PATIENT PREPARATION

Patient preparation is a key factor in ensuring a positive patient outcome. Ideally, patient preparation begins immediately after the patient and the physician have decided to proceed with an office hysteroscopy. Patient preparation includes a review of the procedure, reinforcement of information given by the physician, assessment of the patient's understanding of information given, and a period of time for questions and answers. The patient should also be encouraged to contact the nurse or her physician, should she have further questions about the procedure, once she has had the chance to absorb the information given.

It is helpful for the patient to have the opportunity to discuss any anxiety she may have about the surgery during the preparation phase. Allowing the patient to discuss her anxiety about the procedure provides an opportunity for the nurse to address the patient's concerns before surgery. It also provides the opportunity for the nurse to develop a specific plan of care to minimize the patient's anxiety level on the day of surgery. DeJong, Doel, and Falconer (as cited by Prather & Wolfe [1]) note that women who are anxious while undergoing a hysteroscopy usually experience more discomfort during the procedure. Therefore, if the nurse is able to develop a plan of care that will help to minimize the patient's anxiety, a more positive outcome and an increase in patient satisfaction can be expected.

The nurse explains to the patient what to expect before, during, and after the procedure. Tempesta and Spencer [2] suggest that this explanation should include what the patient will feel, rather than the activity that will take place around her. The patient should be aware that the physician will inform her of what is being done before proceeding and that vital signs will be monitored during the procedure. Murdock and Gan [3] note that adequate monitoring during office hysteroscopy is essential because of the potential risks for vasovagal attacks, local anesthesia toxicity, and gas emboli.

Other sensations that the patient may feel during office hysteroscopy include a quick pinch, if a tennaculum is used and mild cramping as the uterus is being distended. The patient should be encouraged to remain as relaxed as possible during this phase of the procedure, as remaining relaxed helps to minimize these discomforts. The patient can be taught deep breathing as a method of maintaining relaxation.

If carbon dioxide (CO_2) is used to distend the uterus, the patient should be aware that she may experience some shoulder pain during or after the procedure secondary to the CO_2 instillation. In instances where a low viscosity fluid is used to distend the uterus, the patient should know that she may feel the fluid coming from the vagina. It is important that the patient is aware of this sensation so that the sensation is not mistaken for vaginal bleeding [2]. It is also important to assure the patient that the procedure can be aborted at any time if she finds it intolerable.

On the day of surgery the patient may be instructed by her physician to take an analgesic such as ibuprofen, or offered a mild oral sedative, such as Valium, before the procedure to help alleviate any discomfort or anxiety [4]. Once she arrives at the office, the nurse again reviews what is being done, what to expect during and after the procedure, and allows the patient to ask any last minute questions. The nurse ensures that the informed surgical consent is signed and on the medical record and documents any allergies the patient may have. The patient is instructed to empty her bladder. The nurse then accompanies the patient to the procedure room, instructs her to undress from the waist down and positions her on the examination table in a lithotomy position, ensuring that she is adequately draped to maintain privacy. During the procedure, the nurse provides emotional support to the patient and assistance to the physician as needed. The nurse also communicates the patient's tolerance of the procedure to the physician.

The patient should remain recumbent for a short period of time after the procedure is completed. During this time, the nurse continues to monitor vital signs and observe the patient for any adverse reactions arising from the procedure or from administration of the local anesthetic. The nurse observes the patient for increased abdominal pain, paleness, nausea, diaphoresis, or change of vital signs. Any of these symptoms should be reported immediately to the physician. In the event that shoulder pain from CO_2 instillation is significant, the nurse may place the patient in shallow Trendelenburg position for a short period of time. This position may reduce the amount of discomfort the patient experiences. The shoulder discomfort will resolve. However, Siegler (as cited by Prather & Wolfe [1]) states that complete resolution may take several days.

The nurse reviews discharge instructions with the patient once she has recovered. The nurse also provides a written copy of the discharge instructions reviewed. The patient signs the instruction sheet and the nurse documents in the medical record that verbal and written discharge instructions were given.

Discharge instructions should include what to expect immediately after the hysteroscopy and during the first few days following the procedure. The patient is advised that she may experience mild cramping and vaginal spotting, and that she may experience shoulder pain 1–3 days postoperatively. A non-steroidal anti-inflammatory drug (NSAID) is often prescribed to control discomfort. The patient is instructed to notify the physician immediately if she notices excessive or bright red vaginal bleeding, severe abdominal pain, vaginal discharge with odor, or if she develops a fever >100°F (37.7°C) [1]. Activity may or may not be restricted, depending on whether or not cervical dilatation is required. For instances where little or no cervical dilatation is required restrictive activity, such as no tampons, no douching, or no intercourse may not be necessary. However, when cervical dilatation is required, restrictive activity may be warranted. The physician will determine what activity is prohibited. The nurse will convey these restrictions to the patient when postoperative instructions are given.

PROCEDURE PREPARATION

Preparation for office hysteroscopy includes preparing instruments, supplies, and equipment necessary for the procedure. The nurse checks equipment, instruments, and supplies before the patient arrives at the office on the day of surgery, to ensure these items are in proper working condition and are readily available. This includes confirming that there is sufficient CO_2 in the reservoir of the hysteroflator (if CO_2 is the distending medium of choice), checking to ensure that stopcocks move freely and that tubing and adaptors required to connect equipment and instruments are present.

Several factors must be considered when preparing the procedure room for an office hysteroscopy. Hysteroscopes can be either rigid or flexible and range in size from 3 to 5.5 mm in diameter [5]. Likewise, CO_2 gas or fluid may be utilized to distend the uterus. Administration of a local anesthetic is not usually required when a small diameter or flexible hysteroscope is used. Although a video system is commonly used during office hysteroscopy, it is not an essential component. Therefore, preparation of instruments, supplies, and equipment for office hysteroscopy will depend upon the type of hysteroscope and distending medium used, whether or not a video system will be used, and whether or not a local anesthetic will be administered. There are, however, some supplies, instruments and equipment that are universal for any office hysteroscopy (Figure 1). These include sterile gloves, a

Figure 1
Set up of universal office hysteroscopy instruments.

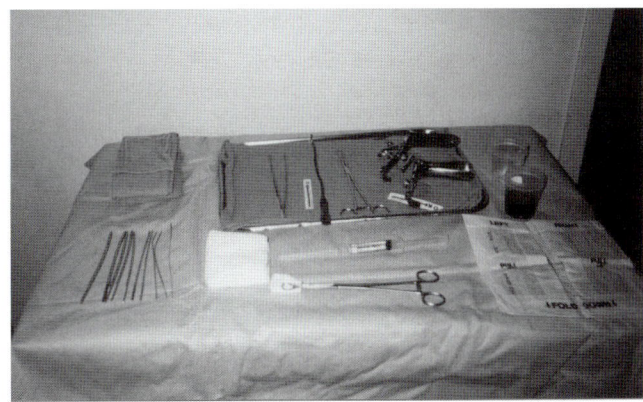

drape sheet or sterile towels, an antiseptic prepping solution, supplies necessary to apply the antiseptic, a vaginal speculum, a uterine sound, and a tissue forcep. A nonadhesive pad (divided into thirds), 4 × 4 gauze sponges, and a specimen container should also be readily available in the event that tissue samples are obtained during the procedure. An endometrial curette or pipelle may also be used to obtain tissue samples.

Equipment in universal use for office hysteroscopy includes the fiberoptic light cable and light source. Video cameras have universal couplers and can be used with any hysteroscope; therefore, the video system is also considered universal equipment even though it is not an essential component of office hysteroscopy.

The nurse prepares the procedure room for the hysteroscopy before the patient arrives. A sterile field is created with instruments and supplies arranged in the manner in which they will be used. A drape sheet or sterile towels are used to drape the operative site. Although the vagina is not sterile, Prather and Wolfe [1] note that office hysteroscopy should be performed as aseptically as possible to reduce the risk of infection. A vaginal speculum is placed on the sterile field and will be used to provide exposure of the cervical canal. An open-sided vaginal speculum may also be included as part of the sterile set up. The open-sided speculum is required if the speculum will be removed from the vagina once the hysteroscope is in place. Commercially prepared cotton tip applicators pre-saturated with povidone-iodine or a container with prepping solution that will be used to clean the cervix are also placed on the sterile field. Xylocaine 1% or a comparable topical anesthetic with a 10-ml Luer-Lok syringe and 3.5-inch, 22-g hypodermic needle may also be placed on the sterile field if a local anesthetic is necessary.

When a rigid hysteroscope is utilized, a single-toothed tenaculum may be required to grasp the cervix. Cervical dilators, ranging in half-size increments from 1 mm to 8 mm, should be readily available in the event that cervical dilatation is required. The rigid hysteroscope, with a diagnostic and operative sheath, fiberoptic light cable, and operative instruments are included on the sterile field as well. For instances where a flexible hysteroscope is utilized, it is placed on the sterile field along with the fiberoptic light cable and flexible operative instruments. Atraumatic tissue forceps may also be added to the sterile field and used to add rigidity to the flexible end of the hysteroscope as it is passed through the cervical canal. The video camera, if used, is placed in close proximity to the sterile field so that the hysteroscope can be attached to the camera before it is advanced through the cervical canal.

The uterus can be distended with CO_2 or a low viscosity fluid (Table 1). Normal saline 0.9% or lactated Ringer solution are the low viscosity fluids most commonly used. However, CO_2 is the medium most often used for hysteroscopies performed in the office setting [4].

CO_2 is instilled using an insufflator specially designed for hysteroscopic surgery. The physician dictates the pressure settings and CO_2 gas flow rate for the hysteroflator and the nurse initiates flow from the unit. Pressures between 40mmHg and 80 mmHg and flow rates between 40 ml/min and 60 ml/min are required to adequately distend the uterus [6]. The patient is informed

Table 1
Supplies needed to instill distending medium

CO_2 gas	Low viscosity fluid
Hysteroscope with sheaths	Hysteroscope with sheaths
Light cable	Light cable
Hysteroflator	IV pole
Insufflation tubing	IV tubing
	Extension tubing
*Extension tubing	1-Liter bag of 0.9% normal saline or lactated Ringer solution
*Luer-Lok syringe	Pressure cuff with pressure gauge
*Saline irrigation fluid	Fluid collection pouch or container
	or
	60-ml Luer-Lok syringe
	Extension tubing

*These items may be needed for irrigation to clean lens

when the CO_2 gas flow begins and is reminded that she may feel mild cramping as the uterus is distended. During this phase of the procedure, it is important for the nurse to keep the patient as relaxed as possible. This can be accomplished by talking with the patient, by encouraging the patient to use breathing techniques reviewed before the procedure, and by keeping the patient informed as to how the procedure is progressing. The video system, when used, is also a valuable tool. The nurse can re-direct the patient's attention to the video monitor and identify anatomy while the physician is performing the hysteroscopy.

Mucus from the cervix and/or bubbles from CO_2 gas that mix with blood creating a type of foam sometimes impair visualization when CO_2 is used as the distending medium. Visualization can also be impaired due to poor distension when CO_2 escapes from the cervix. Cervical suction cups, a four-pronged tenaculum placed on the cervix, and petroleum jelly gauze packed at the cervix are methods employed to maintain distension. The nurse can help maintain adequate visualization and distension by having supplies readily available to remove blood or debris that can collect on the objective lens and by ensuring that connections between the instillation tubing and the hysteroscope are tight.

Two methods can be used to instill low viscosity fluid. One method is continuous pressure. Continuous pressure is accomplished by inflating a pressure cuff around a hanging bag of intravenous fluid connected to the inflow port of the hysteroscope with IV tubing (Figures 2 and 3). The fluid regulator on the IV tubing is opened and the cuff pressure causes fluid to flow downward through the hysteroscope. An absorbent pad is placed under the patient to catch fluid that spills from the vagina. Tubing is also connected to the outflow port of the hysteroscope and allowed to drain into a fluid collection pouch or connected to a container so that it can be measured (Figure 4). A 60-ml syringe filled with fluid, attached to extension tubing that is connected to the

Figure 2
Supplies required for low viscosity fluid using continuous pressure. Included are IV pole, 1-liter bag of IV fluid, pressure bag with pressure gauge, absorbent underbuttock pad, and fluid collection pouch.

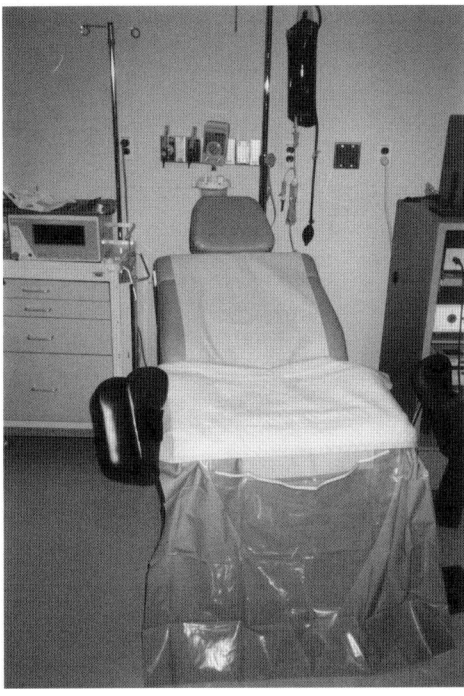

Figure 3
Close-up of continuous pressure method for instilling low viscosity fluid. Included are IV pole, 1-liter bag of IV fluid, and pressure bag with pressure gauge.

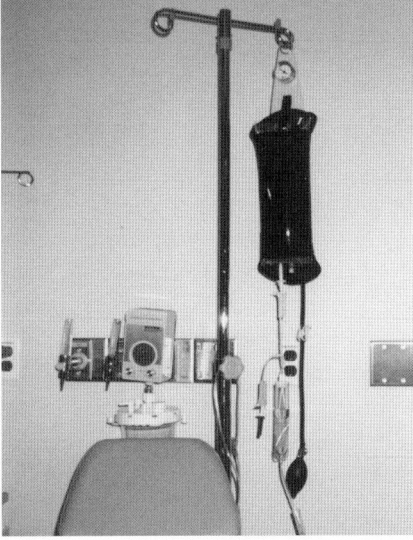

Figure 4
Close-up of fluid collection pouch for use with continuous pressure low viscosity fluid instillation set up, including absorbent underbuttock pad and fluid collection pouch.

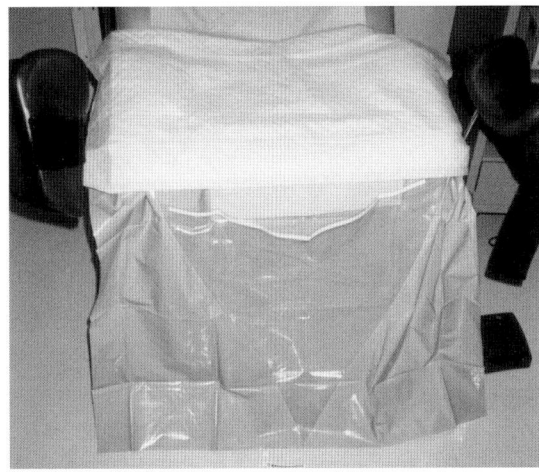

inflow port of the hysteroscope, is another method that can be used to instill a low viscosity fluid. Distension is achieved by slowly advancing the plunger of the syringe once the hysteroscope has been placed into the cervical canal.

Figure 5
Emergency cart.

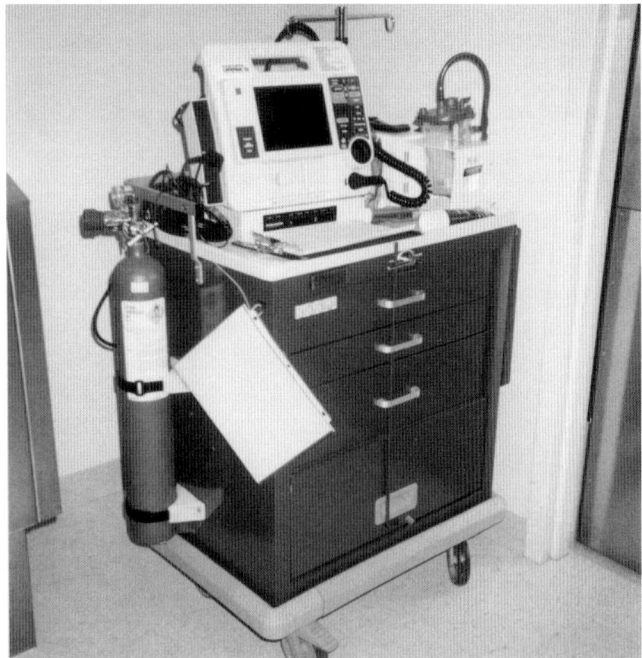

Figure 6
Close-up of emergency cart.

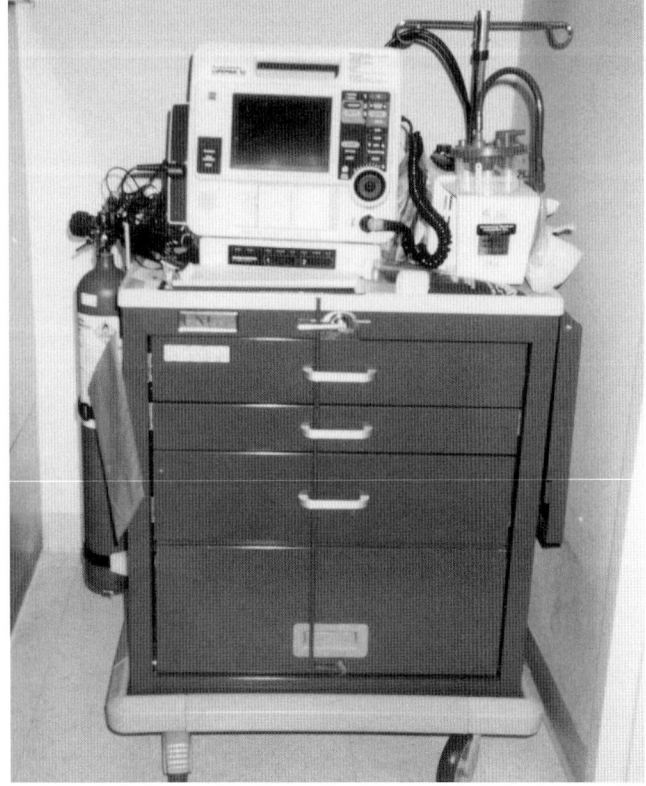

Preparation for emergency situations

Complications from office hysteroscopy are rare and are usually resolved in the office setting. However, when complications do occur, the nurse must be able to work along with the physician in an efficient manner to minimize morbidity (Figures 5 and 6 show an emergency cart). Office personnel must also be familiar with established guidelines in the event that resolution of complications involves transport of the patient to an off-site health-care facility. Guidelines should be a collaborative effort between the physician, the nurse, and the office manager with input from a representative of the health-care facility that will receive the patient.

Uterine perforation is a traumatic complication that can occur during hysteroscopy. Some perforations will not require additional intervention while others may require immediate laparoscopy or necessitate that the patient be observed for several hours. The nurse should be able to recognize uterine perforations so that appropriate intervention can be initiated upon the physician's instruction.

Cervical lacerations, which can create significant bleeding, can occur while dilating the internal os when a tenaculum is used to provide traction on the anterior lip of the cervix. A heavy absorbable suture on a large taper cut needle should be readily available to repair the laceration. It is also advisable to have ring forceps available, which can be used to apply pressure to the cervix, and/or silver nitrate sticks to treat oozing from the tenaculum site.

A review of literature reveals that complications from CO_2 gas instillation are theoretical when appropriate equipment and safety parameters for gas instillation are followed. It is well documented that laparoscopic insufflators must never be used to instill CO_2 gas for hysteroscopic procedures. These insufflators deliver gas in liters per minute at pressures that exceed recommended pressures for intrauterine instillation: 100 ml/min and 100 mmHg are the maximum flow rate and CO_2 pressure, respectively, allowed to ensure safe gas delivery [6]. The nurse must be familiar with safety parameters associated with using CO_2 gas as the dissention medium.

Vasovagal response and adverse reactions to local anesthetics are complications that require immediate resolution. Emergency equipment including atropine, oxygen, adrenaline, diphenhydramine hydrochloride (Benadryl) ammonia to inhale, and a ventilating device must be readily available in the procedure area where hysteroscopies are preformed [1]. (See the chapter on Anesthesia.)

CONCLUSION

The nurse plays a vital role in ensuring that patient safety, comfort, and satisfaction are achieved and maintained throughout office hysteroscopy procedures. Proper preparation, assurance that the physician has all the necessary equipment and instruments, and a patient who is relaxed and educated about the procedure that is about to take place are factors that facilitate successful completion of an office procedure that is well received and well tolerated.

REFERENCES

1. Prather C, Wolfe A. The nurse's role in office hysteroscopy. *J Obst Gynecol Neonatal Nurs* 1995; **24**: 813–816.
2. Tempesta SO, Spencer MP. Nursing implications for hysteroscopy in an outpatient setting. In: Isaacson KB, ed. Office Hysteroscopy. St Louis: Mosby, 1996: 38–44.
3. Murdoch JAC, Gan TJ. Anesthesia for hysteroscopy. *Anesthesiol Clin North Am* 2001; **19**: 125–140.
4. Valle RF. Office hysteroscopy. *Clin Obstet Gynecol* 1999; **42**: 276–289.
5. Isaacson KB. Selecting the proper equipment for office rigid hysteroscopy. In: Isaacson KB, ed. Office Hysteroscopy. St Louis: Mosby, 1996: 17–29.
6. Porter MB, Brumsted JR. Uterine Distention. In: Isaacson KB, ed. Office Hysteroscopy. St Louis: Mosby, 1996: 45–53.

6 Techniques for approaching the uterus: classic and vaginoscopical

Stefano Bettocchi

> **Take Home Message**
> The vaginoscopic technique makes it possible to approach the uterine cavity without a speculum and without a tenaculum. This reduces the anxiety of the patient and allows for maximum relaxation. The absence of the speculum allows a greater maneuverability of the scope. This is an advantage when the uterus lies in an extreme anteversion or retroversion. Vaginoscopy is possible with a 0° scope but is easier with a 30° fore-oblique scope. The learning curve is rapid.

CLASSIC APPROACH

Described at the end of the 1970s, this technique was strictly related to the technology available at that time – simple 5-mm 30° diagnostic hysteroscopes – and no endoscopic cameras were available. Therefore, the endoscopic view was obtained only by looking through the eyepiece of the scope. Thus, it is clear that each movement of the hysteroscope must be followed by a similar movement of the operator's head. This was not a comfortable situation, especially if wide movement of the scope was required. The only way for the hysteroscopist to visualize the portio easily was to insert the speculum while the scope was introduced in the cervical canal, and in the uterine cavity this was achieved by first positioning a Potzi-Collins forceps (tenaculum).

By using a counter-traction on the tenaculum to reduce the angle between the cervix and the uterine body, the scope was inserted blindly into the cervical canal. The endoscopist's view started, by applying the eye to the scope's eyepiece, only when the hysteroscopist had the feeling that the tip of the scope had reached the uterine cavity. The cervical canal was observed during the withdrawal of the scope. With this technique the movements of the scope, and thus of the hysteroscopist's head, were limited to exploration of the uterine cavity.

It is easy to appreciate that for a long time the two nightmares of endoscopists have been perforation of the uterus and the vagal reflex. It was not uncommon, when using the above technique, to place heavy traction on the tenaculum to force the introduction of the scope in a stenotic cervix, stimulating the sensitive uterine innervations (by the traction) and scratching the myometrial fiber (with the tip of the scope), or to perforate a soft uterine wall.

For a long period of time, the widespread use of local or general anesthesia was related to the difficulties of carrying out this technique and the high degree of patient compliance required.

VAGINOSCOPICAL TECHNIQUE

At the beginning of the 1990s, endoscopic cameras – together with the new generation of small diameter hysteroscopes – became widely available at reasonable prices. Only then did hysteroscopists finally have the opportunity to work comfortably, seated on a small chair, and able to observe the endoscopic monitor. The movements of the scope were no longer related to the difficulties of following it with the body, looking through the eyepiece. It was no longer necessary to visualize the cervix and to produce counter-traction with a tenaculum.

In 1995 a different approach to the uterus was described [1], without the use of the speculum and the tenaculum – the vaginoscopical approach [2]. The vagina is a cavity, collapsed, like the uterine cavity, but easily distensible with minimal pressure. The portio and the external cervical os can easily be visualized with the same distension media and the same pressure as used to distend the uterine cavity. Insertion of the hysteroscope without a tenaculum requires a good knowledge of the physics of instrumentation and dexterity on the part of the operator. Without the aid of the tenaculum, the insertion of the hysteroscope into the cervical canal through the internal cervical os may be difficult if the operator does not understand the correlation between what appears on the screen and the exact position of the scope in the cervix typical of the 30° fore-oblique view.

TECHNIQUE

Before starting the examination, the patient's history is carefully collected, with particular attention to clinical/subclinical signs of vaginal infections. If there is any doubt, vaginal bacteriology is performed. In the presence of an infection the procedure is postponed until specific treatment has been carried out. If the history is negative, the patient is seated on a comfortable gynecological chair or bed and the hysteroscope (30° fore-oblique) is positioned on the vaginal introit, separating the labia with the fingers, without any disinfection of the area. The vagina is distended with the same distension medium used for the uterine cavity (saline solution) and with the same pressure (around 20 mmHg automatically controlled by an electronic suction/irrigation pump). The tip of the scope must remain 1 cm away from the mucosa in order to obtain a panoramic view. When the hymen is visualized the scope is driven in the posterior fornix to readily visualize the portio and then slowly backwards with narrow lateral movements to locate the external cervical os. Once this is correctly visible the tip of the scope is introduced into the cervix and then into the cavity, following the uterine anatomy and relating the movements of the hands to the deflected 30° view on the monitor.

REFERENCES

1. Bettocchi S, Selvaggi L, Porreca M, Loverro G. The vaginoscopical technique: a new approach to hysteroscopy. *J Am Assoc Gynecol Laparosc* 1995; **2** (Suppl): 76.
2. Bettocchi S, Selvaggi L. A vaginoscopical approach to reduce the pain of office hysteroscopy. *J Am Assoc Gynecol Laparosc* 1997; **4**: 255–258.

Figure 3

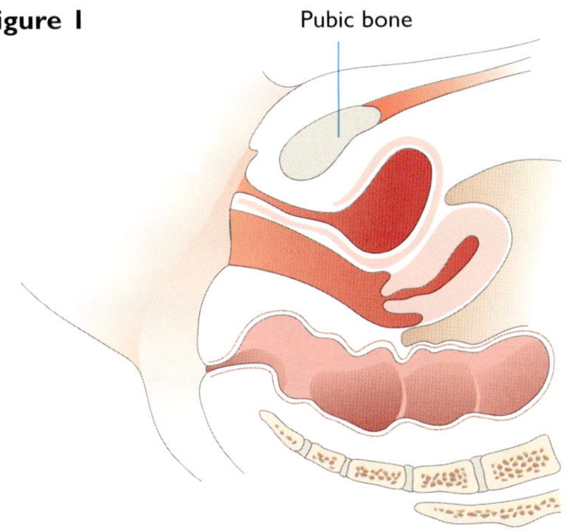

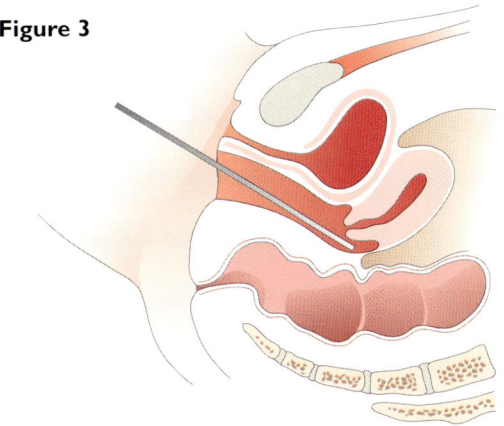

Figure 4

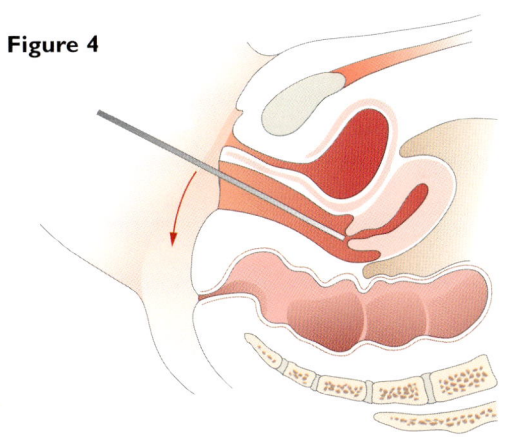

Figure 1

Figure 2

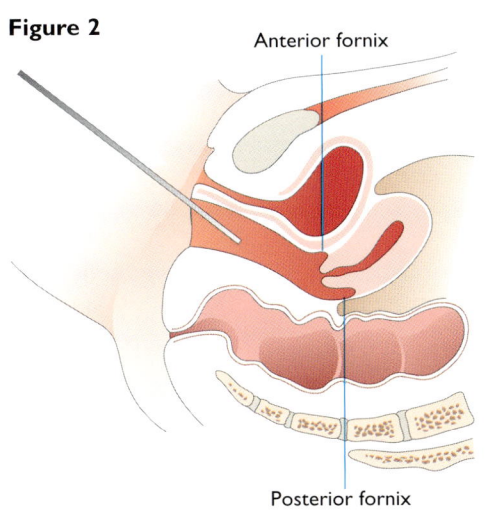

Figure 5

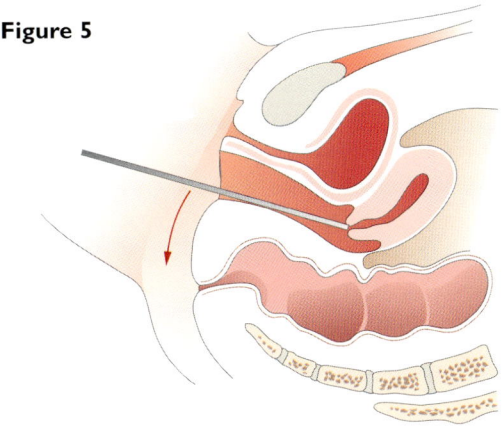

7 Distension media in diagnostic hysteroscopy

J. Hamou

> **Take Home Message**
> When one is embarking on ambulatory hysteroscopy, there are two ways to distend the uterine cavity. The classic method employs CO_2 and the more commonly used method employs low molecular weight fluid distension media. The classic gas distension gives better, clearer images, as the refractory index of the gas is the same as the surrounding air. The use of gas as a distension medium requires more experience, and the examination takes longer. The learning curve is somewhat slower when gas is used. A specific gas insufflator is required, according to the indications given in this chapter. In the vaginoscopic approach, the vagina is the first chamber to be distended, therefore gas cannot be used. Low molecular weight distension media are used in this situation. The different approaches produce differences in the interpretation of the visual findings, as with gas the endometrial structures are glued to the wall, whereas these structures are flooded in the liquid media. A gravity bag is sufficient for fluid distension. CO_2 gas is extremely safe, whereas – if not used carefully – liquid distension carries the risk of infection and cell transportation towards the abdomen.

Correct distension of the uterine cavity is a fundamental precondition of the proper hysteroscopic technique. Several methods can be used to distend the uterine cavity. The methods used for diagnostic hysteroscopy differ from those used in classical surgical hysteroscopy with the patient under general anesthesia. The use of a hysteroresectoscope for intrauterine electrosurgery requires additional safety measures and preconditions. This technique is only feasible with electrolyte-free liquid distension media to prevent the electricity from spreading.

The most common distension media are divided into two categories: gases used only in diagnostic hysteroscopy and liquids used in both diagnostic and operative hysteroscopy.

CARBON DIOXIDE DISTENSION

The use of an insufflator with automatic pressure control was introduced into practice by H.J. Lindemann in 1972. The technical innovations of recent years have been accompanied by greater reliability and safety, so that CO_2 distension is currently considered the method of choice in diagnostic hysteroscopy. The initial fear of gas embolism was definitively dispersed when Lindemann and Rubin reported 90,000 complication-free insufflations performed by 380 different authors. Indeed, the doses required to induce the first signs of CO_2 intoxication are much higher than those used for the entire hysteroscopic procedure performed with the application of proper insufflation criteria, i.e. with an insufflation system able to keep the pressure within the 100–120 mmHg range and a flow of 30–60 ml/min (corresponding to an intrauterine pressure of 40–80 mmHg). Therefore, CO_2 has proved to be the most suitable distension medium. Since it does not distort the intrauterine view in any way, it permits extremely fine, detailed evaluation of the endometrial physiology, i.e. provides a natural view of the uterine cavity which otherwise would not be possible with a liquid distension medium. Theoretically, it is even possible to perform minor surgery using CO_2, although a liquid medium is preferable in all forms of surgical hysteroscopy.

THE ELECTRONIC VARIABLE PRESSURE/VARIABLE FLOW INSUFFLATOR

The electronic variable pressure/variable flow insufflator (Hamou Hysteroflator) (Figure 1) is controlled by an electronic molecular counter that eliminates the requirement for a number of mechanical circuits and allows for programmed control of both the flow and the pressure of the CO_2. This ensures complete safety and avoids any additional excesses in pressure or flow.

It can be preset to provide the optimal gas delivery for each of the applications of microhysteroscopy including panoramic microhysteroscopy, microcolpohysteroscopy, salpingoscopy, and tubal insufflation. In this latter case, the surgeon can vary the flow as dictated by the permeability and functional status of the tube.

The regulation of the CO_2 flow is entirely automatic. As pressure gradually increases, the flow gradually decreases until it reaches 0 when a pressure of 180 mmHg is attained.

Because pressure and flow are always in equilibrium there is no risk of momentary excess and any loss of gas through the tubes or the cervix is immediately compensated. This gentle approach markedly reduces any myometrial peristalsis. The pressure and the flow rates are displayed digitally.

The device combines the advantages of earlier instruments and is better adapted to the anatomic and physiologic conditions of the genital tract. The total quantity of gas delivered to the uterine cavity is about 40–50 ml.

Whatever insufflator is used, the quantity of gas needed to perform a microhysteroscopic examination is less than that needed for tubal insufflation [1] or conventional panoramic hysteroscopy [2,3]. This small amount of CO_2 offers several advantages. First, the low flow produces a gradual uterine distension, thereby lessening the patient's pain by not inducing peristaltic contractions. Second, there is no need to apply the cumbersome cervical occlusive cap [4,5]; therefore, the unobstructed cervical canal can act as a safety valve if pressures do become excessive. Third, there is a very limited passage of CO_2 into the peritoneal cavity, leading to a very low incidence of shoulder pain. If shoulder pain does occur it is usually transient. Finally, there is little risk of intravascular absorption of CO_2. Lindemann and Bercy [4] have demonstrated that the direct introduction of CO_2 into the femoral vein in quantities that were twenty times greater than that used by the authors is well tolerated. As CO_2 is less soluble than oxygen in blood it is rapidly eliminated by the lungs without any prolonged alteration in the PCO_2 [6].

TOLERANCE AND SECURITY EVALUATION WHEN USING GAS MEDIA

The parameters that have been measured are the $PaCO_2$, total CO_2, and pH. The results are shown in Table 1. For those patients undergoing microhysteroscopy without anesthesia, examination time was from 6 to 15 minutes, and we did not notice any significant modifications in pH or $PaCO_2$. Many patients presented with hyperventilation with a mean frequency of 22/min and tachycardia of 100–110/min. These changes were attributed to the apprehension preceding the examination and the various investigations.

For the 10 patients who received an anesthetic using spontaneous ventilation, the pH tended toward acidosis after 5 minutes of general anesthesia and although the pH fell during the performance of the hysteroscopy, the critical level was reached in only one patient. The main value of the pH was 7.368. In nine patients with assisted ventilation, modifications in gas, tension, and hemodynamics were noted in one case and followed an episode of cyanosis at the time of intubation. $PaCO_2$ and CO_2 were reduced and pH was increased. These variations occurred following hyperventilation. Therefore, it can be said that if hysteroscopic examination is undertaken with meticulous attention to technique, there are very minimal clinical, hemodynamic, or blood gas changes that expose the patient to very small risk. In contrast, there have been some severe accidents where the pressure or flow of CO_2 was not kept under surveillance or where a laparoscopic insufflator was used. Almost all of these accidents, the most serious of which occurred six times in 1973, were caused by faulty control of the rate or pressure of insufflation. In one fatal case [7] 30–50 liters of gas were insufflated without control of volume or pressure.

THE USE OF FLUIDS IN OFFICE HYSTEROSCOPY

The use of fluid for office hysteroscopy is more convenient for flexible endoscopes. It is useful for less invasive office hysteroscopy, especially when confronted with stenosis of the cervical canal or postmenopausal narrow internal os. We prefer to use the small 2.9-mm hysteroscope with a convenient double sheath (promoted by S. Bettocchi). The inner sheath of 4.3 mm may be used alone with CO_2 insufflation. This inner sheath in conjunction with the

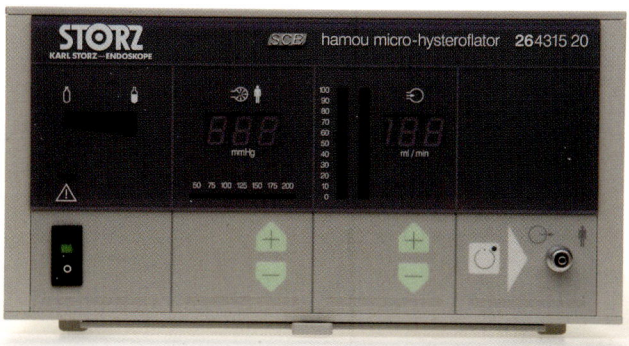

Figure 1
The Hamou electronic insufflator. From the left the first set of dials give the content of the CO_2 reservoir. The second column from the left gives an indication of the intrauterine pressure expressed in mmHg. The third column from the left indicates the inflow pressure. Both the second and the third column can be regulated by pressing the + and − signs, while the diode in the last column gives the operator the ability to shut down the flow, while the insufflator remains on standby.

continuous flow outer sheath of 5 mm, has double continuous flow as for the resector double flow sheath. Saline solution is appropriate, as no electricity is involved. The systems used to control pressure and flows are described below.

GRAVITY FALL SYSTEM

Raising the bag to an adequate height (90–100 cm above the patient's perineum is sufficient to achieve a pressure of approximately 70 mmHg) causes the liquid to flow down by gravity force. Irrigation is achieved by connecting the tubing of the resectoscope outflow connector to a collection basin. This outlet can also be connected to a suction pump, although in such cases it can prove difficult to maintain a good balance between outflow and suction pressure.

PRESSURE CUFF

These devices, similar to a sphygmomanometer, are insufflated around the bag, exerting pressure on it. An assistant must keep the pressure at approximately 80 mmHg, since the outflow pressure drops as the bag is gradually emptied. Irrigation is generally achieved in the same way as described for the gravity fall system.

ELECTRONIC SUCTION AND IRRIGATION PUMP
(Figure 2)

Automatically controlled suction and irrigation are very important to maintain a clear field of view in hysteroscopic surgery and constant dilatation of the uterine cavity. As an alternative to pre-setting flow rate, suction, and irrigation pressure, there are other system versions available that allow for monitoring and control of the pre-set volume difference between irrigation liquid inflow and outflow and the change in this parameter per minute. The following settings are generally used: flow rate of approximately 200 mmHg, outflow pressure of 75 mmHg, and suction pressure of 0.25 bar. The Hamou Endomat® can be used both in hysteroscopy and laparoscopy by simply changing the irrigation set.

Table 1
Variation in arterial pH, $PaCO_2$, and CO_2 during ambulatory hysteroscopy without anesthesia

	Basal status				During hysteroscopy			
Patient	pH	Total CO_2	$PaCO_2$	PaO_2	pH	Total CO_2	$PaCO_2$	PaO_2
1	7.439	19.5	28	109.2	7.429	19.3	28.3	107
2	7.379	24.4	40.0	84.2	7.423	26.2	38.9	107.6
3	7.341	17.7	31.8	104.3	7.401	24.3	37.9	103.3
4	7.413	17.8	27.1	119.2	7.441	18.8	26.8	106.8
5	7.382	23.4	36.2	104.2	7.379	22	36.1	111.3
6	7.478	21.1	27.6	138.3	7.435	19.6	24.8	189.2
7	7.387	19.9	32.2	115	7.394	22.1	35.1	95.9
8	7.367	187.5	27.8	106.5	7.366	17.5	29.6	102
9	7.414	21.1	32	132.2	7.452	22.2	30.9	126
10	7.381	19.1	31.2	96.7	7.414	22.7	34.4	111.2
11	7.380	19.4	35.4	122	7.374	22.9	38.1	100.5
12	7.367	16.2	26.8	159	7.406	18.7	29.1	146
13	7.356	21.5	37.2	113.8	7.370	19.2	38.3	154.2
14	7.384	22.2	36	100.8	7.391	24.1	38.5	114.8
15	7.368	22.9	38.6	114.2	7.378	21.7	35.9	114.8
Average	7.390	20.18	32.667	114.76	7.403	21.486	33.51	117.96

REFERENCES

1. Rubin IC. Uterine endoscopy, endometroscopy with the aid of uterine insufflation. *Am J Obstet Gynecol* 1925; **10**: 313.
2. Lindemann HJ. Eine neue Untersuchungsmethode für die Husteroskopie. *Endoscopy* 1971; **4**: 194.
3. Siegler AM. A comparison of gas and liquid for hysteroscopy. *J Reprod Med* 1975; **15**: 73.
4. Lindemann HJ, Bercy G. Endoscopy. New York: Appleton-Century-Crofts, 1976: 493–501.
5. Porto R. La pneumo-hysteroscopie. *Acta Endosc* 1973; **3**: 84.
6. Salat Baroux J, Hamou JE, Maillard J, Chouraqui A, Verges P. Complications from microhysteroscopy. In: Siegler AM, Lindemann HJ, eds. Hysteroscopy, Principles and Practice. Philadelphia: Lippincott, 1984: 112–118.
7. Siegler AM, Kemman EK, Gentle GP. Hysteroscopic procedures in 257 patients. *Fertil Steril* 1976; **27**: 1267.

BIBLIOGRAPHY

Antoine T. Der heutige stand der ausslichtmicroskopie in der Gynekologie. *Arch Gynekol* 1961;180–162.

Antoine T, Grunberger V. Atlas der Kolpomikroskopie. Stuttgart, 1956.

Baggish MS. Contact hysteroscopy: a new technique to explore the uterine cavity. *Obstet Gynecol* 1979; **54**: 350–354.

Bercy G. Endoscopy. New York: Appleton Century Crofts, 1976: 222–242.

Hamou JE. Hystéroscopie et microhystéroscopie avec un instrument nouveau : le microhystéroscope. *Endosc Gynecol* 1980; **2**: 131.

Hamou JE. Microhysteroscopy. *Acta Endosc* 1980; **10**: 415.

Hamou JE. Hystéroscopie et microhystéroscopie avec un instrument nouveau: le microhystéroscope. In: Albano V, Cittadini E, Quatararo P, eds. Endoscopia Ginecologica. Palermo: COFESE Publishers, 1980.

Hamou JE, Salat-Baroux J, Henrion R. Hystéroscopie et microhystéroscopie. In: Encyclop Med Chir. Paris: Masson, 1985; 11.

Hopkins HH. Optical principles of the endoscope. In: Bercy, ed. Endoscopy. New York: Appleton, 1976.

Lindemann HJ. Historical aspects of hysteroscopy: *Fertil Steril* 1973; **24**: 230.

Lindemann HJ. Hysteroscopy today and tomorrow. *Endoscopy* 1978; **10**: 234.

Lindemann HJ. Gynakologische und geburtshilfiche endoskopie. *Arch Gynecol* 1985; **238**: 1.

Lindemann HJ, Mohr J. CO_2 hysteroscopy: diagnosis and treatment. *Am J Obstet Gynecol* 1976; **124**: 129.

March CM, Israel R, March AD. Hysteroscopic management of uterine adhaesions. *Am J Obstet Gynecol* 1978; **130**: 653–657.

Neuwirth RS, Levine RV. Evaluation of a method of hysteroscopy with the use of 30% Dextran. *Am J Obstet Gynecol* 1972; **114**: 696.

Nitze M. Uber eine neue Behandlungs Methode. Med Press Wien, 1879.

Ohkawa K, Ohkawa R. Hysteromicroscopy. In: Siegler AM, Lindemann HJ, eds. Hysteroscopy: Principles and Practice. Philadelphia: JB Lippincott, 1984.

Paille F. Magnifying endoscopy. *Acta Endosc* 1980; **10**: 233.

Palmer R. Un nouvel hysteroscope. *Bull Fed Soc Gyn Obst* 1975; **40**: 3.

Porto B, Gaujoux J. Une nouvelle methode d'hystéroscopie: instrumentation et technique. *J Gynecol Obstet Biol Reprod* 1972; **1**: 691.

Quinones RG. Hysteroscopy: choosing distention media. *Int J Fertil* 1984; **29**: 129.

Salat Baroux J, Hamou JE, Uzan S, Antoine JM. Notre experience sur 744 hystéroscopies. In: Netter A, Gorins P, eds. Actualités Gynecologiques. Paris: Masson, 1980.

Siegler AM, Kemman EK. Hysteroscopy. *Obstet Gynecol Surv* 1975; **30**: 567.

Sugimoto O. Hysteroscopy: current and future status of hysteroscopy. *Sanfujinka Jissai* 1972; **21**: 377.

Sugimoto O. Diagnostic and Therapeutic Hysteroscopy. Tokyo: Igaku-Shoin, 1978.

Valle RF, Sciarra JJ. Hysteroscopy: a useful diagnostic adjunct in gynaecology. *Am J Obstet Gynecol* 1975; **122**: 230.

Vulmiere J, Fourestier M, Gladu A. Hystéroscopie de contact. Perfectionnements à l'endoscopie medicale. *Presse Med* 1972; **60**: 1292.

Vulniere JC, Fourestier M, Gulot GF. Endoscope de contact. Brevet n. 1.370,580 INPI Paris 1962.

Figure 2

The Hamou Endomat® can be used in hysteroscopy and laparoscopy by changing the cuff on the sensor of the apparatus. The sensor is found on the first column from the right under the pump wheel, next to the diode that when pressed and giving a bright green light will start the pump. In the first column from the left is the main switch. The second column from the left indicates the inflow volume in ml/minute. The second column from the left indicates the intrauterine pressure in mmHg. The third column from the left indicates the aspiration pressure in bars. In the third column there is a diode which activates the aspiration when pressed, but can shut down the aspiration pressure without stopping the pump itself. By pressing the + and − signs in the green arrows the pressure needed for each individual patient can be set.

8 The self-retaining office hysteroscope

H. Guedj

> **Take Home Message**
> The self-retaining hysteroscope is the result of the maximal reduction of the different components needed for ambulatory hysteroscopy. The light source and the insufflation pump are reduced to the point that these are easily transportable. The results are optimal and reproducible. In an age where liquid distension media are recommended the self-retaining hysteroscope remains a valid alternative in diagnostic hysteroscopy.

INTRODUCTION

Before 1980 hysteroscopic practice was rather complicated. Hysteroscopes consisted of three parts each connected to a different exterior element:

- The optic connected to a cold light generator by means of fiberoptic cable.
- The cervical cap connected to a pump to ensure the vacuum between the cap and the exterior cervix.
- The sheath around the optic allowing the inflow of the distention medium – CO_2 gas in most cases.

This presumes three distinct entities, three exterior sources and three pieces of the hysteroscope. This instrumentation was complex and heavy; it became difficult to maneuver and cumbersome to transport. This impaired the teaching of the technique and the diffusion of the technique of intrauterine endoscopy between practicing gynecologists.

This is why in 1980 Dr Bernard Parent and myself engaged in the creation of an autonomous panoramic hysteroscope.

The aim of this instrument is to unite in one unit the endoscope, the light source, and the CO_2 insufflator. The advantage is that the unit is portable and can be manipulated with one hand (CO_2 'all-in-one' hysteroscope). It was the first autonomous endoscopic unit that could be used with ease in daily practice for diagnostic purposes in the office. Easy to mount, light to transport, and easy to apply in daily use, it was used more frequently.

DESCRIPTION OF THE SELF-RETAINING HYSTEROSCOPE (Figures 1 and 2)

THE ENDOSCOPE

The center part of the hysteroscope is the Wolf panoramic telescope. The standard telescope has an exterior diameter

Figure 1
Self-retaining hysteroscope. (a) Overall view. (b) Autonomous panoramic hysteroscope: standard optic of 4 mm. Autonomous mini-hysteroscope: small optic of 2.7 mm. A, endoscope (panoramic optic and its sheath); B, security valve; C, rotating infusion volume meter (2 positions); D, light source; E, intermediate piece; F, handpiece (contains the three batteries); G, CO_2 container; H, silicone rubber tubing to deliver the CO_2.

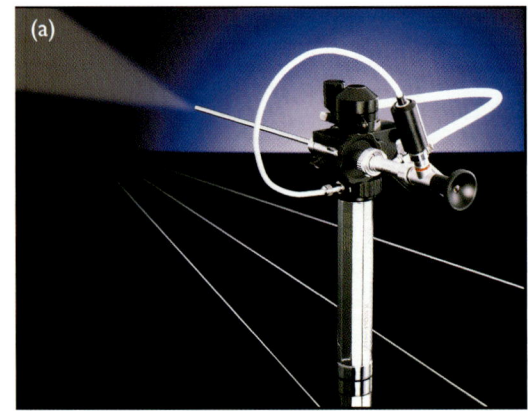

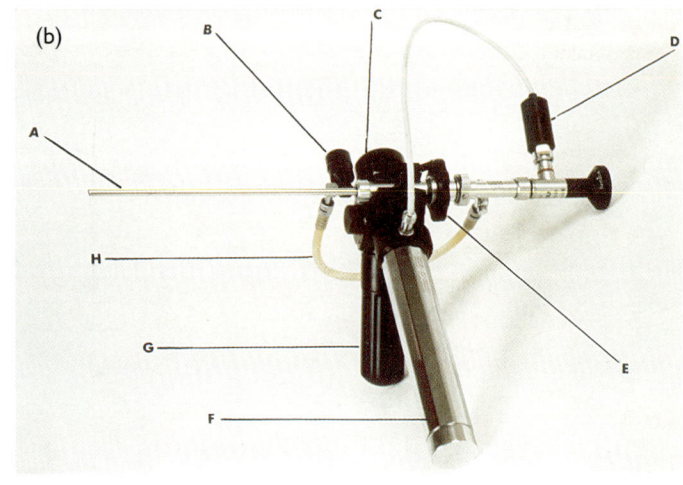

of 4 mm, but a smaller telescope of 2.7 mm can be used so that the examination becomes easy in every patient, even in a nulliparous or a menopausal patient. All these telescopes designed for diagnostic purposes have a forward oblique vision, meaning that the angle of view is of 25° off from the axis of the telescope (Figures 3). The visual field is 80% of this angle of view. In other words, to avoid false passages (Figure 4), the progression of the distal part of the telescope in the endocervical canal has to be done in the axis of the window of the telescope, this means in this angle of 25° off the axis of the telescope. This forward oblique vision allows a simultaneous frontal and sideways view of the uterine cavity. The 0° direct view requires a steep inclination of the scope in the vagina and vulva in order to bring the view in front of the segment for study. This maneuver is often painful for the patient. The forward oblique vision makes it possible, by rotational movements, to view the cavity over 180°. The forward oblique vision means to the rigid scope what the movements of the distal part means to the flexible scope. The telescope is inserted in a sheath (15 charr). This sheath has a stopcock to allow CO_2 insufflation. The gas travels along the sheath and is ejected tangentially on the surface of the distal lens of the telescope, like a wiper blade, and hence always allows a clean field of vision even in cases of uterine bleeding. The sheath carrying the telescope is slipped in an intermediate sheath and coupled to the gas-providing system.

During outpatient hysteroscopy a biopsy can be taken under direct visual control. In this case the 2.7-mm telescope must be used within a sheath with an outside oval form with a diameter of 17 charr, at its largest diameter 5.6 × 3 mm. This sheath has a working channel of 7 charr, which allows the introduction of a biopsy forceps (flexible or semi-rigid) alongside the telescope.

CHARACTERISTICS OF THE TELESCOPES PROVIDED WITH A WIPER BLADE SYSTEM

The special profile at the distal end of the sheath and the particular and precise cut of this profile in proportion to the surface of the telescope allow the liberation of the CO_2 gas flow in the form of a jet tangential to the surface of the telescope due to a small gutter carved in the internal wall of the sheath (Figures 5a and 5b). This causes the 'wiper blade' effect produced by the gas on the surface of the telescope and allows for clear vision even in cases of uterine bleeding.

Figure 3
Sharacteristics of the forward oblique 4-mm telescope.

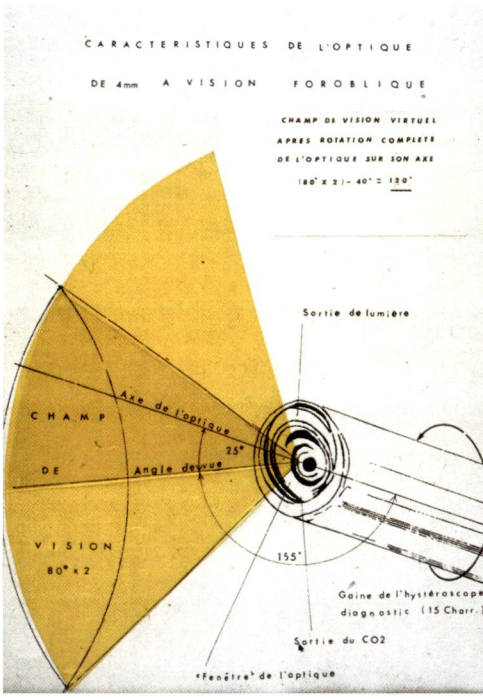

Figure 4
Potential problem during the examination of the cervical canal: the false passage, a pseudo canal excavated in the mucosa.

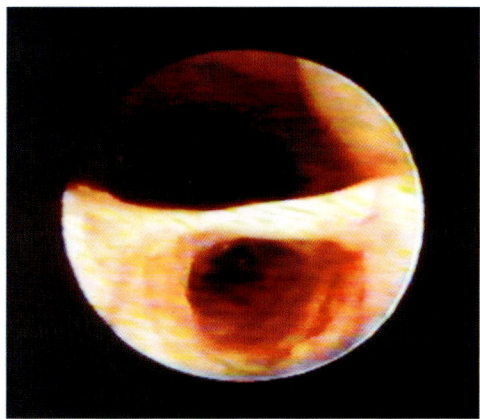

Figure 2
Self-retaining hysteroscope with sheath for biopsy forceps.

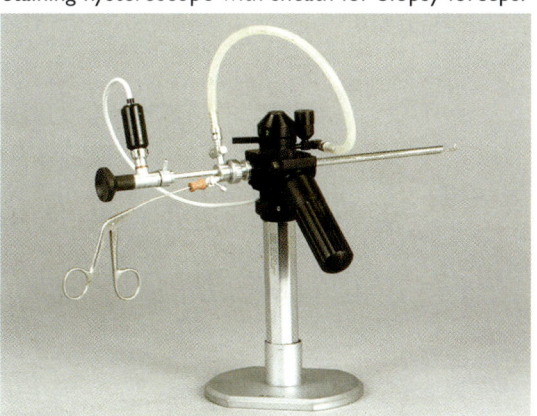

THE CO₂ INSUFFLATION UNIT

This unit consists of:
- A CO_2 cartridge.
- An expansion cylinder in two stages: the system regulating the gas expansion.
- A security valve (Figure 6).

Functioning.

The expansion cylinder, situated on the upper part of the handpiece of the instrument, brings the CO_2 pressure down from the original pressure in the cartridge to 200 mb (150 mmHg), at the same time it limits its maximum flow to 100 ml/min. At the exit of the expansion cylinder there is an integrated safety valve that allows the gas out of the system into the surrounding air when the gas pressure exceeds 226.6 mb (170 mmHg). This integrated safety valve therefore eliminates every risk of excessive pressure. This valve functions on an internal system compressing a spring with an adjusting nut and a small valve. The valve is factory-adjusted on an expansion cylinder of 150 mmHg. Under these conditions the CO_2 gas is brought through a tubing to the sheath around the telescope. The cartridge of gas contains approximately 4 liters of expanded gas. This amount allows for some 10 hysteroscopies. The advantage is that these cartridges are readily available in the drugstores. The revolving flow meter (Figure 7) is situated on the top of the instrument and features two possible positions for the gas flow so as to ensure a rigorous constant flow of gas in both positions. This is made

Figure 5
SMechanism causing the windshield wiper effect of the CO_2. (a) Internal structure of the distal part of the sheath; the canal is elaborated within the thickened part of the sheath, the CO_2 has to flow through this passage. (b) The relationship between the optic and the sheath allows the gas to be blown over the surface of the optic tangentially.

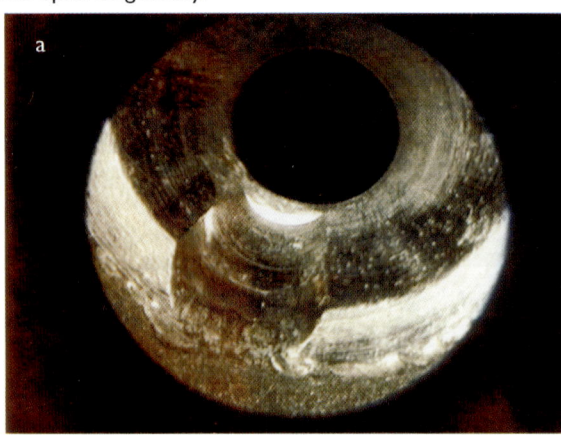

Figure 6
Diagram of a cross-section of the security valve. Security control regulation set at 150 ml or 11 mmHg (5.5 high and 5.5 bar) = 149.6 grams at full aperture.

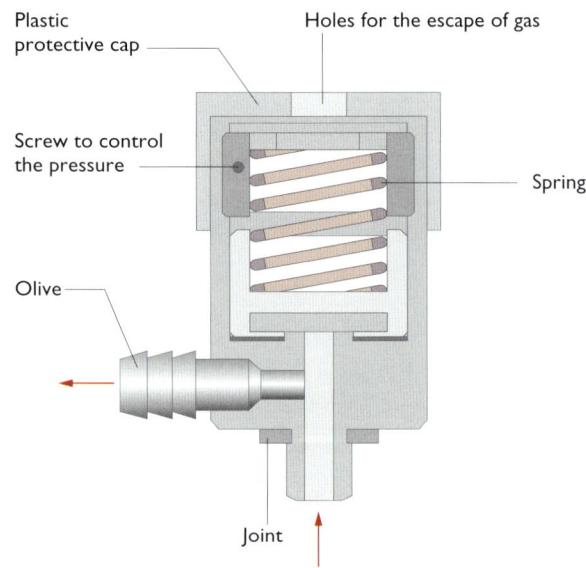

Figure 7
Miniaturized flow meter for use in video hysteroscopy in the private office. It ensures that two flow rates of CO_2 are kept rigorously constant. 1 = 75 ml/min, corresponding to a pressure of 75 mmHg. 2 = 100 ml/min, corresponding to a pressure of 150 mmHg. The integrated security valve lets the gas escape at a pressure of 170 mmHg.

possible by a metal perforated disk that can be rotated. The perforations have different diameters for each selection of gas flow.

Position 1: flow = 75 ml/min
  Pressure at the tip of the instrument = 75 mmHg.
  Under these conditions the reserve of CO_2 is sufficient for 40 minutes.

Position 2: flow = 100 ml/min
  Pressure at the tip of the instrument = 150 mmHg.
  Under these conditions the reserve of CO_2 is sufficient for 40 minutes.

The concept of this flow meter was inspired by the continuous oxygen flow meters of the 'Himalaya' type used in mountain climbing (Figure 8).

COLD LIGHT GENERATOR

The light is provided by a miniaturized projector using a powerful micro halogen lamp. Its weight is <50 g. The projector is connected to an energy source consisting of three nickel cadmium rechargeable batteries. These batteries are placed in a cylindrical container that forms the handpiece of the instrument. It lasts for 1 hour (Figures 9. The different parts of the self-retaining hysteroscope are packed in a carrier case that allows easy transportation from one location to another (Figures 10).

DESCRIPTION OF THE TECHNIQUE USED

The examination takes place during the first half of the menstrual cycle. The preferred day of the cycle is 11. An antispasmodic drug is given (Spasfon®), as is a drug to facilitate a slight dilatation of the cervical canal (Cytotec®). Both are administered the evening before the examination. The location for the examination can be an outpatient department at the hospital or the private office; because of the simplicity of the equipment, both are interchangeable. After the procedure the patient is instructed to remain in the facility for some 10 minutes to be observed for the unlikely event of a vasovagal reaction.

STERILIZATION OF THE HYSTEROSCOPE

The telescope, the internal sheath, and the external sheath are laid down in a self-sealing box containing trioxymethylene tablets (12 hours at room temperature; 10 minutes at 40°C) (Figure 11). Another option is soaking in

Figure 9
Self-retaining hysteroscope, dismantled.

Figure 8
Permanent oxygen flow regulator (Himalaya type).

Figure 10
Carrier case for transporting the different elements of the scope.

a solution of formaldehyde (Detercide®, Cidex®) for 30 minutes (1 dosage in a container of 4.5 liters of sterile water) (Figure 12). If they are soaked both the optic and the sheaths should be rinsed thoroughly with sterile water. On the other hand the remaining parts of the instruments do not need sterilization (flow meter, security valve, CO_2 container, and batteries container).

(Authors note: sterilization techniques concerning the instruments are submitted to the specific rulings in the different countries.)

EXAMINATION TECHNIQUE

After a vaginal examination to evaluate the uterus for its volume and position in the pelvis, the operator washes his or her hands and puts on his or her gloves after disinfection. Once the vaginal speculum is in position the external os is rinsed with Dakin®, care is also taken to rinse the vagina. The telescope and the supporting sheaths are then mounted on the rest of the apparatus. Care is taken not to contaminate the telescope and the sheaths during the process of assembling. The flow rate is regulated at 100 ml/min. A tenaculum is placed on the anterior lip of the cervix to bring the uterine cavity in line with the axis of the cervical canal. The examination is about to start.

The progression into the cervical canal is slow and according to the principles of the forward oblique telescope. The operator halts at the level of the internal os. Here dilatation takes place after 10–20 seconds. The telescope is then advanced towards the center of the opening and enters the uterine cavity. During the passage of the upper part of the cervical canal and the isthmus the position of the telescope and hence the instrument is one of extreme anteversion or extreme retroversion (Figure 13).

The self-retaining hysteroscope reminds us by its 'all-in' principle of the ancestor of the hysteroscopes, the instrument ideated by Desormeaux in 1865. This instrument consisted of a vertical cylinder containing a light source, the light was produced by a flame produced by lighting a mixture of alcohol and turpentine. The remainder consisted of a tube for observation. This tube could be bent into different positions to make the observations easier (Figure 14). This illustrates that there is not such a big difference between the profile of the hysteroscopist of 2002 and that of 1865 (Figure 15).

Figure 11
An airtight box for sterilization of instruments using trioxymethylene tablets.

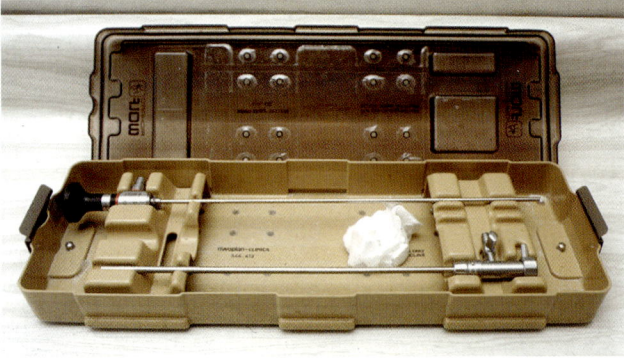

Figure 12
A watertight box for the sterilization of the instruments using formaldehyde.

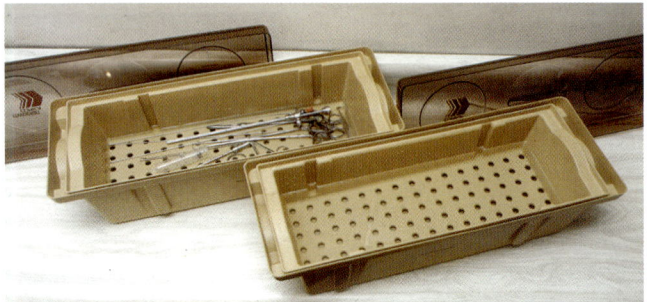

Figure 13
Technique of an examination using the self-retaining hysteroscope.

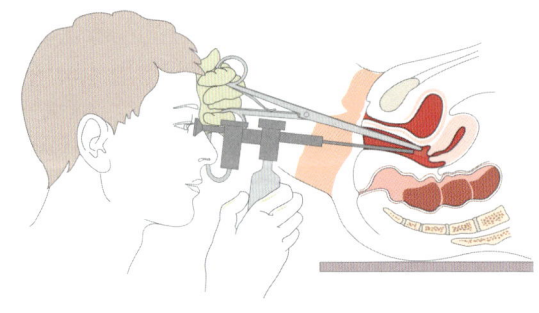

Figure 14
The Desormeaux hysteroscope.

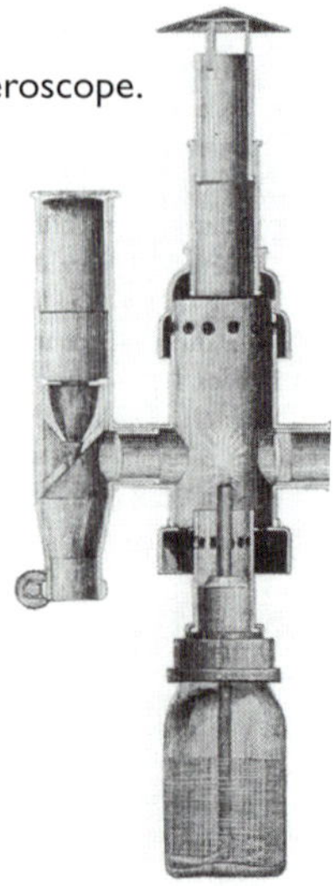

INTEGRATION OF THE SELF-RETAINING HYSTEROSCOPE INTO VIDEO HYSTEROSCOPY

(Figure 16)

When the physician wishes to perform a video documentation, enabling him or her to obtain photo documentation at the same time, the light provided by the miniprojector's halogen lamp has to be replaced by a more powerful cold light source. We use a 250-W halogen lamp or a 175 xenon light source. When the self-retaining hysteroscope is used in this way a number of irreplaceable documents can be added to the patient's file.

- Registration on a video or DVD cassette where comments can be added directly over a microphone.
- Generation of photographs by using a colour printer type Videoprinter.

We store these items on a mini trolley (Figure 17).

We make a written report of the examination and draw the lesions on a pre-printed drawing of the uterine cavity. If the clinician is able to use a computerized system they are then able to have a report on computer in digital imaging, allowing four to six prints showing different incidences of the observed lesions (Figures 18 and 19).

EVIDENCE BASE AND STATISTICS (META-ANALYSIS)

The miniaturization of the different systems, especially of the insufflation unit and the integrated light source, in the 'self-retaining hysteroscope' greatly facilitate the technique for exploring the uterine cavity. This is mainly due to the ease of regulating the flow meter.

This means that costs are greatly reduced, as there is no longer the need for a cumbersome hysteroflator or an external light source. The costs are reduced by a factor of two.

The CO_2 cartridges are readily available in the normal drugstore and cost 7.81 Eur/$6.90 for a box of 10 cartridges. This should be compared with a normal bottle container of 350 liters of CO_2. The volume of the bottle container (320 × 120 × 304 mm) and the legal prescriptions and its weight (c. 6 kg) are elements that should be taken into consideration. Therefore the self-retaining hysteroscope's write off is much shorter than that of classical hysteroscopes. Nowadays hysteroflators cost between 5466.85 and 6246.92 Eur or $4824.9 and $5514. This is the price of the whole of the integrated system of the self-retaining hysteroscope.

Figure 15
Use of the Desormeaux hysteroscope in 1865.

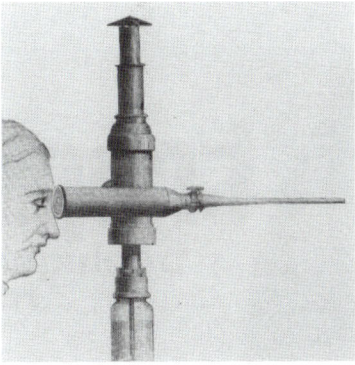

Figure 16
Hysteroscopic examination in the private office using video hysteroscopy.

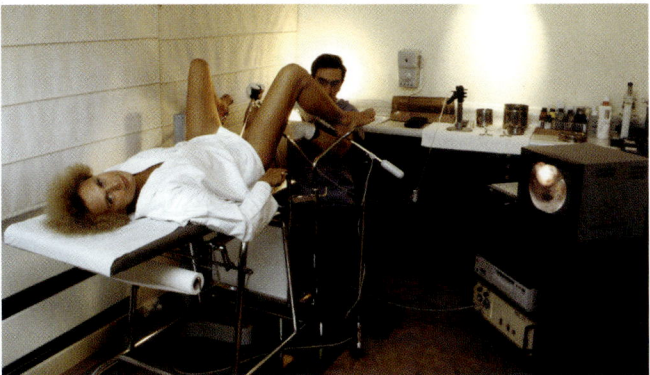

Figure 17
Mini column for video hysteroscopy in the private office. This tower is only half as cumbersome as the tower used in the theater. From top to bottom: mini CO_2 source and its flow meter with incorporated security valve; video monitor and to its left the camera housing; VHS video recorder; video printer; cold light source; foot switch to control the picture capture.

THE DECISION-MAKING TREE (ALGORITHM)

The ease of use of the self-retaining hysteroscope makes it an instrument for daily use. It is so reduced in space (Figure 20) that it can be used alongside the colposcope and the ultrasound in the office (Figure 21) or the outpatient facility.

- In the case of a subfertility exploration it can precede the hysterosalpingogram. Before each attempt at IVFET, exploration of the cavity is a must, especially because of the ease of the technique.
- In the search for causes of spontaneous and repeated miscarriages hysteroscopy is the first step before every other examination, as uterine malformations or intracavitary lesions can be diagnosed and treated, in most cases, in the same session.
- When a patient presents with abnormal uterine bleeding, hysteroscopy can precede the ultrasound examination. The screen wiper effect makes it possible to see even in periods of active intracavitary bleeding.
- In cases of amenorrhea, hysteroscopy can precede the hysterosalpingogram if there is a suspicion of intracavitary adhesions.
- In the case of an abdominal pain syndrome, hysteroscopy in the office can precede laparoscopy.
- When an IUCD is lost, hysteroscopy is superior to ultrasound examination.

All these indications mean that hysteroscopy is the first examination, ahead of suspected intrauterine pathology, as this examination can be decided and performed during the first visit even without premedication.

Figure 18
Report of a hysteroscopic examination with digitalized hysteroscopic images. The theater case. Diagnostic hysteroscopy in a patient aged 35 years presenting with secondary infertility. The examination was performed at cycle day 14 after premedication with Spasfon®. Endocervical canal: normal. Internal orifice: passed through easily. Uterine cavity: size and form normal. Uterine cornua free. Tubal orifices easily visualized. The endometrium has a normal trophic aspect at the level of both the corneal area and on the anterior part of the uterine cavity. The aspect is one of a normal proliferative endometrium in phase with the day of the menstrual cycle. There are two abnormal areas: at the level of the posterior side of the uterine cavity there is a site representing a chronic endometritis characterized by a zone of dark red endometrium and brilliant white spots. On the posterior side right after the isthmus there is a region with an endometrial hyperplasia, rather whitish in colour, distending towards the left border of the uterine cavity. Conclusion: anatomically normal uterine cavity. There is a zone of chronic endometritis on the posterior side of the uterine cavity, where a zone of hyperplastic endometrium was also noted.

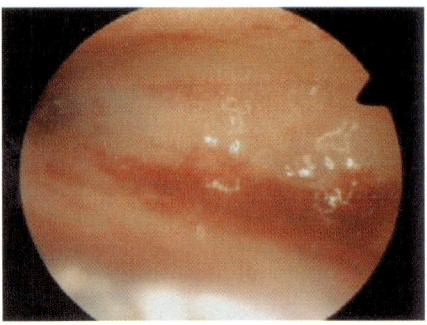
Thursday 7 June 2001 16:01:22
Panoramic view if the uterine cavity: size and format normal

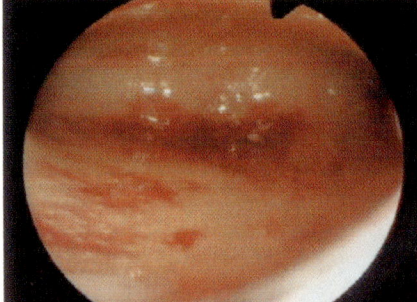
Thursday 7 June 2001 16:01:29

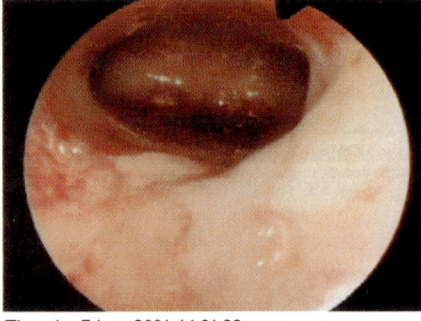
Thursday 7 June 2001 16:01:38
There is a dense zone of endometrial hyperplasia on the posterior side of the region just past the isthmus and extending towards the left lateral border

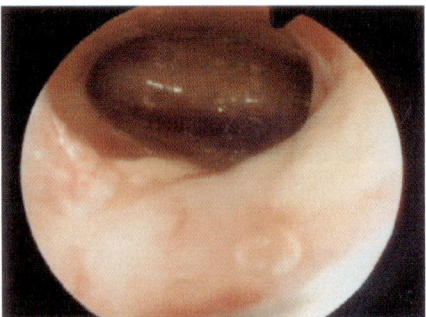
Thursday 7 June 2001 16:01:41
Mucosal hyperplasia on the posterior side and the left lateral border

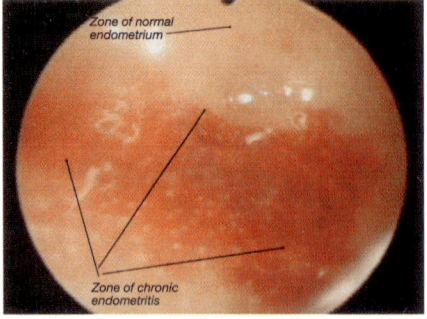
Thursday 7 June 2001 16:02:29
Enlarged image of the zone of chronic infection lying on the posterior side

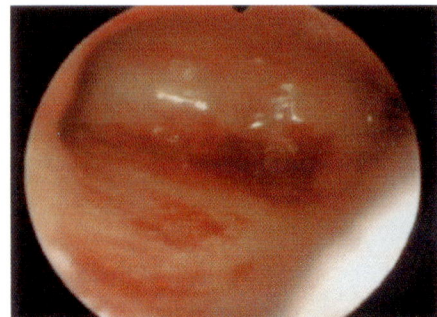
Thursday 7 June 2001 16:02:37
Panoramic view if the uterine cavity: size and format normal

Figure 19

Report of a hysteroscopic examination with digitalized hysteroscopic images. Case report. Diagnostic hysteroscopy in a patient aged 53 years presenting with menorrhagia lasting several months. Endocervical canal: the endocervical canal is deformed by the presence of a mucous polyp inserted on the left side near the internal orifice of the cervix. This polyp did not hamper the passage of the scope towards the uterine cavity. Uterine cavity: in the cavity we observe a large submucous fibroid occupying three-quarters of the visual field. This fibroid has a very distinct superficial vascularization. The fibroid is retained on the wall by a very large pedicle covering the total length of the lateral border to the left of the uterine cavity. The right uterine cornu is accessible and its tubal orifice is readily visible. On the contralateral side the fibroid obstructs the left cornu and its tubal orifice. The uterine endometrial lining looks normal and there are no signs of hyperplasia or adenomyosis. Conclusion: endocervical polyp and a large submucous pedunculate fibroid that bleeds on contact and is implanted over the whole length of the left side of the uterus. An endoscopic resection of the endocervical and endocavitary lesions is necessary.

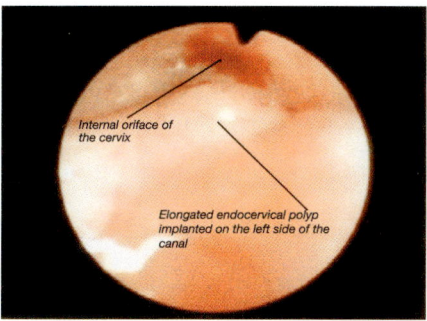

Friday 31 March 2000 11:00:39
The endocervical canal is restricted by the presence of a long polyp implanted on the left side just under the internal oriface

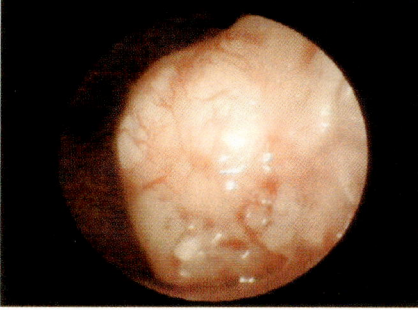

Friday 31 March 2000 11:02:31
Submucous fibroid with distinct superficial vascularization: the lateral side does not hamper access to the right uterine cornu

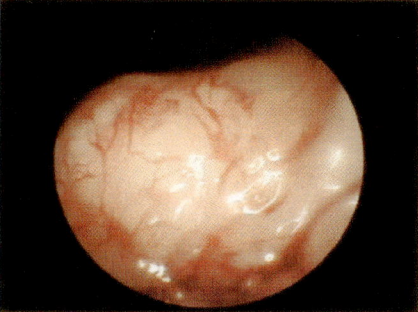

Friday 31 March 2000 11:02:39
Left lateral implantation of the fibroid extends over the total length of the left uterine border

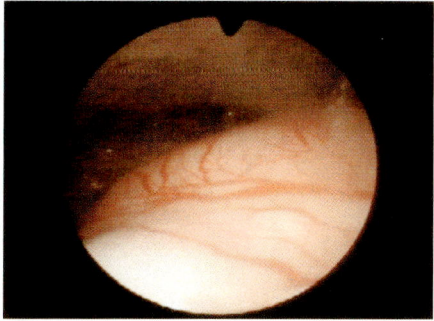

Friday 31 March 2000 11:02:45
Upper side of the submucous fibroid, very corrugated surface with numerous vessels

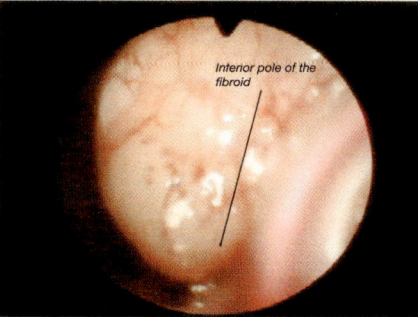

Friday 31 March 2000 11:03:28
Inferior pole of the fibroid and implantation on the proximal side of the uterine cavity border

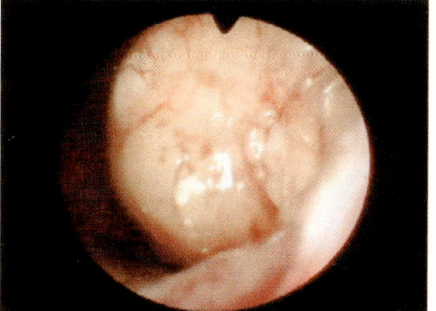

Friday 31 March 2000 11:03:30
Left lateral implantation on the middle part of the left lateral border of the uterus

Figure 20

A self-retaining hysteroscope set up in a physician's office, demonstrating its simplicity and space-saving features.

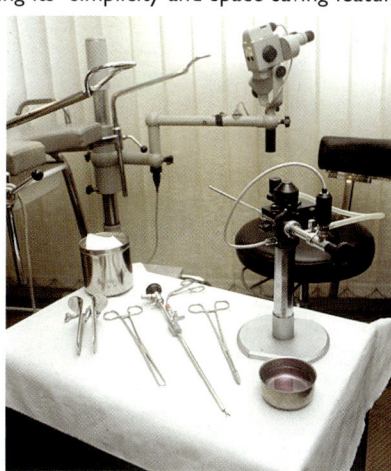

Figure 21

Examination at a private office.

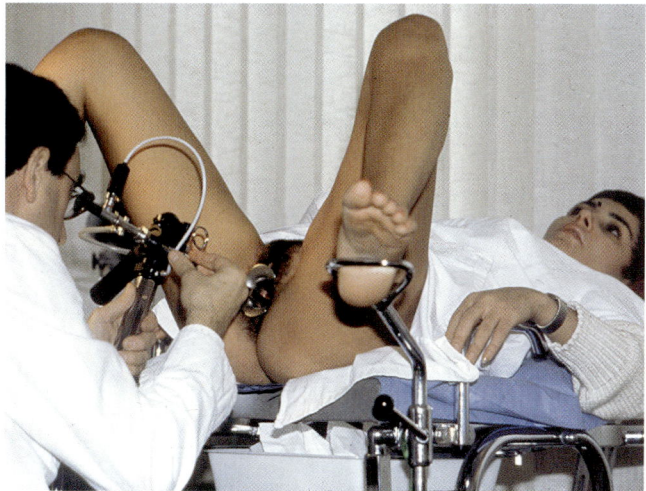

PRACTICAL RECOMMENDATIONS

The self-retaining hysteroscope is safe to use due to the flow control and the control of the CO_2 pressure. The safety of use is at least equal to that of conventional hysteroflators. The self-retaining hysteroscope is considered to be an instrument of daily use for the clinician on condition that it is readily available near the examination couch and that it has been sterilized the night before. CO_2 cartridges should be readily available in sufficient quantities. It is recommended that two optics are kept available – one of 2.7 mm and one of 4 mm – so that these can be interchanged according to the needs of the case. As with all endoscopic instruments it is essential for the quality of the examination that the maintenance of the scopes and the sheaths be optimal. It is therefore recommended that the scopes and sheaths are rinsed with large amounts of clear water immediately after each examination. A cotton swab can be used to avoid blood coagulation in the small gutter at the end of the sheath supporting the telescope (the gutter responsible for the screen wiper effect).

CONCLUSION

The technique of hysteroscopy with the self-retaining hysteroscope can appear somewhat archaic and rudimentary when compared with hysteroscopes connected to automatic hysteroflators. However, the technique has the advantage of greater simplicity and greater ease in its use while providing the same safety features.

It is my belief that making the instrumentation more simple by miniaturizing the different elements involved but maintaining the same safety standards creates a de-dramatization of the hysteroscopy itself. Therefore it will make hysteroscopy more accessible to greater numbers of hysteroscopists not only because the examination itself is easier but also because of the dramatic reduction of the initial investment in the equipment. Fear of problems arising from the use of CO_2 and the burden of the initial investment are the main obstacles for gynecologists considering taking up hysteroscopy.

BIBLIOGRAPHY

Baggish MS, Barbot J, Valle R. Diagnostic and Operative Hysteroscopy, A Text and Atlas, 2nd edn. St Louis: Mosby, 1999: 121–122.

Blanc B, Boubli L. Endoscopie Utérine. Paris: Edition Pradel, 1996: 14.

Blanc B, Boubli L. Manuel d'Hystéroscopie Opératoire. Paris: Edition Vigot, 1991: 28.

Desormeaux AJ. De l'Endoscope et de ses Applications au Diagnostic et au Traitement des Affections de l'Urètre et de la Vessie. Paris: Baillière Edit, 1865.

Gimpelson RJ. Experience with the Autonom 4992 Self-Contained panoramic hysteroscope. *J Reprod Med* 1998; **33**: 11.

Guedj H. Videohystéroscopie diagnostique au cabinet de consultation. Genesis, NUH communication. *Rev Gynecol Obstet Endocrinol* 1994; **6**: 20–25.

Guedj H. Videohystéroscopie: diagnostics. Présence et communications médicales (Laboratories Wyeth France). *Forum Gynecol* 1995; **6**: 9–12.

Guedj H, Valle RF. An Atlas of Hysteroscopy: A Guide to Diagnosis. The Encyclopedia of Visual Medicine Series. Carnforth: Parthenon Publishing, 1997.

Guedj H, Valle RF.A Slide Atlas of Hysteroscopy, An Aid to Diagnosis. Carnforth: Parthenon Publishing, 1997.

Parent B, Guedj H. Qu'est-ce que l'hystéroscopie? *Quotidien Med* 1994; **5330**: 13–14.

Parent B, Guedj H, Barbot J, Nodarian P. Panoramic Hysteroscopy. Baltimore: Williams and Wilkins, 1987: 15–28.

Parent B, Barbot J, Guedj H, Nodarian P. Hystéroscopie Chirurgicale: Laser et Techniques Classiques. Paris: Masson, 1994: 3–7.

Parent B, Barbot J, Guedj H. Hystéroscopie Chirurgicale: Laser et Techniques Classiques, 2nd edn. Paris: Masson, 1997: 3–7.

Sadoul G, Beuret T. L'hystéroscopie: un examen diagnostique réalisé en ambulatoire. *Quotadien Med* 1994; 18–19.

Siegler AM, Valle RF, Lindemann HJ, Mencaglia L. Therapeutic Hysteroscopy, Indications and Techniques. St Louis: CV Mosby, 1990: 18–20.

Indications, contraindications and complications of outpatient hysteroscopy

Rafael F. Valle and B.J. van Herendael

> **Take Home Message**
> The indications for office hysteroscopy are mainly abnormal uterine bleeding, screening before IVF, and confirming the on ultrasound findings. There are very few contraindications except for pelvic inflammatory disease (PID) and excessive uterine bleeding. If the standard technique is used properly the complications are minimal, as the time-span of the procedure is limited.

INTRODUCTION

In 1978 Rafael F. Valle wrote that 'hysteroscopy is indicated in any situation in which intrauterine visualization will enhance diagnostic accuracy and refine therapy' [1]. Over two decades later this statement remains valid when discussing hysteroscopic indications. However, the approach to hysteroscopy in an office setting has changed because of simplification of the technique with the avoidance of cervical dilatation and the use of small caliber instruments that permit the continuous flow system for uterine distention. Also, telescopes manufactured with lenses of the fused fiber bundles allow better utilization of light. Finally, the almost routine use of video systems and the utilization of hysteroscopy in an office setting have been broadened and simplified. Thus there have been major developments in the equipment available, but the indications for hysteroscopy have not changed significantly [2–5].

Table 1
Indications for diagnostic hysteroscopy

- Endocervical canal lesions
- Suspected endometrial polyps
- Suspected submucous leiomyomas
- Abnormal hysterogram/sonogram
- Misplaced intrauterine foreign bodies
- Uterine anomalies
- Intrauterine adhesions
- Evaluation of the endometrium
- Evaluation of the tubal ostia

CURRENT INDICATIONS FOR DIAGNOSTIC HYSTEROSCOPY

The main indication for the utilization of hysteroscopy remains the evaluation of abnormal uterine bleeding; this includes the suspicion of endometrial polyps or submucous leiomyoma. The evaluation of an abnormal hysterosalpingogram is also an indication, as is an abnormal sonogram suggesting an intrauterine lesion. Patients with repetitive pregnancy wastage will benefit from a complete evaluation of the endocervical canal and uterine cavity. Suspected focal adhesions and intrauterine septa are also genuine indications for intrauterine evaluation. Misplaced IUDs, particularly when detected at sonography, become a good indication for direct intrauterine visualization. However, conditions that suggest extensive uterine cavity occlusion, complete uterine septa, large submucous leiomyomas or endometrial polyps, and other pathology that may require extensive intrauterine adhesions are best evaluated at the time of planned surgery – combining the diagnostic hysteroscopic evaluation with the therapeutic approach (Table 1 and Figure 1) [6,7].

INDICATIONS FOR AND LIMITATIONS OF OPERATIVE HYSTEROSCOPY IN THE OFFICE

The refinement of small hysteroscopes, as well as instrumentation that can be manipulated through a 5 Fr operating channel, have made it possible to perform some therapeutic procedures in an office setting under local or no anesthesia. However, these indications or applications of hysteroscopy in the office vary according to the experience of the operator and the instrumentation available. The retrieval of misplaced intrauterine devices (particularly when suspected by ultrasonography to be in the uterine cavity), is an excellent indication for operative hysteroscopy in the office. Similarly, some endometrial biopsies can easily be accomplished in this type of setting, for example, the removal of a small pedunculate polyp (<2 cm) and the removal of small pedunculate submucous leiomyomas (<1 cm). The lysis of focal and filmy or fibromuscular intrauterine adhesions can easily be performed in an office setting. Confirmed uterine septa (no larger than 1–2 cm) can be treated. In addition, evaluation of the intratubal milieu by salpingoscopy guided by hysteroscopy can be performed by trained physicians in an office setting, as can the applications of new reproductive technologies such as GIFT, ZIFT, and tubal insemination. Finally, tubal sterilization (ESSURE™ intratubal devices) is currently being evaluated and has proved feasible in an office setting.

The evaluation of the uterine cavity for abnormal uterine bleeding can easily be accomplished in an office setting with currently available instrumentation that does not require cervical dilatation. However, the performance of operative hysteroscopy requires careful selection of patients and their pathology, as well as adequate training by the practitioner to perform these procedures safely, atraumatically, and efficiently in an office setting (Table 2).

CONTRAINDICATIONS (Table 3)

Pelvic inflammatory disease remains an absolute contraindication to hysteroscopy as, despite the fact that the technique of hysteroscopy has decreased in trauma and manipulation, the possibility of disseminating the infection is real and should be avoided. Patients should be treated appropriately and if necessary hysteroscopy should be performed only after the disease has been completely eradicated. Uterine infection is not a contraindication. The mere fact that we see an infection could suggest that we have to postpone the investigation of the cavity. However,

Table 2
Indications for operative hysteroscopy in the office (vary according to the clinician's experience and available instrumentation)

- Removal of misplaced IUDs and other foreign bodies
- Endometrial targeted biopsies
- Small pedunculate polyps (<2 cm)
- Small pedunculate submucous myomas (<1 cm)
- Lysis of focal and filmy intrauterine adhesions
- Small uterine septa (<1 cm)
- Tubal sterilization (intratubal devices)
- Falloposcopy guided by hysteroscopy
- GIFT, ZIFT, tubal insemination

Figure 1
Algorithm for office hysteroscopic evaluation of abnormal uterine bleeding.

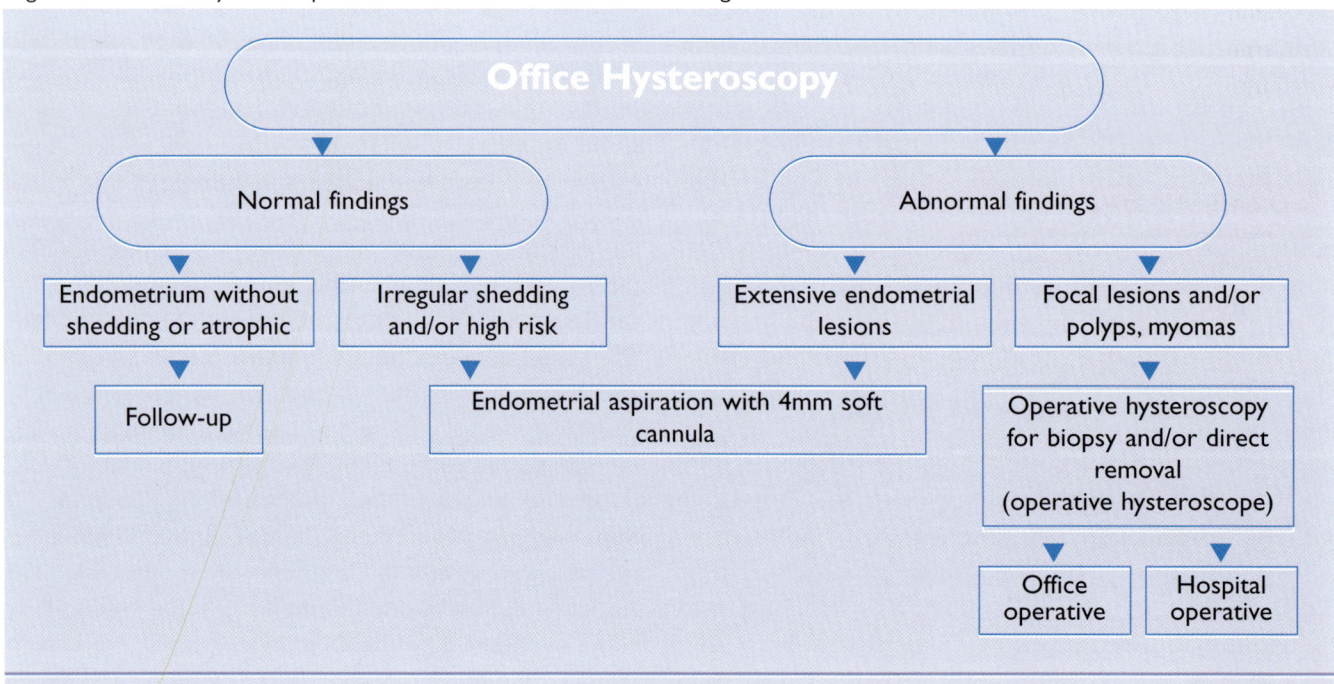

looking into the cavity will reveal details of the seriousness of the infection and the degree of involvement of the endometrium. This could be a considerable help in deciding what treatment to apply and eventually the length of the treatment. There is a difference between a strawberry pattern in the subacute infection of the endometrium and the destruction of the whole of the endometrial lining in acute infections. In the first case the patient should only be treated for a limited period of time; in the second the patient should be treated for at least 12–16 days. Furthermore, the visual involvement of the tubal ostia – indicating that the tube is involved – should alert the physician to consider a longer period of treatment with antibiotics that will also cover *Chlamydia trachomatis* infection and in cases of subfertility lead to consideration of an exploratory laparoscopy to inspect the tubes from the abdominal side. In chronic infections the visual appearance of lymph cell conglomerates in and under the basal layer of the endometrium indicates that these patients should receive treatment with broad-spectrum antibiotics for several consecutive months during the menstrual period.

However, abnormal moderate uterine bleeding has become a relative contraindication that can be bypassed by the use of continuous flow hysteroscopy, which permits evacuation of blood and lavage of clots to allow visualization. Only profuse uterine bleeding will become a real contraindication to the method, despite a continuous flow washing of the cavity.

Other relative contraindications remain unchanged, such as wanted pregnancy, known carcinoma of the cervix or endometrium, severe cervical stenosis, an uncooperative or unstable patient and certainly inappropriate training of the physician and lack of proper instrumentation.

The physical condition of the patient can be a contraindication. In critically ill patients with impaired ventilation carbon dioxide could alter the acid-base balance and cause acute acidosis, less in patients who do not receive general anesthesia.

Finally, a lack of indication also should be listed as a contraindication., as well as the inexperienced physician, and – particularly in the nonanesthetized patient – a lack of training equals inexperience.

Endometrial cancer is not a contraindication, as there is now ample proof that hysteroscopy performed with the usual precautions will only be of help. It will give the clinician some idea of the macroscopic involvement of the higher portion of the cervical canal; thus making the difference between a simple hysterectomy and a hysterectomy with pelvic lymphadenectomy. The only absolute contraindication is overt cervical cancer with an extension high up in the cervical canal, thus creating a possible path for cervical perforation. This would cause the implantation of a large number of cells on the peritoneum and push the cells directly into the blood and lymphatic vessels.

COMPLICATIONS

Possible complications of hysteroscopy and hysteroscopic surgery in the office are markedly reduced as compared with complications related to the use of larger instruments, with selective utilization of energy sources such as electrosurgery, lasers, and vaporizing electrodes, and of treatment that requires extensive dissection and intrauterine manipulation. Nonetheless, even with small instruments the potential for complications exists, albeit to a lesser degree. Uterine perforation will remain the most

Table 1.
Contraindications for office hysteroscopy

Absolute	Relative
Pelvic inflammatory disease (PID)	Endometrial cancer (to be performed only for staging or directed biopsies)
Overt cervical cancer	Infection of the uterine cavity and the tubes
Inexperienced physician	Physical condition of the patient
Lack of sterility in fluid distension	Patient with a known history of vasovagal reaction
	Early pregnancy (to be performed only to perform chorion biopsy or to remove IUCD)

common complication, particularly when operative hysteroscopy is performed. The smaller instrumentation utilized, if not guided with precision and delicacy, can easily perforate the uterus. Complicaitons arising from infection are practically non-existent, owing to a decrease in manipulation of the uterus; nevertheless, all precautions for avoiding contamination should be exercised.

Diagnostic hysteroscopy is certainly almost innocuous and the fact that the endoscope is introduced under direct vision should help to avoid uterine perforation.

When therapeutic hysteroscopy is used, the complications that can occur depend on the pathology encountered. Because only focal adhesions should be treated in this setting, the chances of uterine perforation are practically eliminated, similarly when only small uterine septa are divided. Postoperative bleeding also is markedly decreased, because of selection of the pathology treated; e.g. only small (<1 cm) pedunculate myomas are approached and small (<2 cm) pedunculate polyps are removed. However, if perforation occurs other organs may be injured and, despite the small caliber of the instrumentation, they should be approached cautiously and delicately, as with hysteroscopy in an operative theater and under regional or general anesthesia. The procedures in the office are short: <5 minutes for diagnosis and <10 minutes for therapeutic procedures. Therefore, the chances of fluid overload are practically non-existent, particularly when continuous flow systems are used.

If energy sources are used, then complications related to them could occur at uterine perforation and will not vary from those that occur when larger instrumentation is used in an operating theater. Laser and electrosurgery (unipolar, bipolar) will carry those potential complications inherent to the energy source. Finally, the utilization of vaporizing electrodes should also be carefully monitored, particularly if prolonged time is spent (>10 minutes), in view of their potential for excessive bubbling and production of gas embolism.

These latter methods of operative hysteroscopy in an office setting should be undertaken cautiously, as they have an inherent potential risk, not necessarily directly related to hysteroscopy but rather related to the energy used. They should be used cautiously and with good understanding of their physics and tissue interaction.

LIMITATIONS OF OPERATIVE HYSTEROSCOPY IN THE OFFICE

There are several limitations to performing therapeutic procedures in the office and these are as follows. First, the size of the instruments, as usually small caliber instruments are utilized in the office to avoid cervical dilatation. Anesthesia is limited and extensive manipulation may cause discomfort to the patient. Also, the set up available may not be adequate and may lack ancillary instrumentation. Additional equipment may be required for completion of the procedure.

Alternatives in the office may be limited, should the procedure fail or should any complication arise. Other adjuncts such as concomitant laparoscopy or even ultrasound may not be able to be utilized or not at hand. Finally, when extensive manipulations are required the necessary help, such as assisting nurses and even an anesthesiologist, is not available, therefore limiting the therapeutic procedures.

SUMMARY AND CONCLUSIONS

Abnormal uterine bleeding remains the main indication for intrauterine evaluation in an office setting. When performing office hysteroscopy it is important to avoid contraindications, particularly pelvic inflammatory disease or excessive uterine bleeding. Against the background of good indications and absent contraindications, the performance of meticulous technique and awareness of potential complications, these complications should be practically eliminated and if they occur the physician should be prompt to recognize them and treat them appropriately. No method or technique can ever be free of complications, but following the guidelines of proper indications, absent contraindications, and good technique will certainly provide a safe, effective, and appropriate office-based method for uterine evaluation and treatment.

Office hysteroscopy is therefore mainly a diagnostic procedure aimed at evaluating the uterine cavity in patients complaining of abnormal uterine bleeding and determining the appropriate way to either biopsy or treat any intrauterine pathology discovered.

Success in the performance of office hysteroscopy depends on the appropriate selection of the patient, the outlined indications, absence of contraindications, availability of adequate instrumentation, and a meticulous technique in the performance of the procedure.

Although some minor therapeutic procedures can be performed in the office, these should be appropriately planned, and patients should be selected to avoid failures or complications. Additionally, realistic expectations for these procedures should be kept in mind, defining aims in performing this type of evaluation or treatment and deciding on additional procedures if unexpected difficulties or pathology are encountered.

REFERENCES

1. Valle RF. Hysteroscopy. In: Wynn RM, ed. Obstetrics and Gynecology Annual. New York: Appleton Century Crofts, 1978: 245–283.
2. Valle RF. Office hysteroscopy. *Clin Obstet Gynecol* 1999; **42**: 276–289.
3. Valle RF. Hysteroscopy for gynecologic diagnosis. *Clin Obstet Gynecol* 1983; **26**: 253–276.
4. Valle RF. Indications for hysteroscopy. In: Siegler AN, Lindemann HJ, eds. Hysteroscopy: Principles and Practice. Philadelphia: JB Lippincott, 1986: 21–24.
5. Valle RF. Future growth and development of hysteroscopy. In: DeCherney AH, ed. Hysteroscopy. Obstet Gynecol Clin North Am Series. Philadelphia: WB Saunders, 1988; 15: 107–126.
6. Valle RF, Sciarra JJ. Role of hysteroscopy in the evaluation of menorrhagia. In: Shirish S, Sutton C, eds. Menorrhagia. Oxford: Isis Medical Media, 1999: 43–52.
7. Valle RF. A closer look at the postmenopausal bleeding uterus (editorial). *J Am Assoc Gynecol Laparosc* 2000; **7**: 171–173.

10 Pre-IVF hysteroscopic evaluation of intrauterine cavity

Aygül Demirol and Timur Gürgan

> **Take Home Message**
> As the incidence of structural abnormalities of the uterine cavity is high in patients requiring IVFET (19–50%), it is necessary to perform hysteroscopy before the first attempt. Although the procedure is costly, the costs have to be related to the overall costs of an IVFET procedure and the risk of failure when an obvious and treatable problem is overlooked. The introduction of office hysteroscopy can reduce some of the costs and aggressiveness of the procedure. In the literature, more and more evidence appears to correlate the anatomy of the endometrium and the images of congestion and infection with failure of the embryo to implant.

Despite advances in ovarian stimulation regimens, oocyte collection techniques, and laboratory management over the past 20 years, implantation rates per embryo transferred still remain at a low 10–15% [1]. Most embryos that are transferred during IVF-ET (in vitro fertilization and embryo transfer) procedures fail to implant for unknown reasons. Several key factors responsible for implantation have been described, not the least of which are quality of the embryo and receptivity of the uterus [2–4]. It also appears that a favorable endometrial integrity is necessary for achieving successful pregnancy. Although embryo quality can be assessed by standard embryological techniques, uterine receptivity has been more difficult to evaluate. However, the factors that determine a favorable endometrial milieu are still controversial. Adequate endometrial development is certainly essential for good receptivity, and attempts have been made to identify biochemical markers specific for endometrial function [5–7]. Among the potential uterine predictors for implantation measurable by ultrasonography are endometrial thickness and volume, endometrial pattern, and blood flow in the uterine and (sub)endometrial arteries [8–10].

In this chapter we will discuss whether the diagnosis and treatment of intrauterine lesions with hysteroscopy is of value in improving the pregnancy rates for the success of IVF-ET programmes.

IMPORTANCE OF THE INTRAUTERINE VISUALIZATION

Structural abnormalities of the uterus and endometrial cavity may affect reproductive outcome adversely by interfering with implantation and causing spontaneous abortion [11]. In women undergoing IVF treatment, the incidence of uterine abnormalities has been reported to range from 19% to 50% [12–15]. These abnormalities can have a negative effect on pregnancy rates in these patients. Intrauterine pathologies and structural uterine abnormalities that may be responsible for the failure of IVF can be detected and treated, resulting in improved pregnancy rates in IVF. Thus screening the uterus before proceeding with IVF has been recommended [12–15].

Abnormalities of the uterine cavity are correlated with possible pathologies regarding the implantation of fertilized eggs or with problems concerning the evolution of pregnancy (risk of spontaneous abortion). Some of these abnormalities, for example polyps, submucous tumors or adhesions, can prevent successful nidation of a blastocyst by creating an unfavorable environment for its development.

Abnormalities of the cervical canal are of particular interest for embryo transfer. Cervical stenosis can be resolved by adhesiolysis and dilatation. Endocervical polyps and adhesions can be removed during hysteroscopy. The information gained during the procedure can be used during the ET procedure, preventing traumatic and difficult embryo transfers and contributing to the increase of pregnancy rates.

METHODS FOR THE EVALUATION OF THE INTRAUTERINE ENVIRONMENT

Although other methods of uterine evaluation have been introduced, such as HSG (hysterosalpingography), vaginal sonography, transvaginal hysterosonography, and magnetic resonance imaging, all of them offer specific features that complement each other and are valuable in the appropriate evaluation of selective patients. Since it enables direct visualization of the endometrium, hysteroscopy is the gold standard for the evaluation of the endometrial cavity. Intrauterine pathologies and structural uterine abnormalities which may responsible for failure of embryo implantation can be detected and treated hysteroscopically, resulting in improved pregnancy rates.

Since the World Health Organization (WHO) recommends only HSG for infertility work-up [16], most IVF units perform only HSG to assess the uterine cavity before an IVF cycle, but in the detection of abnormalities HSG is not reliable for precise diagnosis, with low specificity [17–20] and a false-negative rate and it has a high false-positive rate [21]. HSG has a sensitivity of 65–75% in relation to hysteroscopy [22,23].

The use of ultrasonography (US) in conjunction with intrauterine saline infusion sonohysterography is an appealing alternative to hysteroscopy and HSG for uterine screening before IVF. Sonohysterography has been found to be highly sensitive, specific, and accurate in identifying abnormalities such as myomas, polyps, synechiae, septa, and uterine anomalies [24–26]. In comparison with HSG, sonohysterography is superior for evaluation of the uterus, but office hysteroscopy allows the easy treatment of the pathologies at the same time.

OFFICE HYSTEROSCOPY

Office hysteroscopy can be performed without general anesthesia in an ambulatory setting with low cost and minimal inconvenience to the patient, and some lesions diagnosed during the procedure can be operated easily by using different items of equipment through the operative channel of the hysteroscope. This is a suggested technique for the pre-IVF evaluation of the uterine cavity.

Diagnostic hysteroscopes of small caliber (<5 mm outer diameter) are commonly used in office settings. The telescope has a 2–4 mm outer diameter and the encasing sheaths are 4–6 mm. Endoscopes of <3 mm outer diameter encased in a 4-mm outer diameter sheath seldom require cervical dilatation. Because of their size, hysteroscopes with 4-mm or less outer diameter are better used with CO_2 gas or continuous saline infusion systems for distension of the uterus; 180° angle or preferably 30° angle of view telescopes are used. Semi-rigid operative hysteroscopic instruments such as scissors, grasping forceps, and biopsy forceps (5 Fr size) are available for office use with 5–6 mm continuous flow hysteroscopes. 5 Fr vaporizing electrodes may be used in the office for treatment of small intrauterine lesions such as polyps, focal adhesions, small pedunculate submucous myomas, and small uterine septa.

COLLECTED STUDIES RELATED TO HYSTEROSCOPIC EVALUATION AND TREATMENT OF INTRAUTERINE PATHOLOGIES RELATED TO IVF SUCCESS

Some studies have been performed to evaluate the uterine cavity to diagnose the pathologies that may be responsible for IVF failure and to find out if hysteroscopic treatment of intrauterine pathologies increases the success of IVF-ET outcome.

Seinera et al. [27] reported hysteroscopic findings in their IVF program; 360 patients underwent hysteroscopy before IVF, the procedure was successful in 332 patients. The most common findings were cervical stenosis, polyps, and intrauterine adhesions. In all, 148 women were found to have uterine abnormalities (44.5%) but treatment of the pathologies and the analysis of the effect of these pathologies on the IVF outcome was not studied [27].

Shamma et al. [13] assessed the role of hysteroscopy in their IVF program, they included 28 patients undergoing IVF prospectively. They all had normal HSG and HS performed in an office setting without general anesthesia. Group I (16 patients) had normal hysteroscopic evaluation, group II (12 patients) had abnormal hysteroscopic findings including small (<1.5 cm) uterine septa ($n = 3$), small submucous fibroids measuring <2 cm ($n = 3$), uterine hypoplasia with the uterine cavity measuring <5 cm ($n = 4$), and cervical ridges ($n = 2$). There was no significant difference between the groups with respect to the demographic properties and IVF parameters such as number of oocytes retrieved, fertilization rate, and number of embryos transferred. There was a significant difference in the clinical pregnancy rates between patients in groups I and II (37.5% and 8.3% respectively, $p = 0.04$). These authors demonstrated the importance of performing hysteroscopy before IVF-ET [13].

Behjatnia et al. [28] compared hysteroscopic findings in 248 patients with primary infertility with those of 150 women with secondary infertility. The results of hysteroscopy were normal in almost half of the patients in each group, 133 and 68, respectively. The occurrence of septate uterus, endometrial polyps, and ostial diaphragm was not statistically different between the groups. The prevalence of intrauterine synechiae was significantly different ($p<0.01$) and they concluded that diagnostic hysteroscopy should be performed on all patients before IVF-ET.

Varasteh et al. [29] compared reproductive benefits of hysteroscopic myomectomy and polypectomy for infertility to outcomes in fertile couples with normal hysteroscopic findings. Of the 78 subjects, 36 had myomectomies, 23 had polyectomies, and 19 had normal cavities. Among the three groups, there were no significant differences in age, type of infertility, length of infertility, or follow-up after the procedure. Polypectomy subjects had significantly higher pregnancy and live birth rates than women with normal cavities. Women who had myomectomies >2 cm had significantly higher pregnancy and live birth rates, achieving statistical significance at a myoma size of 3 cm or greater for live births. Spontaneous abortion rates among first pregnancies were similar for all patients. Both hysteroscopic polypectomy and hysteroscopic myomectomy appeared to enhance fertility compared with infertile women with normal cavities.

Lass et al. [30] investigated the effect of endometrial polyps on pregnancy outcome in an IVF program and concluded that small endometrial polyps (<2 cm) do not decrease the pregnancy rate but there is a trend toward increased pregnancy loss. They randomized 83 patients in two groups: 49 women (group I) had standard IVF-ET, while 34 women (group II) had hysteroscopy and polypectomy following oocyte retrieval. The suitable embryos were frozen and the replacement cycle took place a few months later. The pregnancy rate in group I was similar to the general pregnancy rate of their IVF unit over the same period (22.4% versus 23.4%), but the miscarriage rate was higher (27.3% versus 10.7%, $p = 0.08$). In group II (women who underwent hysteroscopy and polypectomy), the pregnancy and miscarriage rates were similar to those of frozen embryo cycles. They concluded that small endometrial polyps (<2 cm) do not decrease the pregnancy rate, but a trend toward increased pregnancy loss was shown [30].

La Sala et al. [31] analysed the role of diagnostic hysteroscopy and endometrial biopsy in an IVF program. They studied the incidence of unsuspected endouterine abnormalities in 100 patients who had two failed IVF-ET cycles. In 18 patients (18%), hysteroscopy revealed an important endouterine abnormality. Of the 18 patients who had intrauterine pathologies, 15 did not achieve pregnancy after IVF-ET. Three patients became pregnant but had a spontaneous abortion.

Kirsop et al. [32] investigated the role of hysteroscopy in patients with failed IVF/GIFT transfer cycles. Fifty patients who had undergone two or more failed IVF-ET or GIFT cycles where fertilization had been demonstrated underwent hysteroscopy; 28% were found to have intrauterine abnormalities which may have been responsible for the failure of IVF-ET or GIFT. Patients with an abnormality diagnosed during hysteroscopic evaluation had undergone a significantly higher mean number of failed transfer cycles.

In the study by **Dicker et al.** [33], the value of repeat hysteroscopy was evaluated. They determined if repeat hysteroscopic evaluation after failed IVF-ET cycles is of value in detecting undiagnosed or misinterpreted initial diagnosis, as well as subtle new intrauterine abnormalities. They included 110 women with normal initial hysteroscopic findings who failed to conceive during three or more IVF-ET cycles. In view of the recurrent failures, all patients were re-evaluated and thus underwent a repeat hysteroscopic evaluation. In 20 patients (18.2%) various abnormalities were detected. Fourteen of 20 patients with uterine abnormalities completed 43 IVF-ET cycles that resulted in 6 clinical pregnancies (13.9% per transfer). The women with adhesions, submucous myomas, and endometrial polyps were treated by an operative procedure before the next IVF-ET cycle. Their results indicate that repeat hysteroscopic evaluation, in cases of recurrent IVF-ET failure, is an important adjunctive method for further evaluating and possibly optimizing IVF-ET results [33].

None of these studies was prospectively randomized, especially as regards addressing the impact of treatment of intrauterine pathologies during hysteroscopic procedures on subsequent pregnancy rates in IVF-ET success.

We performed a prospective randomized study to evaluate if the diagnosis and treatment of intrauterine lesions with office hysteroscopy is of value in improving the pregnancy outcome in patients with recurrent IVF failure [34].

In all, 455 patients who had undergone two or more failed IVF cycles in which two or more good quality embryos were transferred participated prospectively in the study. They all had normal HSG. Informed consent was obtained before entry in the study. The patients' ages ranged from 24 to 40 years (mean 32 years), the duration of infertility ranged from 2 to 14 years (mean 6.5 years), and all the patients had primary infertility.

Patients were randomized into two groups. Those in group I ($n = 211$) did not have office hysteroscopic evaluation of uterine cavity and cervix before commencing controlled ovarian stimulation for IVF treatment, whereas patients in group II ($n = 210$) had office hysteroscopy. Patients who had normal hysteroscopic findings were included in group IIa ($n = 154$) and patients who had abnormal hysteroscopic findings were included in group IIb ($n = 56$). Any intrauterine lesions that were diagnosed were operated during the office procedure.

Hysteroscopy was performed in the early proliferative phase with a 2.9-mm, 30°, rigid Bettochi continuous flow operating office hysteroscope (Karl Storz Endoscopy, Tuttlingen, Germany) and saline solution was used for distention.

There was no difference in the mean age, duration of infertility, number of failed cycles, and causes of infertility in the groups.

Among the 210 patients (group II) who had office hysteroscopy 56 (26%) had intrauterine pathologies. The duration of the procedure was usually <10 minutes. In all, 33 patients (15.7%) had endometrial polyps; of these, 30 patients had multiple polypoid lesions in different areas of the endometrial cavity. Filmy or mild intrauterine adhesions involving the uterine cavity were diagnosed and operated in 18 patients. Five patients had cervical adhesions that were easily lysed with scissors.

There was no difference in the mean number of oocytes retrieved, fertilization rate, number of embryos transferred, and first trimester abortion rates between patients in the various groups. Of the 421 patients, 3 were not included in the analysis because of failed ET, poor ovarian response, or the availibity of only poor grade embryos (two in group I and one in group IIb). Clinical pregnancy rates in group I, group IIa and group IIb were 21.6%, 32.5%, and 30.4%, respectively. There was a statistically significant difference in the clinical pregnancy rates between patients in group I and group IIa (21.6% and 32.5%, $p = 0.044$, respectively) and group I and group IIb (21.6% and 30.4%, $p = 0.044$, respectively). There was no significant difference in the clinical pregnancy rate patients in groups IIa and IIb.

Our study demonstrates that 26% of patients with normal HSG had abnormal hysteroscopic findings and that the clinical pregnancy rate can be improved significantly after treatment of mild intrauterine and cervical abnormalities by office hysteroscopy. It is possible that these mild abnormalities alter the uterine environment and hence negatively affect uterine receptivity and ultimately pregnancy outcome.

We suggest that patients with normal HSG but recurrent IVF-ET failure should be evaluated hysteroscopically before commencing an IVF-ET cycle, to improve the clinical pregnancy rates [34].

RECOMMENDATIONS

Hysteroscopy is an excellent tool for the diagnosis and treatment of intrauterine abnormalities but the procedure is costly, invasive, and carries the risk of complications such as uterine perforation, infection, bleeding, burns, and embolism. The available data support the use of office hysteroscopy for the diagnosis and treatment of intrauterine pathologies to increase the success of IVF-ET or ICSI-ET outcome in patients with two or more failed cycles in which two or more good quality embryos were transferred. The value of hysteroscopy for every patient who is a candidate for IVF-ET is questionable, since the low incidence of intrauterine problems in such patients may not warrant hysteroscopy as a routine procedure. However, more data are needed to clarify the uncertainties.

REFERENCES

1. Salle B, Bied Damon V, Benchaib M et al. Preliminary report of an ultrasonography and color Doppler uterine score to predict uterine receptivity in an in-vitro fertilization program. *Hum Reprod* 1998; **13**: 1669–1673.
2. Coulam CB, Bustillo M, Soenksen DM et al. Ultrasonographic predictors of implantation after assisted reproduction. *Fertil Steril* 1994; **62**: 1004–1010.
3. Schwartz LB, Chiu AS, Courtney M et al. The embryo versus endometrium controversy revisited as it relates to predicting pregnancy outcome in in-vitro fertilization-embryo transfer cycles. *Hum Reprod* 1997; **12**: 45–50.
4. Meyer WR, Catselbaum AJ, Somkuti S et al. Hydrosalpinges adversely affect markers of endometrial receptivity. *Hum Reprod* 1997; **12**: 1393–1398.
5. Kobl BA, Najmabadi S, Paulson RJ. Ultrastructural characteristic of the luteal phase endometrium in patients undergoing controlled ovarian hyperstimulation. *Fertil Steril* 1997; **67**: 625–630.
6. Seppala M, Tiitien A. Endometrial responses to corpus luteum products in cycles with induced ovulation: theoretical and practical considerations. *Hum Reprod* 1995; **10** Suppl 2: 67–76.
7. Macrow PJ, Li TC, Seif MW et al. Endometrial structure after superovulation: a prospective controlled study. *Fertil Steril* 1994; **61**: 696–699.
8. Kupesic S, Bekavac I, Bjelos D et al. Assessment of endometrial receptivity by transvaginal color Doppler and three-dimensional power Doppler ultrasonography in patients undergoing in vitro fertilization procedures. *J Ultrasound Med* 2001; **20**: 125–134.
9. Schild RL, Knobloch C, Dorn C et al. Endometrial receptivity in an in vitro fertilization program as assessed by spiral artery blood flow, endometrial thickness, endometrial volume and uterine artery blood flow. *Fertil Steril* 2001; **75**: 361–366.
10. Contart P, Baruffi RL, Coelho J et al. Power Doppler endometrial evaluation as a method for the prognosis of embryo implantation in an ICSI program. *J Assist Reprod Genet* 2000; **17**: 329–334.
11. Buttram VC, Reiter RC. Uterine leiomyomata: etiology, symptomatology, and management. *Fertil Steril* 1981; **36**: 433–445.
12. Golan A, Ron-El R, Herman A et al. Diagnostic hysteroscopy: its value in an in vitro fertilization/embryo transfer unit. *Hum Reprod* 1992; **7**: 1433–1434.
13. Shamma FN, Lee G, Gutmann JN et al. The role of office hysteroscopy in in vitro fertilization. *Fertil Steril* 1992; **58**: 1237–1239.
14. Goldenberg M, Bider D, Ben-Rafael Z et al. Hysteroscopy in a program of in vitro fertilization. *J In Vitro Fert Embryo Transf* 1991; **8**: 336–338.
15. Dicker D, Golman JA, Ashkenazi J et al. The value of hysteroscopy in elderly women prior to IVF-ET: a comparative study. *J In Vitro Fert Embryo Transf* 1990, **7**: 267–270.
16. Rowe PJ, Comhaire FH, Hargreave TB, Mellows HJ, eds. WHO Manual for the Standardized Investigation and Diagnosis of the Infertile Couple. Cambridge: Press Syndicate of University of Cambridge, 1993.
17. Golan A, Ron-El R, Herman A et al. Diagnostic hysteroscopy: its value in an in vitro fertilization/embryo transfer unit. *Hum Reprod* 1992; **7**: 1433–1434.
18. Shamma FN, Lee G, Gutmann JN, Lavy G et al. The role of office hysteroscopy in in vitro fertilization. *Fertil Steril* 1992; **58**: 1237–1239.
19. Keltz MD, Olive DL, Kim AH, Arici A. Sonohysterography for screening in recurrent pregnancy loss. *Fertil Steril* 1997; **67**: 670–674.
20. Cunha-Filho JSL, de Souza CAB, Salazar CC, Facin AC, Freitas FM, Passos EP. Accuracy of hysterosalpingography and hysteroscopy for diagnosis of intrauterine lesions in infertile patients in an assisted fertilization programme. *Gynaecol Endosc* 2001; **10**: 45–48.
21. Valle RF. Hysteroscopy in the evaluation of female infertility. *Am J Obstet Gynecol* 1980; **137**: 425–431.
22. La-Sala GB, Sacchetti F, DegIncerti-Tocci F et al. Complementary use of hysterosalpingography, hysteroscopy, and laparoscopy in 100 infertile patients: results and comparison of their diagnostic accuracy. *Acta Eur Fertil* 1987; **18**: 369–374.
23. Golan A, Eilat E, Ron-El R et al. Hysteroscopy is superior to hysterosalpingography in infertility investigation. *Acta Obstet Gynecol Scand* 1996; **75**: 654–656.
24. Keltz MD, Olive DL, Kim AH et al. Sonohysterography for screening in recurrent pregnancy loss. *Fertil Steril* 1997; **67**: 670–674.
25. Randolph JR, Ying YK, Mainer DB et al. Comparison of real time ultrasonography, hysterosalpingography, and laparoscopy/hysteroscopy in the evaluation of uterine abnormalities and tubal patency. *Fertil Steril* 1986; **46**: 828–832.
26. Parsons AK, Lense JJ. Sonohysterography for endometrial abnormalities: preliminary results. *J Clin Ultrasound* 1993; **21**: 87–95.
27. Seinera P, Maccario S, Visentin L et al. Hysteroscopy in an IVF-ET program. *Acta Obstet Gynecol Scand* 1988; **67**: 135–137.
28. Behjatnia Y, Mohammad K, Dabirashrafi H et al. Comparative hysteroscopic findings in women with primary and secondary infertility. *J Am Assoc Gynecol Laparosc* 1996; **3** (4 Suppl): S3–S4.
29. Varasteh NN, Neuwirth RS, Levin B et al. Pregnancy rates after hysteroscopic polypectomy and myomectomy in infertile women. *Obstet Gynecol* 1999; **94**: 168–171.
30. Lass A, Williams G, Abusheikha N et al. The effects of endometrial polyps on outcomes of in vitro fertilization (IVF) cycles. *J Assist Reprod Genet* 1999; **16**: 410–415.
31. La Sala GB, Montanari R, Dessanti L et al. The role of diagnostic hysteroscopy and endometrial biopsy in assisted reproductive technologies. *Fertil Steril* 1998; **70**: 378–380.
32. Kirsop R, Porter R, Torode H et al. The role of hysteroscopy in patients having failed IVF/GIFT transfer cycles. *Aust NZ Obstet Gynecol* 1991; **31**: 263–264.
33. Dicker D, Askhenazi J, Felberg D et al. The value of repeat hysteroscopic evaluation in patients with failed in vitro fertilization transfer cycles. *Fertil Steril* 1992; **58**: 833–835.
34. Gürgan T, Demirol A, Aksu T. The effect of the treatment of intrauterine pathologies on IVF-ET outcome: a prospective randomized study. [Submitted for publication.]

Sonography and sonohysterography in outpatient gynecological practice

Leeber Cohen

> **Take Home Message**
> If the ultrasound technique is learned properly, transvaginal ultrasound (TVS) without the addition of saline is a very effective first step in the evaluation of abnormal bleeding. If combined with an endometrium sampling technique it becomes very useful in screening symptomatic menopausal patients. The addition of color Doppler will outline vascularity but frequently is not required. Saline infusion sonography has to be used as an aid in selected cases.

INTRODUCTION

Transvaginal ultrasound (TVS) is a powerful imaging modality that allows for rapid assessment of the uterus and ovaries in the office setting. It is clearly more sensitive than bimanual examination in identifying leiomyomas and adnexal masses [1]. Residency programs in the USA and many other countries are now required to document appropriate training of residents in both transabdominal and transvaginal ultrasound (TVS). The availability of relatively inexpensive high resolution transvaginal probes and machines has also made it possible for many obstetric and gynecologic practices to obtain their own equipment. That being said there remain many physicians who are untrained or uncomfortable as regards performing TVS.

TRAINING

Courses approved by the American Institute of Ultrasound in Medicine (AIUM) or the International Society of Ultrasound in Obstetrics and Gynecology (ISUOG) are ideal for physicians who are unfamiliar with the physics, safety, and technology of ultrasound. Studying the premenopausal nonpregnant patient is the ideal way for inexperienced physicians to improve their skills. The presence of a well-defined endometrial stripe and ovarian follicles makes proper identification of the uterus and ovaries easier. The examination is well tolerated by most patients.

PROBE PREPARATION

Ultrasound probes should be properly cleaned between uses. All visible contamination should be removed. Vaginal probes should be disinfected in solutions such as Cidex (Advanced Sterilization Products, Johnson and Johnson) – no longer allowed in the European Union as from 2000 – or T-Spray II (Pharmaceutical Innovations) for at least 10 minutes and then rinsed with tap water. An ultrasound gel should be applied to the transducer face and a condom or probe cover should be applied. External lubricant can then be applied to ease insertion and improve imaging.

ORIENTATION

The orientation of the screen should then be checked. In the USA it is routine to place the front of the transducer on the left side of the screen. Most manufacturers place a longitudinal groove on the vaginal probe to identify the front of the transducer. As shown in Figure 1, the vagina will be identified in the superior midline aspect of the image. The bladder will be identified superior and to the left. An anteverted uterus will be identified as rotated towards the bladder and a retroverted uterus away. Once

Figure 1
A midline sagittal picture shows an antroverted uterus. The front of the transducer is displayed on the left side of the screen. The endometrium is mid-cycle.

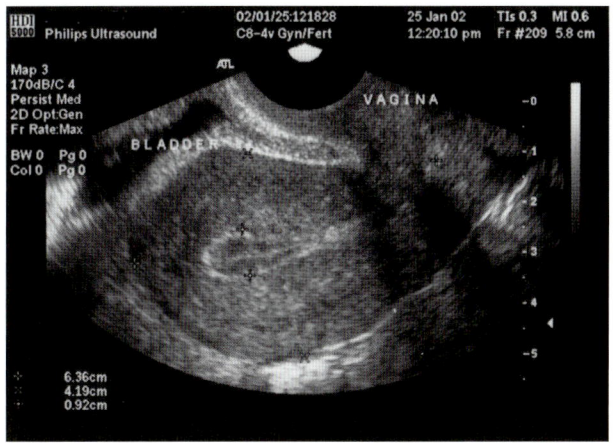

the midline sagittal picture is obtained, the transverse image can be obtained by rotating the transducer 90°, with the front of the transducer to the patient's right (Figure 2). Ovaries can usually be identified by the iliac vessels by following the blood vessels of the broad ligament laterally (Figure 3). Measurements of the ovaries and uterus should be obtained in three dimensions.

NORMAL ENDOMETRIAL ARCHITECTURE

During a normal menstrual cycle the endometrium can usually be described by one of four echo patterns: (1) single-line endometrium, (2) three-line endometrium, (3) transitional endometrium, and (4) hyperechoic endometrium. (Figures 4–6) [2]. The end of the menses is

Figure 2
An axial image of the same patient as in Figure 1. The front of the transducer is turned to the patient's right side. The right side of the uterus is displayed on the left side of the screen. The left side of the uterus is displayed on the right of the screen.

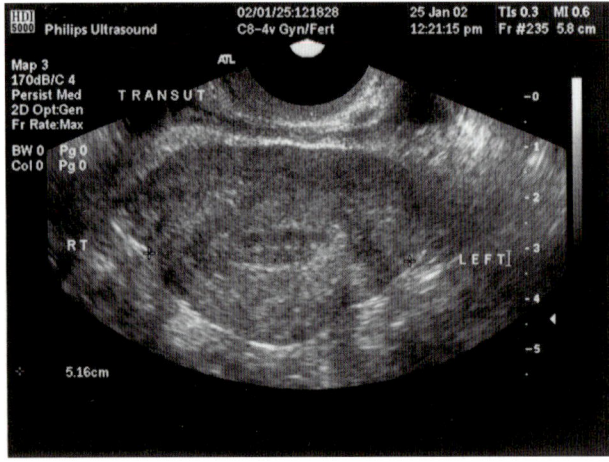

Figure 3
The ovary is easily identified beside the iliac vein. A corpus luteum is outlined by Doppler flow in a circumferential pattern.

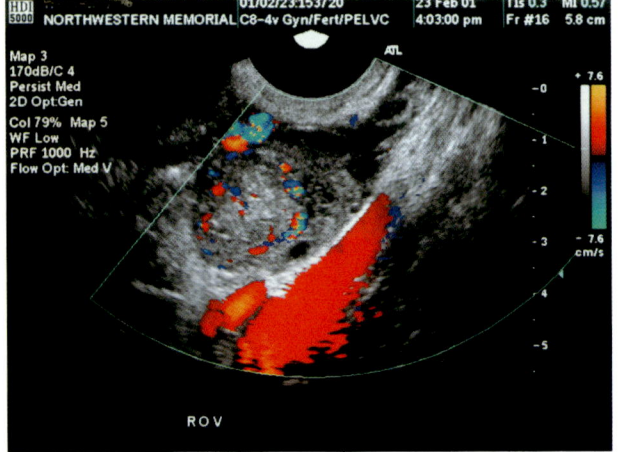

Figure 4
A single line endometrium is noted on day 5 of the menstrual cycle. It measures 3 mm in the A-P direction.

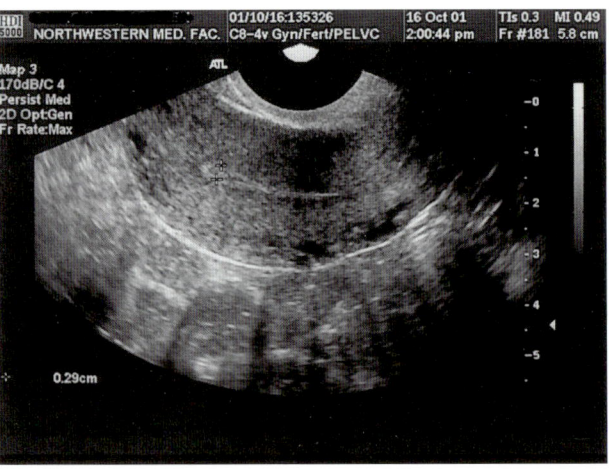

Figure 5
A typical mid-cycle three-line endometrium. The endometrium measures 11 mm in the A-P direction.

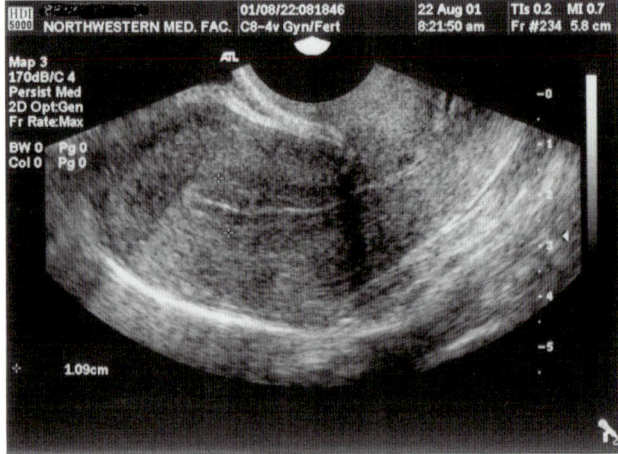

Figure 6
A transitional endometrium is noted in the third week of the cycle. The endometrium has become more echogenic but the midline stripe can still be identified.

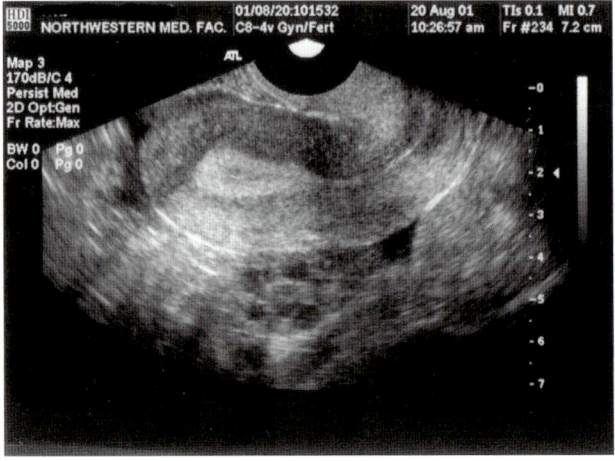

an ideal time to scan the patient, since the endometrial stripe typically measures <4 mm at this time. A normal endometrial thickness at this time excludes most endometrial polyps and submucous leiomyomas. The appearance of a typical mid-cycle endometrium in a birth control pill user is shown in Figure 7.

Submucous leiomyomas, which are usually iso-echoic, similar in echogenicity to the uterine myometrium, can be well outlined by the hyperechoic secretory endometrium (Figure 8) Endometrial polyps are frequently densely echogenic and may be poorly demarcated from a surrounding densely echogenic endometrium (Figure 9a) [3,4]. Scanning at mid-cycle can significantly improve visualization (Figure 9b).

SUBMUCOUS LEIOMYOMA

It rapidly became apparent in the late 1980s and early 1990s that TVS was a powerful tool in the diagnosis of abnormal uterine bleeding. In a series reported by Fedele et al submucous leiomyomas were identified by TVS without saline infusion at 100% sensitivity [5]. However, when both submucous leiomyomas and endometrial polyps are considered, diagnostic accuracy is less than ideal. A recent study of 470 premenopausal women with abnormal uterine bleeding found that TVS was 92% sensitive and 62% specific for the identification of endometrial polyps and submucous leiomyomas [6]. Furthermore, expertise is required. A disturbing study by Towbin et al of 149 patients with excessive uterine bleeding found that transvaginal ultrasound without infusion performed by resident physicians was only 54% sensitive in identifying space-occupying lesions of the uterine cavity [7]. In comparison, office hysteroscopy was 78% sensitive.

Figure 7
A typical mid-cycle 5-mm endometrium seen in a patient who is using an oral contraceptive pill.

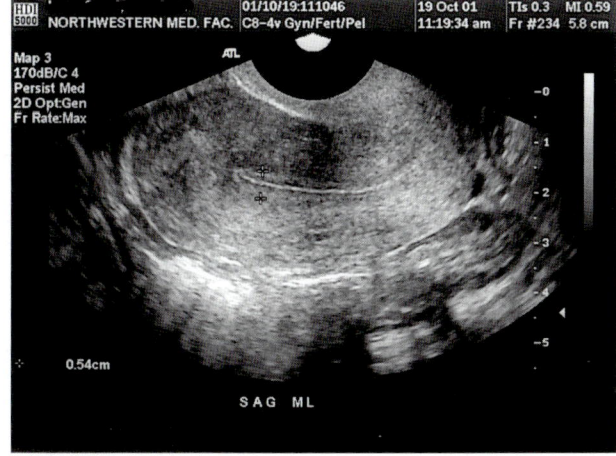

Figure 8
This coronal image from a 3-D study clearly identifies a submucous leiomyoma disrupting the endometrial cavity. The leiomyoma extends within 8 mm of the serosa. The echogenic endometrium can help outline the anatomy.

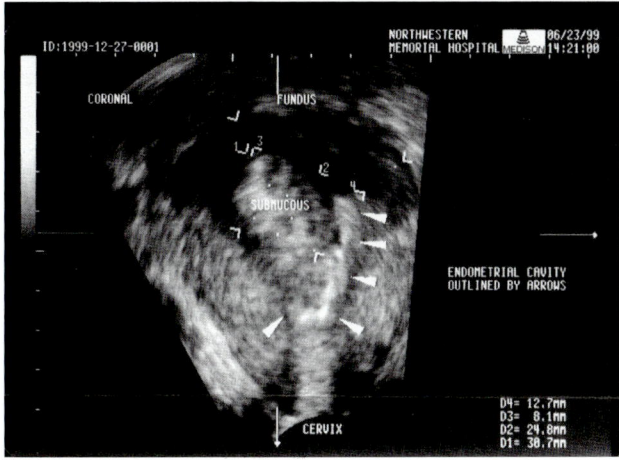

Figure 9a
A 12 _ 8-mm polyp is identified within a transitional endometrium during the third week of the cycle.

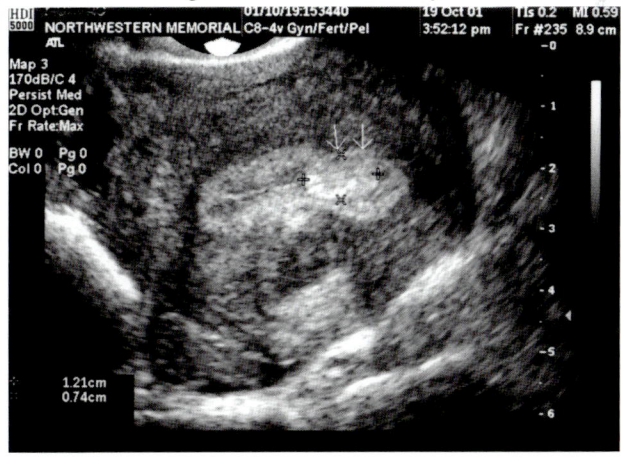

Figure 9b
The same patient was re-scanned 3 weeks later at mid-cycle. The polyp is easily seen within a 3-line endometrium. Doppler confirms an arteriolar vessel entering the polyp.

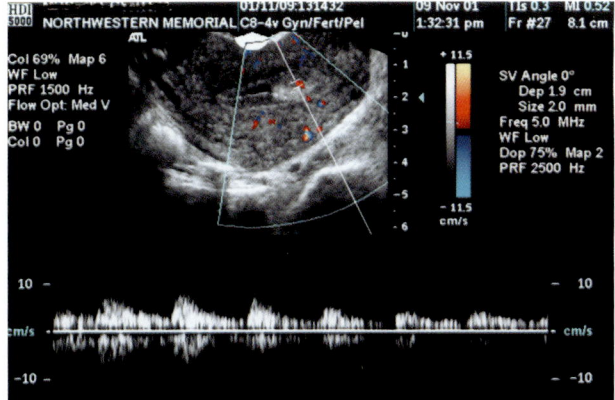

SONOHYSTEROGRAPHY

Many researchers have advocated the addition of saline contrast to improve accuracy. Bernard et al studied a group of 162 women with abnormal uterine bleeding – 109 were premenopausal and 53 were postmenopausal. The sensitivity of saline contrast sonohysterography was 90% for submucous leiomyomas and 89% for endometrial polyps [8]. Unfortunately, this paper did not measure the improvement by adding saline, and did not differentiate between the pre- and post-menopausal groups.

Dueholm et al, in the previously mentioned study [6], with the addition of saline, found 99% sensitivity and 72% specificity for the prediction of submucous leiomyomas and endometrial polyps. The authors note that 21% of the endometrial polyps would have been missed without the addition of saline. This study suggests that saline studies should be performed selectively. Thus if pathology is obvious in TVS without infusion, saline could be deferred.

Saline sonohysterography in menopausal women can be technically difficult and can yield poor image quality. A recent study by Epstein et al found that the procedure was unsuccessful in 20% of patients. In successful studies 50% of the studies resulted in suboptimal image quality [9].

MAPPING SUBMUCOUS LEIOMYOMAS

Saline infusion should also be considered if the degree of myometrial penetration by a submucous leiomyoma is difficult to assess. Wamstecker et al have demonstrated clearly that failure to appreciate significant myometrial extension of submucous leiomyomas can lead to poor case selection and complications [10]. Cohen and Valle have reviewed the role of SHSG and magnetic resonance imaging (MRI) in mapping leiomyomas [11].

Two-dimensional saline hysterography is an excellent tool. It requires the operator to take multiple sagittal as well as axial cuts to accurately map a submucous leiomyoma (Figures 10a and 10b). Three-dimensional imaging allows for routine rapid display of orthogonal images of the uterus. The coronal cuts can be scrolled through and rotated so that mapping can be performed easily (Figures 11 and 12). Three-dimensional ultrasound also decreases the need for saline infusion [12] (Figures 13a and 13b) The addition of Doppler to three-dimensional studies can help define feeder vessels entering tumors and polyps (Figure 14a–c).

ROLE OF MRI

For uteri of more than 12–14-week size or containing multiple leiomyomas MRI is clearly a better technique than ultrasound for mapping the size and location of uterine leiomyomata. MRI is also superior to ultrasound in the correct identification of adenomyosis [13–15].

Figure 10a
A centrally located myoma-like echo is noted within the uterus.

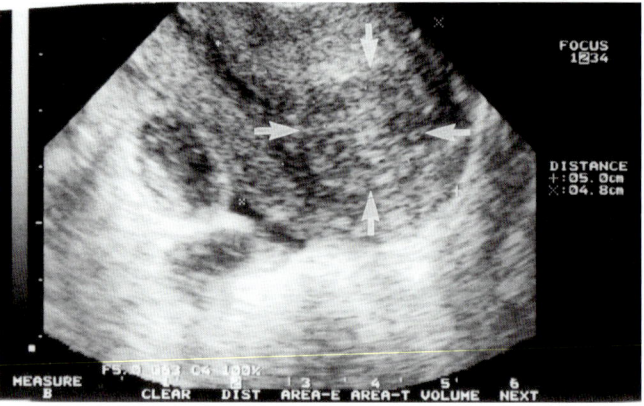

Figure 10b
The 2-D sonohysterogram confirms the presence of a submucous leiomyoma; however, a marked intramural component is noted. Hysteroscopic resection was successful.

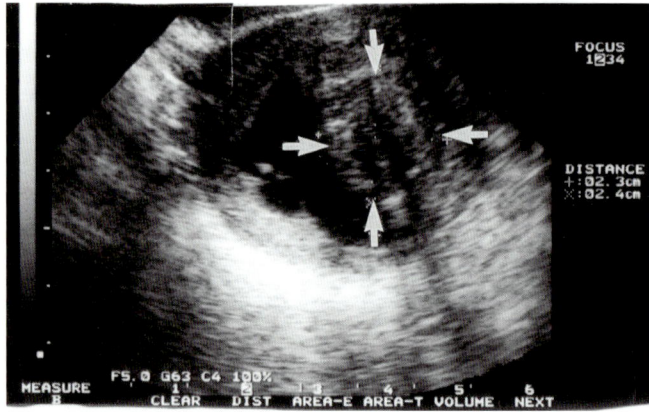

Figure 11
A coronal cut from a 3-D sonohysterogram reveals an echogenic polyp just superior to the catheter.

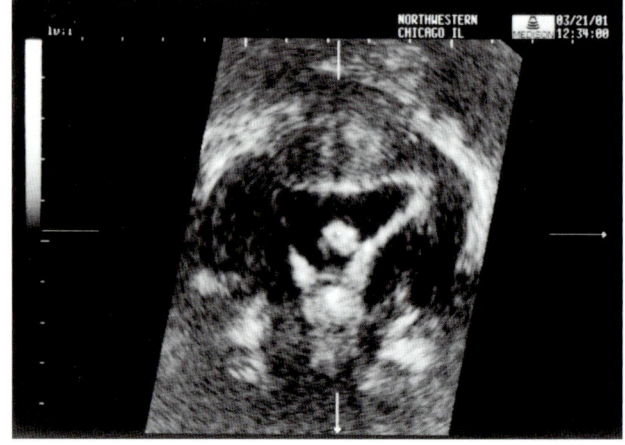

Figure 12
A coronal cut from a 3-D sonohysterogram reveals two submucous leiomyomas. The lower one is predominantly within the cavity. The upper one has mild myometrial extension.

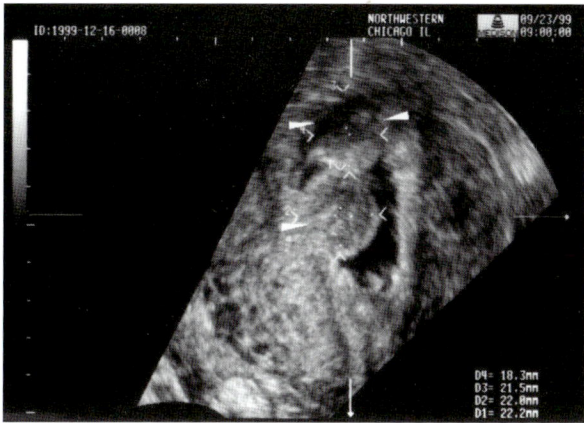

Figure 13 a
A 3-D orthogonal display of a uterus with a centrally located leiomyoma. The study was originally acquired in the sagittal plane. The coronal image was then rotated upright. This resulted in the displayed cuts.

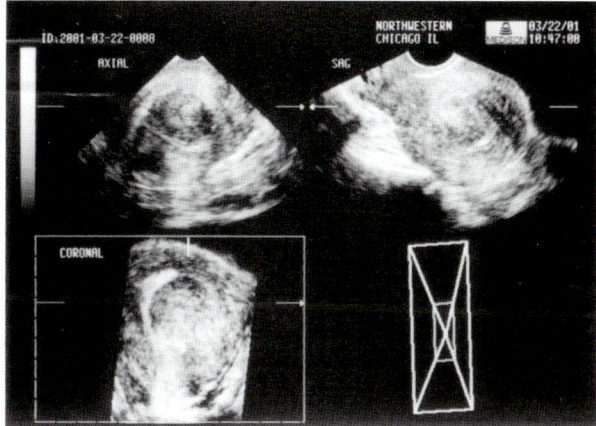

Figure 13b
A magnified view of the coronal image. The relationship of the leiomyoma to the uterine cavity and wall is clearly seen without infusion.

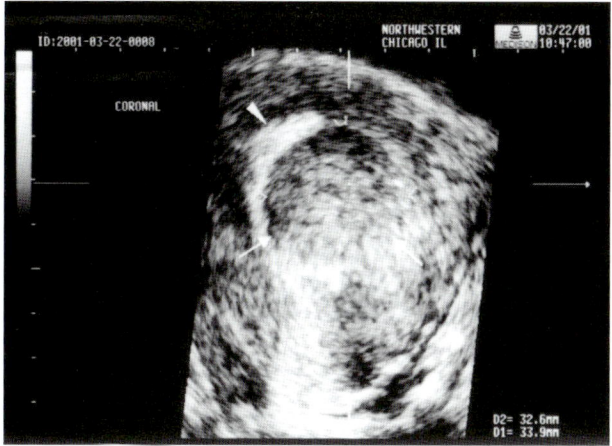

Figure 14a
3-D power Doppler study reveals circumferential flow around the periphery of a leiomyoma.

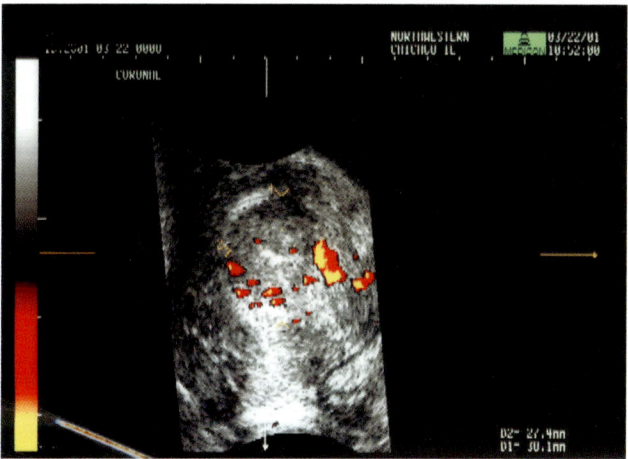

Figure 14b
A 3-D power Doppler study reveals a feeder vessel entering an endometrial polyp.

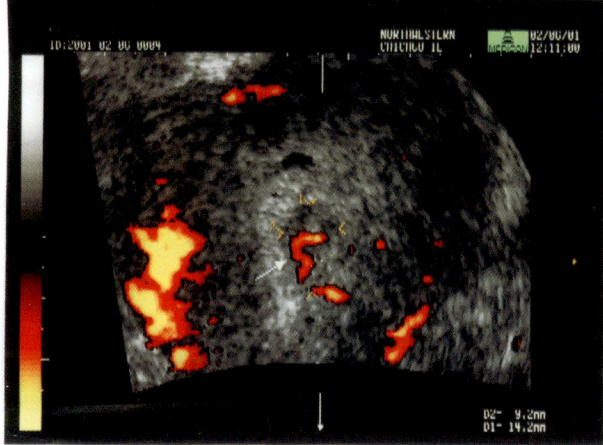

Figure 14c
A 3-D power Doppler study reveals a large vessel entering a very thickened endometrium. This postmenopausal patient had endometrial carcinoma.

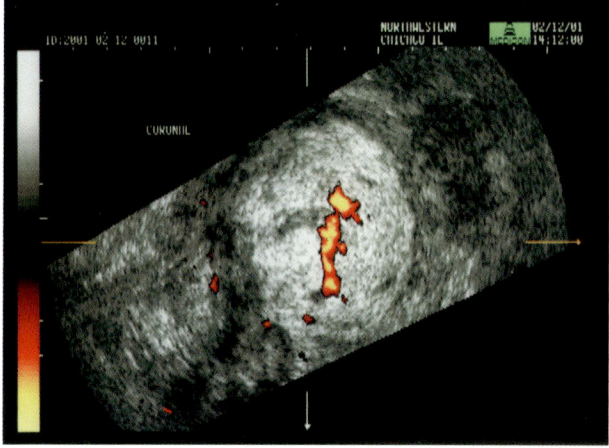

SONOHYSTEROGRAPHY TECHNIQUE

Saline hysterography is easily learned. After insertion of a speculum the cervix is cleaned with betadine. A 7.0 Fr elliptical balloon catheter (Ackrad Labs, Cranford NJ, USA) is placed in the cervical canal or lower uterine segment and the balloon is filled with 1.5 ml of air. The speculum is then removed and the transducer is placed in the vagina. If the catheter is placed in the lower uterine segment slight traction is required to prevent egress of saline. The uterus is then distended with 5–10 ml of fluid. Using the Kretz 3-D probes (KretzTechnik, Zipf, Austria), a motor built into the probe performs the volume sweep in 2–4 seconds, while the hand is held still. If 2-D sonohysterography is performed, multiple sagittal and axial cuts should be taken to fully define the cavity. Reinjection of fluid may be required.

Patients should be premedicated with a non-steroidal anti-inflammatory agent (ibuprofen or a similar product) if not contraindicated. Care should be taken that the patient is not pregnant. Appropriate premedication should be given if there is a history of pelvic inflammatory disease. The practitioner should be prepared to deal with vagal episodes, although they are rare. Informed consent should be obtained.

TUBAL PATENCY

The potential for evaluation of tubal patency with contrast sono-hystero-salpingography was well reviewed by Campbell et al using Echovist (Schering AG, Germany) [16]. The concordance rate with X-ray hysterography was 90%. The false-positive occlusion rate is approximately 10–15%. This technique is achieving increasing acceptance worldwide. Echovist is not FDA-approved for this indication in the USA. Fleischer et al have explored the role of Albunex contrast sonosalpingography in the USA [17]. This product, which is FDA-approved for tubal patency assessment, has been withdrawn from the market, due to poor market share. Three-dimensional power Doppler imaging of fallopian tubes with Echovist appears to promise better evaluation of tubal anatomy than conventional two-dimensional approaches [18].

POSTMENOPAUSAL BLEEDING

Recently a great deal of debate has arisen over whether pipelle biopsy or transvaginal ultrasound is a better initial test for the evaluation of perimenopausal and postmenopausal bleeding. The Nordic multicenter study, which was published in 1995, demonstrated that an endometrial stripe of 4 mm was highly effective in excluding endometrial cancer [19]. The study included 1168 postmenopausal women, 114 with cancer, and 112 with hyperplasias. In 110/112 endometrial cancers were identified with a cut-off value of ≤5 mm. No endometrial cancers were missed when a cut-off value of ≤4 mm was used; however, 8/112 hyperplasias were missed when a cut-off value of ≤5 mm was used. This large series clearly revealed the efficacy of transvaginal scanning without infusion in identifying postmenopausal women who had symptomatic bleeding with endometrial cancer.

CUT-OFF VALUES OF 4 OR 5 MM

The safety of using a 4-mm cut-off value has been reviewed by Gull et al [20]. Combining the three largest published series, 7 of 1361 or 0.5% of women with postmenopausal bleeding and a stripe ≤4 mm had endometrial cancer. Combining 20 published series and using a cut-off value of ≤5 mm, 12 of 14,759 women with postmenopausal bleeding (0.25%) had endometrial cancer. The authors note that this false-negative rate compares favorably with the 2% false-negative rate of dilation and curettage [21].

MEASURING TECHNIQUE

The thickness of the endometrium is usually obtained in the sagittal plane. An A-P measurement incorporating both layers of the endometrium is obtained (Figure 15). It is not uncommon to find small fluid interfaces in the endometrial cavity in postmenopausal patients (Figure 16) Goldstein has found that if the single layer thickness is <3 mm, either no focal abnormalities will be identified or inactive endometrium will be found [22].

PIPELLE BIOPSY

The limitations of pipelle biopsy have been nicely summarized by Goldstein et al [23]. Overall the pipelle technique samples only approximately 3% of the endometrium. Sensitivity for detection of endometrial cancer has ranged from 83% in the series by Guido et al to 97.5% by Stovall et al [24,25]. Goldstein et al note that a significant number of hyperplasias, endometrial polyps, and submucous leiomyomas can be missed by pipelle. The Vabra aspiration technique remains an alternative technique to the pipelle. Rodriguez et al demonstrated in hysterectomy specimens that 41% of the endometrium is sampled by Vabra and 4% by pipelle [26]. The pipelle has achieved great popularity because of its ease of use. The procedure does have limitations that must be recognized by the clinician,

LIMITATIONS OF PIPELLE AND TVS

Direct comparisons of pipelle, transvaginal scan without infusion, and hysteroscopy are revealing. In the series described by Van Den Bosch et al including 140 postmenopausal bleeders, of whom 6 had endometrial cancer, the sensitivitity of pipelle for endometrial cancer was 100% and that for hyperplasia was 63.6% [27]. The detection rate for endometrial polyps and submucous leiomyomas was very poor at 7.1%. In contrast, transvaginal ultrasound without infusion, using a 4-mm cut-off, was also 100% for endometrial cancer, but identified only 82% of benign polyps and submucous leiomyomas.

Several other limitations of the TVS assessment of postmenopausal bleeding need to be mentioned. In the Nordic series an endometrial stripe could not be measured in 3% of cases. Furthermore, the ovaries may be difficult to identify in menopausal patients using TVS. Our experience in the Northwestern Ovarian Cancer Early Detection Program has shown that ovaries in postmenopausal women can be identified more frequently transabdominally with a filled bladder than transvaginally, 95% versus 80%, respectively (unpublished data) There can also be considerable inter-observer variation if inexperienced physicians measure endometrial stripes [28].

SOCIETY OF RADIOLOGISTS IN ULTRASOUND-CONSENSUS CONFERENCE STATEMENT

As summarized by the SRU-Consensus report it would appear that either TVS or pipelle may be acceptable for initial evaluation of postmenopausal bleeding since the number of endometrial cancers missed is small [29]. Clearly, any postmenopausal women with *persistent* unexplained uterine bleeding should undergo hysteroscopic evaluation even if the pipelle or TVS is normal. It is likely that the endometrial cancers, endometrial polyps, and hyperplasias missed by pipelle will eventually be identified because of persistent bleeding.

The fundamental question is, are we hurting patients by this delay in diagnosis? Using the numbers from the series of Gull et al [20], if we take a woman with postmenopausal bleeding, there is only a 0.25–0.5% chance that she will have an endometrial cancer that is missed by triage with TVS. Assuming a 10% risk of endometrial cancer in a woman with postmenopausal bleeding and 98% sensitivity for pipelle biopsy there is a similar chance of missing an endometrial cancer. Fortunately, the clinical history of most of these cases is that the patient will continue to bleed and the diagnosis will be made by hysteroscopy and biopsy. Unless an aggressive tumor is encountered, a delay of several months is unlikely to effect staging and nodal status. The major advantages of office pipelle and TVS infusions are immediate availability in most offices and ease of performance. The tests are also a cheaper initial alternative than surgi-center or hospital-based hysteroscopy dilation and curettage.

If TVS is chosen as the primary screening tool and the endometrial stripe is thickened, ≥5.0 mm, two major options are available. The SRU Consensus Conference algorithm suggests triage to either hysteroscopy D&C or SIS (saline infusion sonohysterography). In the previously noted study by Epstein et al [9] hysteroscopy was clearly superior to both TVS and SIS in differentiating benign from malignant disease. In our laboratory we have also similarly found SIS studies in postmenopausal women to be frequently unsatisfactory or suboptimal. As there are many highly skilled hysteroscopic surgeons in our department, SIS is rarely performed in menopausal patients.

Figure 15
This midline sagittal view reveals a thin 2-mm stripe in a postmenopausal patient.

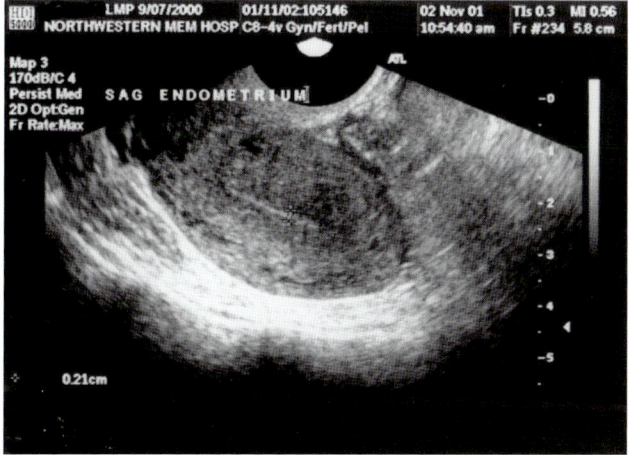

Figure 16
This midline sagittal picture reveals a fluid interface within the endometrial cavity. The one-sided measurements of the endometrium measure 1.3 mm anteriorly and 1.9 mm posteriorly. This was an incidental finding in a postmenopausal patient without bleeding.

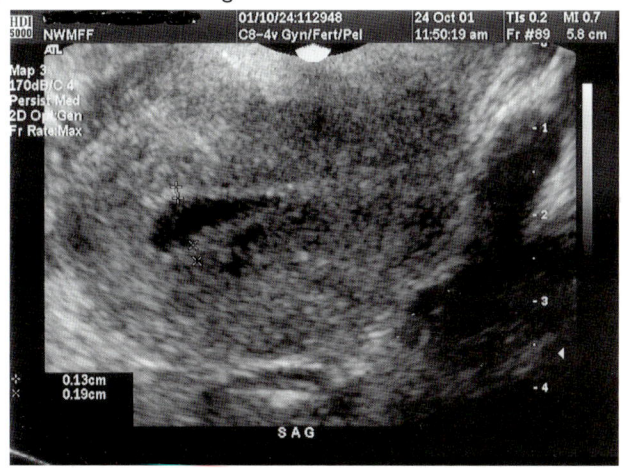

EFFECTS OF TAMOXIFEN

The effects of tamoxifen on the endometrium have been reported extensively. It is not uncommon to encounter large endometrial polyps in postmenopausal women (Figure 17). Pseudo-thickening with subepithelial vacuoles has been described by Goldstein [30]. For asymptomatic patients on tamoxifen, routine surveillance with screening ultrasound examination is not recommended by the American College of Obstericians and Gynecologists [31]. Patients with irregular bleeding or postmenopausal bleeding should be evaluated. If multiple polyp-like echoes are noted on scan, hysteroscopy D&C is our procedure of choice.

ROLE OF COLOR AND POWER DOPPLER IMAGING

Early reports by Kurjak and Zalud [32] and Bourne et al [33] suggested that color Doppler might be useful in differentiating benign from malignant endometrial pathology. Subsequent papers by Carter et al [34] and Chan et al [35] have not confirmed the utility of color Doppler evaluation. Doppler imaging can be useful in displaying the vascular supply of the uterus and performing pulsatility studies. As mentioned it can identify 'feeder vessels' entering tumors and polyps. It may have a role in tubal patency studies.

CONGENITAL UTERINE ANOMALIES

Three-dimensional ultrasound is an excellent technique for identifying and classifying uterine anomalies. Infusion is rarely required [36] (Figures 18–20).

Figure 17
This midline sagittal image reveals the appearance of a typical tamoxifen-stimulated polyp. Multiple small vessels are not infrequently identified within these polyps.

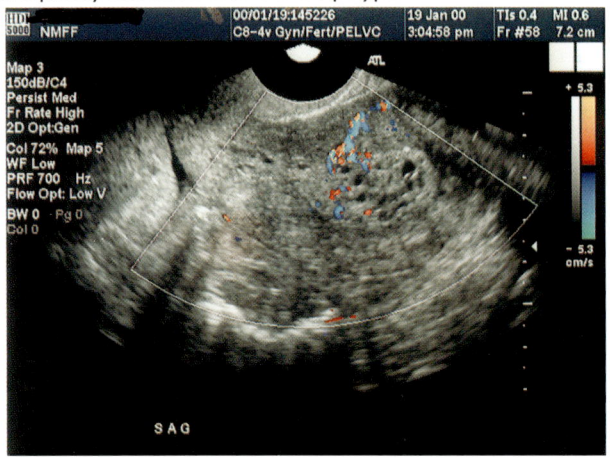

Figure 18
This 3-D study beautifully demonstrates the ability of 3-dimensional orthogonal imaging to differentiate between a septate uterus and an arcuate uterus. As seen in the top left frame, two endometrial stripes are identified (arrows). On the coronal frame in the bottom left, an arcuate cavity is clearly identified.

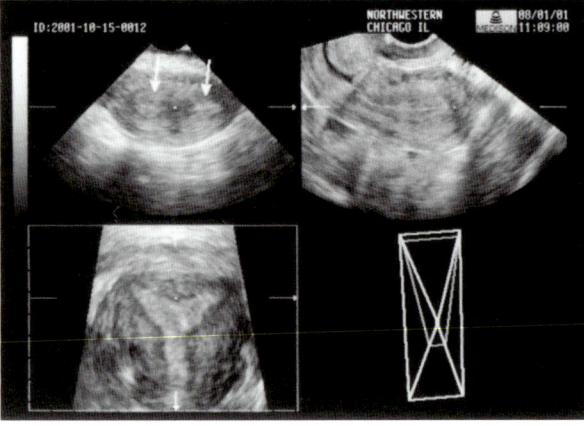

Figure 19
This coronal cut from a 3-D study reveals a complete septation of the uterus and cervical canal.

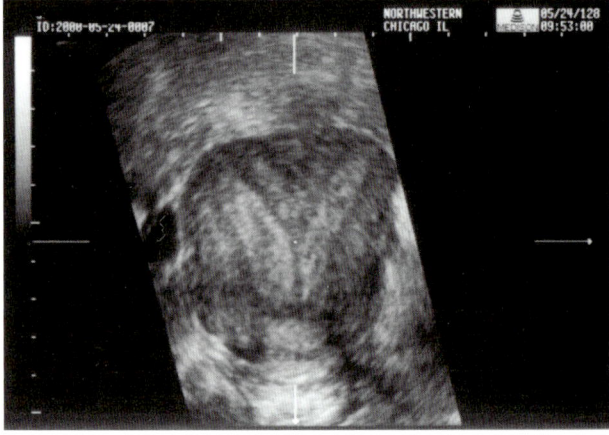

Figure 20
This 3-D study reveals a typical case of a bicornuate uterus.

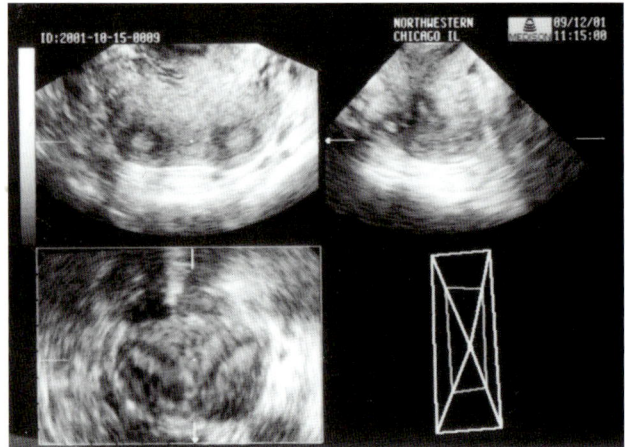

REFERENCES

Padilla L, Radosevich DM, Milad MP. Accuracy of pelvic examination in detecting adnexal masses. *Obstet Gynecol* 2000; **96**: 593–598.

Dodson MG. Use of transvaginal ultrasound in diagnosing the etiology of menometrorrhagia. *J Reprod Med* 1994; **39**: 362–372.

Goswamy RK, Narayan, R. Transvaginal sonography of the uterine cavity with hysteroscopic correlation in the investigation of infertility. *Ultrasound Obstet Gynecol* 1993; **3**: 129–133.

Kupfer MC, Schiller VL, Hansen GC, Tessler FN. Transvaginal sonographic evaluation of endometrial polyps. *J Ultrasound Med* 1994; **13**: 535–539.

Fedele L, Bianch S Dorta M et al. Transvaginal ultrasonography versus hysteroscopy in the diagnosis of uterine submucous myomas. *Obstet Gynecol* 1991; **77**: 745–748.

Dueholm M, Forman A, Jensen ML et al. Transvaginal sonography combined with saline contrast sonohysterography in evaluating the uterine cavity in premenopausal patients with abnormal uterine bleeding. *Ultrasound Obstet Gynecol* 2001; **18**: 54–61.

Towbin NA, Gviazda IM, March C. Office hysteroscopy versus transvaginal ultrasonography in the evaluation of patients with excessive uterine bleeding. *Am J Obstet Gynecol* 1996; **174**: 1678–1682

Bernard JP, Lecuru F, Darles C. Saline contrast sonohysterography as first-line investigation for women with uterine bleeding. *Ultrasound Obstet Gynecol* 1997; **10**: 121–125.

Epstein E, Ramirez A, Skoog L, Valentin L. Transvaginal sonography, saline contrast sonohysterography, and hysteroscopy for the investigation of women with postmenopausal bleeding and endometrium > 5mm. *Ultrasound Obstet Gynecol* 2001; **18**: 157–162.

Wamsteker K, Emmanuel MH, de Kruif JH. Transcervical hysteroscopic resection of submucous fibroids for abnormal uterine bleeding: results regarding the degree of myometrial extension. *Obstet Gynecol* 1993; **82**: 736–740.

Cohen LS, Valle RF. Role of vaginal sonography and hysterosonography in the endoscopic treatment of uterine myomas. *Fertil Steril* 2000; **73**: 197–204.

Cohen LS, Buckley A, Valle RF. The role of three-dimensional ultrasound in the evaluation of premenopausal abnormal uterine bleeding. *J Gynecol Surg* 2000; **16**: 69–77.

Arnold LL, Ascher SA, Schrufer JJ, Simon JA. The nonsurgical diagnosis of adenomyosis. *Obstet Gynecol* 1995; **86**: 461–465.

Dueholm M, Lundorf E, Hansen ES et al. Magnetic resonance imaging and transvaginal ultrasonography for diagnosis of adenomyosis. *Fertil Steril* 2001; **76**: 588–594.

Dueholm M, Lundorf E, Hansen ES, Ledertoug S, Olesen F. Accuracy of magnetic resonance imaging and transvaginal ultrasound in diagnosis, mapping, and measurement of uterine myomas. *Am J Obstet Gynecol* 2002; **186**: 409–415.

Campbell S, Bourne H, Tan SL, Collins WP. Hysterosalpingo-contrast sonography (HyCoSy) and its future role within the investigation of infertility in Europe. *Ultrasound Obstet Gynecol* 1994; **4**: 254–263.

Fleischer AC, Vasquez JM, Cullinan JA, Eisenberg E. Sonohysterography combined with sonosalpingography: correlation with endoscopic findings in infertility patients. *J Ultrasound Med* 1997; **16**: 381–384.

Sladkevicius P, Ohja K, Campbell S, Nargund G. Three-dimensional power Doppler imaging in the assessment of Fallopian tube patency. *Ultrasound Obstet Gynecol* 2000; **16**: 644–647.

Karlsson B, Granberg S, Wikland M et al. Transvaginal ultrasonography of the endometrium in women with postmenopausal bleeding – a Nordic multicenter study. *Am J Obstet Gynecol* 1995; **172**: 1488–1494.

Gull B, Carlsson SA, Karlsson B et al. Transvaginal ultrasonography of the endometrium in women with postmenopausal bleeding: is it always necessary to perform an endometrial biopsy? *Am J Obstet Gynecol* 2000; **182**: 509–515.

MacKenzie IZ, Bibby IG. Critical assessment of dilation and curettage in 1029 women. *Lancet* 1978; **2**: 566–568.

Goldstein SR. Postmenopausal endometrial fluid collections revisited: look at the doughnut rather than the hole. *Obstet Gynecol* 1994; **83**: 738–740.

Goldstein SR, Zeltser I, Horan CK et al. Ultrasonography based triage for perimenopausal patients with abnormal uterine bleeding. *Am J Obstet Gynecol* 1997; **177**: 102–108.

Guido RS, Kanbour A, Ruhn M, Christopherson WA. Pipelle endometrial sampling sensitivity in the detection of endometrial cancer. *J Reprod Med* 1995; **40**: 553–555.

Stovall TG, Photopulos GJ, Poston WM et al. Pipelle endometrial sampling in patients with known endometrial cancer. *Obstet Gynecol* 1991; **77**: 954–956.

Rodriguez GC, Yaqub N, King ME. A comparison of the pipelle device and the Vabra aspirator as measured by endometrial denudation in hysterectomy specimens: the Pipelle device samples significantly less of the endometrial surface than the Vabra aspirator. *Am J Obstet Gynecol* 1993; **168**: 55–59.

Van Den Bosch T, Vandendael A, Schoubroeck et al. Combined vaginal ultrasonography and office endometrial sampling in the diagnosis of endometrial disease in postmenopausal women. *Obstet Gynecol* 1995; **85**: 349–352.

Karlsson B, Granberg S, Ridell B, Wikland M. Endometrial thickness as measured by transvaginal sonography: interobserver variation. *Ultrasound Obstet Gynecol* 1994; **4**: 320–325.

Goldstein RB, Bree RL, Benacerraf BB et al. Evaluation of women with postmenopausal bleeding. Society of Radiologists in Ultrasound-Sponsored Consensus Conference. *J Ultrasound Med* 2001; **20**: 1025–1036.

Goldstein SR. Unusual sonographic appearance of the uterus in patients receiving tamoxifen. *Am J Obstet Gynecol* 1994; **170**: 447–451.

ACOG Committee on Gynecologic Practice: Tamoxifen and endometrial cancer. Committee Opinion. No. 232. Washington, DC: ACOG.

Kurjak A, Zalud I. The characterization of uterine tumors by transvaginal color Doppler. *Ultrasound Obstet Gynecol* 1991; **1**: 50–52.

Bourne TH, Campbell S, Steer CV et al. Detection of endometrial cancer by transvaginal ultrasonography with color flow imaging and blood flow analysis. *Gynecol Oncol* 1991; **40**: 253–259.

Chan F-Y, Chau M-T, Pun T-C et al. Limitations of transvaginal sonography and color Doppler imaging in the differentiation of endometrial carcinoma from benign lesions. *J Ultrasound Med* 1994; **13**: 623–628.

Carter JR, Lau M, Saltzman AK et al. Gray scale and color Doppler chracterization of uterine tumors. *J Ultrasound Med* 1994; **13**: 835–840.

Jurkovic D, Geipel A., Gruboeck K et al. Three-dimensional ultrasound for the assessment of uterine anatomy and detection of congenital anomalies: a comparison with hystersalpingography and two-dimensional sonography. *Ultrasound Obstet Gynecol* 1995; **5**: 233–238.

Saline infusion sonography: the essentials

Linda D. Bradley

> **Take Home Message**
> The introduction of SIS constitutes one of the most significant advances in ultrasonography during the past decade. SIS differentiates between focal and global processes and improves the overall sensitivity for detecting abnormalities of the endometrium. As it adds a maneuver to the classical TVS it is slightly more time-consuming and adds slightly to the discomfort of the patient. There is a different learning curve as for TVS and the results are more operator-dependent, especially for interpreting the status of the endometrium.

INTRODUCTION

Recently, the clinical tools that have historically been used for evaluation of the endometrium have come under intense scrutiny. The need for rapid and accurate office assessment of menstrual disorders is clearly understandable, when we look at the limitations of traditional endometrial assessment. There are seven methods of evaluating the intrauterine cavity, i.e. endometrial biopsy, abdominal ultrasound, transvaginal ultrasound (TVS), hysteroscopy, hysterosalpingography (HSG), saline infusion sonography (SIS), and magnetic resonance imaging (MRI).

In particular, the traditional 'blind' methods of endometrial surveillance are less than optimal, highlighting the need for more accurate and less expensive uterine surveillance techniques that a gynecologist can perform in the office setting. HSG, historically most often used in the evaluation of infertility, has limitations including pelvic irradiation and iodinated contrast medium, patient discomfort, and lack of agreement up to 30%, when compared with hysteroscopy [1]. When compared to hysteroscopy, HSG has a high sensitivity but low specificity (23%), and elevated false-negative (2–50%) and false-positive results (15–32%). Additionally, there is considerable variability in the interpretation and clinical management of patients with an abnormal HSG.

MRI imaging is equally effective and slightly superior to TVS. MRI is less able to detect endometrial polyps, but more accurate than TVS and hysteroscopy in the evaluation of exact submucous myoma in-growth [2]. Additionally, the size, number, and location of uterine fibroids are better characterized with MRI than ultrasound. Measurements of uterine fibroids are more precise and less subject to inter-rater measurements with MRI than with ultrasound.

Currently, transvaginal ultrasound has replaced abdominal ultrasound in the patient with a normal uterine cavity for evaluation of the endometrium, because of improved image quality with transvaginal scanning.

Additionally, SIS is superior to TVS alone for endometrial assessment. Evaluating the endometrium solely with TVS is limited to indistinct images of endometrial lesions. Overall, TVS has a low sensitivity and specificity in detecting endometrial pathology. Studies have clearly demonstrated the difficulty of localizing and characterizing lesions affecting the endometrium [3–5].

Evaluation of the uterine cavity for menstrual disorders has changed tremendously with the introduction of SIS [6]. Saline injected intracervically not only enhances the view of the endometrium and myometrium but also provides an acoustic view that allows for three-dimensional investigation of the uterine cavity and ovaries [7,8].

SIS overcomes the limitations of traditional TVS for evaluating menstrual and postmenopausal bleeding disorders. It offers the advantages of distending the uterine walls to create a three-dimensional view of the uterus, 'enhancing' the view of the endometrial echotexture, and providing images of structural abnormalities of the endometrium and myometrium. This information helps to determine whether endometrial biopsy is needed, to select the type of surgical procedure, to ascertain the hysteroscopic expertise required to remove the lesions, and to judge the resectability of lesions.

EVOLUTION OF SIS

Saline infusion sonography is a procedure whereby saline is infused into the endometrial cavity during TVS to enhance the endometrial view. Although many terms have been used to describe this technique (e.g. echohysteroscopy, hydrosonography, sonohysterography, sonohysterosalpinogography, sonoendovaginal ultrasonography) the acronym SIS, 'saline infusion sonography' was coined by Widrich et al in 1996, and more clearly defines the technique employed [6].

In 1981, Nannini et al [9] first described the procedure using a rigid catheter and transabdominal scanning method called 'echohysteroscopy'.

Richman et al [10] first used high molecular weight dextran (Hyskon) for SIS to verify tubal patency when a collection of fluid was demonstrated in the cul-de-sac. This method could demonstrate only that at least one tube was patent but could not determine which tube was open. Performed transabdominally, this procedure had a sensitivity of 100% for bilateral tubal obstruction and a specificity of 96% for tubal patency.

Randolph et al [11] then combined intrauterine saline solution with abdominal ultrasonography in 1986, correctly identifying 53 of 54 uterine cavities in patients immediately before hysterectomy. Using a rigid Schultze cannula, Bonilla-Musoles et al [12] evaluated 38 patients with abnormal uterine bleeding and found that the saline-enhanced endovaginal ultrasonography was more useful than the transabdominal approach.

In 1992, Syrop and Sahakian [13] found polyps in 13 of 14 essentially asymptomatic patients who were evaluated for infertility with fluid augmentation. Their study utilized a rigid Reuben's cannula and vaginal probe. Parsons and Lense [7] further modified this technique in 1993 for endovaginal ultrasonography with a 5 Fr insemination catheter. Of 39 patients evaluated for abnormal uterine bleeding with this technique, 16 had endometrial polyps, 4 had endometrial hyperplasia, 2 had stage IA endometrial cancer, and 2 had endometrial 'wrinkles'. All of these diagnoses were confirmed with histological specimens. The 15 remaining patients had fibroids that could not be located before augmentation. When saline was infused, localization of fibroids was possible.

Goldstein reported the benefits of ultrasonohysterography in patients with perimenopausal bleeding. He also recognized the limitations of TVS alone in evaluation of the endometrium in women using tamoxifen [14].

Widrich et al [6] published their findings from 130 patients evaluated for abnormal bleeding. They compared the accuracy and pain rating of SIS with flexible hysteroscopy performed in the physician's office and used hysteroscopy as the gold standard. For all SIS findings combined, sensitivity was 96% and specificity was 88% compared with hysteroscopy. They coined the term SIS.

CLINICAL ROLE OF SIS IN THE EVALUATION OF MENSTRUAL DISORDERS

The following are common indications for performing SIS:
- Evaluation of menstrual disorders in the premenopausal or postmenopausal patient.
- Evaluation of the endometrium when it is poorly visualized, thickened, irregular, or not imaged well by conventional TVS, MRI, or CAT scan studies.
- Evaluation of a bizarre, irregular, or inhomogeneous endometrium in women on tamoxifen.
- Evaluation of patients with recurrent pregnancy loss or infertility.
- Post-surgical evaluation of the endometrium.
- The need to differentiate between sessile and pedunculate masses of the endometrium.

SIS TECHNIQUE

Although SIS can be performed transvaginally or transabdominally, most physicians use the transvaginal approach. This procedure is best scheduled when the patient is not bleeding. Women of reproductive age should ideally be scheduled during the early proliferative phase (days 4–10). The risk of interrupting a viable intrauterine pregnancy is lowest at this time. Additionally, fewer false-positive results, less artifacts, and less shearing of the endometrium would occur during placement of the intrauterine catheter, and improved visualization of endometrial polyps and fibroids is possible during the follicular phase.

PREPARATION

Except for patients who have symptoms or signs of pelvic infection or require antibiotics for procedures, or in whom optional nonsteroidal anti-inflammatory drugs (NSAIDs) are administered before the procedure, SIS requires minimal preparation and no anesthesia.

Voiding before SIS is important. Bladder distention is not required. In fact, it can alter the position of an anteverted uterus to retroverted, making evaluation with a transvaginal probe onerous. After informed consent is obtained, a bimanual examination is performed with the patient in the dorsal lithotomy position. An absorbent towel placed under the patient will minimize fluid accumulation. Conventional TVS is performed using a transvaginal probe covered with a condom and gel. Visualization of the cervix is aided by placing an open-sided speculum in the vagina to facilitate introduction of the intrauterine catheter and permit easy removal of that same speculum without displacing the catheter. The cervix is cleansed with an antiseptic solution, such as Betadine or

Hibiclens. The intrauterine catheter is then inserted. Several flexible intrauterine catheters that provide easy access to the endometrium are currently available [15]. I prefer the 25-cm long, 5.6 Fr Soules intrauterine insemination catheter (Cook Ob/Gyn, Indianapolis, IN, USA), because it is inexpensive and easy to use and place within the uterus. For conditions such as incompetent cervix, Asherman's syndrome, or patulous cervix, a balloon-type catheter is useful to optimize uterine distention and minimize fluid loss.

Before the catheter is inserted, it is flushed with sterile saline to decrease artifacts caused by bubbles. A straight catheter should be introduced with sterile uterine packing forceps until the fundus is reached. If distention is inadequate, it may be helpful to pull the catheter back. When cervical stenosis is encountered, a tenaculum or uterine sound can be used to assist in placing the catheter. After the open-sided speculum is removed, the Soules catheter will protrude from the vagina, allowing easy attachment of a 60-ml plastic syringe containing sterile saline.

SIS is a dynamic procedure, and images are best seen in real time. Excellent images and adequate distention usually are obtained with minimal fluid instillation (5–30 ml); ideally, 5–10 ml/min are infused. If the uterus cannot be distended, placing a balloon-tipped catheter and infusing the saline more slowly may help. Air bubbles may accumulate but rapidly disappear as the injection continues. More fluid can safely be used if the patient is bleeding or has blood clots, or if there is poor visualization.

It is essential to employ a systematic technique for viewing the uterus and to watch the video monitor as the scan is performed. As the endometrial cavity distends on the screen, it is important to view the uterus as a three-dimensional structure that must continually be recreated as scanning continues. This three-dimensional image is achieved by scanning from cornua to cornua in the long axis (sagittal plane) and then turning the probe 90° and scanning from the endocervix to the fundus. The sagittal view permits visualization of the uterine cavity and measurement of the endometrial echo. The adnexa are visualized in the semi-coronal plane. The cervix and cul-de-sac are viewed as the transducer is withdrawn. Uterine symmetry and myometrial or intracavitary lesions are appreciated best by slowly scanning transversely from the external os to the fundus. Fleischer et al [16] recommend measuring both layers of the endometrial echo (which represent the anterior and posterior uterine wall basal layers) in the sagittal view to obtain the most accurate measurement of the endometrium. The hypoechoic subendometrial halo should not be included because it represents the vascular layer of myometrium. Both TVS and SIS can be performed in 10–15 minutes in most patients.

POTENTIAL PROBLEMS, PITFALLS, AND TROUBLESHOOTING OPTIONS

The procedural risks associated with SIS are minimal. A bimanual examination and visual inspection of the cervix should be performed before any instrumentation. If bacterial vaginosis, trichomonas, or other sexually transmitted diseases (STDs) are suspected, the procedure should be abandoned. Antibiotics are prescribed only in patients with prior history of STD, artificial joints, or mitral valve regurgitation.

Cervical manipulation can produce a vasovagal reaction. Patients may rarely experience bradycardia, dizziness, or severe pain; therefore, resuscitative equipment should be readily available.

There are no published reports of uterine perforation with SIS. The procedure causes minimal pain, but NSAIDs can be administered 1–2 hours before the procedure if desired – although this does not appear to significantly decrease the already low pain scores [6].

The possibility of transmitting metastatic endometrial cancer through the fallopian tubes during SIS is purely speculative. The small amounts of fluid used and the low infusion intrauterine pressure minimize risk to the patient. Historical data in patients with endometrial cancer evaluated by hysterosalpingography found no evidence of worse-than-normal outcomes [17].

POSTPROCEDURE INSTRUCTIONS

SIS is associated with few complications. Most patients are able to leave the office within 15 minutes of the procedure and return to work and normal activities. Since narcotics are not usually used, patients may drive alone and do not require an escort. Patients are instructed to refrain from vaginal intercourse for 24 hours. In the event of increased temperature, foul-smelling discharge, or persistent pelvic pain, the patient should contact their physician.

FINDINGS

SIS permits rapid assessment of the endometrial cavity, myometrium, and adnexa. Its superiority over TVS in differentiating causes of increased endometrial thickness is readily apparent. Distinguishing between polyps and fibroids, endometrial hyperplasia, global versus focal disease, and depth of myometrial involvement of uterine fibroids is easy with SIS.

The endometrial cavity is a bioassay of the complex changes that occur within the ovary. The ovary produces endogenous hormones which directly influence the growth, echogenicity, thickness, and overall appearance of the endometrium. When SIS is performed, a normal endometrium during the proliferative and secretory phase appears symmetric and is surrounded by anechoic saline (Figure 1c and d). In the premenopausal patient, the endometrium undergoes rapid growth development, and sloughing on a monthly basis. Specifically, the endometrium is thinnest during the menstrual phase, when total thickness is ≤4 mm. During the proliferative phase, the endometrium ranges between 4 and 8 mm. If the endometrial thickness is >15 mm during any phase of the cycle, the patient has a 15% risk of harboring endometrial hyperplasia. During the secretory phase, the endometrium ranges from 8 to 14 mm. Visualizing the ovary (i.e. corpus luteum) and ascertaining the presence or absence of typical hallmarks for secretory endometrium is instructive. The endometrium typically is very thin (<4 mm) in women using prolonged courses of oral contraception, Depo Provera, DepoLupron, hormone replacement therapy, and in postmenopausal women. An endometrial thickness of <5 mm in postmenopausal women who are not using hormone replacement therapy is associated with a low incidence of endometrial cancer [18].

Most findings are best elucidated during the late follicular stage. Improved visualization appears to be related to the length and tortuosity of the endometrial glands with mucin and glycogen storage [19].

ENDOMETRIAL ATROPHY

An atrophic endometrium is typically observed in menopausal women, prolonged Depo-Lupron, Depo-Provera, and continuous oral contraceptive use. Histologically, sclerotic blood vessels and glands are present. The glands may dilate, thus rendering the appearance of cystic spaces on TVS. In postmenopausal women, atrophic endometrium produces a pencil-thin endometrial echo <5 mm thick [20]. SIS reliably determines atrophic endometrium and facilitates clinical care. In postmenopausal women, true reassurance can be provided that the bleeding is not pathologic. Medical therapy with estrogen, is used to remedy the problem. (See Figure 1a–d.)

Figure 1a
A 54-year-old woman who had been postmenopausal for 3 years; she presented with postmenopausal bleeding.
(a, b)TVS demonstrates a retroverted uterus and a 1.6-mm endometrial echo;

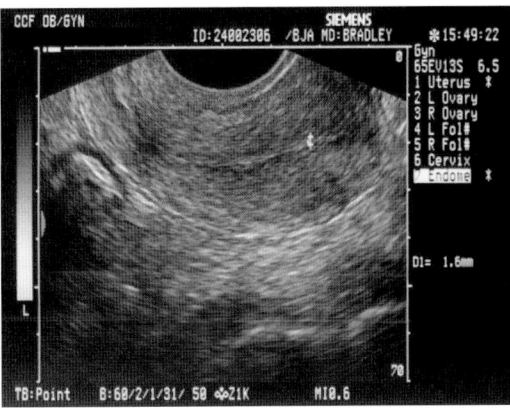

Figure 1b

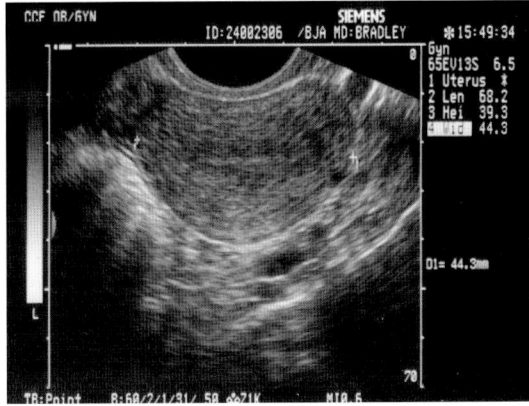

Figure 1c
(c, d) SIS images document thin symmetric endometrium.

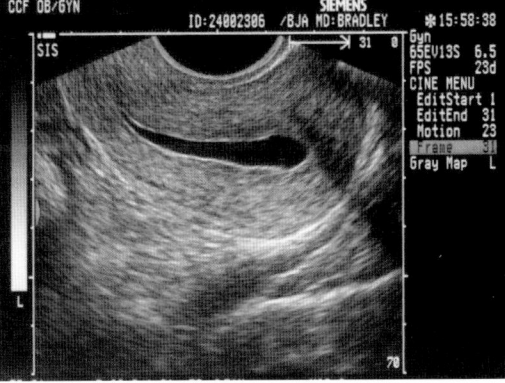

Figure 1d

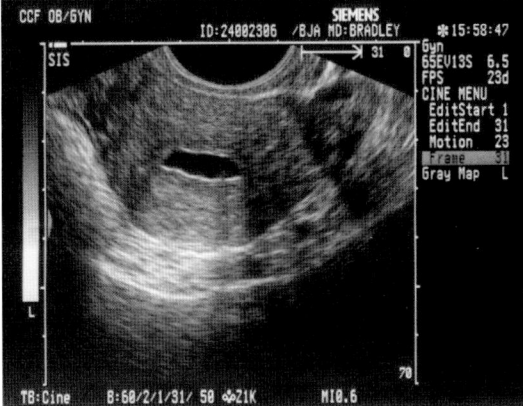

ENDOMETRIAL POLYPS

Endometrial polyps occur frequently in the reproductive and menopausal years. Viewed transvaginally, polyps distort the endometrial echo, creating the impression that the endometrial echo is widened. A mass that is well defined and uniformly hyperechoic suggests a benign endometrial polyp. Retrospectively, in 68 postmenopausal women evaluated by TVS it was found that cystic spaces within an abnormally thickened endometrium tended to be predictive of polyps [21]. Histologic examination of the cystic spaces is due to dilated glands. Because polyps can be camouflaged in secretory endometrium, visualization is best during the proliferative phase.

SIS can differentiate pedunculate from sessile polypoid masses. During SIS fluid instillation, polyps may be seen to undulate. They are surrounded by anechoic fluid and are, therefore, hyperechoic. Polyps may vary in size, location, number, and risk of malignancy. They are usually homogeneous; but they can reveal microcystic changes. Understanding the location of polyps is helpful surgically, since the stalk size and location can be easily determined with SIS. Polyps typically do not distort the endomyometrial complex. Although polyps typically distort the endometrium, creating falsely thickened measurements, the true endometrium can be measured separately from the polyp, once the fluid is instilled. In a retrospective study of 78 women with endometrial polyps treated by hysteroscopic polypectomy nearly two-thirds reported improvement of their symptoms [22]. (See Figure 2a and b.)

INTRAUTERINE FIBROIDS

Fibroids are difficult to locate with conventional ultrasound, because they transmit sound poorly, attenuate the beam, and have ill-defined borders (Figure 3a and b). Fibroids may obscure measurements of the endometrium by creating an irregular endomyometrial interface. They may have varied appearance, including cystic, calcific, hypoechoic, echogenic, isoechoic, and mixed echogenic patterns. Degenerating fibroids often appear cystic. Location of fibroids is improved with SIS. Additionally, location, size, and degree of intramural extension can be

Figure 2a
TVS with indistinct 17-mm endometrial echo.

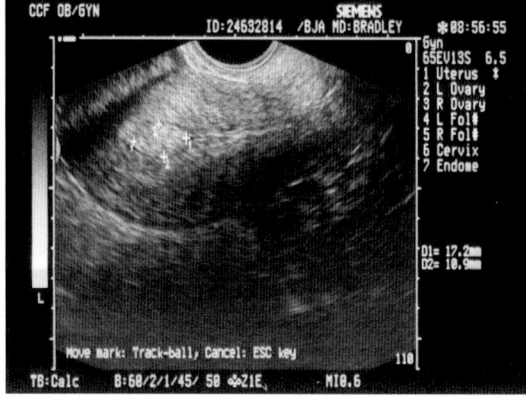

Figure 2b
SIS demonstrates a clearly defined 1.6 cm × 1.1 cm endometrial polyp.

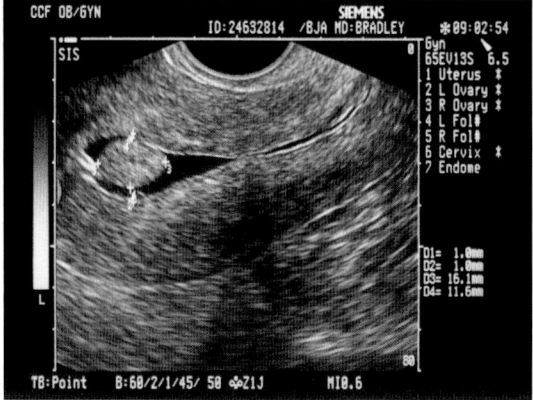

Figure 3a
TVS of ill-defined endometrium in sagittal view.

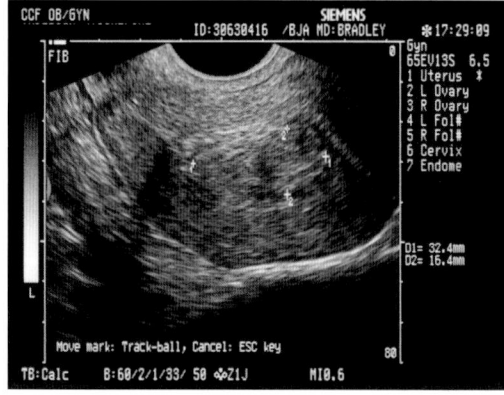

Figure 3b
Coronal view of central hyperechoic fibroid.

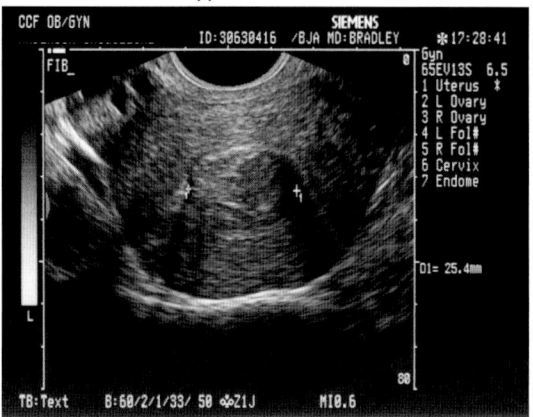

classified with SIS [23]. The following classification of intracavitary uterine fibroids is based on SIS for the purpose of planning surgery:

SIS class 1 fibroids are intracavitary and do not involve the myometrium. The base or stalk is visible with SIS (Figure 4a and b).

SIS class 2 fibroids have a submucosal component that involves <50% of the myometrium (Figure 5a and b).

SIS class 3 fibroids have an intramural component >50%. They can be transmural and located anywhere from the submucosa to the serosa. These fibroids often appear as a bulge or indentation into the submucosa when viewed hysteroscopically (Figure 6a and b).

For a successful surgical outcome, it is important to identify preoperatively the size, number, location, and depth of intramural extension of uterine fibroids. Fibroid size and location are associated with complete respectability, the number of surgical procedures necessary for complete resection, the duration of surgery, and the potential complications from fluid overload [24].

ENDOMETRIAL HYPERPLASIA

Endometrial hyperplasia cannot be definitively diagnosed with SIS; however, endometrial thickness, echogenicity, and appearance may suggest the need for endometrial biopsy for confirmation or hysteroscopy. Truly, endometrial hyperplasia can only be documented by histologic analysis. Hyperplasia may be global, multifocal, focal, or may occur within a polyp. Hyperplasia may produce a uniformly hyperechoic and thickened endometrium [25]. SIS can guide the surgeon to obtain either a hysteroscopically directed biopsy if a focal process is identified, or an endometrial office biopsy if a global process is noted. The ranges of endometrial thickness in hyperplasia and carcinoma overlap. Most hyperplasias widen the endometrium to 0.6–1.3 cm in postmenopausal women, with a mean thickness of 1 cm [26]. Hulka et al [21] evaluated 68 postmenopausal women and noted that endometrial hyperplasia often appeared hyperechoic, with the endomyometrial interface intact. Possible causes of increased endometrial thickness are summarized in Table 1 and Figure 7a and b.

Figure 4a
Schematic representation of SIS class 1 fibroid.

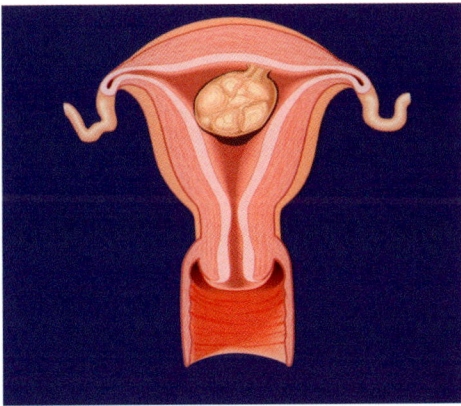

Figure 4b
SIS class 1 demonstrating an intracavitary fibroid; it does not involve the myometrium.

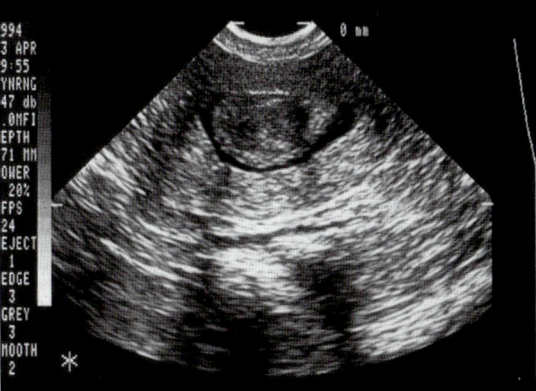

Figure 5a
Schematic representation of SIS class 2 fibroid.

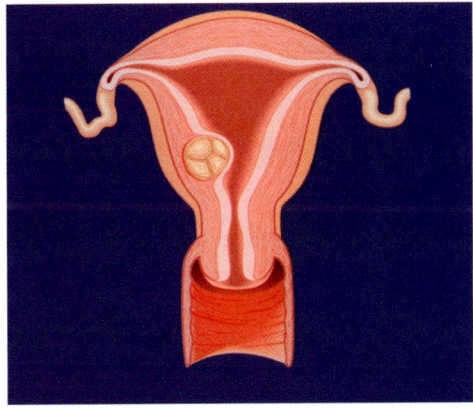

Figure 5b
SIS class 2 fibroid involving <50% of the myometrium.

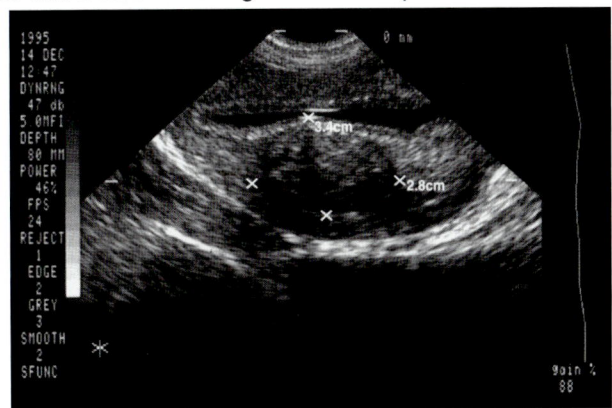

ENDOMETRIAL CANCER

Endometrial cancer requires a histologic analysis; however, it can be suspected by the increased endometrial thickness as determined by TVS or characteristic appearances obtained with SIS. Endometrial cancer is difficult to distinguish from hyperplasia unless the endometrial thickness is increased or associated with a disruption of the endomyometrial interface. Most studies report that the endometrium is thicker in patients subsequently noted to have endometrial pathology than in patients with benign conditions, although there may be an overlap [27].

The endometrial echo has a myriad of appearances in patients with endometrial cancer, including an irregularly thickened, ill-defined endometrium; a heterogeneous pattern; and mixed echogenicity with variable hypoechoic texture. The endomyometrial junction may be intact or irregular (Figure 8a and b).

INTRAUTERINE ADHESIONS

Shalev et al [28] demonstrated better appreciation of intrauterine adhesions during mid-cycle compared with menses. Intrauterine adhesions appeared as hyperechoic, irregular, linear echoes, with cord-like features, and

Table 1
Uterine abnormalities detectable by saline infusion sonography

- Intrauterine fluid accumulation due to cervical stenosis
- Endometrial cancer
- Endometrial hyperplasia
- Endometrial polyps
- Dyssynchronous endometrium
- Uterine fibroids: intraluminal, submucosal
- Tamoxifen-induced changes
- Intrauterine synechiae

Figure 6a
Schematic representation of SIS class 3 fibroid

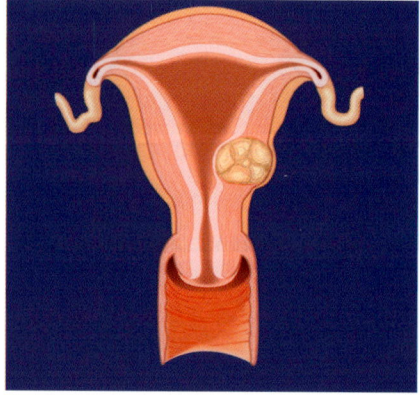

Figure 6b
SIS class 3 fibroid demonstrating >50% intramural component; the transmural component abuts the posterior endometrium.

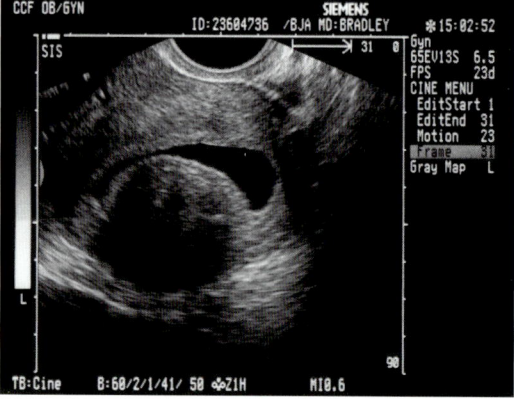

Figure 7a
TVS of a hyperechoic 21.9-mm endometrial echo.

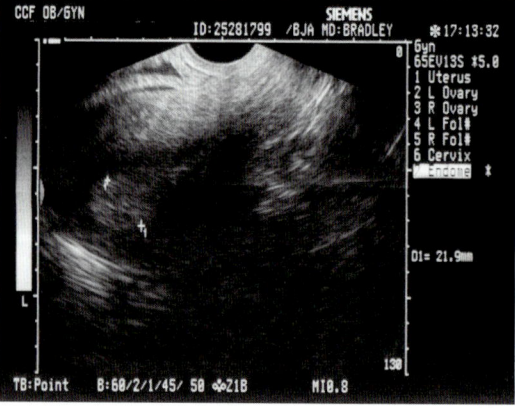

Figure 7b
SIS view of an irregular and asymmetric endometrium with the anterior endometrium 12.9 mm and the posterior endometrium 9.9 mm. Endometrial biopsy was consistent with complex endometrial hyperplasia without atypia.

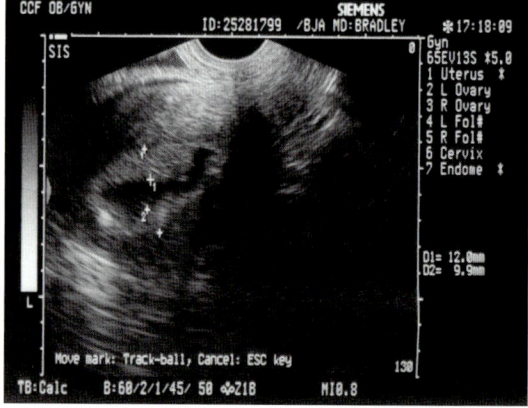

endometrial foci and could be differentiated from polyps by their irregular shape and more precise location Adhesions interrupt the continuity of the endometrial layer. During the early follicular phase, adhesions appear as irregular central lines in the endometrium. In patients with Asherman's syndrome, the adhesions appear as thin, bridging bands that may distort the endometrium. In addition, the uterus may be difficult to distend [29].

TAMOXIFEN-INDUCED CHANGES

Patients using tamoxifen do not require routine endometrial surveillance. They should be evaluated comprehensively like any woman on hormone therapy who presents with abnormal uterine bleeding. Although most long-term tamoxifen users develop an inactive endometrium, some demonstrate increased endometrial hyperplasia, and hysteroscopically appear to have marked hypervascularity and endometrial polyps, hyperplasia, and rarely cancer.

Figure 8a
TVS of a 'naturally occurring' SIS. An indistinct endometrial shadow is noted.

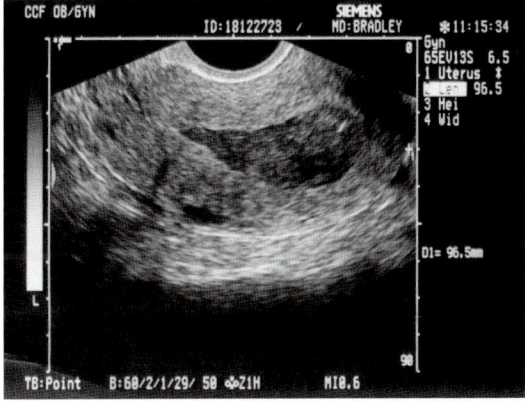

Figure 8b
A 4.6 cm _ 2.1 cm intracavitary mass. Biopsy was consistent with a carcinosarcoma (mixed mesodermal) heterologous type.

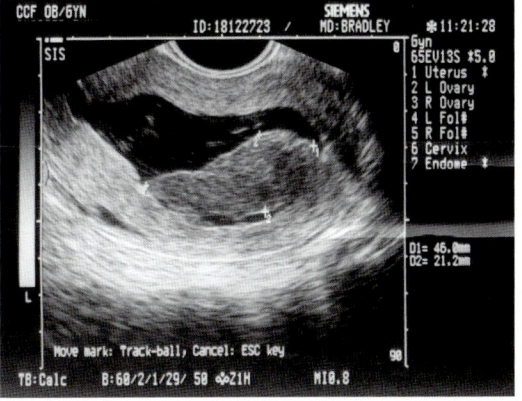

Goldstein [30] has advocated SIS to better clarify bizarre, heterogeneous, or centrally located uterine changes noted on conventional TVS. Saline infusion can reveal the true location of the abnormalities, i.e. the subendometrial layer. These abnormalities were thought to represent a 'reactivation of the foci of adenomyosis' in the form of microcysts. When viewed microscopically, the endomyometrial junction in tamoxifen users is irregular and nonlinear as compared with a linear junction in nonusers [31].

LIMITATIONS

Although the authors generally prefer SIS for endometrial evaluation, Widrich et al [6] were unable to complete the procedure in patients with a cavernous uterine cavity of 12–14 weeks in gestational size, submucosal fibroids measuring >4 cm, large endometrial polyps that fill the entire endometrial cavity, and large transmural fibroids that put greater downward pressure on the endometrium. Difficulty in placing the intrauterine catheter may occur in patients with cervical stenosis, isthmic synechia, a markedly retroverted uterus, or intrauterine septa. Patients with cervical stenosis may benefit from placement of laminaria for 1–3 hours or oral or vaginal Misoprostol, and uterine sounding may sufficiently disrupt synechiae. Cervical traction with a single-toothed tenaculum can straighten the uterine axis in cases of marked retroversion.

Additional limitations include the inability to thread the catheter, the presence of endometrial pseudo-polyps, the introduction of air bubbles into the uterus, and the inability to distend the uterine cavity in cases of a patulous cervix. In addition, endometrial thickness varies in premenopausal women owing to the ovarian cycle. Therefore, observing patients through several cycles to verify the presence of cyclic ovarian activity and endometrial sloughing may obviate endometrial biopsy. If there is no change in thickness, endometrial biopsy should be performed to rule out disordered proliferative endometrium, hyperplasia, and malignancy.

Although SIS overcomes many of the limitatations of TVS, sometimes the endometrium just cannot be visualized, is indistinct, and indeterminate findings occur. If the endometrium is not well seen, then hysteroscopy plays a definitive role in ascertaining endometrial morphology. Indistinct imaging may occur with larger intramural fibroids, synechiae, malignancy, and large intracavitary lesions.

On occasion it may be difficult to distinguish between a sessile polyp or submucosal fibroid if the typical characteristics of a polyp or fibroid are not apparent.

Luckily, however, treatment with operative hysteroscopy is the same for both procedures.

Finally, more false positives may occur if SIS is performed in the presence of active uterine bleeding. Endometrial clots may be thought to be polyps, fibroids, or hyperplasia. Some authors have suggested that if a lesion <10 mm is detected, SIS should be repeated when the patient is not bleeding, before taking a patient to the operating room for operative hysteroscopy, to decrease the likelihood of a negative hysteroscopic view.

Currently, SIS cannot determine tubal patency. This limitation may soon be history, as newer products that are injectable may permit accurate detection of tubal patency, and thereby avoid the need for HSG with all its inherent problems [33].

COSTS

The development of clinical algorithms incorporating SIS – particularly in premenopausal versus postmenopausal women – may decrease costs by eliminating unnecessary endometrial biopsy and D&Cs (see algorithm in Figure 9). The Nordic trial suggested that approximately 50% of biopsies of bleeding postmenopausal patients with an endometrial echo of <5 mm are unnecessary [18]. Goldstein's algorithm (developed after analysing >400 perimenopausal evaluations) concluded that hysteroscopically directed endometrial biopsy is best for women with focal processes, while endometrial aspiration biopsy is best for those with global disease [34]. The elimination of unnecessary biopsies and hysteroscopy will further reduce the costs associated with the evaluation of abnormal uterine bleeding. Generally, SIS is less costly than hysteroscopy.

CONCLUSION

The introduction of intracervical SIS during TVS constitutes one of the most significant advances in ultrasonography during this past decade. It can provide a wealth of information about the uterus and adnexa in patients with abnormal bleeding. Given the disparity between endometrial biopsy results and ultrasonographic findings, histologic reports of 'insufficient tissue', 'atrophic endometrium', or 'scant tissue' on biopsy are no longer sufficient to rule out pathology. SIS provides a view of the endomyometrial complex that cannot be obtained with TVS alone. SIS differentiates between focal and global processes and improves the overall sensitivity for detecting abnormalities of the endometrium.

The continuing challenge for gynecologists is to provide patients with cost-effective, minimally invasive evaluation and directed therapy for menstrual dysfunction. SIS identifies patients who need biopsy, directs the surgical approach, and minimizes office diagnostic hysteroscopy – all with a quick office procedure. For patients, the benefits include minimal discomfort and an enhanced understanding of their condition through viewing the ultrasound monitor. Women also appreciate the scheduling flexibility, the rapid recovery that enables them to return to work sooner, and the fact that they do not need an escort because the effects of the anesthesia or analgesic are minimal.

Figure 1a
Clinical algorithm incorporating SIS.
(Reproduced with permission from Widrich et al. Am J Obstet Gynecol 1996; 174: 1327–1334.)

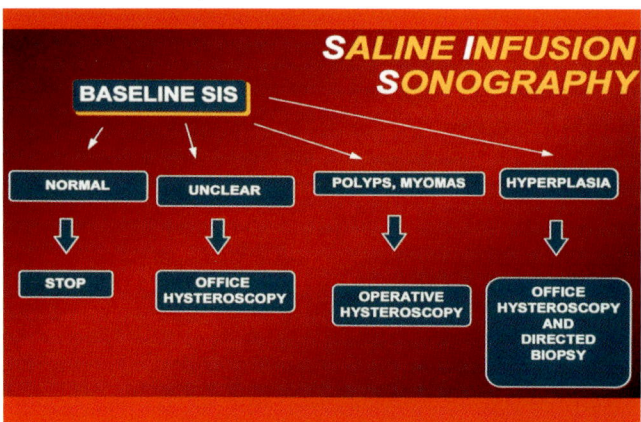

REFERENCES

Brown SE, Coddington CC, Schnorr J, Toner JP, Gibbons W, Oehninger S. Evaluation of outpatient hysteroscopy, saline infusion hysterosonography, and hysterosalpingography in infertile women: a prospective, randomized study. *Fertil Steril* 2000; **74**: 1029–1034.

Dueholm M, Lundorf E, Hansen E, Ledertoug S, Olesen F. Evaluation of the uterine cavity with magnetic resonance imaging, transvaginal sonography, hysterosonographic examination, and diagnostic hysteroscopy. *Fertil Steril* 2001; **76**: 350–357.

Fedele L, Bianchi S, Dorta M. Transvaginal ultrasonography versus hysteroscopy in the diagnosis of uterine submucous myomas. *Obstet Gynecol* 1991; **77**: 745–748.

Goldstein SR, Nachtigal M, Beller U. Endometrial assessment by vaginal ultrasound prior to endometrial sampling. *Am J Obstet Gynecol* 1990; **163**: 119–123.

Fleischer AC, Mendelson EB, BohnVelez M. Transvaginal and transabdominal sonography of the endometrium. *Semin Ultrasound CT MR* 1988; **9**: 81–101.

Widrich T, Bradley L, Mitchinson AR, Collins R. Comparison of saline infusion sonography with office hysteroscopy for the evaluation of the endometrium. *Am J Obstet Gynecol* 1996; **174**: 1327–1334.

Parsons AK, Lense JJ. Sonography for endometrial abnormalities: preliminary results. *J Clin Ultrasound* 1993; **231**: 87–95.

Goldstein SR, Zeltser I, Horan CK et al. Ultrasonography-based triage for perimenopausal patients with abnormal uterine bleeding. *Am J Obstet Gynecol* 1997; **177**: 102–108.

Nannini R, Chelo E, Branconi F et al. A new diagnostic technique in the study of female infertility. *Acta Eur Fertil* 1981; **12**: 165–171.

Richman TS, Viscomi GN, DeCherney A et al. Fallopian tubal patency assessed by ultrasound following fluid injection. *Radiology* 1984; **152**: 507–510.

Randolph JR, Ying YK, Maier DB et al. Comparison of real-time ultrasonography, hysterosalpingography, and laparoscopy/hysteroscopy in the evaluation of uterine abnormalities and tubal patency. *Fertil Steril* 1984; **46**: 828–832.

Bonila-Musoles F, Simon C, Serra V et al. An assessment of hysterosalpingosonography as a diagnostic tool for uterine cavity defects and tubal patency. *J Clin Ultrasound* 1992; **79**: 104–143.

Syrop Ch, Sahakian V. Transvaginal sonography detection of endometrial polyps with fluid contrast augmentation. *Obstet Gynecol* 1992; **79**: 104–143.

Goldstein SR. Unusual ultrasonographic appearance of the uterus in patients receiving tamoxifen. *Am J Obstet Gynecol* 1994; **170**: 447–451.

Dessole S, Farina M, Capobianco G, Nardelli GB, Ambrosini G, Meloni GB. Determining the best catheter for sonohysterography. *Fertil Steril* 2001; **76**: 605–609.

Fleischer AC, Kalemeris GC, Machin J et al. Sonographic depiction of normal and abnormal endometrium with histopathologic correlation. *J Ultrasound Med* 1986; **5**: 445–452.

DeVore GR, Schwartz PE, Morris JM. Hysterography: a 5 year follow up in patients with endometrial carcinoma. *Obstet Gynecol* 1982; **60**: 369–372.

Karlsson B, Granberg S, Wiklan M et al. Transvaginal ultrasonography of the endometrium in women with postmenopausal bleeding – a Nordic multicenter study. *Am J Obstet Gynecol* 1995; **172**: 1488–1494.

Grunfeld S, Wickland M, Karlsson B. High resolution endovaginal endometrium: a noninvasive test for endometrial adequacy. *Obstet Gynecol* 1991; **78**: 200–205.

Gaucherand P, Piacenza JM, Salle B, Rudigoz RC. Sonohysterography of the uterine cavity; preliminary investigations. *J Clin Ultrasound* 1995; **23**: 339–348.

Hulka CA, Hall lDA, McCarthy K, Simeone JF. Endometrial polyps, hyperplasia, and carcinoma in postmenopausal women: differentiation with endovaginal sonography. *Radiology* 1994; **191**: 755–758.

Jones H. Treatment of endometrial polyps. *Obstet Gynecol Surv* 2001; **56**: 142–143.

Bradley LD, Falcone T, Magen A. Radiographic imaging techniques for the diagnosis of abnormal uterine bleeding. *Obstet Gynecol Clin North Am* 2000; **27**: 245–276.

Emanuel MH, Verdel MJ, Wamsteker K. A prospective comparison of transvaginal ultrasonography and diagnostic hysteroscopy in the evaluation of patients with abnormal uterine bleeding: clinical implications. *Am J Obstet Gynecol* 1995; **172**: 547–552.

Weigel M, Friese K, Strittmatter HJ. Measuring the thickness – is that all we have to do for sonographic assessment of endometrium in postmenopausal women? *Ultrasound Obstet Gynecol* 1995; **6**: 97–102.

Wikland M, Granbert S, Karlsson B, Norstrom A. Endometrial thickness as measured by endovaginal ultrasound; a reliable parameter for excluding endometrial pathology in women with postmenopausal bleeding. *Ultrasound Obstet Gynecol* 1991; Suppl: 51.

Sheth S, Hamper UM, Kurman RJ. Thickened endometrium in the postmenopausal woman: sonographic correlation. *Radiology* 1993; **187**: 135–139.

Shalev J, Meizner I, Bar-Hava I, Dicker D, Mashiach R, Ben-Rafael Z. Predictive value of transvaginal sonography performed before routine diagnostic hysteroscopy for evaluation of infertility. *Fertil Steril* 2000; **73**: 412–417.

Cullinan JA, Fleischer AC, Kepple DM, Arnold AL. Sonohysterography; a technique for endometrial evaluation. *Radiographics* 1995; **15**: 501–514.

Goldstein SR. Unusual ultrasonographic appearance of the uterus in patients receiving tamoxifen. *Am J Obstet Gynecol* 1994; **170**: 447–451.

Goldstein SR. Saline infusion sonohysterography. *Clin Obstet Gynecol* 1996; **39**: 248–258.

Schwartz LB, Snyder J, Horan C, Porges RF, Nachtgall LE, Goldstein SR. The use of transvaginal ultrasound and saline infusion sonohysterography for the evaluation of asymptomatic postmenopausal breast cancer patient on tamoxifen. *Ultrasound Obstet Gynecol* 1998; **11**: 48–53.

Schlief R, Deichert U. Hysterosalpingo-contrast sonography of the uterus and fallopian tubes: results of a clinical trial of a new contrast medium in 120 patients. *Radiology* 1991; **178**: 213–215.

Goldstein SR, Zelster I, Horan CK et al. Ultrasonography-based triage for perimenopausal patients with abnormal uterine bleeding. *Am J Obstet Gyencol* 1997; **177**: 102–108.

13 Observations on the anatomy of the endometrium

As seen through the microhysteroscope on an outpatient basis: reflections on physiology and pathophysiology

Bruno J. van Herendael and Stefano Bettocchi

> **Take Home Message**
> Observation of the endometrium is an easy and reproducible method providing that a scope is used that has the facility to sharpen the image at 60–80 times enlargement. Correlation with pathology is as high as 90%. The interpretation of the anatomy can alter the clinical management and guide the clinician to a more refined diagnosis on a see and treat basis.

INTRODUCTION

It has been demonstrated over and over again that anatomical causes such as myoma, polyps, and adhesions are a not-so-silent minority, as far as causes for abnormal uterine bleeding (AUB) or infertility are concerned. Their presence accounts for some 18–20% of demonstrable problems. This leaves 80% of causes unaccounted for. Therefore, in the mid-1980s we started studies to gain understanding of the problems, mainly of subfertility and later of AUB. The pathological samples were viewed by Maurizio Colafranceschi and in a later phase Stefano Bettocchi added new definitions and observations.

These studies were made possible because Jacques Hamou developed a new generation of scopes [1–3], with an outer diameter of only 6 mm, so that observations of the endometrium could be made during the menstrual cycle without the need for patients to undergo general anesthesia. Antonio Perino and Ettore Cittadini in Palermo developed a chorionscope of 3 mm diameter and an oval sheath with the same possibilities for performing contact studies and making observations at ×60 magnification. This latter development, the ability to contact and magnify, created by Jacques Hamou, made it possible to adapt the knowledge of the vasculature gained at the level of the cervix by colposcopy to the uterine cavity and more especially to the endometrium. We now are able to explore at the cellular level and at the vascular level. The magnification used is normally ×60. The ×150 magnification is suitable for cytological studies at the level of the ectocervix, and even in this location a great deal of expertise is needed. As staining of the endometrial cells is very difficult and the only stains used are vital stains (such as methylene blue) the whole procedure becomes time-consuming and this means that the very high magnifications are not used very much.

The most striking changes in the endometrium are at the level of the vessels. The red blood cells make observation easy. A specific pattern in the development of the endometrial vessels corresponds with a well-defined phase of the menstrual cycle. This implies that a microhysteroscopic dating of the endometrium can be carried out, based on the vascular pattern and appearance of the individual vessels [4]. The scope is passed through the endocervical canal without prior dilatation and introduced into the uterine cavity. By bringing the scope in contact with the anterior part of the fundus uteri a ×60 magnification is obtained. The vascular pattern of the endometrium is thus visualized. Care is taken to turn off the gas flow so as not to cause hyperemia as a result of the interaction of the CO_2 gas with the red blood cells in the arterioles. By determining the specific pattern of the vessels it is possible to obtain a dating of the endometrium. At first there will be a correlation with pathology of 70% but after a short learning curve the correlation will be as high as 94%.

Table I
The different phases of the endometrium as seen through the hysteroscope

Phase	Days
Early proliferative phase (EPP)	3–8/28
Late proliferative phase (LPP)	9–13/28
Ovulation phase (OP)	14–16/28
Early secretory phase (ESP)	17–22/28
Late secretory phase (LSP)	23–25/28
Premenstrual-menstrual (PM-MP)	26–2/28

EARLY PROLIFERATIVE PHASE (EPP)

At the conclusion of the menstrual period only the basal layer of the endometrium remains, within it are the remaining portions of the basal arteries. New vessels grow from the stumps of the old vessels (Figure 1) [5–8]. Arterioles, the coiled arteries from the basal arteries, come off at right angles and are directed towards the surface of the endometrium. These are very small and very straight in the first part of their course [5,7]. Therefore the main vessels seen hysteroscopically in this period are the basal arteries, which run perpendicular to the endometrial surface. Small coiled arteries that run perpendicular to the endometrial surface are seen as interrupted or punctuated lines (Figures 2 and 3) [9].

LATE PROLIFERATIVE PHASE (LPP)

This phase is marked by the rapid growth of the coiled arteries. These get more and more convoluted and their spiralization is easily visualized (Figure 4) [10].

OVULATION PHASE (OP)

The endometrium gives no clue as far as the exact day of ovulation is concerned. This is logical, as morphologic changes follow the endocrine changes. Before the features that are characteristic of the early secretory phase appear there is a gap of some 36–48 hours [11].

EARLY SECRETORY PHASE (ESP)

The coiled arteries reach the superficial layer of the lamina functionalis of the endometrium and form a network of

Figure 1
Diagrammatic representation of the changes in the endometrium in the various phases.

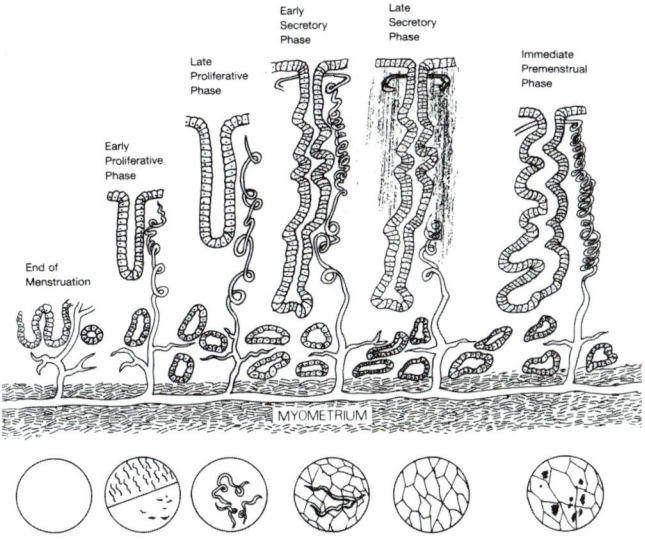

Figure 2
Figures 2 and 3 early proliferative phase (EPS). The main vessels seen hysteroscopically in this period are the basal arteries, which run perpendicular to the endometrial surface. Small coiled arteries that run perpendicular to the endometrial surface are seen as interrupted or punctuated lines.

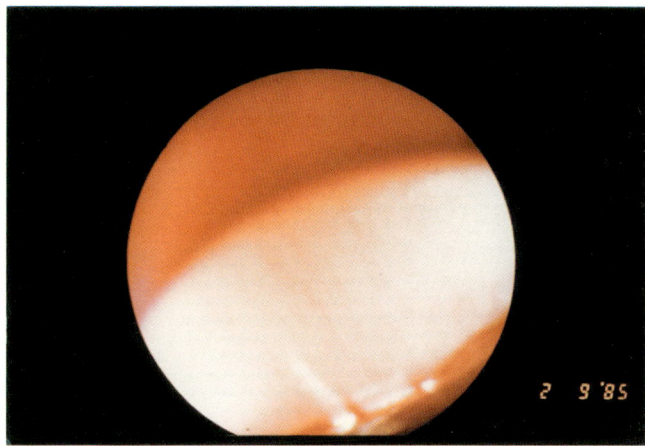

Figure 3

Figure 4
Late proliferative phase (LPP). This phase is marked by the rapid growth of the coiled arteries, their spiralization is easily visualized.

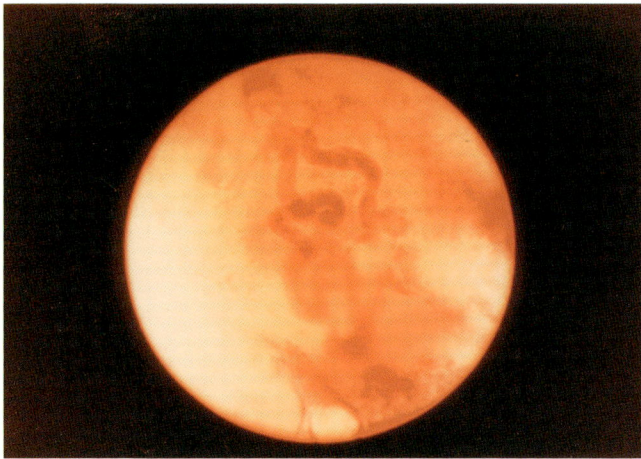

capillaries around the glandular openings. As there is no densification of the stroma in between the glands at this stage of the menstrual cycle it is possible to see capillaries in two different planes. These planes tend to shift over one another under the pressure of the final lens of the scope. This is the main feature of the ESP – a two-layered endometrium – a deeper layer where the coiled arteries can be seen and a superficial layer composed of the capillaries forming the fine reticulum around the glands just beneath the epithelial surface (Figure 5) [5].

LATE SECRETORY PHASE (LSP)

The endometrium has now reached its maximum height of 7–8 mm. The densification of the functional layer starts in this phase owing to the accumulation of secretions, stromal edema, and predecidual reaction [11,12]. This densification is the important factor in this period of the cycle. The underlying coiled arteries are no longer visible. Hysteroscopically only the superficial network of capillaries can be seen. The ivory color of the endometrium is characteristic of this period (Figure 6).

PREMENSTRUAL-MENSTRUAL PHASE (PM-MP)

The superficial network of capillaries still exists, but blood collections are formed near the endometrial surface [5,13]. Menstruation does not rule out hysteroscopy. In this phase it can be seen that, at the onset of the menstruation, the menstrual shedding starts at the level of the cornual parts of the fundus uteri and runs in a circular way towards the isthmus (Figure 7).

Figure 8 shows the different phases of the cycle.

PSEUDOFUNCTIONAL DYSVASCULAR ENDOMETRIUM (PFDE)

In 1991 Stefano Bettocchi (who was working in the Department of Obstetrics and Gynaecology of the Jan Palfijn General in Antwerp, Belgium at the time), first drew attention to an alteration of the vascularization, an abnormal vascular framework with more complex branching, during contact microhysteroscopy at ×60 magnification [14–17]. The main difference from the classical dating of the endometrium lies in the superficial layer, where large convoluted vessels are seen together with the coiled arteries. On panoramic hysteroscopy the uterine cavity appears normal, as does the endometrium at macroscopic evaluation, when the superficial network of large vessels cannot be seen. We have classified this pattern as pseudofunctional dysvascular endometrium (PFDE). The term was chosen because it describes an endometrium that appears normal on panoramic view (pseudofunctional), but has an abnormal vascularization

Figure 5
Early secretory phase (ESP). The main feature of the ESP is a two-layered endometrium – a deeper layer containing the coiled arteries and a superficial layer composed of the capillaries forming the fine reticulum around the glands just beneath the epithelial surface.

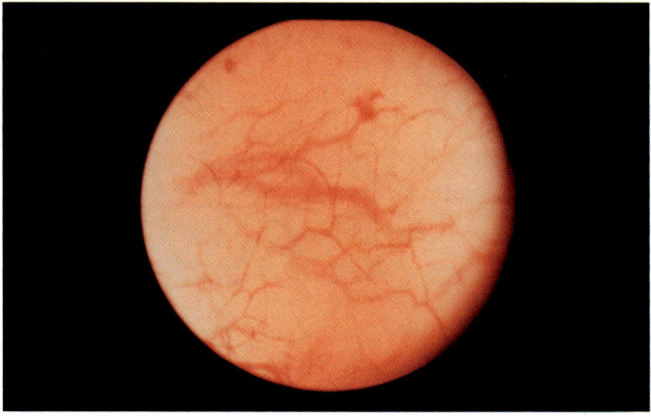

Figure 6
Late secretory phase (LSP). The underlying coiled arteries are no longer visible. Hysteroscopically only the superficial network of capillaries can be seen. The ivory color of the endometrium is characteristic of this period

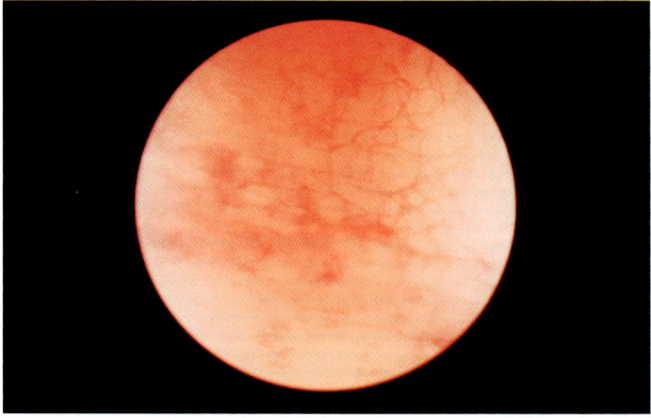

Figure 7
Premenstrual-menstrual phase (PM-MP). The superficial network of capillaries still exists, but blood collections are formed near the endometrial surface.

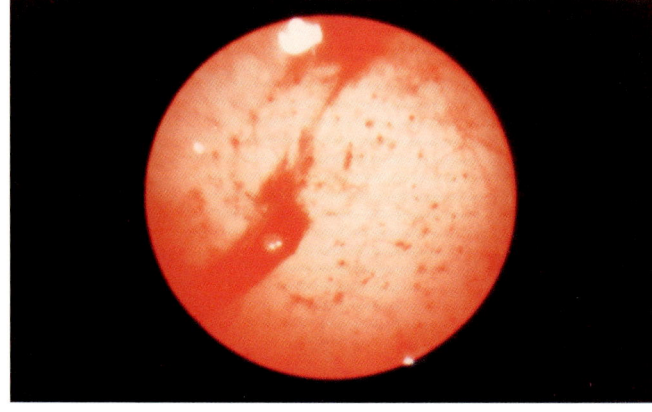

Figure 8
The different phases of the cycle:
(a) EPP;
(b) a later image of EPP;
(c) LPP;
(d) ESP;
(e) LSP;
(f) PM-MP;
(g) bleeding during menses.

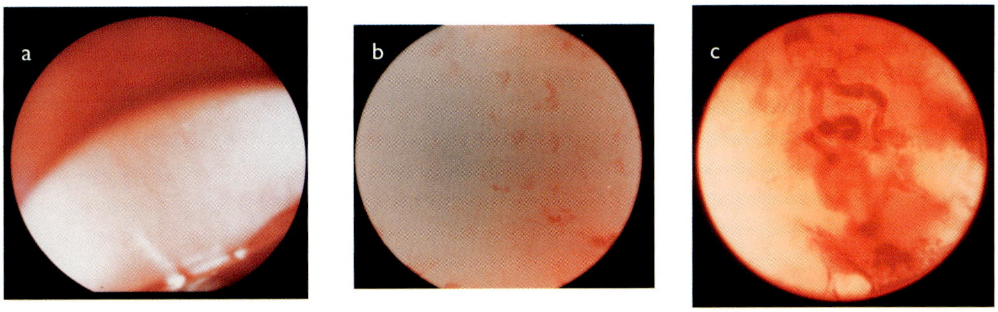

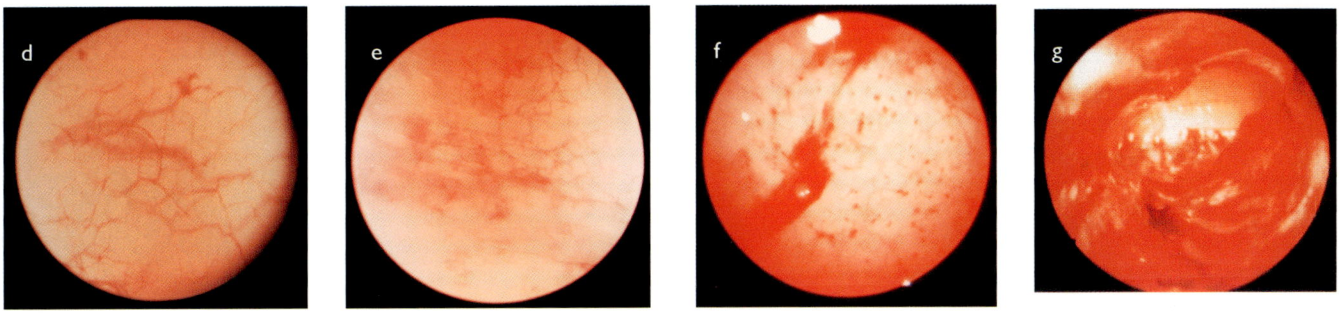

when observed by contact microhysteroscopy (dysvascular) (Figure 9).

As compared with the normal vessels in the peripheral area of the endometrium, an abnormal vascular pattern, composed of irregular engorged arterioles with a complex branching pattern, would suggest a hyperplasia if the gross changes of hyperplasia were also present (Figure 10). As the panoramic view was normal, the existence of a previously undescribed hysteroscopic pattern was recognized. PFDE was found in 49.2% of the patients in the series studied. AUB was the most frequent symptom (65.5%). When the different pathologic diagnoses are considered PFDE is classified as a syndrome in which suppressed endometrium or endometrial hyperplasia prevail (Table 2). Comparing the hysteroscopically well-recognized hyperplasia with the hyperplasia diagnosed under PFDE as a pathological subtype, no differences can

Figure 9
Pseudofunctional dysvascular endometrium (PFDE). (a) The endometrium appears somewhat thickened but normal. (b, d) Engorged vessels with peculiar but normal branching pattern (the branching arterioles have a normal diameter and do not change in appearance but they are present in large numbers and run with a peculiar complex pattern). (c) The superficial vessels are seen to run over longer distances than normal (in the normal cyclic endometrium the terminal arterioles in the superficial layer just surround the glandular openings).

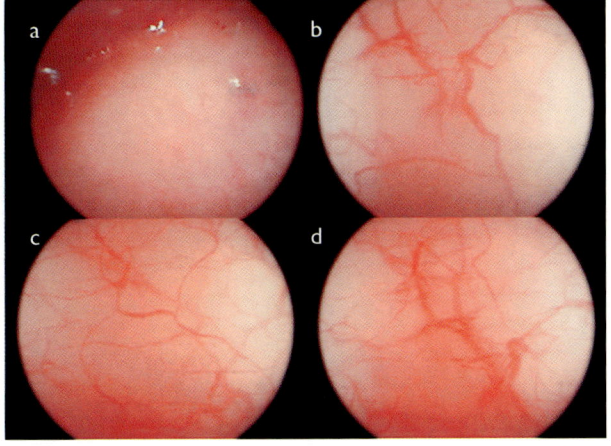

Figure 10
The branching is complex in all these images (taken on the anterior side of the uterine cavity) and the peripheral vessels run over long distances.

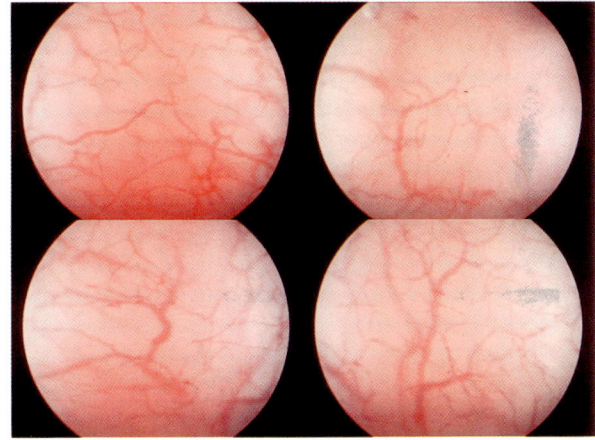

be found except for the lack of atypical hyperplasia in the group of patients with PFDE (Table 3). The possible correlation between the use of oral contraceptives and PFDE is shown in Table 4. We believe that the changes in the vascular pattern are an early sign of endometrial dysfunction or are related to minor or regressing dysfunctional conditions. The hysteroscopic pattern of PFDE can be assumed by cryptic forms of endometrial hyperplasia, such as early and regressing types. This is also true for patients using the last generations of contraceptive pills. The detection of PFDE in these patients, before they become symptomatic, can be clinically significant; therefore these patients can be monitored and eventually treatment can be instituted at an early stage.

Table 2
Frequency of PFDE according to pathologic diagnosis

Pathologic diagnosis	Number with PFDE/Total number of patients	%
Atrophy	3/7	42.9
Proliferative endometrium	4/5	80.0
Secretory endometrium	8/26	30.8
Out-of-phase endometrium	2/6	33.3
Mixed dysfunctional endometrium	5/5	100
Suppressed endometrium	14/26	53.9
Simple hyperplasia	14/27	51.9
Complex hyperplasia	5/4	75
Atypical hyperplasia	0/2	–
Regressive hyperplasia	5/10	50
Total	58/118	49.2

Table 3
Distribution of endometrial hyperplasia by pathological subtype according to hysteroscopic pattern

Subtype	Number (%) with characteristic non-PFDE pattern	Number (%) with PFDE pattern
Simple	13 (61.9)	14 (63.6)
Complex	1 (4.8)	3 (13.6)
Atypical	2 (9.5)	–
Regressive	5 (23.8)	5 (22.8)
Total	21 (100)	22 (100)

Table 4
Frequency of PFDE in women taking oral contraceptives

PFDE	Number (%) taking oral contraceptives	Number (%) not taking oral contraceptives
Yes	26 (70.3)	32 (39.5)
No	11 (29.7)	46 (50.5)

The vascular pattern of the endometrium changes during the menstrual cycle, very specific patterns of blood vessels correspond with well-defined phases of the menstrual cycle. The results are reproducible. The EPP, LPP, ESP, and PM-MP are easy to recognize. The LSP is the most difficult vascular entity to recognize. Here errors are often seen, as most of the dysfunctional entities appear in this phase of the menstrual cycle. The diagnosis of ovulation cannot be made hysteroscopically. There is no histopathologic pattern that gives a clue to the exact moment of the ovulation [18] because the anatomical changes follow the hormonal changes. The pathologist has to wait for the first signs of secretion to be able to confirm ovulation. Contact observation of the vascular pattern of the endometrium is part of the diagnostic hysteroscopic examination, not an independent technique. In the presence of an anatomically normal uterine cavity and in the absence of other systemic diseases the physician should focus on the functional aspects of the endometrium. Contact hysteroscopy is able to identify modifications of the endometrial vasculature suggestive of a local disorder, especially in women with AUB. PFDE is not diagnostic in AUB since it is present with the same frequency in other endometrial diseases such as hyperplasia. PFDE could represent a vascular rearrangement induced by unknown factors. The presence of this abnormal vascular pattern is a confirmation of the hypothesis that modification of the vascular reactivity is the main physiopathological factor in AUB.

ENDOMETRITIS

Chronic endometritis is one of the causes of irregular bleeding and infertility [19–21]. It may be suspected clinically but histological and bacteriological investigations are considered decisive for the diagnosis. The problems are that on the one hand the pathologist has to make the diagnosis according to very strict criteria and on the other hand it is very difficult to obtain uncontaminated specimens from the uterine cavity. The culture swab has to be protected during its passage through the cervical canal. In analogy to specific hysteroscopic patterns that were observed in patients using an IUCD and experiencing AUB we started to look at the infertile patients and found the same hysteroscopic pattern. No dilatation is used. First a

Table 5
Relationship between hysteroscopic results and laboratory findings

Positive cultures	Positive histology	Negative histology
Escherichia coli	2	–
Staphylococcus epidermidis	1	2
Streptococcus milleri	1	1
Streptococcus sanguis	1	–
Streptococcus morbillorum	–	1
Streptococcus bovis	–	1
Ureaplasma urealyticum	1	4
Candida albicans	–	1
Chlamydia trachomatis	1	–
One or more of the above micro-organisms	5	9

Table 6
Histological patterns in patients with hysteroscopic suspicion of infection

Histology	Number of cases	%
Endometritis	17	35
Hypotrophic endometrium	5	10
Early proliferative phase	14	30
Late proliferative phase	4	8
Early secretory phase	6	13
Decidual transformation	2	4
All patterns	48	100

panoramic view is obtained. Thereafter the scope is placed in contact with the fundal endometrium and an assessment of the vascularization is obtained. We have to distinguish between acute and chronic infection. Acute infection is characterized by edema and destruction of the superficial layers of the endometrium. The hysteroscopic panoramic appearance is one of a thick endometrium with an abnormal mucus, seen as significant reflections in the light of the scope. When the scope is brought into contact there are no vessels visible. On the pathological slide the destruction in depth becomes visible and the pathognomonic feature are the polymorphonuclear inclusions in the glandular lumina. The glands are dilated and the interstitial tissue is permeated by granulocytes (Figure 11). Chronic infection has a very different appearance. The typical appearance is called 'strawberry endometrium' (Figures 12 and 13) [22], and is characterized by a reddish endometrium with some dark red patches where small white dots are present at irregular intervals. Some cavities present with patches over the whole of the cavity separated by patches of macroscopic normal endometrium. When the scope is brought into contact a dating of the endometrium is not possible, as the vessels are very fragile and tend to rupture because of the hyperemia caused by the CO_2 gas. If the vessels do not rupture vessels of different cycle periods can be seen within the same visual field. The typical 'strawberry' appearance is caused by the hypotrophy of the interglandular tissue and therefore relative hyperplasia of the glands. The hypotrophy of the interglandular stroma also causes the implantation pattern of the glands to be disrupted. Pathology reveals an

Figure 11

Histopathology of endometritis (H&E).
(a) Acute endometritis. A diffuse infiltrate, mainly composed of polymorphonuclear cells, destroys and fills the gland lumina.
(b) Chronic nonspecific endometritis. A small lymphatic cell aggregate is present in the endometrial stroma. A dilated endometrial gland lumen is filled with debris.
(c) Chronic endometritis, particularly rich in plasma cells. This finding, although nonspecific, may suggest a Chlamydia trachomatis infection.
(d) Tuberculous endometritis (chronic specific endometritis). A non-necrotizing granuloma containing a Langhans' giant cell is easily identifiable on the left side, supporting the histological diagnosis of tuberculous endometritis.
(e) Chronic endometritis caused by IUD insertion. Note the aggregate of lymphocytes near the endometrial surface and the spindle-shaped stromal cells.

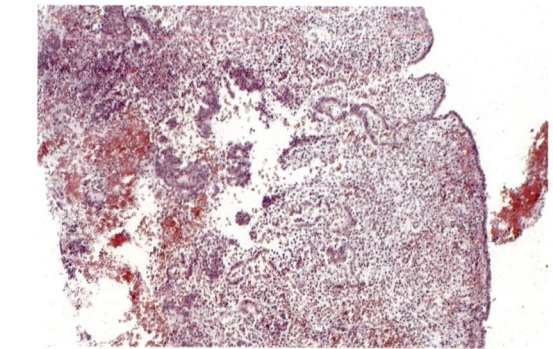
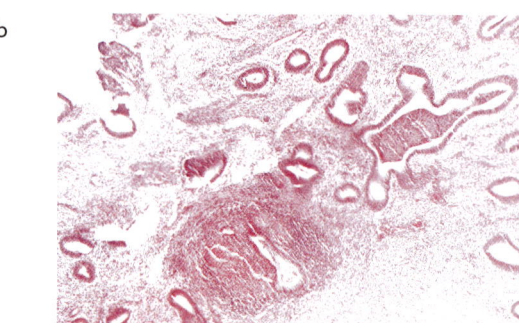
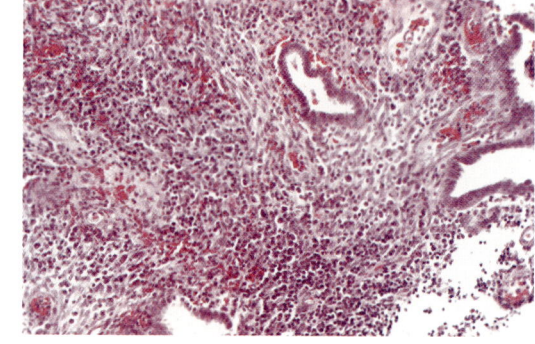
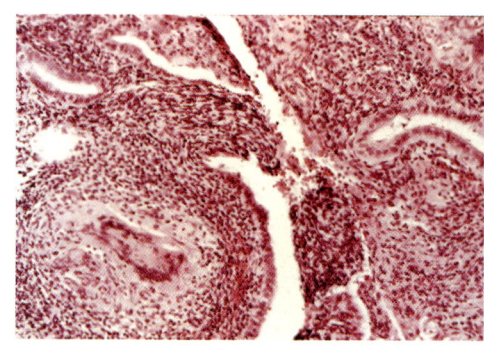
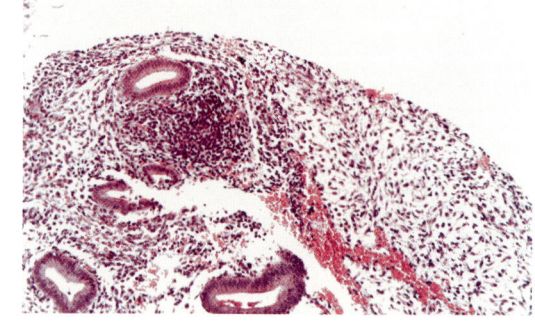

infiltration of granulocytes and lymphocytes in the interglandular stroma. Polymorphonuclear elements remain present in the glands. These are distorted and dilated. The glandular openings protrude towards the cavity. Lymphocyte collections are only seen above the basal membrane in very chronic infections, and are seen by the hysteroscope as white dots under the surface of the endometrial layer.

Chronic endometritis is a difficult diagnosis because no relevant clinical symptoms are generally present, a number of inflammatory cells are commonly found in the endometrium and samples for microbiological testing are often contaminated, as noted above. The basic histologic criterion is the presence of plasma cell infiltration of the endometrial stroma [19]. Two elements emerge from our observations:

- A number of endometria, more importantly those revealed by biological testing, may be hysteroscopically recognized as chronically inflamed.
- There is no relationship between hysteroscopic, pathologic, and microbiological findings. The hysteroscopical examination, combined with contact hysteroscopy, reveals more pathology than the other two techniques. Whenever a dysfunctional endometrium is diagnosed by pathologic studies, and a hysteroscopic pattern of endometritis is found, clinical endometritis is probably present.

Figure 12
A panoramic view of the uterine cavity in a case of chronic endometritis. The typical 'strawberry pattern' is clearly visible on the posterior wall and the left side wall.

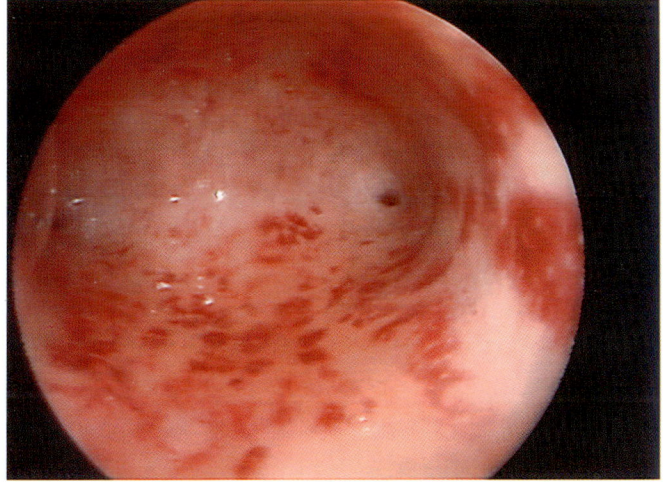

Figure 13
Chronic endometritis. (b) An overview and (d) detailed view. The ostium with an edematous appearance is seen in (a). (c) A contact view demonstrates that dating of the endometrium is no longer possible as no vessels are seen.

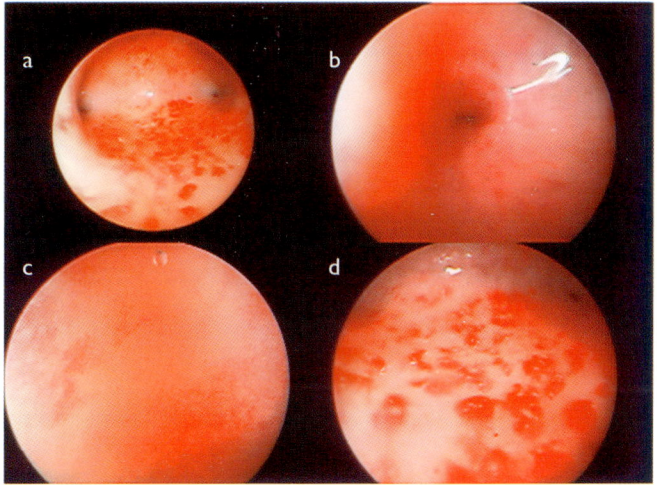

References

1. Hamou J. Microhysteroscopy: a new procedure and its original applications in gynaecology. *J Reprod Med* 1981; **26**: 375–382.
2. Hamou J. Hysteroscopy and microhysteroscopy with a new instrument: the microhysteroscope. *Acta Eur Fertil* 1981; **12**: 29
3. Hamou J. Microhysteroscopy. *Acta Endoscop* 1980; **10**: 29.
4. Van Herendael BJ, Stevens MJ, Flakiewicz-Kula A, Hansch Ch. Dating of the endometrium by microhysteroscopy. *Gynecol Obstet Invest* 1987; **24**: 114–118.
5. Jeffcoate TNA. Principles of Gynaecology, 3rd edn. London: Butterworth, 1967: 91–100.
6. Baggish MS. Contact hysteroscopy: a new technique to explore the uterine cavity. *Obstet Gynecol* 1979; **54**: 350–354.
7. Symmers WStC. Systemic Pathology, 2nd edn, vol 4. Edinburgh: Churchill Livingstone, 1970: 1661–1667.
8. Fox H. The endometrium. In: Anderson JR, ed. Muir's Textbook of Pathology, 11th edn. London: Edward Arnold, 1980: 947–948.
9. Vancaillie T. Hysteroscopic evaluation of hormonal influence on the endometrium. In: Van der Pas H, van Herendael BJ, Van Lith D, eds. Hysteroscopy. Lancaster: MTP Press, 1983: 101–113.
10. Gompel A. Anatomie Pathologique: Gynecologique Obstetricale. Brussels: Arscia, 1963: 198–199.
11. Blauastein A. Normal Menstrual Cycle. Interpretation of Biopsy of the Endometrium. New York: Raven Press, 1980: 13–30.
12. Junquera LC, Carneiro J, Contopoulos A. The female reproductive system. In: Basic Histology, 2nd edn. Los Altos: Lange, 1977: 437–439.
13. Di Fiore MSH. Uterus. In: Atlas of Human Histology, 3rd edn. Philadelphia: Lea & Febiger, 1972: 210–213.
14. Loverro G, Bettocchi S, Porreca M, Selvaggi L. Dysfunctional uterine bleeding: the role of contact microhysteroscopy in the assessment of endometrial vascularization. *J Gynecol Surg* 1996; **12**: 47–53.
15. Bettocchi S, van Herendael BJ, Colafranceschi M. Un nuovo quadro in isteroscopia diagnostica: lo pseudo functional dysvascular endometrium. *G Ital Obstet Ginecol* 1993; **15**: 592–595.
16. Colafranceschi M, Bettocchi S, van Herendael BJ. A new topic in diagnostic hysteroscopy: pseudofunctional dysvascular endometrium. Endometrial hyperplasia and the use of oral contraceptives. In: Malouk FA, Affandi B, Trounson AO, eds. Advances in Human Reproduction. London: Parthenon Publishing, 1993: 273–276.
17. Bettocchi S, Loverro G, Pansini N, Selvaggi L. The role of contact hysteroscopy. *J Am Assoc Gynecol Laparosc* 1996; **3**: 635–641.
18. Noyes RW. Normal phases of the endometrium. In: The Uterus. Baltimore: Williams & Wilkins, 1973.
19. Cadena D, Cavazano FJ, Leone CL, Taylor HB. Chronic endometritis: comparative clinicopathologic study. *Obstet Gynecol* 1973; **41**: 733–738.
20. Greenwood SM, Maran JJ. Chronic endometritis: morphologic and clinical observations. *Obstet Gynecol* 1961; **58**: 176–183.
21. Paavonen J, Kiviat N, Brunham RC. Prevalence and manifestations of endometritis among women with cervicitis. *Am J Obstet Gynecol* 1985; **152**: 280–286.
22. Stevens MJ, van Herendael BJ, Slangen T, Haensch Ch. Hysteroscopic diagnosis of chronic endometritis: which role. *The Cervix and the Lower Female Genital Tract* 1988; 333–336.

Endometrial receptors

Hugo Maia Jr, Amélia Maltez, Célia Athayde, Genevieve Coelho and Elsimar M. Coutinho

> **Take Home Message**
> Although not of immediate use to clinicians dealing with patients, it is important to understand the processes at their basic biochemical level. The future of controlling the pathological processes lies in understanding cellular biology and figuring out solutions at this level.

STEROID RECEPTORS IN THE ENDOMETRIUM

Most of the cyclic events that occur in the endometrium throughout the menstrual cycle are regulated by changes in circulating levels of ovarian steroid hormones [1]. Cyclic changes in this tissue in response to gonadal hormones have historically been studied histologically and more recently immunohistochemical methods have been used to detect the presence of steroid and peptide growth factor receptors [2–4]. Under the influence of estrogens there is a rapid growth of both stroma and glandular epithelium, followed by an increase in vascularization. Figures of mitosis are frequent during the proliferative phase and a great number of cells are positive for Ki-67, a proliferation marker expressed by cells just prior to undergoing mitosis. On the other hand, mitosis comes to a halt in the glandular epithelium during the luteal phase in response to progesterone produced by the corpus luteum, whereas in stroma cell division mitosis persists until decidualizzation begins [5,6].

The levels of estradiol receptor in the endometrium show marked variations in both glandular epithelium and stroma throughout the menstrual cycle, peaking at ovulation and decreasing during the luteal phase, especially in the glands (Figure 1) [7]. The induction of estrogen receptors (ER) in the endometrium is upregulated by their own ligand at transcriptional level and constitutes a sensitive sign of estrogenic action in this tissue [8]. Immunohistochemistry can detect the presence of estrogen receptors even in the atrophic endometrium of postmenopausal patients, which indicates that the endometrium does not age, at least with respect to estrogen-induced proliferation.

The induction of progesterone receptors (PR) in the endometrium is upregulated at transcriptional level by estrogens [9]. PR levels reach a maximum in both glandular epithelium and stroma during the late proliferative phase of the menstrual cycle in response to the rising levels of estrogens produced by the growing follicle. Following ovulation and the concomitant rise in progesterone production by the corpus luteum, there is a marked decrease in the concentration of progesterone receptors in the glandular epithelium and to a lesser degree in the stroma, although they can be detected by immunohistochemistry even when the process of decidualization has begun (Figure 2) [7–9]. Progesterone receptors exist in most tissue in two isoforms, A and B, which play different physiologic roles in the regulation of gene transcription. In the endometrium during the luteal phase, however, only the A receptor persists [10,11]. These post-ovulatory events in steroid receptor concentration are regulated in the endometrium by progesterone at transcriptional level [10]. However, in

Figure 1

Estrogen receptors in endometrial gland and stroma during late proliferative phase.

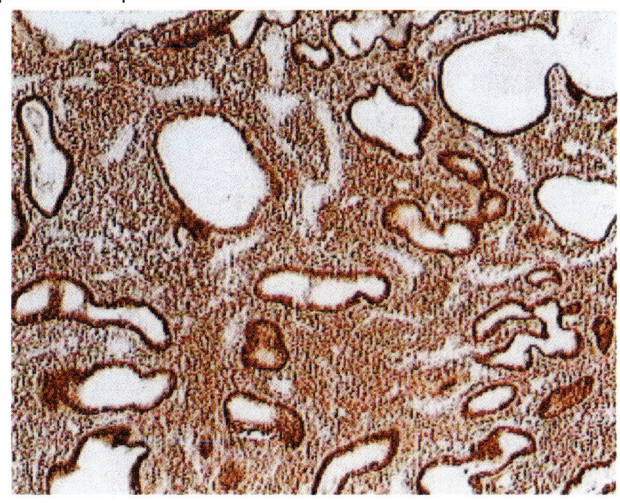

endometrial stroma, cells undergoing mitosis can be detected by immunohistochemistry during the late luteal phase by using antibodies to Ki-67 proliferation at a time when they are virtually absent in the glandular epithelium (Figure 3), indicating that progesterone acting through its stromal receptors can stimulate both proliferation and differentiation in this tissue. Progesterone also stimulates stromal cells to produce numerous hormones, growth factors and their binding proteins, which play an important physiologic role in the process of nidation and placentation [12,13]. The unabated presence of progesterone receptors in the stroma throughout decidualization signals the importance of this hormone for endometrial function during pregnancy.

Figure 2
Progesterone receptors in the endometrium during the luteal phase. Note their presence in stroma and their absence from the glands.

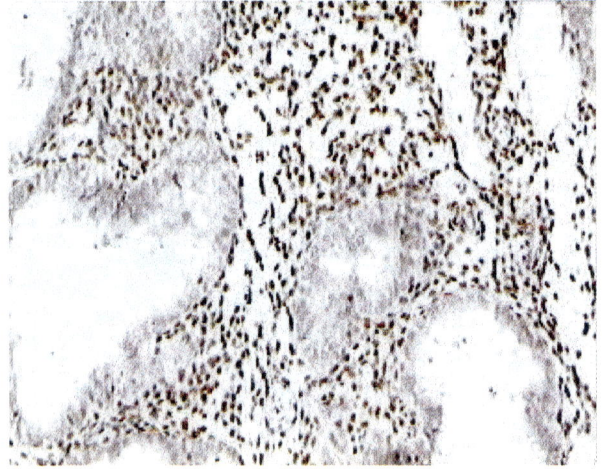

Figure 3
Ki-67-positive cells in endometrial stroma during the luteal phase.

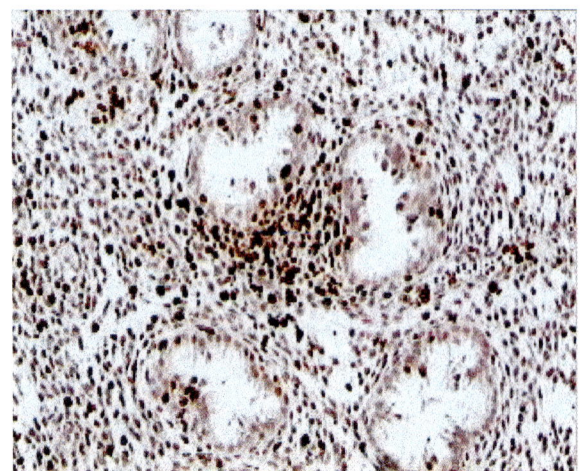

Testosterone receptors (TR) in the endometrium can be detected by immunohistochemical methods and their levels are also upregulated by estrogens. However, in contrast to ER and PR, TR are mainly detected in the stroma cells and practically no staining reaction is detected by immunohistochemistry in the glandular epithelium (Figure 4) [14]. The presence of mRNA transcripts for TR is also much higher in stroma than in glandular cells, which is in accordance with the immunohistochemical data [15]. The presence of androgen receptors in the stroma is consistent with the observation that testosterone is capable of exerting effects on those cells, such as the stimulation of prolactin production and decidualization, that are indistinguishable from progesterone. Testosterone is also devoid of any proliferative effects on endometrial glands and the continuous activation of its receptor leads to glandular atrophy rather than hyperplasia, even in the presence of normal blood levels of estrogen [16]. However, a physiologic role for testosterone receptors in the regulation of endometrial function is not yet known.

ENDOMETRIAL CARCINOMA AND RECEPTORS

Most endometrial carcinomas can be divided into two different types. Type I carcinomas are associated with unopposed estrogens and endometrial hyperplasia. They are low-grade, steroid receptor-positive and occur in younger patients. Type II carcinomas, on the other hand, are unrelated to estrogens, are usually receptor-negative, occur in older patients and are usually of high grade [17]. These different forms of endometrial carcinomas evolve through different pathways and they show marked differences at molecular level. While the type I carcinomas include most of the endometrioid forms, the type II

Figure 4
Testosterone receptors in endometrial stroma.

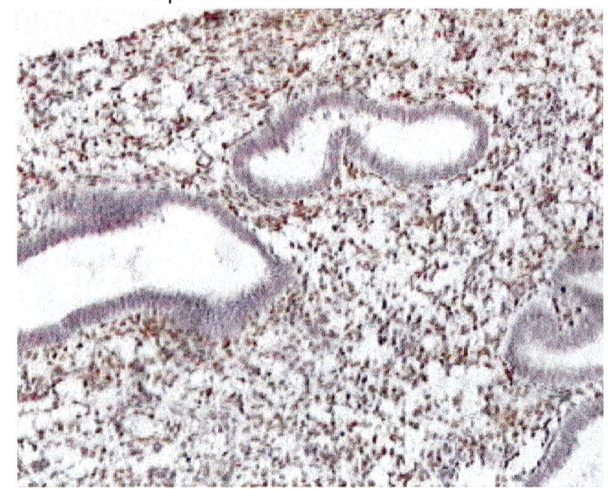

carcinomas include uterine serous papillary carcinoma (UPSC), clear-cell carcinoma, and undifferentiated carcinoma. Immunohistochemical and molecular studies have shown that UPSC are associated with mutations in p53 tumor suppressor gene, which gives them an aggressive biological behavior [18]. Endometrioid carcinomas, on the other hand, do not usually have mutations in p53 gene but they harbor other genomic abnormalities such as micro-satellite instability, alterations in mismatch repair genes, and PTEN mutations that are not shared by type II endometrial carcinomas [19]. The presence of p53 over-expression is therefore a unique feature of serous papillary carcinomas that can be detected in early focal lesions still confined to endometrial polyps (Figure 5) [20]. The transition between the benign epithelium in the polyp and the carcinoma is abrupt with no intermediate stages of progressively complex and atypical hyperplasia. In type I carcinomas, on the other hand, p53 mutations are detected only in G2-G3 carcinomas, being absent in hyperplasia and G1 carcinomas [21–24]. Receptors for estradiol and progesterone are usually present in well-differentiated carcinomas [22]. Testosterone receptors are also detected in type I carcinomas and they are usually present in the malignant epithelium with little staining reaction in the stroma [14]. The reason for the presence of testosterone receptors in the malignant endometrial epithelium and their absence in the benign glands is not yet completely understood. One possible explanation would be binding and concentration of androgens in the tumor for their subsequent aromatization to estrogens. Testosterone receptors could also give a proliferative advantage to neoplastic cells when activated. However, this is still speculative at the moment.

Both estradiol and testosterone receptors were absent in type II carcinomas [14,21–23]. It is noteworthy that p53 mutation with its consequent over-expression is associated with de-differentiation and loss of steroid receptors. The loss of steroid receptors following p53 mutation is associated with poor prognosis. However, this is primarily due to p53 mutation rather than to the loss of steroid receptors, which is only a consequence of the de-differentiation that follows the inactivation of this tumor suppressor gene. In cases of endometrioid carcinomas (type I), the presence of PTEN mutations in precursor lesions can predict the progression to carcinoma even in the absence of significant cell atypia (Figure 6).

STEROID AND EGF RECEPTORS IN THE ENDOMETRIUM

The effects of estrogens on the endometrium are mediated by growth factors whose synthesis is regulated at transcriptional and post-transcriptional level by this hormone [24]. Both estrogens and androgens increase the synthesis of epidermal growth factor (EGF) and its receptor in the endometrium, which is involved in the subsequent mediation of some of the growth-promoting effects of these hormones on this tissue [25,26]. The receptors of the epidermal growth family (EGFR) are transmembrane proteins whose intracellular domain has an intrinsic tyrosine kinase enzymatic activity and an extracellular domain that binds not only to EGF but also to other ligands such as transforming growth factor alpha [27]. Almost all of the growth factors of the EGF family are mitogenic in the endometrium, whereas they play an important role as mediators of estrogen-induced

Figure 5
p53 over-expression in a uterine serous papillary carcinoma.

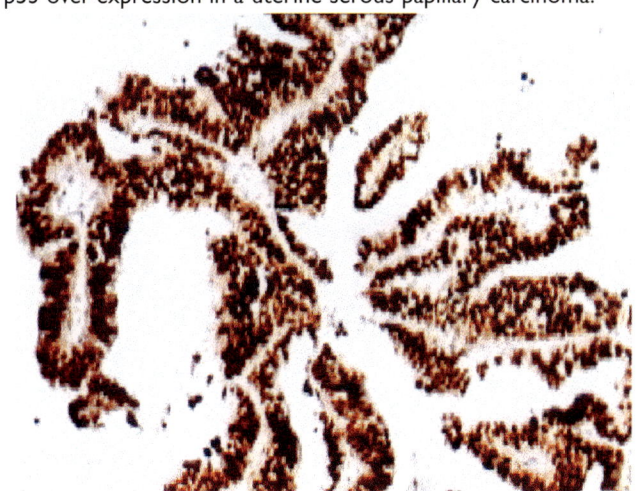

Figure 6
PTEN-negative gland in the endometrium. The patient developed an endometrial carcinoma 1 year later.

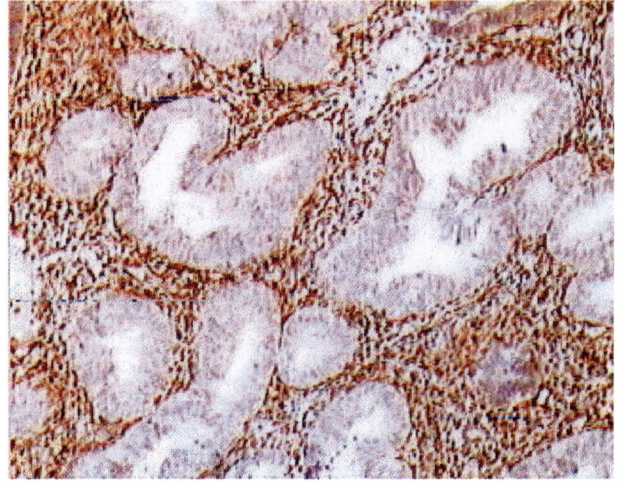

proliferation [28]. One such receptor is c-erbB2, which shares functional and morphologic homologies with the EGFRs. Activation of these receptors in the endometrium leads to epithelial cell proliferation [29]. The intrinsic tyrosine kinase activity of the EGF receptors makes them capable of phosphorylating estrogen receptors, rendering them more active in stimulating gene transcription [30–32]. Therefore, the level of expression of these receptors in the endometrium may regulate estrogenic action in this tissue under normal and pathologic conditions. Receptor phosphorylation leads to a two-fold increase in gene transcription induced by estradiol or to a change from antagonist to agonist action of partial estrogen antagonists such as tamoxifen, as reviewed by Speroff [31]. Thus, the presence of c-erbB2 over-expression in the endometrium may potentiate the effects of exogenous estradiol in the endometrium, leading to the development of endometrial hyperplasia with a higher number of cells undergoing proliferation.

Various studies have revealed that EGFR can activate the estrogen receptor in the absence of its ligand through mechanisms that involve a phosphorylation cascade that starts at membrane level and terminates in the nucleus [28,31,32]. The end result of the EGFR activation will be the phosphorylation of estrogenic receptors with their subsequent dimerization and binding to estrogen-responsive elements in the DNA [31]. This indicates that estrogenic effects can be initiated in target tissue in the absence of estrogens through the activation of EGFR family or they can be augmented by the expression of these growth factor receptors in this tissue. Because estrogens upregulate the receptors of the EGF family and their ligands, the estrogenic effects on the endometrium can be enhanced by the expression of these transmembrane receptors, including the c-erbB2 receptor (Figure 7).

The role played by these tyrosine kinase receptors in the genesis of endometrial proliferative disorders is not yet completely understood but it is possible that c-erbB2 over-expression in the endometrium may phosphorylate the estrogen receptor, resulting in greater estrogenic effects and higher proliferation rates, as previously reported for tamoxifen-treated endometrium [33]. Thus, the presence of c-erbB2 in endometrial hyperplasia may modulate estrogenic action by upgrading the response of the endometrium to this hormone. This mechanism may also play a role in the development of endometrial hyperplasia unassociated with the use of exogenous hormones during menopause [34,35].

ROLE OF c-erbB2 RECEPTORS IN ENDOMETRIAL POLYP GROWTH

The role of growth factor receptors in the pathogenesis of endometrial polyps is not yet completely understood. Studies carried out using transgenic mice that constitutively express the TGF-2α gene have revealed that the rate of genital malignancy is not increased by the continuous expression of this gene. However, when these animals were treated with a synthetic estrogen, diethylstilbestrol, there was an increased incidence of polyps and hyperplasia in their uteri [36]. These studies revealed that there was a synergistic effect between estrogen exposure and TGF-α gene expression in stimulating endometrial polyp development and this was not accompanied by an increase in the incidence of malignancy.

In humans, the role played by TGF-α in the genesis of endometrial polyps is not completely understood. TGF-α binds to EGF receptors and one of the most extensively studied receptors of this family is c-erbB2 [27]. The use of immunohistochemical methods to detect the presence of c-erbB2 over-expression in the endometrium has revealed that a number of benign pathologies such as endometrial polyps already show c-erbB2 over-expression and this was not associated with loss of estrogen receptors or the presence of malignancy [37]. In menopausal patients, the detection of c-erbB2 over-expression in endometrial polyps showed a positive correlation with the number of cells positive for Ki-67 [38]. These findings suggest that the growth of endometrial polyps during menopause may be regulated by the level of c-erbB2 expression which stimulates the phosphorylation of estrogen receptor activation, making them more responsive to the low levels of estrogen found during menopause, while the adjacent c-erbB2-negative endometrium remains unresponsive and atrophic.

Figure 7
C-erbB2 over-expression in a case of endometrial hyperplasia.

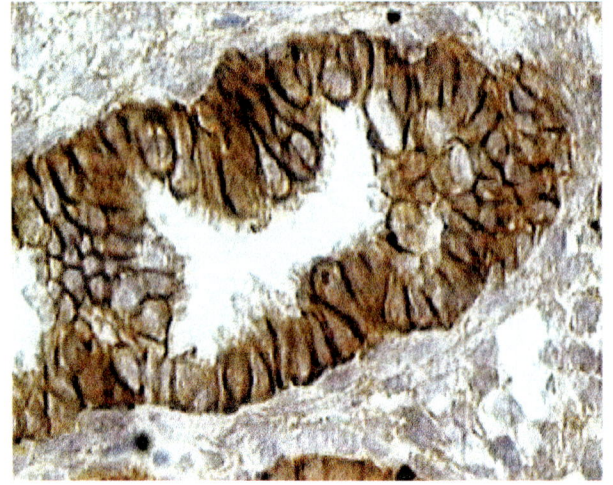

The upregulation of TGF-α action or other related growth factors on endometrial polyps, achieved through the amplification and/or over-expression of c-erbB2 receptors, may also render them more sensitive to partial estrogen antagonists such as tamoxifen. In this respect, it is important to mention that tamoxifen activates the TGF-α gene in the endometrium and one of the most common side effects of tamoxifen therapy in the endometrium is the development of endometrial polyps [33]. The presence of c-erbB2 over-expression has been detected in polyps removed from tamoxifen-treated patients but not in the adjacent endometrium (Figure 8). In cases of diffuse endometrial hyperplasia following tamoxifen therapy, the presence of c-erbB2 over-expression was invariably detected in the glandular epithelium. These preliminary observations may suggest that the presence of c-erbB2 over-expression in endometrial polyps may render them more sensitive than the adjacent negative endometrium to the mitogenic effects of TGF-α whose synthesis is induced by tamoxifen therapy. The presence of estradiol receptors in endometrial polyps and in the atrophic endometrium suggests that tamoxifen may act on both tissues. However, the response in terms of proliferation is more pronounced in the polyp than in the atrophic endometrium owing to the presence of c-erbB2 over-expression in the former [31,32].

Figure 8
C-erbB2 over-expression in a case of endometrial hyperplasia.

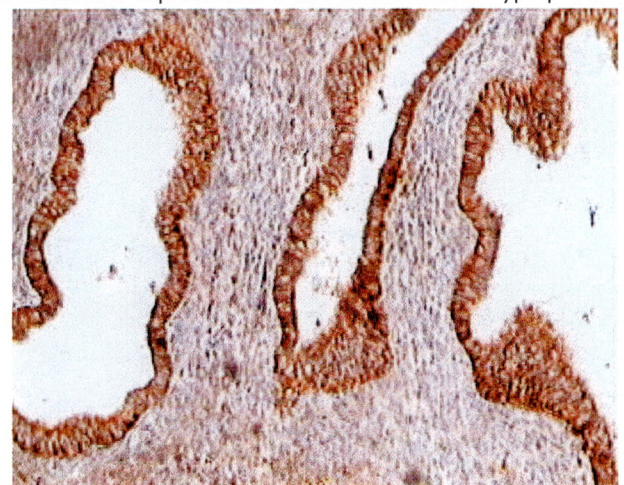

REFERENCES

1. Good RG, Moyer DL. Estrogen-progesterone relationships in the development of secretory endometrium. *Fertil Steril* 1968; **9**: 37.

2. Healy DL, Hodgen GD. The endocrinology of human endometrium. *Obstet Gynecol Surv* 1983; **38**: 509–530.

3. Horowitz GM, Scott RT, Drews MR. Immunohistochemical localization of transforming growth factor alpha in human endometrium, decidua and trophoblast. *J Clin Endocrinol Metab* 1993; **76**: 786–792.

4. Maia H Jr, Maltez A, Fahel P, Oliveira M, Athayde C, Coutinho EM. Hysteroscopic and immunohistochemical findings in endometrial lesions unresponsive to medroxyprogesterone acetate: a report on four cases. *Gynecol Endosc* 2001; **10**: 183–191.

5. Ferenczy A, Bergeron C. Histology of the human endometrium from senescence. *Ann NY Acad Sci* 1991; **622**: 6–27.

6. Ferenczy A, Bertrand G, Gelfand A. Proliferation kinetics of human endometrium during the normal menstrual cycle. *Am J Obstet Gynecol* 1979; **133**: 859–867.

7. Lessey BA, Killam AP, Metzger DA, Haney AF, Greene GL, McCarthy KS. Immunohistochemical analysis of human uterine estrogen and progesterone receptors throughout the menstrual cycle. *J Clin Endocrinol Metab* 1988; **67**: 334–340.

8. Speroff L. The estrogen receptor: changing concepts. Clinical lessons from molecular biology. In: Coutinho EM, Spinola P, eds. Reproductive Medicine: A Millennium Review. London: Parthenon Publishing, 1999: 1555–1561.

9. Savourat JF, Bailly A, Misrahi M et al. Characterization of hormone responsive element involved in the regulation of the progesterone receptor gene. *EMBO J* 1991; **10**: 1875–1883.

10. Feil PD, Clarke CL, Satyaswaroop PG. Progestin-mediated changes in progesterone receptor forms in the normal human endometrium. *Endocrinology* 1988; **123**: 2506–2513.

11. Wiehle RD, Mangal R, Poindexter AN, Weigel NL. Human progesterone receptor A and B expression during menstrual cycle. *Endocr Soc* 1995; Abstr P1-446.

12. Chen GA, Huang JR, Mazela J, Tseng L. Long term effects of progestin and RU 486 on prolactin production in human endometrial stromal cells. *Hum Reprod* 1989; **4**: 355–358.

13. Lockwood CJ, Emerson Y, Guller G, Krikun M, Alvarez V, Schatz F. Progestational regulation of human endometrial stromal cell tissue factor expression during decidualization. *J Clin Endocrinol Metab* 1993; **76**: 231–236.

14. Maia H Jr, Maltez A, Fahel P, Athayde C, Coutinho EM. Detection of testosterone and estrogen receptors in the postmenopausal endometrium. *Maturitas* 2001; **38**: 179–188.

15. Adesanya-Famuyiwa OO, Zhou J, Wu G, Brondy C. Localization and sex steroid regulation of androgen receptor gene expression in rhesus monkey uterus. *Obstet Gynecol* 1999; **9**: 265–270.

16. Floyd WS. Danazol: endocrine and endometrial effects. *Int J Fertil* 1980; **25**: 75–80.

17. Bockman JT. Two pathogenetic types of endometrial carcinoma. *Gynecol Oncol* 1983; **15**: 10–17.

18. Zheng W, Cao P, Zheng M. p53 over-expression and bcl-2 persistence in endometrial carcinoma. Carcinoma of papillary serous and endometrioid sub-types. *Gynecol Oncol* 1996; **61**: 167–174.

19. Sun H, Enomoto T. Mutational analysis of PTEN gene in endometrial carcinoma and hyperplasia. *Am J Clin Pathol* 2001; **115**: 32–38.

20. Maia H Jr, Maltez A, Oliveira M, Fahel P, Coutinho EM. Endometrial polyps and the development of type II form of endometrial carcinoma. In: Coutinho EM, Spinola P, eds. Current Knowledge in Reproductive Medicine. Amsterdam: Elsevier ICS, 2000: 63–69.

21. Maia H Jr, Maltez A, Fahel P, Coutinho EM. Hysteroscopy and immunohistochemical findings in type I and type II endometrial carcinomas. *J Am Assoc Gynecol Laparosc* 2001; **8**: 222–230.

22. Maltez A, Maia H Jr, Oliveira M, Marques D, Coutinho EM. Clear cell carcinoma arising in an endometrial polyp. *Gynecol Endosc* 1998; **7**: 51–53.

23. Kohler MF, Nishii H, Humphrey PA. Mutations of p53 tumor suppressor gene is not a feature of endometrial hyperplasia. *Am J Obstet Gynecol* 1993; **3**: 690–694.

24. DeCecco L, Leone M, Gerbaldo D, Venturini PL, Rissone R, Messeni Leoni M. Steroid therapy and the endometrium: biological and clinical implications. *Ann NY Acad Sci* 1991; **622**: 296–301.

25. Watson H, Franks S, Bonney RC. Regulation of epidermal growth factor receptor by androgens in human endometrial cells in culture. *Hum Reprod* 1998; **13**: 285–291.

26. Mukku VR, Stancel GM. Regulation of uterine epidermal growth factor receptors by estrogen. *J Biol Chem* 1985; **260**: 9820–9824.

27. Connely PA, Stern DF. The epidermal growth factor receptor and the product of the neu proto-oncogene are members of a receptor tyrosine phosphorylation cascade. *Proc Natl Acad Sci USA* 1990; **87**: 6054–6057.

28. Nelson KG, Takahashi T, Bossert NL, Walmer DK. Epidermal growth factor replaces estrogen in the stimulation of female genital tract growth and differentiation. *Ann NY Acad Sci* 1991; **88**: 21–25.

29. Markogiannakis E, Georgoulias V, Margioris AN, Zoumakis E, Stournaras C, Gravanis S. Estrogens and glucocorticoids induce the expression of c-erbB2/NEU receptor in Ishikawa human endometrial cells. *Life Sci* 1997; **61**: 1083–1095.

30. Ishihara S, Taketani Y, Mizuno M. EGF rapidly stimulates tyrosine phosphorylation in cultured endometrial cells. *Asia Oceania J Obstet Gynaecol* 1991; **17**: 363–367.

31. Speroff L. The estrogen receptor: changing concepts. *Climacteric* 2000; **3** (Suppl 1): 2–13.

32. Murphy LC. Antiestrogen action and growth factor regulation. *Breast Cancer Res Treat* 1994; **31**: 61–67.

33. Hachisuga T, Hideshina T, Kawarabayashi T, Eguchi F, Emoto M, Shirakusa T. Expression of steroid receptors, Ki-67 and epidermal growth factor receptor in tamoxifen-treated endometrium. *Int J Gynecol Pathol* 1999; **18**: 297–303.

34. Rasty G, Murray R, Lu L, Kublis P, Benrubi G, Masood S. Expression of HER2 Neu oncogene in normal, hyperplastic and malignant endometrium. *Ann Clin Lab Sci* 1998; **28**: 138–143.

35. Czerwenka K, Lu Y, Heuss F. Amplification and expression of the c-erbB2 oncogene in normal, hyperplastic and malignant endometria. *Int J Gynecol Pathol* 1995; **14**: 98–106.

36. Gray K, Bullock B, Dockson R, Raszmann K, McLachlan J, Merlino G. Mechanism of DES carcinogenicity: effects of the TGF alpha transgene. *Prog Clin Biol Res* 1997; **396**: 217–231.

37. Maia H Jr, Maltez A, Fahel P, Coutinho EM. Histochemical detection of c-erbB2 over-expression in endometrial polyps removed by hysteroscopy. *Gynecol Endosc* 2000; **9**: 253–258.

38. Maia H Jr, Maltez A, Athayde C, Coutinho EM. Proliferation profile of endometrial polyps in post-menopausal patients. *Maturitas* 2001; **40**: 273–281.

Interpretation of visual appreciation of intrauterine pathology

Ramón Labastida, Alicia Ubeda and José Manuel Traver

> **Take Home Message**
> Growth, surface, and vessels are the main landmarks in the evaluation of endometrial changes. Uterine organic pathologies are better screened under direct view, in order to achieve not only an accurate diagnosis, but also the appropriate surgical management. Endometrial hyperplasia is, without doubt, the most difficult diagnosis, because of its similarity to both normal and neoplastic endometrium. In contrast, the high diagnostic efficacy of hysteroscopy allows an early diagnosis of both patterns of endometrial cancer (diffuse or tumor-like).

INTRODUCTION

Hysteroscopy is now a fundamental diagnostic method in daily gynecological practice. On the basis of the advantages of this procedure – that is, to perform a comprehensive direct visualization of the uterine cavity – it seems that other techniques, in particular dilatation and curettage, have been replaced by hysteroscopy for diagnostic assessment of intrauterine lesions [1]. However, difficulties in interpreting hysteroscopic images related to morphological modifications of the endometrial mucosa according to the date of the cycle, the influence of systemic disorders or the effect of hormonal therapies, make biopsy of the endometrium indispensable to establish a definite diagnosis [2]. On the other hand, the feasibility of endometrial biopsy is limited by a number of specific problems, such as in cases of incipient, focal, or pedunculate mobile lesions, as well as the presence of suspicious lesions in areas of difficult accessibility. For this reason, hysteroscopic examination combined with endoscopic-guided biopsy is considered the most reasonable approach for proper evaluation of the endometrium and a better knowledge of intrauterine lesions [3–5]. The most common indications for hysteroscopic examination are shown in Table 1.

It is essential to know the physiology of the endometrium and the hysteroscopic appearance related to the different phases of the cycle in order to recognize abnormal images [6]. During the normal cycle, the endometrial mucosa proliferates progressively and uniformly up to a height of 1 cm. Visual observation of endometrial features should include assessment of the height, surface, and vascular structure of the endometrium.

The *height* of the endometrium becomes readily manifest under hysteroscopic vision. Endometrial mucosa usually shows a regular, uniform surface. Endometrial thickness can be evaluated by pressing the tip of the instrument into the endometrium. Hyper-estrogenic stimulus is usually associated with increased endometrial thickness resulting in a wave-like surface with pseudopolypoid appearance, whereas uniform decrease in endometrial thickness is a distinctive feature of inadequate estrogenic stimulus.

The *surface* of the endometrium is the second parameter to be evaluated during visual inspection of the uterine cavity. The hormonal response of the endometrium as well

Table 1.
Most common indications for hysteroscopy of the uterine cavity

- Functional changes of the endometrium
  - Endometrial hypertrophy
  - Endometrial hypotrophy
  - Endometrial atrophy
- Inflammatory conditions (chronic endometritis)
- Endometrial polyps
- Myomas
- Congenital anomalies
- Synechiae
- Retained products of conception
- Tamoxifen therapy
- Adenomyosis
- Endometrial hyperplasia
- Endometrial carcinoma

as the correlation with the menstrual cycle can be judged by the presence (or absence) of glands and glandular features including number, size, proximity to each other, raised areas, etc. On the other hand, the appearance of cysts, cystic openings, vascularized protrusions, microcalcifications, areas of necrosis, etc., is also indicative of previous endometrial activity. Careful and detailed visualization at high magnification will reveal hypertrophy, uneven or thin areas, bleeding points and/or hypervascularized endometrial surface, which reflect changes or hyperactivity of the underlying tissue and, in some cases, make endometrial biopsy advisable.

Thirdly, it is important to pay attention to the *vascular architecture* of the endometrium. Vascularization typically shows three distinctive patterns: (a) abundant vessels of medium to large caliber with a clear and regular trajectory in a straight line, corresponding to persistent estrogen excess; (b) chorionic vessels of medium and short courses, with diffuse margins and frequently ending abruptly, whose brightness decreases and caliber increases over the course of the normal menstrual cycle; and (c) angiostructure of endometrial pathologic conditions characterized by hypertrophic vascular pattern related to increased focal estrogen activity. Distorted U-shaped angiostructures are frequently seen in high-risk endometrial hyperplasia, or in well-differentiated adenocarcinoma derived from hyperplasia, whereas abnormalities in the caliber, trajectory or endings of the vessels – particularly if accompanied by hypertrophy of the endometrium – are common findings in more atypical lesions.

FUNCTIONAL CHANGES OF THE ENDOMETRIUM

Menstrual cycles under normal hormonal stimulus result in endometrial mucosa of uniform and smooth appearance, homogeneous color, and distinctive features and thickness corresponding to the phase of the cycle at which hysteroscopic examination is perfomed. In case of hormonal derangements, the severity and duration of hormonal abnormalities will determine the main hysteroscopic features of the endometrial mucosa.

ENDOMETRIAL HYPERTROPHY

Excessive mucosal growth is not necessarily accompanied by qualitative abnormalities of the endometrial mucosa [7]. Hypertrophy is usually characterized by avascular pseudopolypoid raised areas that vary in number (Figure 1); more rarely, an hypertrophic area localized in one lateral side may resemble submucous myoma under hysteroscopic vision. At times, there are separated hypertrophic endometrial areas, possibly resulting from inadequate maturation of the stroma. The appearance of the endometrial surface is homogeneous and generally without vascularization. In selected cases or when a polyp is suspected, this makes the postmenstrual phase of the cycle preferable for hysteroscopic examination in order to confirm the persistence of hypertrophy or the presence of a polyp.

ENDOMETRIAL HYPOTROPHY

Endometrial hypotrophy is characterized by a uniform decrease in endometrial thickness in the proliferative phase, except when hormone replacement therapy is given during the menopause. The hysteroscopic appearance includes a poorly vascularized endometrium with a dull and slight irregular surface (Figure 2) and with a lower number of glands than the normal endometrium during the proliferative phase of the cycle. Hysteroscopic features of long-standing endometrial hypotrophy include the presence of glands that are decreased in number and progressively hardly observed as well as interglandular hemorrhagic zones. Endometrial hypotrophy that has developed on a previous hyperplasia of the endometrium gives rise to cystic hypotrophy in which images of cysts,

Figure 1
Hypertrophic endometrium showing pseudopolypoid raised areas.

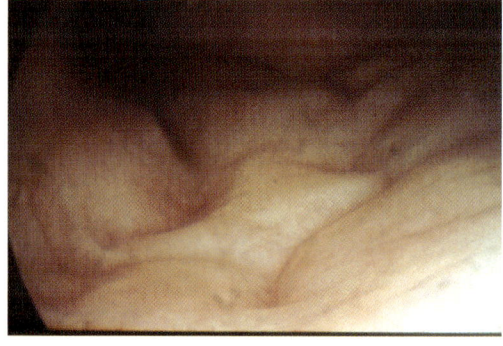

Figure 2
Endometrial hypotrophy with glandular microcyst.

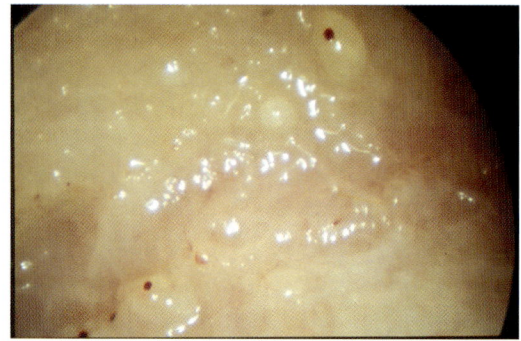

craters, synechiae, etc. are observed as sequelae of previous estrogen hyperactivity.

ENDOMETRIAL ATROPHY

The disappearance of estrogen stimulus will lead to endometrial mucosal atrophy, with thinning of the epithelial lining and of the mesh superficial capillary vessels. These morphological modifications are associated with rarefaction of glandular structures and increased fragility of the stroma (Figure 3). In severe atrophy, the epithelium is smooth and whitish, somewhat like porcelain (Figure 4).

INFLAMMATORY CONDITIONS (CHRONIC ENDOMETRITIS)

Although the uterine cavity has been considered sterile [8] and studies showing infection have been criticized because of the possibility of contamination through the lower genital tract, resolution of chronic endometritis after antiobiotic therapy and of some cases of infertility after prophylactic treatment with tetracyclines strongly support the pathogenetic role of endometrial infection [9,10]. Chronic endometritis may be pictured as follows: the endometrium is flat and the glandular orifices are usually clearly visible but the most distinctive feature consists of a red congestive-bleeding plaque with a whitish irregular punctation formed by glands in diverse stages of secretion (Figure 5). On other occasions, the glands are enlarged, in contact with each other, showing an irregular pattern very similar to glands in maximal secretion but surrounded by a flat, congestive, non-edematous stroma resembling a mosaic (Figure 6).

ENDOMETRIAL POLYPS

Endometrial polyps are exophytic mucous lesions which differ greatly in shape, number, and appearance (Figure 7). The surface epithelium of the polyp is similar to that of the surrounding endometrium and soft in consistency upon contact with the tip of the hysteroscope. Large polyps may be falsely confused with generalized endometrial hypertrophy of one side of the endometrium or with a submucous myoma covered with normal endometrium. The cystic variant, which is characteristic of the menopause, shows retention cysts that differ in number and size. Cystic polyps are highly vascularized and are difficult to distinguish from myomas or endometrial neoplasia

Figure 3
Endometrial hypotrophy preceding endometrial atrophy.

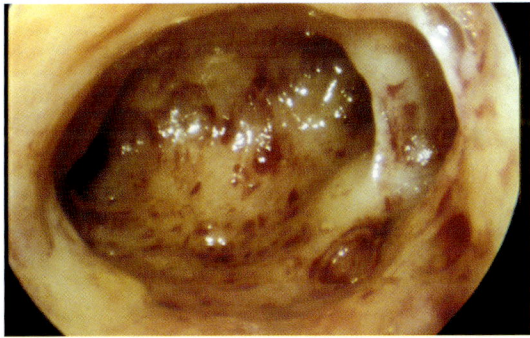

Figure 4
Definite endometrial atrophy, with loss of distinctive features of the mucosa.

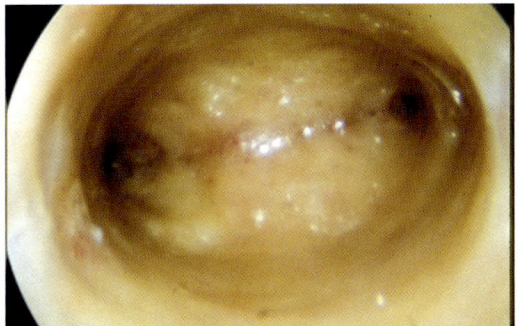

Figure 5
Irregular glandular maturation on a thinned and congestive endometrial stroma.

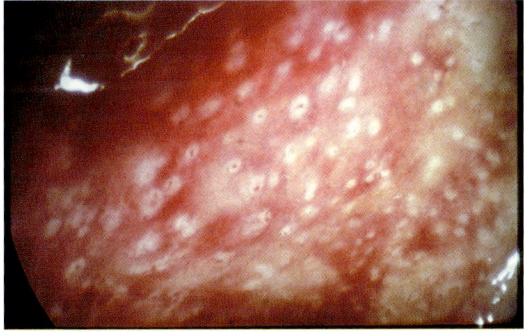

Figure 6
Image of glandular mosaic with raised area due to underlying edema.

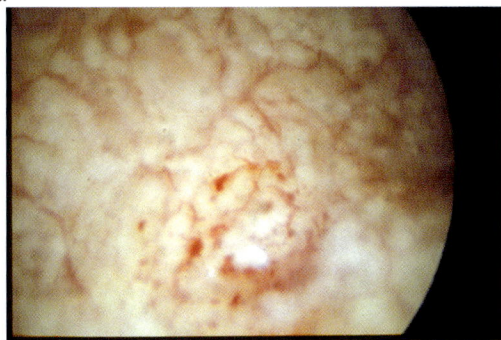

(Figure 8). Polyps with a fibrous component are almost indistinguishable from fibromas, although these fibrotic polyps have a more pearly appearance and scarce vascularization compared with fibromas (Figure 9) [11,12].

MYOMAS

The appearance of these structures under hysteroscopic vision can vary from a regular, smooth surface covered by a homogeneous endometrium similar to that of the remaining uterine cavity to pedunculate endocavitary myomas that can protrude more or less into the cavity. In the majority of cases, however, hysteroscopy reveals a round, regular tumor with abundant and pronounced superficial vascularization of medium and/or large blood vessels (Figure 10) [11,13]. Myomas are usually covered by atrophic endometrium. Hysteroscopic diagnosis of large myomas may be especially difficult in fertile women with regular cycles and scant tumor protrusion. The preservation of the endometrial mucosa and the flattening of the tumor with wide implant base at the time of distension of the uterine cavity may make it difficult to localize them even by pressing the tip of the instrument into the endometrium.

CONGENITAL ANOMALIES

The proper hysteroscopic technique in patients with uterine malformations is further complicated by the irregular distension of the uterine cavity and the decreased tone of the internal cervical os and the isthmus, making passage of the endoscope difficult because of an unequal distension of two hemi-cavities. The definite diagnosis of an abnormal uterus is established when a single right or left tubal ostium is observed. In these cases, hysteroscopic examination of the other hemi-cavity should be performed in an upward direction, so at this point, it is necessary to withdraw and redirect the hysteroscope, which is advanced towards the other tubal ostia (Figure 11) [14].

SYNAECHIAE

Synechiae are classified into marginal or central according to their location, and into endometrial, myofibrous, and connective adhesions according to their consistency. Endometrial synechiae are tiny, delicate, mostly avascular adhesions, lacking any structure. Myofibrous synechiae consist of an axis of muscular tissue covered by a thin layer of endometrial tissue, and connective adhesions consist of extreme dense, avascular, fibrous scar tissue with typical irregular shape and white, shiny appearance [11,15].

Figure 7
Endometrial polyp.

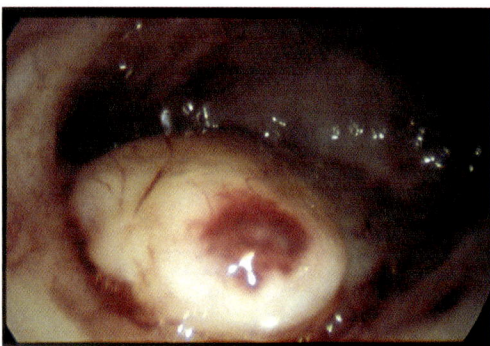

Figure 8
Hypervascularized cystic polyp.

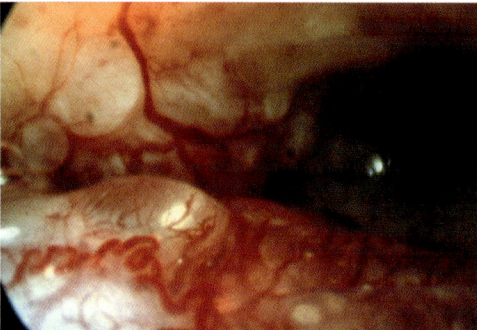

Figure 9
Fibrous polyp resembling a myoma but with less pronounced vascularization.

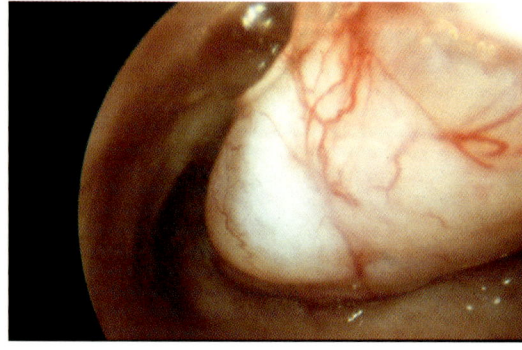

Figure 10
Submucous myoma; increased vascularization.

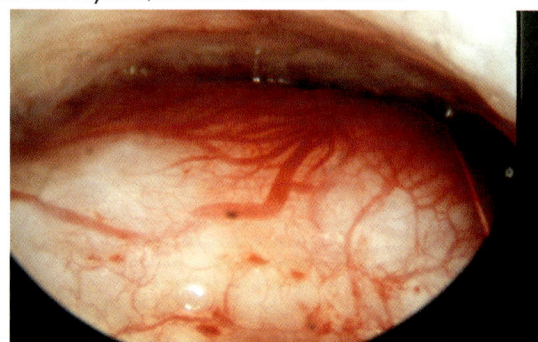

Connective and myofibrous adhesions are tough and not easily ruptured. Contact between two healing zones of the endometrial surface, when favored by an underlying infection, creates mucous bridges which become firm and fibrous beyond 50–60 days. Thus, uterine cavity walls appear to be joined by columns of varying number, width, and strength (Figure 12).

Occasionally, a generalized superficial fibrosis occurs, more markedly in angled points: the uterine fundus and lateral walls. This condition provides a tubular shape to the uterine cavity (Figure 13).

RETAINED PRODUCTS OF CONCEPTION

Retained intrauterine decidual tissue after an incomplete miscarriage appears as irregular masses of yellowish-brown color (characteristic of necrosis) alternating with blue or black areas that vary in size and shape [11]. These masses are firmly attached to the uterine wall and need to be removed by surgery (Figure 14).

TAMOXIFEN THERAPY

Endometrial pathology in tamoxifen users includes an increase in the proportion of stroma, which may explain the cystic aspect of the endometrium. The thickness of the endometrium increases significantly. Nevertheless, histologically the endometrium is atrophic or has slight to moderate estrogenic changes. The presence of superficial glandular cysts with a marked superficial long vascularization and a reddish color of the superficial stroma gives the characteristic intrauterine appearance (Figure 15) [16].

ADENOMYOSIS

Hysteroscopy is not the most appropriate technique for the diagnosis of adenomyosis. Nevertheless, visualization of

Figure 11
Partition of a septate uterus.

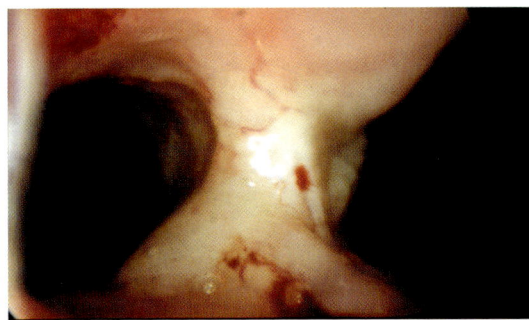

Figure 12
Anteposterior and central musculofibrous synechia dividing the uterus into two cavities.

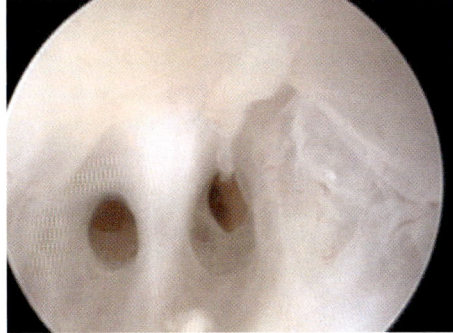

Figure 13
Concentric fibrous synechiae with reduced longitudinal and transverse diameters of the uterine cavity.

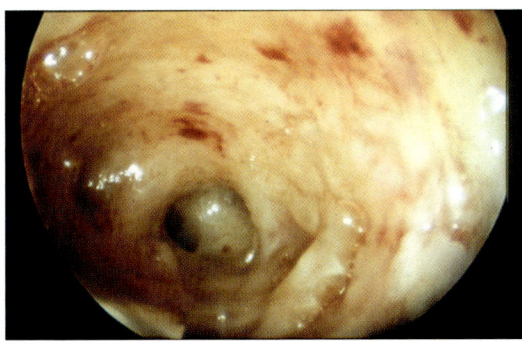

Figure 14
Retained decidual tissue.

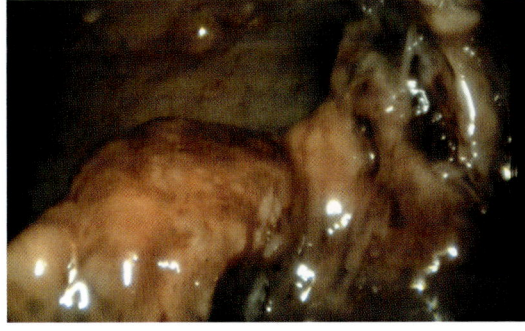

Figure 15
Irregular cystic endometrial surface induced by tamoxifen.

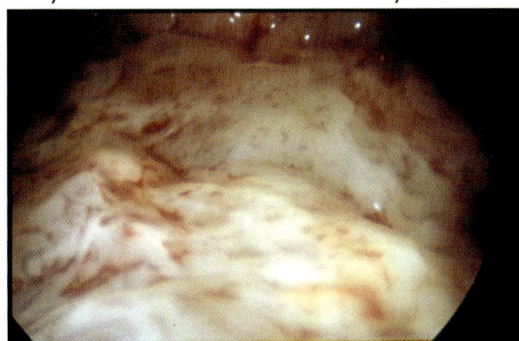

orifices in the endometrial mucosa is an unequivocal sign of adenomyosis, usually accompanied by endometrial hypervascularization (Figure 16) [17].

ENDOMETRIAL HYPERPLASIA

Endometrial hyperplasia is characterized by an increase in the size and volume of glands in association with varying degrees of architectural distortion and stratification, and epithelial atypia. Hyperplastic lesions are classified into atypical and non-atypical simple and complex endometrial hyperplasia. It has not been possible to find a corresponding hysteroscopic image for every histological aspect of endometrial hyperplasia.

The hysteroscopic appearance of simple endometrial hyperplasia includes varied and often multiple hysteroscopic changes [5,18], such as increased endometrial thickness, polypoid formations, increased vascularization, wave-like endometrial surface, and irregular arrangement of the glandular orifices. Although hyperplasia may develop in normal, hypertrophic, hypotrophic or atrophic endometrium, in a series of 502 patients with endometrial hyperplasia undergoing hysteroscopic examination at our institution, endometrial hypertrophy was observed in 49.6% of cases (Table 2).

Increased vascularization of polypoid formations is a distinctive feature of endometrial hyperplasia (Figure 17). On the other hand, hysteroscopic images in complex endometrial hyperplasia are not so extremely varied. There are architectural distortions and vascularization of polypoid aspects is clearly visible and pathological. Hysteroscopic images of multiple gland orifices scattered over the endometrial surface, widened glandular ostia showing a vascularized perimeter, or cystic glandular formations are characteristic findings in adenomatous hyperplasia. The presence of areas of necrosis, hemorrhage, or irregularities of the epithelium together with abnormal hypervascularization or microcalcifications is highly suggestive of endometrial carcinoma.

ENDOMETRIAL CARCINOMA

Hysteroscopy is an extremely reliable technique in the diagnosis of endometrial neoplasia. The endoscopic images are so clear and obvious to interpret that they are rarely confused with other lesions [19]. Endometrial hypertrophy is not invariably present and in a third of cases of endometrial carcinoma, atrophy of the endometrium is observed. Irregular excrescences appearing on an atrophic

Figure 16
Orifice in the fundus due to adenomyosis.

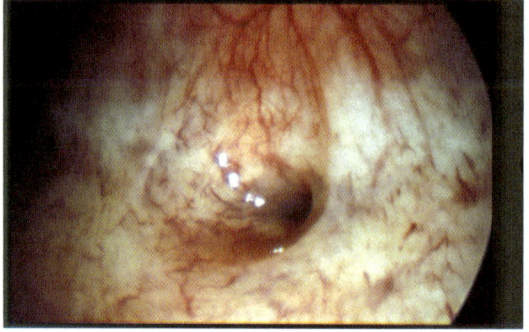

Figure 17
Endometrial mucosal hypertrophy with vascularized pseudopolypoid formations.

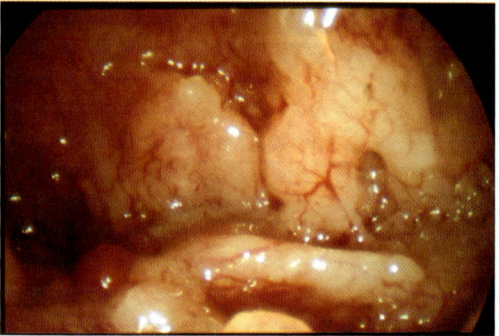

Table 2
Hysteroscopic appearance of endometrial hyperplasia in 502 patients

	Simple hyperplasia (%)		Complex hyperplasia (%)	
Endometrium	Non-atypical, n = 423	Atypical, n = 3	Non-atypical, n = 37	Atypical, n = 39
Normal	111 (26.0)	3 (100)	5 (13.5)	6 (15.3)
Hypertrophic	211 (49.8)	–	14 (37.8)	24 (61.5)
Hypotrophic	77 (18.3)	–	13 (35.1)	4 (10.2)
Atrophic	24 (5.6)	–	5 (13.5)	5 (12.8)

mucosa may be found in the initial stages (Figure 18). Areas of atrophic or hypotrophic endometrium with irregular surface, increased irregular or anarchic vascularization, and microcalcifications are suggestive of malignant endometrial pathology [2]. However, in case of endometrial hypertrophy it is very difficult to differentiate either atypical or non-atypical complex hyperplasia from endometrial carcinoma, especially in the initial stages. Superficial vascularization taking a cerebroid appearance, finger-like proliferations with a central vessel (Figure 19) or the existence of hemorrhagic zones, irregular proliferations, necrosis or microcalcifications on the surface will increase the diagnostic accuracy with respect to endometrial neoplasia.

The hysteroscopic appearance of endometrial carcinoma at advanced stages includes irregular, polylobular masses with erratic vascularization (the vessels typically show abrupt variations in caliber and course), microcalcifications, and hydrometra or hematometra [11,20]. Pseudopolypoid excrescences are frequently coated with areas of necrosis with fibrin (Figure 20).

In carcinomas unrelated to endometrial hyperplasia (Table 3), hysteroscopic vision reveals a free uterine cavity with endometrial atrophy in which the distinctive feature is a mass, morphologically similar to a polyp or a myoma, with abnormal vascularization and irregular surface, necrosis or microcalcifications similar to those observed in pseudopolypoid formations derived from endometrial hyperplasia.

Figure 18
Small neoplastic mass in an atrophic septate uterus.

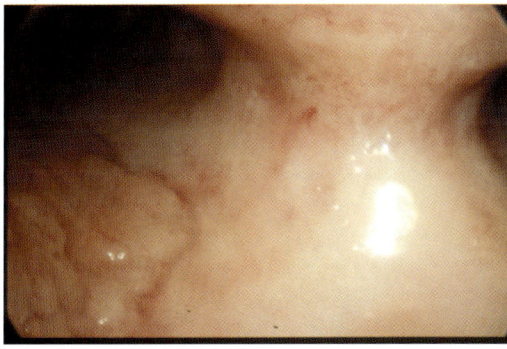

Figure 19
Finger-like hypervascularized proliferations in endometrial adenocarcinoma.

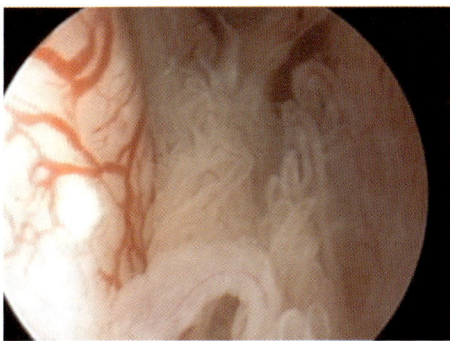

Figure 20
Malignant pseudopolypoid tumor with atypical vascularization in a cystic endometrium.

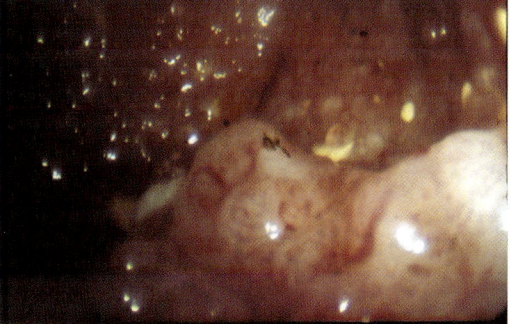

Table 3.
Hysteroscopic features of endometrial carcinoma

Related to hyperplasia
  Polypoid surface
  Atypical vascularization
  Necrosis
  Microcalcifications (corneal pearls)
  Hydrometra or hematometra

Not related to hyperplasia.
  Isolated solid mass resembling a polyp or a myoma
  Hypertrophic vascularization
  Absence of necrosis
  Endometrial atrophy

REFERENCES

1. Van der Pas H, Vancaillie T. Manual of Hysteroscopy. New York, NY: Elsevier Science, 1990.
2. Garuti G, Sambruni I, Colonnelli M, Luerti M. Accuracy of hysteroscopy in predicting histopathology of endometrium in 1500 women. *J Am Assoc Gynecol Laparosc* 2001; **8**: 207–213.
3. Wieser F, Tempfer C, Kurz C, Nagele F. Hysteroscopy in 2001: a comprehensive review. *Acta Obstet Gynecol Scand* 2001; **80**: 773–783.
4. Kochli OR, Wallwiener D, Brandner P et al. Consensus of diagnostic and operative hysteroscopy. Consensus statements of a joint-meeting of the Societies of Gynecological Endoscopy of Switzerland, Germany and Austria, October 1999. *Contrib Gynecol Obstet* 2000; **20**: 182–187.
5. Lindemann HJ. The modern role of hysteroscopy in the care of women. *J Am Assoc Gynecol Laparosc* 2000; **7**: 307–309.
6. Finikiotis G. Hysteroscopy: a review. *Obstet Gynecol Surv* 1994; **49**: 271–278.
7. Corfman RS. Indications for hysteroscopy. *Obstet Gynecol Clin North Am* 1988; **15**: 41–49.
8. Ansbacher R, Boyson WA, Morris JA. Sterility of the uterine cavity. *Am J Obstet Gynecol* 1967; **99**: 394–396.
9. Møller BR, Kristiansen FV, Thorsen P, Frost L, Mogensen SC. Sterility of the uterine cavity. *Acta Obstet Gynecol Scand* 1995; **74**: 216–219.
10. Greenwood SM, Moran JJ. Chronic endometritis: morphologic and clinical observations. *Obstet Gynecol* 1981; **58**: 176–184.
11. Mencaglia L, Hamou JE. Manual of Gynecological Hysteroscopy. Diagnosis and Surgery. Tuttlingen, Germany: Endo-Press, 2000.
12. Fay TN, Khanem N, Hosking D. Outpatient hysteroscopy in asymptomatic postmenopausal women. *Climateric* 1999; **2**: 263–267.
13. Labastida R, Cararach M, Dexeus S, Montesinos M, Julve X, Fábregas R. Tratado y Atlas de Histeroscopia. Barcelona: Editorial Salvat, 1990.
14. Brusco GF, Arena S, Angelini A. The role of diagnostic hysteroscopy in infertile women. *Minerva Ginecol* 2001; **53**: 313–319.
15. Al-Inany H. Intrauterine adhesions. An update. *Acta Obstet Gynecol Scand* 2001; **80**: 986–993.
16. Garuti G, Grossi F, Cellani F, Centinaio G, Colonnelli M, Luerti M. Hysteroscopic assessment of menopausal breast-cancer patients taking tamoxifen; is there a bias from the mode of endometrial sampling in estimating endometrial morbidity? *Breast Cancer Res Treat* 2002; **72**: 245–253.
17. Keckstein J. Hysteroscopy and adenomyosis. *Contrib Gynecol Obstet* 2000; **20**: 41–50.
18. Loverro G, Bettochi S, Cormio G et al. Diagnostic accuracy of hysteroscopy in endometrial hyperplasia. *Maturitas* 1996; **25**: 187–191.
19. Narchetti M, Litta P, Lanza P, Lauri F, Pozzan C. The role of hysteroscopy in early diagnosis of endometrial cancer. *Eur J Gynaecol Oncol* 2002; **23**: 151–153.
20. Gordon AG, Lewis BV, DeCherney AH, Sciarra J. Atlas of Gynecologic Endoscopy, 2nd edn. London: Times Mirror International Publishers, 1995.

Endometrial cell transportation during hysteroscopy

Stefano Bettocchi

> **Take Home Message**
> The type of hysteroscope, the method of distending the uterine cavity, the duration of the procedure, and the pressure required to visualize the endometrial cavity are all variables that may influence the passage of viable cells into the abdominal cavity. During office hysteroscopy saline is the medium of choice and a lower pressure than the contra pressure of the isthmic part of the fallopian tube is the standard. Considering these facts the possibility of spilling endometrial cells is extremely low in office hysteroscopy.

Abnormal uterine bleeding is the most common presenting symptom in patients with endometrial carcinoma [1] and, in the last decade, in order to improve the sensitivity of dilatation and curettage (D&C), hysteroscopy has been established as a feasible and widely accepted procedure for the diagnosis of this condition [2]. However, several case reports have suggested that hysteroscopy may transport endometrial cells into the peritoneal cavity. In particular, distension and irrigation of the uterine cavity during hysteroscopy with fluid distension was suspected to cause tumor cell dissemination into the abdominal cavity in patients with endometrial carcinoma [3–7].

In a multicenter retrospective analysis involving seven Austrian hospitals between 1996 and 1997, of 113 consecutive patients with endometrial carcinoma limited to the inner half or less of the myometrium, the only factor significantly associated with positive peritoneal cytology was a history of hysteroscopy ($p = 0.04$). The authors concluded that hysteroscopy with fluid distension facilitates intra-abdominal dissemination of endometrial cancer cells [8].

Moreover, Arikan and colleagues studied 24 uteri obtained at hysterectomy in patients with stage IA-IB endometrial carcinoma with 'in vitro' hysteroscopy with fluid distension. They proved that transtubal fluid dissemination occurs in 83% of cases and that in 42% of cases the disseminated tumor cells were functionally viable [9].

Considering the potential of hysteroscopy to push cancer cells through the fallopian tubes and into the uterine spaces, a number of papers conclude that the use of this diagnostic modality should be limited to cases in which a diagnosis is not forthcoming by the standard procedures.

On the other hand, Creasman and Lukeman suggested that intraperitoneal dissemination might occur at anatomic sites other than the fallopian tubes, as malignant cells were discovered in the peritoneal cavity in 3 of 44 patients with endometrial carcinoma. One of these three patients had had bilateral salpingectomy and two patients had a tubal ligation before hysterectomy [10].

In fact, the term hysteroscopy is used to describe a wide range of different endoscopic procedures; there is no standard method of performing this diagnostic procedure. The type of hysteroscope, method of distension of the uterine cavity, duration of the procedure, and pressure required to visualize the endometrial cavity are all factors that may influence the final results of the examination. Probably, intrauterine pressure could be considered the most important factor associated with transtubal spillage of endometrial cells. A possible explanation of the results of the Austrian multicenter study [8] is that the authors reported a surprisingly high intrauterine pressure (150 mmHg) [11]. Details of how these pressures were measured and whether high pressures are required for complete distension of the uterine cavity are difficult to discern from the literature. This information is important to the development of a liquid system in which it would be desirable to distend the uterine cavity completely but maintain pressures low enough to prevent spillage from the fallopian tubes into the peritoneal cavity.

In 1990, Siegler and colleagues reported that the usual intrauterine pressure required to visualize the endometrial cavity during hysteroscopy is approximately 40 mmHg; with a higher pressure (around 100/110 mmHg), tubal ostia will be visualized with a consequent intra-abdominal liquid spillage [12].

In 1995, Baker and Adamson determined that 100 mmHg was the median intrauterine pressure for spill of dye from both tubes; no spillage occurred at pressures <70 mmHg, and the threshold pressure of spillage was highest in patients with laparoscopic evidence of tubal disease [13].

More recently, the same authors determined the minimum pressure required to distend the uterine cavity by attaching a Cobe CDX III pressure transducer kit to a 5-mm 0° or a 3-mm 30° hysteroscope. A liquid line was connected from a bag of normal saline to the pressure transducer tip such that saline flowed through the transducer to the hysteroscope. The transducer was attached to a Datascope 2002 pressure monitor (Datascope Corporation, Paramus, NJ, USA), and the lowest intrauterine perfusion pressure necessary for uterine distension ranged from 25 to 50 mmHg (median 40 mmHg) [14].

In conclusion, these studies suggest that normal saline may distend the cavity at a lower pressure than that required to produce spillage from the fallopian tubes. However, additional studies are needed to establish definitive hysteroscopic perfusion pressure guidelines. This information could be important, not only to prevent cell dissemination into the abdominal cavity in patients with endometrial carcinoma, but also the possibility of performing hysteroscopy at pressures low enough to prevent spillage from the fallopian tubes into the peritoneal cavity could be useful in preventing pelvic inflammatory disease (PID) or endometriosis.

REFERENCES

1. Bakarat RR, Park RC, Grisby PW et al. Corpus: epithelial tumors. In: Hoskins WJ, Perez CA, Young RC, eds. Principle and Practice of Gynecologic Oncology. Philadelphia: Lippincott-Raven, 1997: 859–896.
2. Nagele F, O'Connor H, Davies A et al. 2500 outpatients diagnostic hysteroscopies. Obstet Gynecol 1996; **88**: 87–92.
3. Romano S, Shimoni Y, Muralee D et al. Retrograde seeding of endometrial carcinoma during hysteroscopy. Gynecol Oncol 1992; **44**: 116–118.
4. Shmitz MJ, Nahhas WA. Hysteroscopy may transport malignant cells into the peritoneal cavity. Eur J Gynaecol Oncol 1992; **2**: 121–124.
5. Egarter C, Krestan C, Kurz C. Abdominal dissemination of malignant cells with hysteroscopy. Case report. Gynecol Oncol 1996; **63**: 143–144.
6. Rose PG, Mendelsohn G, Kornbluth I. Hysteroscopic dissemination of endometrial carcinoma. Gynecol Oncol 1998; **71**: 145–146.
7. Lo KW, Cheung TH, Yim SF et al. Hysteroscopic dissemination of endometrial carcinoma using carbon dioxide and normal saline: a retrospective study. Gynecol Oncol 2002; **84**: 394–398.
8. Obermaier A, Geramou M, Gucer F et al. Does hysteroscopy facilitate tumor cell dissemination? Cancer 2000; **88**: 139–144.
9. Arikan G, Reich O, Weiss U et al Are endometrial carcinoma cells disseminated at hysteroscopy functionally viable? Gynecol Oncol 2001; **83**: 221–226.
10. Creasman WT, Lukeman J. Role of the fallopian tube dissemination of malignant cells in corpus cancer. Cancer 1972; **29**: 456–457.
11. Bettochi S, Di Vagnio G, Cormio G et al. Intra-abdominal spread of malignant cells following hysteroscopy (Letter). Gynecol Oncol 1997; **66**: 165–166.
12. Siegler AM, Valle RF, Lindemann HJ et al. Therapeutic Hysteroscopy: Indications and Techniques. St Louis: CV Mosby, 1990.
13. Baker VL, Adamson GD. Threshold intrauterine perfusion pressure for intraperitoneal spill during hydrotubation and correlation with tubal adhesive disease. Fertil Steril 1995; **64**: 1066–1069.
14. Baker VL, Adamson GD. Minimum intrauterine pressure required for uterine distention. J Am Assoc Gynecol Laparosc 1998; **5**: 51–53.

Part II
OPERATIVE PROCEDURES

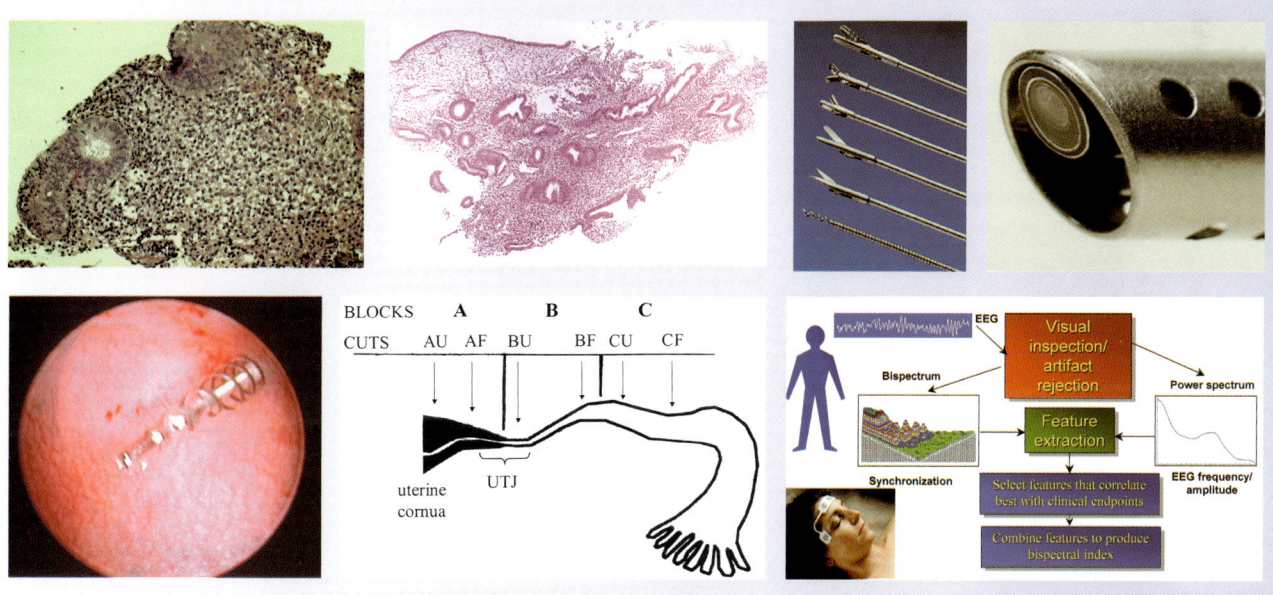

17a Instrumentation and biopsies
The reliability of eye-guided biopsies (EGB)

Stefano Bettocchi

> **Take Home Message**
> The classical punch biopsy technique delivers only the amount of tissue within the confinement of the jaws of the forceps, hence there is often insufficient material for diagnosis (2.5 mm² on average). The technique of grasp biopsy performed with 5 Fr crocodile forceps allows for more material to be extracted in a sufficient volume (5.7 mm²) for adequate pathological examination.

INTRODUCTION

The suggestion that dilatation and curettage (D&C) does not ensure adequate, representative sampling of the endometrial cavity in the detection of intrauterine pathologies is widely supported in the literature [1–5]. Furthermore, focal endometrial lesions such as endometrial hyperplasia and adenocarcinoma can easily be missed with this technique [3,6–8]. Endometrial sampling devices, such as the Vabra, Pipelle or Novak, lead to the same problems owing to their 'blind' nature [9].

In the last few years the development of the new generation of small diameter operative office hysteroscopes (Bettocchi Office Hysteroscopes sizes 4 and 5; Karl Storz, Tuttlingen, Germany) with an operative channel of 5 Fr has allowed physicians to perform more frequent targeted hysteroscopic biopsies to confirm the 'visual' diagnosis. A number of papers have reported the reliability of such biopsies compared with blind procedures [1,3,5, 7–9].

CLASSIC 'PUNCH' TECHNIQUE

The technique used is defined as a 'punch' biopsy. The biopsy forceps bites into the endometrium and is then closed; the mucosa remains inside the jaws and partly around them. The instrument is then extracted through the operative channel while the hysteroscope remains inside the uterine cavity. Thus, the small diameter of the operative channel shaves the surrounding material away from around the tip of the forceps and so the final amount of tissue to be sent to the pathologist is strictly related to the volume of the two jaws of the forceps. The critical point in this procedure is the difficulty in obtaining an adequate amount of tissue for histological diagnosis. With small 5 Fr biopsy forceps and the 'punch' technique, Colafranceschi et al [10] calculated an adequate amount of tissue to be not less than 0.8 mm².

'GRASP' TECHNIQUE

In order to routinely obtain enough material for histological diagnosis, we have modified the technique and perform a so-called 'grasp' biopsy: the biopsy forceps are placed, with the jaws open, against the endometrium to be biopsied. The forceps are then pushed into the tissue and along it for 0.5–1 cm. Once a large portion of mucosa has been detached, the two jaws are closed and the whole hysteroscope is pulled out of the uterine cavity, without pulling the tip of the instrument back into the channel. In this way, not only the tissue inside the forceps, but also the surrounding tissue, protruding outside the jaws, can be retrieved.

COMPARATIVE STUDY

Bettocchi et al [11] have reported a study which evaluated the efficacy of the two techniques described above, with reference to the different biopsy forceps used. The study analysed the amount of tissue obtained in 1276 procedures performed in an office setting during the proliferative phase of the menstrual cycle. The biopsy forceps (Karl Storz) have a diameter of 5 Fr and the jaws of the punch biopsy forceps (Figure 1a) are 2.5 mm long, while the crocodile forceps (Figure 1b) are 5 mm long. The latter instrument also has small teeth on both sides of the jaws to keep hold of the material obtained. These instruments were used together with the Bettocchi Office Hysteroscope size 5 (Karl Storz), with liquid distension (saline solution).

The comparison of the mean quantity of tissue (in mm²) obtained with the different forceps and different techniques used for endometrial sampling is shown in Table 1.

EGB is clearly the most accurate procedure, and in our experience the grasp technique – together with the new generation of biopsy forceps – was the most satisfactory way to obtain a sufficient quantity of endometrial tissue for histology.

REFERENCES

1. Brill AI. What is the role of hysteroscopy in the management of abnormal uterine bleeding? *Clin Obstet Gynecol* 1995; **38**: 319–345.
2. Smith JJ, Schulman H. Current dilatation and curettage practice: a need for revision. *Obstet Gynecol* 1985; **65**: 516–518.
3. Grimes DA. Diagnostic dilation and curettage: a reappraisal. *Am J Obstet Gynecol* 1982; **142**: 1–6.
4. Loffer FD. Hysteroscopy with selective endometrial sampling compared with D&C for Abnormal Uterine Bleeding: the value of a negative hysteroscopic view. *Obstet Gynecol* 1989; **73**: 16–20.
5. Dijkhuizen FPHLJ, Mol BWJ, Brolmann HAM, Heintz APM. The accuracy of endometrial sampling in the diagnosis of patients with endometrial carcinoma and hyperplasia. *Cancer* 2000; **89**: 1765–1772.
6. Lerner HM. Lack of efficacy of prehysterectomy curettage as a diagnostic procedure. *Am J Obstet Gynecol* 1984; **148**: 1055–1056.
7. Valle RF. Office hysteroscopy. *Clin Obstet Gynecol* 1999; **42**: 276–289.
8. Stock RJ, Kanbour A. Prehysterectomy curettage. *Obstet Gynecol* 1975; **45**: 537–541.
9. Agostini A, Cravello L, Rojat-Habib MC et al. Evaluation of two methods for endometrial sampling during diagnostic hysteroscopy. *J Gynecol Obstet Biol Reprod (Paris)* 1999; **28**: 433.
10. Colafranceschi M, van Herendael B, Mencaglia L et al. Reliability of endometrial biopsy under eye-directed hysteroscopic control. *Eur J Gynaecol Oncol* 1991; **12**: 109–110.
11. Bettocchi S, Di Venere R, Pansini N, Pellegrino A, Santamato S, Ceci O. Endometrial biopsies using small-diameter hysteroscopes and 5F instruments: how can we obtain enough material for a correct histologic diagnosis? *J Am Assoc Gynecol Laparosc* 2002; **9**: 290–292.

Figure 1
Biopsy forceps (Karl Storz).

(a) Punch biopsy forceps: jaws are 2.5 mm long.

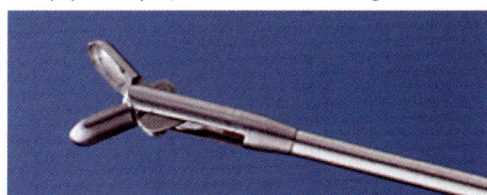

(b) Crocodile forceps: jaws are 5 mm long.

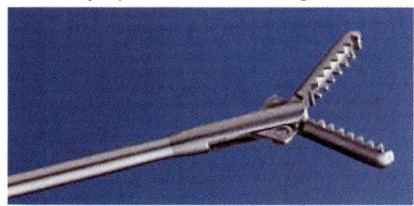

Table 1
Comparison of punch technique and grasp technique

	Punch biopsy forceps (581 patients)	Crocodile forceps (695 patients)
Punch technique		
Number of patients (%)	377 (64.8)	436 (62.7)
Mean amount of tissue	0.8 mm²	2.5 mm²
Grasp technique		
Number of patients (%)	204 (35.2)	259 (37.3)
Mean amount of tissue	1.7 mm²	5.7 mm²

17b Instrumentation and biopsies
Endometrial cytology and endometrial sampling

René Marty

> **Take Home Message**
> The use of hysteroscopy, both flexible and rigid, allows for adequate sampling in the field of cytology and pathology, provided that the specific area in the uterus is located and communicated to the pathologist. The advantage is the de visu interpretation of the lesions that can also be communicated to the pathologist. A certain degree of experience and the use of adequate technique will increase the accuracy of the sampling.

Even for an experienced hysteroscopist, visual diagnosis is hazardous and requires a pathologic confirmation. After years of blind biopsies, hysterosalpingography allowed the gynecologist to more specifically locate pathologic lesions, but the high number of false-positive (32%) and false-negative results made this approach less than ideal [1]. Even the addition of sonographic guidance did not eliminate false-positive and false-negative results.

A great advance in providing an accurate diagnosis of endometrial pathology has been made with the use of the rigid hysteroscope, and more recently with the fibrohysteroscope. A targeted endometrial biopsy under direct vision greatly increases the accuracy. The three major features of a flexible hysteroscope – flexibility, bending tip, and frontal view – allow the endoscopist to pass over obstacles, permitting access to hidden or obscure areas and allow a frontal approach to the selected area to be biopsied (Figure 1 and Table 1).

DIRECTED ENDOMETRIAL CYTOLOGY
Sampling is easy, using a 3 Fr cytobrush pushed inside the uterine cavity in the operative channel of the fibrohysteroscope. This sampling may be focused on a small area. The major application is the early detection of endometrial carcinoma and its precursors (Figures 2 and 3).

The cytobrushing may be associated with a targeted endometrial biopsy. It may be useful to collect samples separately from each uterine wall and fundus and spread the cells on separate slides. The fixation is the same as that for a Pap smear. We usually obtain 30% negative smears. A good concordance was reported by Musssuto [2].

CHARACTERISTICS OF THE MICROBIOPSIES
They are taken with a small flexible forceps (3 Fr) (Table 2). This means that the volume of each endometrial sample is small, ranging between 0.85 mm³ (with Cook forceps) (Figure 4) and 1.3 2mm³ (with Leisegang forceps). So, the difficulty lies in obtaining enough tissue to allow adequate histologic interpretation. This is why we have developed a protocol that makes it possible to produce good reliability and a low rate of rejected biopsies.

Figure 1
The HYF X2 fibrohysteroscope.

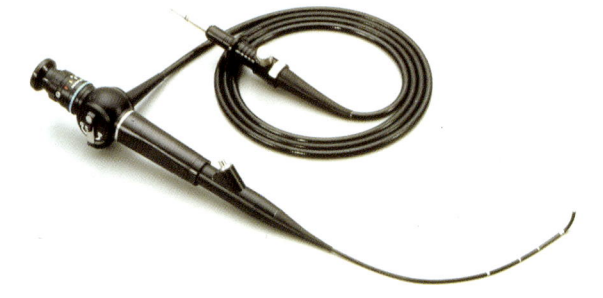

Table 1
Features and benefits of flexible hysteroscopes

• Thinner outer diameter 3.6 mm (HYF-P) × 3.1 mm	*Easy insertion*
• High quality images Number of fibers is approximately double the number in HYF-P	*Accurate diagnosis*
• Wide field of view 90° (HYF-P) × 100°	*Easy orientation*
• Bigger image size Approximately three times bigger than HYF-P	*Easy observation*

PRACTICAL CONSIDERATIONS

To collect the biopsy, when the sample is taken, the best way is to open the forceps jaws and shake the contents inside a small cup filled with sterile water. Sometimes it is useful to collect a microbiopsy by aspiration with a needle. The specimen must be placed in the fixation medium immediately: Bouin is best, because it causes minimal shrinkage and allows the best interpretation of the glycogenic charge inside the epithelial cells.

To conclude, targeted endometrial biopsy performed during fibrohysteroscopy is a reliable procedure if the endoscopist follows a suitable protocol and the greatest accuracy is achieved when the hysteroscopist and the pathologist are skilled and have considerable experience with this technique.

The guidelines for microbiopsies are listed in Table 3.

Figure 2
Endometrial cytobrushing (original magnification ×400).

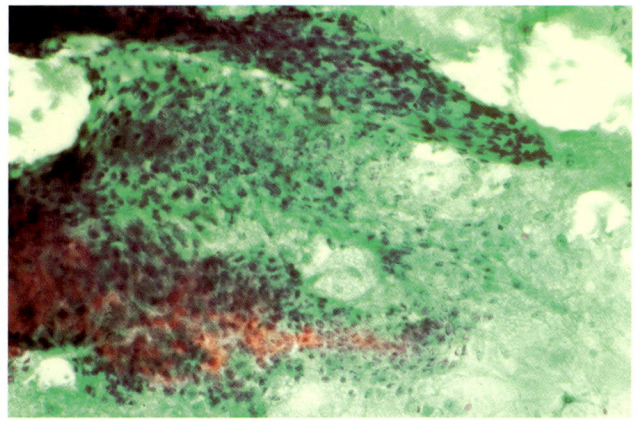

Figure 3
Endometrial smear: postmenopausal bleeding.

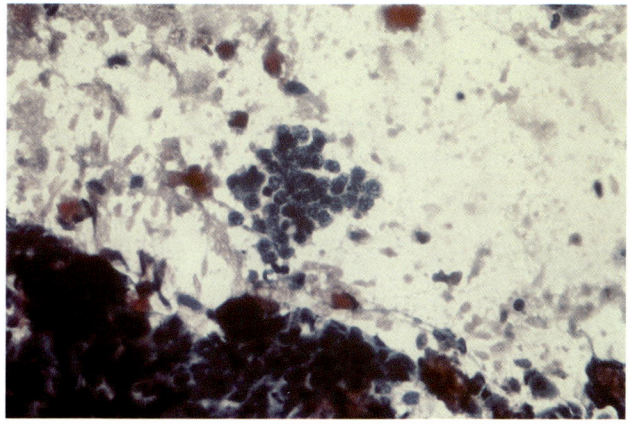

Table 2
Biopsy forceps

Manufacturer	Shaft(Fr)	Biopsy head (jaws)	Volume of specimen (mm^3)	Disposable (single use)	Reusable	Sterilization method
Cook	3	Oval cup	0.85	No	Yes	Steam or ETO
Cook	3	Oval cup	0.85	Yes	No	Not applicable
Olympus	3	Cup (rat tooth)	0.98	No	Yes	Steam or ETO
Leisegang	3	Cup	1.32	No	Yes	Steam or ETO

Table 3
Guidelines for microbiopsies: protocol

- The hysteroscopist should be experience and skilled
- The hysteroscopist should possess good knowledge of the macroscopic appearance of intrauterine pathology
- The hysteroscopist should choose the most appropriate forceps for each individual case
- The hysteroscopist should obtain tissue for biopsy from a selected area in each pathologic lesion
- The hysteroscopist should perform at least three biopsies
- The hysteroscopist should select a pathologist who is well trained in gynecology and microbiopsy
- The hysteroscopist should complete a sheet with a good description of the hysteroscopic findings, including the gross appearance, location of the pathology, and sites of the biopsies

RELIABILITY OF TARGETED ENDOMETRIAL BIOPSIES

We have conducted three successive analyses over 5 years to evaluate the reliability of targeted endometrial biopsies during fibrohysteroscopy [3–5]. When three biopsies are performed, the accuracy is over 94.4% with a rate of 2.7% rejected biopsies (Figures 5 and 6).

The selection of the flexible biopsy forceps must be done according to the specific procedure (Table 4). A polyp may require a biopsy (Figure 7) and a myoma may be discovered at the same time (Figure 8). A substantial improvement in sensitivity is widely linked to the accurate choice of the biopsy forceps. The hysteroscopist must keep in mind that the reliability of targeted endometrial biopsy depends greatly on the area chosen to take the tissue sample. This means that the operator must have a good knowledge of each gross pathology.

This can be clarified by giving two examples:

- Example 1: determining hormonal status. The sample must be taken essentially from the fundus. The uterine walls and isthmus do not respond as well as the fundus to hormonal impregnation.

- Example 2: if a pediculated polyp is discovered, the operator must avoid taking the sample in the area of the tip, one must choose the base and, if possible, straddle the normal and pathologic endometrium. In fact, the tip is often infected, leading to an unreadable biopsy.

The quality and the readability of the pathological specimen are demonstrated in Figures 9 and 10. These biopsies were performed with a 3 Fr biopsy forceps (Leisegang).

Figure 4
Cook 3 Fr biopsy forceps.

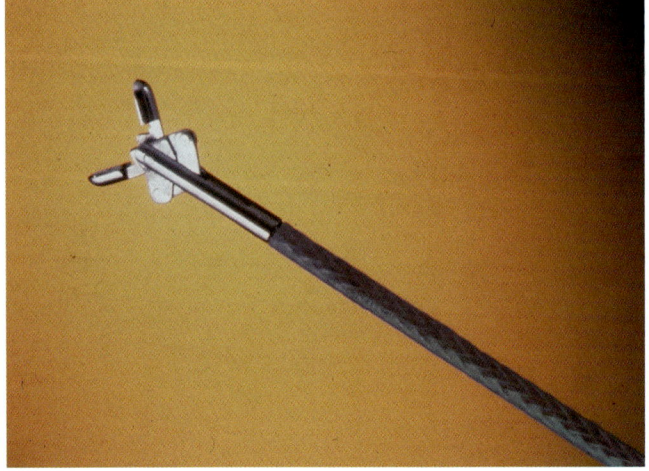

Figure 5
Frequency of rejected biopsies.

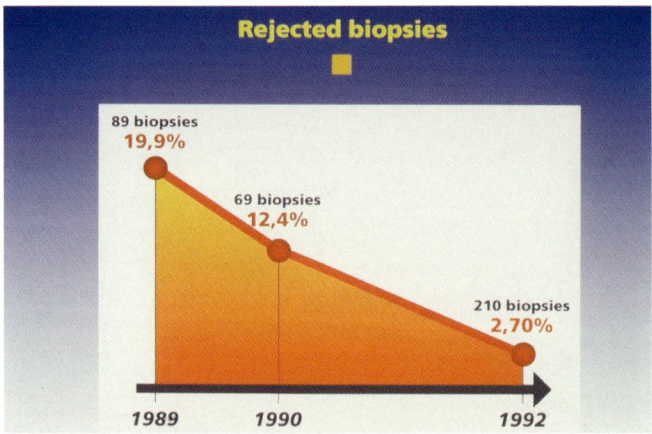

Figure 6
Accuracy of targeted endometrial biopsies.

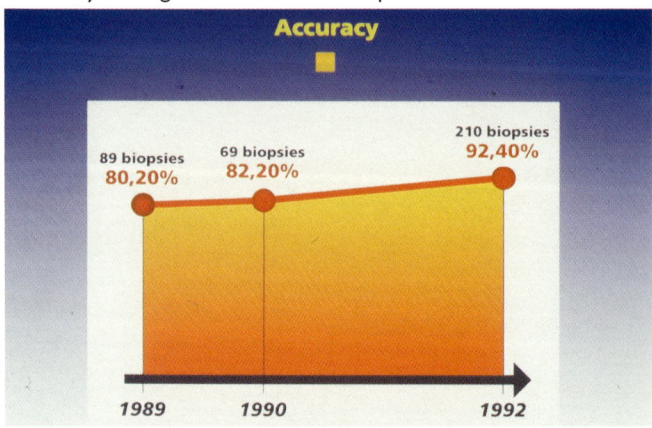

Table 4
Biopsy forceps

Type of procedure	Frontal approach	Oblique approach	Mobile target	Biopsy exeresis
Type of forceps	Standard cup	Rat tooth	Mouse tooth	Alligator
Example	Suspect area	Myoma	Residual products of conception	Polypectomy

THE BASIC IMPORTANCE OF HISTOPATHOLOGY

Endometrial pathology comprises polyps, hyperplasia, and endometrial cancer. Hysteroscopy is the best way to detect a focal lesion and to obtain a good targeted endometrial biopsy.

Because the diagnosis of endometrial hyperplasia can be made only by histology, reliable endometrial sampling is extremely important. As endometrial hyperplasia with cytologic atypia is often very localized, a biopsy under direct hysteroscopic vision is the most reliable way to detect it [6]. In specific cases, it is useful to complete with a suction curettage after the biopsy has been done. If an endometrial cancer is discovered, only hysteroscopy allows the clinician to stage the cancer and determine whether it should be classified as differentiated or not.

A decision tree is suggested to manage a suspicious area of endometrial lining (Figure 11).

Figure 7
Biopsy of polyp.

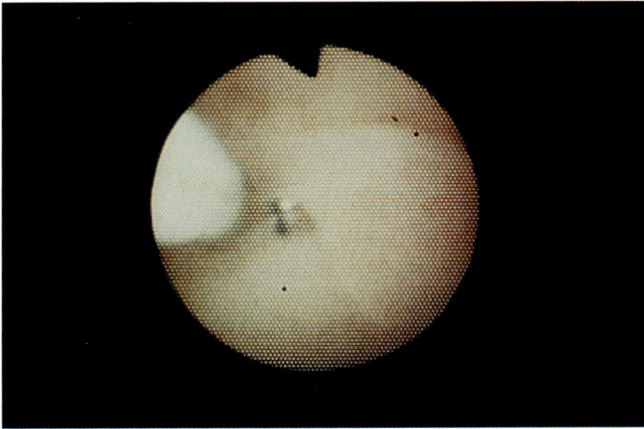

Figure 8
Myoma and sessile polyp.

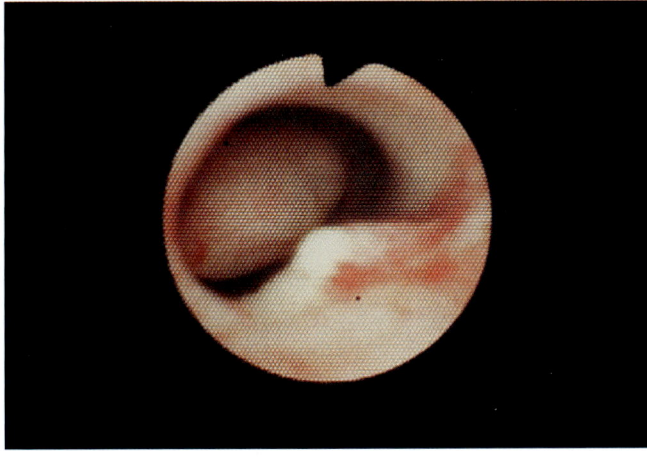

Figure 9
Endometrial biopsy taken with 3 Fr biopsy forceps during the proliferative phase.

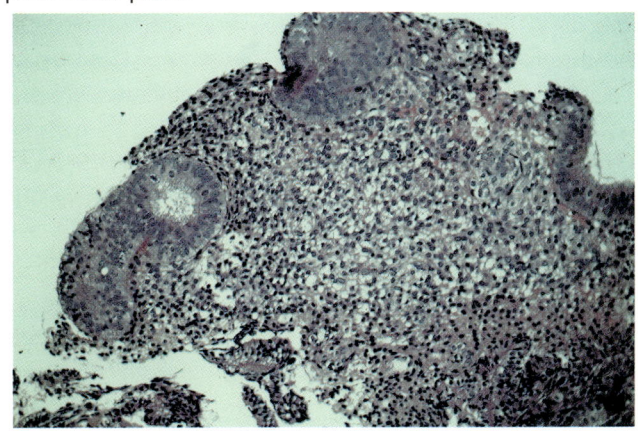

Figure 10
Endometrial biopsy (taken with 3 Fr biopsy forceps): postmenopausal hypotrophia.

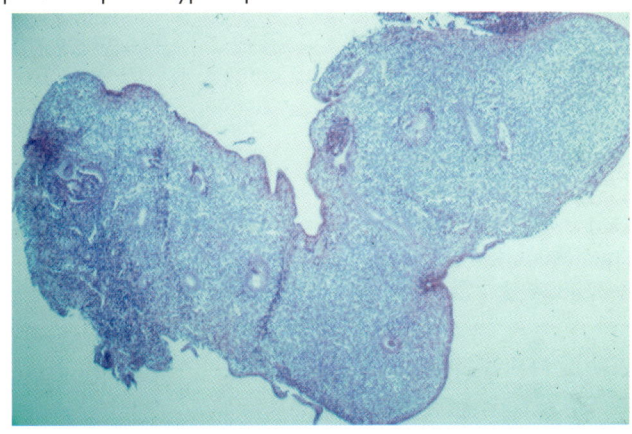

Figure 11
Endometrial cytology and sampling algorithm

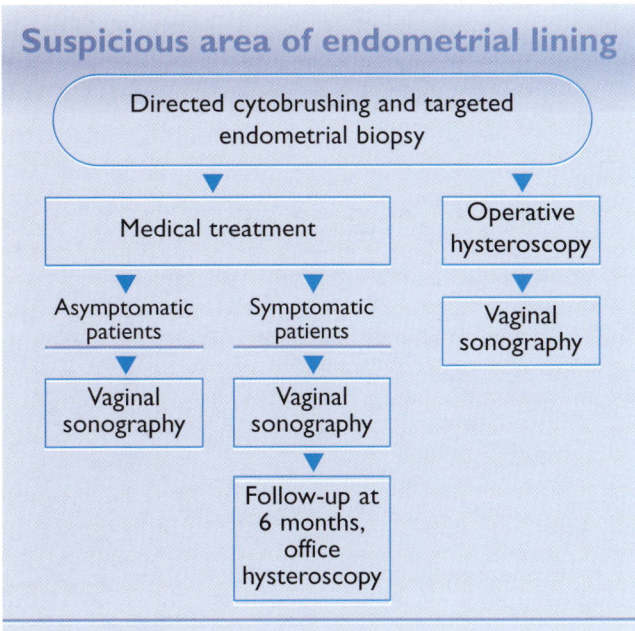

PATIENTS' TOLERANCE OF THE PROCEDURE

An American study was conducted to evaluate patients' tolerance during office hysteroscopy [7]. In 84% of the patients, the procedure was rated as easily accepted discomfort, accepted discomfort, or tolerated discomfort. The results are similar to those we have obtained [8].

OFFICE HYSTEROSCOPY AND ANESTHESIA

As the procedure is very well tolerated, there is no need to use any sedative or premedication. In our experience, the rate of local anesthesia is around 2% with the HYF-XP instrument. If necessary, we perform a paracervical block.

NATIONAL FRENCH SURVEY (35,289 PROCEDURES)

We have coordinated a National French Survey to evaluate the use of fibrohysteroscopes in ambulatory patients without anesthesia for diagnostic evaluation and minor operative procedures.

This survey was conducted for the Club Gynecologique d'Endoscopie Flexible.

Questions and the survey forms were sent to gynecologists who carried out office procedures only, or office and private hospital practice, or university hospital practice only. The total number of procedures reported was 35,289. Two types of fibrohysteroscopes were used. One was the HYF-1T Olympus 4.9 mm with an operating channel of 2.2 mm ($n = 9235$ procedures; 12%). The other hysteroscope was the HYF-P 3.6 mm with an operating channel of 1.2 mm: 27,132 procedures were reported (77%). Both endoscopes were used in 3882 procedures (11%). These data were presented at the AAGL International Meeting held in San Francisco November 2001.

The method of distension was normal saline in 66% (23,095) of procedures. The distribution was 51% university hospital, 38% office, and 11% private hospital. Cervical dilatation before hysteroscopy was necessary in 11% of the cases.

As regards the various indications for hysteroscopy, bleeding and infertility cases cover 50% of the indications. Abnormal hysteroscopy and abnormal ultrasound cases represented 10% and 4%, respectively.

As for combined procedures, they were 56% versus 44% of only visual observation of the uterine cavity. There was a high rate of targeted endometrial biopsies (34%), which is one third of the procedures that were supported by histological proof.

Hysteroscopy combined with diagnostic procedures was reported. Tolerance was rated as good in 90% and medium in 8% of procedures.

The average duration of the procedure was less than 5 minutes in 71% and 5–10 minutes in 27%.

A summary of the 31,844 procedures performed without anesthesia is given in Table 5.

REFERENCES

1. Parent E, Guedj H, Barbot J, Nodarian P. Panoramic Hysteroscopy. Paris: E. Maloine, 1985: 118.
2. Mussuto P. Les défis de la fléxibilité en hystéroscopie. Ses apports diagnostiques et thérapeutiques en gynécologie obstétrique: des perspectives d'avenir. Thesis, Doctorat en Médecine, 1993.
3. Marty R, Mussuto P, Amouroux J, AL. Endometrial biopsy during office hysteroscopy with a 3-French flexible biopsy forceps: evaluation over 69 cases. AAGL International Congress 1990, Book of Abstracts, p. 157.
4. Marty R, Haouet S, Amouroux J. The reliability of endometrial biopsy performed during hysteroscopic evaluation of 89 cases. *Int J Gynaecol Obstet* 1990; **34**: 151–155.
5. Marty R. The targeted endometrial biopsy during flexible hysteroscopy. Technique and results. International Congress of Gynecological Endoscopy, Seoul, Korea, 1992. Abstracts, p. 61.
6. Bergeron C. Histopathologie appliquée à l'hystéroscopy. Gynécologie Internationale. Cours Européen d'Imagerie Gynécologique, 1995. Abstracts, p.19.
7. Bradley L, Widrich T. State-of-the-art flexible hysteroscopy for office gynecologic evaluation. *J Am Assoc Gynecol Laparosc* 1995; **2**: 265.
8. Marty R. Nine years experience with flexible hysteroscopy. In: Isaacson KB, ed. Office Hysteroscopy. St Louis: Mosby Year Book, 1996: 70–71.

Table 5
Fibrohysteroscopy: National French Survey 2001

31,444 procedures without anesthesia	
Normal saline uterine distension	75%
Combined procedures: diagnostic or surgical	55%
5 minutes duration	71%
Good tolerance by patients	90%
Only one type of complication: bleeding	<2%

Blind and hysteroscopically guided endometrial sampling: a pathologist's point of view

Maurizio Colafranceschi

> **Take Home Message**
> The assertion by R.D. Soloway et al (1971) [13] that blind sampling was probably a greater source of error than observer variability has found its solution. Sampling error, which may affect blind endometrial biopsy as well as D&C, can be reduced or removed if hysteroscopy is used with either directed or orientated sampling. If inadequate luteal phase or anovulatory cycle are suspected sampling should be performed at day 22 or later. Only 0.6% of samples demonstrate interruption of pregnancy. AUB sampling at day 5–7 of the bleeding is feasible. Specimens should be taken from the lesion itself. As much information as possible should be given to the pathologist.

INTRODUCTION

For a long time, dilatation and curettage (D&C) has been the standard procedure for obtaining endometrial samples from women with abnormal uterine bleeding (AUB) or infertility. However, the procedure has a high cost matched up to the high prevalence (about 60%) of non-pathologic endometria which are so detected, suggesting that indications for D&C may have been too broad [1]. It should also be noted that a D&C may confer a false sense of security as regards emptying the uterine cavity. De facto, less than half of the uterine cavity is curetted in 60%, less than a quarter in 16%, and less than three-quarters in 84% of patients [2]. In a review of the literature, Gimpelson and Rappold [3] found that D&C failed to detect an intracavitary lesion in 10–35% of patients. The overall sensitivity of D&C was found to be as low as 65% by Loffer [4], and the false-negative rate for the diagnosis of endometrial carcinoma was estimated to be 82.5% by Stock and Kanbour [2]. In Lerner's series [5] comprising five endometrial cancers discovered in uteri excised for benign pathology, only one carcinoma had been recognized previously through curettage. Consequently, D&C is not an accurate diagnostic tool, as it misses large areas of endometrium, frequently fails to detect polyps and myomas, and does not provide the pathologist with selected tissue. In addition, D&C carries an anesthetic risk and a hospital cost.

Endometrial biopsy is a minor operative procedure which does not require cervical dilatation nor anesthesia, causes minimal to moderate discomfort to the patient, and can be performed in the outpatient setting. Novak curette for endometrial biopsy as well as biopsy techniques that use suction to obtain the endometrial sample (such as Vabra and Pipelle), may furnish results equal to D&C without requiring hospitalization. The accuracy of Vabra diagnosis for carcinoma varies from 86.2% [6] to 96% [7] or 98% [8]. According to Grimes [7], specimen adequacy for Vabra aspirates was 85–99% compared to a 77–94% accuracy for D&C, with a lower or null incidence of perforations, hemorrhages, and infectious complications in the Vabra group.

The sensitivity of the Pipelle for the diagnosis of endometrial carcinoma was estimated to be 97.5% by Stovall et al [9]. Comparing Pipelle with Novak curette, these authors found that sample adequacy was approximately 90% for both, and concordance with the diagnosis in excised uteri occurred in 96% of cases [10]. A slightly larger number of patients diagnosed through Novak curette considered sampling to be painful (17% vs 6.7%). In a study by Silver et al [11], pain of moderate to severe intensity was caused by the Novak curette in 76.4%, and by the Pipelle in 45.5% of patients.

As measured by endometrial denudation in hysterectomy specimens, the Pipelle device samples significantly less (4.2%) of the endometrial surface than the Vabra aspirator (41.6%), although the diagnostic accuracy is about the same for both methods – 83.3% for the Pipelle and 84.6% for the Vabra aspirator [12].

In conclusion, sampling devices for endometrial biopsy do not differ significantly in their diagnostic accuracy, although their advantages and disadvantages vary. The inexpensive Novak curette may be easily oriented in the uterine cavity according to necessity, giving a well-preserved strip of full-thickness endometrium. Suction methods allow a more extensive sampling (especially the Vabra aspirator) and are comparatively less painful than the Novak curette, although they are more expensive and may produce suction artifacts in the sampled endometrial fragments (especially Vabra).

HYSTEROSCOPY AND ENDOMETRIAL SAMPLING

Advances in endoscopic biopsy techniques have led to a more thorough understanding of many pathological processes and have significantly enhanced the role of the modern histopathologist in the care of patients with disorders amenable to both medical and surgical treatment. In recent years, hysteroscopy has grown to be an important additional method for assessing the uterine cavity, mainly owing to the fact that, because of their small caliber, diagnostic hysteroscopes do not require cervical dilatation or anesthesia. However, although the hysteroscopic findings can provide a presumptive diagnostic opinion, the hysteroscopic assessment should always be supported by the histological diagnosis, with the possible exception of endometrial atrophy. At present hysteroscopy, accompanied when needed by biopsy or other aspiration techniques, is rapidly replacing D&C in the investigation of endometrial pathology; thus saving time and money and minimizing the patient's discomfort and risks. When biopsy (whatever method is used) is associated with hysteroscopy, diagnostic accuracy is superior to D&C, and sensitivity reaches 98%, with 100% positive predictive value and specificity [4]. The assertion by Soloway et al [13] in 1971 that blind sampling was probably a greater source of error than observer variability has now found a solution.

Generally speaking, biopsy should be a compromise between the volume of tissue required for a reliable interpretation and that which can be removed with acceptable safety and levels of discomfort for the patient [14]. Pathologists are now requested to make accurate diagnoses on smaller and smaller fragments of tissue, given that sampling techniques and hysteroscopy are pushing in this direction. The statement by Dallenbach-Hellweg and Poulsen in 1996 [15] that 'a complete curettage is the ideal method for optimal diagnostic evaluation of the endometrium', while 'for functional diagnosis in infertile patients, endometrial biopsies will usually suffice if properly taken' actually sounds dated, when hysteroscopy is carried out as an outpatient procedure. Histopathology, not unlike medical science, has to be flexible and fine-tuned to changing circumstances [16], rather than confine itself to merely traditional methodology.

Usually, the term biopsy is used in two ways: first, to describe the procedure of tissue removal for diagnostic purposes; second, to describe the tissue that has been removed [14]. Diagnostic hysteroscopy has introduced important modifications to gynecological sampling according to both senses. In fact, in addition to the possibility of orientating the sample after the withdrawal of the instrument depending on the site of the abnormal area, hysteroscopy can be used to perform biopsy under direct vision by introducing the forceps through the sheath of the hysteroscope.

Sampling error, which may affect blind endometrial biopsy as well as D&C, can be reduced or removed if hysteroscopy is used with either directed or orientated sampling. Nonetheless, directed endometrial biopsy, hampered by the very small amount of material that can be sampled in this way, has not gained wide acceptance by gynecologists and pathologists because of the problem of its diagnostic accuracy. It is commonly affirmed that an inadequate amount of tissue yields an unsatisfactory or limited diagnosis [17], and that only in a few diseases (i.e. cancer) is there a pathognomonic pattern imprinted on such small pieces of tissue that, alone, the histopathologist can make a diagnosis [14]. Since atypia is frequently focal in the context of complex endometrial hyperplasia, an extensive sampling is required when complex/atypical hyperplasia is suspected in order to reassure the pathologist in excluding atypia. Moreover, the difficulties in discriminating between atypical endometrial hyperplasia and well-differentiated endometrioid carcinoma may be significant even in curettings, especially in young women.

Therefore, a well-trained pathologist is needed to make a reliable diagnosis on a square millimeter or even smaller area sampled by directed biopsy, which includes a few endometrial glands only [18]. Modern histopathology calls for both an intimate knowledge of biopsy appearances and the ability to interpret biopsies in the context of contemporary clinical practice; therefore, the confidence of the pathologist in the reliability of the sample increases with practice and communication with the clinician. Where is the boundary for specimen inadequacy? For pathologists with an old-fashioned mindset, accustomed to the abundance of material and supposedly adequate pattern of endometrial curettings, dismissal of the biopsy as inadequate and unsuitable for diagnosis is tempting [19]. Surely these small specimens are not always appropriate for a definitive diagnosis and exclusion of pathology? However, when the histological assessment is consistent with the hysteroscopic pattern, diagnostic credibility is greatly increased. Hence, after an unprejudiced evaluation of the histological picture in the first instance, the pathologist has always to consider (i.e. be informed about) the hysteroscopic pattern before making the definite diagnosis. Feinstein's opinion [20] that pathologists should make their diagnoses simply by looking, without exercising inference, not to be influenced by clinical data, should be discarded as potentially unsafe for both the patient and the pathologist. In fact, interpreting the biopsy demands a logical approach that should consider many factors, including patient history and the specific needs of the clinician [21].

TIMING OF SAMPLING

When inadequate luteal phase or anovulatory cycle are suspected, sampling should be performed on cycle day 22 or later (POD 8 or M-7, that is ≤7 days before the onset of the upcoming menstrual period). Endometrial histomorphology may then reveal postovulatory out-of-phase secretory changes or persistent proliferative endometrium. With this exception, blind endometrial sampling is generally advocated at the onset of the uterine bleeding [22], owing to the dilatation of the external os and the lower uterine segment which facilitate the introduction of the sampling device, while the risk of interfering with an unknown pregnancy is avoided. However, endometrial biopsy in infertility patients does not appear to result in increased fetal wastage – which, paradoxically, may be reduced – even if performed in the cycle of conception [23,24]. However, according to Kaminski and Lyon [25], approximately 0.6% of the samples obtained for investigation of infertility demonstrated interrruption of a pregnancy.

The diagnosis of irregular shedding, which is attributed to a persistent function of the corpus luteum, is feasible on days 5–7 of bleeding.

Hysteroscopic examination is best performed in the postmenstrual phase because a clear view is obtained when traumatic bleeding from secretory endometrium is avoided and the endocervical transit is easier. In patients with abnormal uterine bleeding, waiting until the bleeding ceases may cause the temporary loss of the diagnostic tissue, such as endometrial hyperplasia.

SELECTION OF BIOPSY SITE AND DIRECTED BIOPSY (Figures 1–4)

Specimens should be taken from the lesion itself, or from the body on the anterior wall or fundus region when diffuse endometrial pathology is suspected. Apart from directed biopsy – where the volume is rather regular (0.6–1.0 mm^2) [18] – the amount of tissue obtained by sampling is often related to the clinical situation, varying from scant (atrophy) to abundant (secretory endometrum, hyperplasia, carcinoma).

Since small fragments from an endometrial polyp may resemble endometrial hyperplasia or even a well-differentiated adenocarcinoma, directed sampling of the suspected lesion may help in resolving this diagnostic uncertainty. When directed biopsy is performed, multiple samples (three or more) should be collected from the selected site to increase the diagnostic accuracy. Colafranceschi et al [18] noted that, if multiple directed

Figure 1
Well-performed directed endometrial biopsy showing proliferative endothelium (H&E, ×50).

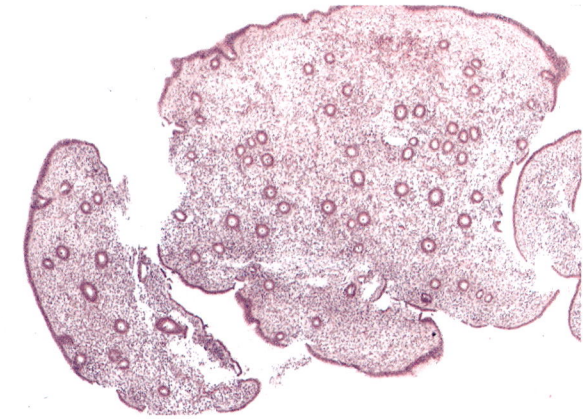

Figure 2
Directed endometrial biopsy showing secretory endometrium (H&E, ×50).

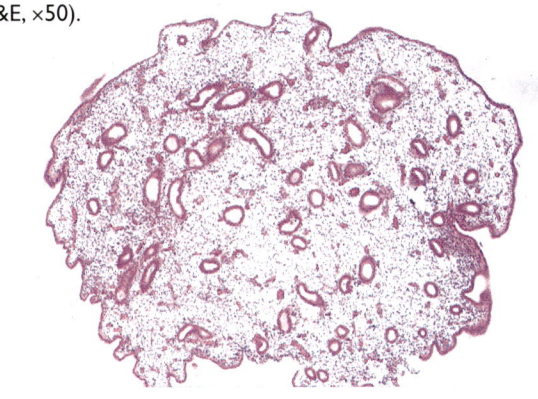

Figure 3
'Stripped' directed endometrial biopsy performed by Bettocchi's technique. Proliferative endothelium can be easily recognized (H&E, ×50).

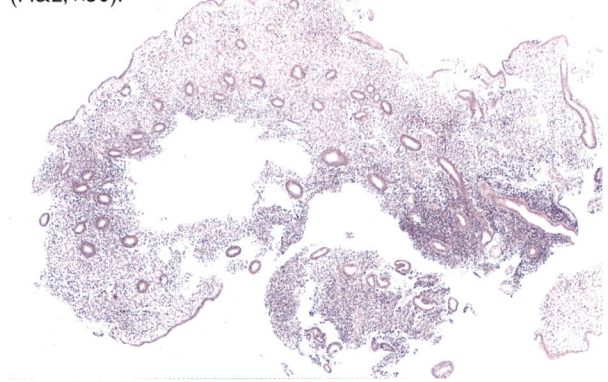

biopsies were taken, the amount of inadequate samples decreased from 9.1% to 1.3% and the agreement of directed biopsy with the reference histological diagnosis rose from 78.8% to 94.8%. In fact, the overall diagnosis is best achieved by integration of multiple findings, because the distinctive features of endometrial hyperplasia may not be present in all specimens owing to focality or regressive changes. In the same study, the diagnostic reliability of directed biopsies was shown to be influenced by the endometrial pattern, the highest rate of disagreement pertaining to proliferative endometrium and hyperplasia, while the diagnosis of endometrial atrophy or suppressed endometrium (oral contraceptive effect) was centered in all cases.

Considering the limits of directed sampling, the practice of orientating the sampling device according to prior hysteroscopic examination appears preferable, especially in diffuse endometrial pathology. The results are usually satisfactory and there is a consistent advantage over blind sampling even when focal pathology is present. The advantage of directed sampling is limited to very small lesions and to the need for correlating the hysteroscopic pattern with the histological pattern with maximal accuracy.

Whatever the sampling method, the final fragment(s) are always irregularly orientated, and frequently mixed with blood and mucus. Endometrial sampling of the isthmic mucosa should be avoided, because it may cause a misinterpretation, suggesting an endometrium responsive to cyclic hormonal stimuli or a fragment of a polyp if the pathologist does not recognize the particular site. Likewise, fragments of the basalis, which does not cycle with the functionalis, may lead to the erroneous diagnosis of a weakly proliferative endometrium.

Figure 4
Directed endometrial biopsy. The diagnosis of simple endometrial hyperplasia may be suggested despite the small size of the sample (H&E, ×80).

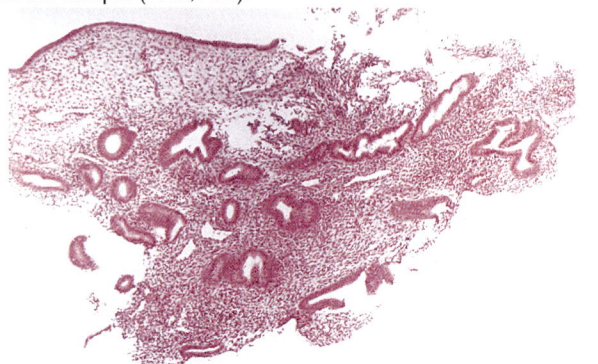

INFORMATION TO BE GIVEN TO THE PATHOLOGIST

Given that the indications for endometrial biopsy are identification of the cause of abnormal uterine bleeding, endometrial evaluation in infertile patients, and assessment of endometrial response to hormonal treatment, the knowledge of an adequate clinical history is mandatory for the pathologist. This includes the patient's age, menstrual/menopausal status (last menstrual period), pattern and amount of bleeding, any hormonal treatment or contraceptive use, pertinent medical history, and reason for endometrial sampling [17]. A brief description of the hysteroscopic appearance with the presumptive diagnosis should be referred to the pathologist when hysteroscopy with biopsy is performed. A synoptic checklist, coding the regions of the uterine body, may be useful for easy identification of the sampled areas.

Unfortunately, part of the aforementioned information is frequently lacking in the clinical forms, and the pathologist must be prepared to address many endometrial specimens with a minimal amount of information [21].

Patient age is important for assessing the risk of endometrial carcinoma in patients with abnormal uterine bleeding (AUB). In a multicenter study coordinated by the author in 1988 for the European Society of Hysteroscopy (ESH), endometrial carcinoma caused the bleeding in 13.8% (82/447) of postmenopausal and in 0.9% (6/628) of premenopausal patients [26]. In a series of 1075 AUB patients collected in the Florentine Department of Pathology, the risk of detecting endometrial carcinoma was as high as 50% in patients older than 80 years of age. In 1974 Hofmeister [27] reported that 17% of endometrial carcinomas diagnosed by routine office biopsy occurred in asymptomatic perimenopausal women. In a review by Caspi et al [28], the finding of a gynecological malignancy ranged from 17% to 63% as a cause of postmenopausal AUB.

Although hysteroscopy is not a substitute for histological diagnosis, endometrial atrophy shows a higher probability of validation by the pathologist compared with other hysteroscopic diagnoses. In the ESH multicenter study, the hysteroscopic assessment of endometrial atrophy had to be upgraded to the diagnosis of simple endometrial hyperplasia in only 7.2% (13/180) of postmenopausal AUB patients [26]. Endometrial atrophy was diagnosed in 40.4% of postmenopausal AUB patients in the ESH series [26] (and in 38.9% of the Florentine series), while this diagnosis was neglible in premenopausal women. The same degree of confidence was not reached by the hysteroscopic assessment of endometrial hyperplasia: in 217 histologically proven cases of hyperplasia, the positive predictive value of hysteroscopy was 58.1%, sensitivity 60.8%, negative predictive value 90%, and specificity 88.9%.

While these data confirm that the hysteroscopic diagnosis should remain presumptive until confirmed by histology, it has to be stressed that only the possibility of correlating the biopsy pattern with the clinical history can provide the most accurate final diagnosis. Direct verbal communication between the pathologist and the gynecologist (and vice versa) may greatly enhance the diagnostic accuracy in difficult or controversial cases.

INFORMATION TO BE GIVEN TO THE CLINICIAN

With the exception of a few cases, it is essential for the pathologist to avoid the statement that the specimen is inadequate for histological assessment, because this assertion may compel the gynecologist to repeat the procedure [19]. Therefore, it is advisable to report the tissue components that are present and let the gynecologist choose the modus operandi, being aware that these scanty specimens cannot be awarded the same degree of credence and infallibility that is generally attributed to the tissue diagnosis. Nevertheless, the histological diagnosis of endometrial atrophy often relies on very small specimens containing few atrophic glands on a fibrous stroma, and these should be considered representative enough to assess the reliability of the final diagnosis.

In the report, the pathologist should also note the absence of findings consistent with the concern of hyperplasia or carcinoma in order to reassure the gynecologist or, vice versa, alert the gynecologist to repeat the sampling. Likewise, the diagnosis of dysfunctional uterine bleeding in a premenopausal patient requires that the absence of organic lesions is substantiated in both histological and hysteroscopic investigations.

PREPARATION OF THE ENDOMETRIAL SPECIMEN

The specimen should be fixed immediately after removal to avoid autolytic artifacts, which develop rapidly and may hamper an accurate morphologic interpretation. The sampled material should be placed in 10% neutral buffered formalin or in Bouin's solution. This latter tissue fixative yields comparatively better cytological details, but it must be freshly prepared. Moreover, the operator should avoid contact between the cutting edge of the sampling instrument and the solution, owing to the highly corrosive properties of glacial acetic acid. For general purposes, when subtle endometrial changes do not need to be preserved, the widely used formalin fixative is more convenient for storage, and is more practical for use. Care should be taken that the container is tightly closed to avoid leakage of the fixative resulting in rapid autolysis of the specimen.

HANDLING OF THE SAMPLES

Great care must be exercised in handling endometrial biopsies, as they are characteristically scant. The tip of the curette or the forceps, when one biopsy is performed, can be passed through the formalin fixative to remove small fragments that might remain adhered to the instrument. Placing the specimen on a surgical sponge or gauze pad is not advisable, because these may absorb and hide from view the tiny fragments of tissue [29].

The whole sample should be submitted to the laboratory for complete processing, leaving it to the pathologist to carry out selection of the abundant material obtained.

In the laboratory, the entire biopsy specimen should be wrapped in nonabsorbent tissue paper before enclosing it in a labelled cassette, to avoid losing small fragments during processing. The pathologist should be accustomed to cut the paraffin block at multiple levels to prevent inadequate sectioning.

Generally, endometrial samples do not require special staining techniques for diagnosis, as routine hematoxylin and eosin (H&E) will suffice in most cases. When required, H&E staining may be accompanied by additional methods: van Gieson's solution for demonstrating the stroma of endometrial polyps and hyalinized placental villi; reticulin impregnation for demonstrating the lysis of reticulin fibres in collapsed endometrial stroma; periodic acid-Schiff reaction (PAS) for detecting glycogen or mucopolysaccharides in glandular cells. Immunohistochemical stains may occasionally be useful to evaluate estrogen/progesterone receptors in the endometrium of infertility patients and proliferation markers in malignant neoplasms.

ARTIFACTS

Artifacts can be rather confounding for inexperienced pathologists, especially when present in small specimens. Endometrial artifacts range from gland/stroma retraction (fixation artifact) to telescoping (intussusception) (Figure 5) or crowding of endometrial glands caused by squeezing of the tissue and disruption of the stroma (sampling artifacts). Hence, biopsy-induced artifacts may occasionally be mistaken for endometrial hyperplasia, while autolytic artifacts – such as clear spaces around the glands – may be a problem for accurate endometrial dating when the biopsy is taken for functional interpretation (i.e. to confirm ovulation or to diagnose luteal phase defect). The suction artifact induced by aspiration techniques may mimic the cyclic stromal edema of phasic endometrium.

In operative hysteroscopy, coagulation necrosis of resected chips caused by thermal damage may hamper the histological assessment in such a way that no diagnosis is further possible (this happened in 3.1% of the patients in the study reported by Colafranceschi et al [30]). Therefore, the risk of a previously undiagnosed endometrial carcinoma remaining undetected following resection should be taken into account [31]. Proper instrument setting and the operator's ability, as well as the volume and thickness of the samples (the more, the better), all combine to reduce the degree of thermal damage in endometrial chips [30].

Figure 5
Directed endometrial biopsy, showing secretory endometrium with evident telescoping artifact in some gland lumina (H&E, ×50).

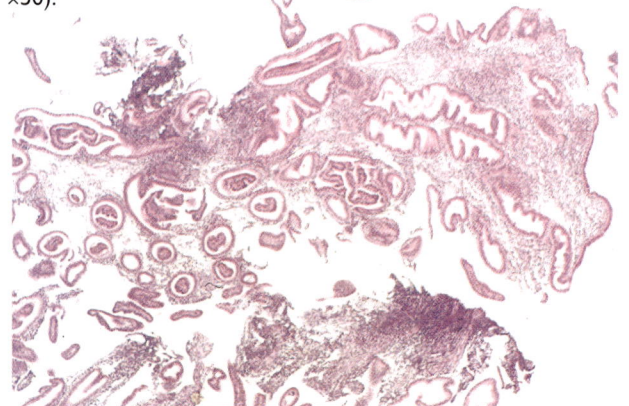

REFERENCES

1. Smith JJ, Schulman H. Current dilatation and curettage practice: a need for revision. *Obstet Gynecol* 1985; **65**: 516–518.
2. Stock RJ, Kanbour A. Prehysterectomy curettage. *Obstet Gynecol* 1975; **45**: 537–541.
3. Gimpelson RJ, Rappold HO. A comparative study between panoramic hysteroscopy with directed biopsies and dilatation and curettage. A review of 276 cases. *Am J Obstet Gynecol* 1988; **158**: 489–492.
4. Loffer FD. Hysteroscopy with selective endometrial sampling compared with D&C for abnormal uterine bleeding: the value of a negative hysteroscopic view. *Obstet Gynecol* 1989; **73**: 16–20.
5. Lerner HM. Lack of efficacy of prehysterectomy curettage as a diagnostic procedure. *Am J Obstet Gynecol* 1984; **148**: 1055–1056.
6. Vuopala S. Diagnostic accuracy and clinical applicability of cytological and histological methods for investigating endometrial carcinoma. *Acta Obstet Gynecol Scand Suppl* 1977; **70**: 1–72.
7. Grimes DA. Diagnostic dilation and curettage: a reappraisal. *Am J Obstet Gynecol* 1982; **142**: 1–6.
8. Lutz MH, Underwood PB, Kreutner A, Mitchell KS. Vacuum aspiration: an efficient outpatient screening technique for endometrial disease. *South Med J* 1977; **70**: 393–395.
9. Stovall TG, Photopulos GJ, Poston WM, Ling FW, Sandles LG. Pipelle endometrial sampling in patients with known endometrial carcinoma. *Obstet Gynecol* 1991; **77**: 954–956.
10. Stovall TG, Ling FW, Morgan PL. A prospective, randomized comparison of the Pipelle endometrial sampling device with the Novak curette. *Am J Obstet Gynecol* 1991; **165**: 1287–1290.
11. Silver MM, Miles P, Rosa C. Comparison of Novak and Pipelle endometrial biopsy instruments. *Obstet Gynecol* 1991; **78**: 828–830.
12. Rodriguez GC, Yaqub N, King ME. A comparison of the Pipelle device and Vabra aspirator as measured by endometrial denudation in hysterectomy specimens: the Pipelle device samples significantly less of the endometrial surface than the Vabra aspirator. *Am J Obstet Gynecol* 1993; **168**: 55–59.
13. Soloway RD, Baggenstoss AH, Schoenfield LJ, Summerskill WH. Observer error and sampling variability tested in evaluation of hepatitis and cirrhosis by liver biopsy. *Am J Dig Dis* 1971; **16**: 1082–1086.
14. Underwood JCE. Introduction to Biopsy Interpretation and Surgical Pathology. Berlin: Springer-Verlag, 1981.
15. Dallenbach-Hellweg G, Poulsen H. Atlas of Endometrial Histopathology, 2nd edn. Berlin: Springer-Verlag, 1996: 1.
16. Kornberg A. Pathology, pathologists, and the new biology. *Arch Pathol Lab Med* 1977; **101**: 397–399.
17. Heller DS. Histopathology of the endometrium – an overview. In: The Endometrium – A Clinicopathologic Approach. Tokyo: Igaku-Shoin, 1994: 43–55.
18. Colafranceschi M, van Herendael B, Perino A et al. Reliability of endometrial biopsy under direct hysteroscopic control. *Gynaecol Endosc* 1995; **4**: 119–122.
19. Anderson MC, Robboy SJ, Russell P, Morse A. The normal endometrium. In: Robboy SJ, Anderson MC, Russell P, eds. Pathology of the Female Reproductive Tract. London: Churchill Livingstone, 2002: 241–265.
20. Feinstein AR. Clinical Judgement. Baltimore: Williams and Wilkins, 1967: 80.
21. Mazur MT, Kurman RJ Diagnosis of Endometrial Biopsies and Curettings – A Practical Approach. New York: Springer-Verlag, 1995: 1–6.
22. Arronet GH, Bergquist CA, Parekh MC, Latour JP, Marshall KG. Evaluation of endometrial biopsy in the cycle of conception. *Int J Fertil* 1973; **18**: 220–225.
23. Cove H. Surgical Pathology of the Endometrium. Philadelphia: JB Lippincott, 1981: 5.
24. Taddei GL, Colafranceschi M, Coccia E, Pellegrini S, Pieri A, Tantini C. Does endometrial biopsy performed during the cycle of conception interfere with pregnancy? In: ESH 5th European Congress on Hysteroscopy and Endoscopic Surgery, Hamburg, Germany, 3–6 June 1992: abstract 54, p. 30.
25. Kaminski PF, Lyon DS. Implications of sampling the implantation site in the endometrial biopsy for infertility. *J Reprod Med* 1990; **38**: 208–210.
26. Colafranceschi M. Hysteroscopy in abnormal uterine bleeding: a multicentric study. In: 3rd European Congress on Hysteroscopy and Endoscopic Surgery, Amsterdam, The Netherlands, 14–17 September, 1988: abstracts, p. 30.
27. Hofmeister FJ. Endometrial biopsy: another look. *Am J Obstet Gynecol* 1974; **118**: 773–777.
28. Caspi E, Perpinial S, Reif A. Incidence of malignancy in Jewish women with post-menopausal bleeding. *Isr J Med Sci* 1977; **13**: 299–304.
29. Hernandez E, Atkinson BF. Clinical Gynecologic Pathology. Philadelphia: WB Saunders, 1996: 280.
30. Colafranceschi M, van Herendael B, Mencaglia L, Bettocchi S, Bolis GB, Hänsch O. Endometrial resection: histological study. In: 5th European Congress on Hysteroscopy and Endoscopic Surgery, Rome, Italy, 15–18 June 1994: abstracts, p. 5.
31. Colafranceschi M, Bettocchi S, Mencaglia L, van Herendael BJ. Missed hysteroscopic detection of uterine carcinoma before uterine resection: report of three cases. *Gynecol Oncol* 1996; **62**: 298–300.

18 Liquid distension media and their complications

Rafael F. Valle

> **Take Home Message**
> The office or the outpatient set up should not be mistaken for an operating theater. The procedures should be simple and limited in duration. It is important to maintain the osmolality of the plasma at 280–300 mOsmol/L. Low viscosity fluids without electrolytes are more dangerous than fluids with electrolytes. In case of excessive fluid absorption with the latter pulmonary edema may occur but hyponatremia is the exception. Close monitoring of the fluid is mandatory to avoid the TURE syndrome (the equivalent of the TURP syndrome in urology). If the syndrome occurs hyponatremia should be corrected slowly.

INTRODUCTION

Office hysteroscopy, whether diagnostic or operative, should be a relatively easy, quick, and complication-free procedure. The fact that cervical dilatation is avoided and the introduction of small caliber hysteroscopes is performed under direct view, practically should eliminate any chance of uterine laceration or perforation. Similarly, because operative procedures should be relatively simple and expeditious, problems of fluid overload should be nonexistent. Unfortunately, despite these warnings, serious complications have occurred when the office method is extended far beyond its capabilities, confusing the office with the operating theater. Clinical judgment and common sense sometimes get mixed up with the idea of attempting the performance of difficult procedures in the office setting with the false premises of saving time, inconvenience to the patient, and cost. None of these premises should ever replace safety, efficacy, and adequate treatment. With this in mind, this chapter is written so that the physiologic principles of these fluids and their interactions are well understood and therefore their possible complications can be avoided.

The frequency of operative hysteroscopy has increased remarkably in the last two decades. This is due partly to better instrumentation and partly to physicians' awareness of the value of treating endoscopically many gynecologic conditions that in the past required a hysterectomy or extensive blind transcervical manipulations that only occasionally were able to treat pathologic conditions adequately. In the early 1980s, new applications were introduced for hysteroscopic surgery and the resectoscope was adapted for gynecologic use, providing the capability of using electrosurgery within the uterine cavity. These changes included the use of low viscosity fluids to distend the uterus, with or without electrolytes, depending on the instrument used. Some hysteroscopic operations require extensive dissections, resections of the endometrium or removal of submucous leiomyomas that partially penetrate the uterine wall. This has meant that the time and exposure of open endometrial and myometrial vessels to this fluid brings about a problem not frequently seen before with hysteroscopy, i.e. the excessive absorption of low viscosity fluids, which sometimes leads to pulmonary edema and hyponatremia, if the fluids are devoid of sodium. As gynecologists became aware of these problems, attempts were made to prevent these conditions before they occurred, and when they did, to treat them appropriately [1–6].

PHYSIOLOGIC CONSIDERATION OF LOW VISCOSITY FLUIDS AND ELECTROLYTES

When fluids are administered parenterally to patients, it is important to maintain the osmolality of the plasma, which is 280–300 mOsmol/L. Most parenteral fluids upon injection maintain this osmolality by containing substances that permit their infusion. Maintenance of osmolality is particularly achieved with electrolytes, should the infused fluid require electrolytes, and when devoid of electrolytes other substances or solutes are used. However, in this latter situation these substances (glycine, sorbitol, or mannitol) may not remain in the vascular system for long, and therefore fluid free of these substances used for maintaining osmolality may decrease the overall serum osmolality, thus triggering fluid overload [7].

When fluids with electrolytes are used – such as Ringer lactate, normal saline, dextrose 5% in half normal saline –

the serum osmolality is maintained by sodium and its associated chloride or bicarbonate. Therefore, when excessive fluid absorption occurs, while the patient may develop pulmonary edema, hyponatremia does not occur. However, when fluids devoid of electrolytes such as glycine 1.5%, sorbitol 3%, or mannitol 5% are used, free fluid may remain in the intravascular tree, triggering early fluid overload and hyponatremia because of the lack of electrolytic components.

Glycine 1.5% is a nonelectrolytic irrigating fluid commonly used for transurethral surgical procedures. It is a sterile, nonpyrogenic, hypotonic solution of the amino acid glycine. It is a nonelectrolytic solution with an osmolality of 200 mOsmol/L. Its degradation will produce ammonia and oxalate crystals as byproducts, which can cause problems of mental confusion and/or precipitation of oxalate crystals in the kidney should excessive degradation occur.

Sorbitol 3% solution also can be used to distend the uterus. It is a nonelectrolytic solution, electrically nonconductive and with an osmolality of 165 mOsmol/L. Because it is a reduced form of dextrose, it is metabolized to carbon dioxide and water and/or excreted by a normally functioning kidney.

Finally, mannitol 5% is an inert substance with an osmolality of 270 mOsmol/L that acts as a diuretic and helps in the removal of free water if excessive amounts have been absorbed. About 6–10% of the absorbed mannitol is metabolized and the remainder is filtered by the kidney. The half-life of mannitol in the plasma is 15 minutes. However, being an intravascular osmol, when administered, it may increase the intravascular volume as well [7].

High viscosity fluids such as dextran 32% or Hyskon were used frequently in the late 1970s and early 1980s, as a medium to distend the uterine cavity. At present its use has decreased significantly owing to the poor recovery when infused in the uterine cavity, as no continuous flow can be established with the instrumentation available; therefore, its use has decreased as compared with low viscosity fluids. Nonetheless, it is still a good alternative as a distending medium owing to its high viscosity, which means that only small amounts are required to perform minor procedures. However, because of its osmotic properties, if it is not recovered after injection in the uterus, it may trigger pulmonary edema by increasing the vascular osmotic pressure. Furthermore, if excessive amounts (>500 ml) are absorbed it may also trigger changes in coagulation factors, producing intravascular coagulation that may cause alarming bleeding, with changes in fibrinogen, clotting factors V, VIII and IX, and the factor VIII-Von Willebrand complex. It has been calculated that the fluid accumulated in the intravascular tree by osmotic absorption will be about 10 times the amount of dextran absorbed. Additionally, because of its large molecular weight (>70,000), it may not be well filtered by the kidney and because of its long half-life in the intravascular tree (up to 6–7 days), plasmapheresis may be required on occasion in cases of excessive intravascular absorption, if the patient fails to respond to appropriate ventilation and diuretics [8,9].

FLUIDS AND ELECTROLYTES: FLUID OVERLOAD AND HYPONATREMIA

Because sometimes electrosurgery is not required in the uterine cavity, operative hysteroscopy is performed with mechanical instruments or with lasers. These methods do not imply conduction, therefore, it is important to use fluids with electrolytes. Ringer lactate, normal saline, or dextrose 5% in normal saline are most appropriate for these procedures. Nonetheless, fluid overload may still occur despite the fact that the threshold or limits for toxicity have changed. Therefore, appropriate monitoring of both inflow and outflow is most important and if intravasation of >1.5–2 liters of fluid occurs, immediate diuresis should be established to prevent pulmonary edema (Tables 1 and 2) [10].

Three factors should be taken into consideration when administering fluids into the uterus under pressure: (a) control of intrauterine pressure to no more than 100 mmHg, so as not to over-ride the mean arterial pressure (MAP), (b) expedite the procedure, limiting the time taken to usually no more than 1 hour, and (c) avoid or limit extensive intramyometrial dissections [11–13].

Although electronic pumps have been introduced on the market that can provide a controlled intrauterine pressure, it is also important to bear in mind the type of procedure that is performed and to be very cautious about surgical invasion into the myometrial wall, because if the myometrium is invaded at 3–4 mm depth from the surface the intrauterine pressure required for intravasation will certainly be much lower than 100 mmHg. Therefore, these procedures should be expedited and an accurate record of the amount of fluid infused and recovered should be available, so that the deficit can be calculated (Table 3) [11,12].

Many methods have been proposed to maintain an adequate balance of fluids during operative hysteroscopy, in addition to the measuring of inflow and outflow. These include mixing the fluids with ethanol 1%, analysing the content of alcohol in the fluids by a breath analyser, and thus deriving the amount of fluid absorbed. However, while

Table 1
Water and sodium chloride concentration per liter (electrolytes in millimoles)

Product	Calories	Na	Cl
Sodium chloride (NaCl) 0.45%	–	77	77
Dextrose 5% in 0.45% NaCl	170	77	77
Dextrose 10% in 0.45% NaCl	340	77	77
Normal saline (0.9% NaCl)	–	154	154
Dextrose 5% in 0.9% NaCl	170	154	154
Dextrose 10% in 0.9% NaCl	340	154	154
Sodium chloride 3% in water*	...	513	513
Sodium chloride 5% in water*	...	855	855

* Hypertonic solutions, not for regular IV use.

Table 2
Water and sodium chloride concentration per liter (electrolytes in millimoles)

Product	Calories	Na	Cl	K	Ca	Lactate
Lactated Ringer solution (Hartmann's)	9	130	110	4	1.5	28
Dextrose 5% in lactated Ringer solution	179	130	110	4	1.5	28
Dextrose 5% and lactated Ringer solution with 20 KCl	179	130	129	24	1.5	28
Dextrose 5% and lactated Ringer solution with 40 KCl	179	130	149	44	1.5	28

Table 3
Factors influencing intravasation of distending media

- Type of medium: CO_2, Hyskon, low viscosity fluids
- Intrauterine pressure: >MAP; myometrial invasion >4 mm
- Length of procedure (>1 hour)
- Amount of fluid used
- No outflow, no continuous flow
- Tubes tied
- No cervical leakage
- Type of procedure: > if damage to endo/myometrium
- Partial perforation
- Excessive IV fluid infusion

Table 4
Hysteroscopic myomectomy: avoiding fluid overload

- Discuss with anesthesiologist: complexity of procedure, IV fluids, patient's risks, etc.
- Consider epidural anesthesia in high risk patients
- Indwelling catheter to monitor urine output
- Accurate account of fluid deficit (inflow–outflow)
- Look for signs of decompensation: vital signs, decreased oxygenation (pulse oximetry), hypothermia (esophageal probe), EKG, etc.
- If deficit is >800 ml: evaluate electrolytes (Na), status of procedure, patient's condition, etc.
- STOP the procedure if: deficit is >1000 ml, electrolytes (Na) decreased, + signs of decompensation, extended time is needed to complete the procedure

this method may be another adjunct to monitoring the deficit, it may not give an accurate account of total fluids absorbed, particularly interstitial fluids; therefore, it should be used as an adjunct and not as the only method to monitor the fluid lost during hysteroscopic surgery [14,15].

Because the most threatening situations of fluid overload may occur with fluids devoid of electrolytes, it is important to monitor electrolytes, specifically sodium, serially during an operation. At present there are systems involving micro-chip computers that can provide instant results or point of care results of tested electrolytes, that require a minimal amount of whole blood and determine the level of electrolytes, specifically sodium, in <2 minutes. These methods are most useful for operative hysteroscopy and will provide point of care testing for prevention rather than monitoring electrolytes for treatment, as has been traditionally done.

Because the threshold of toxicity is greater with fluids devoid of electrolytes, it is important to be meticulous in the monitoring of inflow and outflow. Should a deficit of ≥1 liter occur, immediate monitoring of electrolytes (sodium), should be done and then diuresis and electrolyte replacement should be instituted. Additionally, all anesthesia monitoring devices must be rigorously observed (particularly with patients under general anesthesia), such as pulse oximetry, esophageal temperature, vital signs, and urine output (Tables 4–6) [10].

THE 'TURP' SYNDROME ('TURE' SYNDROME IN GYNECOLOGY)

The post-TURP syndrome is a constellation of symptoms and signs associated with absorption of large volumes of nonelectrolytic distending media. Patients develop bradycardia and hypertension followed by hypotension, nausea, vomiting, headache, visual disturbances, agitation, confusion, and lethargy. The symptoms are a result of hypervolemia, dilutional hyponatremia, and decreased osmolality. If unrecognized and untreated the syndrome may result in seizures, cardiovascular collapse, and death [7]. This syndrome is well known by both urologists and anesthesiologists. Because women, particularly menstruating women, are apparently at greater risk of developing this problem – due perhaps to some derangement of ATP-ase, a brain enzyme that helps in extruding water and solutes to protect itself – the transuterine resection (TURE) syndrome is more dangerous in these women and increases their likelihood of dying if treatment is not provided early in its development [16]. The brain extrudes solutes in defense of fluid overload and hyponatremia. However, should hyponatremia become chronic (usually >48 hours) then the treatment of sodium replacement should be more cautiously undertaken to avoid brain demyelinization. This is because the solutes that have been extruded may take a longer period of time to be replaced. Therefore, if a rapid correction of hyponatremia is instituted, there will be a

Table 5
Correlation of glycine 1.5% intravasation and lowering of serum sodium

Fluid absorption (ml)	Serum sodium (mOsm/L)
<500	0–2.5
500	4–5
1000	8–10
2000	16–20
>2000	>20

Table 6
Management of fluid overload during hysteroscopy

Serum sodium deficit (mOsm)	Fluid deficit (ml)	Corrective measures (Rx)
0.5	≤500	No measures
8–10	1000	Careful observation (Na, diuresis)
16–20	2000	DC procedure (serial Na determination replacement, diuresis)
>20	>2000 dangerous zone, could be fatal	ICU (consultation, Na replacement, diuresis)

shifting of fluids towards the vascular system, producing brain desiccation upon a rapid treatment of hyponatremia, which will remove fluids from the brain to correct the transient hyperosmolality produced by the infusion of excessive amounts of sodium. In the acute state this may be resolved by adding 1–2 mOsmol per hour with a total of no more than 12 mOsmol in 24 hours to correct acute onset of hyponatremia. Nevertheless, patients will require monitoring in an intensive care unit, with serial determination of electrolytes and urine output. Usually hypertonic saline solutions for correction of hyponatremia are not required and normal saline may be sufficient [17,18]. This condition usually resolves in 12–24 hours.

It is for these reasons that when extensive dissections in the uterus are foreseen, regional anesthesia may be the anesthetic of choice, as the patient will remain awake and the first signs of intoxication will show with some confusion and tremor and/or nausea and headache.

No attempt should be made to normalize serum sodium rapidly, but only to achieve a level where serious secondary problems will not occur; therefore, 130–135 mOsmol/L should be the goal.

MONITORING SYSTEMS (PROTOCOLS) TO PREVENT FLUID OVERLOAD

The occurrence of fluid overload will be more common when extensive dissections are carried out in the uterus, such as the removal of submucous leiomyomas (particularly those that have a large intramural component), endometrial resection, division of a large wide uterine septum, and dissection of extensive intrauterine adhesions.

Several scoring systems have been introduced in an attempt to predict which patients are more prone to absorb >1 liter of fluid. Molnar et al [19] proposed a scoring system for patients undergoing endometrial resection in an attempt to select those patients who were more at risk of absorbing >1 liter of fluid during a hysteroscopic procedure. For endometrial resection they propose a score that divides patients into low, medium, and high risk categories for fluid overload with scoring assigned to different features: parity from 0 to 3, when parity existed the score was 0 and when no parity existed the score was 3. Endometrial preparation with GnRH analogs score 0 when not given and 1 when given. Uterine cavity length <8 cm was assigned a score of 0; 8 cm length a score of 1, 9–10 cm a score of 2 and >10 cm a score of 3. The presence of a submucous fibroid added a score of 3 to the scoring system and 0 when not present (Tables 7 and 8). While this and other scoring systems may be helpful, it is important (rather than assigning different scoring numbers) to remember that the larger the uterine cavity the more time may be utilized in performing the procedure. The presence of a large submucous leiomyoma also may increase not only time but dissection of the uterine wall; and similarly the lack of endometrial suppression may make the procedure more difficult and more lengthy (and vice versa). Also, the vascular constriction produced by GnRH analogs may decrease the fluid intravasated during any procedure.

NEW OPERATING INSTRUMENTS SIMULATING BIPOLAR SYSTEMS

There has been great interest in introducing electrosurgical electrodes that can be operated under saline solution. While not truly bipolar, they simulate a bipolar system by bypassing the electrical current from one electrode to another and increasing the current density, creating a vapor chamber that activates the energy and destroys the tissue by vaporization. These methods, such as the Endometrial Resection Ablation (ERA) Sleeve, the VersaPoint, and other similar electrodes that may be activated under saline solutions are being used now in clinical practice. Nevertheless, it is important to remember that excessive saline solution, if not monitored, may still produce pulmonary edema. Furthermore, when excessive saline solutions are used and the urine output is not well

Table 7
Preoperative fluid overload risk score for endometrial ablation

	Score			
	0	1	2	3
Parous	Yes	…	…	No
Endometrial preparation	Yes	No	…	…
Cavity length (cm)	<8	8	9–10	>10
Submucous fibroid	No	…	…	Yes

Table 8
Fluid overload risk-score for endometrial ablation (>1 liter absorption)

Risk	Score
Low	0–2
Medium	3–7
High	≥8

Adapted from Molnar et al. [19].

monitored, the patient may excrete hypertonic saline and produce what is known as a desalination process. This involves the excretion of hypertonic urine, usually accompanied by sodium and potassium and the liberation of free water in the intravascular tree that not only may contribute to pulmonary edema but may also produce a delayed hyponatremia. This process has been observed in patients who receive only isotonic solutions such as saline and later on develop delayed hyponatremia that may also result in death [20]. Therefore, it is important to maintain similar monitoring systems to those outlined earlier for fluids containing electrolytes and, specifically, to monitor the inflow and outflow and calculate the deficit. There should be specific defined limits as to when to stop the procedure or institute active diuretic therapy in those patients who absorb >1.5–2 liters of saline solution.

SUMMARY AND CONCLUSIONS

It is undeniable that hysteroscopy and hysteroscopic surgery have increased in the last two decades. This increase has been the result of gynecologists learning these techniques and the introduction of new applications for operative hysteroscopy, as well as the interest of industry in manufacturing better systems for hysteroscopy, particularly continuous flow hysteroscopes and resectoscopes. These have been adapted with a variety of electrodes that permit electrosurgery inside the uterus. Low viscosity fluids have become the method of choice to distend the uterine cavity during operative hysteroscopy, either with electrolytes when no electrosurgery is required or without electrolytes when electrosurgery is used. Because therapeutic hysteroscopic procedures usually require more time than diagnostic procedures, the use of low viscosity fluids may favor excessive absorption by the patient and therefore expose these patients to pulmonary edema and possible hyponatremia, if the fluids do not contain electrolytes. Therefore it is important to establish close monitoring of the fluids used, particularly to avoid excessive deficits and also to establish teamwork with anesthesiologists, assisting nurses and physicians. All members of the team need to be aware of the possibility of excessive fluid absorption and need to attempt to avoid this problem. When this problem occurs it must be diagnosed at an early stage, and treated appropriately to avoid serious sequelae. The establishment of specific protocols for all operative hysteroscopic procedures is of utmost importance for the avoidance, early detection, and appropriate treatment of these conditions when they occur.

In the office setting, as noted at the beginning of this chapter, these complications should be prevented by selecting operative procedures that are suitable for the office setting, by the use of strict protocols, and by the avoidance of prolonged and difficult manipulations when unexpected pathology is encountered. The latter require larger instruments and regional or general anesthesia.

REFERENCES

1. Witz CA, Silverberg KM, Burns WN, Schenken RJ, Olive DL. Complications associated with the absorption of hysteroscopic fluid media. *Fertil Steril* 1993; **60**: 745–756.
2. McLucas B. Hyskon complications in hysteroscopic surgery. *Obstet Gynecol Surv* 1991; **46**: 196–200.
3. Loffer FD. Complications from uterine distention during hysteroscopy. In: Corfman RS, Diamond MP, DeCherney A, eds. Complications of Laparoscopy and Hysteroscopy. Oxford: Blackwell Scientific Publications, 1993: 177–186.
4. Peterson HB, Hulka JF, Phillips JM. American Association of Gynecologic Laparoscopists 1988 Membership Survey on Operative Hysteroscopy. *J Reprod Med* 1990; **25**: 590–591.
5. Hulka JF, Peterson HB, Phillips JM, Surrey MW. Operative Hysteroscopy. American Association of Gynecologic Laparoscopists 1991 Membership Survey. *J Reprod Med* 1993; **38**: 572–573.
6. Arieff AI, Ayres JC. Endometrial ablation complicated by fatal hyponatremic encephalopathy. *JAMA* 1993; **270**: 1230–1232.
7. Baggish MS, Brill AF, Rosenweig B, Barbot JE, Indman PD. Fatal acute glycine and sorbitol toxicity during operative hysteroscopy. *J Gynecol Surg* 1993; **9**: 137–143.
8. Garry R, Hasham F, Kokri MS, Mooney P. The effect of pressure on fluid absorption during endometrial ablation. *J Gynecol Surg* 1992; **8**: 1–10.
9. Baggish MS, Davaluri C, Rodriguez F, Camporesi E. Vascular uptake of Hyskon (Dextran 70) during operative and diagnostic hysteroscopy. *J Gynecol Surg* 1992; **8**: 211–217.
10. Hasham F, Garry R, Kokri MS et al. Fluid absorption during laser ablation of the endometrium in the treatment of menorrhagia. *Br J Anaesth* 1992; **68**: 151–154.
11. Indman PD, Brooks PG, Cooper JM, Loffer FD, Valle RF, Vancaillie TG. Complications of fluid overload from resectoscopic surgery. *J Am Assoc Gynecol Laparosc* 1998; **5**: 63–67.
12. Valle RF. A Manual of Clinical Hysteroscopy. New York: Parthenon Publishing Group, 1998: 41–46.
13. Vulgaropulos SP, Haley AC, Hulka JF. Intrauterine pressure and fluid absorption during continuous flow hysteroscopy. *Am J Obstet Gynecol* 1992; **167**: 386–391.
14. Hahn RG. Ethanol monitoring of irrigating fluid absorption. *Eur J Anaesthesiol* 1996; **13**: 102–115.
15. Molnar BG, Magos AL, Kay J. Monitoring fluid absorption using 1% ethanol-tagged glycine during operative hysteroscopy. *J Am Assoc Gynecol Laparosc* 1997; **4**: 357–362.
16. Taskin O, Buhur A, Birincioglu M et al. Endometrial Na +, K+-ATPase pump function and vasopression levels during hysteroscopic surgery in patients pretreated with GnRH agonist. *J Am Assoc Gynecol Laparosc* 1998; **5**: 119–124.
17. Istre O, Skajaa K, Schjoensby AP, Forman A. Changes in serum electrolytes after transcervical resection of endometrium and submucous fibroids with use of glycine 1.5% for uterine irrigation. *Obstet Gynecol* 1992; **80**: 218–222.
18. Istre O, Bjoennes J, Naess R, Hornbaek K, Forman A. Postoperative cerebral oedema after transcervical endometrial resection and uterine irrigation with 1.5% glycine. *Lancet* 1994; **344**: 1187–89.
19. Molnar BG, Broadbent JAM, Magos AL. Fluid overload risk score for endometrial resection. *Gynecol Endosc* 1992; **1**: 133–138.
20. Steele A, Gowrishanker M, Abrahamson S, Mazer CD, Feldman RD, Halperin ML. Postoperative hyponatremia despite near-isotonic saline infusion: a phenomenon of desalination. *Ann Intern Med* 1997; **126**: 20–25.

Bipolar energy

Stefano Bettocchi

> **Take Home Message**
> Even if bipolar instruments are not truly bipolar, they represent a real revolution in the use of energy within the confinement of the uterine cavity. The electrical energy created between the metal electrode of the instrument and the return electrode allows the use of nonionic solutions. This indicates that the only problem that can arise is an overloading problem with hyponatremia. However, as outpatient procedures are of limited duration, and the conscious patient will alert the physician when she feels pain, the risk is minimal and operative procedures are very safe.

1997 was the year of the great revolution in office hysteroscopy. After a very long period when only mechanical instruments were available for the so-called operative hysteroscope, and electricity (monopolar) was the prerogative of the resectoscope, the first bipolar electrode that was perfectly compatible with existing office hysteroscopes was introduced onto the market. Afterwards other companies presented similar products.

VERSAPOINT

This instrument (produced by Gynecare, Ethicon Inc., NJ, USA) is composed of a dedicated bipolar electrosurgical generator (Figure 1), a connection cable, disposable electrodes, and a footswitch.

The electrode is 5 Fr (1.6 mm, the same as most of the operative channels) and the tip has two poles (active and return) separated by 2 mm at the distal shaft by a ceramic insulator (Figure 2). Three different electrodes are available (Figure 3): Spring (thick and short, for rapid tissue vaporization and desiccation), Twizzle (thin and long, for vaporization and needle-like cutting), and Ball (spherical, for precise vaporization and desiccation). The Spring and Twizzle tips have a spiral-like design formed by two metal wires twisted together.

Only tissue in contact with the active electrode in the electrical path circuit will be desiccated or vaporized. The instrument works only in saline solution, producing a 'vapor pocket' (Figure 4): the pattern of the electrical field dictates behavior and depth of penetration. Na and Cl ions migrate to complete the circuit and the electrosurgical generator determines the electrosurgical endpoint by controlling a locally produced high impedance micro environment. The generator also tailors output to changes in impedance at the active electrode.

Figure 1
Dedicated bipolar electrosurgical generator (Gynecare, Ethicon).

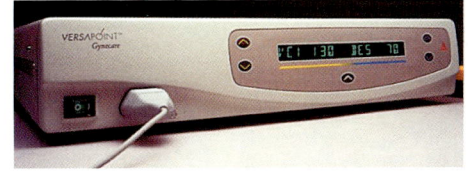

Figure 2
Schematic representation of the shaft and tip of the Versapoint.

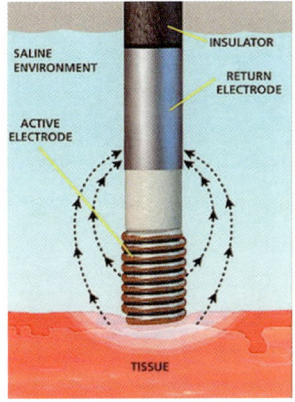

Figure 1
Dedicated bipolar electrosurgical generator (Gynecare, Ethicon).

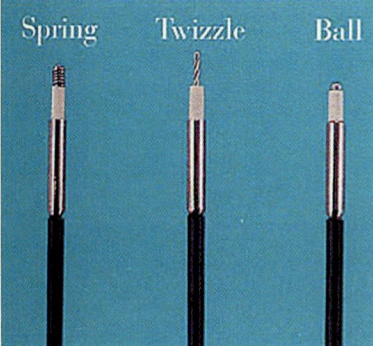

The generator provides different modes of operation (waveform) (Figure 5): the vapor cut waveform, resembling a cut mode (the acronyms are VC1, VC2, VC3, where VC3 corresponds to the mildest energy flowing into the tissue), the blend waveform (BL1, BL2), and the desiccation waveform, resembling a coagulation mode (DES). The generator is connected to the 5 Fr electrode via a flexible cable. Once connected, the generator automatically adjusts to the default setting (VC1 and 100 W).

BIPOLAR ELECTRODE BY KARL STORZ

Recently, a 5 Fr bipolar electrode has been presented by Karl Storz (Tuttlingen, Germany). The tip's design is similar to a needle, and it is made entirely of metal, unlike the Versapoint Twizzle electrode. It has the great advantage of being reusable and can be connected to any bipolar generator available on the market.

CLINICAL EXPERIENCE

Since 1995 we have performed 7256 hysteroscopic office-based procedures at the University Center of Endoscopy in Bari, Italy. Institutional review board approval was obtained for this study. All the procedures were performed during the proliferative phase of the cycle, using the transvaginal approach, without tenaculum and speculum, using saline distension medium and a 5-mm continuous flow office hysteroscope (Bettocchi Office Hysteroscope size 5; Karl Storz). The scope is based on a rod lens system with a diameter of 2.9 mm and a 30° view. The continuous flow sheath has an oval profile and maximum 5-mm diameter with an incorporated 5 Fr working channel. The mechanical instruments used were grasping forceps with teeth and scissors (Karl Storz). Intrauterine pressure was kept constant at 25/35 mmHg, using an electronic pump for irrigation and aspiration (Endomat; Karl Storz).

The electrosurgical instrument was the Versapoint Bipolar Electrosurgical System (Gynecare, Ethicon Inc.), consisting of a dedicated bipolar electrosurgical generator and two types of electrodes: the Twizzle, specifically for precise and controlled vaporization (resembling cutting) and the Spring, indicated for diffuse tissue vaporization, as described above.

INSTRUMENT SETTINGS

After a test period we concluded that the default settings of the Versapoint bipolar electrical generator were incompatible with our techniques (performed without any type of anesthesia or analgesia), and therefore decided to use the mildest vapor cutting mode (VC3) and to reduce the power setting by half, to 50 W. For the same reasons, we chose the Twizzle electrode rather than the Spring electrode, as in our experience the Twizzle electrode is a more precise 'cutting' instrument, and with lower power settings it can work closer to the myometrium with less discomfort.

PATIENTS

Since 1998, and up to April 2002, we have treated 501 patients (age range 18–79 years) with single or multiple benign intrauterine pathologies observed during hysteroscopy, by the Versapoint 5 Fr procedure [1]. These included 445 endometrial polyps, 49 submucosal myomas <2 cm and 21 partial intramural myomas with a submucosal section not exceeding 1.5 cm. Larger myomas were treated with the resectoscope, as in our experience, use of the 5 Fr Versapoint electrodes to treat these larger myomas (> 2 cm) is time-consuming and yields poorer quality final results. The patients came to our center with abnormal uterine bleeding, abnormal ultrasound findings, sterility/infertility problems, or for evaluation before or during hormone replacement therapy (HRT). They underwent an office hysteroscopic procedure, without any analgesic pretreatment, in the proliferative phase of the cycle (day 6 up to day 11) as well as transvaginal

Figure 4
Schematic representation of production of vapor pocket by Versapoint.

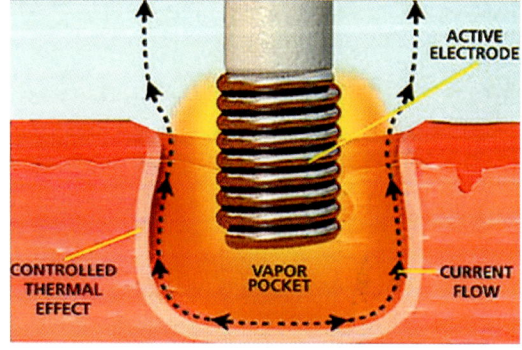

Figure 5
Schematic representation of vapor cut waveforms.

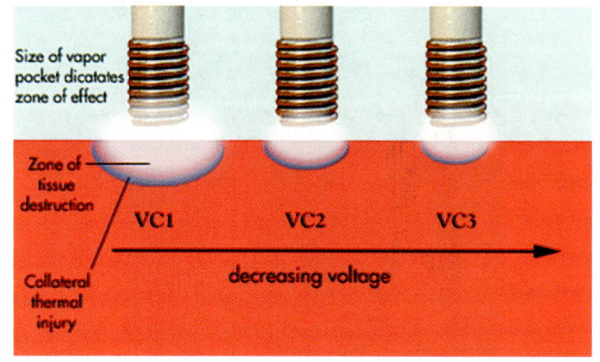

ultrasound (TV-US). Infertile patients presenting a partially intramural myoma ($n = 21$), were pretreated with 3 months of Gn-RH analogs to shrink the fibroids. In all cases the removed tissue was sent to the pathologist for histological confirmation.

To verify patient compliance, a visual analog score of pain was proposed immediately after the procedure. Patients were asked to fill out privately an anonymous questionnaire assessing the maximum amount of pain suffered during the procedure, by marking a cross on a 10-cm line. The following classification was proposed: 0–1 = no discomfort; 2–4 = discomfort equivalent to normal menstrual pain; 5–7 = moderate pain equivalent to heavy menstrual pain; 8–10 = severe pain.

OPERATIVE TECHNIQUE

All polyps <0.5 cm were removed using 5 Fr mechanical instruments (sharp scissors and/or crocodile forceps), largely for cost reasons. Larger polyps were removed intact, with the Versapoint Twizzle electrode, only if the internal cervical os size was wide enough for their extraction. Otherwise, they were sliced, from the free edge to the base, into two or three fragments small enough to be pulled out through the uterine cavity using 5 Fr grasping forceps with teeth (Fig. 6). To remove the entire base of the polyp without going too deep into the myometrium, in some cases the Twizzle electrode was bent by 25–30°, enough to produce a kind of hook electrode. A similar technique was applied to submucosal myomas with the difference that, due to their higher tissue density, they were first divided into two half-spheres and then each of these was sliced as described above (Fig. 7). Particular attention was paid to the intramural part of the myoma, if present. To avoid any myometrial stimulation or damage, the myoma was first gently separated from the capsule using mechanical instruments (grasping forceps or scissors) as already described for resectoscopic myomectomy [2,3]. Once the intramural section became submucosal it was sliced with the Versapoint Twizzle electrode. The unpaired Student's *t* test was used for statistical analysis; a *p* value < 0.05 was considered statistically significant.

RESULTS

All patients were treated without anesthesia or analgesia. The 445 endometrial polyps ranged between 0.5 and 4.5 cm in size and the average operating time was 17 minutes. Two hundred and six polyps (46.3%) were removed intact while the rest ($n = 239$, 53.7%) were removed by the slicing technique. Endometrial polyps <0.5 cm were removed using mechanical instruments.

The 49 submucosal myomas were between 0.5 and 2.0 cm and average operating time was 22 minutes. A longer operating time was required because of the need to slice the myoma at different angles before removal, as discussed above. The 21 partially intramural myomas, all pretreated with 3 months Gn-RH analog therapy, ranged between 0.6 and 1.5 cm and the average operating time was 31 minutes. The time taken was even longer because of the special operative technique required (a combination of mechanical and electrical instruments, as described above) and the need to avoid any myometrial stimulation (particularly difficult in view of the location of the myoma).

The rate of successful procedure, in terms of compliance by the patients, was higher for endometrial polyps than for intramural and submucosal myomas ($p < 0.05$), due to the difficulty of establishing a reliable technique that could be performed without anesthesia or analgesia, together with the small number of cases treated.

Histological examination of the removed tissue showed a correspondence with the hysteroscopic diagnosis in all cases except one. This was a menopausal patient taking HRT who presented abnormal uterine bleeding. TV-US showed an endometrial thickness of 7 mm. At hysteroscopy, a 1.5-cm polyp on the anterior uterine wall was discovered and removed during the same procedure. The macroscopic aspect at hysteroscopy was normal, without any sign of necrosis, degeneration or vascular

Figure 4
Slicing technique used to treat large endometrial polyps.

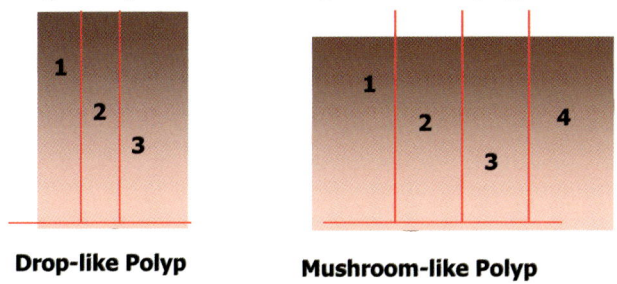

Figure 5
Slicing technique used to treat submucous and partially intramural myomas <2 cm in size. Segments 1a–4a refer to the first half-sphere, while 1b–4b refer to the second half-sphere.

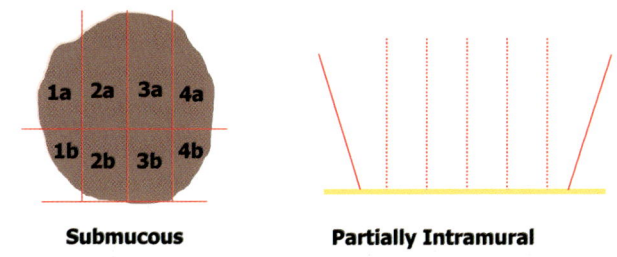

abnormalities, but histology showed a focal carcinoma located at the base of the polyp. The patient underwent hysterectomy 2 weeks later and the final histological examination of the whole uterus showed no sign of malignancy.

No failures or major complications (i.e. severe pain, vagal reflex, intravasation, uterine perforation, etc.) occurred during the procedures.

Follow-up was performed after 3 months, or after two spontaneous cycles in patients who had had Gn-RH pretreatment ($n = 21$). All the hysteroscopic procedures were performed during the proliferative phase of the cycle (day 6 up to day 11) to avoid endometrial thickness. Only one patient underwent hysterectomy, as described above. No recurrence of the pathologies was observed at follow-up in any of the patients. In those operated for myomas, the uterine wall had a normal aspect with no scar tissue.

REFERENCES

1. Bettocchi S, Ceci O, Di Venere R et al. Advanced operative office hysteroscopy without anaesthesia: analysis of 501 cases treated with a 5 Fr. bipolar electrode. *Hum Reprod* 2002; **17**: 2435–2438.
2. Mazzon I, Sbiroli C. *Manuale di Chirurgia Resettoscopica in Ginecologia.* Milan: UTET Edizioni. 1997.
3. Gimpelson RJ. Hysteroscopic treatment of the patient with intracavitary pathology (myomectomy/polypectomy). *Obstet Gynecol Clin North Am* 2000; **27**: 327–337.

Mechanical instruments for operative hysteroscopy

Rafael F. Valle

> **Take Home Message**
> Not all hysteroscopic operations can be performed with mechanical instruments. Their availability broadens the versatility of operative hysteroscopy. Semi-rigid instruments allow for easier and faster interventions. The correct application and use of mechanical instruments will require clinical judgment about the feasibility of removing the pathology. 5 Fr instrumentation is the standard.

INTRODUCTION

Hysteroscopy has been extended from a diagnostic procedure to a therapeutic one for a variety of intrauterine conditions. New and improved instrumentation has also facilitated the performance of extensive intrauterine dissections.

The original therapeutic applications of hysteroscopy, such as targeted biopsies and removal of foreign bodies and polyps, have been expanded to include those previously performed by hysterotomy and laparotomy. These include dissection of extensive and severe intrauterine adhesions, removal of submucous leiomyomas, division of uterine septa, tubal cannulation for tubal obstruction, and ablation of endometrium for patients with intractable uterine bleeding, who are not candidates for a hysterectomy [1–3].

Because the majority of these operations require delicate dissections, accessory hysteroscopic operative instrumentation such as flexible, semi-rigid, and rigid forceps and scissors are most useful to complete some of these operations safely, duplicating with endoscopes the standard open abdomen surgery. Certainly not all hysteroscopic operations can be performed with mechanical instrumentation, and the need for a resectoscope is obvious, particularly for endometrial ablation, resection of submucous leiomyomas of the sessile type and those that are partially intramural. However, the use of mechanical instruments remains necessary for many other conditions and their availability when performing hysteroscopy is not only important but broadens the versatility of operative hysteroscopy.

HYSTEROSCOPES

The original operative hysteroscopes with a 7 Fr operating channel are now only used in the operating theater, because they require cervical dilatation for introduction. However, with the introduction of small-caliber diagnostic/operative hysteroscopes with a 5 Fr operating channel, the instrumentation has also been adapted for these types of hysteroscopes. These instruments are semi-rigid scissors, biopsy forceps, and grasping forceps. The original flexible instruments have been replaced by semi-rigid ones, because the former were difficult to manipulate while dissecting tissue. Similarly the completely rigid instruments cannot be inserted easily through a 5 Fr operating channel.

The hysteroscopes most commonly used in the office setting are those of the rigid type. Furthermore, because cervical dilatation should be avoided, instruments of <5.5 mm outer diameter are preferable. These instruments are usually fitted with a 5 Fr operating channel, therefore, instrumentation should be of the 5 Fr caliber. Occasionally, larger hysteroscopes are used with an outer diameter (OD) of 6–7 mm. These instruments provide a 7 Fr operating channel and larger instrumentation is used (Figures 1–3).

The flexible fiberoptic hysteroscopes permit use of flexible mechanical instrumentation of 2 mm diameter, and in general are longer than those required for rigid hysteroscopes, i.e. 50–60 cm long. However, they are somewhat more difficult to manipulate than the semi-rigid instrumentation used with the rigid hysteroscope (Figure 4) [4,5].

MECHANICAL ANCILLARY HYSTEROSCOPIC INSTRUMENTS

The mechanical instruments available for operation with small caliber hysteroscopes (3.5–4.5 mm OD), are similar to those of 7 Fr designed for operative hysteroscopes with 7 mm OD. While originally the mechanical instruments were of the flexible type, they were difficult to manipulate and not sturdy enough to perform extensive dissections. So as not to add other components to the hysteroscopes, that could admit rigid instruments, semi-rigid instruments were introduced. These include scissors, biopsy forceps, grasping forceps, catheters, etc. These semi-rigid instruments are somewhat flexible, like a saber, but cannot completely bend in 90° angles because they will break. However, there is slight flexibility that permits them to be introduced like wires through the operating channels of the hysteroscope. Therefore manipulation becomes easier and faster, with the ability to target easily the lesion to be treated or biopsied. However, because of their small caliber (5 Fr), they require delicacy in their use otherwise they can be easily bent or even break. The 7 Fr mechanical instruments are sturdier, but cannot be used with a 3.5–4.5 mm OD hysteroscope, which is the most commonly used hysteroscope in the office setting. Therefore, 5 Fr instrumentation of a similar design to the 7 Fr equipment must be used. At present, almost all manufacturing companies that provide hysteroscopes have developed this type of instrumentation. However, flexible instruments are required when using flexible hysteroscopes, their shafts are longer because of the length of these hysteroscopes, which are larger than the rigid ones. Several sets of each type should be at hand when attempting hysteroscopic surgery with these instruments, in view of their fragility and possible breakage during a procedure [4–6].

To facilitate their manipulation, these instruments are better maneuvered with the handle up, with the thumb and index fingers only, rather than by attempting to grasp them like a pistol. This facilitates manipulation and the to-and-fro movement usually required when operating. Catheters of 1 mm OD can be inserted into the 5 Fr operating channel of a small caliber hysteroscope, such as the Novy catheter to evaluate possible tubal obstruction and the ESSURE micro-insert for tubal sterilization. The nipple used in the hysteroscope should have a pinhead size opening to avoid reflux of the distending medium while performing operative hysteroscopy (Figures 5–7).

Figure 1
Continuous flow, diagnostic and operative hysteroscope with semi-rigid forceps in place (Storz).

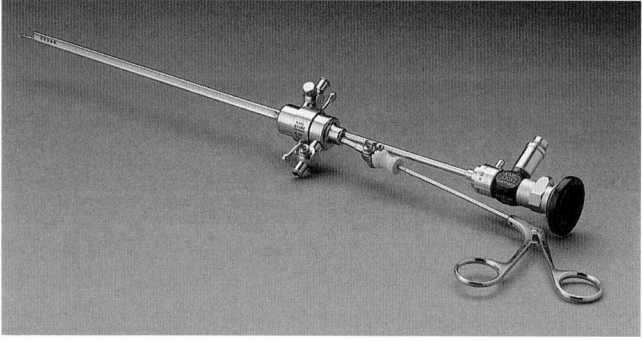

Figure 2
Close-up view of distal end of continuous flow hysteroscope with grasping forceps in place (Storz).

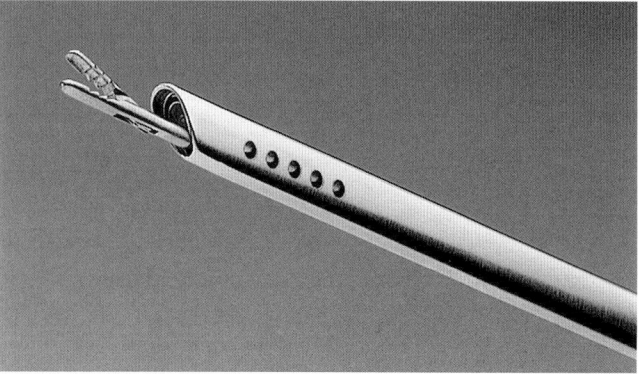

Figure 3
Distal tips of various 5 Fr mechanical instruments. From left to right: cork-screw to fix myomas, sharp scissors, blunt scissors, punch biopsy forceps, spoon biopsy forceps, and grasping forceps.

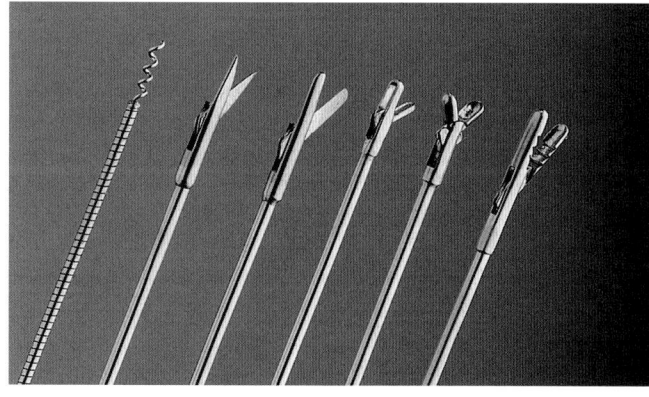

Figure 4
Flexible hysteroscope (Fujinon).

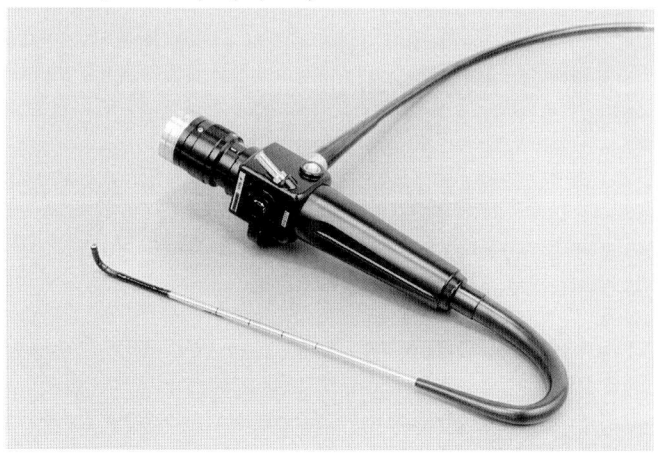

ADVANTAGES AND DISADVANTAGES OF MECHANICAL INSTRUMENTATION

The advantages of this type of instrument in dissecting or removing tissue at hysteroscopy are obvious. They can be inserted easily and dissection is fast and precise, particularly when continuous flow hysteroscopes are used. Fluid with electrolytes can be used, as no conducting energy is utilized.

Figure 5
Close-up view of 7 Fr semi-rigid mechanical instruments (Storz).

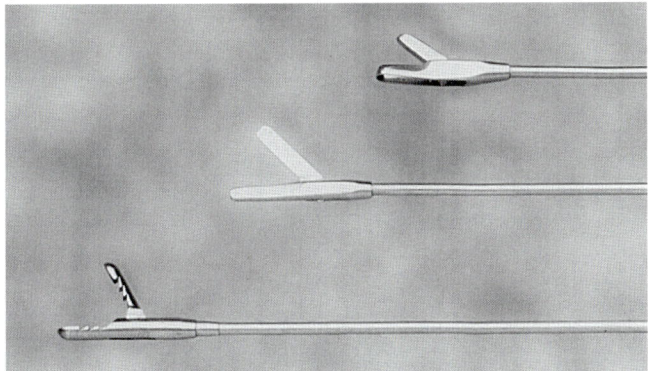

Figure 6
Close-up view of 7 Fr flexible mechanical instruments (Storz).

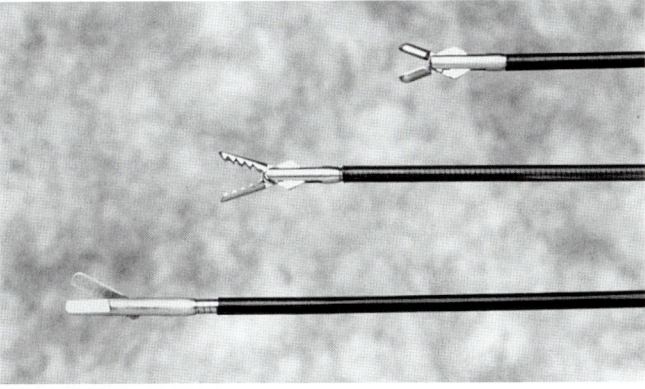

Figure 6
Close-up view of flexible wireguide encased in a 1mm catheter for tubal cannulation (Cook OB/GqN).

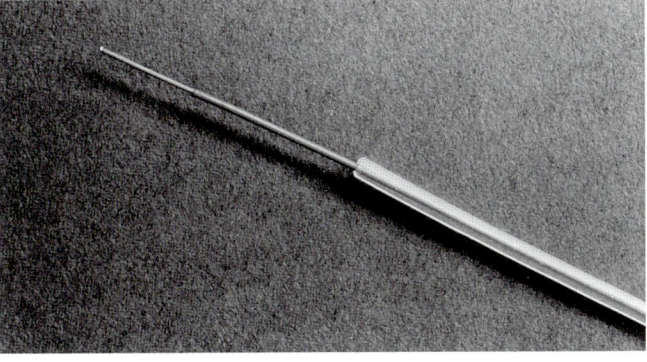

The disadvantages are that the small caliber of these instruments does not permit major dissections and they can easily get dull or worn out with use. Therefore, a back-up system is important should this occur.

APPLICATIONS
TARGETED BIOPSIES
Because the instrumentation for taking biopsies is small, particularly if a 5 Fr instrument is used, multiple biopsies of the lesion are required in order to obtain adequate tissue for pathologic evaluation. Once the tissue is grasped with each sample the hysteroscope is removed with the biopsy forceps in place so as not to lose the tissue while passing it through the small operating channel. Several re-entries are therefore necessary.

POLYPS
Polyps, particularly those of the pedunculate type, can also be removed during office hysteroscopy if the diameter does not exceed 1 cm. Morcellation may be required and this is done with scissors in order to retrieve larger portions of the polyp rather than utilizing only the biopsy forceps [7].

SUBMUCOUS LEIOMYOMAS
Although at present submucous leiomyomas are best treated with the resectoscope, small (<1 cm) pedunculate submucous leiomyomas may be encountered during ambulatory office hysteroscopy. In this situation the dissection of these myomas is relatively easily accomplished with hysteroscopic scissors. The total removal will depend on the cervical dilatation, as usually removal is accomplished by traction in multiparous patients. Patients with this type of leiomyoma usually complain of abnormal uterine bleeding and the cervix is already somewhat dilated. Should the extraction of the myoma not be accomplished, morcellation with a monopolar or bipolar electrode will accomplish reduction in size by simple bisection. Another alternative is to leave the myoma already transected in the uterine cavity and wait for a spontaneous atraumatic expulsion. Some leiomyomas with a small intramural component (<25%), with a size not exceeding 1 cm can also be dissected with hysteroscopic scissors. The technique of using the scissors not only to dissect but to mechanically elevate the myoma off its attachment to the uterine wall of course, serving as a leverage to accomplish this task, is most useful [8].

INTRAUTERINE ADHESIONS
Intrauterine adhesions, particularly those that are focal and thin, can easily be divided with hysteroscopic scissors. The division is best performed at the middle of the adhesion and

by reviewing the symmetry of the uterine cavity at the level of the internal os, once the adhesions are divided, particularly if they are fundal or are in the uterotubal cones [9].

UTERINE SEPTA

The division of small and thin uterine septa is done by cutting the septum from side to side and maintaining this plane of division in the middle of the septum to avoid bleeding [10].

IUDS

The thread of an IUD misplaced in the uterine cavity is grasped and by retrieving the hysteroscope with a fixed IUD by the forceps, the IUD is easily removed [11].

TUBAL CANNULATION

Tubal cornual occlusion that is diagnosed at hysterosalpingography requires further evaluation with laparoscopy, to rule out spasm encountered in about 30% of these patients. However, despite the lack of true fibrotic tubal obstruction, a mucus plug made of proteinaceous material may still impede the tubal passage of indigo carmine at laparoscopy. To diagnose or rule out true tubal obstruction, tubal cannulation is added by utilizing Novy catheters guided under hysteroscopy, which permit the insertion of a flexible guidewire of <0.5 mm diameter and encased in a 1-mm diameter catheter. When cannulation is completed, bypassing the intramural portion of the tube, the guidewire is removed and indigo carmine is injected through the catheter. The majority of these patients will show tubal patency [12].

TUBAL STERILIZATION

New methods of tubal occlusion for sterilization purposes have been developed, such as the placement of a Conceptus ESSURE micro-insert. This new hysteroscopic application is an easy procedure to perform in the office utilizing a small endoscope. The deploying catheter is inserted into a 5 Fr channel and delivered to each tubal opening; a device is deployed in each tube. Despite the fact that tubal cannulation is performed and the device is deployed by expansion, the procedure is well tolerated by patients with the use of a paracervical block anesthesia only (see the chapter on Sterilization).

OTHER SPECIFIC APPLICATIONS

Specific uses of the mechanical instruments include targeted biopsies, polypectomy when the polyp is relatively small (<2 cm) and pedunculate, and myomectomy for some pedunculate myomas (<1 cm). Semi-rigid scissors with sharp tips are most useful in the division of intrauterine adhesions, as the adhesions are only divided and not removed. Additionally with uterine septa, this type of instrumentation becomes the method of choice, particularly when the septa are thin. These two latter applications can also be carried out in the office setting, but with certain limitations. The intrauterine adhesions should be focal and well defined, not occluding the uterotubal cones and of the mild or moderate type. Similarly, when dividing septa it is preferable to confine the application of division to small uterine septa which do not completely occlude the uterine cavity.

The removal of misplaced IUDs can easily be accomplished in an office setting with this type of instrumentation. Finally, tubal cannulation for sterilization purposes may become one of the most used therapeutic applications of operative hysteroscopy in the office.

Operative hysteroscopy continues to require mechanical tools and the method should be tailored to the pathology and its easy resolution.

DISTENDING MEDIA

It is important to realize that when mechanical tools that do not require conductive energy are employed, the liquids used in the distension of the uterus may contain electrolytes – specifically normal saline. Certainly, because any procedure in the office setting should be brief, no major problems of fluid overload can occur, as the method should be rapid and expeditious. However, even in this setting any electrolyte inbalance should be completely avoided. The performance of operative hysteroscopy in this setting should not be improvised but should be learned progressively from proper and successful use as the patient is only under local anesthesia or is not receiving any anesthesia.

SUMMARY AND CONCLUSIONS

It is obvious that operative hysteroscopy in the office setting can be extended to many conditions that were previously only attempted with the large (>7 mm OD) operative hysteroscope. Today, with the advent of small caliber continuous flow hysteroscopes and a 5 Fr operating channel, new instrumentation has been adapted to perform some of these procedures in the office setting. Mechanical instruments certainly add versatility to operative hysteroscopy when performed in an office setting. The appropriate application and use will require clinical judgment about the feasibility of removing the specific pathology in this setting. To add versatility to operative hysteroscopy this type of instrumentation should be available any time the treatment is necessary to be provided in the same setting.

The hysteroscopic approach to intrauterine surgery has added major benefits, not only in avoiding more traumatic manipulations with its subsequent sequelae, but in decreasing morbidity, hospitalization costs, and most importantly equalling if not surpassing the efficacy of previous treatments performed more invasively in the uterus.

REFERENCES

1. Valle RF. Hysteroscopy for gynecologic diagnosis. *Clin Obstet Gynecol* 1983; **26**: 253–276.
2. Valle RF, Baggish MS. Instrumentation for hysteroscopy. In: Baggish MS, Barbot J, Valle RF, eds. Diagnostic and Operative Hysteroscopy. A Text and Atlas, 2nd edn. St Louis: Mosby, 1999: 97–126.
3. Valle RF. Accessory instruments for operative hysteroscopy. In: Baggish MS, Barbot J, Valle RF, eds. Diagnostic and Operative Hysteroscopy. A Text and Atlas, 2nd edn. St Louis: Mosby, 1999: 127–138.
4. Bettocchi S. Office Hysteroscopy. Tuttlingen, Germany: Endo Press, 1999.
5. Valle RF. General principles and instrumentation. In: A Manual of Clinical Hysteroscopy. New York: Parthenon Publishing Group, 1998: 15–21.
6. Valle RF. Diagnostic hysteroscopy in the office. In: A Manual of Clinical Hysteroscopy. New York: Parthenon Publishing Group, 1998: 47–53.
7. Valle RF. Hysteroscopy: diagnostic and therapeutic applictions. *J Reprod Med* 1978; **20**: 115–118.
8. Valle RF. Hysteroscopic removal of submucous leiomyomas. *J Gynecol Surg* 1990; **6**: 89–96.
9. Valle RF, Sciarra JJ. Intrauterine adhesions: hysteroscopic diagnosis, classification, treatment, and reproductive outcome. *Am J Obstet Gynecol* 1988; **1158**: 1459–1470.
10. Valle RF. Hysteroscopic treatment of partial and complete uterine septum. *Int J Fertil* 1996; **41**: 310–315.
11. Valle RF, Sciarra JJ, Freeman DW. Hysteroscopic removal of intrauterine devices with missing filaments. *Obstet Gynecol* 1977; **49**: 55–60.
12. Valle RF. Tubal cannulation. In: Siegler AM, ed. Hysteroscopy. Obstet Gynecol Clin North Am Series. Philadelphia, PA: WB Saunders, 1995; 223: 519–540.

Indications and limitations of operative hysteroscopy in the office setting

Stefano Bettocchi

> **Take Home Message**
> The indications are directly related to the new generation of office operative hysteroscopes with a continuous flow system and the possibility of using mechanical and electrical instruments of 5 Fr diameter. As the nerve endings are situated in the myometrium it is important that the surgeon respects the endometrial lining. The instrument should be held in close vicinity to the final lens of the scope and the scope should be moved very gently.

For a long time, indications and limitations have been strictly related to available technology, and the technique used. A procedure performed under local or general anesthesia, or with a high level of discomfort for the patient, cannot be used routinely. Also, CO_2 distension cannot be used in the presence of blood or dense mucus. Therefore, the indications, if the technique is performed in the 'classic' way, must be limited.

In contrast, if the procedure is performed with the latest technology (small diameter scopes with operative channel, liquid distension, automatic control of the intrauterine pressure) and by the vaginoscopical approach, the final result will be a simple, painless procedure that can be performed in an ambulatory setting.

Hysteroscopy is the gold standard procedure for the examination of the uterine cavity, for whatever purpose.

Therefore, abnormal uterine bleeding (AUB), dysfunctional uterine bleeding (DUB), suspected pathology at ultrasound examination (US), endometrial thickness at US, sterility/infertility, repetitive abortions, uterine malformation and Mullerian abnormalities, endometrial carcinoma, foreign bodies, and lost IUDs are all indications for hysteroscopy.

INDICATIONS AND LIMITATIONS FOR CLASSIC SURGERY

All the intrauterine benign pathologies can be treated with the resectoscope, even if for some of them the use of mechanical instruments can successfully solve the problem. Adhesions, septae, occlusion of the uterine cavity (Aschermann), and anatomical impediments can be treated with scissors. The use of this instrument is more indicated

Figure 1
Scheme of treatment indications for office operative hysteroscopy, before (a) and after (b) the introduction of bipolar tools.

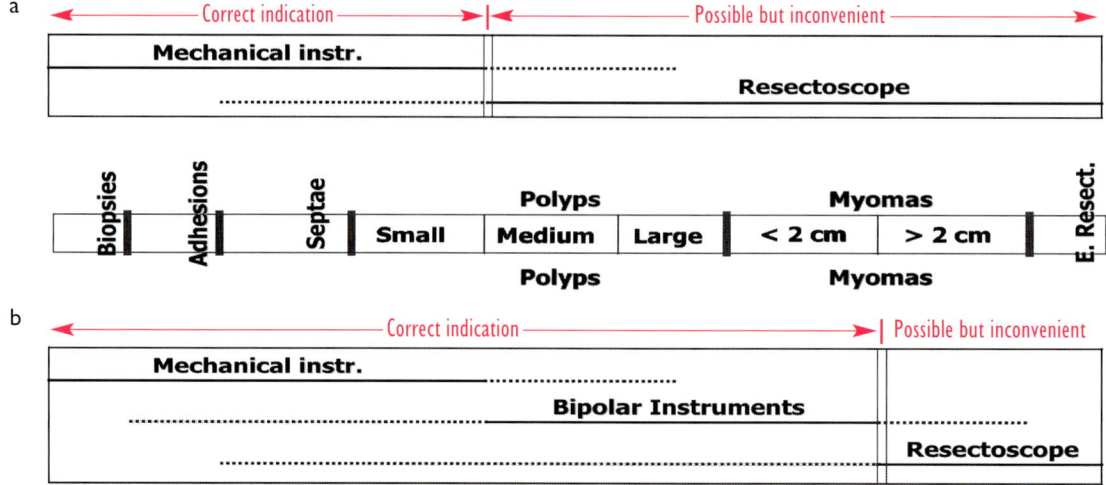

than electrosurgery because the surgeon can avoid causing thermal damage in the nonpathologic tissue.

The only limitation is the presence of some uterine abnormalities that can reduce the volume of the uterine cavity, impeding the introduction of these large instruments.

INDICATIONS AND LIMITATIONS FOR AMBULATORY SURGERY

Ambulatory surgery is strictly related to the use of the new generation of office operative hysteroscopes and to the availability of mechanical and electrical instruments with a diameter of 5 Fr (the size of the operative channel, corresponding to 1.6 mm). As the scope's diameter is not bigger than 5 mm and sensitive innervations of the uterus start from the myometrium out, it is easy to understand that most (or all) of these procedure can be performed easily without any analgesia or anaesthesia in an ambulatory setting. It is very important that the surgeon respect the uterine muscle, performing narrow movements of the scope and taking care to avoid touching, scratching, or cutting the muscle fibers. Furthermore, we suggest working with the active area of the instrument (scissor blades or forceps jaws) very close to the tip of the scope: this will avoid losing the depth of view. The indications depend on the instrument used (Figure 1).

MECHANICAL INSTRUMENTS (Figure 2)

Sharp scissors can be used, as mentioned before, to treat adhesions, septae, and fibrotic tissues that produce anatomic impediment to the insertion of the hysteroscope. The main problem for the surgeon is to distinguish between fibrotic tissue and muscle and mucosa: fibrotic tissue is normally whitish, nonvascularized, and not innervated, while the muscle is pinkish, well vascularized, and sensitively innervated. Scissors can also be used to treat cervical polyps, normally characterized by a strong fibrotic base, whereas grasping forceps may leave some well-vascularized tissue (the base of the polyp) that can provoke the re-growth of the pathology.

In contrast, strong grasping forceps (like the Karl Storz crocodile forceps; Figure 3) are successfully used to perform endometrial polypectomy, to retrieve lost IUDs and to remove foreign bodies from the uterine cavity. The only limit to this surgery is the diameter of the internal cervical os (ICO). Sometimes it is easy to detach a large endometrial polyp from its implant on the myometrium but then it could be impossible to get it out of the cavity because of a small ICO. We suggest that endometrial polyps of a size not bigger than the ICO are mechanically treated and the rest are left for electrosurgery.

ELECTRICAL INSTRUMENTS

In the USA in 1997 a revolutionary bipolar instrument was presented for operative hysteroscopy, the VersaPoint (Gynecare, Johnson & Johnson, NJ, USA) (Figure 4). The great advantage in ambulatory procedures was the diameter of the probe (5 Fr, the same as the operative channel of the majority of the operative scopes) and the required distension media (saline solution, the same as used for normal procedures). Thanks to the availability of two different electrodes (the thick 'Spring' electrode indicated for tissue vaporization, and the thin 'Twizzle' electrode for cutting tissue) the possibility of treating a larger amount of benign pathologies in an ambulatory setting increased

Figure 2
Selection of mechanical instruments.

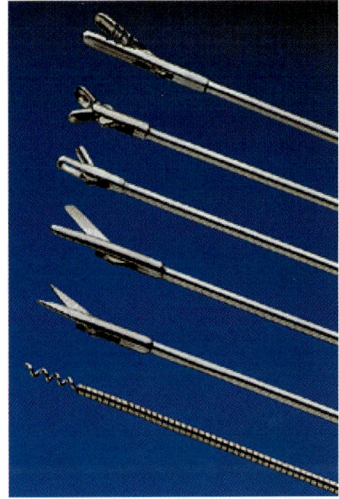

Figure 3
Schematic representation of vapor cut waveforms.

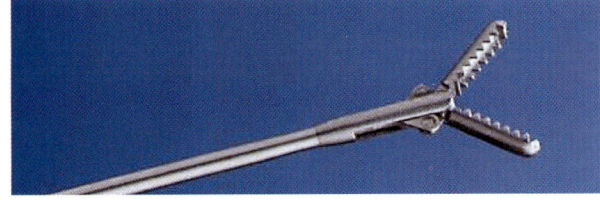

Figure 4
VersaPoint bipolar instrument for operative hysteroscopy (Gynecare, Johnson & Johnson).

dramatically. Recently a similar bipolar electrode was released by Karl Storz Company (Tuttlingen, Germany). It is also 5 Fr, and needs saline solution to work, but it is reusable and can work with any bipolar generator, unlike the VersaPoint.

We personally prefer to use the Twizzle electrode with low energy to obtain a cutting effect on the tissue. The indications for this kind of surgery are very similar to those suggested for the resectoscope, with the exception of myomas larger than 1.5–2 cm and endometrial resection/ablation. For these two procedures the use of the resectoscope is still indicated: it is faster and the final result is better than with the VersaPoint.

The most exciting results with these 5 Fr bipolar probes are obtained when treating cervical and endometrial polyps, as well as submucous and partially intramural myomas <1.5–2 cm. They are sliced, from the free edge to the base, into two or three fragments large enough to be pulled out through the uterine cavity using 5 Fr grasping forceps with teeth (Figure 5). To remove the entire base of the polyp without going too deep into the myometrium, in some cases the Twizzle electrode is bent by 25–30°, enough to obtain a kind of hook-electrode. A similar technique is applied to submucosal myomas with the difference that, due to their higher tissue density, they must first be divided into two half-spheres and then each of these must be sliced as described above (Figure 6). Particular attention is paid to the intramural part of the myoma, if present. To avoid any myometrial stimulation or damage, the myoma is first gently separated from the capsule using mechanical instruments (grasping forceps or scissors), as already described for resectoscopic myomectomy [1,2]. Once the intramural section becomes submucosal it is sliced with the Versapoint Twizzle electrode.

As mentioned above, we still prefer to use mechanical scissors to treat adhesions and uterine septa.

REFERENCES

1. Mazzon I, Sbiroli C. *Manuale di Chirurgia Resettoscopica in Ginecologia*. Milan: UTET Edizioni. 1997.
2. Gimpelson RJ. Hysteroscopic treatment of the patient with intracavitary pathology (myomectomy/polypectomy). *Obstet Gynecol Clin North Am* 2000; **27**: 327–337.

Figure 5
Slicing technique for treating large endometrial polyps.

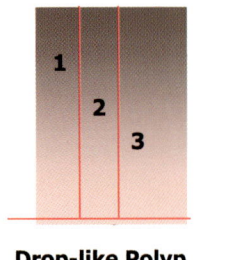
Drop-like Polyp

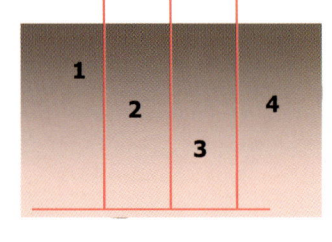
Mushroom-like Polyp

Figure 6
Slicing technique for treating submucous and partially intramural myomas <2cm.

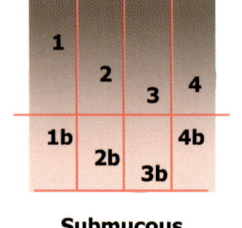
Submucous

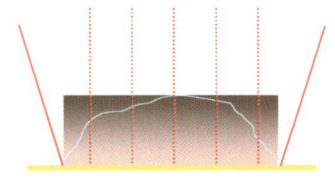
Partially Intramural

New indications for hysteroscopy: sterilization

Rafael F. Valle and B.J. van Herendael

> **Take Home Message**
> An ambulatory, office-based, non-incisional method of sterilization has been sought for over the years that hysteroscopy has been used as a technique. The simplest and easiest method, although with unproven efficacy, has been the use of Hamou nylon plugs. These were never approved by the FDA. The principle is to occlude the tubal intramural lumen by ingrowth of the body's own cells, ingrowth caused by mini-trauma to the tubal epithelium. The ESSURE coil combines new technological advances in instrumentation and design. The design allows the device to be locked in the intramural part of the tube for the period necessary for the ingrowth of cells to be realized. These types of sterilization are irreversible. The patients should be counselled and made aware of this fact. The technicality is reduced to a minimum. Hysteroscopical skills are mandatory.

INTRODUCTION

Tubal sterilization using intratubal occlusive devices was widely explored in the early 1970s with the aim of accomplishing this method of sterilization in an ambulatory setting [1,2]. However, despite the enthusiasm and variety of methods proposed, the feasibility, effectiveness, and safety of these methods was never realized. While hysteroscopy was used to deliver these initial devices under direct vision into the fallopian tube openings, the hysteroscopes available then were too large (7 mm OD) to be introduced atraumatically without previous cervical dilatation. Furthermore, most of the devices introduced could not be anchored acutely to avoid subsequent dislodgement and the complete occlusion of the fallopian tubes could not be guaranteed in a significant number of patients. Therefore, when clinical trials of some of these tubal plugs began, these problems were immediately observed. Furthermore, with some methods, particularly those relying on electrosurgical coagulation, serious complications occurred. Consequently, this approach to tubal sterilization was abandoned [3]. A quarter of a century later, the idea has been revised with the advantage of new technology providing better devices that can be introduced easily through a 5 Fr hysteroscopic channel of a small caliber, 3.9–5.9mm OD hysteroscope. Great advances have been made in the manufacture of instrumentation, providing hysteroscopes with continuous flow systems and optical lenses that offer better utilization of light. Furthermore, the routine use of video systems greatly facilitated these procedures in an office setting without the need for general anesthesia [4,5].

A new intratubal device, the ESSURE pbc micro-insert (previously called the STOP device), has been introduced by Conceptus (San Carlos, CA, USA) and evaluated in vitro and in vivo for acute anchoring as well as chronic retention and tubal occlusion.

DESCRIPTION OF ESSURE™ INSERT

The ESSURE™ insert is a coil that consists of a stainless steel inner coil, an outer coil made from nitinol and polyethylene terephthalate (PET), Dacron fibers. The inner coil attaches the device to a guidewire used in its placement. The outer coil anchors the device in the fallopian tube upon deployment. For insertion, the device is maintained in a low profile position through the use of a release catheter. A hydrophilic catheter to facilitate the access to the tube accompanies the guidewire, the release catheter, and the device. The entire system is attached to a handle, aligned for one-hand release of the device. The device is delivered through a 5 Fr operating channel of a small caliber hysteroscope.

The PET fibers have had widespread clinical use for >40 years, and have been demonstrated to produce an immediate local inflammatory response characterized by macrophages, fibroblasts, foreign body giant cells, and plasma cells. A moderate foreign body inflammatory reaction is elicited by the PET fibers. This inflammatory response peaks between 2 and 3 weeks, after which the inflammatory response slowly resolves over a 10-week period. Extensive fibrosis results, causing occlusion and chronic anchoring of the PET material and any associated medical device (Figures 1–5).

TECHNIQUE OF INSERTION AND DEPLOYMENT

The patient is placed in the dorsal lithotomy position and the vaginal area and cervix are cleansed with an antiseptic solution. A paracervical block is performed with a local anesthetic. Any local anesthetic can be used to perform a paracervical block, nonetheless, because of its low toxicity an ester type of anesthesia is preferable, such as chloroprocaine, (Nesacaine) 1% solution, injecting 4–6 ml of the solution superficially at the base of each uterosacral ligament. A small amount of anesthetic (0.5 ml) can also be injected on the anterior lip of the cervix to place a tenaculum without discomfort to the patient.

A small caliber, 3.9–5.9 mm OD hysteroscope with continuous flow system is used. The tenaculum is optional, placed on the anterior lip of the cervix, and hysteroscopy is performed without previous cervical dilatation (Figures 6–9).

Low viscosity fluids such as normal saline are preferable when using the hysteroscopic method with a continuous flow system. The normal saline is warmed to room temperature to avoid discomfort to the patient by cooling.

Figure 1
Components of ESSURE™ micro-coil system (image courtesy of Conceptus Inc.).

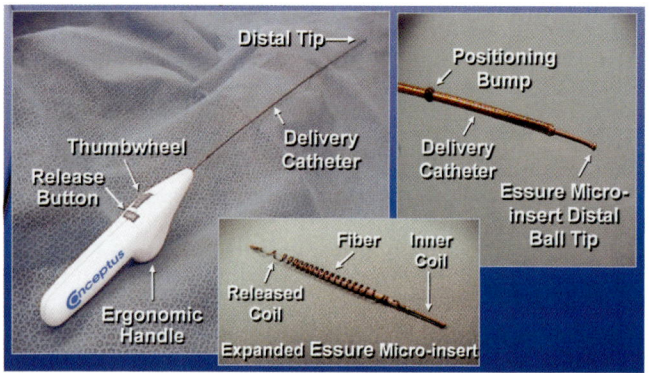

Figure 4
Isolated expanded micro-coil (image courtesy of Conceptus Inc.).

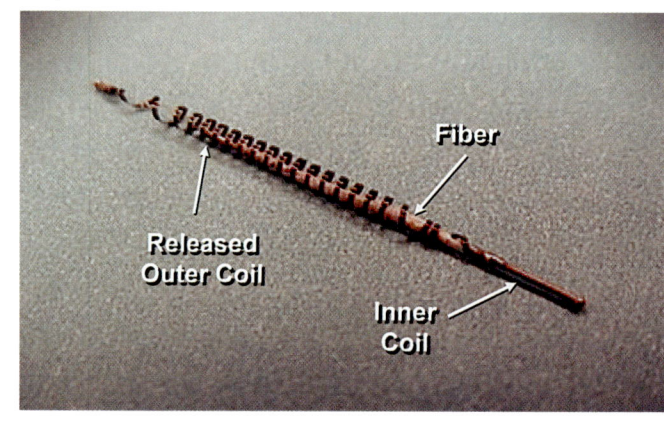

Figure 2
Diagrams of wound down and expanded micro-coil.

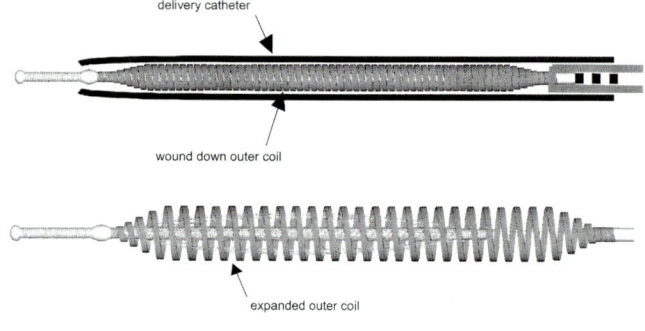

Figure 5
Close-up diagrammatic view of ESSURE™ micro-coil.

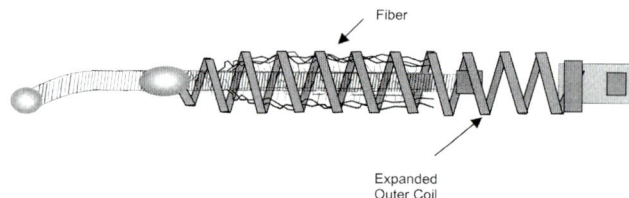

Figure 3
Diagram of micro-coil with delivery catheter.

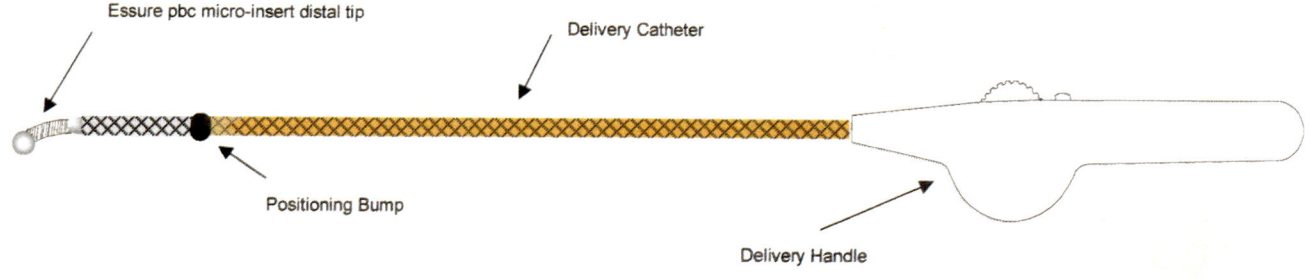

The uterine cavity is evaluated and both tubal openings are observed. The ESSURE™ micro-insert is fed through the 5-Fr operating channel of the hysteroscope and gently guided into the tubal opening until a dark circle of the outer catheter comes into view. The wheel in the handle is activated until a stop occurs showing the micro-insert in the tubal lumen, still undeployed in its inner catheter. A metal marker comes into view signifying good placement and, by pressing the small button in the handle, the micro-insert is deployed. Further thumb turning of the wheel in the handle will demonstrate the anchoring of the micro-insert by expansion of the spring outer metal. Several counter-clockwise turns finally detach the delivery system and the insert proximal end is evaluated by hysteroscopy to be sure that 5–10 mm of trailing insert are in the uterine cavity. The same procedure is performed in the opposite fallopian tube (Figures 10–13).

Figure 6
ACMI Slimline™ operative hysteroscope outer sheath and operative bridge, 5.5 mm diameter, 1.7 mm working channel with ACMI M3™ 12° autoclavable telescope.

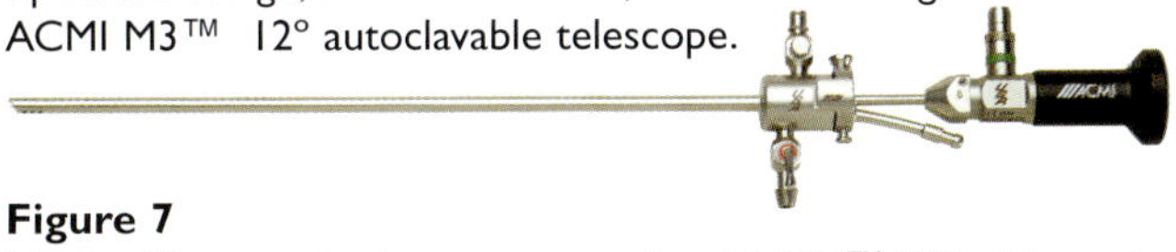

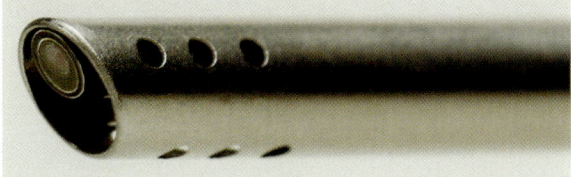

Figure 7
Slimline™ operative hysteroscope tip with M3™ 30° wide angle autoclavable telescope.

Figure 8
ACMI Slimline™ operative hysteroscope, port detail.

Figure 9
ACMI Slimline™ semi-rigid alligator forceps, 1.7 mm diameter, 42 cm length.

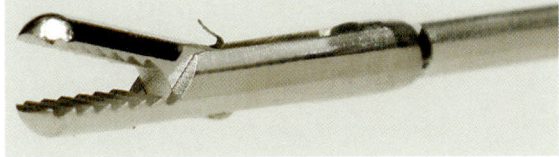

Figure 10
Delivery handle of deploying catheter showing turning wheel for release of catheters and button for micro-coil deployment.

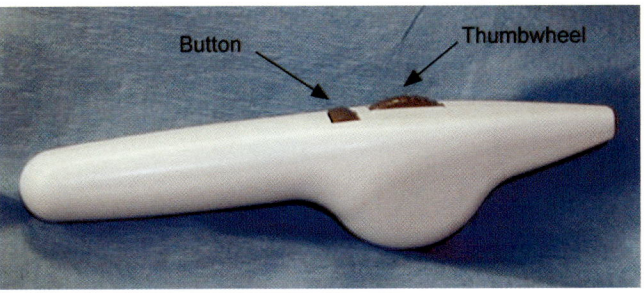

Figure 11
Delivery handle with thumb on thumb wheel.

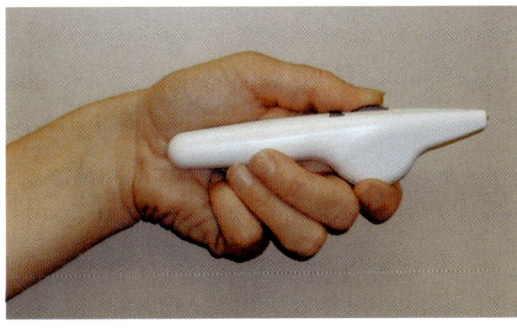

Figure 12
ESSURE™ micro-coil introduced in fallopian tube with deploying catheter.

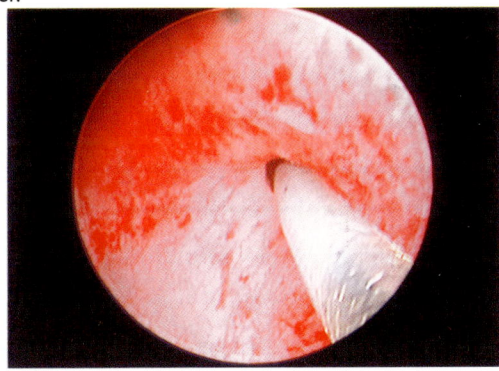

Figure 13
ESSURE™ micro-coil introduced in fallopian tube with deploying catheter.

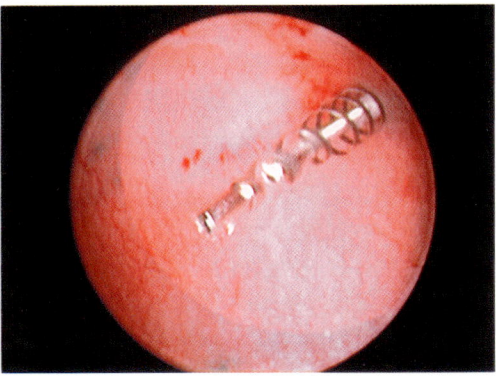

EVALUATION OF THE ESSURE™ MICRO-INSERTS IN A PREHYSTERECTOMY STUDY

To evaluate the feasibility of insertion, anchoring, and complete tubal occlusion produced by the ESSURE™ micro-inserts, studies were designed to insert these devices in women who required a hysterectomy and were willing to delay the procedure for at least 3 months after the tubal devices were inserted. At hysterectomy, the portions of the fallopian tubes containing the devices were removed for histologic evaluation. Forty-three patients underwent device placement with the ESSURE™ micro-inserts.

Forty-one patients had device placement in both fallopian tubes and two patients each had device placement in one tube, with a total of 84 tubes treated with device placements. Successful placement of the device occurred in at least one tube in 43 patients or 57/84 (68%) attempts. Because of the uterine pathology present in this patient population, the device placement rate was significantly less than that experienced in the population with intended sterilization. Failure to place the device was considered to be device-related in only one tube (1%). In this case, the catheter failed to retract from the device. The cause of this failure was identified and resolved by design change. In those patients with uterine myomas or thickened endometrium that permitted visualization of the tubal ostium, placement of the device was achieved. The average procedure time was 15 minutes. No intraoperative adverse effects were noted during placement.

The patients in this study were followed until their hysterectomy, which was done between 24 hours and 14 weeks after device placement. The majority of the hysterectomies were done at the completion of almost 3 months. Tubal occlusion was evaluated by hysterosalpingogram before the hysterectomy and all tubes (50/50, 100%) were found to be occluded. Histologic evaluation in 27 patients accounting for 47 tubes was also carried out, with an 80% occlusion rate in those patients with devices that had been in place for >4 weeks and consistent with 100% functional occlusion noted by the hysterosalpingogram done before hysterectomy (Tables 1 and 2) [6].

Table 1
Length of device wearing by device iteration

Length of device wearing	Number of patients
<2 weeks	2
2–5 weeks	5
5–7 weeks	1
7–9 weeks	0
9–11 weeks	2
11–13 weeks	6
13–15 weeks	16
>15 weeks	1
Pending hysterectomy	0
Total	33

Table 2
Histology results by tube

	Wearing time (weeks)					
	1–4	4–8	8–12	12–16	>16	Total
Tissue reaction	n = 9 tubes	n = 5 tubes	n = 3 tubes	n = 8 tubes	n = 1 tube	n = 23 tubes
Moderate/extensive acute inflammation	7/9	2/5	0/3	17/29	0/1	26/47
Moderate/extensive chronic inflammation	8/9	4/5	3/3	26/29	1/1	42/47
Moderate/extensive loose fibrosis	7/9	3/5	3/3	26/29	1/1	40/47
Moderate/extensive dense fibrosis	7/9	2/5	3/3	25/29	1/1	38/47
Moderate/extensive disruption of epithelium	7/9	4/5	3/3	29/29	1/1	44/47
Moderate/extensive disruption of lamina propria	7/9	4/5	3/3	28/29	1/1	43/47
80–100% obliteration of tubal lumen	4/9	5/5	3/3	26/29	1/1	39/47
Overall reaction to device = extensive	3/9	1/5	3/3	26/29	1/1	34/47
Overall reaction to device = moderate	2/9	3/5	0/3	1.29	0/1	6/47
Overall reaction to device = mild	4/9	1/5	0/3	2/29	0/1	7/47

HISTOLOGICAL EVALUATION

PATIENT POPULATION

To evaluate patient safety and comfort during device wearing, and to obtain histologic information on the ESSURE™ device to confirm the theoretical mechanism of action Conceptus conducted a study of the ESSURE™ micro-coil in patients scheduled to undergo a hysterectomy 24 hours to 12 weeks after micro-insert placement. In all, 47 patients were enrolled and implanted with devices in the pre-hysterectomy trial.

DEVICE WEARING – LONG-TERM

As noted above, patients in this study were followed until their hysterectomy, which was usually scheduled between 24 hours and 12 weeks after device placement. Table 1 details the length of device wearing for each of the device iterations in this study.

There were no reports of pain during device wearing. No pain was reported during pelvic examinations conducted just before the hysterectomy in any of the patients.

There was no evidence of inflammation, ulceration, or hemorrhage on gross examination of the uterus, except one patient with adenomyosis who was noted to have ulceration and hemorrhage in the uterine cavity; both fallopian tubes in this patient were unremarkable.

HSG RESULTS

Tubal occlusion was evaluated just before the hysterectomy by HSG. In tubes in which device movement or perforation did not occur, occlusion was noted in 50/50 (100%) tubes evaluated.

METHODOLOGY

Fallopian tubes of all patients enrolled in the study underwent both gross and microscopic examination. Care was taken at the time of hysterectomy to remove the uterus and tubes en bloc, without cutting into the device or using electrosurgery on the tubes. Once the tubes were removed, the uterus and tubes were X-rayed to determine the position of the devices in the tubes. Markers were placed at the uterotubal junction (UTJ) as a landmark. The uteri were then bi-valved and the uterine end of the device was evaluated for position as well as to examine any local response to the device in the uterus. The uterine cornua and tubes were then excised and placed in formalin. An independent histopathologist then conducted gross examination of the tubes. Subsequent to the gross examination, the tubes were sent for processing at a core laboratory and then returned to the independent histopathologist for microscopic evaluation. The tubes were processed at the core laboratory as follows:

1. The tubes were X-rayed to determine the placement of the device within the tube.
2. The specimens were then dehydrated in alcohol and xylene and embedded in methyl methacrylate (MMA) until polymerized.
3. The resulting block was then compared to the X-ray and the embedded fallopian tube was divided into three blocks according to the device position, using a diamond blade saw:
   a. block A included the uterine cornua up to the UTJ,
   b. block B included the UTJ to the proximal isthmic portion of the tube, and
   c. block C included the proximal isthmic portion to a point within 5 mm distal to the end of the device.
4. Two cross-sectional sections were then taken from the uterine end of blocks A, B, and C (designated the prefix U), and the fimbrial end of block C (designated the prefix F), using a diamond saw. (See Figure 14 for the locations of histological sectioning.)
5. These sections were ground down to a thickness of approximately 50–100 microns for microscopic evaluation.
6. The slides were then prepared from each section: one was stained in H&E and the other with Goldner's trichrome.

The MMA embedding process and the diamond saw cutting were undertaken to preserve the integrity of the relationship between the device and the tissue.

Figure 14
Diagrammatic representation of cut locations for histological sectioning. AU, the cut at the proximal portion of the device near the uterine cavity; AF, the cut near the fimbrial end; BU, the cut with the device in the intramural isthmic portion; BF, the cut at the distal portion of the isthmic tube; CU, the section at the distal end of the device.

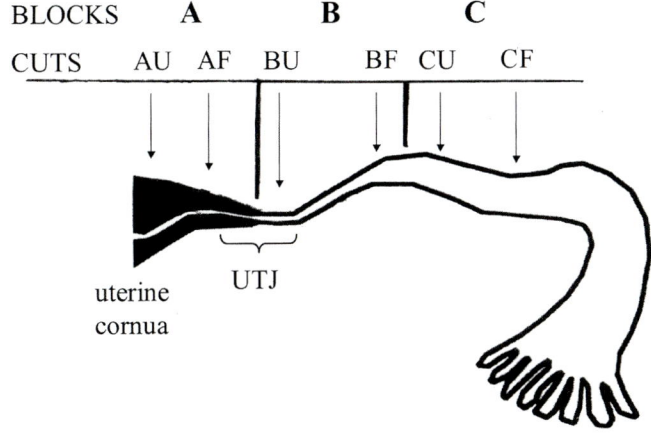

HISTOLOGICAL EVALUATION – RESULTS

Patients wore the device for periods of time ranging from 8 days to 14 weeks. The distribution of wearing times is noted in Table 1. Table 2 provides some of the quantitative information derived from the histology slides. This information is presented by wearing time to more clearly view the increasing tissue response seen over time.

PET fibers have been in widespread clinical use for approximately 40 years and tissue responses to this material in humans are relatively well characterized. The histologic response to the ESSURE micro-insert is characteristic of the histologic response observed with the use of PET fibers in other anatomic sites. Specifically, the PET fibers appear to elicit a strong fibrous and inflammatory tissue response that extends into the space between the inner and outer coils of the ESSURE micro-insert. The tissue response consists predominantly of macrophages and mononuclear cells, with some foreign body-type giant cells and acute inflammatory cells. The fibrous response consists of both loose and dense fibrous tissue. In the cases studied with 3 months of wearing time, smooth muscle cells were also observed migrating from the fallopian tube wall into the space between the inner and outer coils. This response is clearly demonstrated when comparing cross-sections of tubal segments from patients with and without devices (Figures 15 and 16).

In addition, the fibrosis and tissue reaction were noted to be localized to the inner portions of the fallopian tube wall. There is no evidence that the fibrosis induced by the device will extend beyond the wall of the fallopian tube, or cause peritubal adhesions or serositis.

Normal tubal architecture was present within 5 mm distal to the end of the device. The histologic analysis revealed normal tubal segments; inflammatory cells were absent. This can be observed in specimens collected that were distal to the device (see human histology specimens) (Figure 17).

An independent histopathologist for the study concluded that the tissue response to the ESSURE™ micro-insert is occlusive in nature and should provide for long-term anchoring of the device as well as pregnancy prevention. The study demonstrated that the tissue reaction is predictable, occurred in all specimens that contained fiber, and is localized to the device Figures 18–20).

PRELIMINARY CLINICAL RESULTS

In all, 871 women with documented fertility who selected investigational hysteroscopic permanent contraception with the ESSURE™ micro-inserts were recruited; 269 women were involved in phase II and 602 women in a

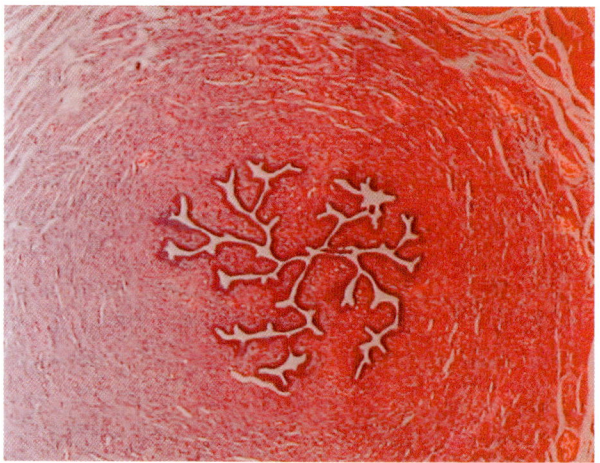

Figure 15
Cross-sectional appearance of normal fallopian tube.

Figure 16
Cross-sectional view of fallopian tube with implanted ESSURETM micro-insert. Inner metallic ring is the ESSURETM micro-insert's outer coil. Complete absence of normal architecture and infiltration of tissue throughout the ESSURETM micro-insert structure is demonstrated.

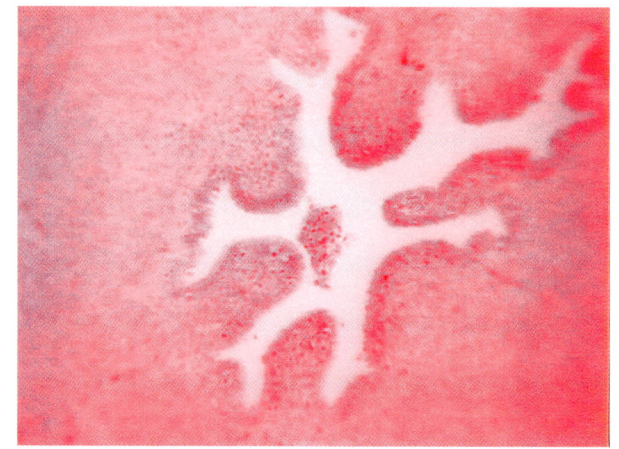

Figure 17
Cross-sectional view of tube 5 mm distal to micro-insert. Note absence of inflammatory cells. Tissue response is localized to the device.

pivotal study. A total of 227 (84%) women in phase II were attempted and 518 (86%) in the pivotal study. It was found that 187 of 193 women (96.4%) in the phase II study had bilateral occlusion at 3 months and 416 of 433 women (96.1%) in the pivotal study. Bilateral occlusion at 6 months was demonstrated in all 194 patients (100%) in the phase II study and 420 of 433 (97.7%) in the pivotal study. In the phase II study 143 women were relying on the ESSURE device for more than a year. No pregnancies have occurred in either study. The procedure was well tolerated by the great majority of patients (>90%); on average it lasted 13–18 minutes, and resulted in little or no postoperative discomfort. Local anesthesia (43.8%), IV sedation and/or analgesia (52.4%), were the anesthesia used for these procedures in 93.0% of patients in the phase II study and 92.8% in the pivotal study (Tables 3–5) [7,8].

Based on this information, clinical trials have been extended and are underway to use the ESSURE™ micro-inserts as a permanent method of contraception in women requiring tubal sterilization. However, on the basis of the above information, it is expected that the transcervical method of tubal sterilization utilizing the ESSURE micro-coils will be an excellent alternative for permanent contraception in women.

SUMMARY AND CONCLUSIONS

An ambulatory, office-based, non-incisional method of sterilization has been elusive. New technological advances in instrumentation and design of intratubal occlusive devices have permitted the introduction of a promising new method of transcervical sterilization utilizing modern intratubal devices. The ESSURE™ micro-insert is a flexible micro-coil that can be deployed transcervically in

Figure 18
Cross-sectional microscopic views of fallopian tube containing the ESSURE™ micro-coil. Histology 8 days after device placement: fibrosis and acute inflammatory cells migrating into device. AU, cross-section of device near uterine cavity, note fiber on inner coil; CU, cross-section taken at distal end of device; CF, cross-section of fallopian tube 5 mm distal to device location; BU, cross-section with the device in the intramural isthmic portion.

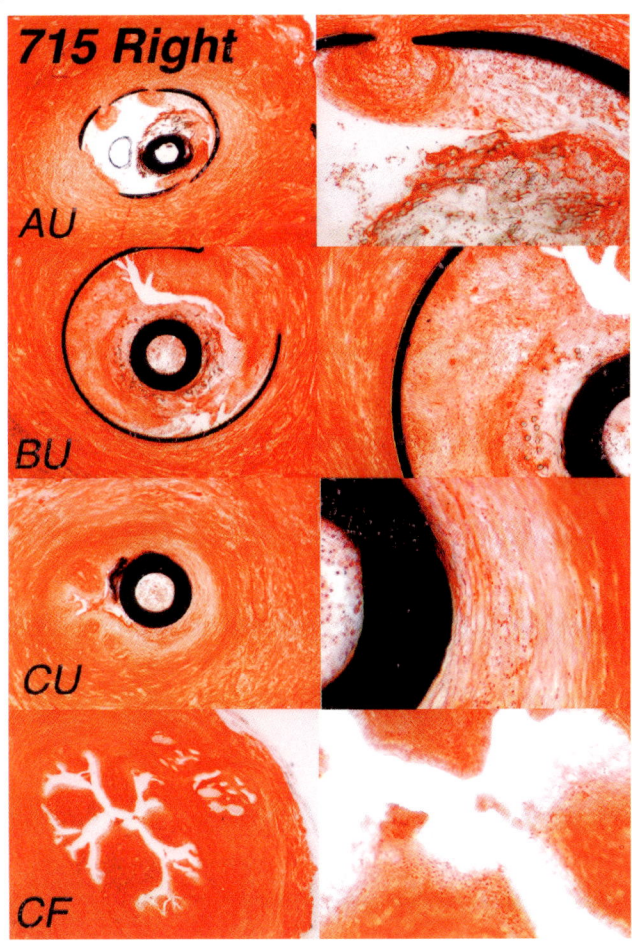

Figure 19
Human histology 5.5 weeks after device placement: fibrosis replacing tube. Acute and chronic inflammatory cells are present. AU, cross-section of device near uterine cavity, note fiber on inner coil; BU, cross-section with the device in the intramural isthmic portion; CU, cross-section taken at distal end of device; CF, cross-section of fallopian tube 5 mm distal to device location.

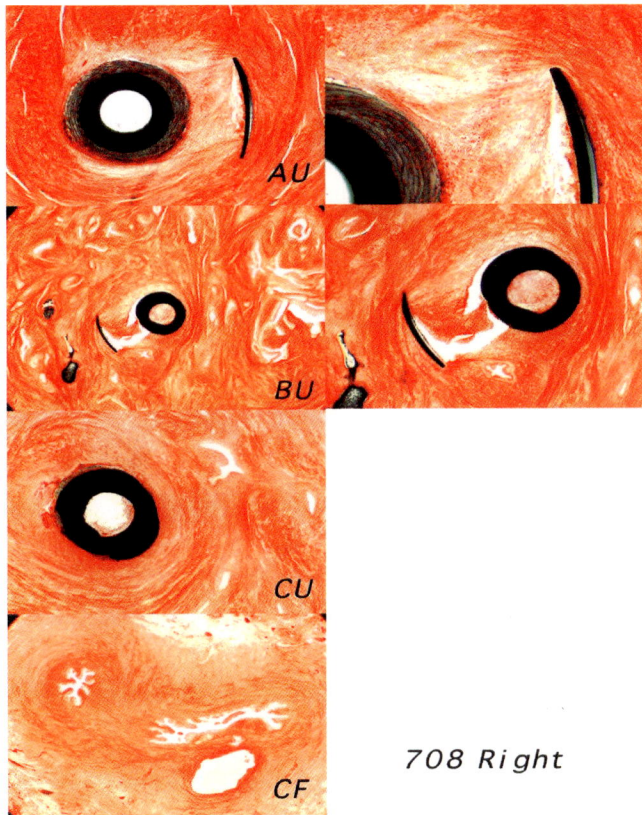

the fallopian tube, utilizing small caliber hysteroscopes with a 5 Fr operating channel. This method of deployment avoids cervical dilatation and permits its use and performance in an office setting under local anesthesia. In vitro and in vivo studies demonstrated the feasibility and the occurrence of complete tubal occlusion when these devices were placed before patients underwent a hysterectomy. The tubal occlusion demonstrated complete fibrosis of the lumen and paved the way to clinical trials to evaluate the use of these devices for permanent contraception. The avoidance of general anesthesia, incisions, and their associated cost and morbidity makes this method of contraception an excellent alternative for women seeking permanent contraception. Because its performance is a truly ambulatory office procedure, it decreases morbidity, cost, and inconvenience to the patient. Hopefully the ongoing clinical trials will demonstrate its true long-term safety and effectiveness as a contraceptive method.

Table 3
Demographics of clinical study

Parameter	Phase II	Pivotal study
Patients enrolled	269	602
Patients attempted	227 (84%)	518 (86%)
Average age (years)	35	32
Age range (years)	23–45	21–40
Height (inches)	64.17	64.45
Weight (lbs)	154.0	159.49
Gravidity	2.6	3.0
Parity	2.2	2.3

Table 4
Clinical effectiveness

Parameter	Phase II	Pivotal study
Bilateral occlusion at 3 months	96.4% n = 187/194	96.1%* n = 416/433
Bilateral occlusion at 6 months	100% n = 194/194	97.7%† n = 420/433
Woman months of wearing	3974	3462
Woman months of effectiveness	3057	1360
Number of women relying on ESSURE pbc for >1 year	143	NA
Number of pregnancies	0	0

NA, not applicable.
*Of the 17 patients not occluded at 3 months, only 4 had undergone repeat HSGs at the time of this data analysis.
†5 of 13 patients have undergone repeat HSGs at 6 months, 8 patients are awaiting evaluation.

Table 5
Adverse events

Parameter	Phase II	Pivotal study
Patients experiencing adverse events	5.7% (13/227)	4.2% (22/518)*
Type of adverse event		
Expulsion	0.4% (n = 1)	2.7% (n = 14)
Perforation	1.8% (n = 4)	0.8% (n = 4)
Proximal band detachment	1.3% (n = 3)	0.4% (n = 2)
Undesirable device location	1.3% (n = 3)	0.2% (n = 1)
Others	0.9% (n = 2)	0.6% (n = 3)

*Of 14 patients experiencing expulsion, 8 had reattempts resulting in successful replacement of the device. Three patients were also found to have patency but underwent sterilization before reattempts were considered. One patient was found to be occluded despite expulsion.

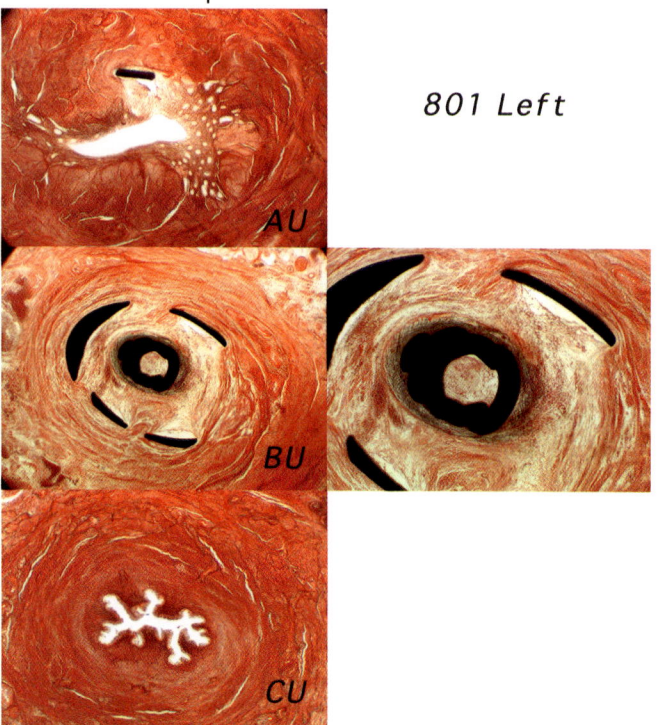

Figure 20
Human histology almost 13 weeks after device placement. Dense fibrous tissue is present, and inflammatory cells are scant. AU, proximal portion of device near uterine cavity; BU, device in intramural-isthmic portion, fiber is visible on inner coil; CU, cross-section of fallopian tube 5 mm distal to device location.

REFERENCES

1. Sciarra JJ. Hysteroscopic approaches for tubal closure. In: Zatuchni GI, Labbock MH, Sciarra JJ, eds. Research Frontiers in Fertility Regulation. Hagerstown, MD: Harper and Row, 1980: 270–286.
2. Zatuchni GI, Shelton JD, Goldsmith A, Sciarra JJ. Female Transcervical Sterilization. Philadelphia, PA: Harper and Row, 1983.
3. Darabi K, Richart R. Collaborative study on hysteroscopic sterilization procedures: preliminary report. *Obstet Gynecol* 1977; **49**: 48–54.
4. Valle RF. Tubal catheterization for sterilization purposes. In: Gleicher N et al. Tubal Catheterization Procedures. New York, NY: Wiley, 1992: 139–160.
5. Valle RF, Read T. Hysteroscopic sterilization. In: Baggish MS, Barbot J, Valle RF, eds. Diagnostic and Operative Hysteroscopy: A Text and Atlas, 2nd edn. Boston, MA: Mosby, 1999: 353–366.
6. Valle RF, Carignan CS, Wright TC and the STOP Prehysterectomy Investigation Group. Tissue response to the STOP microcoil transcervical permanent contraceptive device: results from a prehysterectomy study. *Fertil Steril* 2001; **76**: 974–980.
7. Kerin JF, Carignan CS, Cher D. The safety and effectiveness of a new hysteroscopic method for permanent birth control: results of the first ESSURE™ pbc Clinical Study. *Aust NZ J Obstet Gynaecol* 2001; **41**: 364–370.
8. Valle RF, Cooper JM, Kerin JF. Hysteroscopic tubal sterilization with the ESSURE™ non-invasive permanent contraception system: preliminary results. *Obstet Gynecol* 2002; **99** (Suppl 4): 11S.

22 Anesthesia and monitoring in an outpatient set up

Bruno Lasters and B.J. van Herendael

> **Take Home Message**
> Most patients undergoing diagnostic hysteroscopy do not need an anesthetic and can be hysteroscoped without any form of premedication or anesthesia. The surgeon should have knowledge of the possible complications and should be able to treat these on the spot. If more advanced procedures are tackled, the necessary monitoring equipment should be available. The requirement for this equipment to be available is dependent on local law. An overview of the most recent equipment is provided, as are schemes for the use of local anesthetic agents and schemes for dealing with both common and rarer complications.

INTRODUCTION

Although today most hysteroscopic procedures are performed using vaginoscopy as a technique without any form of anesthesia for both diagnosis and operative procedures, there are still some circumstances that require premedication or local anesthesia. The different circumstances can be catalogued as follows:

- Known stenosis of the cervical canal.
- Manipulation of the tubal ostium and the intramural region.
- Need to overdilate the uterine cavity.
- Need to manipulate or extract volumes of >2 cm in diameter.

Experience indicates that the major pain points are the isthmus and the distal part of the cervical canal, just before the scope passes into the uterine cavity and the fundal area. Dilating the intramural region sometimes causes a vasovagal reaction, but this does not happen with every patient. Because of the different nature of pain stimuli in the different pain points, different treatments or a combination of different treatments are required.

CERVICAL STENOSIS

In cervical stenosis there are two entities:

- Pure anatomic stenosis
- Functional stenosis.

In cases of anatomic stenosis such as DES influence on the cervix in cases of uterine hypoplasia, or cervical trauma, i.e. after a difficult cesarean section and in the advanced menopause a pharmacologic means should be used to soften the cervical canal before the examination. The most universally used drugs are those based on prostaglandins, such as vaginal tablets of Sulprostone or Cytotec®. Ideally the drug should be applied intravaginally the night before the hysteroscopy. The vaginal tablets or ovules should be inserted at least 2 hours before the actual examination to let the drug act on the connective tissues of the cervix.

Historically mechanical dilators have been used. Mechanical dilators are not as appropriate for outpatient hysteroscopy, as they need mechanical insertion into the cervical canal the night before the hysteroscopy. As manipulation is required this makes the examination less outpatient in nature. Natural laminaria have no memory of swelling and hence tend to swell more where there is less resistance. This means that they will swell more at the tip inserted into the uterine cavity and hence are more difficult to remove. Artificial swelling bodies such as Lamicel® have a memory of swelling. This means that these elements swell homogeneously over the entire length of the device. Once again, manipulation is required the night before hystereoscopy is due to be carried out, and these aids are expensive.

In the case of an anatomic cervical stenosis it is better to give an appropriate premedication to avoid unnecessary pain sensation.

The cases of functional stenosis are confined to the upper part of the cervical canal in the very anxious patient. Here there is a need for local anesthesia and for premedication to avoid excessive neuro-vegetative reactions, i.e. generalized abdominal cramping accompanied by nausea and generalized tremor.

MANIPULATION OF THE TUBAL OSTIUM AND THE INTRAMURAL REGION

The tubal ostium and the intramural region are very sensitive and can cause an intense pain sensation. The patient will relate this as a cramping pain that can occur even several hours after the manipulation. When an object has been left in the intramural region the pain remains for some 24–48 hours and sometimes there is an exacerbation of the cramp-like pain during the first 2 days of menstruation and during orgasm.

This kind of pain is due to direct contact with the tissues and to muscle spasms, which need a specific treatment. When manipulation of the tubal ostia or in the intramural region is mandatory, we combine a potent analgesic with the premedication and the eventual local anesthesia. This NSAID (nonsteroidal antiinflammatory drug) should also be given immediately after the hysteroscopy and repeated some 3–5 hours afterwards. This will prevent most of the cramp-like pain episodes during the 24 hours following the examination. After 24–48 hours there seems to be a habituation to the stimulus and the patient does not experience pain any more, except in acute circumstances such as the beginning of menstruation and the immediate pre-orgastic contractions of the uterine musculature.

NEED TO OVERDILATE THE UTERINE CAVITY

In cases where we need to distend the uterine cavity to a maximum, or over the maximum for a particular cavity, a cramping of the uterine muscle will automatically follow. This is believed to result from a release of prostaglandins caused by the stretching of the myometrium. These cramps start at the distal cornual end and roll towards the internal os of the cervix. As these muscle contractions are similar in pattern to the menstrual cramps for the patient the pain sensation is exactly that of menstrual cramping. In retrograde experimentation in vitro Thierry Van Caillie proved that the opening pressure for the isthmic part of the tube is 50 mmHg. He proved that in vitro all tubes are open at a retrograde infusion pressure of 50 mmHg, whereas at 30 mmHg some isthmic parts still resisted. If we transpose these experiments in vivo and translate the figures in antegrade pressure we should not induce muscular contractions when we work under the dilatation pressure of 30 mmHg. This is difficult to evaluate when we are working with a pressure bag. Gravity inflow seldom exceeds 30 mmHg dilatation pressure and a mechanical pump device is ideal as we can then preset the pressure. If we really need to exceed 30 mmHg we need to give premedication including a muscular relaxant to avoid vasovagal reaction and we should combine the regime with a NSAID. The analgesic drug needs to be repeated once or twice at intervals after the procedure.

NEED TO MANIPULATE OR EXTRACT VOLUMES OF >2 cm OUT OF THE UTERINE CAVITY

If we need to manipulate large volumes (>2 cm in diameter) we overdistend the cavity, resulting in the same process of uterine muscle contraction as described above. The uterine cavity is a virtual cavity confined by a relatively thick muscle coat, which is larger than that in other hollow organs. The maximum dilatation capacity of the nonpregnant uterine cavity is 4 cm from myometrial to myometrial layer. We also have the endometrium between 2 and 11 mm depending on the cycle day. This means that both layers of the endometrium can be between 3.6 and 3 cm distant from each other, taking into account the compression of the endometrial layers at maximum dilatation in the normal sized uterus. The consequence is that when volumes >2 cm are manipulated there will be a mechanical stimulation of one or both myometrial layers, initiating the sequence of rhythmic contractions, starting at the distal cornu and propagating towards the internal cervical os. When we try to remove volumes of >2 cm in diameter we will directly stimulate the surrounding myometrium, starting the process of contractions. Therefore we should try to avoid extracting volumes >2 cm through the cervix in the outpatient situation. When performing such extraction, local anesthesia of the cervix and preferably of the cervical canal should be utilized, and premedication including a muscular relaxant and a NSAID should be given before the hysteroscopy and repeated afterwards at regular intervals (3–4 hours) to avoid cramp-like sensations occurring in the following 24–48 hours.

LOCAL ANESTHESIA

In modern outpatient hysteroscopy there is no longer the need for the systematic use of local anesthesia; indeed, there are a few disadvantages connected with local anesthesia. The patient is already anxious and the sight of a syringe with needle advancing towards her vagina does not really help. The anesthesia effects last much longer than the hysteroscopy and the numbness is comparable to the numbness felt after anesthesia for dental work. The patient will experience that numbness for a few hours after the examination. Systemic effects are rare and in principle only occur when the anesthetic is injected directly into a vessel. Systemic effects can be severe. They can consist of neurological and cardiovascular phenomena such as convulsions, respiratory depression, arrythmia and cardiac insufficiency.

Local anesthesia is given in a paracervical block or even better in a combination of intracervical and paracervical block. The intracervical injections consist of 3 ml of a 1% solution at 10 and 14 hours. The paracervical injection comprises 5 ml of a 1% solution at the insertion of the sacro-uterine ligaments. It is crucial to insert the needle only a few millimeters into the tissues just under the mucosa. To avoid intravascular injections it is mandatory to aspirate, with the needle in place, just before injecting the product. If blood is aspirated the injection site should be changed and the procedure restarted.

PRODUCTS (Table 1)

The advice is to stick with one of the products. This will mean that you will know the product, its effects, and possible side effects thoroughly in a very short period of time, so the likelihood of making mistakes becomes very small.

The anesthetic effect starts within 2–3 minutes. Good anesthesia and hence procedure time is 15–20 minutes. When a vasoconstrictor is added the duration of the effect is prolonged by a factor of three – some 45 minutes up to 1 hour.

Take care not to exceed the maximum dosage allowed. Xylocaine without a vasoconstrictor has a maximum dosage of 200 mg at 10 mg/ml; this comes to a maximum of 20 ml!!!

Vasoconstrictors (Tables 2 and 3)

The advantages of vasopressins are that the vasopressin derivates give vasoconstriction without the reactive vasodilatation. This is the case when adrenaline (epinephrine) is used.

COMPLICATIONS OF LOCAL ANESTHETICS

If one keeps in mind the indicated maximum dosages the complications will be very rare.

Three main complications:

1. The inhibiting effect on the conductive system of the heart can result in
   - arrythmia
   - hypotension, collapse and cardiac arrest.
2. Drowsiness, respiratory arrest, epileptic convulsions and collapse, followed by cardiac arrest.
3. Allergic reactions (mostly due to the stabilizers used).

The first two are related to rapid absorption, allergic reactions are independent of dose.

TREATMENT OF COMPLICATIONS

It is important to know what has caused the complication (Tables 4–7). Allergic reactions can be treated with adrenaline 0.5 mg IMI stat. Other problems can be treated with assisted ventilation and atropine 0.5–1.0 ml IV (of a 1:1000 solution).

Tables 4–7 demonstrate that it is necessary to have a resuscitation kit with respiratory support and the necessary medication available when you perform hysteroscopy in a private or outpatient setting.

PREMEDICATION

With the exception of patients undergoing diagnostic hysteroscopy, all patients should have premedication (see Table 8). In the event that the diagnostic hysteroscopy reveals a pathology that needs an operative procedure the patient should be rescheduled if she has not had sufficient premedication. This is to avoid the possibility of a vasovagal reaction. The symptoms are bradycardia followed by nausea and cold sweats followed by convulsions and loss of consciousness. This is definitely not a situation we want in the private office or in the out-patient department; to avoid it we should discuss the problem with the patient and continue the hysteroscopy only if the patient is in agreement and does not experience pain. If we even suspect that the procedure will convert from diagnostic to operative we should give the patient premedication.

SEDATION

Since the introduction of the '2001 JCAHO' regulations on sedation, new and more precise definitions have come into

Table 1
Possible maximum dosages of different products

Local anesthetic	Maximum dosage without vasoconstrictor	Maximum dosage with vasoconstrictor
Lidocaine® (1% or 2%) (Xylocaine)	200 mg	500 mg
Mepivacaine® (1% or 2%) (Scandicain, Carbocain)	300 mg	500 mg
Citanest® (1% or 2%) Prilocaine	400 mg	600 mg

practice. (JCAHO = Joint Commission on Accreditation of Healthcare Organisations.)

1. Minimal sedation: ANXIOLYSIS

The patient is able to respond normally to verbal commands. Vital parameters do not change.

2. Moderate sedation: SEDO-ANALGESIA

The patient experiences a slight depression of consciousness and will respond purposefully to verbal commands or to light tactile stimulation. Spontaneous ventilation stays adequate and no manipulation of the upper airway is necessary to keep a patent airway.

3. Deep sedation: SEDO-ANALGESIA

Only repeated or painful stimuli can arouse the patient from their depressed consciousness. Airway interventions are mostly mandatory, such as chin lift. Spontaneous ventilation can be compromised, the patient can become hypoxic. Meanwhile cardiovascular functions are maintained.

4. Anesthesia

During general anesthesia the patients are no longer arousable, even by painful stimulation. All vital parameters need appropriate supportive measures by an anesthetist. This topic is beyond the scope of this chapter.

Table 2
Characteristics of POR 8®

Generic name	Ornipressin (8-ornithine-vasopressin) Polypeptide with vasopressin-like properties
Dosage	1 IU in 12–20 ml local anesthetic solution 1 IU in 12–20 ml saline
Maximum dosage	5 IU in 60–100 ml of diluent
Contraindications	Coronary heart disease Severe hypertension Advanced arteriosclerosis Epilepsy Hypersensitivity to the drug
Side effects	Pallor of the skin (face) Less common: – Rise or fall in blood pressure – Cardiac arrhythmias – Anginal pain

Table 3
Characteristics of adrenaline (epinephrine)

Contraindications	Coronary heart disease Severe hypertension Advanced arteriosclerosis Epilepsy Hypersensitivity to the drug
Dosage	1 : 200,000
Side effects	Unrest, anxiety Pallor Perspiration Tachycardia Extra systole

Table 4
Inhibiting effects on the conductive system of the heart

Dosage
- Rapid absorption from the injection site
- Accidental intravascular injection
- Exceeding maximum doses

Treatment
- Atropine 0.5 mg IV
- Mayo tube, oxygen 4–6 liters/min
- Intravenous line
- Adrenaline 0.5–1.0 ml IV (of 1:1000 solution) or 5–10 ml of a 1:1000 ml solution
- Respiratory and cardiac support

Table 5
Stimulating effects on the central nervous system

Causes
- Rapid absorption from the injection site
- Accidental intravascular injection
- Exceeding the maximum doses

First symptom: paresthesia of the tongue and the perioral region, metallic taste. Auditory disturbance (tremor and convulsions)

Treatment in case of convulsions
- Diazepam (Valium®) 10–20 mg IV
- Respiratory support

Inadequate sedation occurs in up to 15% of cases. The following factors can be taken in account:

- The procedure does not match the sedation; too many painful stimuli with inadequate pain relief.
- Abnormal or even paradoxical reactions to the sedation, e.g. agitation, inhibited behavior.
- No cooperation with the patient, e.g. language barrier.
- Respiratory problems resulting in hypoxia (hypoxia is defined as a saturation below 90%)
- Airway obstruction.
- Unstable circulating parameters, especially in patients with ASA >3.
- Unexpectedly prolonged procedures.

MONITORING FACILITIES

1. Saturation meter
2. 5-Lead ECG (including precordial lead V 5)
3. Respiratory rhythm
4. NIBP (noninvasive blood pressure monitoring)
5. BIS (bispectral analysis).

BIS monitoring (Figures 1–3) is the only scientific equipment available for correct measurement of the depth

Table 6
Allergic reactions and anaphylactic shock

Cause
- Hypersensitivity to the local anesthetic used

Symptoms
- Agitation
- Flushes
- Palpitations
- Paresthesia and pruritus
- Coughing and breathing difficulties (bronchospasm and laryngeal edema)
- Followed after a few minutes by shock and convulsions

Treatment
- Adrenaline 0.5 ml (1:1000) SC or IM
- Clemastin (Tavegyl®) 2 mg (= 2 ml) IV
- Prednisolone-sodium succinate 40 mg IV
- Supportive measures: IV line and oxygen
- In cases complicated by bronchospasm, insufficient reaction on adrenaline R/Aminophylline 240 mg (= 10 ml) (Euphyllin®) SLOWLY IV

Table 7
Treatment of acute local anesthetic toxicity

Airway
- Ensure clear airway; suction if required

Breathing
- Face mask and oxygen can help
- Aim for adequate ventilation
- If necessary use artificial ventilation

Circulation
- Elevate the legs
- Increase the IV fluids if blood pressure drops
- CVS support drug if low blood pressure persists

Drugs of choice

CNS depressive
- Diazepam 5–10 mg IV
- Thiopental 50 mg IV in incremental doses until seizures cease

Muscle relaxant
- Thiopental 50 mg IV if control of ventilation is inadequate with above measures (requires artificial ventilation and may necessitate intubation)

CVS support
- Atropine 0.6 mg IV if there is a drop in heart rate
- Ephedrine 12.5–25 mg IV to restore adequate blood pressure
- Ephedrine for profound cardiovascular collapse

Adapted from: Neural Blockade. In: Cousin MJ, Bridenbauch PO, eds. Clinical Anaesthesia and Management of Pain, 2nd edn, with permission of the publishers, JB Lippincott, Philadelphia.

of anesthesia or sedation. Far too often in the past sedation changed into a form of general anesthesia because of incorrect appreciation of the dosage of medication needed to achieve the desired effect. In traditional anesthesia practice blood pressure, heart rhythm, respiratory frequency and depth, degree of muscle tone, diameter of the pupil, presence of tears and cold sweat are all indirect and nonspecific signs for determining the level of anesthesia. Great variation of the parameters is possible because of comorbidity, associated medication, and surgical techniques. Patient intervariability may be an even greater problem in correct evaluation. Therefore, the optimal depth

Figure 1
Sensor XP application.

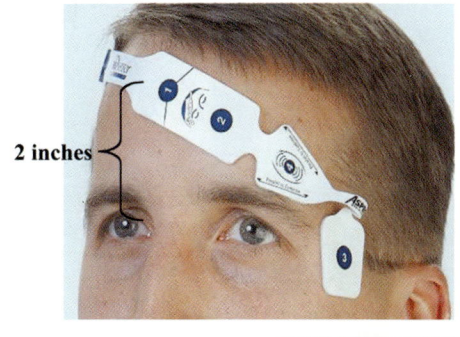

- **Apply sensor on forehead at angle**
  - Circle no 1: centered, 2 inches above nose
  - Circle no 4: Above/adjacent to eyebrow
  - Circle no 3: Either temple between corner of eye and hairline

- **Press edges of sensor**
  - Circle all 4 elements

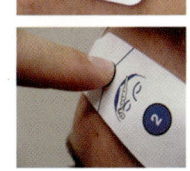

- **Press each circle for 5 seconds**
  - Use fingertip
  - Press firmly

Figure 2
Measurement principle.

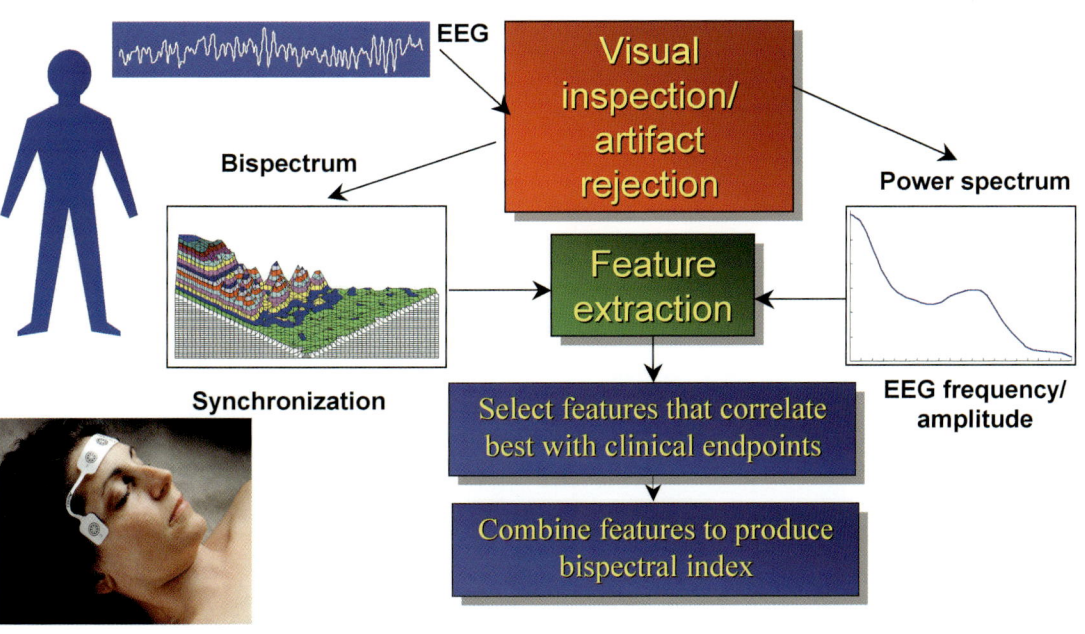

of sedation will not be reached by underdosage or overdosage of medication.

The final BIS index (Figure 4) is the result of the reduction in the first step of the EEG artefacts. In the second step there is the identification of the EEG with an analysis of the suppression, near suppression, and non-artefact undulating EEG. In the last step the different indices of the EEG are mapped to the hypnotic level and result in a BIS value.

The range guidelines shown in Figures 5–9 are used in the clinical endpoints and sedation ranges.

The BIS spectral index gives a *direct* measurement of the anesthetic effect. This means that the hypnotic endpoints are no longer influenced by the patient or by the medication. The index correlates well with brain metabolism (Figure 10).

This indicates that conditions that do have an effect on brain metabolism can interfere with the bispectral index value (see Further reading section).

FURTHER READING

Alkine MT. Quantitative EEG correlations with brain glucose metabolic rate during anesthesia in volunteers. *Anesthesiology* 1998; **89**: 323–333.

Rampil IJ. A primer for EEG signal processing in anesthesia (review). *Anesthesiology* 1998; **89**: 980–1002.

Figure 3
BIS® generation.

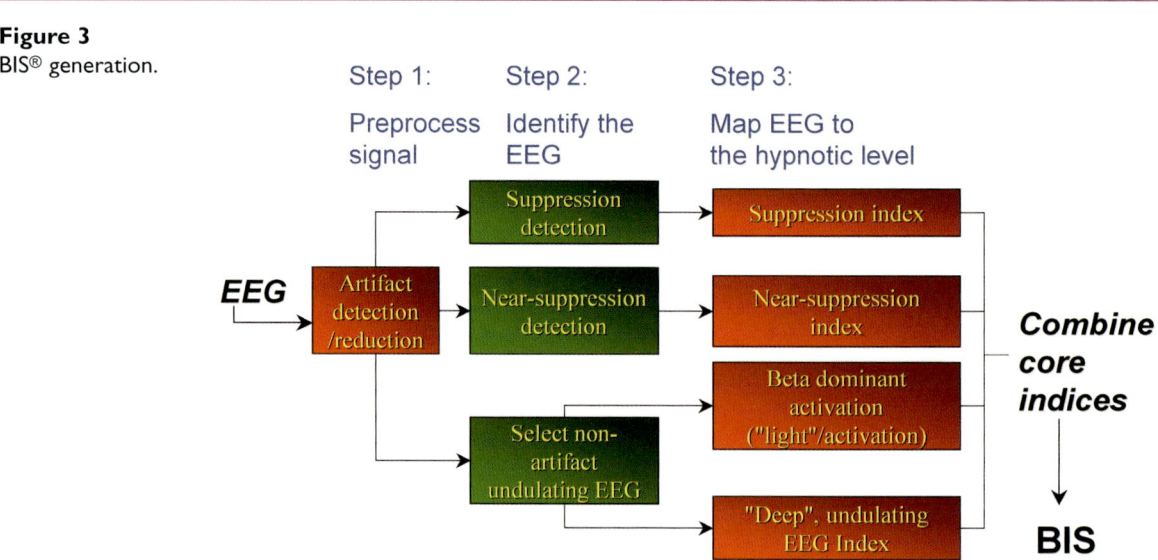

Figure 4
Components of the bispectral index.

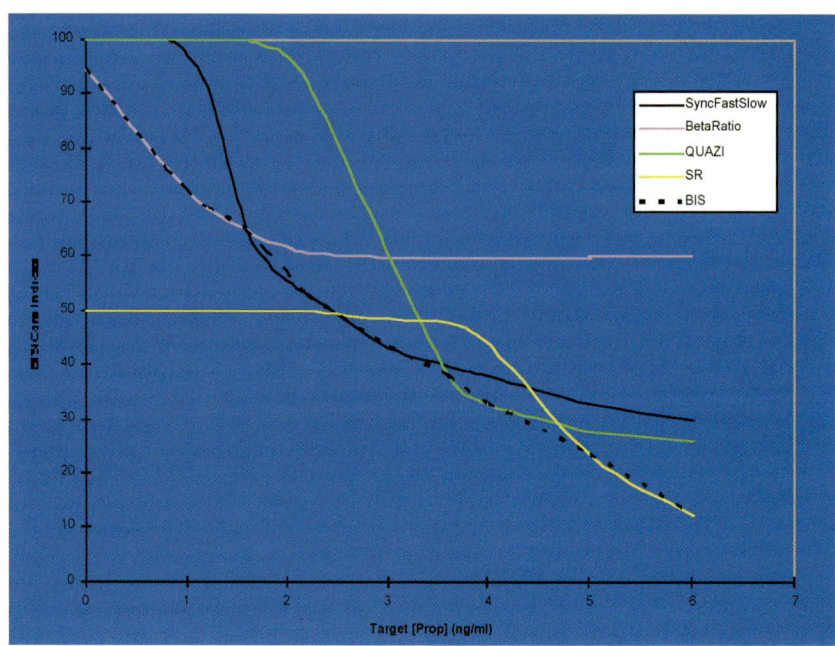

Figure 5
EEG patterns during anesthesia.

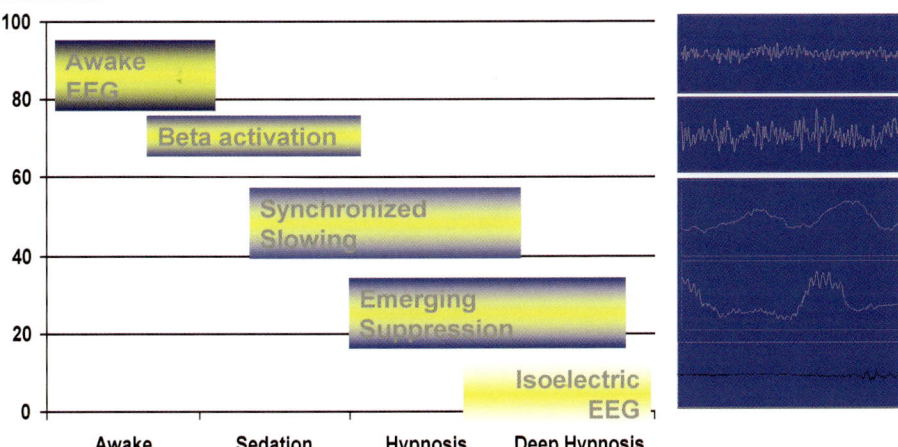

Figure 6
EEG frequency patterns.

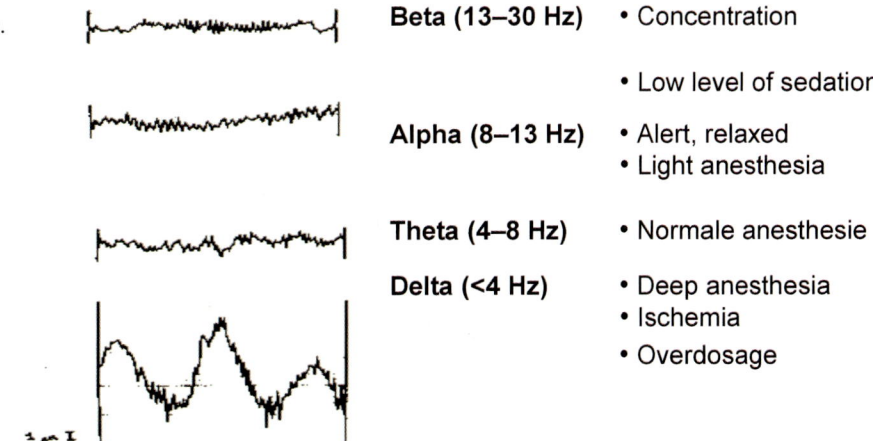

- **Beta (13–30 Hz)**
  - Concentration
  - Low level of sedation
- **Alpha (8–13 Hz)**
  - Alert, relaxed
  - Light anesthesia
- **Theta (4–8 Hz)**
  - Normale anesthesie
- **Delta (<4 Hz)**
  - Deep anesthesia
  - Ischemia
  - Overdosage

Figure 7
Very 'deep' EEG patterns.

- Delta
- Light suppression
- Total suppression

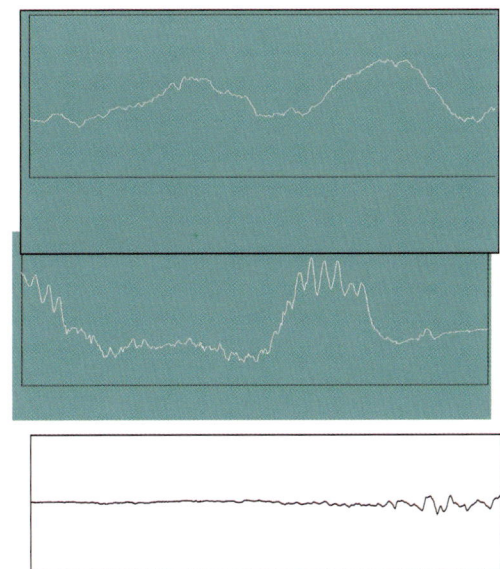

159

Figure 8
EEG patterns during anesthesia.

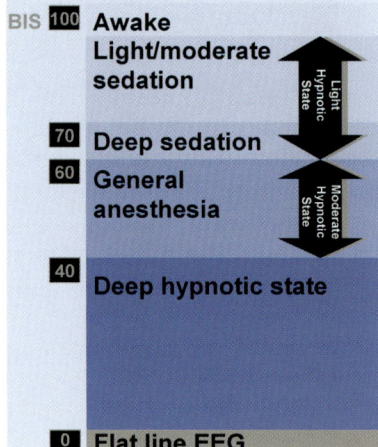

Figure 9
EEG frequency patterns.

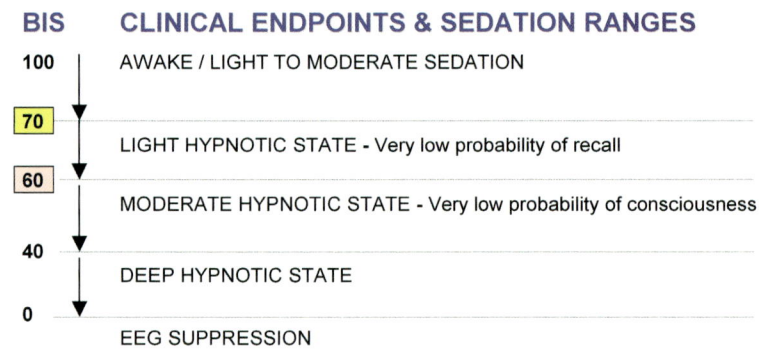

Figure 10
Very 'deep' EEG patterns.

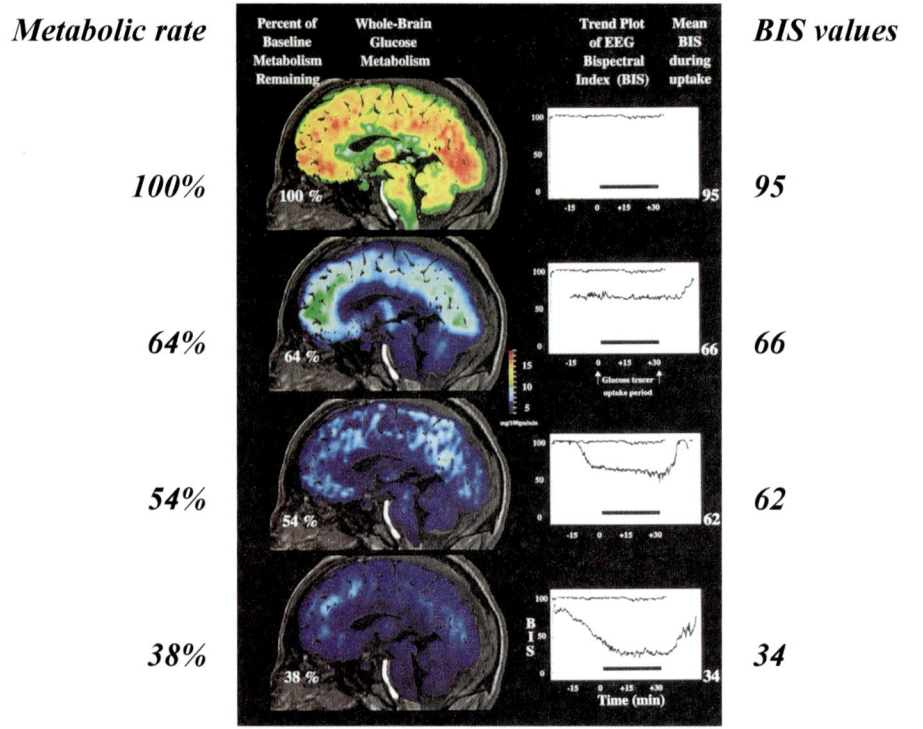

Part III
PRACTICAL ASPECTS

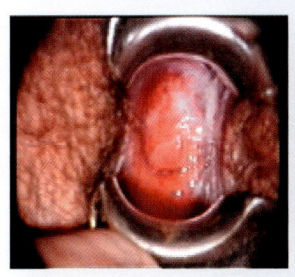
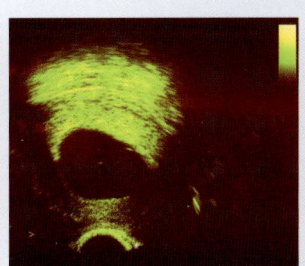
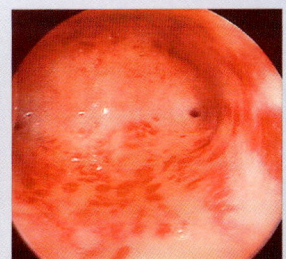
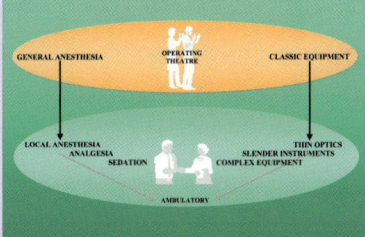
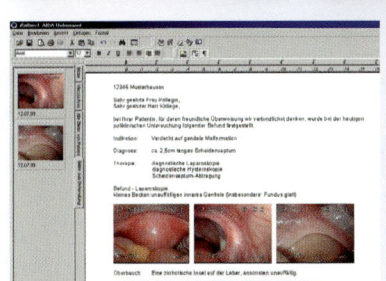
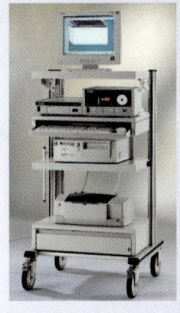
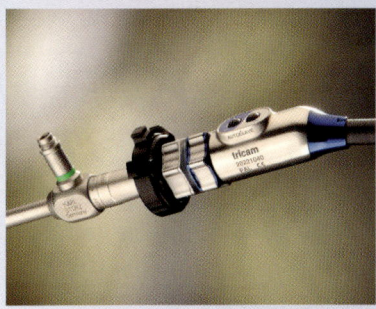
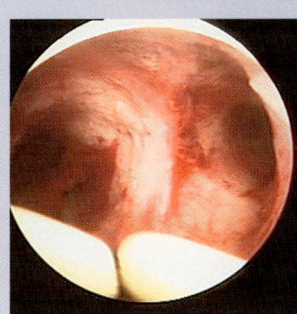

23a Disinfection, sterilization, and maintenance of instruments: Europe

Sabine Taylor

> **Take Home Message**
> It is essential that hysteroscopes and associated equipment are disinfected strictly according to European regulations and the individual country's laws. The surgeon has to be acutely aware of the possible risk of infection to the patient and of the risk due to intoxication by the products used for disinfection or sterilization. Each patient has to be considered as potentially contaminated and thus capable of contaminating other individuals. All the instruments must be decontaminated; the canals of the scope are rinsed with a sterile syringe and a disinfecting agent and are left in this solution for some 15 minutes. After this cycle the instruments are rinsed with fresh cold running water. The third phase is a 1-hour cycle in a disinfectant containing glutaraldehyde 2%. The instruments are immersed completely. The last cycle comprises rinsing with sterile water. In France there is a legal obligation to record in a register the different steps of the cycles.

INTRODUCTION

Hysteroscopy in the private office or the operating room has to meet safety criteria, not only for the patient, but also for the nursing staff and the surgeon.

Personnel need to know and carefully manage both the risk of infection and the risk of intoxication by the maintenance products [1].

A written protocol describing in detail step by step the disinfection, rinsing, decontamination, and rinsing even after the final storage must be readily available [2]. Indeed, each patient has to be considered as potentially contaminated and thus capable of contaminating other individuals.

The emergence of infectious pathologies, caused by viruses such as HIV, HBS, HBC, and agents such as those of Creutzfeldt-Jakob disease, mean that the utmost care must be taken to avoid inter-individual contamination and also nosocomial infection [3,4].

Hysteroscopy requires vigilance as regards the following factors:

- Maintenance of instruments
- Decontamination and disinfection of instruments
- Manipulation of materials
- Protection of the nursing staff
- Tracing of instruments
- Formation of the nursing staff.

In France, the prevention of risk of infections due to endoscopic interventions has been the subject of circular letters produced by the Ministry of Health: 'A *savoir la direction general de la santé direction des hôpitaux*' (circular letter DGS/DH no. 236 of 02/04/96 and circular letter DGS/DH no. 672 of 20/10/97).

There are two types of hysteroscopes to consider:

- Hysteroscopes that are *heat-stable* and *autoclavable*
- Hysteroscopes that are *heat-sensitive* and *non-autoclavable*.

Two distinct procedures are required, depending on the type of instrument involved. The description of these procedures is indeed a synthesis of what is actually done in Europe. We can say that for the majority of European ensdocopists the procedure followed is almost identical. The only difference is that in France there is an obligation to produce written documentation so that all invasive acts relative to the patient, the surgeon, the date, and the material used are traceable [5].

Recommendations by the authorities are not systematically found in each country of Europe. Nevertheless almost all surgeons have adopted the same procedure, validated by the most of them [6].

ESSENTIAL MATERIALS

The performance of hysteroscopy in the outpatient office needs the manipulation of the soiled hysteroscopes, their cleaning and disinfection, the exact timing of each adequate soaking bath, and finally the linking of the instruments to the insufflator and the cold light source.

It is convenient to have skilled personnel for all these different tasks; ideally a nurse executing this function next to the surgeon [7].

Whatever the type of instrument used, it is necessary to have four soaking boxes of 6–8 liters at your disposal. (These boxes have to be cleaned and autoclaved at 125°C after each change of product.) The disinfecting solutions have to be changed at least every day to maintain their bactericidal and virusciidal properties [8].

As regards the environment, the room where endoscopic materials are treated has to be clean, well-ventilated and, ideally, equipped with a hood to eliminate the aldehyde vapors.

Qualified hygienists should carry out regular control checks by bacterial sampling of air and water, and the cleaning and disinfection procedures for the endoscopes.

The early phases of decontamination and rinsing concern all the equipment and then, if the equipment is heat-stable it must be autoclaved at 134°C for 18 minutes. If the material is not autoclavable, a disinfection phase with a product containing glutaraldehyde 2% is required.

Endoscopes are very fragile and very expensive instruments. Staff must always take into account the manufacturer's recommendations regarding the functioning and operation of the scope, as well as the accessories, so that degradation of the instruments is limited as far as possible, and their technical and hygienic reliability can be maintained [9].

The essential equipment comprises:
- Nonsterile, protective, single-use gloves
- Protective glasses
- Mask with active carbon
- Bib
- Apron
- Nonsterile swabs
- Wipes
- Flexible brush
- Irrigation apparatus for hysteroscope channels
- Syringe (20 ml)
- Timer.

DECONTAMINATION CYCLE

Before any single use a decontamination cycle should be performed, after washing of hands, and with nonsterile, protective single-use gloves.

It is sufficient to aspirate the disinfection liquid in a sterile syringe and to pass this disinfectant liquid through the channels of the hysteroscope before total immersion of the hysteroscope in a disinfectant bath (Bodedex type) for at least 15 minutes to clean and decontaminate. A quaternary ammonium compound, a proteolytic enzyme, and a detergent make up this decontamination. The bactericidal-fungicidal-viruscidal action is obtained after contact for at least 10 minutes. Sporicideal action is obtained after at least 45 minutes (Tables 1 and 2).

Table 1
Cleaning and decontamination products for instruments and materials before sterilization

Products	Properties	Efficacy	Preparation for efficient dilution	Contact time/ directions	Conservation	Incomptabilities	Precautions
Bodedex	Cleaner Decontaminator	– Bactericidal – Fungicidal – Viruscidal	Powder with measure 1 dose of 25 g for 5 liters lukewarm water	– 15 minutes – Cleaning – Meticulous rinsing	24 hours	Detergents	Gloves required
Hexanios G + R	Cleaner Decontaminator	– Bactericidal – Fungicidal – Viruscidal (HIV + HBV) – Tuberculocidal	Packs of 25 ml 5 liters of cold water for 25 ml	– 15minutes – Brushing – Cleaning – Rinsing – Drying	24 hours		Gloves required

RINSING CYCLE

After soaking, careful rinsing with cold water is advisable, making sure that all the channels of the hysteroscope are dismantled, cleaned, and rinsed separately from the sheath.

After soaking, all the sheaths must be dried with a soft swab and the irregular parts must be thoroughly brushed. No organic traces can be allowed to remain, as glutaraldehyde fixes protein particles [10].

DISINFECTION CYCLE

The material must be totally immersed, after irrigation of the channels with disinfectant solution containing glutaraldehyde 2%, for 1 hour.

The glutaraldehyde is a bactericidal, fungicidal, viruscidal, and tuberculocidal disinfectant in 15 minutes. It is sporicidal in 1 hour. It is not corrosive, but instruments should not be soaked for more than 2 hours.

FINAL RINSING CYCLE

Sterile gloves should be worn to remove the hysteroscope from the disinfectant bath and then it should be totally immersed in a bath containing sterile water. Meticulous rinsing includes irrigating all the channels in the instruments by injection of sterile water. Afterwards the material is reusable.

STORAGE

It is not advisable to store the hysteroscopes, ready for use straight after these different steps; ideally they should be packed in sterile material and then stored away from sources of contamination. Soaking for 10 minutes in a glutaraldehyde solution is the only requirement for pretreatment at the start of activities to eliminate any microbiological contamination that may result during storage.

Completion of the phases described above takes 90 minutes per soiled endoscope. When there are a significant number of procedures to do this lengthy process necessitates a large number of scopes.

As far as heat-stable material is concerned the different steps of decontamination, cleaning, and rinsing are the same. After rinsing with cold water the hysteroscopes are autoclaved at a temperature of 134°C for 18 minutes and then they are ready to use.

TREATMENT OF THE ACCESSORIES

Serilization of the accessories has to be done after decontamination and rinsing. For those accessories that cannot be sterilized the procedure of disinfection, rinsing, and drying described above must be carried out.

VIGILANCE AND TRACEABILITY

We consider that the French directions have to be followed where traceability is concerned.

'The need for traceability is equated with the function of the appliances. The traceability of the sterilized medical appliances in health instances is a part of the quality system and has to be done in combination with the material vigilance.' [Article 2.2.8, circular DGS/DH no. 672 of 20/10/97.]

'The decree no. 96-32 of 15/0/96 on the material vigilance of the medical appliances defines the obligation to declare all incident or risk that could happen to the medical appliances as part of the material vigilance. These could be linked to the sterilization. So the responsible of the sterilization is obligated to work in close collaboration with the local representative of the material vigilance.' [Article 3, circular DGS/DH 672 of 20/10/97.]

The providers of care have to ensure the possibility of finding, if necessary, all the sterilization parameters for a medical appliance used for a particular patient.

Table 2
Disinfection by soaking nonautoclavable instruments and utensils

Products	Properties	Efficacy	Preparation for efficient dilution	Contact time/ directions	Conservation	Incomptabilities	Precautions
Korsolex NF	Disinfectant	– Bactericidal – Fungicidal (Aspergillus) – Viruscidal (HIV + HBV) – Tuberculocidal	300-ml bottle 1 bottle (300-ml) for 10 liters of cold water	– 15 minutes – Cleaning – Preceding rinsing	8 days maximum 24 hours	Avoid soaking for more than 2 hours	Gloves required
		– Sporicidal		– 1 hour	8 days maximum		

CONCLUSION

From the surgeon's point of view, hysteroscopy requires knowledge of the disinfection protocols.

Rigorous follow-up of the different steps guarantees the safety of patients. The appropriate maintenance of hysteroscopes and their accessories is indispensable for good quality practice.

All these recommendations have to be available on a written document validated by the provider of care or by a group of experts.

The formation of the staff and their education as regards the risks of contamination by patients and the products used will lead to respect for the given orders.

REFERENCES

1. Le traitement des hystéroscopes. Réalisé par un groupe de travail. AP-HP. Editions DOIN. Février 1990
2. Marchetti MG, Salvatorelli G, Finzi G, Cugini P. Endoscope washers – a protocol for their use. *J Hosp Infect* 2000; **46**: 210–215.
3. Mencaglia L, Tiso E, Tantini C, Bianchi R. Risks of virus transmission during diagnostic hysteroscopy. *J Am Assoc Gynecol Laparosc* 1996; **3** (4 Suppl): S30.
4. Ayliffe G. Minimal access therapy decontamination working group. Decontamination of minimally invasive surgical endoscopes and accessories. *J Hosp Infect* 2000; **45**: 263–277.
5. Cravello L, Cailleux J, Roger V, Bretelle F, Blanc B. La désinfection des hystéroscopes non autoclavables en Gynécologie – proposition d'une protocole et organisation de son encadrement. *J Gynecol Obstet Biol Reprod* 1999; **28**: 381–383.
16. Buckx MJ, Dankert J, Beenhakker MM, Harrison TE. Decontamination of laryngoscopes in The Netherlands. *Br J Anaesth* 2001; **86**: 99–102.
7. Prather C, Wolfe A. The nurse's role in office hysteroscopy. *J Obstet Gynecol Neonatal Nurs* 1995; 24: 813–816.
8. Von Rheinbaben F. Viruscidal disinfection in gynecology [in German]. *Zentralbl Gynakol* 1992; **114**: 265–269.
9. Holland P, Soop N. Flexible endoscopes: structure and function – the air and water system. *Gastroenterol Nurs* 2000; **23**: 264–268.
10. Knieler R. Manual cleaning and disinfection of flexible endoscopes – an approach to evaluating a combined procedure. *J Hosp Infect* 2001; **48** Suppl A: S84–S87.

23b Disinfection, sterilization, and maintenance of instruments: USA

Donna M. Morrison

> **Take Home Message**
> Guidelines developed by the Association for Professionals of Infection Control and Epidemiology (APIC) and recommended practices developed by the Association of Perioperative Registered Nurses (AORN) should be followed when writing policies and procedures to ensure that standards of care are met. The instruments have to be thoroughly cleaned and decontaminated in a controlled area before they are disinfected or sterilized. Normal saline should be avoided; it has ionizing properties. It is very important to blow-dry all the channels to prevent formation of toxic byproducts when ETO is used and to prevent dilution of the disinfecting agent. Paracetic acid and hydrogen peroxide gas-plasma are the low temperature sterilization methods of choice. High-level disinfection is the method of choice in the office setting. Glutaraldehyde 2% is the most commonly used disinfectant. Safety precautions and guidelines determined by the Occupational Safety and Health Administration (OSHA) must be followed to prevent injury to health-care workers.

INTRODUCTION

Proper care and maintenance of instruments and equipment used during office hysteroscopy is essential in ensuring patient safety. Maintenance of equipment is required to ensure proper functioning and to prolong the useful life of the equipment. Meticulous cleaning and high-level disinfection or sterilization of instruments is required to prevent infection of the uterus or bloodstream from instruments contaminated with colonizing micro-organisms from the vaginal tract, exogenous micro-organisms from contaminated hysteroscopy equipment, or contamination from the environment or health-care workers involved in the procedure [1]. External surfaces of hysteroscopic equipment must be wiped with an approved germicidal agent immediately after use to prevent transfer of micro-organisms from contaminated equipment between patients.

Policies and procedures that provide detailed step-by-step instructions for cleaning and disinfection or sterilization of hysteroscopic instruments and equipment should be developed. Manufacturer's instructions are followed to ensure that specific instruments and equipment are properly cleaned and to ensure that the appropriate high-level disinfectant or sterilization method is used. Guidelines developed by the Association for Professionals in Infection Control and Epidemiology (APIC) and recommended practices developed by the Association of Perioperative Registered Nurses (AORN) should be followed when writing policies and procedures to ensure that standards of care are met.

CARE AND MAINTENANCE OF EQUIPMENT

Hysteroscopic equipment such as the hysteroflator, light source, and video camera can be considered low maintenance equipment. However, preventative maintenance should be performed according to the manufacturer's recommendations to ensure that electronic calibrations that regulate pressure and flow rate are accurate, to ensure that adequate lighting is available for the procedure, and to prevent interruption in visualization due to alterations in the image projected on the monitor. Gas intravasation due to increased flow rates and pressures can occur when equipment is miscalibrated or malfunctions [2]. Likewise, light transmission can be interrupted abruptly when recommended hours of bulb use are exceeded. Images projected on the monitor can also be altered when camera cables and couplers are not maintained appropriately.

CARE AND MAINTENANCE OF INSTRUMENTS

Instruments used for office hysteroscopy include the telescope, diagnostic and operative sheaths, operative instruments, fiberoptic light cable, vaginal speculum, tennaculum, and dilators. These instruments must be maintained to facilitate adequate visualization. The telescope is inspected for damage by holding it up to the light and looking at the shape and sharpness of the image.

Any shape other than round indicates that there is internal damage to the scope. Likewise, a foggy or blurred image signifies that either the lens is dirty, fluid invasion has occurred, or fiberoptic bundles in a flexible hysteroscope or glass rods that make up a rigid hysteroscope have been damaged. The telescope should be thoroughly cleaned, dried, and inspected again. If fogginess or a blurred image is still present, the scope should be sent for repair.

The telescope, diagnostic and operative sheaths, operative instruments, and light cables should be separated from heavier instruments. These items are very delicate and can easily become damaged if one of the heavier instruments is inadvertently placed on top of any of them. Advancing instruments or the telescope through a sheath that has become damaged should be avoided as this may cause further damage to the sheath and may also damage the telescope. Telescopes should be handled by the eyepiece to avoid slippage and should be inserted into the sheath perpendicularly to avoid damage to the objective lens. Movable parts on sheaths should be lubricated regularly to ensure that they move freely during operation. Sheaths should also be checked to ensure that they are free from nicks or burrs. The vaginal speculum should be checked to ensure that it opens and closes smoothly, and dilators should be inspected to ensure that they have the same length, curvature, and weight (solid or hollow).

Light cables are inspected for damage by holding both ends of the cable up to the light and looking for discolored spots or blackened areas on either end. The cable should be replaced when several discolored spots or large blackened areas are seen, as these findings indicate that the fiberoptic bundles are damaged and light transmission will be compromised. Allowing the end of the light cable to fall to the floor once removed from the light source can also severely damage the cable. The light cable should be disconnected from the light source by holding it by the handle. The light cable should be coiled loosely for storage to avoid damage to fiberoptic bundles.

PREPARING INSTRUMENTS FOR DISINFECTION OR STERILIZATION

It is imperative that instruments are thoroughly cleaned and decontaminated in a controlled area, using universal precautions, before they are disinfected or sterilized. AORN recommended practices [3] state that debris, mucus, and tissue impede the effectiveness of the disinfectant or sterilization method used, and list cleaning and decontamination as the first and most critical steps in breaking down the chain of disease transmission.

Instrument cleaning should begin at the point of use. Lumens of diagnostic and operative sheaths and instrument channels should be flushed with water to remove any residual tissue or debris immediately after the procedure. Flushing with normal saline should be avoided as normal saline has ionizing properties that can cause rusting and pitting of the metallic sheaths. After instruments have been moved to the decontamination area, multiple parts must be disassembled to ensure that all crevices, joints, and inner channels are properly cleaned.

Manual cleaning of hysteroscopic instruments is recommended owing to the delicacy of these devices. A solution that contains water with an enzymatic cleaner is used to begin the manual cleaning process. An enzymatic cleaner is added to water to help break down organic and inorganic soiling and bioburdens from instrument surfaces. Once instruments have gone through the presoaking process, they are washed with a mild detergent that has a neutral pH of 7. A detergent with a neutral pH is required to avoid damage to instrument surfaces [3]. Instruments are carefully immersed in the cleaning solution and the external surfaces are scrubbed with a sponge or soft cloth. Instrument channels are cleaned by nserting an instrument channel brush through the port and brushing the entire channel. The instrument channel is then irrigated with clean water, alternating with cleaning solution to remove debris loosened during the brushing procedure [3].

It is equally important to rinse and dry instruments thoroughly after cleaning, before proceeding to the disinfection or sterilization process. Instruments are carefully immersed in a bin of clean water and rinsed thoroughly to remove any residual detergent. Residual detergent is removed from instrument channels by irrigating the channels with copious amounts of clean water. Instrument surfaces, lumens, and instrument channels must be thoroughly dried to prevent the formation of toxic byproducts when ethylene oxide gas (ETO) is the sterilization method and to prevent dilution of the disinfecting agent when instruments are placed in the solution [3,4].

STERILIZATION TECHNIQUES

Until recently, ETO has been the method of choice for sterilization of heat-sensitive items. However, restricted regulations related to the use of ETO have prompted health-care facilities to look at alternative sterilization processes. Peracetic acid and hydrogen peroxide gas-plasma are low-temperature sterilization technologies that have been proven to effectively eliminate all forms of microbial life, including spores, thus rendering the item sterile.

Sterilization utilizing peracetic acid is accomplished with the use of an automated endoscopic reprocessing system designed to remove debris and residue through a high agitation process that takes 30 minutes to complete [1]. The automated endoscopic reprocessing system dilutes 35% peracetic acid, which is a balanced mixture of acetic acid, hydrogen peroxide, and water, to a final concentration of 0.2%. A buffer and anticorrosive agent are added during the process [1], making it safe to use on heat-sensitive instruments that can be completely immersed in liquid.

Hydrogen peroxide gas-plasma is a low-temperature sterilization technique that accomplishes sterilization by creating a vacuum and automatically injecting 58% hydrogen peroxide around items that have been placed in a sterilization chamber. At the end of the 1-hour sterilization process, active components are recombined to form oxygen and vaporized water [5]. Therefore, unlike ETO, aeration is not required with this process, as hydrogen peroxide gas-plasma does not leave toxic residues or emissions. The system is designed to sterilize metal, non-metal, and most heat- and moisture-sensitive instruments. Rigid hysteroscopic instrumentation with channels or lumens that are 31 cm or less and at least 6 mm in diameter are examples of items that may undergo this method of sterilization. However, this sterilization process is not recommended for items wrapped in linen or other paper materials, powders, liquids, and devices that have long, narrow, or dead-end lumens [1]. The instrument manufacturer should confirm material compatibility before instruments are initially sterilized by this method.

Saturated steam under pressure is the preferred sterilization method for items that can withstand high pressure, heat, and moisture [4]. Hysteroscopic instruments fall into this category. Until recently telescopes were not compatible with this sterilization process. However, today many rigid hysteroscopes are heat-stable and can be sterilized with pressurized steam. The manufacturer should confirm that their product is compatible with this form of sterilization. Flexible hysteroscopes are not compatible with the steam sterilization process.

Although ETO, low-temperature sterilization techniques, and steam are methods that can be utilized to sterilize endoscopic instruments, these methods are usually impractical for the office setting. Therefore, high-level disinfection is the method most commonly used to prepare hysteroscopic instruments for patient use in the office setting.

HIGH-LEVEL DISINFECTION

The Spaulding classification system is used to determine the level of disinfection required for medical devices based on the nature of the item and the manner in which it is to be used [4]. The hysteroscope is considered a semi-critical medical device, according to this classification system, because it comes into contact with mucous membranes. Spaulding's classification system stipulates that semi-critical items should either be sterilized or at least receive high-level disinfection, utilizing a liquid sterilant/disinfectant that has been approved by the Food and Drug Administration (FDA). High-level disinfection is defined as the inactivation of all vegetative bacteria, mycobacteria, fungi, and viruses, but not necessarily all bacterial endospores [5].

Agents used as chemical disinfectants must have certain properties. These chemicals should have microbicidal properties that will not be significantly decreased in the presence of organic matter. Likewise, these chemicals should not be toxic to personnel and should not cause damage to the endoscope. Unfortunately, the number of high-level disinfectants that meet these criteria is limited. Other factors also influence the efficacy of germicidal agents used as high-level disinfectants. The type and number of micro-organisms; precleaning, rinsing, and drying of the item before disinfection; the concentration, active ingredients, and exposure time of the chemical agent; the physical configuration of the item to be disinfected; the temperature and pH of the chemical agent; hardness of the water; and the presence of surfactants all have a bearing on how effective the germicidal agent will be in achieving high-level disinfection [4].

Glutaraldehyde 2% is the chemical germicide most often used when high-level disinfection and/or cold sterilization are desired. This germicidal agent is non-corrosive to metals and does not damage endoscopes. It is also highly resistant to neutralization by organic soil [5]. All internal and external surfaces and channels of an item must have contact with the glutaraldehyde for at least 20 minutes to achieve high-level disinfection. To facilitate contact of the disinfecting agent with the internal surfaces of instrument channels, the lumens should be flushed with the agent to eliminate air pockets before immersing the instrument in the disinfecting solution.

Instruments that have been disinfected with glutaraldehyde must be rinsed thoroughly with sterile water to remove residual toxins and irritating residue that can cause adverse reactions in patients. Chemical colitis has been documented as a complication associated with inadequate rinsing of glutaraldehyde from endoscopes. Sterile water must be used to prevent recontamination that can occur if tap water is used. In the event that sterile water is unavailable and tap water is used, it must be followed with a 70% alcohol rinse and forced-air drying to achieve an acceptable level of disinfection [3].

Written instructions from the manufacturer for preparing glutaraldehyde, testing efficacy of the solution, and determining when the solution should be discarded must be followed to ensure that high-level disinfection is obtained for each item placed in the disinfecting agent. Safety precautions and guidelines determined by the Occupational Safety and Health Administration (OSHA) must be followed to prevent injury to health-care workers exposed to the disinfecting agent. Glutaraldehyde is irritating to the skin, eyes, and nasal mucosa when exposure levels are >0.3 ppm. Therefore, OSHA has mandated 0.2 ppm as the ceiling limit for the level of glutaraldehyde that is permitted in the air [5]. To achieve this, glutaraldehyde should be used in a well-ventilated area, care should be taken to limit manipulation of the liquid during use, and the solution should be stored in covered plastic containers. Likewise, personal protective equipment, which includes eyewear, gloves, masks, and an impervious gown or apron should be worn when use of glutaraldehyde is anticipated.

CONCLUSION

Proper care and maintenance of endoscopic equipment and instruments is imperative for patient safety. Equipment is maintained to make sure that it functions properly when needed. Meticulous cleaning with proper disinfection or sterilization is required to prevent transfer of bacteria and micro-organisms between patients.

Several methods may be employed to disinfect or sterilize instrumentation used for office hysteroscopy. Manufacturer's guidelines are followed to prevent damage to specific instruments. Regulatory guidelines that have been mandated by agencies such as APIC, AORN, and OSHA must be followed to ensure that both patients and health-care workers are safe.

REFERENCES

1. Tempesta SO, Spencer MP. Nursing implications for hysteroscopy in an outpatient setting. In: Isaacson KB, ed. Office Hysteroscopy. St Louis: Mosby, 1996: 38–44.
2. Morrison DM. Management of hysteroscopic surgery complications. *AORN J* 1999; **69**:194–209.
3. Recommended practices for high-level disinfection. In: AORN Standards, Recommended Practices, and Guidelines. Denver: Association or Perioperative Registered Nurses, 2000: 221–227.
4. Recommended practices for sterilization in the practice setting. In: AORN Standards, Recommended Practices, and Guidelines. Denver: Association or Perioperative Registered Nurses, 2000: 267–278.
5. Alvarado CJ, Reichelderfer M, and the 1997, 1998, and 1999 APIC Guidelines Committees. APIC guideline for infection prevention and control in flexible endoscopy. *Am J Infect Control* 2000; **28**: 138–155.

24 Office hysteroscopy: reimbursement

Joseph J. Houser

> **Take Home Message**
> In the USA managed care has changed the way medical practice is conducted. A successful practice depends upon developing more attention to the business portion of the medical practice. This not only applies to the USA but also to the rest of the world, because of the emphasis on maintaining a healthy business aspect. Evidence-based medicine is here to stay and ICD-9 codes for diagnosis and CPT-4 codes for treatment are now used all over the world. Office hysteroscopy provides savings to the health-care system and meets the patient's demand for prompt diagnosis and treatment. The investment to obtain a hysteroscope and video system for the office are not insignificant but should be weighed against the cost of leaving the office and performing the procedure elsewhere. Proper patient encounter documentation combined with adherence to reimbursement guidelines should allow clinicians to claim an accurate reimbursement, provide better patient management and increase patient and procedure volume.

INTRODUCTION

There is little doubt that managed care has dramatically changed the way that medical practice is conducted. To provide optimal patient care, physicians must now adjust the way they view their office practice in light of the changes brought about by managed care. Today's successful medical practice depends upon developing efficiencies in operations as well as attention to the medical business aspects. This includes providing insurance companies with evidence-based charges when contracting for fees, patient marketing of the value of office procedures, and developing a revenue approach to office staffing decisions.

Reimbursement issues for medical professionals continue to evolve under the 2002 RBRVS (relative based relative value scale), which summarizes the average value of factors affecting a specific procedure for all physicians performing that procedure. As medical costs differ for every locale, and for every practice, understanding how to set the proper fees for maximum reimbursement requires that a number of factors be taken into consideration. The key to proper reimbursement for office procedures is an evidence-based approach for the medical services provided, coupled with fee negotiation based on the value each procedure brings to a payer and comperable cost savings to the payer.

EVIDENCE-BASED MEDICINE APPROACH

Reimbursement is based on evidence. The physician submits a claim for charges defined by a diagnosis, using the ICD-9 codes, and treatment, using the CPT-4 codes. These accepted codes provide the basis for reimbursement based on RBRVS. Combined with Evaluation and Management (E/M) codes, together they represent the evidence for reimbursement.

ICD-9 (International Classification of Diseases, 9th revision) is the coding classification system that groups related disease entities and procedures for reporting diagnosis and provides evidence for treatment. It has been established as a benchmark for quality review and services as part of the function for reimbursement payments.

CPT-4 (Current Procedural Terminology, 4th edn) is a descriptive listing of codes for reporting medical procedures. It provides a uniform language for reporting medical, surgical, and diagnostic services that provides an accepted format for describing medical services for reimbursement. CPT was developed, and is maintained, by the American Medical Association (AMA). CPT-4 is currently under revision by the AMA. CPT-5 is projected to replace the CPT-4 coding system gradually, beginning in late 2002, and be fully phased in by the end of 2003. These changes are intended to clear up some of the ambiguity related to certain procedures. It is important to remain current on changes in CPT terminology and procedural codes, in order to monitor reimbursement changes.

RBRVS standardizes fees for medical practice and is the basis for establishing practice fees for both private payers and Medicare. Reimbursement using this standard is based on factors mentioned earlier and changes periodically.

Reimbursement requires a review of current reimbursement rates using this system for the medical services provided, as values change periodically.

RBRVS uses the following factors to determine the relative value payment compared to other performed procedures: 1) physician time for the procedure; 2) technical skill component; 3) health risk the condition presents to the patient; 4) health risk the procedure presents to the patient; 5) medical/legal risk to the physician (malpractice expense).

Reasonable and customary fees set by physicians are normally established with good intentions to account for practice expenses and to provide reasonable reimbursement that allows survival of the medical practice. In today's environment of reimbursement limits, it is important to establish fees that are based on the value of services provided so that they also provide evidence for reimbursement and appeal if necessary.

E/M codes (Evaluation and Management Services) define the face-to-face encounter as a professional services consultation. By utilizing the newly established E/M system, the physician provides the evidence required to request reimbursement. E/M services are documented evidence that there was a clear clincal-based evaluation of the patient's condition, that decisions were based on sound clinical data, and that recommended treatment has been evaluated based on its validity and usefulness in clinical practice.

Reimbursement should to be straightforward, considering the amount of documentation required by payers. However, reimbursement can be a two-way street, with fee schedules that may be out of sync with the maximum allowable reimbursement from payers. As office-based procedures occur without the huge overheads associated with hospitals or outpatient surgery centers, they provide a higher relative value in relation to the costs of providing such services, or at the very least, the same value at a reduced cost. When negotiating fees with payers, reimbursement for office procedures should be based on the evidence of the value of these services and the reduced cost to the payer as compared to a hospital based procedure. Evidence-based cost saving is a valuable tool in requesting and contracting for appropriate fees with payers. It is important to know, as well as to document, the cost savings of performing a procedure in the office rather than in a hospital or outpatient surgery facility.

Capturing appropriate reimbursement requires attention to the documentation required to perform the medical service and the requirements to operate the office cost-effectively. Many medical offices receive only 54% of their billed receivables and only 65–75% of what they are entitled to from contracted payers [1]. This is often due to inadequate or missing evidence and information regarding the services performed. Collecting full reimbursement requires adequate documentation and an office staff dedicated to ensuring that every event is properly coded and that reimbursement is received promptly.

Fee schedules should be reviewed annually. Updated fee schedules from contracted carriers should be obtained to compare allowable payments against billed services to ascertain if full reimbursement is being captured. Reasonable and customary fees should be calculated using an activity-based cost method, where all resources involved in providing the service can be measured and the service can be adjusted accordingly. Without periodic review, the reimbursement requested may actually fall short of the reimbursement allowed [2].

OFFICE HYSTEROSCOPY

This chapter will deal with hysteroscopy performed in the office environment. Office hysteroscopy not only provides savings to the health-care system, but also meets the combination of patient demand for prompt diagnosis and financial stringency [3]. Hysteroscopy offers the physician and the patient a real-time image of intrauterine conditions and can lead to both improved patient management and compliance. Diagnostic hysteroscopy is a simple and safe office procedure that permits direct visualization of the uterine cavity. The outpatient success rate reaches almost 100% [4]. Yet, hysteroscopy is too often overlooked as a primary diagnostic and patient management tool for the office.

Almost 30% of premenopausal and 75% of postmenopausal gynecological consultations in the office are related to abnormal uterine bleeding (AUB) [5]. In premenopausal women with symptoms of AUB, 40–85% of these will have a uterine abnormality [6]. In postmenopausal women, 88% of those with AUB will demonstrate uterine pathology [7]. Numerous studies have provided the clinical evidence and validity of the usefulness of hysteroscopy, particularly as it relates to AUB. Hysteroscopy with biopsy is considered the gold standard and most comprehensive evaluation for the diagnosis of AUB, and is recommended for any patient with equivocal findings from previous biopsy or ultrasonography [8].

Hysteroscopy can also be used in conjunction with either saline-assisted sonography (SIS) or vaginal ultrasound to provide superior clinical predictive diagnosis. A clinical study demonstrated that when compared to findings at operative hysteroscopy, 72% of abnormalities were correctly identified by outpatient hysteroscopy, 60% by ultrasound, and 52% by SIS. However, the specificity increased to 68% for ultrasound when it was followed by hysteroscopy and to 64% for SIS when it was followed by hysteroscopy. Transvaginal ultrasonography, with or without saline enhancement, complements but does not replace hysteroscopy [9].

Hysteroscopy takes a relatively short time to perform when compared with other office-based procedures, the technical skills can be learned quite easily, equipment costs are often similar to other office investments, and the complication rate is low [10]. In addition, it provides prompt visual diagnosis without the time delay necessary for interpretive confirmation (except in the case of biopsy results). Based on its lower cost and greater diagnostic accuracy, office hysteroscopy with suction biopsy should be the method of choice for evaluating gynecologic conditions such as AUB [11].

UNDERSTANDING REIMBURSEMENT

One of the first papers on evidence-based costs analysis of performing hysteroscopy in the office versus the hospital was published in 1996 by Dennis Hidlebaugh, while at the Fallon Clinic (Worcester, MA, USA). The Fallon Clinic remains one of the country's highest rated HMOs. He concluded that based on a comparison of costs, diagnostic accuracy, and minimal complications, office hysteroscopy with biopsy offers a method of choice for evaluating AUB. The cost saving from moving hysteroscopy from an outpatient facility to the office has been calculated at between $900 and $1000 per patient [10]. This information is useful in establishing that there is a financial benefit to the healthcare system and an evidence-based history of justification for performing hysteroscopy as a diagnostic tool for the treatment of AUB.

The AMA has assigned specific CPT-4 codes that reflect the value of each procedure. There are five factors that make up the relative value units for each procedure: the physician's time; technical skills; the severity of the patient's illness; risks to the patient; and medical/legal risk to the physician.

COMMON PROCEDURAL CODES FOR OFFICE HYSTEROSCOPY

The CPT codes used in the office for hysteroscopy are:

- 58555   Hysteroscopy, diagnostic (separate procedure). Local anesthesia is included in this service; however, this procedure may be performed under general anesthesia depending on the age and/or condition of the patient.

- 58558   Hysteroscopy, surgical; with sampling (biopsy) of endometrium and/or polypectomy, with or without D&C.
Local anesthesia is included in this service; however, this procedure may be performed under general anesthesia depending on the age and/or condition of the patient.

Based on the 2001 current RVUs, hysteroscopy provides better differential reimbursement than other commonly performed office procedures (Table 1).

Under the correct coding initiative, certain procedures are considered as being performed at the same time as the primary procedure and cannot be billed separately unless it is a significant and separate procedure. For example, surgical hysteroscopy always includes diagnostic hysteroscopy. Table 2 provides information on those procedures that may be paid either through utilization of a

Table 1
Relative value of common gynecologic office procedures

Procedure	CPT	RVU	RVU $
Transvaginal ultrasound	76830*	2.48	90.00
Colposcopy	57452	2.78	101.00
Colposcopy with biopsy	57460	5.28	191.00
Cystourethroscopy	52000	5.58	202.00
Endometrial biopsy	58100	3.16	114.00
Hysteroscopy	58555	6.62	240.00
Hysteroscopy with biopsy	58558	8.79	318.00

*76830 represents both the technical and interpretation portions. If only the professional component is being reported use 76830-26. The interpretation is then billed separately by the radiologist.
*58340 is used for catheterization and introduction of saline or contrast material for hysterosonography.

modifier or by indication of a separate ICD-9 diagnosis code, while other procedures are never paid under the same billing as the primary procedure.

Although supplies and materials for hysteroscopy are considered part of the procedure reimbursement, CPT-4 code 99070 may sometimes be used when the materials used are greater than would normally be used for the procedure. Some states (e.g. Massachusetts) and private payers recognize the added equipment cost and allow for code 99070 to be included as long as there is a documentation sheet attached to the reimbursement claim that categorizes the costs for each of the supplies used.

REIMBURSEMENT CODING

The key to obtaining appropriate reimbursement is good medical business office management. Success depends on an efficient accounts receivable plan coupled with accurate billing procedures. Providing the evidence of services rendered is not only good medicine but good business practice as well.

There are 32 ICD-9 codes that support performing diagnostic hysteroscopy, CPT 58555, and hysteroscopy with biopsy, CPT 58558. In addition, there are another 18 ICD-9 codes for CPT 58555, and another 18 codes specific for CPT 58558.

An example of correct coding for evaluation of a patient seen in the office for AUB might require several coding steps to be undertaken to receive proper reimbursement. A separate ICD-9 code would be used that is evidence of a need to perform an ultrasound (76830), i.e. metorrhagia (626.6). If an abnormality is found during ultrasound, another ICD-9 code would be used to identify the need for a hysteroscopically directed biopsy (55558), i.e. leiomyoma of the uterus, unspecified (218.9).

If the physician also performs a significant and separately identifiable E/M service at the same visit due to the findings, the physician would then need to report a modifier (−25) with the E/M code. Modifier −25 indicates that a significant, separately identifiable evaluation and management service was performed by the same physician on the same day as the procedure or other service.

According to CPT 2001 of the AMA Current Procedural Terminology, both the E/M and the procedure should be reported if a patient's condition requires a 'significant, separately identifiable E/M service'. 'Significant' implies that the E/M service required some level of history taking, examination, and/or medical decision-making; 'separately identifiable' means that the visit is distinct from the procedure. In other words, the E/M service should be above and beyond the usual care associated with the procedure.

When E/M services are provided on the same day as a procedure, the physician must identify the additional service on the insurance claim form. CPT 2001 instructs the provider to append the −25 modifier to the E/M service to confirm that distinct services were performed [12]. The CPT brief descriptor for the −25 modifier reads 'Significant, separately identifiable evaluation and management service by the same physician on the same day of the procedure or other service'.

CPT 2001 further states in its instructions for using the −25 modifier: 'The E/M service may be prompted by the symptom or condition for which the procedure and/or service was provided. As such, different diagnoses are not required for reporting of E/M services on the same date'. Therefore, in the case of the patient with dysfunctional uterine bleeding, the diagnoses for both the E/M service and the hysteroscopy with endometrial biopsy (58558) would probably be the same. Both services also could correctly be reported. In other situations, the visit might be prompted by a condition unrelated to the procedure.

In general, report both the E/M service and the procedure if:

- The decision to perform the procedure was made at the same encounter as the E/M service (even if for the same diagnosis); OR

- The diagnosis for the E/M service is different from the one for the procedure.

Table 2
Correct coding initiative

58555					
	May be paid	57100	57410	58100	...
	Never paid	57800	69990	...	...
58558					
	May be paid	57100	58100	58555	...
	Never paid	57410	57800	58120	69990

Generally, report only the procedure if:
- The decision to perform the procedure was made at another visit; OR
- The E/M service provided on the same day did not require significant history taking, physical exam, and/or decision-making.

DOCUMENTING THE ENCOUNTER

It is important to document a visit clearly whenever a procedure is reported on the same day as a consultation. Since all procedures include some element of patient evaluation, it is necessary to provide evidence of additional services. It is helpful, in the event of a review by or appeal to the insurance company, to physically document separate notes on both the office visit and the procedure. This does not mean that they have to be on different pieces of paper or that a lengthy note is required. Simply skipping a space and labeling the procedure portion can help to distinguish the services.

Since each CPT code represents a separate element of work and reimbursement, payers expect complete documentation of all services for which reimbursement is requested. The level of E/M service that represents a 'significant, separately identifiable' work is debatable. It has been suggested that a problem-focused encounter, such as a 99212 (established E/M service representing a problem-focused history and exam and straightforward medical decision-making), may not be indicative of a significant visit. At minimum, there should be some level of history taking, performance of an examination, medical decision-making, and/or the amount of time involved. The procedure note should clearly describe the service identified by the selected CPT code.

Although proper coding does not guarantee reimbursement, it is important to apply the CPT guidelines consistently for all types of payers. Understanding the rules can improve the chances for reimbursement while protecting the practice from potential audit liability.

DOCUMENTATION

It is important that patient encounter records allow for inclusion and billing for the complete scope of services performed. Documentation should be prepared so that when the patient enters the office there is an automatic documentation that occurs:
1. Patient registration
2. Patient information tools (consent information for procedures)
3. E/M encounter forms for documenting the visit allowing both ICD-9 and CPT entries
4. Patient history and physical charts
5. Medical supplies chart for use with CPT 99070
6. Superbill and charge tickets.

Maintaining proper documentation for reimbursement claims is a vital function of every member of office staff. A practice-wide mindset should be in place that emphasizes the philosophy that reimbursement is integral to a successful medical practice, and is, thus, everyone's job. Both the billing and accounts receivable employee must be aware of and familiar with the following information [13].
1. Written policies and procedures for patient encounters and billing
2. The necessity to keep all third party contract charges and coding issues current
3. The importance of conducting periodic routine audits to match reimbursement requests and received payments in order to identify potential problems
4. Fee schedule
5. Profiles of what each insurance company in the area allows
6. Proper claims information for each payer
7. Practice letter to accompany charges out of the ordinary or extraordinary circumstances for modifiers.
8. Instructions for collection procedures if the payer is not prompt in payment or an immediate appeal letter to be filled upon denial of payment.

HCPCS/CPT codes are updated annually by the AMA in order to change, add, or delete codes based on current practice. Although most payers use these codes, it is important to establish this fact with each insurer. This can best be accomplished by having a prepared form letter that indicates the CPT codes used in the practice, as well as the physician's reasonable and customary fees for each procedure. This letter requests that the insurer confirm that it utilizes the same AMA coding system and that rates reflect reasonable and customary charges for the specific geographical area.

Reasonable and customary reimbursement for a geographical area can often be obtained through a variety of on-line Internet sources. Some of these sources also provide claims assistance services to capture proper reimbursement. In addition, most states have laws and regulations that define reasonable reimbursement timelines for payers, some of which allow for fines if the payer is not prompt on a reasonable and nondisputed claim.

UNDERSTANDING OPPORTUNITY COSTS

Further investigation demonstrates that performing diagnostic hysteroscopy in the office avoids the lost economic costs of performing the same procedure away from the office – in a hospital or outpatient surgery center. Every office has a flow of patients and even a planned procedure for ensuring optimal patient care and office time management; the necessity of having the physician away from the office for the performance of a certain procedure changes the average receivables that support the office. This is due to the loss realized as a result of the number of patients not seen during the time spent away from the office. This includes not only the time spent at the outside facility, be it hospital or outpatient surgery center, but also the incurred travel time. This loss in revenue can be more than the value of reimbursement for the procedure. Since a hysteroscopic procedure can easily be built into the existing office routine with little disruption of normal patient scheduling, the revenue loss that ensues when a physician performs this procedure outside the office is nonexistent.

Performing hysteroscopy in the office provides an increase in value to the office practice and can be scheduled around the normal patient schedule (Table 3).

The patient arrives at the office and is escorted to the treatment room area.

A nurse answers any initial questions the patient has, and prepares both the patient and the equipment for the procedure (10 minutes).

The physician enters the procedure room and, after greeting the patient and ascertaining that she has no further questions or concerns, performs the procedure (5 minutes).

The nurse cleans up after the procedure and escorts the patient to the consultation room while the physician sees the next patient.

The physician discusses the recommended course of action based on the hysteroscopic findings with an informed patient and then proceeds to the next patient.

Once learned, office hysteroscopy takes less than 5 minutes to perform and allows both the physician and the patient direct visual confirmation of uterine pathology.

Since physician reimbursement is basically the same for diagnostic hysteroscopy, whether performed in the hospital or office, optimal reimbursement for medical services remains at the office level.

Given the practicality of performing hysteroscopy in the office, the speed at which proficiency can be obtained, and the introduction of smaller hysteroscopes for diagnosis, understanding reimbursement becomes the key to developing this office component of medical practice.

Performing a diagnostic hysteroscopy in the office avoids the economic opportunity costs of taking the patient to the hospital. Since a hysteroscopic procedure can easily be built into the daily office routine without disrupting the normal patient flow, leaving the office to go to the hospital or outpatient facility to perform a hysteroscopy may not be productive in terms of time and cost-efficiency.

COSTS OF HYSTEROSCOPY EQUIPMENT

One reason often stated for not performing hysteroscopy is the cost of the investment to obtain a hysteroscope and video system for the office. While the cost of obtaining a hysteroscopic set up is not insignificant, this cost must be weighed against the cost of leaving the office to perform a hysteroscopy procedure elsewhere.

Equipment costs should be examined, as physicians performing office hysteroscopy can choose between a basic hysteroscope set up or a hysteroscope with a video system. The addition of a video system allows better communication with the patient, since the patient can more fully understand the recommendations for medical or surgical intervention.

A basic hysteroscope system consists of a hysteroscope and light source; the cost ranges between $7500 and $9500. A full system, including video and documentation, ranges between $14,000 and $20,000.

The cost of performing hysteroscopy in the office should include the cost of disposables, equipment costs, and personnel time. The cost per procedure for performing hysteroscopy in the office, examining five or six patients

Table 2
Patient flow for hysteroscopy

Event 1	Normal office					
Event 2	Hysteroscopy	Patient preparation	Hysteroscopy	Clean up	Consultation	Involvement
Time	5 minutes	10 minutes	5–10 minutes	5 minutes	10 minutes	
Nurse	Patient A	Patient A	Patient A	Patient A	Other patients	25–30 minutes
Physician	Other patients	Other patients	Patient A	Other patients	Patient A	15–20 minutes

per month, would be about $74 per procedure for the equipment, with an average reimbursement of $228 for diagnostic hysteroscopy [14] (code 58555, nonparticipating, nonfacility fee). This would provide approximately $27,270 of revenue for the office over the term of a 3-year lease. With more utilization of hysteroscopy and an average of 10–15 patients per month, and considering that 50% of the patients might require a biopsy (code 58558), the return to the practice improves the contribution to the office to $120,650 over the 3-year lease and reduces the cost per procedure to $37.00.

Most companies that provide hysteroscopy equipment offer advanced financial tools that provide acquisition options other than outright purchase. For example, some permit leasing the instruments with an option to purchase after 2–3 years. This is the most economical equipment acquisition method and ensures that reimbursements can be matched to practice costs and, thus, preserves the capital funds of the practice. The physician should decide which is the best economic vehicle to use based on the individual tax situation and expected patient volume.

SUMMARY

Hysteroscopy bears the evidence of experience as a valued office procedure. Performing hysteroscopy in the office has proven to be an effective and reliable clinical method for diagnosing the cause of AUB. In this new age of smaller hysteroscopes, financial vehicles for obtaining equipment, and an opportunity for significant cost advantages, the use of hysteroscopy as the procedure of choice for AUB now represents not only optimal patient care, but also optimal financial practice care.

Office hysteroscopy provides a point of service benefit in terms of office time management, increased revenue, and potentially an increase in surgical services due to increased recognition of uterine abnormalities. Proper patient encounter documentation combined with adherence to reimbursement guidelines will allow timely and accurate reimbursement for medical services for this valuable procedure.

REFERENCES

1. Floreen N. Understanding Today's Reimbursement, Medical Practice Reimbursement Manual. New York: McGraw-Hill, 1998: 1.
2. Floreen N. Understanding Today's Reimbursement, Medical Practice Reimbursement Manual. New York: McGraw-Hill, 1998: 32–33.
3. Isaacson KB. Office hysteroscopy. St Louis: Mosby Year Book, 1996: 14.
4. Towbin NA, Gviazda IM, March CM. Office hysteroscopy versus transvaginal ultrasonography in the evaluation of patients with excessive uterine bleeding. *Am J Obstet Gynecol* 1996; **174**: 1678–1682.
5. Mencaglia L, Perino A, Hamou J. Hysteroscopy in perimenopausal and postmenopausal women with abnormal uterine bleeding. *J Reprod Med* 1987; **32**: 577–582.
6. Lapensee L, Cooper JM, Caplinger PA. Indications and contraindications for office hysteroscopy. In: Isaacson KB, ed. Office Hysteroscopy. St Louis: Mosby, 1996.
7. Townsend DE, Fields G, McCausland A et al. Diagnostic hysteroscopy in the management of persistent postmenopausal bleeding. *Obstet Gynecol* 1991; **77**: 745–748.
8. Oriel K, Schrager S. Abnormal uterine bleeding. American Academy of Physcians, Problem-Oriented Diagnosis, October 1999.
9. Valle RF. Office hysteroscopy. *Clin Obstet Gynecol* 1999; **42**: 276–289.
10. Hidlebaugh D. A comparison of clinical outcomes and cost of office vs. hospital hysteroscopy. *J Am Assoc Gynecol Laparosc* 1996; **4**: 39–45.
11. Michael L, Kettel MD. Abnormal uterine bleeding. Best practice of medicine. NIH: Office of Management Assessment, 2002.
12. National Fee Analyzer. Salt Lake City: Ingenix Publishing Group, 2002: 15.
13. Floreen N. Understanding Today's Reimbursement, Medical Practice Reimbursement Manual. New York: McGraw-Hill, 1998: 1–3.
14. Yale Wasserman DMD. RBRVS E-Z Fees®. Milwaukee, WI: Wasserman Medical Publisher, 2001.

CODING AND REFERENCE SOURCES

HEALTHCARE CONSULTANTS OF AMERICA, INC. [(800) 253-4945]

Physicians Fee and Coding Guide
Information about national charge data with geographic conversion factors to allow calculation of a fee range for a particular area.

Codes, Fees, Modifiers, and more
Information about national charge data plus information to help code claims according to Medicare rules.

Fees on Disk
Customized fees for the individual practice for all CPT codes, Medicare relative values, and billing tips.

MEDICODE [(800) 765-6995]

Customized Fee Analyzer Software
Analyses practice fee data, assesses the current fee schedule in the light of Medicare and fee-for-service data, and allows a practice to estimate 'what if' scenarios with different fee schedules.

Customized Fee Analyzer Book
Contains information on charges for the majority of CPT codes. They will provide information at the 50th, 75th, and 95th percentiles.

National Fee Analyzer
Contains national charge data. Gives information about fee pricing strategies for new and seldom performed procedures, and includes information about Medicare considerations and positions on modifiers.

PMIC [(800) 633-7467]

Custom Fees for Physicians
Provides information about charge data in US zip codes. Information is provided about the 30th, 50th, 65th, 80th, and 95th percentiles.

Medical Fees in the United States 1999
Contains national fee data at the 50th, 75th, and 90th percentiles, the Medicare fee schedule, and RVUs.

WASSERMAN MEDICAL PUBLISHERS LTD [(800) 669-3337]

Physician Fee Reference
Provides 50th (median), 75th, and 90th percentile fees for all US geographic areas, Medicare RBRVS, full CPT descriptions, and global periods.

CARL AYERS, PUBLISHER [(800) 929-4824, EXT. 2363]

Managed Care Fee Watch
Provides lowest and highest managed care fees in a particular market, average, reasonable and customary fee, indemnity reimbursement, and RBRVS fee.

ST ANTHONY'S [(800) 632-0123]
Provides numerous sources for developing practice fees, capitation, and other fee reference data.

25 Evidence-based comparison of the different diagnostic techniques to approach the cervix and the uterine cavity

B. J. van Herendael

> **Take Home Message**
> When the different techniques currently used for diagnosis are compared it becomes clear that the traditional technique, hysterosalpingography, is of very little value because of the very high rate of false-positive findings. Transvaginal sonography is very useful; the addition of saline in saline infusion sonography (SIS) does not add benefit in such a way that the technique of SIS becomes the standard of care. Doppler ultrasound is good, but not necessary in the office and at the moment still more of a research tool. CT scan of the uterus is not better than transvaginal sonography and is not readily available. MRI is a superb technique but not available and very expensive – as is CT scan. For intracavitary lesions office hysteroscopy utilizing the vaginoscopic technique gives the best results in this setting.

Introduction

Knowledge of the anatomic condition and the functional condition of the cervix and the uterine cavity is of utmost importance before starting a treatment. In infertility even minor anatomic deformations have important consequences (Table 1). The Algorithm illustrates the possible approaches to examination of the cervix and uterine cavity.

If we look at the infertile population there is a prevalence of uterine cavity malformations of 32–64%. (Figure 1 shows diagrammatic representations of the classical pictograms of possible congenital anomalies at the level of the uterine cavity.).

THE UTERINE CERVIX

There are very few data on the level of the uterine cervix. However, there is evidence that an anatomically normal cervix is essential to the proper functioning of the genital tract. There are a number of traditional diagnostic methods that have been used to inspect the cervix (Table 2).

Figure 1
Diagrammatic representation of the classical pictograms of possible congenital anomalies at the level of the uterine cavity. Hysteroscopically it is important to diagnose the subseptate cavity, as this condition is responsible for a fair number of reproductive and gynecological problems. The septate uterus can be treated in the outpatient environment.

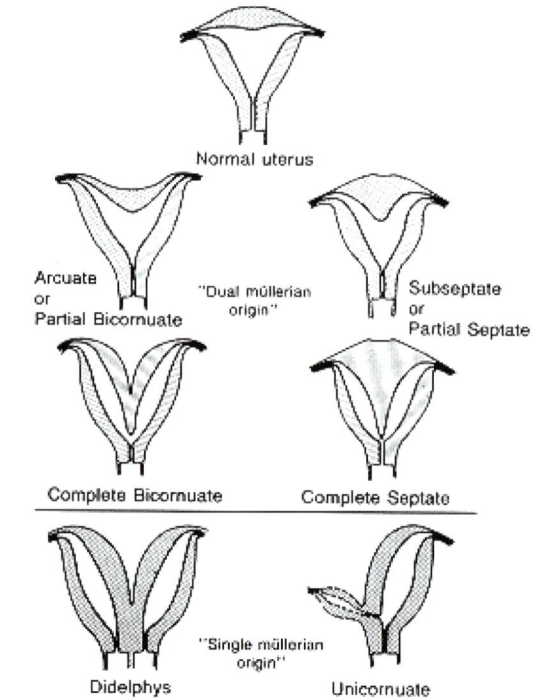

Table 1
Literature survey of the consequences of minor and major anatomic abnormalities at the level of the uterine cavity

Serious reproductive problems	20–25%
Increased risk of abortion	20–45%
Abnormal presentation at birth	20–50%
Retentio placentae	10–20%
Postpartum hemorrhage	10–32%

COLPOSCOPY

Colposcopy gives a visual impression of the outer cervix (Figure 2). The blood vessels can be appreciated and interpreted. The presence of the columnar epithelium on the outside, the so-called erosions, often the cause of abnormal glandular secretions, and abnormal uterine bleeding (AUB) can be evaluated. Only the first few centimeters of the cervical canal can be visualized with a special cervical spreader but this maneuver is painful in most patients, particularly in nullipara.

HYSTEROGRAPHY

Hysterography gives no information on the lower part of the cervical canal as the cone – designed to seal off the cervix and to prevent back flow of the contrast medium – prevents the visualization of this part of the canal. The isthmic part is very well visualized, especially when the filling of the cavity with contrast medium is performed very slowly under controlled pressure, in a uterus that is straightened in the anteroposterior axis of the body. The length of the canal that becomes interpretable depends on the length and form of the cone that is used to seal off the cervix.

TVS

TVS with a vaginal probe of 5–10 MHz gives images of high quality as regards the anatomy of the cervix and the canal. Information on the physiology is difficult to gather with this technique. The location and volume of secretory cysts, so-called Nabothian cysts, can only be assessed by TVS. Adding saline to TVS (SIS) does not have advantages at the level of the cervix and the canal because of the presence of the catheter and if the catheter is withdrawn we fall back on classical TVS.

HYSTEROSCOPY

Hysteroscopy with a mini hysteroscope (<5 mm outer diameter) gives the best diagnostic possibilities. When the vaginoscopic technique is used the outer part of the cervix, the portio, can be observed with the same precision as with the colposcope. The enlargement is even better with the mini hysteroscope, as the enlargement varies from 20× to 80×. The physical properties of the endoscope allow for enlargement of 20× at 1 cm of the cervical surface to 60× in the contact mode. Once the canal entered it is possible to map the entire canal precisely. This is especially important in cases of caesarean section scar or intracervical obstructive adhesions. Hysteroscopy is the only diagnostic tool that allows for a precise localization of the lesions and with the tip of the scope many of the adhesions can be operated on in the same diagnostic session without changing technique and with the patient as a witness. Hysteroscopy offers the advantage that physiological and pathological conditions at this level can be recognized – such as infections, 'Nabothian cysts', and stenosis after currettages. These findings can be incorporated into the fertility plan and treated.

THE UTERINE CAVITY

At the level of the uterine cavity we can propose the same comparison between the different diagnostic techniques (Tables 3 and 4).

HYSTEROGRAPHY

The use of this technique is very limited; it has been proved that there are too many false-positive results. The technique is also too dependent on the physician or technician performing the actual procedure. A great deal of

Table 2
Diagnostic accuracy of inspection of cervix: scored from 0 (very poor) to 10 (very accurate)

Diagnostic method	Portio	Cervical canal	Proximal part of the isthmus
Colposcopy	10/10	0/10	0/10
Hysterosalpingography	0/10	1–2/10	2–3/10
Transvaginal sonography (TVS)	1–2/10	3–4/10	3–4/10
Saline infusion sonography (SIS)	0/10	2–3/10	3–4/10
Hysteroscopy	10/10	10/10	10/10

Figure 2
This image gives an impression of the ectocervix as seen through a videocolposcope at a small enlargement. This is a classical examination. All gynecologists have some training as how to interpret what they see.

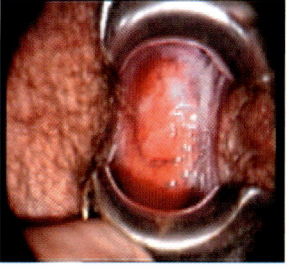

experience is needed and the contrast medium should be injected very slowly to get the maximum amount of information. This implies that the gynecologist should always perform the technique her or himself. On the other hand this technique allows for the detection of difficult-to-diagnose intramural defects, such as adenomyosis. The crypts of adenomyosis in the uterine wall can be demonstrated if the proper technique is used; i.e. stretching the uterus with the tenaculum positioned on the cervix to the point of hurting the patient, combined with very slow injection of the dye under direct radioscopic control until the cavity is nearly completely filled. Very subtle cavity defects can be revealed. Søren Stampe Sørensen [1] published a beautiful monograph on the subject where he proved that small defects at the level of the fundus uteri can be responsible for infertility, prematurity, abnormal fetal position, and even amenorrhea. (Figures 3 and 4).

TVS

TVS is the most popular diagnostic tool (Figure 5). The technique scores well for the detection of anatomical defects. The changes in the endometrium during the menstrual cycle can be evidenced and abnormal endometrial growth (such as in hyperplasia) can be recognized. It is the best diagnostic tool for intramural pathology [2,3]. The use of Doppler in combination with TVS does not offer great advantages in interpreting most of the problems and should be considered with a close look at cost-effectiveness.

SIS

Adding a saline solution to TVS undoubtedly adds to the value of the ultrasound technique as a diagnostic tool, especially in the case of anatomic changes at the level of the uterine cavity [4,5]. When we want to study the

Figure 3
The classic textbook example as to what diagnoses can be made by hysterography. Note that this technique gives an indication of tubal patency, something hysteroscopy cannot do. Note also that the cervix is obscured by the tenaculum and the cone inserted but also by the projection of the pubic bone. Therefore it becomes difficult to interpret the cervical canal.

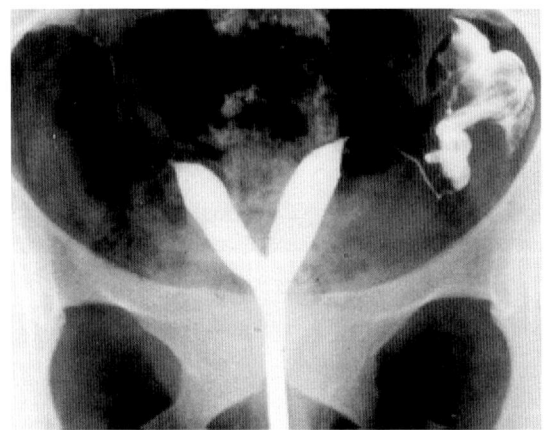

Figure 4
Only very accurate observations can lead to the right interpretation of the uterine cavity and give a clue to the consequences for fertility and gynecological disturbances. Sören Stampe Sörensen was the first to draw conclusions from his personal observations and a review of the literature in his thesis of 1988 [1]. He observed that when the ratio between the height of the fundal excavation (H) and the length of the line connecting the summit of the uterine horns (L) was 0.100 (H/L = 0.100) this was the limit between normal and abnormal uterine contours.

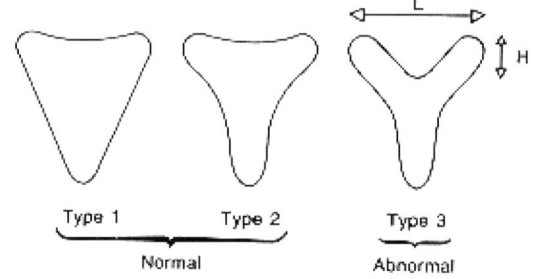

Table 3
Comparison of the diagnostic possibilities of the different techniques at the level of the uterine cavity on a scale of 1–10: 1 very limited, 10 very accurate

Diagnostic method	Cavum uteri anatomy	Cavum uteri physiology	Tubal ostia anatomy	Tubal ostia physiologyy	Intramural pathology
Hysterography	6/10	3/10	3/10	1/10	2/10
TVS	8/10	6/10	1/10	1/10	10/10
SIS	9/10	2/10	2/10	1/10	10/10
Hysteroscopy	10/10	10/10	10/10	10/10	1/10

physiology of the endometrium this becomes more difficult than with the classic TVS technique, as much depends on the infusion pressure used (Figure 6). This means that a great deal of experience is needed and a limited amount of saline has to be injected very slowly. In routine conditions it is difficult to measure the precise dilatation pressure and this pressure is critical for the interpretation of the physiology and the pathology of the endometrium. So, to be evaluated at its maximum value the technique is rather more time-consuming than classic TVS and is in need of a more experienced physician than classic TVS. Therefore, in view of evidence-based evaluation the technique should be reserved for cases where classic TVS leaves room for doubt in diagnosis.

HYSTEROSCOPY

When used in combination with vaginoscopy this diagnostic technique is the best for the evaluation of intracavitary problems, whether at the anatomic, physiologic, or pathologic level. The reason for emphasizing the vaginoscopic technique is that by using the vagina as a first cavity to be dilated before entering the cervical canal and from there the uterine cavity, this technique eliminates the use of a tenaculum and of local anesthesia. Therefore, the anxiety of the patient and the pain sensations are reduced to a point where it becomes possible to perform painless diagnostic hysteroscopy in almost all patients. The restriction of the technique is that it allows only for evaluation of intracavitary disease with the exception of the openings into the cavity of the

Figure 5
TVS of the uterine cavity. Adding saline as in SIS does not greatly enhance the diagnostic capacity of the TVS. It allows for better location of the lesion. Adding Doppler ultrasound only occasionally adds to the diagnostic capability of the technique. These techniques are more accurately described in Chapters 11 and 12.

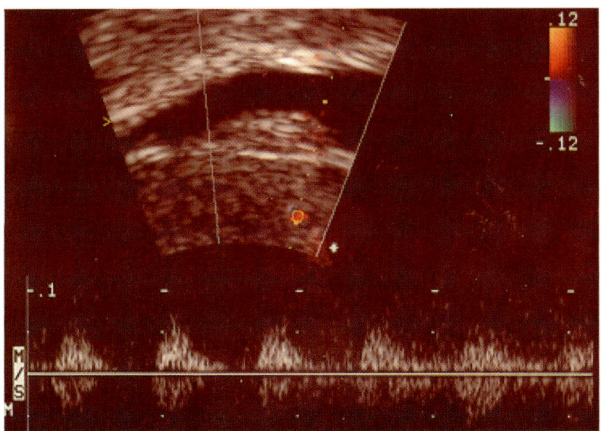

intramural adenomyosis crypts. The latter are best seen immediately after the end of the menstrual flow. In the cavity hysteroscopy is the best diagnostic technique not only for anatomical problems – e.g. myoma formation, polyps, and adhesions – but also for interpreting physiologic changes in the endometrium and the pathologic changes in the advent of infection [6].

This is because the technique allows for a direct visual interpretation of the problem (Figure 7). The same direct visualization also makes it possible to determine a correct topographic location for the anatomic problems and to relate the volume of the problem to the total volume of the uterine cavity. This is possible but very difficult with the indirect techniques [7,8]. It is the only technique that allows a good interpretation of the tubal ostia – not only of the anatomic integrity but also of the physiology, e.g. endosalpingitis or edema of the first millimeter of the intramural part due to adenomyosis of the tube. It also allows for an interpretation of the function of the intramural part of the tube. When the intrauterine pressure exceeds the counter pressure of the isthmic part of the tube the intramural part of the tube will 'open' to allow the

Figure 6
(a) and (b) The importance of the infusion pressure in SIS. In a uterus with very thick endometrium, as seen in (a), the endometrium can be compressed against the walls and is therefore no longer interpretable.

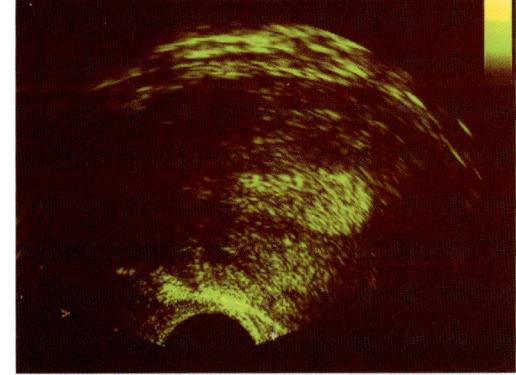

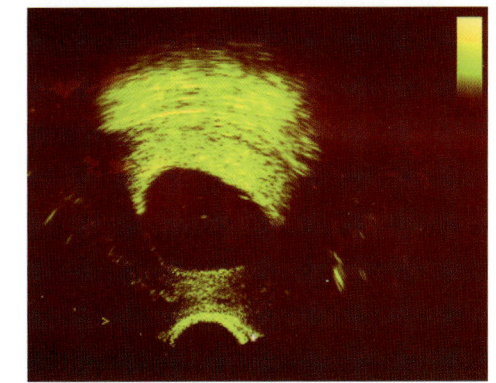

passage of distension medium to the abdominal cavity. Our group described this phenomenon as the 'flap valve' mechanism in the early 1980s. It should be noted that if a thin-walled hydrosalpinx exists the flap valve phenomenon will continue until the tube is fully dilated.

CT scan and *MRI* are not included in the tables as these techniques are not routinely available in the standard outpatient department or in private facilities. In the literature it has been shown that a CT scan is inferior to TVS with vaginal probes of 5 and 7.5 MHz for the detection of small uterine lesions.

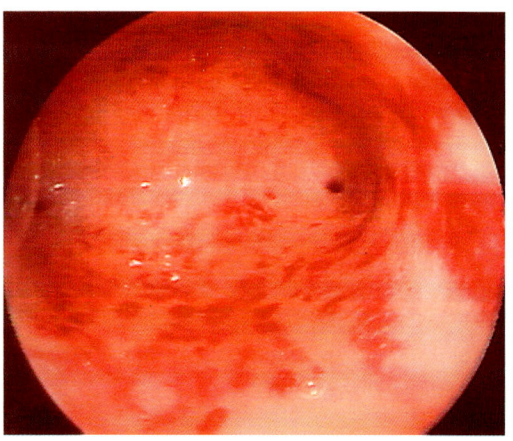

Figure 7
Hysteroscopic view of the uterine cavity covered with the typical strawberry pattern as described by Stevens et al in 1988 [6]. This feature can not be diagnosed by any other diagnostic method.

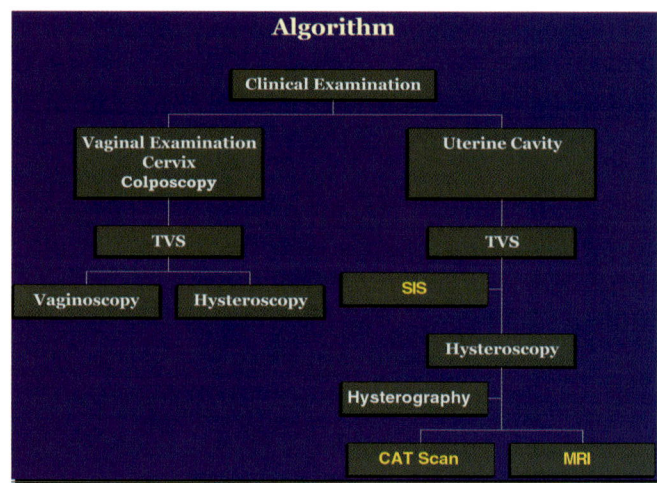

Figure 8
Possible approaches to the cervix and uterine cavity.

Table 1
Data from a literature search on sensitivity, specificity, and false-positive results concerning anatomical changes in the uterine cavity (the reference value is always operative hysteroscopy)

Technique	Sensitivity	Specificity	False-positive results
Hysterosalpingography		23%	15–32%
Hysteroscopy	79–96%	93%	6–15%
Saline infusion sonography	44–96%	91%	6–24%
Transvaginal ultrasound	54–60%	90%	10–19%

REFERENCES

1. Søren Stampe Sørensen. Minor Mullerian Anomalies and Oligomenorrhea in Infertile Women. København: L?geforeningens Forlag, 1988.
2. Towbin NA, Gviazda IM, March CM. Office hysteroscopy versus transvaginal ultrasonography in the evaluation of patients with excessive uterine bleeding. *Am J Obstet Gynecol* !996; **174**: 1678–1682.
3. Wieser F, Tempfer C, Kurz Ch, Nagele F. Hysteroscopy in 2001: a comprehensive review. *Acta Obstet Gynecol Scand* 2001; **80**: 773–783.
4. Epstein E, Ramirez A, Skoog L, Valentin L. Transvaginal sonography, saline contrast sonohysterography and hysteroscopy for the investigation of women with postmenopausal bleeding and endometrium > 5 mm. *Ultrasound Obstet Gynecol* 2001; **18**: 157–162.
5. Krampl E, Bourne T, Hurlen-Solbakken H, Istre O. Transvaginal ultrasonography, sonohysterography and operative hysteroscopy for the evaluation of abnormal uterine bleeding. *Acta Obstet Gynecol Scand* 2001; **80**: 616–622.
6. Stevens MJ, van Herendael BJ, Slangen T, Haensch Ch. Hysteroscopic diagnosis of chronic endometritis: which role! *Cervix and Lower Female Genital Tract* 1988; **6**: 333–336.
7. Sousa R, Silvestre M, Ameida e Sousa L et al. Transvaginal ultrasonography and hysteroscopy in postmenopausal bleeding: a prospective study. *Acta Obstet Gynecol Scand* 2001; **80**: 856–862.
8. Brown SE, Coddington CC, Schnorr J, Toner JP, Gibbons W, Oehninger S. Evaluation of outpatient hysteroscopy, saline infusion hysterosonography and hysterosalpingography in infertile women: a prospective, randomised study. *Fertil Steril* 2000; **74**: 1029–1034.

26a Training and accreditation: USA

Hysteroscopy and operative hysteroscopy: learning, training, proctoring, and credentialing

Rafael F. Valle

INTRODUCTION

As hysteroscopy and hysteroscopic surgery have been adapted by gynecologists, the number and complexity of hysteroscopic procedures performed have increased markedly. However, because these procedures are just beginning to be taught in residency programs to physicians completing their training programs, not all physicians already practicing gynecology have had the opportunity to learn these procedures formally. Therefore, they sometimes find themselves with a vacuum that is difficult to fill with short training sessions or postgraduate courses [1].

Furthermore, as with any procedure that is initiated and clinically applied, there is a learning curve that requires a systematic approach to learn these procedures in a progressive manner (from easy to difficult) and to use the initial experience as a method of improving step by step in the acquisition of skills, confidence, and overall safety. A systematic didactic approach to acquiring skills is an important task of a program that should be available to all gynecologists requiring this type of training. Fortunately, today these types of programs have already been designed and can help the practitioner to simplify the learning process by profiting from the accumulated years of experience of tutors and by the availability of modern instrumentation that can facilitate the performance of hysteroscopic procedures [2].

THE LEARNING CURVE

A systematic approach to learning should begin with a thorough knowledge of the instrumentation with its different components that can then be tried in inanimate models, animal models, extirpated uteri, or other simulated models, to acquire dexterity, hand–eye coordination, and familiarity with endoscopic views. It is also important to have some fundamental theoretical background on the indications, contraindications, and possible complications of hysteroscopy. This process of learning can be achieved easily by attending seminars, workshops, and tutorials, and by reviewing different books and atlases published on the subject [3–7].

Advancing to the stage of performing hysteroscopy in patients, it is best done while the patient is under general anesthesia, to avoid the frustrations and problems that can occur at the beginning. This will make the transition to regional anesthesia and finally local anesthesia or conscious sedation easier. As with any surgical method that requires dexterity, the transition should be planned from diagnostic to therapeutic procedures. Different methods of hysteroscopic surgery should be reviewed, always maintaining a systematic approach from easy to difficult procedures (Tables 1–4).

Table 1.
Learning hysteroscopy

- Familiarize with instrumentation
- Know the techniques
- Review indications, contraindications, possible complications
- Attend seminars, workshops, tutorials
- Have reasonable expectations
- Use documentation, photography, video

Table 2
Anesthesia for hysteroscopy

1. Begin with general anesthesia
2. When proficient, may use local anesthesia with/without sedation
3. Sedation alone with small endoscopes

Table 3
Learning diagnostic applications

- Uterine models
- Extirpated uteri
- Before D&C (multiparous, postmenopausal)
- Before vaginal hysterectomy
- At tubal sterilization

Therefore it is important to review books, slides, video demonstrations and CD ROMs (now readily available), that can pave the way to obtaining knowledge of hysteroscopy and hysteroscopic surgery before the procedures are performed in patients. Clinical judgment and common sense are paramount in the appropriate selection of cases, and systematic knowledge of uterine anatomy and physiology is needed to distinguish clearly normal from abnormal conditions [8–10].

The multiplicity of teaching aids now available, particularly video demonstrations and CD ROMs, can promote interactive learning to resolve clinical problems and adapt various hysteroscopic methods to intrauterine treatment [11].

It is a realistic hope that virtual reality models will soon be available that will help physicians in acquiring dexterity and appropriate manipulation of instruments that perhaps will replace many of the models that simulate human uteri currently used for training.

PROCTORING AND PRECEPTORSHIPS

As many physicians now practice diagnostic and operative hysteroscopy efficiently, they can help beginners by acting as tutors, helping to establish appropriate set ups to facilitate the logistics and ergonomics of displaying the instrumentation and other necessary equipment such as pumps, light sources, video monitoring, cameras, etc. This is most helpful, not only for physicians, but also for the relevant team performing endoscopic procedures such as assistants, nurses, and anesthesiologists [12].

For diagnostic procedures, after practicing on special models, initial supervision is important – to correct mistakes, encourage achievement, and share specific practical tips that the beginner can easily adopt.

For therapeutic procedures, different models for hysteroscopic surgery are available and the beginner can practice before attempting them on a live patient. These teaching models simulating real, clinical situations are available for trainees, and the transition to clinical situations can be facilitated. Here, supervision is most important, following the basic philosophy of going progressively from easy cases to difficult ones [13].

ACCREDITATION AND CREDENTIALING

Because of the need to assure the safety and efficacy of carrying out new procedures, hospitals are beginning to credential physicians in new procedures necessitating the fulfilment of several requirements needed to learn and acquire new skills. Lectures, seminars, workshops, and practical sessions are part of the component with accreditation from specially formed councils, such as the American Council of Gynecologic Endoscopy recently formed in the USA that will review basic credentials and operative cases performed to assess these requirements. While accreditation only ensures that these requirements have been fulfilled, accreditation councils cannot assure credentialing, which will be the responsibility of each institution that is to grant privileges to physicians to perform these or other surgical procedures [14] (Tables 5–7).

These monitoring methods will also ensure that those physicians who want to perform new procedures that they have not performed before should undergo initial supervision until competency has been demonstrated.

Most credentialing institutions in the USA have adopted the guidelines for obtaining privileges in Gynecologic Operative Endoscopy proposed by the Society of

Table 4
Learning therapeutic applications

- From easy to difficult (IUCDs, polyps, biopsies)
- Adhesions, septa, myomas, ablation (when proficient)
- Fiberoptic lasers (endometrial ablation, septa, adhesions, myomas)
- Use of resectoscope (myomas, septa, adhesions, endometrial ablation)
- Tubal cannulation
- Experimental applications (sterilization, chorionic villus sampling, GIFT, ZIFT, etc.)

Table 5
Establishing credentials for hysteroscopy: requirements

- Privileges in gynecologic surgery
- Didactic course
- Practical workshop (laboratory setting)
- Tutorial by qualified hysteroscopist
- Supervision of first cases, particularly operative cases
- Advanced procedures require preceptorship
- Laser and resectoscope (special requirements)
- Experimental techniques: approved informed consent and protocol by institutional review board

Reproductive Surgeons and the American Society of Reproductive Medicine (ASRM) – formerly known as the American Fertility Society – in 1994 [3].

Two levels of competency have been proposed for hysteroscopy:

Level 1: Simple procedures
- Diagnostic hysteroscopy with targeted biopsies
- Removal of small (<2 cm) polyps
- Removal of intrauterine contraceptive devices (IUCDs)
- Minor Asherman's syndrome
- Removal of a small (<1 cm) pedunculate fibroid.

Level 2: More complex operative procedures requiring additional training
- Division/resection of uterine septum
- Endoscopic surgery for major Asherman's syndrome
- Endometrial resection/ablation
- Resection of submucous myomas (>1 cm) or myomas with intramural component
- Repeat endometrial resection/ablation
- Tubal cannulation.

RESIDENCY TRAINING

The training of hysteroscopy and hysteroscopic surgery in a residency program is similar to that being offered for other types of surgery, i.e. progressive learning under close supervision with increased responsibility as experience is acquired. Because of the increased variety and number of surgical cases, residency programs are in an enviable position to offer residents experience with a variety of pathologic conditions that will help them better learn and understand hysteroscopic surgery. Formal residency programs usually have competent and dedicated instructors who will ably guide the trainees in achieving competency. This training program is now needed as part of the overall requirements for specialty Boards in Obstetrics and Gynecology. It is envisaged that eventually this training program will be incorporated in all training programs all over the world and then competency in gynecologic endoscopy will be an essential requirement for all gynecologic surgeons [8].

SUMMARY AND CONCLUSIONS

As endoscopic surgery advances and physicians learn new procedures, it is important to offer a comprehensive and systematic program of learning. This program should include fundamental requirements in learning diagnostic hysteroscopic procedures and advanced surgical and therapeutic procedures. This program is most valuable, needed, and should be encouraged for all beginners and physicians who continue their learning process to maintain skills and dexterity. While many courses and workshops are available all over the world, the university-approved ones should be encouraged, as they have the academic recognition and capabilities for teaching that will facilitate the learning curves of all physicians. For operative hysteroscopy, preceptorships are most useful, as physicians will have the opportunity of observing and listening to accomplished surgeons who can correct mistakes, encourage success, and share their accumulated experience and practical pearls of wisdom while supervising.

Once training is established at the residency level, or similar settings, updating and maintaining proficiency will be required to continue to perform hysteroscopic procedures safely and efficiently.

Table 6
Credentialing for laser hysteroscopy

- Training in diagnostic and operative hysteroscopy
- Formal didactic laser course (physics, safety, tissue interaction)
- Laser laboratory experience (especially with fiber lasers)
- Laser hysteroscopy preceptorship
- Supervision by qualified laser surgeon at the beginning
- Continued surgical practice

Table 7
Credentialing for use of resectoscope

- Training in diagnostic and operative hysteroscopy
- Knowledge of electrosurgery principles
- Knowledge of appropriate media for uterine distension for use of electrosurgery
- Laboratory experience with resectoscope
- Preceptorship in use of resectoscope
- Supervision by qualified hysteroscopist at the beginning
- Continued surgical experience

REFERENCES

1. Siegler AM. Learning and teaching hysteroscopic tubal sterilization. In: Sciarra JJ, Butler JC, Speidel JJ, eds. Hysteroscopic sterilization. New York: Intercontinental Medical Book Corporation, 1974: 133–143.
2. Keye WR. Hitting a moving target: credentialing the endoscopic surgeon. *Fertil Steril* 1994; **62**: 1115–1117.
3. Society for Reproductive Surgeons. Guidelines for attaining privileges in operative endoscopy. *Fertil Steril* 1994; **62**: 1118–1119.
4. American College of Obstetricians and Gynecologists. Credentialing guidelines for new operative procedures. ACOG Committee Opinion 142, August 1994.
5. Chapron C, DeVroey P, Dubuisson JB, Pouly JL, Vercellini P. ESHRE Guidelines for Issuing Accreditation and Monitoring in Gynecologic Endoscopy. *Hum Reprod* 1997; **12**: 867–868.
6. Tulandi T. Canadian guidelines for training in operative endoscopy (letter). *Gynaecol Endosc* 1995; **4**: 69.
7. American College of Surgeons. Statements on Emerging Surgical Technologies and the Evaluation of Credentials. *ACS Bulletin* 1994; **79**: June.
8. Sanmmarco MJ, Youngblood JP. A residency teaching program in operative endoscopy. *Obstet Gynecol* 1993; **81**: 463–466.
9. Glawocki GA. An in-hospital teaching program in gynecologic laser therapy. *J Reprod Med* 1985; **30**: 93–96.
10. Wolfe WM, Levine RL, Sanfilippo JS, Eggler S. A teaching method for endoscopic surgery, hysteroscopy and pelviscopic surgery. *Fertil Steril* 1988; **50**: 662–664.
11. Levy JS, Gillio RG, Fenner DE, Cornman-Levy D. Maximizing learning potential for health care providers: sound educational principles coupled with computer technologies. *J Gynecol Surg* 1998; **14**: 141–147.
12. Hidlebaugh D. The role of a surgical preceptor in learning resectoscopic endometrial ablation. In: Jordan MP, Hunt RB, Loffer FD, eds. Hysteroscopy update. Proceedings of the World Congress of Hysteroscopy, Miami, FL, February 9–11, 1996. Published 1997.
13. Lefebvre Y, Cote J, Lefebvre L. Teaching hysteroscopy by virtual simulation. In: Jordan MP, Hunt RB, Loffer FD, eds. Hysteroscopy update. Proceedings of the World Congress of Hysteroscopy, Miami, FL, February 9–11, 1996. Published 1997.
14. Valle RF. Learning hysteroscopy for credentialing. In: A manual of clinical hysteroscopy. New York: Parthenon Publishing Group, 1998: 99–102.

26b Training and accreditation: USA

Training and credentialing in operative hysteroscopy

Toufic Nakad and Keith Isaacson

INTRODUCTION

The field of operative endoscopy is developing very rapidly. The introduction of new techniques and equipment has allowed the operating gynecologist to carry out endoscopically many cases that previously would have required a laparotomy. However, this rapid evolution of surgical endoscopy has created concerns for physicians who are applying these new technologies, especially gynecologists who did not have the appropriate training during their residency years. As a result of these developments, the need for a formalized system of training and credentialing in gynecologic operative endoscopy has become obvious.

Proper training and certification are important to ensure the highest quality of health care, to maximize successful outcomes, and to minimize morbidity. Furthermore, documentation of appropriate surgical skills is essential for the medicolegal protection of parent institutions, operating room personnel, and surgeons. Although complications are an accepted risk of surgery, the surgeon's credentials in the application of these techniques will minimize his or her liability in the event of a malpractice suit. Some surgeons have been concerned that implementing a uniform and fair credentialing process for operative endoscopy, either in a hospital or outpatient facility, will result in an increased risk of litigation. The courts, however, have found hospitals and staff members negligent when a negative outcome occurs and no appropriate and reasonable quality control measures have been instituted. For example, in *Gonzales v. Nork*, the Superior Court in Sacramento County, California concluded on November 19, 1973:

> 'The hospital has the duty to protect its patients from malpractice by members of its medical staff when it knows or should have known that malpractice was likely to be committed upon them ... It was negligent in not knowing, because it did not have a system for acquiring knowledge.'

The training and credentialing of endoscopic surgeons has become a pressing and immediate issue; immediate because poor surgical training has a negative and potentially fatal impact on patient outcomes and pressing because nonmedical agencies are taking rapid steps to implement credentialing guidelines. An example of this is the 1992 guidelines issued by the New York state health department specifying 'that surgeons must perform at least 15 laparoscopies under supervision' before a hospital may issue privileges permitting them to do a laparoscopic cholecystectomy independently. This was triggered by events from August 1990 through June 1992 when at least 7 patients died and 185 others suffered serious or life-threatening complications from the procedure in that state. Officials went on to include laparoscopically assisted vaginal hysterectomy (LAVH) and other endoscopic procedures as well. This decision was, at that point, a breakthrough in the establishment of guidelines governing the utility of endoscopic surgery in patients' treatment because it originated from a governmental agency and not a medical society. It was also the trigger for many societies around the country to take the initiative and come up with nationwide credentialing and training guidelines in operative endoscopy.

GENERAL CREDENTIALING GUIDELINES FOR OPERATIVE HYSTEROSCOPY

In 1992 the American College of Obstetrics and Gynecology (ACOG) published its guidelines for departmental qualifications of gynecologists requiring privileges to perform operative hysteroscopy. These guidelines are summarized as follows:

1. Each applicant must be a member in good standing of the institution's department of obstetrics and gynecology.
2. Each applicant must have extensive experience of utilizing the hysteroscope for diagnostic procedures.
3. Each member must have documented resident education and experience or must have completed a course in operative hysteroscopy, which has been approved for AMA category 1 credits or ACOG cognates.
4. Each applicant should initially be supervised in his or her own operative hysteroscopic cases. The supervisor should make a written recommendation to the department head.
5. Gynecologic surgeons should restrict their activities to equipment for which they are qualified and procedures for which they are credentialed.

One year later in 1993, the Council on Resident Education in Obstetrics and Gynecology (CREOG) established a training program to teach academicians how to establish endoscopic surgery modules in their residency training programs. This has lead to the establishment of a reproductive surgery fellowship program sponsored by the Society of Reproductive Surgeons (SRS), which is a division of the American Society for Reproductive Medicine (ASRM). The society also came up with a set of principles, a framework to be used by those who desire or must prepare specific requirements for credentialing of endoscopic surgeons. These were quite similar to the ACOG guidelines, with the introduction of some new concepts. The principles presuppose the following:

1. The applicant must be eligible or certified by the American Board of Obstetrics and Gynecology and is a member in good standing of the institution from which the privileges are being requested.
2. The applicant has been granted privileges to perform any and all of the prerequisite procedures (diagnostic hysteroscopy) and has demonstrated the ability to perform these safely, efficiently, and effectively.
3. Privileges will be granted for individual procedures or a group of related procedures as deemed to be appropriate.
4. Training to perform a procedure should consist of the following steps:
   a. A formal didactic course or series of lectures supplemented by a review of pertinent literature and technical information.
   b. Supervised experience in a laboratory that provides the opportunity to rehearse the techniques required at surgery.
   c. The observation of an experienced surgeon who has been granted privileges to perform the procedures in question.
   d. Performance of several procedures under the supervision of a credentialed surgeon until the applicant and supervisor agree that the applicant can perform the procedure independently in a safe, efficient, and effective manner.
5. That the performance of the surgeon be monitored and that each surgeon be required to demonstrate continuing expertise. The requirements for renewal of privileges by the institution may vary depending on the procedure and/or institution.
6. A letter from the director of an approved residency training program can be enough if the required training criteria have been fulfilled during residency.
7. If there are no surgeons on the staff of the parent institution who can act as preceptors, then supervised preceptorship can be arranged by scheduling a number of appropriate cases in conjunction with other interested surgeons and inviting a visiting expert, an appropriate consultant to serve as the preceptor.

The same concerns were shared by international gynecologists. In Europe in 1997, for example, the European Society of Human Reproduction and Embryology (ESHRE) organized a Committee of Special Interest Group on Reproductive Surgery, which has written its own guidelines for training, accreditation, and even monitoring in gynecologic endoscopy. The criteria proposed by the committee are similar to those already described by SRS and ACOG as regards the phases of training (didactic, observational, and preceptorship) and the institutional accreditation procedures. However, they went further in proposing continuous monitoring for surgeons who wish to maintain ESHRE accreditation. They set up certain requirements that must be met every 3 years. These include:

1. Attendance at workshops, updates, and postgraduate courses organized or approved by ESHRE.
2. Compilation of a list of endoscopic surgical procedures performed in a calendar year, specifying any complications.
3. Acceptance of quality control and auditing activity by ESHRE.
4. Compilation of a list of studies performed and papers published on endoscopic procedures.
5. Participation in multicenter studies.

It is recommended that procedures be performed in well-organized operating theaters where an experienced team and the necessary technical equipment are available. ESHRE will, on the other hand, provide continuing information in workshops and training courses.

These guidelines represent the basic principles governing the development of a protocol addressing training and credentialing of gynecologists in operative endoscopy. However, there are legal issues surrounding the liability of the credentialing surgeon if the person credited has a maloccurrence. Also, unlike training for laparoscopic surgery, there are no good animate models for learning advanced hysteroscopic techniques. The challenge, therefore, is not only to establish credentialing guidelines that require laboratory training, but to continue the exploration of inanimate training modules that optimize hysteroscopic teaching. There is optimism that new simulation technologies can revolutionize the whole training and certification system.

TRAINING FOR OPERATIVE HYSTEROSCOPY

Traditionally, residents are trained by exposure to multiple surgeries with subsequent accumulation of knowledge allowing them to develop skills to perform complex procedures. Initially, this is done under supervision and later on independently. Even though this system is effective, it takes several years to consider a trainee well trained. With advancing technology, however, the pendulum is rapidly swinging towards the performance of more cases endoscopically, making it difficult for the practicing gynecologic surgeon to stay up-to-date. Hence it is necessary to devise a training system that will address the needs not only of residents but also, and equally importantly, those of gynecologists in private practice.

Training is the step where a practitioner acquires the knowledge to correctly select the patient for surgery, the type of approach, and the necessary instrumentation. It is also the stage where skills are developed to appropriately counsel and consent the patient, perform the procedure, and minimize and control intraoperative complications. Generally, a sequential approach has been recommended by major societies to train practitioners to perform operative hysteroscopy. It consists of didactic, laboratory experience, observational, and preceptorship phases.

1 *Didactic phase*. A series of lectures or presentations (audiovisual) addressing the theoretic aspects of hysteroscopic surgery, including patient selection, preoperative evaluation, instrumentation, surgical techniques, complications, and clinical outcomes. Due to time restrictions and enhanced convenience, this level of training will likely be web-based in the near future.

2 *Laboratory experience*. This provides the trainee with 'hands-on' experience using hysteroscopic equipment to simulate surgical techniques before applying them in real patients. This could be done in a 'dry lab' on a pelvi-trainer model, which is currently inadequate. A better alternative is to use a wet lab utilizing the pig bladder as a substitute for the human uterus in a continuous flow environment. The disadvantages of these models lie in their limitations in simulating full surgical cases. However, these models do provide training in hand–eye coordination when using the hysteroscopic equipment. Recently, hysteroscopic computer simulation has been developed by specialists in this field. Simulators, especially those equipped with haptic or tactile feedback, allow the trainee to practice a full procedure. While the graphics are still somewhat cartoonish, there is tremendous growth potential for these tools in the training and credentialing arenas. Sitting at the screen, a resident or the practitioner can perform a hysteroscopic myomectomy by manipulating a joystick. As mentioned, these simulators are still far from representing real life surgery, where complications like bleeding, perforation, electrolyte imbalance, and air or gas embolism, etc. often dictate the outcome of surgery.

3 *Observational phase*. The trainee is required to observe real-time surgery performed in the operating suite, and get a sense of how different instruments are used on a real patient. Viewing pretaped procedures is not an acceptable substitute for this phase.

4 *Preceptorship phase*. This is the final and most important phase in training, where the trainee is ready to do the surgery himself or herself under direct supervision. The preceptor should have proven expertise and should allow the trainee to do most if not all the surgery, while keeping the surgeon and the patient out of trouble. Not only should the trainee be responsible for the preoperative patient selection and preparation, but postoperative management as well.

A training program or course that incorporates all the above-mentioned phases should take on average 2–3 months for the average practitioner, and could easily be incorporated in the obstetrics and gynecology 4-year residency curriculum.

CREDENTIALING AND ACCREDITATION

After the fulfilment of the training schedule, the course director will document the trainee's attendance and the supervisor will evaluate their surgical skills. Credentialing then becomes the responsibility of the operating facility. Assignment of operating privileges in the hospital is often procedure-specific, meaning the surgeon will ask for privileges to perform certain procedures such as endometrial ablation or hysteroscopic polypectomy after fulfilling their training requirements. However, this process sometimes becomes cumbersome, particularly in a rapidly changing field like hysteroscopy.

Alternatively, many societies such as the ASRM, ACOG, and ESHRE advocate credentialing based on skill level. They propose a scheme linking the procedures to their appropriate training level. An example of this tier system is one published in 1997 by the ESHRE Committee of Special Interest Group on Reproductive Surgery. It is summarized by the following:

Level I: diagnostic hysteroscopy

Level II: polypectomy, removal of pedunculate myomas, section of partial septa, lysis of mild synechiae, endometrial ablation, tubal cannulation

Level III: lysis of severe synechiae, section of complete septa, removal of myomas with intramural extension.

Based on this, the surgeon will get privileges to perform all the surgeries pertaining to the same skill level.

A fairly similar credentialing scheme implemented in 1996 at the Northwestern Memorial Hospital was associated with a significant reduction in the rates of surgical complications as well as operating times.

Finally, it should be noted that accreditation by formal or informal boards does not guarantee lifetime surgical competence. This is why follow-up on surgeons' performance (case list) and medical education (CME credits) every few years should be recommended to revalidate their certificate.

Conclusion

There is little doubt that the increasing trend of performing minimally invasive therapies in gynecology will continue. The benefits of reduced morbidity and improved outcomes will fuel this growth. Despite these advantages, 'open surgery' still accounts for the majority of benign cases treated in the USA, partly if not mainly due to the lack of expertise in the former techniques among practitioners.

Faced with this challenge, medical societies have advocated the implementation of training and certification programs for residents during their 4 years of residency, as well as for active practitioners. The task is very difficult owing to the scarcity of resources such as certified trainers, centers equipped to carry out the training programs, practitioners' time and how much of that can be spared to obtain adequate training. In addition, the cost of training gynecologists is substantial, and partnerships with industry should be explored to help defray these costs.

An alternative to training is the development of new 'blind' procedures that eliminate the need for hand–eye coordination development. The 'global ablations' technologies are just one example of creating new technology instead of training for the standard techniques. What we should be advocating is the creation of training tools that will enhance our surgical skills and can be applied to all endoscopic procedures.

27a Training and accreditation: Europe

Walter Costantini

INTRODUCTION

During the last half of the twentieth century, in the aftermath of a terrible world war, it became more and more important to safeguard the quality of life of the human race. This included both the physical and relational integrity.

Confronted with the rapid and excellent progress of medical science – which allows insights into the reasons for the problems that interfere with human well-being and provides us with solutions to these very problems – we would increasingly like to know how to deal with a particular problem, especially when this directly involves patient satisfaction (Figure 1).

This striving explains the explosive growth of mini-invasive techniques. These techniques respect the physical integrity of the person to the full and in an even more recent development of thoughts they tend to respect to the full the personal environment and the professional activity of the patient.

The 1970s and 1980s witnessed an explosion of this particular way of thinking. Advances in biotechnology and medical engineering made treatments possible in a way that was unthinkable just a few years earlier. This evolution was not always to the liking of the medical profession but has definitely been a driving force within the complex world of medicine [1,2].

This large input of nonmedical disciplines into medicine has led to an identity crisis within the profession, afflicting even the highest levels to such a degree that the whole structure of the system had to be rethought.

There is another factor, namely the division within the medical act between the *what to do* and the *how to do it* fraction of the act. This principle has been the foundation of medical thinking up to now and is still the foundation of current medical education. Although not recommendable, the diffuse mechanism of delegation of the operative act has caused delay in the integration of new technologies into the medical profession. Above all, it has made it very difficult (up to the late 1990s in a lot of European universities) to update the teaching, a teaching based on useful but illogical subdivisions in the knowledge required by registrars [3].

In this way a subspecialism of endoscopy has been created. In gynecology, particularly in the fields of laparoscopy and hysteroscopy, at the same level there are subspecialisms in gynecological oncology, gynecological endocrinology (human reproduction), fetal medicine and uro-gynecology. Only the last four are recognized by the European Board (EBCOG) within the area of gynecology and obstetrics [4–6]. The incongruity of this fact is obvious. Where the different recognized subspecialities depend on a complete clinical curriculum (epidemiology, semeiology, diagnosis, indications, and treatment) to claim their purpose, only endoscopy (which straddles the different subspecialities) does without the clinical premises and focuses on the therapeutic modalities. This means that there is a great risk that training a pure endoscopist will lead to the creation of a simple technician of a surgical therapy. This in turn would severely damage both the medical profession and endoscopy.

There seems to be no simple solution, because the technique has to be learned from this overwhelming majority of surgeons who have no cultural and technical background that includes the 'endoscopic' way of thinking and working.

Training and accreditation will have to be obtained:

1. In a short period of time because of the pressing demands of the patients.
2. With strong deontological guarantees of operative safety; this will also standardize the acquisition of learning.

Figure 1
Dealing with a particular problem, especially when this directly involves patient satisfaction.

3 With emphasis on a strong theoretical-practical foundation to create the possibility for the widespread teaching of future generations and spontaneous personal updating by experienced surgeons.

These are the aims that endoscopy wants to achieve immediately, while two or three generations of teachers will pass through universities all over Europe, and more adequate teaching that conforms to the new realities of surgery will be developed. This requires a political will on the part of the providers involved in medical organization within a united Europe and a precise engagement of the different national scientific societies to institute and control standardized teaching and accreditation of this particular form of surgery. This will facilitate the diffusion of the technique rapidly and on a large scale. Here lies a task with a limited timespan that will be finished within the next 30–40 years, then once again the different notions of *why, what and how to do* will be reunited within every subdiscipline.

Within the field of endoscopy not all techniques have followed the same direction and not all present the same problems. For example, by definition hysteroscopy has only one subject – gynecology. Here we gather visual images – which cannot be obtained by any other technique – of the uterine cavity, an essential organ for any gynecologist [7]. This technique allows unique access into the uterine cavity to perform conservative treatments. These three unique and irreplaceable characteristics of hysteroscopy influence its use in gynecological practice. The use of the technique cannot be considered as a valuable alternative for the classic diagnostic and therapeutic techniques. It becomes an inevitable and irreplaceable complementary tool [8].

Hysteroscopy is the first of the endoscopic techniques that is in need of a rapid and thorough diffusion within the limits of security and control as stated earlier. There is a particular need to introduce the technique into all gynecologic teaching programs with compulsory practical execution of the technique under preceptorship conditions during the actual training period at the universities [9,10].

Within the specific period of time when classic hysteroscopy was diffused we witnessed a specific form of hysteroscopy – ambulatory hysteroscopy – forging its own specific place [11,12]. This specific autonomous place can be explained by the complex approach required when a patient is awake and by the expected reduction in time for postoperative observations. This approach is the reason why there is no excessive hurry to diffuse the technique and its introduction can be done under strict conditions and with the necessary precision. Today these conditions are necessary to evaluate the introduction of new surgical procedures. Although these procedures improve and widen the scope of the assistance we can give there is always the need to evaluate the risk-benefit included in the medical act [13,14].

THE EUROPEAN SITUATION

It is better to consider the general problem only in this section. In my opinion the European regulations concerning training and accreditation, even now, show many differences.

Classification, teaching, and credentialing of endoscopic procedures are all aspects of one issue, namely training in endoscopy. In the 1990s authors such as Sciarra, Azziz, Chapron, and Luciano highlighted this fact (Table 1). Many societies – the European Association for Endoscopic Surgery, the former European Society of Hysteroscopy, the American and European Colleges of Obstetrics and Gynaecology, the Canadian Society and the AAGL, the ESHRE, and the ESGE faced the challenge [15–19].

All these societies have worked out guidelines for training. They suggested classifications of endoscopic procedures according to the skills of the surgeon. They suggested didactic measures to teach and evaluate. Only the American Accreditation College for Gynecological Endoscopy has succeeded in achieving a voluntary system where the physician is accredited on the basis of evidence of procedures performed [20–24].

However, when considering the different guidelines there is a common trend. All of them want endoscopic surgery to be carried out only by experienced surgeons and

Table 1
Principal training and accreditation guideline promoters

EAES	European Association for Endoscopic Surgery
ACOG	American College of Obstetricians and Gynecologists
EBCOG	European Board and College of Obstetrics and Gynaecology
SOGC	Society of Obstetricians and Gynaecologists of Canada
AFS	American Fertility Society
SRS	Society of Reproductive Surgeons
AAGL	American Association of Gynecologic Laparoscopists
ESHRE	European Society for Human Reproduction and Embriology
ESGE	European Society for Gynaecological Endoscopy

the training always consists of three phases: a theoretical and hands-on course followed by an observational period and ending with a one-to-one supervision of the surgeon's own cases (Table 2).

Some guidelines define characteristics and minimum standards for each of the training phases.

The trainee is often asked to perform a specified procedure by the conventional method before approaching the problem by the endoscopic route.

Most schemes for hysteroscopy (Table 3) ask for a theoretical course of 12–15 hours and 4–6 hours of hands-on practice. Here dry or organic models are preferred. The trainee has to witness 10–20 surgical procedures and is finally asked to perform 5–15 surgical procedures under one-to-one supervision (Table 4).

Where continuous formation and prolongation of accreditation are concerned there are two different trends [25]. The first is a procedure-specific training and accreditation leading to a permanent and procedure-specific accreditation (Table 5). The second is related to the full list of endoscopic procedures but leads to a temporary accreditation that has to be renewed after a number of years under specified conditions (Table 6). As one can imagine the first trend does not match the rapid evolution of endoscopy. The second system is based on a professional reality but its implementation requires rigorous checking and frequent updating.

These different kinds of classification for the procedures depend on the different societies who created them. When we use a multi-level classification we create a precise but doubtful grading for surgeons. This is because grading the different complex surgical procedures is difficult and not always feasible. On the other hand we can adhere to a system of proven skill levels, adopted by the majority of guidelines. Here we have a better quality system compliance (Table 7).

A distribution in levels should be specific enough to distinguish the skilled from the less skilled surgeons without creating artificial differences that can complicate a surgeon's professional life. We must remember that for the moment training and accreditation are voluntary choices,

Table 2
Common trends in diverse training guidelines

Trainee	Experienced laparotomic surgeons
Training phase 1	LABORATORY. Theory and hands-on practice
Training phase 2	PRECEPTORSHIP. Surgical observational period
Training phase 3	TUTORSHIP. Supervised own surgical performance

Table 3
Suggested characteristics and minimum standards for training courses (1)

Theoretical teaching for physical principles, patient selection, surgical technique, morbidity, and clinical outcomes	12 – 15 hours
Hands-on practice with dry, organic, or live models	4 – 6 hours

Table 4
Suggested characteristics and minimum standards for training courses (2)

PRECEPTORSHIP Observation of training level operations carried out by an experienced surgeon	10 – 20 operations
TUTORSHIP Training level performance supervised by an experienced surgeon	5 – 15 operations

Table 5
Types of training agreement and accreditation (1)

ARGREEMENT →	TRAINING →	PRIVILEGES
One or few procedures with/out its variants (E.G.: Hysterectomy, Miomectomy)	General information Specific laboratory	To perform some specific procedures
Particular instrument or device using (E.G.: Electrosurgery, Laser, Gasless Laparoscopy, etc.)	Specific preceptorship Specific tutorship	To use a specific instrument or surgical device

all over Europe, so interpretation should be clear and easy to understand and comply with. This has been the choice of the American Accreditation College (Table 8). Here only one level is listed for endoscopic procedures, as other levels are considered insufficient or too experimental for credentialing.

In Europe there is a need for such a system that is common to all member states. This will require, more than ever, hard work from the member states to set up a register of surgeons and to assure continuous checking by an authorized local body of the surgeons carrying out endoscopy (Figure 2).

PRINCIPLES OF HYSTEROSCOPIC TRAINING

To use the hysteroscopic technique we cannot refer to a classic surgical technique. So the surgeon has only to adapt to the anatomic conditions of the cervix and the uterine cavity and carry out procedures based on his knowledge of the pathology in this region including anatomo-pathological data. He also has to consider what classical techniques offer as results compared to the endoscopic treatment. The clinical training should be inherent to the development of the individual gynecologist. On the other

Figure 2
In Europe there is a need for a system that is common to all member states.

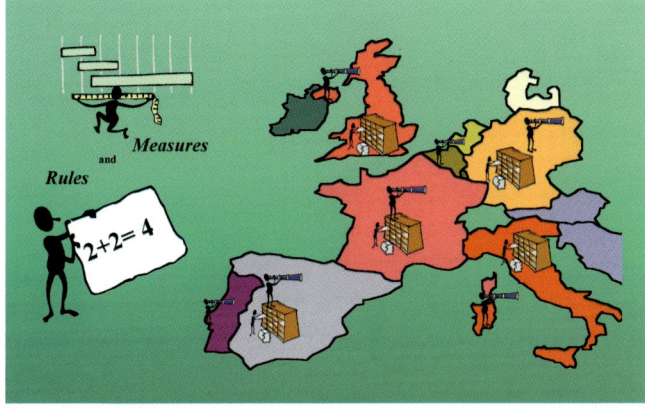

Table 6
Types of training agreement and accreditation (2)

ARGUMENT	TRAINING	PRIVILEGES
A group of same complexity procedures (E.G.: Procedures from a defined classification level)	General information Basic laboratory	To perform a group of procedures
A kind of endoscopy (E.G.: Laparoscopy, Hysteroscopy, etc.)	Random preceptorship Random tutorship	To perform a kind of endoscopy

Table 7
Azziz skill level outlines for laparoscopic training and certification [15]

Level 1	Basic Laparoscopy	Diagnosis Ablation/Removal of mild Endometriosis Salpingo/Ovarolysis of mild Adhesions Ectopic Pregnancy Treatments
Level 2	Advance Operative Laparoscopy	Resection of moderate/severe Endometriosis Resection of Ovarian/Paraovarian Cysts Salpingectomy/Ovariectomy Neosalpingostomy and Fimbrioplasty Moderate and severe Adhesiolysis Pedunculated Fibroids removal LUNA Appendectomy
Level 3	Innovative or Experimental Operative Laparoscopy	All other Procedures including Presacral Neurectomy Intramural Myomectomy Hysterectomy

hand the anatomo-pathological components require that knowledge of the macro-diagnostic examination of the uterine cavity must be updated. This last aspect can be resolved by studying endoscopic images of the region concerned alongside comments by an expert [26].

To acquire the basic technique to perform hysteroscopy leading to its correct use we have to pass though three different successive steps. These steps coincide with the three components of the hysteroscopic surgical act: the organization of the instruments, organization of body posture and movements, and last but not least coordination in space.

Organization of the instruments

Some authors mention that the quality of the instruments accounts for up to 25–30% of the quality of hysteroscopy. If we add to this number the 10–15% due to the nurse factor where instrument maintenance is concerned we can easily state that instruments and their maintenance have as big a part to play as surgeons in the quality of the hysteroscopic examination.

The training therefore has to consider all instrumental and mechanical details that can influence the dynamics of the procedure and its overall quality [27].

The following list of data can be proposed:

- The position of the patient on the couch and her physical position with respect to the operator and the instrumentation.
- The assistance that the personnel give to the surgeon.
- Knowledge of the components, function, assembly, principal usages, pitfalls, and risks of the various instruments that will be used during surgery.
- Knowledge of the various sources of energy and other aids that will be used during surgery.
- Thorough knowledge of the distension media, their pros and cons, which are used to distend a well-vascularized organ.

These data should make up the inbuilt 'database' of every gynecologist so that they can be automatically retrieved to steer the act of hysteroscopy so that the attention of the surgeon can be focused on the problem at hand.

To produce optimal function within the examination room, all staff who will be involved in the procedure require training on the theoretical and practical aspects of hysteroscopy.

SURGEON'S BODY POSITION

Surgery is not different from any other physical activity. The surgeon's body translates a specific idea. To achieve this preconceived idea the body needs a specific osteo-arthro-muscular tone. The level of this body posture is in direct relation to the complexity of the idea to be achieved. There is also a direct relationship between the decline of the quality of every intense human effort and the duration of the effort. The same can be said of the relation between the length of an effort and the amount of caloric use demanded by this effort. It is also common knowledge that training can enhance body resistance and the quality of the task performed. This because of the strengthening of specific muscles and articulations needed to accomplish a specific act and the relaxation of other muscles and articulation not necessary for this particular movement. It is because of this automatization of particular movements,

Table 8
Accreditation unique level certified by the American Accreditation Council for Gynecological Endoscopy

PROCEDURES		Excluding because too easy
TUBAL	All Procedures	Sterilisation
ADNEXAL	All Procedures	Ovarian drilling
UTERUS	Cornual Resection, Myomectomy	Myoma < 3 cm
HYSTERECTOMY	LAVH, TLH, SLH	Adnexal isolation only
ADHESIOLYSIS	All Procedures	Minimal or mild adh.
ENDOMETRIOSIS	All Procedures	AFS stage 1 – 2 Endometrioma < 3 cm
COLPOSUSPENSION	Burch, Pelvic Reconstruction	-
MISCELLANEOUS	Appendectomy, Lymphnode sampling or dissection	-

the hypertrophy of some muscles, and an intelligent development of their own resources, that athletes are able to enhance their performance. In the discipline of 'surgical athletics' the same principles are valid. Therefore we have to establish the essential components of the physical requirements for the best results in hysteroscopy, namely:

- The body posture and dynamics needed for an ideal operation
- Specific exercises to increase the body posture and dynamics.
- Methods to evaluate the levels reached.

The hysteroscopic approach demands significant adaptations of our normal body posture, more especially at the level of the agonist-antagonist forces, the fixed body parts, and the balance of the system (Figure 3). The most significant points can be listed as follows:

- The absence of supports within the limits of the operating field.
- Distended arms increase the gravity force effect on the agonist muscles in an already high-level balance.
- Reduced action of the antagonist muscle with less balance for the fine movements of the hands.
- There is a more pronounced necessity to bring the upper body in equilibrium towards the back because the gravity centre of the system moves anteriorly.

These elements require specific preparations to become a good hysteroscopist.

- The operator has to find an optimum individual position, taking into account the relative heights and distances between the operator and the perineum of the patient. This position has to reduce the necessary tonus of the muscular mass of the scapulo-humeral system as much as possible.
- The position of the monitor and other essential apparatus should be organized in such a way that these can be used to eliminate prolonged rigidity of the upper limb articulation and excessive extension of the neck.
- A personalized training scheme that enhances the strength of the muscles of the back and the deltoids (Figure 4).

COORDINATION IN SPACE

Every single interaction between our selves and the surrounding world necessitates a constant noting and integration of our position within this environment. This is called our coordination in space.

Coordination in spaces comes to us without effort as our cerebellum has acquired this faculty from our early childhood. This means that we can integrate all proprioceptive information from the osteo-articular-muscular system and capture this information in an integrated image that lets us know moment by moment our own position in space (Figure 5).

A voluntary movement or intervention on the other hand can only be successful when we have a sensory perception of the presence and the relative location in space of the object that we want to work on. This information is given to us by impulses that we receive through the cerebral cortex by all our senses, particularly visual impulses. This information is processed by our brain and will eventually allow us to intervene. This is the end result of a dialogue between the voluntary and the involuntary centers within the brain.

Figure 3
The hysteroscopic approach demands significant adaptations of our normal body posture, especially at the levels of the agonist-antagonist forces, the fixed body parts, and the balance of the system.

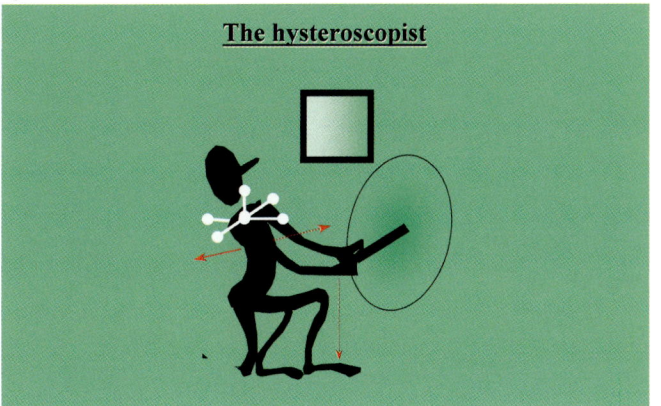

Figure 4
A personalized training scheme that enhances the strength of the muscles of the back and the deltoids.

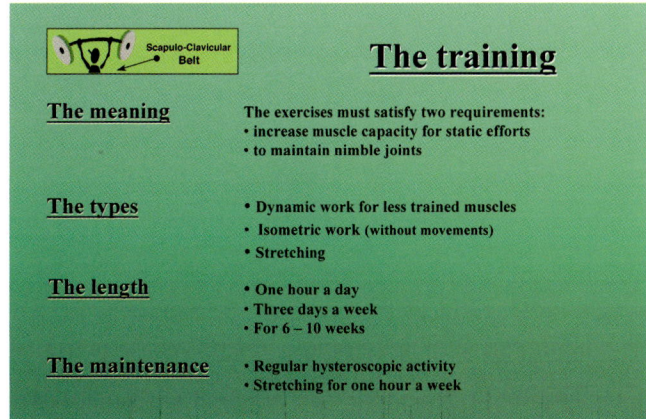

This intervention will be more efficient, fluid, coherent, and economic if the interaction between the voluntary and involuntary centers is at its highest level. This supposes that the number of confirmations, needed to be able to continue to act, between the different centers is at the lowest level.

The endoscopic approach in general requires a very high level of coordination. Hysteroscopy in particular, as a technique, enhances our visual capacities and reminds us constantly of the contradictions between the interpretation of our position in space by our brain and indirect perception, i.e. 'non-real', of the space we work in and how it is revealed to us by the monitor.

This can lead to serious mental fatigue and reduces the speed of the surgical procedure. This cannot be related to the intensity of our brain function (consciousness) but rather to our cerebellar function (automatic). Therefore we must work on this last function in order to improve our performance.

The teaching about this coordination in space will require training to reproduce repetitive movements within the boundaries of a virtual organ along the same principles that we used as newborn children to acquire our coordination in space.

The creation of short circuits in the execution of movements therefore requires specific very simple exercises than can be repeated very frequently, so that eventually interference by the brain, which slows down the movements and consumes a great deal of energy, can be minimized (Figure 6).

TRAINING IN OUTPATIENT AND OFFICE HYSTEROSCOPY

The specific requirements for outpatient techniques do not differ in essence from those used in in-patient hysteroscopy. The teaching is the same except for some specific notions on how to approach the conscious patient (Figure 7) [28].

The surgeon should be even more attentive, for the following reasons [29]:

- The optics used to perform hysteroscopy in outpatient conditions tend to be reduced in diameter and therefore more delicate and sometimes more complex. The surgeon should therefore be very attentive to the more fragile instruments and the costs of the system.
- The reduced weight of the system does not demand too much in terms of the surgeon's overall balance. It requires more attention to the small movements, as the system allows for an atraumatic approach. This requires more energy from the lateral and anterior muscles of the deltoid and pectoral region.
- As we proceed along natural cavities (vagina and cervical canal) there has to be a perfect alignment so as

Figure 5
Reality management.

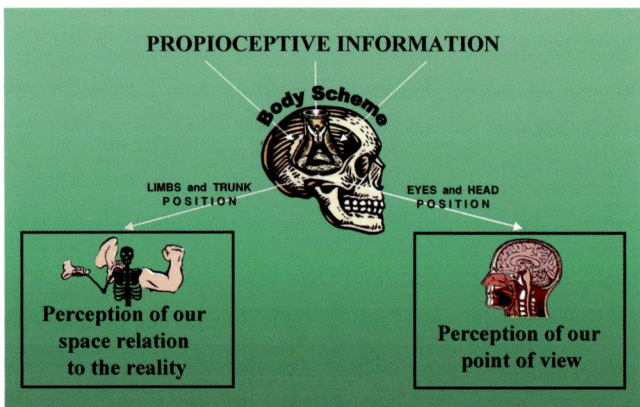

Figure 6
Coordination in space will require training to reproduce repetitive movements.

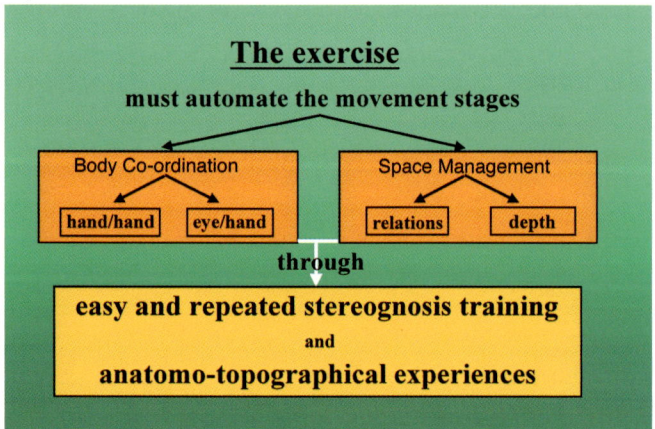

Figure 7
Reducing the invasive aspects of procedures.

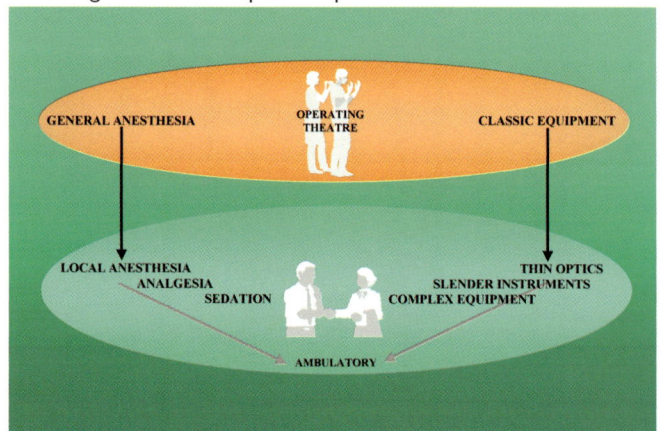

not to traumatize the walls of the different sections. Hitting the structures causes pain to the patient. Therefore this requires even greater coordination in space; the importance of the cerebellar automatisms becomes even greater during all the different steps of the examination.

Learning the technique is not the greatest obstacle for the hysteroscopist who would like to use it in the outpatient setting. More important than the ability to perform the task is the ability to communicate with the patient, so that the patient can follow the diagnostic process and be informed about the different points [30]. Here we have to put into practice the true significance of 'informed consent', as it is essential to have the patient's full cooperation before, during, and after the procedure.

Here the surgeon has to carry out the procedure with a deontological attitude, not as a qualifying optional, but as an integrated part of the examination and the therapy.

The above points emphasize the complexity of the ambulatory hysteroscopic approach.
This complexity confirms how important it is for the surgeon to have an extensive gynecological and endoscopic knowledge and a broad range of experience in the ambulatory approach.

REFERENCES

1. Liaison Committee for Obstetrics and Gynecology. The definition of the obstetrician/gynaecologist. Bulletin of American Board of Obstetrics and Gynecology. March 1979.
2. Rainey JB, Ruckley CV. Work of a day-bed unit 1972-8. *BMJ* 1979; **2**:714–717.
3. Bulletin for 1983 for the Division of Gynecology, Oncology, Maternal Fetal Medicine, Reproductive Endocrinology: American Board of Obstetrics and Gynecology, 1983: 16.
4. Assemblèe Général de la Section UEMS de Gynècologie-Obstetrique, 1992.
5. Templeton A. Subspecialty training and academic careers. *Bailliere's Clin Obstet Gynecol* 1999; **13**: 423–434.
6. Pearse WH, Gant NF, Hagner AP. Workforce projections for sub specialists in obstetrics and gynecology. *Obstet Gynecol* 2000; **95**: 312–314.
7. Hamou J, ed. Hysteroscopy and Microhysteroscopy. Palermo: CoFeSe, 1984.
8. Dexeus S, Labastida R, Marques L. Hysteroscopy in daily gynaecologic practice. *Acta Eur Fertil* 1986; **17**: 423–425.
9. Loffer FD, Bradley LD, Brill AI, Brooks PG, Cooper JM. Hysteroscopic fluid monitoring guidelines. The ad hoc committee on Hysteroscopic training guidelines of the American Association of Gynecologic Laparoscopists. *J Am Assoc Gynecol Laparosc* 2000; **7**: 167–168.
10. Loffer FD, Bradley LD, Brill AI, Brooks PG, Cooper JM. Hysteroscopic training guidelines. The ad hoc committee on Hysteroscopic training guidelines of the American Association of Gynecologic Laparoscopists. *J Am Assoc Gynecol Laparosc* 2000; **7**: 165.
11. Gubbini GP, Linsalata I, Stagnozzi R et al. Outpatient diagnostic hysteroscopy: 14,000 cases. *Minerva Ginecol* 1996; **48**: 383–390.
12. Habiba MA. Diagnostic accuracy of outpatient hysteroscopy [comment] *Am J Obstet Gynecol* 1997; **176**: 1399–1400.
13. Zupi E, Luciano AA, Valli E et al. The use of topical anesthesia in diagnostic hysteroscopy and endometrial biopsy. *Fertil Steril* 1995; **63**: 414–416.
14. Boey WK. Challenges in ambulatory surgery: discharge criteria. *Ann Acad Med Singapore* 1995; **24**: 906–909.
15. Azziz R. Training, certification and credentialing in gynaecologic operative endoscopy. *Clin Obstet Gynecol* 1995; **38**: 313–318.
16. Baker R. Outpatient hysteroscopy versus day case hysteroscopy. What exactly is patient satisfaction? *BMJ* 2001; **322**: 48.
17. Cooper MJW, Fraser I. Training and accreditation in endoscopic surgery. *Curr Opin Obstet Gynecol* 1996; **8**: 278–280.
18. Fraser IS, Petrucco OM. Guidelines for training in advanced operative laparoscopy *Gynecol Endosc* 1994; **3**: 133–134.
19. Keye WR Jr. Hitting a moving target: credentialing the endoscopic surgeon. *Fertil Steril* 1994; **62**: 1115–1117.
20. Peel KR. The implications of the changing nature of gynaecological surgical practice on training. *Br J Obstet Gynaecol* 1995; **102**: 177–178.
21. American Fertility Society: Guidelines for attaining privileges in gynecologic operative endoscopy. *Fertil Steril* 1994; **62**: 1118–1119.
22. Tulandi T. Canadian guidelines for training in operative Endoscopy. *Gynaecol Endosc* 1995; **4**: 69–72.
23. Chapron C, Devroey P, Dubuisson JB, Pouly JL, Vercellini P. ESHRE guidelines for training, accreditation and monitoring in gynaecological endoscopy. European Society for Human Reproduction and Embryology. Committee of Special Interest Group on Reproductive Surgery. *Hum Reprod* 1997; **12**: 867–868.
24. Hasson HM, Getzels J. A system of credentialing physicians in advanced gynaecologic endoscopy. *J Am Assoc Gynecol Laparosc* 2001; **8**: 214–217.
25. Sciarra JJ, Boike GM. Teaching gynecologic endoscopy: an international challenge. In: Gynecologic Endoscopy Surgery. CIC Edizioni Internazionali, 1994: 95–100
26. Anonymous. Credentialing guidelines for operative hysteroscopy. ACOG Committee Opinion: Committee on Gynecologic Practice *Int J Gynaecol Obstet* 1992; **39**: 246.
27. Chin KA, Penketh RJ. Training in endoscopic surgery in gynaecology. *Hosp Med* 1998; **59**: 242–244.
28. Bert JM. Pros and cons of practice-owned and office-based ambulatory surgery centers. *Am J Knee Surgery* 2000; **13**: 245–248.
29. Lindheim SR, Kavic S, Shulman SV, Sauer MV. Operative hysteroscopy in the office setting *J Am Assoc Gynecol Laparosc* 2000; **7**: 65–69.
30. Paschopoulos M, Paraskevaidis E, Stefanidis K, Kofinas G, Lolis D. Vaginoscopic approach to outpatient hysteroscopy. *J Am Assoc Gynecol Laparosc* 1997; **4**: 465–467.

Training and accreditation: Europe
European point of view

B.J. van Herendael

BACKGROUND

The basic problem is that there are no European guidelines for training in endoscopy. The European Union (EU) has not published directives as to the specific standards that the training of physicians in internal medicine, surgery, and gynecology, should attain. Various European societies therefore have tried or are trying to set up their own standards for training but these are rather a help to get to a Good Clinical Practice (GCP) for the individual member of the specific society. These standards have no legal significance and therefore do not have be followed. The different societies – European Society of Gynaecological Endoscopy (ESGE), European Society of Human Reproduction and Embryology (ESHRE), and the local national societies – therefore do not have the ability to intervene when there is an obvious problem, even medicolegal, due to insufficient training of the physician. As there are no official rulings the individual medical schools do not have the obligation to train physicians in endoscopy, as it is not an official part of the curriculum of the speciality concerned. In Europe, at the moment, there is no official system of accreditation for the different specialities in medicine let alone for endoscopy. The degrees are recognized throughout the EU but a long and trying procedure is necessary to be able to practice in one of the individual member countries and an official residence in the specific country is necessary to obtain privileges to practice in the specific country of choice. The different European Boards of specialities are trying to come to consensuses but do not foresee a rapid complete integration. The conclusion of this introduction is that because of the lack of official ruling there is a great number of not-so official rulings, even within different specialities, creating confusion in different specialities.

However, because of increasing legal pressures the different societies have to set some rules for their members, so as to help an individual member when they are faced with a claim concerning an alleged medical fault or malpractice. In Flanders, the Vlaamse Vereniging voor Gynaecologie en Obstetrie (VVOG) started, through its board for professional quality and defence (Werkgroep Beroeps Belangen VWBB), a register of all the claims against gynecologists in Belgium in order to have an idea of what problems are most prone to engender legal actions on the one hand and to try to get to a better quality of practice and defence on the other hand. The tendency in the EU is to move to a nonfault policy. The example has been set by the Scandinavian countries and has been followed by most other individual countries because of the fact that an increasing number of physicians are working without any form of medical insurance. In view of the approaching enlargement of the EU with former eastern block countries the fear is that here no member state, even the core member states, will have the economical resources to continue paying for the national health schemes and will not have enough physicians remaining in the national health services if no care is taken regarding the level of measures to prevent irrational claims from patients.

In endoscopy we are confronted with very specific challenges. From the experience of different training centers we know that about 9% of all physicians embarking in endoscopy with the aim of performing surgery will never be able to do so. The main reason is what I have called the 'SEBCOH principle' (Miami 2000). What we see on the Screen with our Eye has to be transported to our Brain to be able to interpret the findings and to Coordinate the Handheld instruments to operate. The SEBCOH principle is even more important in hysteroscopy, as the orientation is more difficult than in other fields of endoscopy. There are very few markers in the uterus – the isthmus and both tubal ostia. Therefore when one or the other is missing it becomes very difficult to determine the orientation. Thus, very good and experienced laparoscopic surgeons do not want to operate hysteroscopically. In addition, the dilatation capacity of the uterus is reduced to some 4 cm maximum, decreasing the space even more. A reduced space does not allow for large movements and reduces the speed of even a simple operation. In hysteroscopy without anesthesia or with local anesthesia the maximal dilatation, the distance between the two layers of endometrium at full distension, is even more reduced, as is the ease of carrying out the different movements. This is because the patient will experience a classical maximal dilatation as very painful and will ask to discontinue the procedure.

TRAINING STANDARDS

To overcome these different problems and to provide the individual physician with the necessary experience to be able to practice hysteroscopy with the necessary confidence, the former European Society for Hysteroscopy (ESH) – now incorporated in the ESGE – published training requirements as early as 1992. In my opinion these are currently still the best training requirements, although there is not much difference between what the ESGE and the ESHRE put forward. These requirements are rather tough but I do believe that a certain degree of toughness is required to develop good endoscopic, hysteroscopic surgeons because of the above-mentioned reasons.

A 250 diagnostic hysteroscopies should be performed; 20 are to be performed under one-to-one supervision. This seems a tremendously high number but if hysteroscopies carried out immediately before D&Cs are included this is a reasonable number.
B 25 minor interventions should be performed; 10 are to be performed under one-to-one supervision.
C 25 intermediate interventions should be performed; 10 are to be performed under one-to-one supervision.
D 25 major interventions should be performed; 10 are to be performed under one-to-one supervision.

DIAGNOSTIC HYSTEROSCOPY

A total of 250 diagnostic hysteroscopies was accepted as reasonable; 20 had to be performed under preceptorship or one-to-one supervision.

This seems like a very significant number, but hysteroscopies carried out immediately before curetage in anesthetised patients were accepted. A very high number is required if a physician wants to perform hysteroscopies under local or no anesthesia, so as to get experience with the instruments and visualization of the cavity. These rules were set out in the days of CO_2 hysteroscopy. This type of distension medium requires a very high level of skill and is time-consuming. The change to liquid distension media made diagnostic hysteroscopy easier, although the imaging suffered, and therefore the initial number can safely be reduced to 100 with 10 under direct supervision.

One hundred hysteroscopies with liquid distension medium are required, of which 10 must be performed under one-to-one supervision. Hysteroscopies carried out under general anesthesia before curettage are accepted.

OPERATIVE HYSTEROSCOPY

The main difference between operative and diagnostic procedures is the manipulation of the different instruments in a reduced space and the use of different types of energy in this space. The use of normal saline does not protect the patient from fluid overload, therefore a training course should always have a part dedicated to the possible problems and complications and to the treatment of the latter. The danger of the fluid overload is the free water in the circulation and this can also occur when ionic solutions are used if the amount of intravasation into the circulation is too high.

One of the main factors responsible for fluid overload is the length of the intervention. It can be stated that difficult procedures and procedures that require the elimination of large amounts of tissue from the uterine cavity require more time and hence have the potential to become dangerous. The different operative procedures have been classified into different categories based on the difficulty and thus the length of the procedure (Tables 1–3). As the first two classes of procedures can be carried out under local or no anesthesia there is a case for also adhering to these rulings for operative procedures carried out in an office setting.

Each of the categories requires a qualification in diagnostic hysteroscopy and 25 procedures should be performed with 10 under one-to-one supervision in each of the categories shown in Tables 1–3.

Table 1
Interventions classed as minor

- Eye-directed biopsies
- Small polyps
- IUCD removal in the nonpregnant uterus

Table 2
Interventions classed as intermediate

- Hysteroscopic tubal catheterization
- Balloon salpingoplasty
- Hysteroscopic sterilization
- Local treatments
- Adhesiolysis grades I and II (according to ESH classification)

Table 3
Major interventions

- Adhesiolysis grades III and IV (acccording to ESH classification)
- Myomectomy
- Large polyps
- Resection of uterine septum
- Endometrial resection and ablation
- IUCD removal in the pregnant uterus

28 Training and accreditation: Australia

Peter J. Maher

OVERVIEW

'Recently, experiments with hysteroscopy, such as those that were repeatedly undertaken in the past, but which never reached their goal, have been taken up again, this time with greater success. The results now are so positive that hysteroscopy must be recognized as a valuable method for diagnosis within the uterine cavity as well as for influencing tubal function' [1]. Although the concept of hysteroscopy had been accepted for more than 60 years before the above revelation, many problems had been encountered. Firstly, there was the lack of sophistication of the optics used. The instrument had a large diameter, which in turn made insertion near impossible without dilatation of the cervix. The medium used to visualize the cavity also contributed to less than perfect vision. With water, the possibility of absorption brought with it the potentially severe complication of hemolysis if absorption occurred. The concept of constant irrigation lessened this to a degree. Rubin in 1925 [2] had suggested CO_2 gas for performing the test that now bears his name. This medium was proposed for hysteroscopy in 1971 [3]. It was at this time, as a gynecological registrar (3rd year post graduation) in the gynecological department of St Vincent's Hospital in Melbourne, that I was first introduced to hysteroscopic examination of the uterine cavity. The instrument had an 8-mm diameter outer sheath and general anesthesia was required to allow passage of this instrument through the cervix. The optics, although the best available at the time, were totally inadequate. The resultant examination was therefore far from satisfactory. The technological advances that occurred during the 1980s in optical systems resulted in smaller telescopes with much better resolution. This improvement was also enhanced by the improvement in light sources. Despite these technical advances, hysteroscopy in this country was confined to only a small number of enthusiasts.

Early reports of endometrial ablation [4] failed to make an impact on the therapeutic use of hysteroscopy in this country until the author and his colleague reported their first experience in 1989 [5]. Within 2 years of this publication, nearly 5000 cases of endometrial resection had been performed in the private sector of medical care in Australia. Today this figure stands at approximately 1500. This rapid decline over the last decade is, in fact, a reflection of the unacceptable failure rate of endometrial ablation that has occurred. The author believes that the failure resulted, not from the inadequacy of the procedure itself but from the lack of expertise in hysteroscopy – a necessary prerequisite to performing complex intrauterine surgery. In 1996, Molloy et al [6] reported on national trends in endoscopic surgery in Australia. They did this using the Medicare database, which allowed access to the number of procedures in the private practice sector using specific 'item numbers' for each procedure. At that time, just under half of the population had private health insurance and therefore an extrapolation of the data could be used to cover the whole population. Between 1991 and 1992, there were >80,000 episodes of dilatation and curettage, which decreased by 45% by 1995. Over the same 4 years, there was a 19% increase in office hysteroscopies performed and an overall increase by 4% of all hysteroscopies. This rather anomalous outcome had resulted from the Medicare number being removed for hysteroscopy and curettage when performed together. Interestingly, from the same database over the same 4 years, there was a 248% increase in operative hysteroscopy, not including endometrial ablation, from 1164 to 2888 episodes. This rapid rise in the uptake of both diagnostic hysteroscopy and minor operative hysteroscopy paralleled the uptake of endometrial ablation. It is therefore interesting to note that it was only in the early part of the 1990s that the first hysteroscopic courses were held on a regular basis.

The Royal Australian and New Zealand College of Obstetricians and Gynaecologists, the body responsible for training the consultants of the future, has no specific guidelines with respect to technique or number of cases performed when considering hysteroscopy. It is necessary for the trainee to be able to perform hysteroscopy and operative procedures [7]. The number is the responsibility of the training institution! The technique will therefore obviously depend on the trainee's mentor – a person who may or may not support both hysteroscopy and operative hysteroscopy over more traditional procedures, e.g. hysterosalpingogram, dilatation and curettage, and even hysterectomy. As previously mentioned, endometrial resection, not hysteroscopy, came under scrutiny from the learned College. Guidelines were drawn up in consultation with the Australian Gynaecological Endoscopy Society (AGES) which has been in existence for more than 10 years. These guidelines have been reviewed recently for both bodies by the author.

'Hysteroscopic endometrial ablation has been used as an alternative to hysterectomy for treatment of menorrhagia since 1989 in Australia. The operation requires special skills which are known to be associated with a steep learning curve. The uptake over the last decade has not been as prolific as expected. The surgical manufacturing industry has turned its attention to the development of "global" systems which have a short learning curve necessary to acquire the skill in their use. All gynaecologists should fulfill the guidelines before embarking on this type of surgery. In general, it is expected that the gynaecologists would be formally accredited to undertake this procedure by an appropriate hospital credentialling committee' [8].

The newly recommended training requirements are set out below:

1. Good diagnostic hysteroscopy skills (preferably more than 100 procedures). This is often obtained at registrar (pre-qualification) level. (In this author's opinion, the problem with this approach is that there has been no didactic teaching specific to hysteroscopy undertaken before this level of expertise is reached.)
2. Training in endometrial ablation requires hands-on experience under supervision, with a normal sized anteverted uterus in the first instance. (It is hard today to justify in vivo training before having spent adequate time on a hystero-trainer.)
3. Training will be effected by observing a number of cases, performing further cases under supervision and then performing cases without supervision. For recently graduated Fellows, this level should be achieved at registrar level. Alternatively, attendance at training courses is recommended. (The courses that our unit conducted in the early and mid 1990s were stopped due to the lack of attendances. To this day, I am concerned as to who is conducting training sessions in this country.)
4. Initial learning curve probably depends both on technique used and natural ability and caution of the surgeon. At least five cases should be observed before starting. The following should be regarded as the absolute minimum experience required under the supervised training phase:
   (i) Resection – 10 cases
   (ii) Rollerball – 5 cases.
   The actual learning curve is much longer than this and some surgeons never develop a coordination to perform difficult cases. (This is an important observation. Such doctors would be readily identified during didactic teaching sessions that also include laboratory operating sessions. Our first priority must be our patients!!)
5. Training of nursing and other members of the operating theatre team is also essential.
6. Training supervisors should have completed at least 50 cases which include technically difficult cases and uterine abnormalities. (It is difficult to see how this could be possible when one considers that approximately 3000 cases are spread over nearly 600 practising gynecologists in this country on an annual basis.)
7. Gynaecologists training in endometrial ablation should have a nominated supervisor who is well recognized as having adequate experience and skill in this field.
8. The gynaecologist should be aware of all the potential complications of the procedure, in particular the risk of fluid overload. Nursing staff should be instructed to monitor excess fluid loss and report it to both the surgeon and the anaesthetist. Any fluid imbalance of >1,000 ml should be considered significant. (Rather than including this information in training guidelines, such data should be gleaned from didactic teaching sessions in the classroom.)
9. Difficult cases should only be attempted by the experienced surgeon. These include the markedly retroverted uterus, the uterine cavity >10 cm, the presence of intrauterine or sub-mucous fibroids, the nulliparous uterus and the congenitally abnormal uterus.
10. Sub-mucous or intra-cavity fibroid removal should not be attempted during the course of endometrial ablation until the operator is totally comfortable with the primary procedure. (Such a situation should not arise if the patient has been appropriately investigated with high resolution ultrasound. This is a simple preoperative investigation that would be taught during training sessions.)

These training guidelines are in stark contrast to those recommended by the Ad Hoc Committee on Hysteroscopic Training Guidelines of the American Association of Gynecologic Laparoscopists [9]. This Committee is committed to four separate aspects of hysteroscopic training. These include didactic lectures, hands-on laboratory training, case observation, and preceptorship. It recommends that the didactic portion should include diagnostic and operative hysteroscopy and be a minimum of 6 hours.

It was with this in mind and the knowledge that no formal training was presented by the Royal Australian College of Obstetricians and Gynaecologists that, in a joint venture with Olympus Australia, the Endosurgery Unit at Mercy Hospital for Women commenced formal courses in diagnostic and operative hysteroscopy. The course had three components:
- a series of didactic lectures,
- pelvic trainers for both diagnostic and operative procedures and
- live surgery demonstrating diagnostic hysteroscopy, endometrial resection, and hysteroscopic resection of fibroids..

The demonstration of resection of a uterine septum or lysis of adhesions was dependent on the availability of an appropriate case at the time of each course.

The lectures covered the following topics including:
- Instrumentation
- Distension media
- Indications for hysteroscopy
- Office hysteroscopy, operative hysteroscopy, myoma resection, ablation, and other techniques
- Complications.

Studies have clearly shown the benefit of hysteroscopy over dilatation and curettage, particularly in the investigation of abnormal bleeding [10,11]. There are accepted indications for hysteroscopy (Table 1).

Table 1
Indications for hysteroscopy

Diagnostic hysteroscopy
- Abnormal uterine bleeding
- Suspected intrauterine pathology on vaginal ultrasound
- Investigation of infertile patient
- Tracking of endometrial hyperplasia
- Contact hysteroscopy – abnormal cytology

Operative hysteroscopy
- Lost intrauterine device
- Ablation/resection of the endomyometrium
- Lysis of intrauterine adhesions
- Resection of intrauterine fibroid/septum
- Hysteroscopic tubal occlusion

Further discussion about most of the above indications is outside the brief of this chapter. The author will confine his comments to some important principles taught in the didactic lectures of his course which include complications and resection techniques for both endometrium and fibroid removal.

COMPLICATIONS

Complications are more commonly associated with operative rather than diagnostic hysteroscopy. Complication rates in general exceed those reported by 'experts' in large series [12]. Complications that can occur include perforation of the uterus with resultant damage to surrounding structures. If perforation occurs during diagnostic hysteroscopy this does not normally cause significant problems. On the other hand, pelvic structures can be damaged, particularly when electrosurgical or laser energy is activated at the moment of perforation. The unfavorable outcomes result from hemorrhage, water intoxication, damage to other pelvic structures, infection, hematometra, and pregnancy.

In a series of 850 hysteroscopic operative procedures Hill et al [13] reported the following complications: perforation 0.8%, hemorrhage 0.8%, infection 0.5%, hematometra 1.8%, and pregnancy 0.02%. The authors were surprised by the small number of perforations in their series and the lack of association with the learning curve of hysteroscopic surgery. They recommended preliminary diagnostic hysteroscopy under general anesthesia in any case where cervical narrowing is contemplated. If this was still not possible, then Cervagem® pessaries should be inserted 3–4 hours before the surgery [14]. Additionally, we consider it safer to use graduated dilators and allow time between each increase in dilator size. Once the cervix is dilated to Hegar 11, the resectoscope can safely be placed in the cervical canal and then advanced under direct vision into the uterine cavity. We recommend overdilation of the cervix to avoid unnecessary force being used when inserting the resectoscope.

COMPLICATIONS ASSOCIATED WITH DISTENSION MEDIA

Fluid

Excessive absorption of fluid distension media is one of the most frequent complications of operative hysteroscopy. Although most patients recover without long-term sequelae, there are cases of permanent morbidity and death recorded from this complication [15]. Uterine distension is necessary for two reasons. It must create an intra-cavity space to allow enough room for operative maneuvers. The second important function is to inhibit bleeding into the operative field and thus allow continuation of surgical procedures. Complications arise from intravasation of the medium into the patient's bloodstream, with resultant hypo-osmolality, hyponatremia, and hemolysis, depending on the medium used. This latter complication was seen during urological transurethral resection of the prostate when water was used. It is no longer used in hysteroscopic urological resectoscopic surgery. Now the most commonly used fluid solutions are Ringer's solution, normal saline or 1.5% glycine. Solutions used for intrauterine electrosurgical procedures must not be conductive and therefore electrolyte-containing solutions cannot be used. Hyskon (32% dextran 70) was used initially as it was non-miscible with blood. This is an unsuitable solution for continuous flow resectoscopes and is also known to caramelize rapidly with the passage of electric current. The hypo-osmolality and hyponatremia mentioned above present the surgical team with a life-threatening problem known as water intoxication or TURP (transurethral resection of prostate) syndrome. It is characterized by disorientation, nausea, vomiting, and fitting, with the possibility of permanent brain damage and death. Intrauterine pressure is the single most important variable that the surgeon can control [16]. A value greater than the mean arterial pressure significantly increases the risk of intravasation [17]. Although fluid has been known to intravasate through the intact endometrium, this is uncommon. High risk situations arise during endometrial, myoma, and septum resection when large vascular spaces are opened. Agents such as oxytocin have been suggested to be of value in preventing intravasation [18].

If hyponatremia associated with water intoxication does occur, it is reported that premenopausal patients are 25 times more likely to die or have permanent brain damage than men or postmenopausal women [19]. Careful attention to fluid balance should avoid such a catastrophe. A negative fluid balance of >1500 ml should alert the surgeon to the possibility of this complication and the operative procedure should be completed as soon as possible. A fluid loss of >2 litres demands immediate cessation of the surgical procedure. Serum sodium estimation should be performed in all patients when 1500 ml or more of glycine are believed to have been absorbed.

Gas

Carbon dioxide is the safe distension gas for hysteroscopic diagnosis. It is unsuitable for all but simple intrauterine surgery, e.g. the removal of a simple polyp. To minimize the risk of absorption, we limit the intrauterine pressure to 100 mmHg and the flow rate of insufflation to <100 ml/minute. If large volumes of CO_2 are intravasated, either due to excessive pressure or through open vascular sinuses, then embolization and death may occur. Cardiac irregularities may occur following intravasation, due to an induced metabolic acidosis [20]. Small volume embolization with CO_2 is not harmful. On the other hand, air embolism in small volumes can be dangerous. For this reason, flushing of the tubing with CO_2 is mandatory before the hysteroscope is inserted into the cervical canal. This avoids direct flushing of the volume of air that occupies the dead space in the tubing being forced under pressure into the uterine cavity. If embolization does occur, the procedure must be stopped immediately and measures instituted to ensure restoration of cardiopulmonary equilibrium. Where there is a suspicion of intravasation of large volumes of CO_2, gas may accumulate in the right side of the heart. This is a potentially fatal occurrence and immediate action must be undertaken to avert cardiopulmonary collapse. Hemodynamic stability may be increased by turning the patient onto her left side.

HYSTEROSCOPIC SURGERY

Attendees at our courses are introduced to the principles of operative hysteroscopy with particular attention to endometrial ablation and intra-cavity myoma resection. A sound knowledge of instrumentation is essential before either in vitro or live surgery is attempted. All participants take a hands-on role in a laboratory setting using a purpose-built trainer to get the feel of resection and to learn the hand-eye coordination needed to perform intrauterine resection successfully. Hysteroscopic surgery has been very slowly adopted in this country and, as previously mentioned, it still is performed in relatively small numbers. The first report of a series of endometrial ablations in this country by Maher and Hill [21] in 1990 was one of the factors that influenced the rapid rise in interest in learning this new technique. This interest continued until the introduction of the newer 'global' ablation systems and now the older techniques appear to be on the decline again. Even the authors of this publication were, themselves, some 14 years late in adopting the procedures that Neuwirth and Assin first published in 1976 [22].

The technique used to perform resection of the endometrium is well described elsewhere [23]. Certain style changes adopted by experienced surgeons performing endometrial resection are incorporated into the teaching. The author prefers to use the rollerball on the fundus and the cornua and then resect the anterior and posterior walls of the uterus. Some experts prefer to perform the whole operation with the rollerball [24]. Others perform total resection. We emphasize the importance of endometrial suppression with an appropriate agent if rollerball only is used. Endometrial thinning is also an advantage for the surgeon during the learning curve of resection. It is easy to 'lose one's way' in the uterine cavity if vision is obscured by multiple chips of resected endomyometrium.

Resection does have one important advantage over the ablation technique. There are many pieces of endomyometrium available for sending to the pathologist for histological assessment should a neoplasm be missed during the preoperative work-up.

In Australia during the 1990s, laser energy was limited in its use in endometrial destruction to very few centers. The high cost of both Nd:YAG and argon laser energy sources limited their use to general hospitals with gynecological departments. The author attended many laser courses during the late 1980s and early 1990s but never used these devices in a clinical setting for endometrial ablation. Electrosurgery proved to be an excellent alternative and was the modality chosen by most of the gynecologists in this country.

MYOMA RESECTION

Many of the techniques required for resection of intracavity myomas are the same as those for resection of the endometrium. As mentioned, there is an increased risk of fluid absorption during resection of myomas. The risk of fluid absorption directly relates to the size of the fibroid, its vascularity, and the length of the surgery, which may reflect the degree of difficulty, the skill of the surgeon, or both [25]. Cooperation between the surgeon, the anesthetist, and the operating theatre staff is essential to ensure correct assessment of fluid balance and avoid fluid overload. We recommend, in line with others, that a fibroid diameter of 5 cm is the maximum size suitable for hysteroscopic resection. We also advise a maximum operating time of 45 minutes, which may mean that the patient requires a two-stage procedure.

Grade II fibroid patients (Table 2) are at highest risk of excessive intravasation of fluid [26].

We also teach that laparoscopy has a real place during the resection of the fibroids. If, during the course of the resection, the fibroid penetrates further into the uterine wall than was assessed preoperatively, a laparoscopic view of the serosal surface may be necessary to alert the operator to impending perforation. There are no real rights or wrongs when performing myoma resection. Very great care must be taken if the surgeon operates away from himself when using a passive action resectoscope, because of the increased risk of fundal perforation. Such a technique is permissible but should be reserved for the highly skilled hysteroscopic surgeon.

Bleeding can be a problem after fibroid resection, particularly where it is not possible to resect all the tumor. Several vasoconstrictor agents injected either directly into the fibroid or into the uterine wall have met with variable success. Laparoscopic injection of a vasoconstrictor agent into the uterine wall may decrease the amount of blood loss. In the event of excessive bleeding at the completion of myoma resection, we recommend inserting a Foley catheter with a 30-ml balloon into the uterine cavity and inflating the balloon to its capacity. The patient can return to the ward and have the catheter removed any time from 6 to 24 hours later without the need for general anesthesia. This technique has been successfully used in our unit on several occasions over the last 10 years.

SUMMARY AND CONCLUSIONS

The governing body of specialist gynecologists in this country has no formal training and accreditation process in place. Residents in training learn surgical techniques from their senior colleagues using the same 'old' principles that have been in place since surgical training began, i.e. watch and do a little under supervision and when the confidence level is high, fly solo! The problem with this technique is that it is unsatisfactory for new surgical procedures, in that both the trainer and trainee learn together. Unless there is a structured learning process involving theory, laboratory 'hands-on', and then supervised live surgery, bad surgical practice will slowly be accepted as 'best practice'. The sad thing is that hysteroscopic surgery is relatively simple, effective, and has a low complication rate when performed by an experienced surgeon. In properly selected patients, careful precise endomyometrial surgery will help many women avoid the need for hysterectomy. I believe that the ever-decreasing number of hysteroscopic surgeries (not diagnostic) being performed in this country reflects the unacceptably high failure rate which, in turn, is a reflection of poor understanding of the principles involved.

Dedicated centers, such as ours, have taken the lead in offering both junior and senior doctors both theory and practice in hysteroscopic surgery.

Table 2
Intracavity fibroids: European Society of Hysteroscopy Classification [26]

Grade	Characteristics
Grade 0	Pedunculated
Grade I	<50% intramural and >50% intracavity
Grade II	<50% intracavity and >50% intramural

REFERENCES

1. Stoekel W. Lehrburch der Gynakologie, 4. Leipzig: Aufl. Hirzel, 1933 (S.103).
2. Rubin IC. Uterine endoscopy, endometroscopy with the aid of uterine insufflation. *Am J Obstet Gynecol* 1925; **10**: 313.
3. Linderman HJ. Eine neve Untersuchung methode fur die Hysteroskopie. *Endoscopy* 1971; **4**: 194.
4. Goldrath MH, Fuller TA, Segal S. Laser photovaporisation of endometrium for the treatment of menorrhagia. *Am J Obstet Gynecol* 1981; **140**: 14.
5. Hill D, Maher P. Transcervical endometrial resection for abnormal uterine bleeding. *Med J Aust* 1989; **151**: 418.
6. Molloy D, Crosdale S. National trends in gynaecological endoscopic surgery. *Aust NZ J Obstet Gynaecol* 1996; **36**: 27.
7. Training Program Handbook. RANZCOG Publications, 2001: 43–44.
8. Resource Manual. RANZCOG Publications, 1992.
9. Loffer F, Bradley L, Brill A, Brooks P, Cooper J. Hysteroscopic training guidelines. *J Am Assoc Gynecol Laparosc* 2000; **7**: 165.
10. Gimpleson RJ, Rappold HO. A comparison study between panoramic hysteroscopy with directed biopsies and dilatation curettage. *Am J Obstet Gynecol* 1988; **158**: 489–492.
11. Loffer FD. Hysteroscopy with selected endometrial sampling compared with D & C for abnormal uterine bleeding. The value of a negative hysteroscopic view. *Obstet Gynecol* 1989; **73**: 16-20.
12. Smith DC, Donohue LR, Waszak SJ. A hospital review of advanced gynaecological endoscopic procedures. *Am J Obstet Gynecol* 1994; **170**: 1635–1642.
13. Hill D, Maher P, Wood C, Lawrence A, Downing B, Lolatgis N. Complications of operative hysteroscopy. *Gynaecol Endosc* 1992; **1**: 185–189.
14. Lawrence AS, Healy DL, Hill DJ, Paterson P. Management of submucous fibroids with buserilin, gemeprost and hysteroscopic resection. *Med J Aust* 1991; **154**: 280–282.
15. Indman P, Brooks P, Cooper J, Loffer F, Valle R, Van Caillie T. Complications of fluid overload from resectoscopic surgery. *J Am Assoc Gynecol Laparosc* 1998; **5**: 63–67.
16. Loffer F. Complications of hysteroscopy – their cause, prevention and correction. *J Am Assoc Gynecol Laparosc* 1995; **3**: 11–26.
17. Garry R, Hasham F, Kobri M et al. The effect of pressure on fluid absorption during endometrial ablation. *J Gynecol Surg* 1992; **8**: 10.
18. Garry R, Mooney P, Hasham F et al. A uterine distension system to prevent fluid absorption during Nd:YAG laser endometrial ablation. *Gynecol Endosc* 1992; **1**: 23–27.
19. Ayus JC, Wheeler JM, Arieff AI. Post operative hyponatraemic encephalopathy in menstrual women. *Ann Intern Med* 1992; **117**: 891–897.
20. Corson SL, Hoffman JJ, Jackowski J et al. Cardio-pulmonary effects of direct venous CO_2 insufflation in ewes. A model for CO_2 hysteroscopy. *J Reprod Med* 1988; **33**: 440–444.
21. Maher P, Hill D. Transcervical endometrial resection for abnormal uterine bleeding. Report of 100 cases and review of literature. *Aust NZ J Obstet Gynaecol* 1990; **30**: 357–360.
22. Neuwirth RS, Assin HK. Excision of submucous fibroids with hysteroscopic control. *Am J Obstet Gynecol* 1976; **126**: 95–99.
23. Holt E, Gilmer MD. Endometrial resection. In: Endometrial ablation. *Clin Obstet Gynecol* 1995; **9**: 279–299.
24. Van Caillie TG. Electrocoagulation of the endometrium with the ball end resectoscope. *Obstet Gynecol* 1989; **74**: 425.
25. Wood C, Maher P. Endoscopic treatment of uterine fibroids. In: Uterine fibroids. *Clin Obstet Gynecol* 1998; **12**: 289–316.
26. de Blok S, Dijkman AB, Hemrika DJ. Transcervical resection of fibroids (TCRM): results related to hysteroscopic classification. *Gynecol Endosc* 1995; **4**: 243–246.

29 Training and accreditation: The Far East

Bao-Liang Lin

Hysteroscopy has become a standard method for diagnosis and treatment of some intrauterine diseases. This kind of endoscopic surgery has many advantages over the traditional treatment and has allowed many women to avoid a hysterectomy or uterotomy.

I started to perform diagnostic hysteroscopic examinations with a rigid hysteroscope in 1983 and developed a partly soft and partly rigid flexible diagnostic hysteroscope in 1985, and a partly soft and partly rigid flexible operating hysteroscope in 1987. Afterwards, I performed >12,000 cases of diagnostic hysteroscopy (including 9500 cases of flexible hysteroscopy). In addition, I began performing resectoscopic operations in 1985 and operated on 2000 cases (including 1400 cases of submucous myoma), employing a variety of procedures. Our group published the first paper on rollerball endometrial ablation in 1988 [1].

Nevertheless, currently hysteroscopy is not a popular procedure in Japan. Many large hospitals do not have a hysteroscopic training program because of a lack of good teachers or of hysteroscopic instruments; even though a lot of gynecologists are interested and are looking for ways to familiarize themselves with this new technique. One of the reasons that physicians would like to take up this new procedure is that official insurance already covers several types of hysteroscopic operation. Also, at present hysteroscopy is not popular in other Asian countries. I have seen some physicians performing hysteroscopic operations after merely studying papers and video films. Consequently, the patient could not be woken after the procedure and was transferred directly to the ICU because of hyponatremia [2]. Furthermore, I have heard that in some countries hysteroscopic complications were more frequent and more serious than laparoscopic complications. The complications were sometimes fatal and, because of legal problems, these cases were not reported publicly. As a result, education in the field of hysteroscopy became a big problem. Unfortunately, so far, most endoscopic workshops held in Japan have been concerned with laparoscopy only.

I have been invited to participate in endoscopic workshops in many other Asian countries to teach hysteroscopy. On September 2000, an Asian hysteroscopic training center was set up in Beijing Fuxing hospital, an affiliated hospital of the Capital University of Medical Sciences, in Beijing, China. Professor Enlan Xia, who has a lot experience of operative hysteroscopy and is enthusiastic about teaching hysteroscopy, is the chairman of the department. Every year many gynecologists, including foreign doctors, go to Fuxing hospital to receive training in endoscopic techniques. As a visiting professor, I regularly participate in the training program.

The basic hysteroscopic training (some points were suggested by the American Association of Gynecological Laparoscopists [3]) includes:
1 Didactic training in both diagnostic and operative hysteroscopy.
2 Observation of various hysteroscopic video films.
3 Hands-on laboratory training using a Wallwiener-Bastert Hystero Trainer (Karl Storz).
4 Case observation.
5 Preceptorship.

Flexible hysteroscopy is rather more difficult to learn than rigid hysteroscopy. Physicians should master diagnostic hysteroscopy first and then familiarize themselves with operative hysteroscopy. It is also important to use a Hystero Trainer for learning the operative techniques including resection, coagulation or excision of a specimen using scissors, laser, and high frequency electrosurgery. Because there is no finer way to transmit surgical skill, preceptorship is the most effective way of training.

In summary, to avoid serious and possibly even fatal complications, a strict training program in hysteroscopy is necessary. Completion of a 2- or 3-day workshop may not provide an adequate qualification. Preceptorship is the most important and highly recommended method of training.

REFERENCES

1 Lin BL, Miyamoto NH, Tomomatu MH et al. The development of a new hysteroscopic resectoscope and its clinical applications on transcervical resection (TCR) and endometrial ablation (EA). *Japanese Journal of Gynecologic and Obstetric Endoscopy* 1998; **4**: 56–61.
2 Carter JE. Hysteroscopic surgery – avoid the complication of hyponatraemic encephalopathy. *Minimal Invasive Therapy & Allied Technology* 1997; **6**: 241–248.
3 Loffer FD, Bradley LD, Brill AI et al. Hysteroscopic training guidelines. *J Am Assoc Gynecol Laparosc* 2000; **7**: 165.

Training and accreditation in hysteroscopy: an overview

Arnold Gillespie

In this chapter seven distinguished gynecological endoscopists have summarized the current state of training and accreditation in their countries. Hysteroscopy has been practiced in isolated centers for decades but practical hysteroscopy did not reach the gynecological armamentarium until the late 1980s. At that time the majority of currently practicing gynecologists had finished their training; a training in which hysteroscopy had played no part.

Professor Costantini has encapsulated the main problem for these gynecologists by writing 'There seems to be no simple solution, because the technique has to be learned from this overwhelming majority of surgeons who have no cultural and technical background that includes the "endoscopic" way of thinking and working.' He further states that 'It is the needs of these gynecologists which now need to be addressed.' Sadly none of the articles in this chapter indicates that this has been done effectively in the last decade in any of the countries represented.

Dr Valle expresses the situation slightly differently in the USA but acknowledges that the problem is the same in that physicians (who have not had training in their residency program) can '... find themselves with a vacuum that is difficult to fill with short training sessions or postgraduate courses'. Dr Nakad and Professor Isaacson add to the gloom by saying 'The task is very difficult owing to the scarcity of resources such as certified trainers, centers equipped to carry out the training program, practitioners' time ...' while Professor Maher further darkens the scene by pointing out the near impossibility of there being enough recognized trainers in Australia and New Zealand when training guidelines in these countries recommend that, despite the relatively small clinical availability, training supervisors should undertake 50 cases which include 'technically difficult cases and uterine abnormalities.'

Professor Costantini is less troubled by the urgency in solving the problem than the other authors in that he believes that, with the passage of time, a solution will emerge as '... two or three generations of teachers will pass through universities and more adequate teaching that conforms to the realities of surgery will be developed.' He further states 'Here lies a task with a limited time-span that will be finished within the next 30–40 years.' There is no strong evidence from the articles that this desirable solution is inevitable. Professor van Herendael does not sound optimistic that the problem is self-limiting because of changes in teaching as he points out that in Europe '... individual medical schools do not have the obligation to train physicians in endoscopy ...' In the USA, Dr Valle points out that while residency training programs '*usually* have competent and dedicated instructors' he further indicates that 'these procedures are just *beginning* to be taught in residency programs ...' Dr Nakad's and Professor Isaacson's assessments of the difficulty of the task and scarcity of resources have already been referred to above. Professor Maher does not gain joy from the situation in Australia and New Zealand. He tells us that while the Royal Australian and New Zealand College of Obstetricians and Gynaecologists is the body responsible for training in those countries, it has no specific guidelines as regards the technique of training or the number of cases that must be performed while in training. That task remains the responsibility of the trainee's mentor who may or may not be an enthusiastic and experienced hysteroscopist. Dr Bao-Liang Lin indicates that in Japan 'Many large hospitals do not have a hysteroscopic training program because of a lack of good teachers or of hysteroscopic instruments.'

Faced with these training difficulties and under the pressure generated by patients keen to avail themselves of the perceived advantages of hysteroscopic techniques, the inevitable happened. Untrained physicians undertook procedures that resulted in disastrous outcomes. In an attempt to minimize this Nakad and Isaacson believe that 'The training and credentialing of endoscopic surgeons has become a pressing and immediate issue; immediate because poor surgical training has a negative and potentially fatal impact on patient outcome and pressing because nonmedical agencies are taking rapid steps to implement credentialing guidelines.'

Thus many societies that champion the use of endoscopy have defined sets of guidelines for training and accreditation. While there is no doubt that the motivation behind the development of the various guidelines was to ensure high standards in hysteroscopy, the desire of the medical profession to avoid being dictated to by nonmedical or government bodies undoubtedly played some part. The guidelines commonly detail training suggestions, ultimately it is usually the institution in which a surgeon works that determines the accreditation. Litigation also played a major role in ensuring the development of guidelines. Litigation is mentioned by van Herendael and by Nakad and Isaacson. Perhaps the high level of litigation consciousness in the USA has played a part in the greater success in achieving accreditation procedures in that country than in other countries.

The details of the guidelines are given by the other authors in this chapter. They vary in their specifications and their surgical requirements. Maher says that the guidelines in Australia and New Zealand are '... in stark contrast to those recommended by the Ad Hoc Committee on Hysteroscopic Training Guidelines of the American Association of Gynecological Laparoscopists.' Van Herendael says '... there is no official system of accreditation for endoscopy' and Costantini believes that '... for the moment training and accreditation are voluntary choices, all over Europe ...'

The universal implementation of guidelines and accreditation procedures remains a logistic and often not solvable problem, in all countries. Guidelines may set a standard; at the moment a somewhat arbitrary and variable standard. Accreditation provides some measure of protection for institutions anxious to minimize their legal and litigable responsibilities. Guidelines and accreditation procedures do nothing to address the basic problem that is training, or more accurately, the difficulty in obtaining timely and adequate training. It is to be hoped that Maher is wrong in attributing the fall in the number of operative hysteroscopies in Australia to the poor outcomes obtained because of inadequate training by the surgeons who undertook the procedures. Diagnostic and operative hysteroscopy have enormous potential for improving patient care. It would be sad indeed if inadequacy of surgical training brought them into disrepute and ultimately caused their demise.

The challenge remains. All of the authors can see the problem; none has the solution. It is well over a decade since practical hysteroscopy was introduced and training problems have been present all of that time. Should we be acting more decisively or can the current *laissez faire* situation continue (which risks the discrediting of hysteroscopy) or shall we just await the Costantini solution over the next 30–40 years?

Record-keeping, documentation, and registry

Photo and video archiving for endoscopy

Luk Rombauts, Scott Pearce and Yves van Belle

> **Take Home Message**
> The electronic eye of the camera produces an electrical signal that is digital in nature. Traditionally this signal has been stored on digital carriers with a great loss of quality. Because of the growing storage capacity of computer memory more and more cameras are now provided with a digital output. Archiving can now be done on digital video recorders without loss of quality. Mini-DVD tapes represent a space saving as well. However, the answer is the ever-expanding computer memory and the multitude of storage devices. The DVD burner is the latest. A DVD disk carries up to 9 Gb per disk. New systems have been developed ranging from software-only products via computer-based systems to modular stand-alone systems. The future is the Picture Archiving and Communication Systems (PACS). Here the advantage is the much improved workflow and possibility for interpretation of the images by several specialists in different locations simultaneously.

INTRODUCTION

The current generation of endoscopic equipment provides us with medical imaging in unsurpassed color depth and resolution. The advent of digital technology now enables us to store and edit this information with virtually no loss of quality.

The endoscopic camera produces an electrical signal which represents the image 'seen' by the CCD (charge-coupled device), the electronic eye of the camera head. This electrical signal is digital in nature, meaning that the information stored within it consists of 0s and 1s. As long as the signal is transmitted digitally throughout the system there is virtually no quality loss. In contrast with an analog signal, signal noise from interfering electrical components or poor video cabling will have little or no impact.

Because archiving of images traditionally has involved analog equipment, such as a VHS recorder or video printer, currently most camera controllers only have analog outputs. This means that the original signal is fed through a digital/analog converter, an important source of quality loss, after which it is relayed to the monitor, video recording, or other imaging device.

With the exponential growth of computer memory, processor speed, and imaging software, high quality images and video can now be archived digitally and this has prompted some manufacturers to include digital output on their camera controllers. This digital communication port is commonly known as 'firewire' (IEEE 1934).

ARCHIVING

Different media can be used to archive images recorded in the operating theater.

Printers, either thermal wax-coated or ink-jet, can be connected to the camera controller to produce a still image record. Although the image quality is generally excellent, no editing of the image is possible once the image is printed.

Digital video recorders enable segments or entire operations to be recorded in digital quality. There are many benefits. Not only is this the best way to store video, the small size of mini-DVD tapes (7 × 5 × 1 cm) is also a great space saver. Multigeneration copying (copies of copies of copies …) can easily be achieved without quality loss. This is a major advantage over analog recordings, where unacceptable quality loss generally occurs after one or two generations. In addition, digital video segments can easily be fed back into a computer for further editing, again without quality loss.

Computers also allow archiving of still images or video. Possibilities continue to expand with hard disk sizes now available over 100 Gigabytes (Gb) at affordable rates. New software is being developed to allow the large computer files associated with the original digital image or video to be dramatically compressed in size with little quality loss. Even so, the largest hard disks inevitably get filled up. Hence, the explosion in storage devices such as CD writers and CD rewriters and, more recently, DVD burners. The enormous storage capacity on a DVD disk (up to 9 Gb/disk) should alleviate any fears of quickly running out of storage space. As computer power has grown and software technology has improved, video editing can now be performed on desktop and even laptop computers. The iMovie software developed by Apple has enabled the novice to edit simple videos with only a 15-minute introduction. The possibilities for outstanding video presentations have now come within the reach of every endoscopic surgeon.

Recognizing the growing need for digital archiving, medical technology companies are now developing new systems for use in the operating theater. These range from software-only products, such as the Health Communication Networks 'Gynaescribe' in Australia, designed to be used on a laptop computer, to total freestanding video or still image archiving units, such as the system produced by Stryker, which can store and record data onto a recordable CD.

AVAILABLE ARCHIVING SYSTEMS

Software-only systems

These systems all require a computer with a video capture card and enough memory. A number of software programs are available, varying between each country. Two typical programs are described below.

Health Communication Network (HCN, Australia) – Gynaescribe

This is a Windows-based software program. Basic system requirements are a Pentium 500 Mhz CPU with 500 Mb hard disk drive and 128 Mb RAM. The Gynaescribe software program has a preformatted database containing three modules – laparoscopy, hysteroscopy, and colposcopy. Patient data can be entered and operation reports and letters can be produced. An image capture card enables still images to be recorded. Some sections allow extra data to be added, but overall the preformatted database does not allow a lot of flexibility. Video segments cannot be stored.

Smith and Nephew Medicap 2000 – version 3

This is available as a software-only program for use on your own computer, or as a complete package including computer, software, digital video camera, and camera controller.

It uses a Windows-based operating system. The basic system requirements for a desktop computer are a Pentium III 550 MHz CPU with 128 Mb RAM, and ideally 10 Gb for video file storage.

The system allows still images and up to 2 hours of video capture. Images are recorded onto either a hard drive or CD ROM. The software program allows recording of patient details and entering of captured images or video. Notes can be attached to images and reports can be printed.

COMPUTER-BASED SYSTEMS

These systems are sold as turn-key systems, complete computer packages with software pre-installed for immediate use in the operating theater.

Karl Storz – Advanced Image and Data Archiving System (AIDA) (Figures 1–5)

This is a Windows-based computer operating system sold as a complete package for use in the operating theater. AIDA allows data collection, storing, and processing of images and the creation of letters and reports. Data can be stored in a preformatted template or customized templates can be created. Images can be inserted into the templates and post-processing of the images can be performed, for example, comments or arrows can be inserted or the image color and contrast can be altered.

Information can be stored on a floppy disk drive, CD ROM, or computer hard drive, or can be sent to a network or e-mailed. AIDA will not run on an Apple Macintosh computer but information can be sent to an Apple Macintosh. Files can be formatted in JPEG, BMP, or TIFF. Video streaming using MPEG-1 and MPEG-2.

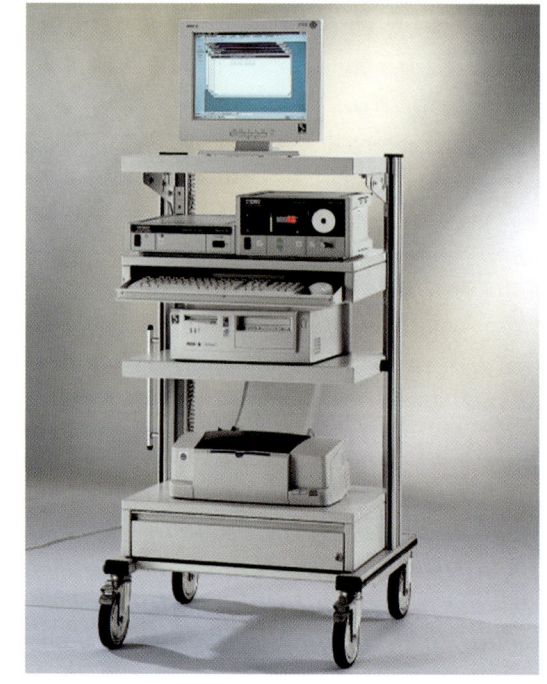

Figure 1
AIDA. The endoscope is connected to a computer. This computer can be stored on the tower and connected to a hard copy writer.

RECORD-KEEPING, DOCUMENTATION, AND REGISTRY

Olympus/rpSzene

In Europe, Olympus is marketing a system manufactured by another company called rpSzene. It is a Windows-based computer system with facilities for database archiving, image capture of both stills and video, video editing, and the creation of reports. The system can be used to replace the operating theater monitor, with the advantages of image capture and personal computer facilities. Templates for patient data are based on Microsoft Word, but custom templates are possible. Video recording speed can be adjusted. Full video editing including cutting, title insertion, copying, and individual picture export is provided. Patient data and images are saved first onto the hard drive or zip drive, then onto CD ROM. With 8× CD recording a 700-Mb CD will take 15 minutes to record. Data can be sent to a network or e-mailed. Satellite computers need to have the same video card as rpSzene to play the video. Write protection can ensure that data cannot be erased easily from the hard drive. Images are stored as BMP, JPEG, or TIFF. High quality MJPEG compression is used for video. Analog S-VHS and VHS ports are provided and optical devices such as endoscopes or microscopes can be connected to the system regardless of the make. Data are managed by the 'volume manager', similar to a file manager in Windows. It follows a 'tree branch' structure with patient data at the top and branches or paths down to 'film' files for each patient with further branches from each film file to the location of

Figure 2
AIDA. The patient's data are brought to a preprogrammed screen and are integrated into the filing system.

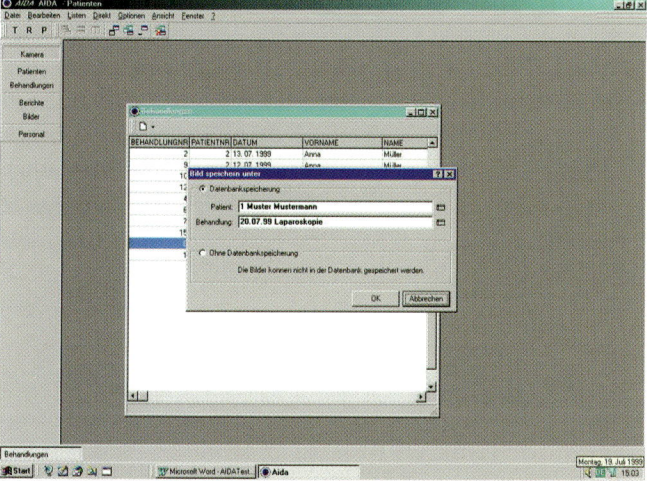

Figure 3
AIDA. The patient's information is put into the computer on a programmed screen working under Windows. The program allows for direct integration of the patient's data into a letter to colleagues or to the patient.

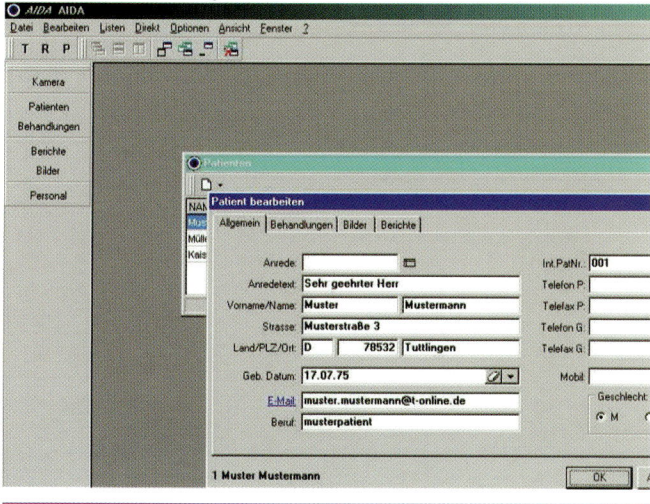

Figure 2
AIDA. The comments and the pictures are recorded on the hard disk and can be reproduced on a data or DVD disk or printed directly with the hard copy writer. This information can be integrated directly into the letter to send out or can be archived.

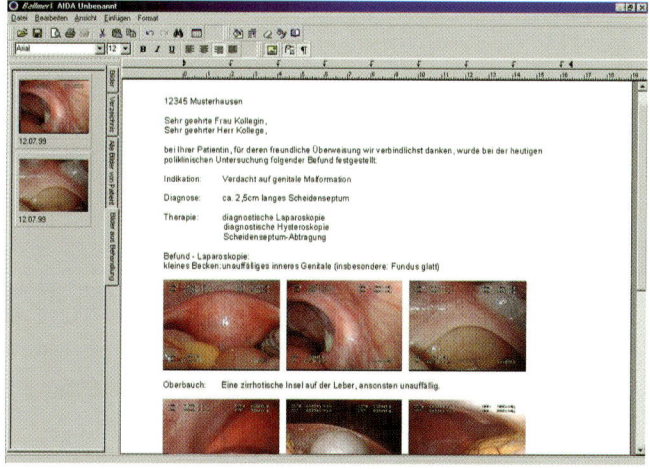

Figure 5
AIDA. The images can be labeled using the keyboard integrated into the digital camera.

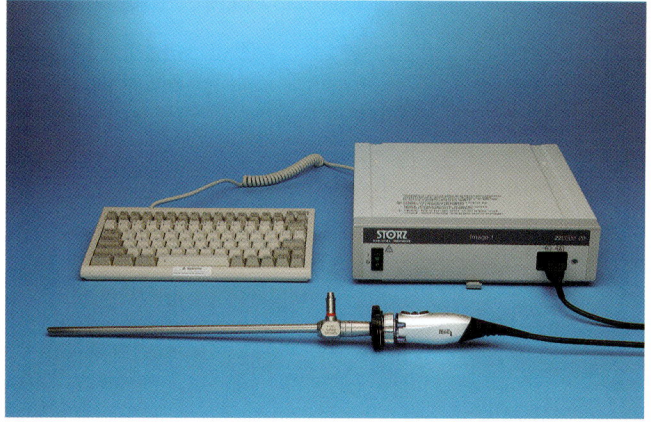

the storage media used for that particular image, e.g. CD ROM, DVD-ROM.

MODULAR SYSTEMS
Stryker (SDC Pro – Stryker Digital Capture)
Unlike the above 'computer systems', Stryker have developed a single unit, not much larger than a video recorder, which is designed to fit onto the operating theater endoscopic 'tower'. It allows for image capture of stills and video. Patient details are entered into the unit then images can be captured using the buttons on the endoscopic camera head, a remote control, or directly from the touch-screen console. Images can then be printed, recorded onto a CD ROM (a DVD version is due to be released soon), or sent to a network. This system is smaller than a full computer system but does not have the full features of a 'personal computer'. Digital images are recorded using JPEG or BMP. Captured images cannot be deleted, but at the end of the procedure individual images can be selected for printing or can be recorded onto a CD ROM. CD ROM writing takes approximately 1 minute for each 1 minute of video taken and occurs at the end of the operation, not as the case progresses. Therefore care is needed to ensure that enough time is allowed for writing before starting the next operation.

The unit is designed to exclusively print directly to a Hewlett Packard HP2000CXI ink-jet printer. Other printers cannot be used.

Video editing cannot be performed on the module itself, but commonly available software for use on personal or laptop computers enables editing and adjustment of images and video. Stryker markets an appropriate software program, SDC software pro 2.0. Images thus displayed on a personal computer can be printed out onto any printer.

FUTURE DEVELOPMENTS
As computer technology makes it easier to store digital information, documenting each patient's history with images and/or video from each endoscopic procedure will eventually become the norm – not just to illustrate to the patient the outcome of the operation at the first postoperative visit, but also as medicolegal evidence. It is easy to see how this could grow into an uncontrollable collection of computer files, especially in a hospital environment. As a consequence, the greatest challenge will inevitably be to retrieve the correct information efficiently when it is required.

The surgeon will expect to retrieve clinical data and relevant medical images concerning a given patient from any given computer workstation in a hospital environment [1]. Picture archiving and communication systems (PACS) have been developed to solve the problem of acquiring, archiving, transmitting, and displaying medical images. PACS technology has not yet found widespread acceptance and the systems that have been installed are generally used for the management of radiologic images.

Table 2
Comparison between available systems

Parameter	Karl Storz AIDA	Olympus rpSzene	Stryker SDC Pro
Computer system' or individual unit	Computer	Computer	Individual unit
Images and/or video	Images only	Images and video	Images and video
File and/or video format	JPEG, BMP, or TIFF MJPEG for video	JPEG, BMP, or TIFF; MJPEG for video	JPEG or BMP
Storage media	Floppy disk, CD ROM, computer hard drive, network	CD ROM, computer hard drive, zip drive, network	CD ROM, network
Video editing from the unit	Not available (but software could be installed)	Available	Available
Software use	Preformatted or custom templates	Preformatted or custom templates	Not applicable (image capture unit only)
Printer	Any printer	Any printer	Hewlett Packard HP2000CXI only

However, there is no reason why the technology could not be applied to store images from endoscopic procedures too.

Although the technology sounds futuristic, filmless hospitals already exist. Again, the dramatic improvements in processing power, storage capacity, network bandwidths, and intelligent software have allowed for efficient storage and soft copy display of medical images [2]. Integrated communication between the PACS database and the hospital information system (HIS), holding all the other clinical information for the patient, is obviously critical to maximize the benefit to the medical practitioner [2].

The main advantages of a PACS relate to the much improved workflow and interpretation of medical images [3]. No more lost or misplaced films, prints, or tapes [4]. Images can also be viewed by several specialists at different locations simultaneously, greatly facilitating a truly multidisciplinary approach. As images are intelligently grouped and chronologically ordered, retrieval of image sets for comparison with previous studies and assessing disease progression is straightforward. When labeling of images includes relevant key words, building educational multimedia applications should now require much less effort [4,5].

The advantages of a PACS may seem quite overwhelming, but with time growing experience with PACS has already pointed out some shortcomings. Although the filmless hospital sounds like a great cost-saver, the obvious savings have been offset by the need for information technology managers and other computer personnel [3]. In addition, the flow-through of radiology reports back to the referring specialist has become much faster, but this has come at a price. The digital environment of PACS has reduced communication between the radiologist and the specialist, with less clinical information being available to the radiologist during the interpretation of the films [6]. Other challenges to the long-term usefulness of the electronic archive include the uncertain lifespan of high-density electronic storage media and the continuous need to upgrade software and hardware that fuels product obsolescence [7].

REFERENCES

1. Ratib O, Ligier Y, Bandon D, Valentino D. Update on digital image management and PACS. *Abdom Imaging* 2000; **25**: 333–340.
2. Arensen RL, Andriole KP, Avrin DE, Gould RG. Computers in imaging and health care: now and in the future. *J Digit Imaging* 2000; **13**: 145–156.
3. Strickland NH. PACS (picture archiving and communication systems): filmless radiology. *Arch Dis Child* 2000; **83**: 82–86.
4. Wiggins RH, Davidson HC, Dilda P, Harnsberger HR, Katzman GL. The evolution of filmless radiology teaching. *J Digit Imaging* 2001; **14** (2 Suppl 1): 236–237.
5. Harrison M, Koh J, Tran S, Mongkolwat P, Channin DS. Research and teaching access to a large clinical picture archiving and communication system. *J Digit Imaging* 2001; **14** (2 Suppl 1): 121–124.
6. Hayt DB, Alexander S. The pros and cons of implementing PACS and speech recognition systems. *J Digit Imaging* 2001; **14**: 149–157.
7. Blado ME. Management of the picture archiving and communication archive at Texas Children's Hospital. *J Digit Imaging* 2001; **14** (2 Suppl 1): 84–88.

31b Record-keeping, documentation, and registry
Documentation of hysteroscopic and endoscopic procedures

T. F. Kruger, I. J. van der Wat, C. F. Hoogendijk and J. P. van der Merwe

> **Take Home Message**
> Office hysteroscopy needs as simple documentation storage as possible. 'A picture is worth more than thousand words.' As data and video images can easily be stored today different methods of storage have been developed. The FotoMaster system is one of them. A personal computer equipped with a video capture card and a snapshot trigger is the FotoMaster Capture Station. The system allows for transfer of data to a secondary administrative computer (view station) where photographs and comments can be edited. It can be used in electronic mail to update colleagues. The system allows for a reduction in administrative workload as reports can be printed directly after the hysteroscopy. 10,000 images can be stored on a 4-Gb disk.

INTRODUCTION

A picture is worth more than a thousand words [1]. This point was clearly demonstrated in a number of textbooks on endoscopic surgery. If one can document and retrieve endoscopic procedures with ease pictures can be used at different levels to explain, carry out research, and use as a teaching aid.

Endoscopic surgery is a well-established entity in gynecology as well as in other disciplines and has made major strides over the last 15 years. The documentation of laparoscopic and hysteroscopic procedures can successfully be done with video recording. However, this method of documentation poses a few problems, e.g. it can be difficult to retrieve specific information and the practical problem of storage of bulky video tapes in the average office set up [2]. The development of digital cameras created a new potential for storing important aspects of any operation and in this chapter emphasis will be placed on this new development to document operations.

35-MM PHOTOGRAPHY

This method was of particular value before digital cameras became freely available. It is still useful in certain conditions. Strong illumination is needed to take quality photographs through the hysteroscope [3]. The use of an electronic flash generator eliminates the need for slow shutter speeds because movement can blur the picture. Several manufacturers make high power xenon light sources with built-in flash capability allowing both video photography and 35-mm still photography using the same light source [3].

Special lenses designed to attach a 35-mm camera body to the eyepiece of the endoscope are ideal. Fixed focal length lenses can also be used with coupling adapters. Indman illustrated that 35-mm photography creates excellent images, but it is not without its drawbacks [3]. Most endoscopic surgery today is monitored by use of a video camera connected to the eyepiece of the endoscope. To take 35-mm photographs it is necessary to interrupt the procedure, remove the video camera from the hysteroscope, and replace it with the 35-mm camera. Although electronic imaging techniques do not produce the image quality of 35-mm, photographs originating from a video image are quite satisfactory and have in many settings replaced routine 35-mm photography [3].

VIDEO PHOTOGRAPHY

This method is of great value not only for teaching but also for patient information and documentation. However, the retrieval of specific captions from the documented material is difficult and sometimes time-consuming, but when edited, this material is of help and real value in the areas mentioned (e.g. resection of a submucous myoma in a step-by-step fashion).

Video endoscopy has become routine for a multitude of reasons that benefit the patient and the physician. When using video, it is not necessary for the operator's eye to be placed against an eyepiece that is in the operative field. Contamination of the surgical instruments is avoided and decreases the potential risk of infecting the surgeon. Operator fatigue is reduced because the surgeon is free to change positions without losing the view of the surgical field. In addition, other staff members involved in surgery, including assistants, nurses, and the anesthesiologist, can view the procedure, enabling more effective assistance. The procedure can be recorded for education of physicians and patients [3].

To select and use video equipment most effectively, a technical understanding of the video process is necessary. Modern video cameras for endoscopic use consist of a lens and one or more solid-state, image-sensing chips. The chip(s) convert the image into an electronic signal that can be processed and sent to a video monitor, a video or still recorder, or stored electronically. Many endoscopic and most home video cameras use a single chip. Whether a single- or three-chip camera is used, the electronic signal produced at this point consists of three components: one for each of the primary colors (red, green, and blue, or 'RGB'). Each color requires a separate cable to transmit the signal.

Figure 1
Digital cameras allow for direct transmission of images and data to the computer linked with the camera housing; there is no loss of information.

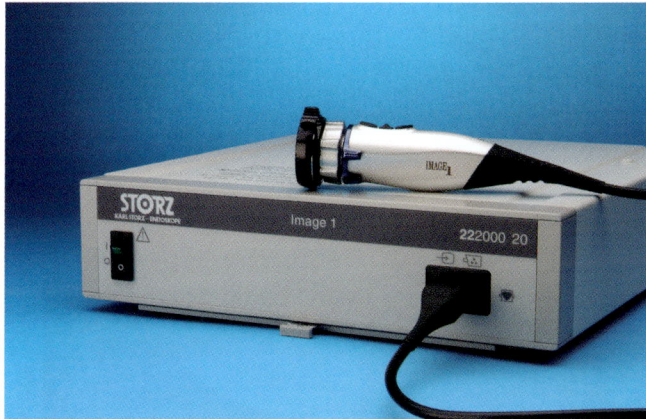

Figure 2
Digital cameras with three chips give more possibilities for color temperature variations and sharpness of the endoscopic image.

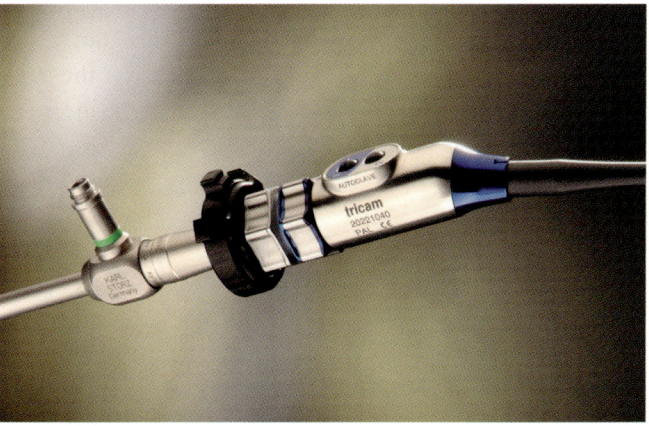

The individual color elements must be translated to a form that can be displayed on a monitor by a process called 'encoding' [3] (Figures 1 and 2).

ELECTRONIC STORAGE

Data/images can easily be stored today. A novel method (FotoMaster) was recently tested and reported on [2].

EQUIPMENT

CAPTURE STATION

A FotoMaster Capture Station is a personal computer (PC)-based system with a video capture card and snapshot trigger. The PC is typically connected to the endoscopic camera, while the snapshot trigger is a small foot-switch controlled by the surgeon to trigger a snapshot photograph. The Capture Station also has full editing and printing capability. Photographs may be annotated with remarks, and unwanted photographs can be removed to streamline the report. A summary of the examination may also be entered. Printing options allow either an abbreviated report with thumbnail photo prints, or detailed full-page color printouts of selected high resolution photographs, which are selected from thumbnail photos and then enlarged. Text only can also be printed.

VIEW STATION

A FotoMaster View Station is a typical personal computer running the FotoMaster software and allows the clinician to view examinations and make report printouts. It can import examinations from a Capture Station on diskette but the View Station cannot capture photographs and cannot create new examinations.

FUNCTION DURING OPERATION

Step one: The existing patient file is accessed or a new patient file is created.
Step two: Photographs of the live video taken by the endoscopic camera are captured by means of a two-button remote control. Written comments are added as required.
Step three: After the examination/surgical procedure, the photographs and comments can be edited and a brief report can be added.
Step four: The examination/surgical procedure data may be printed in the operating theater or transferred, as already explained, to another computer and printouts made of the full report or a summary thereof.

During the 8-month period 6 November 1998 to 30 December 2000, 464 patients were successfully documented: 88 different laparoscopic procedures for endometriosis, 24 neosalpingostomies, 25 salpingolyses, 5 fimbrioplasty procedures, 3 oophorectomies, 62 routine laparoscopic/hysteroscopic procedures, and 17 uterine septa, 9 uterine polyps, and 16 submucosal myomata were removed. Before transfer, 178 embryos were photographed and 25 hysterosalpingograms were performed and documented in the operating theater.

The equipment is easy to use and does not add to operation time. In our set up the surgeon adds comments to the photographs postoperatively. Alternatively the data can be transferred to a secondary administrative computer (view station) where the photographs and comments can easily be edited. The system was also successfully used in electronic mail messages to update colleagues with specific visual images of their referrals. The system (in our unit) also leads to a reduction in administrative load as reports are now printed directly after operation in the theater. We do not print thumbnail pictures or the full size version routinely, only a written report, but in certain cases where needed full color printouts were produced.

Another benefit is that the system can be used during lectures (pre- and post-graduate) by transferring pictures/images to PowerPoint. The system can also be used directly via a data projector to show an entire operation. The research potential is obvious and we are currently documenting cases of endometriosis, looking at adhesion formation at second-look operation after sharp dissection of peritoneum. The same patient folder was used for the second operation and pictures from the same area were carefully and easily reproduced [2]. Investigators have called for a system that provides these specific capabilities [4].

Stored data can be obtained by simply selecting a keyword beforehand and the data for a patient with a specific condition can be retrieved, or the patient's surname can be used. More than one key word can be linked to a single patient, e.g. endometriosis, fimbrioplasty, hydatid of Morgagni, uterine septum (Figure 3). On average, 10–15 pictures were taken per operation to capture the important moments. The advantage of pictures is that less text is necessary to document a case owing to the power and specific details of each picture. We also documented hysterosalpingograms by simply connecting the system to the mobile X-ray equipment (Figure 4). The image quality was good and valuable in training of students. Poor pictures are deleted after each operation. According to the technical specifications 100,000 images can be stored on a 4-Gb hard disk, which gives the capability to store ± 10,000 patient records (based on an average of 10 pictures per operation). Data can be stored on a compact disc at a convenient time once or twice a year.

Taking pictures of embryos in assisted reproduction is also beneficial and can be stored for future evaluation and comparison in pregnant and nonpregnant cycles. The use of this system in dermatology, plastic surgery, and general surgery, by using a different camera system, brings a new dimension to the physician's ability to carefully document and store data and interesting cases.

Although we have only used this system in gynecological procedures, it is apparent that it has the potential to play an important role in all medical specialities where image documentation would be advantageous.

CONCLUSION

The use of video recordings is still of great value today. When edited it can be used to teach students and educate patients regarding specific conditions. However, it is difficult to retrieve specific video data effectively and quickly. The 35-mm camera's role is limited. Static pictures obtained electronically are of great value and if stored in an orderly fashion as outlined above can serve as a valuable databank in an endoscopic unit for years to come.

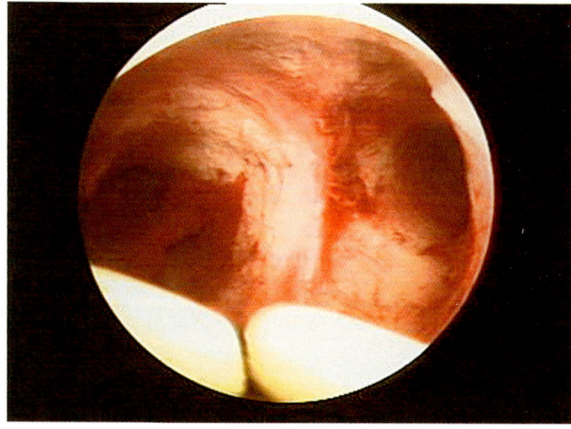

Figure 3
Uterine septum documented with the FotoMaster system.

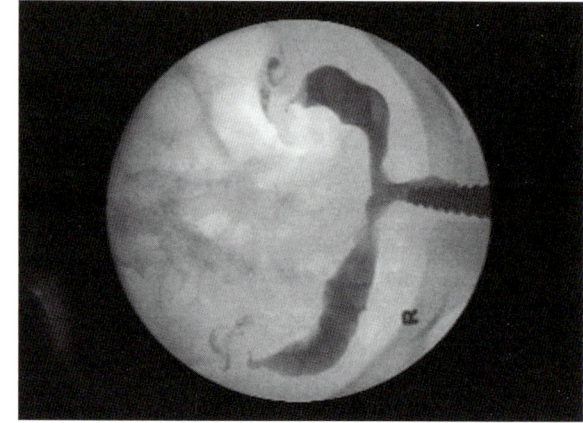

Figure 4
Hysterosalpingogram; uterus bicornus.

We have used the FotoMaster system for this research project; however, most leading equipment manufacturers have now introduced dedicated digital data capturing systems to their product ranges – for example, Karl Storz AIDA (Advanced Image and Data Archiving system) (Figure 5), Stryker SDC Pro (Stryker Digital Capture).

These systems can be added to existing contemporary endoscopic equipment or become part of their recently introduced integrated operating room concepts (Karl Storz or Stryker Hermes) which allow the surgeon full control of devices, lighting, cameras, documentation, and teleconferencing from a central station by manual or voice control.

These digital data capturing systems allow for storage of digital image data and surgical documentation in a similar fashion to the FotoMaster. All these systems allow for teleconferencing and PowerPoint presentations.

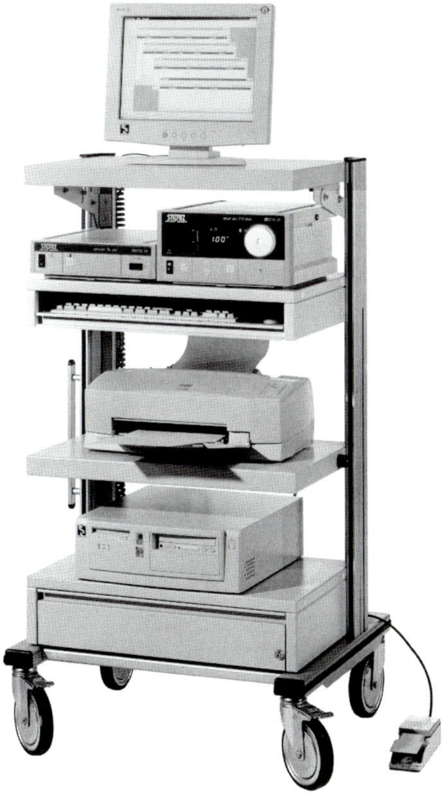

ACKNOWLEDGMENTS

We thank Mrs Helena Krüger for editing the manuscript, Hamilton Thorne Research (Beverly, MA, USA), and PrimeLogic Digital Image Solutions (Somerset-West, South Africa) for placing the FotoMaster system for evaluation.

REFERENCES

1. Donnez J, Nisolle M, eds. An Atlas of Laser Operative Laparoscopy and Hysteroscopy 1994. Parthenon Publishing Group, 1994.
2. Kruger TF, Van der Merwe JP, Marino H, Hoogendijk CF, Du Toit C. A novel method (FotoMaster) of documenting endoscopic surgical procedures. *Fertil Steril* 2000; **74**: 418–419.
3. Indman PD. Documentation in endoscopy. *Obstet Gynecol Clin North Am* 1995; **22**: 605–616.
4. Gudzick DS, Canis M, Silliman NP et al. Prediction of pregnancy in infertile women based on the American Society for Reproductive Medicine's revised classification of endometriosis. *Fertil Steril* 1997; **67**: 822–829.

Figure 5
An integrated system on the tower in the hysteroscopy room gives the physician a variety of choices as to how to control the information gathered. When the images are in direct vision, the better ones can be stored and the others can be rejected.

Part IV
THE OFFICE AND OUTPATIENT TEAM

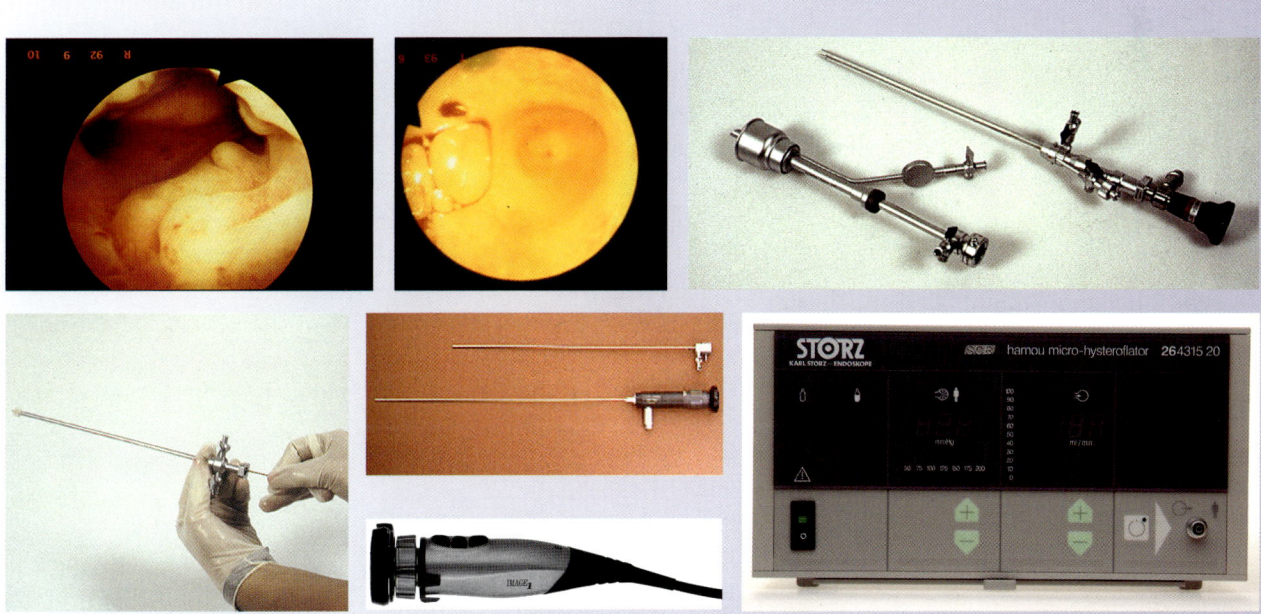

32 The nurse's perspective

Corry G.W.A. Stappers-de Kuijer

> **Take Home Message**
> An office hysteroscopy should be gentle, sophisticated, and patient-friendly. The procedure room should be restful and comfortable for the patient, a separate dressing-room is advisable. Hysteroscopy is teamwork. The patient is the priority but the smooth running of the procedure depends on the condition of the instruments. As the patient is awake she is aware of the whole procedure and all additional activities and discussions. This requires a different attitude from both the physician and the assisting personnel.

A diagnostic hysteroscopy should be gentle, sophisticated, patient-friendly, and reliable.

The procedure room should be restful and comfortable for the patient; a separate dressing-room is advisable. Try to create a friendly atmosphere in which the patient can relax as much as possible.

Specific indications for performing a diagnostic hysteroscopy:

- abnormal uterine bleeding
- abnormal or inconclusive transvaginal sonography (TVS) findings
- secondary dysmenorrhea
- infertility (primary and secondary)
- abnormal or inconclusive hysterosalpingography (HSG) findings in the uterine cavity
- 'lost' intrauterine contraceptive device (IUCD)
- presurgical assessment of endoscopic operability
- follow-up after hysteroscopic surgery
- after complicated intrauterine manipulations related to pregnancy
- abnormal ultrasound or HSG.

Contraindications:

- increased ESR and CRP
- pregnancy
- suspicion of pelvic inflammatory disease (PID)
- abnormal cervical culture.

Possible complications:

- intravasation
- allergic reactions to iodine, local anesthetics, or distension media
- perforations of the uterine wall.

It is very important to schedule the hysteroscopy in the first half of the menstrual cycle. In the secondary phase of the cycle the endometrium is too thick and minor disorders, such as small myomas or fibroids, could easily be missed (Figure 1).

Not every patient will be suitable for an ambulatory procedure; the selection should be made during an office visit before the procedure.

Very nervous and tense patients could better be scheduled for a procedure under general anesthesia at the operating room or a patient may prefer this approach.

Figure 1

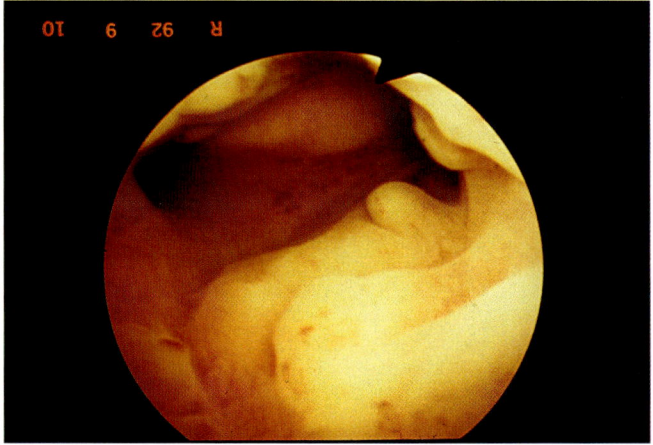

During the procedure the patient could feel some discomfort and menstrual cramping owing to the distension of the uterine cavity, which is one of the reasons that it is beneficial to keep up communication with the patient and try to distract her mind from the actual procedure itself. It can be advantageous to have the patient's partner attend the procedure.

Like all endoscopy, hysteroscopy is teamwork. Cooperation between the gynecologist and the assisting personnel is of great importance. This can only be accomplished with assistants who are involved in the procedure. The first priority is the patient; we should very well be aware of her condition during and after the procedure and when leaving the hospital.

However, it is not only the patient that needs our attention. The use of the various pieces of apparatus and instruments demands a specific know-how and the maintenance of the equipment is very important for smooth procedures. Hysteroscopic instruments are rather vulnerable and should be handled with care.

There is no doubt that the condition of the instruments is very important in the provision of good performance. Personnel should have enough knowledge to recognize minor dysfunctions immediately and if necessary to remedy them at the same time. It is essential to
handle the instruments gently and to observe and follow the instructions given by the manufacturer.

PRACTICAL ADVICE FOR HANDLING EQUIPMENT

VIDEO ENDOCAMERA

Moving parts inside the camera adapter may get stuck due to desiccated particles of the distension medium (Figure 2). In that case it is almost impossible to connect the adapter to the eyepiece. Cleaning the adapter with warm water and a neutral detergent can solve this problem. Do not forget to dry the adapter thoroughly before re-attaching it to the eyepiece. A misty image on the monitor may be caused by moisture between the adapter and the eyepiece of the telescope; this can be removed with a dry cloth.

LIGHT SOURCE AND LIGHT GUIDE CABLE

A good light source and light guide cable are essential for carrying out a good hysteroscopic procedure. There are several light sources available and the supplier should provide instructions for usage. Visualization will be possible with a 150-W halogen light source but in the presence of blood or mucus a 300-W xenon light source is advisable.

Manipulate the light guide cable with care. Forced bending may result in damage or rupture of the glass fibers inside the cable, which will immediately result in reduction of light intensity (Figure 3).

Fiber-glass light guide cables should be checked regularly for ruptured fibers. To check the condition of a light guide cable the front end of it can be pointed to a flat surface with a powered light source. Black spots indicate broken glass fibers. The more dark spots are seen the less the light intensity will be. Most light guide cables can be cleaned in a warm water solution.

PRESSURE CUFF OR ELECTRONIC PUMP

If continuous flow hysteroscopes are used a pressure cuff or electronic pump is needed for administration of the fluid (Figure 4). A pressure cuff in combination with a collection

Figure 2

Figure 3

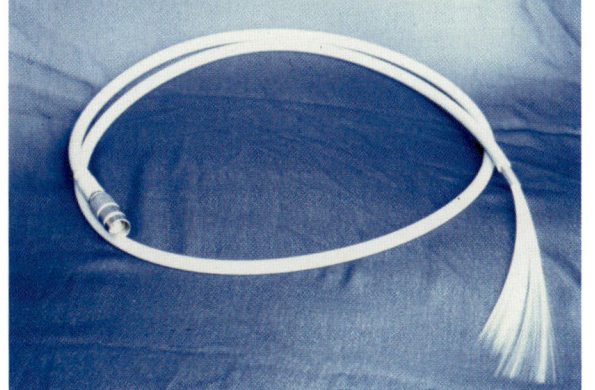

Figure 4

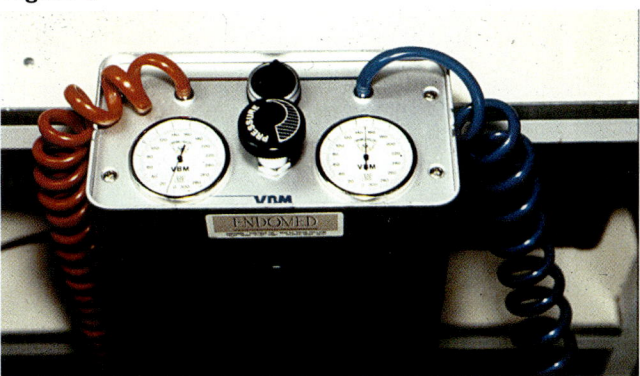

bottle is sufficient for diagnostic or minor surgical procedures. The 'fluid loss' should never be allowed to exceed 1500 ml, in which case the procedure has to be ended. The electronic pump is preferred for major interventions (Figure 5). The use of the scale belonging to the electronic pump is mandatory. Only the combination of these two elements provides for exact data on the inflow and outflow of the distending medium (Figure 6).

When using the pump, take the following precautions:
- prevent the presence of air bubbles in the system
- prevent overflow of the fluid in the bottle
- put the bottle or the scale on a flat surface for proper functioning.

Special tubings for the delivery of the fluid are available.

Figure 5

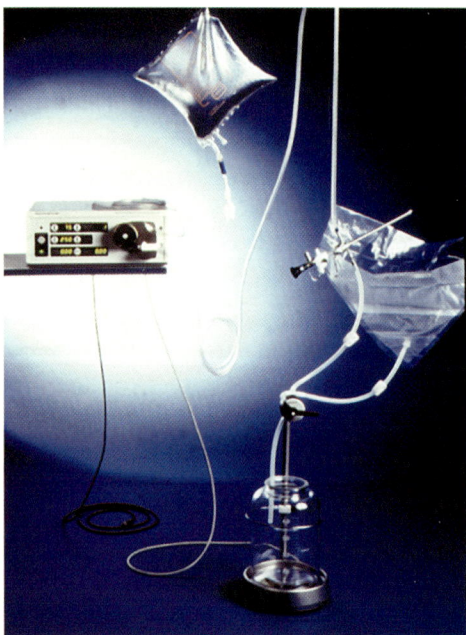

Figure 6

CO_2 INSUFFLATOR

The choice of CO_2 for distension of the uterine cavity usually demands patience, especially when blood or mucus is present (Figure 7).

Only CO_2 insufflators that have been specially developed for hysteroscopy should be used.

Pressure and flow rates have to be adjusted before the procedure. The tubes and the hysteroscope connections must be gas-tight, which must be checked before the start of the procedure. In case of insufficient distension of the uterine cavity – caused by gas leakage through the cervix – a special vacuum portio adapter or a second tenaculum can be applied (Figure 8).

After the procedure the patient may experience some shoulder pain, this is caused by the CO_2 flow through patent tubes into the abdominal cavity.

HYSTEROSCOPES

Continuous flow (CF) hysteroscopes are equipped with separate inflow and outflow channels for transport of the distending medium.

Figure 7

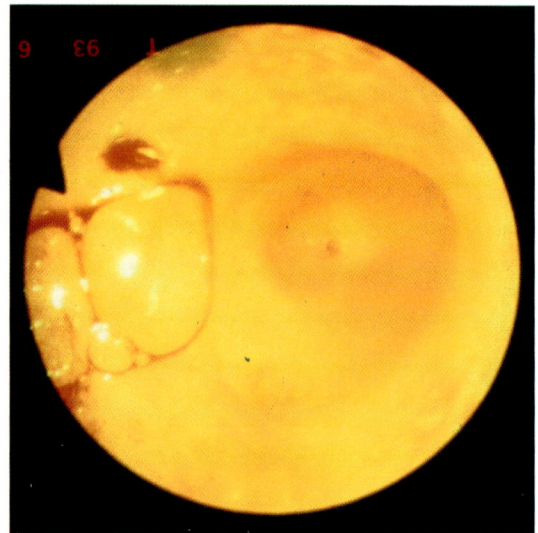

Figure 8

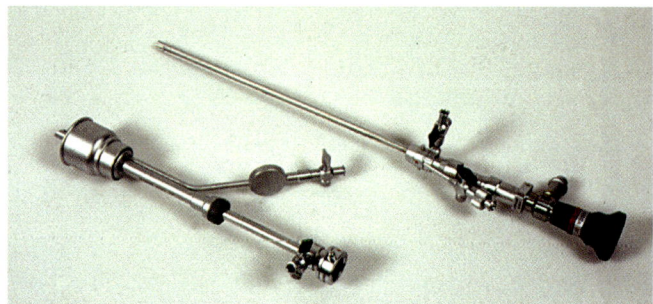

CF hysteroscopes are especially suitable for low viscosity fluids such as sorbitol 5%, glycine 1.5%, or dextrose 5%.

CF hysteroscopy will provide for a very clear image during the whole procedure (Figure 9). Blood or cervical mucus will not obscure the image because of the rapid flow of the distension medium in front of the telescope. The irrigating fluid continuously flushes the tip of the telescope and cloudy fluid is evacuated through the separate outflow channel. The telescope consists of a 3- or 4-mm 30° fore-oblique viewing angle.

Handle the telescope with great care and do not use a forceps with unprotected jaws to move the equipment as this could damage the instruments.

Immediately after the procedure the instruments must be thoroughly cleaned before autoclave sterilization. The hysteroscope should be completely submerged in a neutral detergent. The working channel and the inflow and outflow channels must be flushed with pressure; for example, with a waterpistol or a syringe (Figure 10).

After cleaning the instruments must be stored in a special container for sterilization of the telescopes. Dropping the telescope can result in distorted pictures due to lens fractures or fluid leakage into the telescope.

All moving parts of the surgical instruments must be cleaned meticulously and be checked regularly (Figure 11). Taking good care of your instruments will protect patients against unsuccessful procedures.

CONCLUSION

It is obvious that the main difference between hysteroscopy under general anesthesia and an ambulatory hysteroscopy is the fact that the patient will be aware of the whole procedure and all additional activities and discussions. This requires a different attitude from both the physician and the assisting personnel.

FURTHER READING

Wamsteker K. Hysteroscopy. In: Brosens I, Wamsteker K, eds. Diagnostic Imaging and Endoscopy in Gynecology: A Practical Guide. London: WB Saunders, 1997.

Wamsteker K. Organisation of a hysteroscopic theatre set up and staff.. HTC-NL Syllabus, 1991.

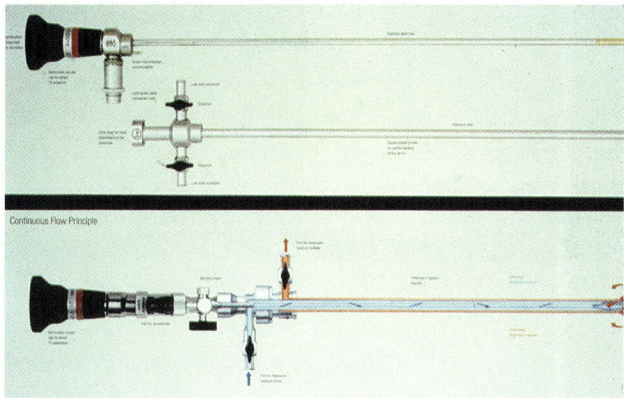

Figure 9

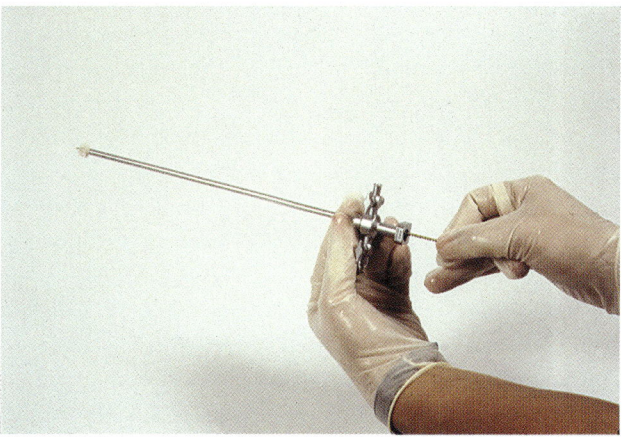

Figure 10

33 Patients' compliance with small diameter scope size

B.J. van Herendael

> **Take Home Message**
> The learning curve to perform diagnostic outpatient hysteroscopy is very steep and does not influence the attitude of the patients. If scopes <3 mm in outer diameter are used, the procedure is still valuable from a clinical point of view as it allows for a diagnosis but is also very well tolerated by the nonprepared patient. The distension medium of choice for small barrel hysteroscopes is liquid medium, as all the problems arising from nonfunctional distension are due to the use of CO_2. Saline provided with a drip is the liquid of choice.

Over a period of three and a half years office hysteroscopy was performed in 279 patients. The hysteroscopies were performed by a first- and a second-year registrar in gynecology under one-to-one supervision of a senior consultant in endoscopic surgery. The patients were seen in the outpatient department and a history was taken if there were any complaints that could warrant an inspection of the cavity [1]. Hysteroscopy was performed immediately after the routine gynecologic examination with a single fiberscope; maximal outer diameter including the sheath was 2.9 mm [2]. The aim was to see what the compliance of the patients would be for this invasive diagnostic procedure. In the early 1990s we used 6-mm diagnostic scopes, the Hamou I scope (Karl Storz, Tütlingen, Germany). A speculum was used to expose the cervix, no tenaculum was used. We never used local anesthesia or any other drug [3]. We observed that a great number of patients had some problems, mostly a sharp pain at the time the progression of the scope reached the upper part of the endocervical canal. This led to stopping the procedure in some 20% of the patients and shortening of the diagnostic procedure in another 15%. If the procedure had to be stopped without being able to perform an eye-directed biopsy the patients had then to be booked for an inpatient hysteroscopy under general anesthesia. Therefore smaller diameter scopes were tried out, and in order to assess the learning curve the procedure was performed by a junior member of staff.

MATERIALS AND METHODS

The patient was installed in the litothomy position as for a classic gynecological examination on a classic gynecological chair. The chair can be maneuvered electrically to alter the height and can be put in the Trendelenburg position by means of a foot-switch. The idea is to position the chair in such a way that the examiner is comfortable and so that the examiner and the patient are able to see the video screen at all times. A Collins speculum was introduced into the vagina to visualize the cervix [4]. The cervix was rinsed with saline and carefully wiped dry with a swab. The single fiberscope (Karl Storz, Tuttlingen, Germany) was an experimental model featuring 0° vision (Figure 1). A camera was attached to the scope. We used a single-chip camera (Telecam®, Karl Storz) (Figure 2). The modern

Figure 1
Single fiberscope (Karl Storz, Tuttlingen, Germany); experimental model featuring 0° vision, a camera was attached to the scope.

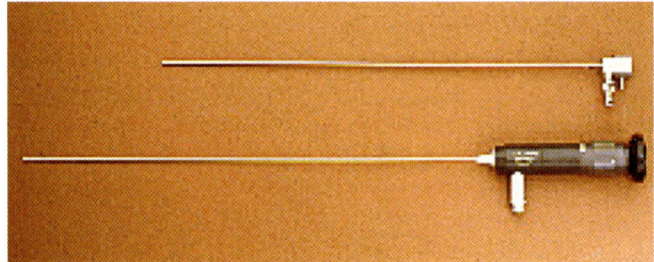

Figure 2
Single-chip camera (Telecam®, Karl Storz).

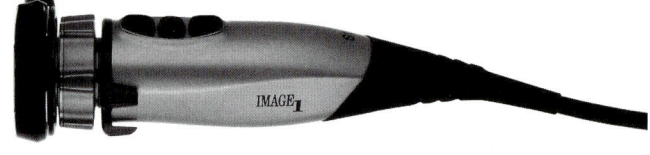

digital cameras are more adapted to the collection of data. Analog cameras tend to lose too much information, especially in fiberscopes. Light was provided by a xenon light source 500° Kelvin (Karl Storz) (Figure 3). CO_2 distension was obtained by an automatic hysteroflator according to Hamou (Karl Storz) (Figure 4).

A saline drip was always available and was prepared in the vicinity if the gas distension was insufficient to obtain a good distension. The fluid container, a bag containing 1 liter of saline, was positioned some 110 cm above the level of the couch. The scope was positioned at the level of the ectocervix to obtain a panoramic view. After light and gas were turned on the scope was advanced through the cervical canal under direct vision. The opening of the cervical canal was kept in the middle of the video screen by maneuvering the hands externally. The scope was gently advanced following the mucus stream into the cavity. The cavity was inspected. An analog visual scale from 0 to 10 was used to evaluate the discomfort of the patient, the ease of the procedure for the examiner, and the clarity of the image.

Figure 3
Xenon light source 500° Kelvin (Karl Storz).

Figure 4
Hamou automatic hysteroflator (Karl Storz).

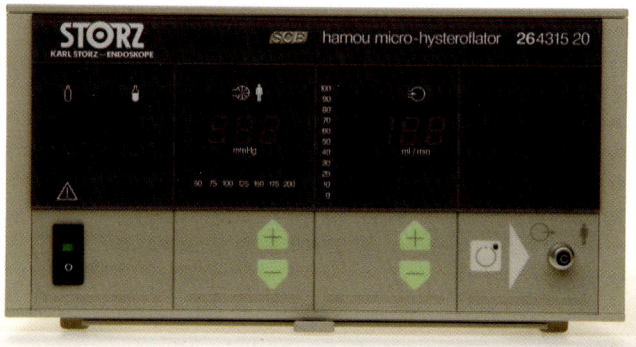

Indications, summarized in Table 1, were mainly abnormal uterine bleeding.

The age of the patients varied from 18 to 75 years. There was no correlation between age and discomfort in any of the patients. In all, 279 patients were examined in the study and of these 184 did not experience any discomfort at all during the entire procedure. Four patients did experience discomfort at the end of the hysteroscopy. Sixty-eight patients experienced marked discomfort at the passage of the cervical canal at the level of the isthmus and scored level 2 in the scale from 0 (no discomfort) to 10 (extreme discomfort). Five patients had extreme discomfort at the start of the procedure, making it impossible to continue, and scored 10. Eighteen patients scored from 3 through to 9, mostly due to abdominal cramping caused by the gas flowing through the tubes into the abdomen.

The clarity of vision was scored at the first attempt (with CO_2 distension). The image quality was scored on a scale from 0 (no visibility) to 10 (very good image). The image quality was scored 190 times at 10 and 46 times at 9 (partially hazy). On only 12 occasions the score was 0, no vision; 12 times the vision was scored between 8 and 6 (fair); and five times at 5 (fair but only just enough to make a visual diagnosis). Two patients scored 3, four scored 2 and one scored 1 (visual image insufficient to make a proper diagnosis). We missed one complete septum, an obvious diagnosis with classic hysteroscopy, in this series of patients. In all these patients the lack of distension due to the sole use of CO_2 was the reason for the poor score and the diagnosis was easy to correct once saline was used as a distension medium in the patients who scored 5 or less. In the one patient whose score was 1 the score was changed to 10 just by using liquid distension medium

Table 1
Indications for hysteroscopy

Indications	%
AUB	28.61
Previous surgery	10.14
Check med	7.24
IUCD	3.98
Failed IVFET	1.44
Abdominal discomfort	1.44
Dysmenorrhea	1.08
Check sonography	0.72

The feasibility or the ease of performing the procedure scored very high on an analog scale from 0 to 10: i.e. 0, no difficulties; 10, impossible to perform the hysteroscopy with CO_2 distension. In all, 199 examinations scored 0, and 42 scored 1. Twelve examinations scored 10, the procedure was not possible with gas distension owing to nondilatation of the cervical canal in menopausal patients. Keep in mind that gas distension was used, and a speculum was used to visualize the cervix. Nine examinations scored 8, 7, or 6; five examinations scored 5 and the other examinations were very difficult – three scored 4, one scored 3, and seven scored 2.

Table 2
Levels of discomfort experienced by patients (0, no discomfort; 10 extreme discomfort)

Discomfort score	Number of patients
0	184/279
1	4/279
2	68/279
3	5/279
4	5/279
5	4/279
6	3/279
7	0/279
8	0/279
9	1/279
10	5/279

Table 3
Scores for clarity of vision with CO_2 distension

Clarity of vision	Number of patients
10	199/279
9	46/279
8	1/279
7	9/279
6	2/279
5	5/279
4	0/279
3	2/279
2	4/279
1	1/279
0	12/279

Table 3
Scores for feasibility of examination

Feasibility score	Number of patients
10	199/279
9	42/279
8	3/279
7	1/279
6	5/279
5	5/279
4	3/279
3	2/279
2	7/279
1	0/279
0	12/279

CONCLUSION

For too many years outpatient hysteroscopy has been perceived as too daunting by many gynecologists, mainly for three reasons. The first is the gynecologist's fear of inflicting pain on their patients [5]. This reason was linked closely to the second reason, the apprehension of the gynecologist at not to being able to perform the examination on an outpatient basis with the patient awake, witnessing and judging the performance. Besides these major reasons there was a third reason related to the optics of the scopes – it was considered that they were not small enough to pass through the cervical canal without anesthesia or that when the scopes were small enough the optical quality was not adequate for an appropriate diagnosis. The optical quality is related to the diameter and until recently there were physical limitations, closely linked to the mechanics of the instrument production, to the reduction in diameter of the classic Hopkins rod lens system. However, excellent small diameter diagnostic scopes (2.9 mm including the sheath) are now available; hence these are even smaller than the scope used in the study described above.

Fiberoptics were the solution to this limitation [1]. The single fiberoptic was an experimental scope to prove that single fiber and reduced diameter gave good results in the sense that images can be obtained that are good enough for clinical diagnosis. We could prove that patients comply with the procedure when performed with a small diameter hysteroscope even if they are not mentally prepared for the procedure. Small diameter hysteroscopy, so-called 'ultra mini hysteroscopy', offers a solution to two of the three reasons that held gynecologists back from performing hysteroscopy in an outpatient set up [6], i.e. the fear of inflicting pain on their patients and the fear that ultra small diameter scopes do not offer sufficiently good images to make a clinical diagnosis. The diameter was so small that we were able to prove this point with our current study, 252 0f the 279 patients experienced no or only very slight discomfort. The fact that it was not possible to link discomfort to the age of the patients indicates that the problem of causing discomfort to the patient is procedure-related rather than due to the condition of the uterus in the different age categories. In this series the major reason for discomfort was CO_2 distension. When the uterus is distended with saline at a low distension pressure the level of discomfort is greatly reduced. It should be noted that the fiberscopes have no fore-oblique lens and that the direction of the vision is 0° degrees. This physical aspect requires more and greater external maneuverability. With a speculum in place and a young inexperienced physician holding the scope this is more difficult than the classic procedure and could more easily lead to the patient experiencing discomfort. It has been proved that eliminating the speculum and using the vagina as a first distension chamber more or less eliminates the discomfort. Indeed when the vagina is used as first chamber a pair of small scissors can be used to open up stenosed cervices without the patient feeling any discomfort.

The fact that local anesthesia can be avoided by using the ultra small diameters reduces the procedure time. The omission of paracervical or cervical anesthesia also reduces the discomfort, as the patients do not have to feel the initial sting and the pain caused by the tissue being dilated by the anesthetic agent.

As regards the technique there is one minus point. The distension of the uterine cavity is more difficult than in classic hysteroscopy, as there is more backflow. The distension medium leaks alongside the outer sheath of the scope in the cervical canal. This is another reason for using the vagina, the vaginoscopic technique, as a first chamber. So if a pump system is used the pressure settings should be adapted and are not the same as for the classic hysteroscopy. When using the Hamou Hysteromat® (Karl Storz GmbH Tütlingen Germany) we use a pressure of 100 mmHg with a flow of 400 ml when dilating the vagina and once in the isthmus the pressure is reduced to 50 mmHg. Keep in mind that the pressures given are an indication only, as the pump has some problems in detecting the exact pressure at the tip of the ultra small diameter scopes.

The single fiberoptics produce a good enough image for anatomic, macroscopic diagnoses in all cases where the distension of the cavity is adequate. Gross disorders related to pathophysiology such as the chronic endometritis 'strawberry' pattern and advanced adenomyotic lesions are detectable [7]. Because we did extensive work on the physiology and pathophysiology of the endometrium with the classical 6-mm diameter hysteroscopes with 30° fore-oblique lenses it was a disappointment not to be able to perform contact hysteroscopy with enlargements to assess the state of the endometrium [8] owing to the physical properties of the fiber. Therefore, in recent years when the ultra small diameter Hopkins rod lens system became available we changed to these scopes.

As quality of vision is directly related to the distension there is a case for advising beginners to use low molecular weight liquid distension media, and the easiest to use is normal saline solution. As an ionic solution there is not so much potential danger of producing TURP syndrome, as it contains sodium, but large amounts in the circulation of the patient will create a dangerous situation. There is certainly no case for persevering with CO_2 distension if the distension is difficult [9,10].

Stenosis of the cervix is the one difficult situation. Before the advent of vaginoscopy these patients had to be operated under general anesthesia so as to be able to dilate the outer cervix and the cervical canal. When vaginoscopy is performed the stenosis can be overcome by using small scissors to cut into the ectocervix to open a path for the scope. This manipulation is painless for the patient. The difficult cervical stenoses are not those at the level of the ectocervix but stenosis of the mid or high portion of the canal, mainly due to previous curettages or caesarean sections. These can also be mastered by using a pair of more sturdy scissors and again in this case the patient will not feel the manipulation even if she watches the screen.

REFERENCES

1. Emmanuel MH, Wamsteker K, Lammers FB. Is dilatation and curettage obsolete for diagnosing intrauterine disorders in the premenopausal patients with persistent abnormal uterine bleeding. *Acta Obstet Gynecol Scand* 1997; **76**: 65–68.

2. van Herendael BJ, Beretta P, Mei L, Pansini N, Bettocchi S. Fibrescopes in outpatient hysteroscopy. *Ital J Gynaecol Obstet* 1997; **9**: 76–79.

3. Cicinelli E, Didonna T, Ambrosia G, Schonauer LM, Fiore G, Matteo MG. Topical anaesthesia for diagnostic hysteroscopy and endometrial biopsy in postmenopausal women: a randomised placebo-controlled double-blind study. *Br J Obstet Gynaecol* 1997; **104**: 316–319.

4. Bettocchi S, Selvaggi L. A vaginoscopic approach to reduce the pain in office hysteroscopy. *J Am Assoc Gynecol Laparosc* 1997; **4**: 255–258.

5. Belligham FR. Outpatient hysteroscopy problems. *Aust NZ J Obstet Gynecol* 1997; **37**: 202–205

6. Lin BL, Iwata Y, Liu KH, Valle RF. The Fujinon diagnostic fibre optic hysteroscope: experience with 1.503 patients. *J Reprod Med Obstet Gynecol* 1990; **35**: 885–889.

7. Cravello L, Porcu G, D`Ercole C, Roger V, Blanc B. Identification and treatment of endometritis. *Contracept Fertil Sex* 1997; **25**: 585–586.

8. Penney G, Valle L, Souter V, Templeton A. Endometrial assessment procedures: an audit of current practice in Scotland. *Hum Reprod* 1997; **12**: 2041–2045.

9. Brooks PG. Venous air embolism during operative hysteroscopy. *J Am Assoc Gynecol Laparosc* 1997; **4**: 399–402.

10. Corson SL. Hysteroscopic fluid management. *J Am Assoc Gynecol Laparosc* 1997; **4**: 375–379.

Counseling patients

Chris Van de Mosselaer

> **Take Home Message**
> It is not necessary for the counselor to be medically educated, as he or she mostly acts as the 'go-between' in the patient–doctor relationship. A visit to the doctor's office is always stressful for the patient. The patient needs communication and attention for various practical issues and special care for her emotions. Unlike men, women tend to want to exchange ideas and feelings, mostly with other women, before making decisions. This is especially so for operative procedures, such as hysteroscopic sterilization. The counselor should have a high degree of empathic capacity and needs to be as 'open' as possible to any kind of question or situation and should know exactly what is going on, before, during, and after the procedure. Time and body language are the key issues.

The presence of a counselor can be of great importance.

It is said that counseling is *'a practice or professional service designed to guide an individual to a better understanding of his problems and potentialities by utilising modern psychological principles and methods especially in collecting history data, using various techniques of the personal interview and testing interests and aptitudes'* (Webster, 1981)

So it is understood that it is not necessary for a counselor to be medically educated, as he or she mostly acts as the 'go-between' in the patient–doctor relationship.

Most of the time, the doctor (gynecologist) is concentrating on the technical or clinical aspects of the problem that is presented. A visit to the doctor's office is always a significant event for the patient, especially when it concerns the basic elements of a person's being.

The patient needs communication, conversation, feedback, and attention for various practical issues and special care as regards emotions involved in the visit. Also, the doctor does not have enough time to talk to all patients extensively, even though they would sometimes want to do so.

Women – as opposed to men – tend to want to exchange ideas or feelings more, mostly with other women before making decisions, or because they want to exchange information on particular minor or major operations. When these operations affect the basic essence of their womanhood, they are even more cautious.

Hence, it is practical, advisable, or even preferable, to have a person who is very close to the doctor and who knows his skills and behavior, and at the same time takes the time to listen to the patient. This person can be a nurse (e.g. in a hospital environment), a personal assistant to the doctor (e.g. in the private office) or a trainee.

The higher the educational level of the patient, the more she tends to want to talk about the problem or her questions with the counselor, because she is used to looking for alternatives, advantages, or disadvantages, or just to discuss or exchange ideas.

Less educated women tend to consider the doctor as the sole source of information.

Before the visit to the doctor's office, women may be nervous. This is especially the case for a first gynecological visit to a particular doctor, for check-up visits when tests have been performed, or when an operation has been performed and the patient needs to come back for a check-up. It is therefore *very important* to treat the patient as an individual, certainly not as a number, however crowded the office may be.

At a first visit, then the patient certainly needs to be put at ease and her possible fears regarding the doctor and/or the clinical investigation should be reduced or removed.

Also, practical issues appear when an operation is due to take place; depending on the personal situation of the patient, various issues have to be dealt with.

a) All women will ask themselves some similar questions in direct relation to their womanhood:

- Does this affect my looks? Will people see what happened to me?
- Will I still be attractive to my partner?
- Will I feel differently afterwards?
- Will this operation affect my emotional or sex life?

Those questions are – almost always – for the doctor in person. However, it is also possible that the patient will ask the counselor these questions.

b) Married women or women with a regular partner have, as compared with women who are single, other preoccupations, mostly linked to their family situation:

- How long will I be away?
- What kind of hospital am I going to?
- Who will help me with registration, room reservation, etc.?
- What documents do I need for insurance, health, etc.?
- What can I do about my children? Who will take care of them?

c) Single women with no children have less practical questions about their home situation, as they mostly live alone and seem more independent. When they do have children, they have similar questions to those in above-mentioned category.

d) Working women have a supplementary dimension to take care of:

- How long will I be away from work?
- Is it normal or acceptable to talk about this operation with colleagues at work?
- Will my professional performance be influenced by what is going to happen?

But there is more: as doctors, under some national legislation, are not allowed to advertise, they sometimes have no influence on patients' behavior concerning visits and/or check-ups.

Hence, an important role for the counselor seems to be to make the patient conscious of the importance of a regular check-up. One very often meets patients who have not visited a doctor for quite a while and are suddenly confronted with a major problem or disease.

Last, but certainly not least, the counselor should have a high degree of *empathic capacity*, and needs to be as 'open' and as flexible as possible for any kind of question or situation. Statistically patients come from all groups of the population, varying from highly qualified to 'uneducated' in the traditional sense. They all need to be treated equally, i.e. on the level they know and are used to.

The openness of the counselor will undoubtedly have an influence on the patient and her behavior, both in general and in terms of her attitude towards the doctor and the techniques and/or operation(s). The counselor can act correctively, if it appears that the patient has inappropriate expectations.

The communication process between patient and counselor will result in a better understanding of the patient and her preoccupations, and hence the doctor can be informed about important or general aspects he was not aware of following the regular (rather short) visit in the office (Figure 1).

CONCLUSION

We can say that the role of the counselor is:

- To make time for the patient, and to make sure that she is at ease.
- To listen carefully, and to use the right body language. When the counselor is nervous, the patient will be even more nervous.
- And, to ask open questions ('How do you feel?' rather than 'Do you feel well?')

Figure 1
Communication scheme.

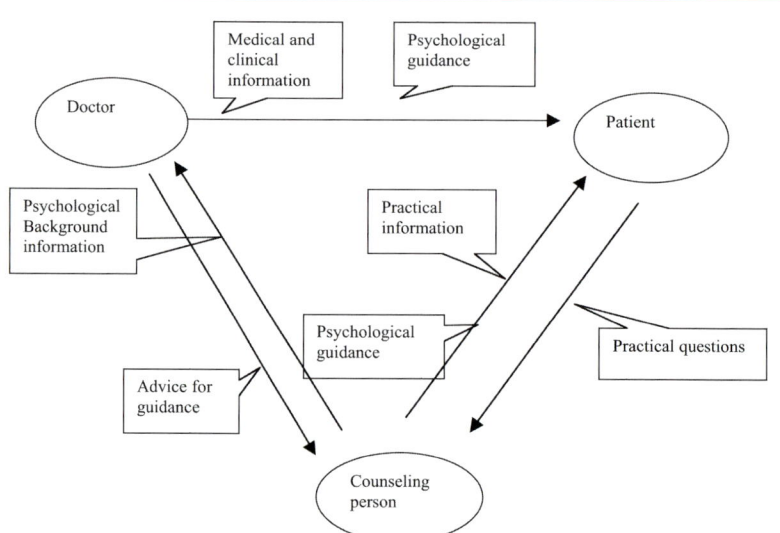

Part V
Epilogue

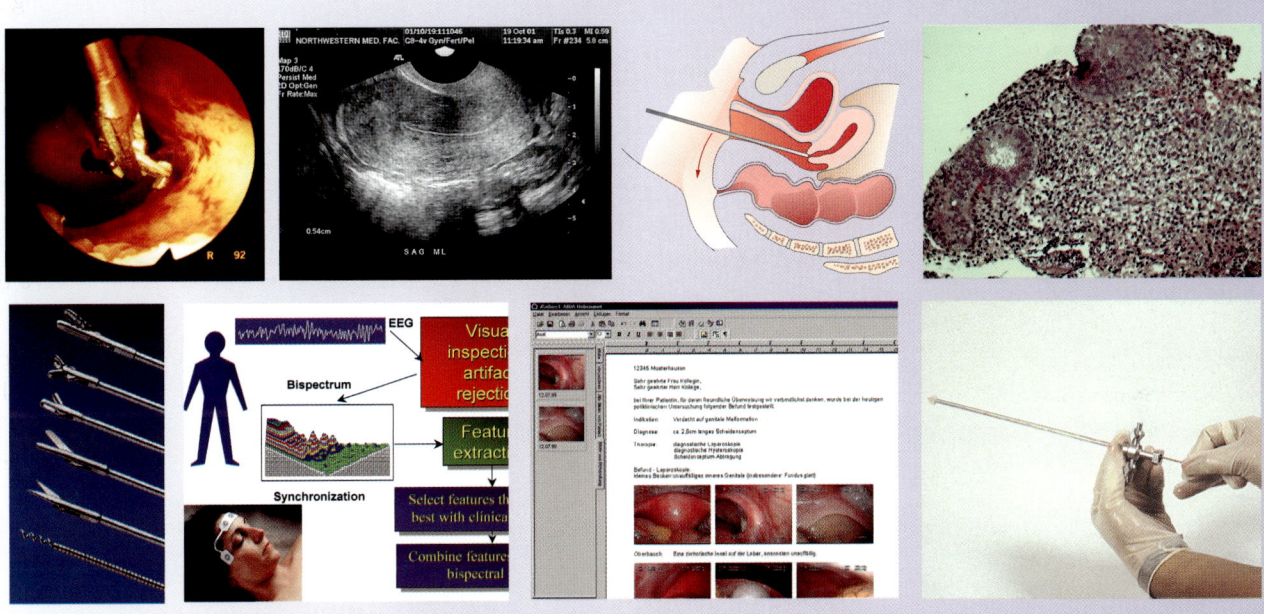

Ambulatory hysteroscopy

The task of gathering together an international group of well-known hysteroscopists to put together and describe their experience in a comprehensive manual is not easy. However, with dedication and cooperation the difficult task becomes easier. We have attempted to offer this unique volume as the text and atlas on the state-of-the-art of ambulatory hysteroscopy, be it diagnostic or therapeutic. We have assembled the different chapters into a comprehensive, logical, and unified volume to guide physicians sequentially in reviewing, understanding, and adapting the most up-to-date information on this exciting field of intrauterine viewing, thus facilitating the diagnosis and treatment of diseases that may affect women. The volume has been specifically geared to procedures performed in an office setting, however, many of the thoughts, guidelines, and new approaches can also be extended to the performance of hysteroscopy in a hospital setting under regional or general anesthesia. We certainly hope that this contribution will serve as a guideline for physicians interested in the subject. We also hope that this publication will add another step in the solid establishment of hysteroscopy as an important method of diagnosis and treatment of uterine conditions that no gynecologists should be able to ignore in their daily practice. Thus all patients requesting this approach can benefit and clinicians can facilitate their treatment and recovery.

Rafael F. Valle
Bruno J. van Herendael
Stefano Bettocchi

Index

Indexer: Dr Laurence Errington

abdominal cavity, endometrial cancer cell dissemination during hysteroscopy into, 107-8
abdominal pain syndrome, 52
accreditation, 209-10
    Australia, 202-7
    Europe, 193
    Far East, 208
    principal guideline promoters, 193
    USA, 190-1
acid—base balance, CO_2 distension, 43
ACMI Slimline™ operative hysteroscope for tubal occlusion with ESSURE insert, 145
adenomyosis, 103-4
adhesions/synechiae (intrauterine), 80-1, 137-8
    cutting/dividing, 23, 137-8
    interpretation of visual appearance, 102-3
    saline infusion sonography, 80-1
adrenaline, 154, 155
adverse events *see* complications
age and endometrial carcinoma risk with abnormal uterine bleeding, 120
allergic reactions, 154, 156
amenorrhea, self-retaining hysteroscope, 52
American Accreditation College/Council, 195, 196
American College of Obstetrics and Gynecology (ACOG), credentialing and the, 188-9
American Society of Reproductive Medicine, 186, 189
analgesia in sedation/anesthesia, 155
anaphylactic shock, 156
anesthesia, 116, 152-6
    general, 155
    learning/training, 184
    local *see* local anesthesia
    semi-rigid hysteroscopy, 10
anxiolysis with sedatives, 155
anxious/nervous patients, 34, 222
archiving, 211-15
Asia, training, 208
atrophy, endometrial, 101, 120, 121
    saline infusion sonography, 77
Australia, training, 202-7, 209, 210
autoclavable hysteroscopes, 162

bacterial cultures, 89
Bettocchi office hysteroscope 2-mm, 27
biopsies (and microbiopsies), 110-23
    blind, 117, 118
    forceps for *see* forceps
    information to be given
        to clinician, 121
        to pathologist, 120-1

    pathologist's point of view, 117-23
    Pipelle, 70-1, 117, 118
    with self-retaining hysteroscope, 47
    site selection, 119
    targeted/directed, 112, 114, 119-20, 137
        reliability, 114
    see also histology; sampling
bipolar systems (and electrodes), 10, 131-4, 141-2
    new operating system simulating, 128-9
bispectral analysis, 156-8
bleeding
    abnormal uterine (AUB), 84, 171
        age and endometrial carcinoma risk with, 120
        contraindicating hysteroscopy, 57
        indicating hysteroscopy, 55
        postmenopausal *see* postmenopausal women
        self-retaining hysteroscope, 52
        see also spotting
    in fibroid resection, 206
blood vessels *see* vasculature
Bodedex, 163
body position *see* position
brush cytology, 112

camera *see* digital recording systems; video photography
cancer (incl. carcinoma), cervical, contraindicating hysteroscopy, 57
cancer (incl. carcinoma), endometrial, 22, 22, 94-5, 104-5
    age and risk of, with abnormal uterine bleeding, 120
    contraindicating hysteroscopy, 57
    cytology (directed), 112
    interpretation of visual appearance, 104-5
    peritoneal dissemination during hysteroscopy, 107-8
    saline infusion sonography in, 80
        risk of spread, 76
    steroid receptors and, 94-5
Capture Station, Fotomaster, 217
carbon dioxide gas (distension with), 42-3
    complications, 38, 205
    insufflator *see* insufflator
    nurse's role, 36-7, 224
    patient explanation, 34
    self-retaining hysteroscope, 48-9, 51
    semi-rigid hysteroscopy, 9
    small diameter hysteroscopy, 227
    tolerance and security evaluation, 43
carcinoma *see* cancer
cardiac effects of local anesthetics, 154, 155

cardiovascular support with local anesthetic toxicity, 156
CD recorder, 23
cell (endometrial) transportation during hysteroscopy, 107-8
central nervous system, excitatory effects of local anesthetics, 154, 155
    drugs reducing, 156
cervical canal (progression inside and examination of)
    in classical approach, 40
    flexible hysteroscope, 14
    self-retaining hysteroscope, 50
        problems, 47
    stenosis, 152
        small diameter hysteroscopy in, 229
    vaginoscopical approach, 40
cervical os, internal (ICO), diameter limiting surgery, 141
cervix
    cancer contraindicating hysteroscopy, 57
    diagnostic inspection techniques
        comparisons, 178-9
        possible options, 182
    lacerations, 38
    surgery, flexible hysteroscopy following, 16
chair, 3-5, 29
    small diameter hysteroscopy, 226
charge-coupled device (CCD), 20, 211
chemical disinfectants, required properties, 168
China, training, 208
chloride concentrations in distension fluids, 126
Chorionscope (Hamou III), 26
Circon diagnostic flexible scope, 20, 21
cleaning of instruments, 163, 167, 225
coagulation necrosis, 122
codes and coding
    procedural *see* procedures
    reference sources for, 177
    reimbursement, 173-4
cold light source *see* light source
color Doppler, 72
color elements of digital images, 217
colposcopy compared with other diagnostic techniques, 179
communication process (counselor–patient–doctor), 232
competency, levels of, 186
compliance (incl. tolerance of discomfort), 116
    with small diameter scopes, 226-30
complications (adverse events), 38, 57-8, 204-5
    distension media, 31, 125-8, 201, 204-5

ESSURE insert for tubal sterilization, 150
glutaraldehyde, 168, 169
local anesthetics (and their treatment), 154, 155, 156
saline infusion sonography, 76
see also emergency situations; safety precautions
computed tomography, 182
computers (for image capture and archiving), 211-12
computer-based systems, 212-14, 217
conception, retained products of, 103
Conceptus ESSURE micro-insert *see* ESSURE micro-insert
congenital uterine anomalies, 178
3D-ultrasound, 72
consequences, 178
interpretation of visual appearance, 102
connective adhesions, 102, 103
continuous flow and pressure (distension fluid), 30, 31, 37, 224-5
contraindications (outpatient hysteroscopy), 7-8, 55-6, 222
absolute, 7, 56
relative, 7, 57
contrast sonohysterography, saline *see* saline infusion sonohysterography
coordination in space, 197-8
costs (economic), 170
equipment, 175-6
opportunity costs, 174-5
saline infusion sonography, 82
see also fees; reimbursement
couch, 3-5
counseling, 231-2
see also information
CPT (Current Procedural Terminology), 170, 172-3, 173, 174
credentialing, USA, 188-9, 190-1
crocodile forceps, 110, 111, 141
cultures, microbial, 89
Current Procedural Terminology (CPT), 170, 172-3, 173, 174
cystic polyps, 101-2
cytology, endometrial
algorithm, 115
directed, 112

D&C, 117, 118
decidual tissue, retained, 103
decontamination, Europe, 163
Desormeaux's apparatus, xv, 50
dextran 70, 29%, 31
dextrose 5% solutions, 126
diagnostic hysteroscopy
indications, 55, 204
outpatient service *see* outpatient service
procedural code 58555 for, 172
training in Europe, 201
diagnostic outpatient service *see* outpatient service
diagnostic techniques/applications (in general)

for cervical and uterine cavity approaches, comparisons, 178-83
learning, 184
didactic phase in training, 190
digital recording systems, 211, 214, 217, 218
fibrohysteroscopy, 13
single fiberscope, 226-7
dilatation and curettage (D&C), 117, 118
discharge (of patient), instructions, 33, 35
disinfection
high-level, 167-8
preparation for, 167
distension media, 31, 42-5, 138
complications, 31, 125-8, 201, 204-5
conventional hysteroscopy, 5
flexible hysteroscopy, 15-16
fluid as *see* fluid
gas as *see* carbon dioxide gas
nurse's role, 36-7, 223-4
patient information, 34
semi-rigid hysteroscopy, 8-9
small diameter hysteroscopy, 229
training, 201
for tubal sterilization, 144
doctor *see* physician
documentation and record-keeping, 211-19
reimbursement and, 171, 174
Doppler, color and power, 72
drugs *see specific (types of) drugs*
drying of instruments, 167
DVD burners, 211-12

E/M (Evaluation and Management) services, 171, 173-4
economic costs *see* costs
EEG, bispectral analysis, 156-8
EGF receptors, 95-6
electrodes, bipolar *see* bipolar systems
electroencephalogram (EEG), bispectral analysis, 156-8
electrolytes (in distension fluids)
disturbances, 125-8, 205
physiologic considerations, 124-5
electronic pump *see* pump
electronic storage of images, 217-18
electronic variable pressure/variable flow insufflator, 42-3
electrosurgery/electrical instruments, 131-5, 141-2
embryo transfer (ET), 17, 60
emergency situations, 38
see also complications; safety precautions
empathy, counselor, 232
employment, questions asked by women in, 232
endocervical polyp, self-retaining hysteroscope examination, 53
Endomat®, Hamou, 44, 45
endometrioid carcinoma, 94, 95
endometritis, 89-91, 101
endometrium
ablation
in Australia, 202, 203
fluid overload risk for, 128

anatomical observations, 84-92
atrophy *see* atrophy
cancer *see* cancer
cell transportation during hysteroscopy, 107-8
in flexible hysteroscopy
cyclical appearance, 16
suspect area evaluation, 14-15
functional changes, 100-1
height, evaluation, 99
hyperplasia *see* hyperplasia
hypertrophy, 100
hypotrophy, 100-1
in menstrual cycle *see* menstrual cycle
in menstrual disorders, saline infusion sonography, 75
pathology *see* pathology
polyps *see* polyps
preparation with GnRH analogs, 128
pseudofunctional dysvascular, 86-9
receptors, 93-8
resection in Australia, 205-6
sampling *see* sampling
specimen preparation and handling, 121
surface, evaluation, 99-100
in ultrasound, normal architecture, 66-7
energy sources, complications, 58
epidermal growth factor (EGF) receptors, 95-6
epinephrine, 154, 155
equipment/instruments/hardware (other than hysteroscope), 29-31, 32-3, 110-16, 223-5
care and maintenance of
Europe, 162-5
USA, 166-9
for cleaning/disinfection/sterilization, 163
conventional hysteroscopy, 5
costs, 175-6
flexible hysteroscopy, 13, 23
nurse's role, 35-6, 223-5
operative hysteroscopy, mechanical *see* mechanical instruments
semi-rigid hysteroscopy, 8-9
training and, 196
see also specific equipment
c-erbB2 receptors, 96, 96-7
ESSURE micro-insert (STOP device), 138, 143-51
clinical results, 148-9
description of insert, 143
evaluation
histological, 147-8
in pre-hysterectomy study, 146
technique of insertions and deployment, 144-5
estrogen receptors, endometrial, 93
cancer and, 95
EGF receptors and, 96
ethylene oxide (ETO) gas, 167, 168
Europe
equipment and instrument care and maintenance, 162-5
training in, 189, 190, 192-202, 210

European Society of Human Reproduction and Embryology (ESHRE) and training, 189, 190
European Society of Hysteroscopy classification, intracavitary fibroid, 206
Evaluation and Management (E/M) services, 171, 173-4
evidence-based medicine
   diagnostic techniques compared for inspection of cervical and uterine cavity, 178-83
   reimbursement issues and, 170-1

fallopian tubes
   occluded, cannulation, 137, 138
   occlusion for sterilization *see* ESSURE micro-insert
   patency, saline (contrast) sonography, 70, 82
Far East, training, 208
fees, 170-1, 171
   reference sources, 177
fertility problems (infertility/subfertility), 17, 60-4
   congenital uterine anomalies associated with, 178
   self-retaining hysteroscope, 52
fiberscope/fiberoptic hysteroscope (in fibrohysteroscopy), 13, 19-20, 26, 135
   development, 25
   progression inside cervical canal, 14
   Storz single fiberscope, 226
   withdrawal, 15
fibrohysteroscopy, 112
   author's preferred equipment, 13
   development, 12
   National French Survey, 116
fibroids *see* leiomyomas
fibrous polyps, 102
fixation of specimens, 121
flexible scopes, 12-24, 32
   equipment/instrumentation, 13, 23
   features and benefits, 112
   historical development, xiv, 12
   mechanical construction, 19-20
   microbiopsies and, 112
   for operative hysteroscopy *see* operative hysteroscopy
   special cases, 16-17
   types available, 20-1
      diagnostic, 20
      operative, 21
flow (distension media)
   with fluid media, continuous (and continuous pressure), 30, 31, 37, 224-5
   with gas (CO_2)
      with self-retaining hysteroscope, 48-9
      variable, 42-3
fluid, distension, 31, 37, 43-4, 124-30, 138
   complications, 31, 125-8, 201, 204-5
   conventional hysteroscopy, 5
   flexible hysteroscopy, 15-16
   high viscosity *see* high viscosity

distension fluid
   low viscosity *see* low viscosity
distension fluid
   nurse's role, 36, 37, 223-4
   semi-rigid hysteroscopy, 8-9
   small diameter hysteroscopy, 229
   training, 201
   for tubal sterilization, 144
fluid overload, 125-7, 201, 205
   management, 127
   prevention, monitoring systems, 128
forceps
   biopsy, 23, 28, 110, 111, 113, 114, 136
      with self-retaining hysteroscope, 47
   grasping, 23, 28, 136, 141
foreign bodies, grasping forceps, 23, 28
formaldehyde (for sterilization), 50
Fotomaster System, 217, 219
France, National Survey, 116
Fujinon flexible scopes
   diagnostic, 20, 21
   operative, 21, 22
functional changes of endometrium, 100-1

gamete intrafallopian transfer (GIFT), 62
gas insufflation *see* carbon dioxide gas; insufflator
general anesthesia, 155
GIFT (gamete intrafallopian transfer), 62
glutaraldehyde, 164, 168-9
glycine 1.5% solutions, 125
   intravasation, 127
GnRH analogs, endometrial preparation, 128
gonadotropin-releasing hormone (GnRH) analogs, endometrial preparation, 128
grasp biopsy, 110
   compared with punch biopsy, 110
   forceps for, 23, 28, 136, 141
gravity pressure/gravity fall system, 30, 44
growth factors, endometrial effects, 95-7
Gynaescribe, 212

Hamou Endomat®, 44, 45
Hamou Hysteroflator (electronic insufflator), 42, 43, 227
Hamou I scope, 25, 26
Hamou II scope, 25, 26
Hamou III scope, 26
hardware *see* equipment
Health Communication Network (Australia) — Gynaescribe, 212
heart, local anesthetic effects, 154, 155
Her2 (c-erbB2) receptors, 96, 96-7
Hexanios G + R, 163
high viscosity distension fluid, 31
   physiologic considerations, 125
histology/histopathology, 115
   with ESSURE micro-insert device, 147-8
   infection and, 89, 90
   see also biopsies; pathology; sampling

historical development, xiv-xv, 2-3
   flexible scopes, xiv, 12
   rigid scopes, 25-6
   saline infusion sono(hystero)graphy, 74-5
hormone replacement therapy and flexible hysteroscopy, 17
hormone status, biopsies and, 114
hydrogen peroxide gas-plasma, 167, 168
hygienists, 163
hyperplasia, endometrial, 104
   carcinomas related/unrelated to, interpretation of visual appearance, 105
   interpretation of visual appearance, 104
   saline infusion sonography, 79
hypertrophy, endometrial, 100
hyponatremia, 125-7, 205
   management, 127-8
hypotrophy, endometrial, 100-1
hysterectomy, ESSURE insert study in patient requiring, 146
Hysteroflator (electronic insufflator), Hamou, 42, 43, 227
hysterography compared with other diagnostic techniques, 179-80
   cervical canal, 179
hysterosalpingography (HSG)
   contrast sonohysterosalpingography, tubal patency, 70
   in subfertility, 60, 61
   in tubal occlusion with ESSURE insert, 147
hysteroscopes
   autoclavable vs non-autoclavable, 162
   costs, 175
   fiberoptic *see* fiberscope
   flexible *see* flexible scopes
   historical development, xiv-xv, 2-3
   nurse's role, 36, 224-5
   rigid *see* rigid scopes
   self-retaining *see* self-retaining hysteroscope
   semi-rigid, 8

iatrogenic trauma, 38, 57-8
ICD-9, 170, 173
image archiving, 211-15
in vitro fertilization (uterine examination)
   failed, flexible hysteroscopy for, 17
   pre-IVF hysteroscopic examination, 60-4
      collected studies, 61-3
      importance, 60
      methods other than hysteroscopy, 60-1
indications (outpatient hysteroscopy), 7, 55-6, 99, 222, 227
   diagnostic hysteroscopy, 55, 204
   operative hysteroscopy *see* operative hysteroscopy
   self-retaining hysteroscope, 52
infection, uterine, 89-91
   not contraindicating hysteroscopy, 56-7

infertility *see* fertility
information/advice (patient), 231-2
    on discharge, 33, 35
    on distension media, 34
    on saline infusion sonography, postprocedure, 76
injury, iatrogenic, 38, 57-8
instruments *see* equipment
insufflation *see* carbon dioxide gas
insufflator (CO_2), 31, 224
    electronic variable pressure/variable flow, 42-3
    with self-retaining hysteroscope, 48-9
    small diameter hysteroscopy, 227
International classification of Diseases 9th revision, 170, 173
interventions *see* procedures
intramural (intracavitary) leiomyomas removal
    bipolar electrosurgery, 132-3, 133, 142
    European Society of Hysteroscopy classification, 206
    training in Australia, 203
    saline infusion sonography, 79
intramural region, manipulation, 153
intraperitoneal dissemination of endometrial cancer cells during hysteroscopy, 107-8
intrauterine devices (IUDs/IUCDs), lost/misplaced
    removal, 23, 28, 138
    self-retaining hysteroscope examination, 52
intrauterine pathology *see* uterine cavity; uterus
intravasation of distension fluid, 31, 125
    factors influencing, 126
    glycine 1.5%, 127
irrigation, pump for, 44
IUDs *see* intrauterine devices

Japan, training, 208

Korsolex NF, 164

laboratory experience for trainees, 190, 194
laser hysteroscopy, credentialing, 186
learning curve, 184-5, 203
leiomyomas (fibroids; myomas)
    biopsy, 114, 115
    interpretation of visual appearance, 102
    MRI, 68-70, 102
    removal/resection/myomectomy, 137, 206
        electrosurgery, 132-3, 133, 134, 142
        fluid overload avoidance, 126
        subfertile patients, 61-2
        training in Australia, 203, 206
    self-retaining hysteroscope examination, 53
    sonography, 67
        saline infusion, 68, 78, 81-2

light-guide cable, 30, 167, 223
light source (cold light), 30, 223
    care and maintenance, 166
    conventional hysteroscopy, 6
    fibrohysteroscopy, 13
    nurses and, 223
    self-retaining hysteroscope, 49
    semi-rigid hysteroscopy, 9
Lin
    giant forceps, 23
    sheaths, 23
liquid distension *see* distension
lithotomy position, 3
litigation, 210
local anesthesia, 153-4
    cervical stenosis, 152
    complications and their treatment, 154, 155, 156
    in small diameter hysteroscopy, avoidance, 229
low viscosity distension fluid, 31, 37
    physiologic considerations, 124-5
luteal phase *see* secretory phase

magnetic resonance imaging, 182
    leiomyomas, 68-70
malformations *see* congenital uterine anomalies
malignancy *see* cancer
mannitol 5% solutions, 125
mechanical instruments for operative hysteroscopy, 28, 135-9, 141
    advantages and disadvantages, 137
    ancillary, 135-6
    applications, 137-8
medico-legal issues, 210
menorrhagia, self-retaining hysteroscope, 53
menstrual cycle, endometrium during, 84-6, 99-100, 100
    flexible hysteroscopy, 16
    steroid receptors, 99
    timing of sampling, 119
    vascular pattern, 84, 89
menstrual disorders, saline infusion sono(hystero)graphy, clinical role, 75
menstruation, endometrium during, 86
metrorrhagia, flexible hysteroscopy, 16
microbial cultures, 89
microbiopsies *see* biopsies
microcolpohysteroscope, xiv-xv
micro-hysteroscopy, operative outpatient, 10
    see also mini endoscopes; small diameter (ultra mini) scopes
mini endoscopes (hysteroscopes), xiv-xv
    flexible hysteroscope, 12
    see also micro-hysteroscopy; small diameter (ultra mini) scopes
miscarriage, spontaneous and repeated, self-retaining hysteroscope, 52
Mochida flexible scopes
    diagnostic, 20, 21, 22
    operative, 21, 23
modular archiving systems, 214

monitoring systems, 156-8
    fluid overload prevention, 128
muscle relaxants with local anesthetic toxicity, 156
myofibrous synechiae/adhesions, 102, 103
myoma *see* leiomyoma
myomectomy *see* leiomyomas

National French Survey, 116
neu (c-erbB2) receptors, 96, 96-7
New Zealand, training, 209
non-steroidal anti-inflammatory drugs (NSAIDs), 153
Novak curette, 117, 118
nulliparous women, flexible hysteroscopy, 16
nurse, role, 34-9, 175, 222-5
nurse facilitator and semi-rigid hysteroscopy, 9

observational phase in training, 190
office *see* operating room
Olympus
    archiving system (rpSzene), 213-14
    flexible scopes
        diagnostic (HYF-FP/HYF-X2), 13, 20, 21, 112
        operative (HYF-IT), 21, 22
operating room (office) and its set up, 29
    conventional hysteroscopy, 3
    semi-rigid hysteroscopy, 8
    see also equipment
operative hysteroscopy, 109-62
    flexible scopes, 135
        types available, 21
    indications, 55-6, 140-1, 204
        in ambulatory surgery, 141
        in classic surgery, 140-1
        new, 143-51
    limitations, 55-6, 58, 140-1
        in ambulatory surgery, 141
        in classic surgery, 140-1
    mechanical instruments *see* mechanical instruments
    micro-hysteroscopy, 10
    procedural code 58558 for, 172
    rigid scopes, 135
        sheaths *see* sheaths
    thermal damage of endometrial chips, 122
    training
        Australia, 205
        Europe, 201
        USA, 184-91
    see also procedures
opportunity costs, 174-5
optics, 25, 26, 228
ornipressin, 155
ostia, tubal *see* tubes (uterine)
outpatient service
    diagnostic, 2-18
        conventional hysteroscopy, 2-6
        flexible hysteroscopy, 12-18
        semi-rigid hysteroscopy, 7-11
    nurse's role, 34-9, 175, 222-5

set up of operating room *see* operating room
training, 10
ovulatory phase, endometrium in, 85

p53 mutations, 95
PACS (picture archiving and communication systems), 214-15
pain
    abdominal pain syndrome, 52
    manipulation of tubal ostium, 153
    see also analgesia
papillary carcinoma, uterine, 95
pathology (uterine/endometrial)
    in flexible hysteroscopy
        evaluation, 14-15
        missed, 15
    interpretation of visual appreciation, 99-106
    see also histology
patient
    compliance and tolerance *see* compliance
    information *see* counseling; information
    physical condition contraindicating hysteroscopy, 57
    position *see* position
    preparation, 34-5
    selection, 222
pelvic inflammatory disease as contraindication, 56
peracetic acid, 167-8
peritoneal dissemination of endometrial cancer cells during hysteroscopy, 107-8
personnel
    conventional hysteroscopy, 5
    semi-rigid hysteroscopy, 9
    see also specific personnel
pH, CO_2 distension, 43
photography
    35-mm, 216
    video *see* video photography
physical condition contraindicating hysteroscopy, 57
physician/doctor
    communication with patient and counselor, 232
    conventional hysteroscopy, 5
picture archiving and communication systems, 214-15
Pipelle biopsy, 70-1, 117, 118
polyethylene terephthalate (PET) of ESSURE micro-insert, 143
    histologic response, 148
polyp(s), endocervical, self-retaining hysteroscope examination, 53
polyp(s), endometrial, 22, 96-7, 101-2
    biopsies, 114, 115
    c-erbB2 receptors and, 96-7
    pregnancy outcome in IVF and effects of, 62
    removal, 137
        bipolar electrosurgery, 133, 142
        by resection *see* polypectomy

saline infusion sonography, 78, 81-2
tamoxifen-stimulated, ultrasound, 72
polypectomy
    snare, 21, 22
    subfertile patients, 61-2
POR 8®, 155
position (body)
    patient, 3-5
        small diameter hysteroscopy, 226
    surgeon, 196
postmenopausal women
    bleeding, 70
        age and endometrial cancer risk with, 120
        endometrial smear, 113
    flexible hysteroscopy, 16
power Doppler, 72
preceptorship, 185, 190, 194
premedication, 4, 154
premenstrual phase, endometrium in, 86
pressure
    continuous flow and (with distension fluid), 30, 31, 37, 224-5
    variable, (with CO_2 insufflator), 42-3
    very low, observation in flexible hysteroscopy at, 16
pressure cuff, 30-1, 37, 44, 223-4
printers/printing, 211, 217
procedures/interventions
    codes, 177
        CPT, 170, 172-3, 173, 174
        reference sources, 177
    length, fluid overload related to, 201
    levels (and their relevance to training), 201
        Europe, 190, 194-5, 201
        USA, 186, 195, 196
    reducing invasiveness, 198
proctoring, 185
progesterone receptors, 93-4
proliferative phase of menstrual cycle, endometrium in, 85
    steroid receptors, 93
    timing of sampling, 119
proprioceptive information, 197, 198
pseudofunctional dysvascular endometrium, 86-9
pseudopolypoid tumor, malignant, 105
PTEN mutations, 95
pump, electronic
    for distension, 30-1, 223-4
    for suction and irrigation, 44
punch biopsy, 110
    compared with grasp biopsy, 110
    forceps, 110, 111

quality of instruments, training and, 196

RBRVS (relative based relative value scale), 170, 170-1
receptors, endometrial, 93-8
record-keeping *see* documentation
reimbursement, 170-7
    evidence-based medicine and, 170-1
    understanding, 172-3
relative based relative value scale (RBRVS), 170, 170-1

resectoscope, credentialing, 186
residency training in USA, 186
resuscitation kit, 154
retained products of conception, 103
rigid scopes, xiv-xv, 25-8, 32
    history, 25-6
    for operative hysteroscopy *see* operative hysteroscopy
rinsing cycle, 164, 167
    final, 164
rod lens system, 25, 26, 228
rollerball, 205-6
rpSzene, olympus, 213-14

safety precautions, 33
    see also complications; emergency situations
saline distension media, 31, 126
    conventional hysteroscopy, 5
    flexible hysteroscopy, 15-16
    for tubal sterilization, 144
saline infusion sono(hystero)graphy (SIS), 68, 70, 74-84, 171-2, 180-1
    compared with other diagnostic techniques, 180-1
    costs, 82
    evolution, 74-5
    findings, 76-81
    limitations, 81-2
    menstrual disorders, clinical role, 75
    postprocedure instructions, 76
    problems/pitfalls/troubleshooting, 76
    technique, 75-6
sampling, endometrial, 110-23
    algorithm, 115
    artifacts, 121-2
    blind, 117, 118
    error, 118
    pathologist's point of view, 117-23
    specimen preparation, 121
    timing, 119
    see also biopsies
scissors, 136, 141
SDC Pro, Stryker, 214
SEBCOH principle, 200
secretory/luteal phase, endometrium in, 85-6
    steroid receptors, 93
    timing of sampling, 119
sedation, 154-6
    inadequate, 156
self-retaining hysteroscope, 46-54
    decision-making tree, 52
    description, 46-9
    evidence base and statistics (meta-analysis), 51-2
    examination technique, 49, 50
    practical recommendations, 54
    sterilization, 49-50
    in video hysteroscopy, 51
semi-rigid hysteroscopy, 2-6
    anesthesia, 10
    indications and contraindications, 2-3
    instruments, 8-9
    operative outpatient
        micro-hysteroscopy, 10

personnel, 9
procedure, 9-10
set up, 8
success/failure rates, 10
septa, uterine, 178
  division, 138
sheaths (outer)
  care and maintenance, 167
  flexible scopes, 23
  rigid scopes, 27-8
    diagnostic 2-mm scopes, 27-8
    diagnostic 4-mm scopes, 27
    operative 2-mm scopes, 28
    operative 2.9-mm scopes, 27
    operative 4-mm scopes, 27
single fiberscope (Storz), 226
slicing technique, polyps and myomas, 133, 142
Slimline™ operative hysteroscope for tubal occlusion with ESSURE insert, 145
small diameter (ultra mini) scopes, 226-30
  patient compliance, 226-30
  see also micro-hysteroscopy; mini endoscopes
Smith and Nephew Medicap 2000 (version 3), 212
snare polypectomy, polyps (endometrial), 21, 22
soaking boxes, 163
Society of Radiologists Ultrasound Consensus report, 71
Society of Reproductive Surgeons (SRS), credentialing and, 185-6, 189
sodium
  concentrations in distension fluids, 126
  low blood levels see hyponatremia
software-only archiving systems, 212
sonography see ultrasonography
sorbitol 3% solution, 125
spaces, coordination in, 197-8
spotting, flexible hysteroscopy, 16
Spring electrode, 10, 132, 141
staff see personnel
staining, 121
standards, training, 194, 200-1
sterilization (of equipment), 167-8
  accessories, 164
  preparation for, 167
  self-retaining hysteroscope, 49-50
sterilization (tubal) with ESSURE insert see ESSURE micro-insert
steroid receptors, endometrial, 93-6
  cancer and, 94-5
  EGF receptors and, 96
STOP device see ESSURE micro-insert
storage
  images
    equipment, 217-18
    media, 214
  instruments, 164, 225
Storz, Karl
  Advanced Image and Data Archiving (AIDA), 212, 214

bipolar electrode, 132, 142
flexible scopes
  diagnostic, 20, 21
  operative, 21
rigid scopes, 25, 26
single fiberscope, 226
see also Hamou
Stryker SDC Pro, 214
subfertility see fertility
submucous leiomyomas
  removal, 137
    electrosurgery, 132-3, 133, 141
    training in Australia, 203
  sonography, 67
    saline infusion, 68, 79, 81-2
suction, pump for, 44
supervisor, training, Australia, 203
surgery
  cervical, flexible hysteroscopy following, 16
  hysteroscopic see operative hysteroscopy
synechiae see adhesions

tamoxifen-treated women, 72
  flexible hysteroscopy, 16-17
  interpretation of visual appearance, 103
  sonography, 72
    saline infusion, 81
teamwork, 223
telescope (of self-retaining hysteroscope), 46-7
  care and maintenance, 167
  with wiper-blade system, 47-8
testosterone receptors, endometrial, 94
  cancer and, 95
TGF-á and endometrial polyps, 96-7
thermal damage of endometrial chips in operative hysteroscopy, 122
35-mm photography, 216
3D-ultrasound, congenital uterine anomalies, 72
traceability, 164
training, 184-202
  Australia, 202-7, 209, 210
  Europe, 189, 190, 192-202, 210
  Far East, 208
  standards, 194, 200-1
  UK, 10
  ultrasound, 65
  USA/America, 184-91, 195, 196, 209
transforming growth factor-α and endometrial polyps, 96-7
transuterine resection syndrome, 127-8
transvaginal ultrasound see ultrasonography
trauma, iatrogenic, 38, 57-8
Trendelenburg position, 4
trioxymethylene tablets, 49-50
tubes (fallopian) see fallopian tubes
tubes (uterine), ostia of
  fiberscope evaluation, 15
  manipulation, 153
'TURP' syndrome (TURE syndrome in gynecology), 127-8

tutorship, 194
Twizzle electrode, 10, 132, 141, 142

UK, training, 10
ultra mini scopes see small diameter scopes
ultrasonography (incl. sonohysterography), transvaginal, 65-83
  comparisons with other diagnostic techniques
    cervical inspection, 179
    uterine cavity inspection, 180
  limitations, 70-1
  normal endometrial architecture, 66-7
  orientation, 65-6
  probe preparation, 65
  saline infusion see saline infusion sonohysterography
  Society of Radiologists Ultrasound Consensus report, 71
  in subfertility, 61
  training, 65
United Kingdom, training, 10
United States of America (USA)
  equipment and instrument care and maintenance, 166-9
  training and accreditation, 184-91, 195, 196, 209
uterine cavity
  diagnostic techniques for comparisons, 179-82
    possible options, 182
  distension see distension
  flexible hysteroscopic evaluation, 14-15
  IVF and examination of see in vitro fertilization
  need to manipulate or extract volumes >2 cm out of, 153
  need to overdilate, 153
uterine cervix see cervix
uterus
  adhesions see adhesions
  bleeding see bleeding; spotting
  classical approach, 40
  congenital anomalies see congenital uterine anomalies
  fibroids see leiomyomas
  infection see infection
  pathology see pathology
  perforation, 38
  resection syndrome (TURE), 127-8
  septa see septa
  vaginoscopical approach, 40-1

Vabra diagnosis, 117
vagal reflex see vasovagal response
vaginoscopical technique, 40-1
vasculature (blood vessels), 100
  alterations (=pseudofunctional dysvascular endometrium), 86-9
  menstrual cycle-related changes, 84, 89
vasoconstrictors, 154
  in myomectomy, 206

vasovagal response/reflex/reaction, 38
    saline infusion sonography, 76
Versapoint, 131-2, 132
video hysteroscopy
    hysteroscope, 20, 21
        integration of self-retaining
            hysteroscope into, 51
video photography, 29-30, 216-18, 223
    conventional hysteroscopy, 5
    digital systems, 211-12, 213, 214, 217-18
    nurses and, 223
    semi-rigid hysteroscopy, 9
View Station, Fotomaster, 217
vigilance with equipment, 162, 164
visual appreciation of pathology, interpretation, 99-106

water, sterile, glutaraldehyde removal with, 168
wiper-blade system, telescopes with, 47-8
withdrawal, fiberscope, 15
working women, questions asked, 232

xenon light source, 9, 13, 223, 227
xylocaine, 154